Theories of
Social Psychology

McGraw-Hill Series in Psychology

CONSULTING EDITOR

Norman Garmezy

Adams: Human Memory
Berlyne: Conflict, Arousal, and Curiosity
Bernstein and Nietzel: Introduction to Clinical Psychology
Blum: Psychoanalytic Theories of Personality
Bock: Multivariate Statistical Methods in Behavioral Research
Brown: The Motivation of Behavior
Campbell, Dunnette, Lawler, and Weick: Managerial Behavior, Performance, and Effectiveness
Crites: Vocational Psychology
D'Amato: Experimental Psychology: Methodology, Psychophysics, and Learning
Dollard and Miller: Personality and Psychotherapy
Ferguson: Statistical Analysis in Psychology and Education
Fodor, Bever, and Garrett: The Psychology of Language: An Introduction to Psycholinguistics and Generative Grammar
Forgus and Melamed: Perception: A Cognitive-Stage Approach
Franks: Behavior Therapy: Appraisal and Status
Gilmer and Deci: Industrial and Organizational Psychology
Guilford: Psychometric Methods
Guilford: The Nature of Human Intelligence
Guilford and Fruchter: Fundamental Statistics in Psychology and Education
Guion: Personnel Testing
Hetherington and Parke: Child Psychology: A Contemporary Viewpoint
Hirsh: The Measurement of Hearing
Hjelle and Ziegler: Personality Theories: Basic Assumptions, Research, and Applications
Horowitz: Elements of Statistics for Psychology and Education
Hulse, Egeth, and Deese: The Psychology of Learning
Hurlock: Adolescent Development
Hurlock: Child Development
Hurlock: Developmental Psychology: A Life-Span Approach
Klein: Motivation: Biosocial Approaches
Krech, Crutchfield, and Ballachey: Individual in Society
Lakin: Interpersonal Encounter: Theory and Practice in Sensitivity Training
Lawler: Pay and Organizational Effectiveness: A Psychological View
Lazarus, A.: Behavior Therapy and Beyond
Lazarus, R.: Patterns of Adjustment
Lewin: A Dynamic Theory of Personality
Maher: Principles of Psychopathology
Marascuilo: Statistical Methods for Behavioral Science Research

Marx and Hillix: Systems and Theories in Psychology
Morgan: Physiological Psychology
Novick and Jackson: Statistical Methods for Educational and Psychological Research
Nunnally: Introduction to Statistics for Psychology and Education
Nunnally: Psychometric Theory
Overall and Klett: Applied Multivariate Analysis
Porter, Lawler, and Hackman: Behavior in Organizations
Robinson and Robinson: The Mentally Retarded Child
Ross: Psychological Disorders of Children: A Behavioral Approach to Theory, Research, and Therapy
Shaw: Group Dynamics: The Psychology of Small Group Behavior
Shaw and Costanzo: Theories of Social Psychology
Shaw and Wright: Scales for the Measurement of Attitudes
Sidowski: Experimental Methods and Instrumentation in Psychology
Siegel: Nonparametric Statistics for the Behavioral Sciences
Steers and Porter: Motivation and Work Behavior
Vinacke: The Psychology of Thinking
Winer: Statistical Principles in Experimental Design

Theories of Social Psychology

Second Edition

Marvin E. Shaw
University of Florida

Philip R. Costanzo
Duke University

McGraw-Hill Book Company

New York   St. Louis   San Francisco   Auckland   Bogotá   Hamburg
Johannesburg   London   Madrid   Mexico   Montreal   New Delhi
Panama   Paris   São Paulo   Singapore   Sydney   Tokyo   Toronto

This book was set in Times Roman by Black Dot, Inc. (ECU).
The editors were Patricia S. Nave and Barry Benjamin;
the production supervisor was Leroy A. Young.
R. R. Donnelley & Sons Company was printer and binder.

THEORIES OF SOCIAL PSYCHOLOGY

1 2 3 4 5 6 7 8 9 0 D O D O 8 9 8 7 6 5 4 3 2 1

ISBN 0-07-056512-0

Library of Congress Cataloging in Publication Data
Shaw, Marvin E.
    Theories of social psychology.

    (McGraw-Hill series in psychology)
    Bibliography: p.
    Includes indexes.
    1. Social psychology.   I. Costanzo, Philip R.
II. Title.   III. Series.
HM251.S47   1982   302   81-12383
ISBN 0-07-056512-0   AACR2

Contents

Preface   xi

1
INTRODUCTION

CHAPTER 1   Social Psychology and Social Theory   3
     The Field of Social Psychology   4
     Theory in Social Psychology   7
     Problems of Theory Construction in Social Psychology   15
     Plan of the Book: An Overview   18

2
THE REINFORCEMENT ORIENTATION

CHAPTER 2   The Reinforcement-Theory Orientation   23
     Brief Historical Introduction   24
     Terms and Constructs   28
     Reinforcement Theory and Social Phenomena   39

CHAPTER 3   Theories of Social Learning and Imitation   41
            A Classical Theory of Social Learning and Imitation   42
            A Vicarious Process Theory of Imitation   53
            Comment and Evaluation   66

CHAPTER 4   Social Reinforcement–Exchange Theories   68
            A Theory of Elementary Social Behavior   69
            A Theory of Interdependence   80
            Equity Theory   102

3

THE FIELD-THEORETICAL ORIENTATION

CHAPTER 5   Basic Concepts and Constructs of Field Theory   111
            The Principal Attributes of Field Theory   112
            The Major Constructs of Field Theory   116
            Applications of the Theory   126

CHAPTER 6   Field Theories in Social Psychology   136
            A Theory of Interpersonal Relations   137
            Social Penetration Theory   153
            Theories of Crowding   162
            A Theory of Hope   170

4

THE COGNITIVE ORIENTATION

CHAPTER 7   Basic Concepts of the Cognitive Orientation   179
            Cognitive Definitions of Basic Terms   181
            Cognitive Explanations of Selected Psychological Processes 185
            Krech and Crutchfield's Cognitive Theory   192
            Summary   196

CHAPTER 8   Cognitive Consistency Theories   198
            The p-o-x Theory   199
            The A-B-X System   204
            The Principle of Congruity   210
            A Theory of Cognitive Dissonance   217
            A Theory of Psychological Reactance   228

CHAPTER 9   Attribution Theory in Social Psychology   232
            A Theory of Correspondent Inferences   234
            A Theory of External Attribution   241

Self-Perception Theory 250
A Postscript and Prospective on Attribution Theory 257

CHAPTER 10 Theories of Social Comparison, Judgment, and
Perception 259
Social Comparison Theory 259
Social Judgment Theory 269
A Theory of Choice 277
Integration Theory 282
A Theory of Attitudes and Behavioral Intentions 285
Inoculation Theory 288

5

THE ROLE-THEORY ORIENTATION

CHAPTER 11 Role Theory 295
The Language of Role Theory 296

CHAPTER 12 Role-Related Theories in Social Psychology 314
Ingratiation Theory 315
Impression Management Theory 328
A Theory of Self-Monitoring 337
A Theory of Objective Self-Awareness 345

6

SPECIALIZED THEORIES

CHAPTER 13 Theories of Group Processes 353
Affiliative Conflict Theory 354
A Theory of Removing and Recruiting Group Members 356
FIRO: A Three-Dimensional Theory of Interpersonal
Relations 360
A Theory of Motives and Goals in Groups 368
A Theory of Group Productivity 377
A Contingency Model of Leadership Effectiveness 382

CHAPTER 14 Single-Principle Perspectives Relevant to Social
Psychology 389
A Theory of Fear of Success 391
A Two-Factor Theory of Emotion 397
A Perspective on Obesity-Prone Behavior 402
An Achievement Attribution Viewpoint 405
The Attitude Similarity–Attraction Paradigm 408

7

CONCLUSION

CHAPTER 15 Epilogue   413
                Current Status of Theories   413
                Theories and Research   417
                A Look to the Future   419

References   421

Glossary   459

Indexes   466
    Name Index
    Subject index

Preface

At the time that we had begun compiling our notes for the revision of *Theories of Social Psychology*, ten years had passed since its first publication. Both of us welcomed the opportunity to sharpen our presentation of social psychology's theories through this revision effort. However, we did not initially anticipate that the theoretical content of the book would require the overhaul that this final product represents. In the first edition of this book we organized our presentation of theories by relating them to five general orientations extant in the study of human psychology (Reinforcement theory, field theory, psychoanalytic theory, cognitive theory, and role theory). In addition, we presented several theories which seemed to significantly cross the conceptual boundaries of these orientations in two "transorientational" theory chapters. We have retained much of this basic organizational framework. The theories presented in the current edition of this book are compiled into four general orientations (reinforcement, field, cognitive, and role). The presentation of the psychoanalytic orientation and three of the four specific theories deriving from it were dropped from the current edition. As in the first edition, two chapters presenting unclassified theories are included but these theories are now referred to as "specialized" rather than "transorientational."

The four chapters which describe general orientations (Chapters 2, 5, 7, and 11) are close facsimiles to the orientation chapters presented in the first edition of the book. Our purpose in these chapters was, and is, to present the forms of thought that characterize theory construction in social psychology. Such general forms of thought change at a much slower pace than their specific theoretical derivatives. Thus, we have judged that much of the basic content of the original orientation chapters would suffice as exemplars of the historical and ideological strains of reasoning evident in social psychological theories. Beyond this close overlap between Theories 1 and Theories 2, the reader will find a considerable divergence in context.

In the first edition of this book, twenty-five separate theories of significance to the social psychology of the sixties were presented. In this edition, fifteen of these theories have been retained, and ten have been removed from the presentation. The ten discarded theories were not shunted for lack of essential adequacy but because they failed to either undergo significant development or to constitute major interpretive devices for the generation or explanation of social psychological research. The fifteen theories that have been retained from the first edition have each been updated by us to reflect their status in the social psychology of the seventies and eighties. Some of these retained theories were put through quite extensive revision owing to important developments in the theorists' perspectives and related research developments (e.g., see attribution theories). Some of the other theories retained from the first edition have been more simply updated by examining recent research applications and by clarifying restatements of the theorists.

In addition to the revisions of the fifteen retained theories, the current edition of this book presents twenty-three theoretical frameworks not represent-ed in the original edition. Thus, nearly as many theories reported in the entire first edition have been added to this second edition. Indeed, approximately 60 percent of the specific theories presented in this edition did not appear in the first edition. While the changing content in this second edition may partly reflect our shortsightedness in the original selection of theories to be presented, the lion's share of the newly presented theories has been proposed since the time that the first edition went to press. The seventies appears to have been a period of significant theoretical proliferation in social psychology. Many new theories of the middle range appeared and were quite prone to be focused upon specific phenomena (e.g., obesity, crowding, hope, manipulative social interaction, achievement, choice, etc.). It is perhaps noteworthy that theories with the potential to provide a general framework for social psychology made their initial appearance in the fifties and sixties (i.e., exchange theory, equity theory, attribution theory, and cognitive consistency theories). These latter models have met with modest success in affording general propositions to the field. The reader will observe that a measure of this success is the degree to which the propositions of the more general frameworks are embedded in models of specific phenomena.

In the preface to the first edition we expressed the hope that by presenting the more promising theories of social psychology in a single volume, we could be instrumental in encouraging students to test theories, and in inspiring theorists to modify and extend their theories in response to new evidence and ideas. Our hopes for this edition remain the same. Our commitment to this project has been sustained by the belief that the advance of our understanding of social psychological phenomena depends upon the adequacy of the theories which govern the search for knowledge.

We are indebted to many people for intended or unwitting contributions to this volume. We would particularly like to thank the theorists whose work we have represented in this book. We do hope that we have not misrepresented their ideas. We are aware that our abbreviated presentations can scarcely do justice to their theories, and we apologize for this inadequacy. Barry Schlenker read and generously commented upon many portions of the original manuscript. Erik Woody and Pamela Slater, former graduate students of the second author, contributed to this project in many direct and indirect ways. Our present and past colleagues at the University of Florida and Duke University have helped provide an atmosphere of inquiry conducive to the pursuit of this work. Rhona Robbin, Pat Nave, and Barry Benjamin from the McGraw-Hill editorial staff have discharged their roles skillfully and with admirable forebearance for our idiosyncrasies. Deborah Earnhardt, Pat Johnson, and Marge Williams graciously typed portions of this manuscript—frequently under the knife of an impending deadline. Finally, to Lilly May, Mike, Susan, Simone, and Adam, our thanks for the anchoring identity that impelled us through the arduous and grump-inducing struggles of authoring.

Aside from these personal acknowledgments we would also like to thank the following publishers and organizations for providing permission to quote from their copyrighted works: Academic press; Addison-Wesley Publishing Co.; Alfred A. Knopf; American Psychological Association; Brooks/Cole Publishing Co.; Center for Advanced Studies in the Behavioral Sciences; Chandler Publishing Co.; Dorsey Press; Free Press; Harcourt Brace Jovanovich Publishing Co.; Harper & Row; Holt, Rinehart and Winston; J. B. Lippincott Co.; John Wiley and Sons; Jossey-Bass, Inc.; Lawrence Erlbaum Associates; Macmillan Publishing Co.; McGraw-Hill Book Co.; Oxford University Press; Prentice-Hall Publishing Co.; Plenum Publishing Co.; Random House; Winthrop Publishing Co.; Yale University Press.

Marvin E. Shaw
Philip R. Costanzo

Part One

Introduction

Chapter 1

Social Psychology and Social Theory

Throughout recorded history man has been deeply interested in social behavior. Even the most casual observer notes that individuals behave differently when in the presence of others than when alone and that behavior varies depending upon which others are present. The patterns of responses to others becomes highly complicated with the formation of social units, such as families, clans, institutions, and nations. Although interest in social behavior is rooted in antiquity, the delineation of social psychology as a specific area of study is a comparatively recent development. For example. the first American textbooks on social psychology appeared less than a century ago (McDougall, 1908; Ross, 1908).

Modern social psychology purports to base its propositions and conclusions on observations in relatively controlled situations. Areas of concern include attitudes and attitude change, person perception, interpersonal attraction, altruism and helping behavior, aggression, social power, social influence, and similar problems. As a result of the empirical approach, a considerable amount of data about social behavior has accumulated. To be useful, such data must be organized in a systematic way so that the meaning and implications of these data can be understood. Such systematic organization is the function of theory. This book is an attempt to present some of the more productive theories and hypotheses proposed by social psychologists.

It is necessary at this point to define two critical terms in the title of this book that are used extensively in the following pages: *social psychology* and *theory*. Each term has been defined in a variety of ways, and some writers express the opinion that "social psychology defies meaningful definition" (Seidenberg & Snadowsky, 1976, p. 3). Nevertheless, we have adopted minimal definitions. *Social psychology is the scientific study of individual behavior as a function of social stimuli.* By "scientific" we mean to imply only that observations are made under controlled conditions; armchair speculations are not acceptable data for social psychology, although such speculations may serve as useful guides for research. The specification of behavior as "individual" is an attempt to emphasize the social psychologist's concern for the individual as the unit of analysis, as opposed to larger units such as groups and institutions. Finally, "social stimuli" refers to humans and their products. Thus, another person is a social stimulus, and the things that he or she creates, such as social groups, norms, and other social products, also serve as social stimuli. It should be clear that social stimuli include the effects of past social experiences to the extent that those effects (the things the individual brings with him or her to the present) are unambiguously derivable from social factors. That is, social psychologists ordinarily study the effects of social stimuli that are mediated by enduring processes (e.g., attitudes and norm internalization). On the other hand, personality characteristics, such as manifest anxiety, self-confidence, and conceptual systems, are usually excluded because the historical antecedents of such characteristics are not clearly social in nature.

A theory is a set of interrelated hypotheses or propositions concerning a phenomenon or set of phenomena. This is indeed a minimal definition of theory, but we believe it encompasses the essential elements of the concept as delineated by the philosophy of science. In the following sections, the meaning of both social psychology and theory is explored more fully.

THE FIELD OF SOCIAL PSYCHOLOGY

The definition of social psychology given in the preceding section does not adequately reflect the wide range of issues and problems encompassed by this field of study. A consideration of the area and scope of social psychology and of its relation to other social sciences may provide a better understanding of this field.

Area and Scope of Social Psychology

The definition of social psychology presented above is only one of many definitions that have been suggested. A review of other formulations may contribute to the understanding of the domain of social psychology.

"Social psychology is the scientific study of human interaction" (Watson, 1966, p. 1).

"Social psychology is a subdiscipline of psychology that especially involves the scientific study of the behavior of individuals as a function of social stimuli" (Jones & Gerard, 1967, p. 1).

"Social psychology: A discipline that attempts to understand, explain, and predict how the thoughts, feelings, and actions of individuals are influenced by the perceived, imagined, or implied thoughts, feelings and actions of others" (Raven & Rubin, 1976, p. 516).

"Social psychology is the study of the way in which individuals are affected by social situations" (Worchel & Cooper, 1976, p. 7).

Social psychology is "the scientific study of the personal and situational factors that affect individual social behavior" (Shaver, 1977, p. 14).

Social psychology is "a scientific attempt to understand and explain how the thoughts, feelings, and behavior of individuals are influenced by the actual, imagined, or implied presence of others" (Vander Zanden, 1977, p. 27).

Social psychology is all of these things; however, it is easy to get the impression that all of human behavior falls within the domain of social psychology. In practice, the field of social psychology is more limited than implied by the various definitions. The areas included in the field may be classified under three major headings: (1) the study of social influences on individual processes, (2) the study of shared individual processes, and (3) the study of group interaction.

The category labeled "social influences on individual processes" includes those phenomena which (1) may be influenced by social stimuli, (2) may also occur in the absence of any social stimulus, and (3) usually are not shared by persons who are not exposed to the immediate stimulus situation. Perception, motivation, learning, and attribution are examples of such phenomena. Many aspects of perception, motivation, and learning are not primarily social in nature; hence they have been studied primarily by non-social psychologists. However, to the extent that social variables are determinants of these processes or that these processes are related to social behavior, the social psychologist must (and does) study them. On the other hand, many of the theories formulated to account for such individual processes have been developed by others and are not social psychological in nature. The theorist merely incorporates the effects of social variables into a more-comprehensive theory.

"Shared individual processes" refers to those phenomena that (1) are basically individual in that their manifestation does not depend upon the immediate presence of social stimuli, (2) derive directly from social stimuli, and (3) are usually shared by others in the same social group. Language and social attitudes are examples of such phenomena. The development of language and social attitudes depends upon interaction with others in the social group, but once they have developed they function more or less independently of the social group. For example, a person who "knows the English language" may make use of this skill to help organize thoughts when alone; he or she is able to speak and write whether others are present or not. Imitation and modeling behavior are also examples of this category, although the degree to which these processes are shared by others in the group is probably less than in the case of language and social attitudes.

The category labeled "group interaction" includes all those processes which (1) depend upon interaction with others and (2) are manifested only when others are present, at least in spirit. Leadership, communication, power relations, authority, conformity, cooperation and competition, and social roles fall into this category. The behavior that occurs is, of course, behavior of individuals, but it is behavior in response to immediate social stimuli. Perhaps because this category is uniquely social in nature, more social theories have been formulated about these phenomena than those of either of the other two categories.

The Place of Social Psychology in the Behavioral Sciences

Among the behavioral sciences, social psychology is most closely related to anthropology and sociology. Anthropology is usually defined as the science of man. It is concerned primarily, but not exclusively, with primitive man. More specifically, anthropology is the study of man in relation to distribution, origin, classification of races, environmental and social relations, physical characteristics, and culture. Thus the province of anthropology is that of entire cultures and their analyses, both singly and in relation to each other. Anthropology is an extremely important field for the social psychologist. We are socialized in a specific culture; and the motives, values, and aspirations of that culture tend to bias our view of the behavior of people in other cultures. The findings of anthropologists can help overcome this bias and can identify the tremendous diversity in human behavior from culture to culture. The social psychologist cannot hope to understand fully the individual's behavior in social situations without an awareness of the culture's influences upon his or her behavior.

Sociology is, of course, closely related to both social psychology and anthropology. It is the science of society, social institutions, and social relationships. More specifically, sociology is the systematic study of the development, structure, and functions of human groups, conceived as organized patterns of collective behavior. Sociologists are interested primarily, but not exclusively, in group behavior, institutions, and intergroup relations. Their major problems concern the ways behaviors of people are similar or different because of group membership influences. Since humans almost inevitably spend much of their waking lives as members of various social groups, the findings of sociologists are of great value to the social psychologist in the attempt to understand social behavior.

Anthropology, sociology, and social psychology thus represent three levels of analysis in the study of social man. Anthropology considers the entire culture; sociology deals with smaller collectivities within the larger culture; and social psychology is concerned with the behavior of the individual in response to social influences. Whereas both sociology and social psychology are interested in behavior within groups, sociology is interested in the fact that all members of the group are subject to the same influences, and social psychology is concerned primarily with the influences which play upon the individuals as members of the group. The social psychologist finds the principles established by anthropologists and sociologists indispensable, but the focus of interest is basically different from that of either the anthropologist or the sociologist. This difference is reflected not only in the unit of analysis but also in the method of study. Although in practice there is considerable overlap across disciplines, sociologists and anthropologists rely more heavily on quasi-experimental designs and descriptive analysis, whereas social psychologists place relatively greater faith in experimental or controlled investigations.

THEORY IN SOCIAL PSYCHOLOGY

Social psychologists, like other scientists, seek to *understand* the phenomena being studied. If a phenomenon is understood, it can be *predicted* to the extent that the relevant variables are known and *controlled* to the extent that one has power over the relevant variables. The converse is not true; a person may be able to predict and/or control a phenomenon without understanding it. For example, it is not difficult to imagine a primitive person who could accurately predict that the sun would rise in the east and set in the west without any understanding of the system producing these events. Similarly, it is quite possible for a man to control an automobile without understanding the causal relationships between his actions and the behavior of the vehicle. Although understanding is the major goal of science, prediction is nevertheless important because it is the process which permits verification of empirical and theoretical generalizations. Control is, of course, highly important in the application of scientific discovery, but its significance for science is limited to situations in which control is necessary for further investigation.

In attempting to understand social behavior, the social psychologist uses both experience and theory. Experience provides the raw data upon which understanding is based; theory organizes experience so that its implications for more-general social behavior are recognized. Not all experience provides acceptable data, however. Only that experience which meets the criteria for admission to the body of scientific knowledge is acceptable. In general, experience that meets these criteria derives from experimentation or, at least, observations under controlled conditions. Thus only propositions that are based upon objective observations that are public and repeatable are admitted to the body of scientific knowledge.

Empirical data are essential for understanding social behavior, but empiricism alone does not lead to major advances in any science. Empirical data must be organized and interrelated so that they can be interpreted and unified. This is the function of theory. The role of theory in advancing science was emphasized by both Campbell (1921) and Conant (1953). Campbell noted that it is unusual for new laws to be suggested merely from experimentation; Conant asserted that all really revolutionary and significant advances that have occurred during the history of science have been the result of new theories. Kuhn (1970) maintained that "normal science" advances only when there is a theory that is *accepted* by members of a scientific community.

The Nature of Theory

In the introduction to this chapter we defined theory as a set of interrelated hypotheses or propositions concerning a phenomenon or set of phenomena. Although this definition is adequate for the purposes of this book, it is by no means the only definition that might be proposed. The following examples are representative:

> "Theories are sets of statements, understandable to others, which make predictions about empirical events" (Mandler & Kessen, 1959, p. 142).

> "A *theory* is a set of systematically related and organized hypotheses which allows a scientist to understand, explain, and predict a wide variety of phenomena" (Severy, Brigham, & Schlenker, 1976, p. 12).

> "But at best an authentic theory should present a set of testable propositions stating the relationship of variables producing a phenomenon" (Hollander, 1976, p. 34).

> "The term *theory* is normally applied to the higher order integration of hypotheses into systematic networks that attempt to describe and predict broader ranges of events by allowing one hypothesis to qualify another or to specify the conditions under which another will be appropriate" (McDavid & Harari, 1968, p. 21).

> "A theory is a symbolic construction" (Kaplan, 1964, p. 296).

Despite the variations in wording, these definitions are not inconsistent with our definition in any essential characteristic, with the possible exception of the one proposed by Kaplan. The bare statement that a theory is a symbolic construction, however, does not do justice to Kaplan's detailed and insightful treatment of the nature of theory. He suggested that a theory is a way of making sense out of a confused set of data; it allows us to use, modify, or discard habits as the situation demands. A theory is thus a device for interpreting, criticizing, and unifying established laws. Theorizing does not mean that a person learns by experience, but rather that he learns from experience. The *from* learning is the process that requires symbolic constructions; these constructions can provide vicarious experience which the person never actually undergoes. The process of symbolic construction makes use of empirical data, but it goes beyond the data and points to new insights. This view of "mental work" in the formulation of scientific propositions is similar to that propounded by Polanyi (1968), although

Kaplan apparently did not interpret this process as reflecting indeterminacy in the real world as Polanyi did.

Theory is thus in part a summary of known "facts" and in part conjecture about the implications of facts and the probable relationships among them. In a sense, it may be regarded as an attempt to map the real world, although theories differ in the degree to which this is true. That is, some theories employ concepts (constructs) that are not assumed to represent any specific thing in the real world. Nevertheless, all theories purport to say something about actual events and phenomena and are not merely fictitious representations of imaginary situations.

For purposes of this book, we shall distinguish between "theory" and "orientation." Our definition of a theory as a set of interrelated hypotheses corresponds to Merton's ". . . *theories of the middle range:* theories intermediate to the minor working hypotheses evolved in abundance during the day-to-day routines of research, and the all-inclusive speculations comprising a master conceptual scheme from which it is hoped to derive a very large number of empirically observed uniformities of social behavior" (Merton, 1949, p. 5). In contrast, *orientation* is similar to Merton's "master conceptual scheme." In this book, orientation refers to a general approach to the analysis and interpretation of behavior. In psychology, these general orientations are often called *systems,* although they are sometimes referred to as theories. Such systematic orientations provide the general framework within which theories are formulated. General orientations that have been most influential in social psychology are the stimulus-response reinforcement approach, the field-theoretical orientation, the cognitive orientation, and the role-theory orientation. As we shall see, many of the theories in social psychology derive from these general approaches, either singly or in combination.

Functions of Theory

We have already indicated that theory plays a very important role in social psychology and pointed to some of the functions performed by theory. It is probably not feasible or desirable to list all the functions of theories in social psychology; however, it may be useful to point to some of the major purposes served by theory. In the first place, theory is a convenient way of organizing experience; it permits us to handle large amounts of empirical data with relatively few propositions. This fact means that theory enables the social psychologist to deal in a meaningful way with information that would otherwise be chaotic and largely useless.

But a theory does much more than this. A second function of theory is that it enables us to go beyond the empirical data and see implications and relationships that are not evident from any datum taken alone. It has been asserted that propositions contain within themselves certain consequences, and no conclusion can be drawn that is not inherent in the propositions under consideration. On the other hand, some philosophers have maintained that, by proper juxtaposition of two or more propositions, it may be possible to discover truths that are not contained in these propositions. The story is told of the priest who told guests at a party that the first person who confessed to him was a murderer. Later a young man entered the room and introduced himself as the first person to confess to the priest. No one would have difficulty in drawing the immediate inference that the young man was a murderer, yet this conclusion is not inherent in either statement taken alone. Regardless of the merits of the two positions, it is clear that interrelated hypotheses can reveal conclusions that are not evident from data considered in isolation.

This function of providing insights beyond the empirical data provides the basis for a third function of theory: it is a stimulus and guide for further empirical investigation. Theory leads to predictions about events not yet observed and encourages the researcher to examine the consequences of these predictions. This leads to further empirical data, which may support the theory or suggest needed modifications or even rejection of the theory.

Mandler and Kessen (1959) suggested that theory also performs an anticipatory function. It indicates the kinds of events that the individual may expect to occur under specified conditions, even if those conditions have not been encountered before. This function can be valuable not only for everyday behavior, but also in guiding the experimentation of the researcher. In a sense, we may say that theory provides a bridge to something "out there" and thus makes our world seem more logical, reasonable, and organized.

Not all theories, of course, are equally effective in fulfilling these functions. Kuhn (1970) argued that only those theories that share two essential characteristics contribute significantly to the advancement of science. First, the achievement of the theory must be sufficiently great to attract a group of adherents, and, second, the theory must be sufficiently open-ended that many problems remain to be solved. Such theories were labeled *paradigms*.[1] Thus to be accepted as a paradigm (and therefore contribute to the advancement of science), a theory must seem better than other theories that purport to explain the same phenomena, but it need not explain all aspects of the phenomena under consideration. Without a paradigm or a candidate for a paradigm, "normal science" does not advance. All facts concerning a particular phenomenon or set of phenomena will appear to be equally relevant and fact gathering is likely to be random activity. The existence of a paradigm identifies problems to be solved; commitment of a group of scientists to a paradigm ensures that concentrated efforts can be directed toward the solution of those problems.

Kinds of Theories

As Marx and Hillix (1963) have pointed out, theories may differ in a variety of ways. Obviously, they differ in regard to subject matter (some deal with leadership, others with attitude change, etc.), generality, precision, rigor of

---

[1] In a later work, Kuhn (1974) concluded that his original usage of paradigm included two distinct concepts: *disciplinary matrixes* and *exemplars*. A disciplinary matrix includes all those shared commitments of a scientific group; an exemplar is a concrete problem solution.

prediction, and origins of postulates (empirical versus rational). But theories also differ in other respects that are perhaps more basic than these. Einstein (1934) distinguished between *constructive* and *principle theories.* Constructive theories attempt to build up a map of more-complex phenomena from the materials of a relatively simple scheme which constitutes the starting point. Principle theories, on the other hand, use the analytic method. The starting point of such theories is a set of empirical data, rather than hypothethically constructed elements, as in the constructive method. The advantages of the constructive method were said to be clarity, completeness, and adaptability; those of principle theories were held to be logical perfection and a secure foundation. Heider's (1946) p-o-x theory (see Chapter 8) is an example of a constructive theory in social psychology, whereas Bandura's (1966) theory of imitation is an example of a principle theory (see Chapter 3).

A somewhat similar classification, reductive versus constructive, was referred to by Marx (1951). *Reductive theories* attempt to explain phenomena by appealing to lower levels of analysis. For example, the theorist may attempt to explain social motivations in terms of physiological needs. *Constructive theories* take the reverse approach; they attempt to explain phenomena by appealing to higher levels of abstraction. This distinction is not very useful for the explication of social theories.

Kaplan (1964) considered several classifications; however, he appeared to prefer the classification which distinguishes between *concatenated* and *hierarchical theories.* This classification is similar to Einstein's distinction between constructive and principle theories. A concatenated theory is one whose component propositions (laws) form a network of relations which constitutes an identifiable pattern. Each proposition typically converges on some central point, and specifies one of the factors which plays a part in the phenomenon that the theory is supposed to explain. In the usual case, a concatenated theory consists of tendency statements that are meaningful only in their joint application. Fiedler's (1964) contingency model of leadership effectiveness (see Chapter 13) is an example of a concatenated theory in social psychology. A hierarchical theory is one whose component propositions are deduced from a set of basic principles. A proposition is explained by showing that it is a logical consequence of the set of principles. Similarly, a phenomenon is explained if it can be shown to follow from the principles, given a set of specified initial conditions. In its ideal form a hierarchical theory consists of (1) a calculus whose sentences contain names and meanings for the theoretical entities being considered, (2) a set of definitions couched in observational terms, and (3) an interpretative model that specifies the conditions under which the postulates of the calculus are true. There is probably no theory in social psychology that meets the requirements of an ideal hierarchical model, but French's (1956) theory of social power (see Chapter 5) fits the general class.

The types of theories that we have considered so far are based upon the form of the theory. It is also possible to classify theories on the basis of content. Kaplan (1964) noted that every theory demarcates an explanatory shell for the phenomena with which it deals. This shell contains all that is necessary and sufficient to explain the phenomena, according to the theory. The classification of theories as *molar* or *molecular* is based on the radius of the explanatory shell. In psychology, a molar theory might refer to the person as a whole, whereas a molecular theory might consider neural connections within the organism. In social psychology, theories referring to group phenomena, such as those described in Chapter 13, might be considered molar theories; consistency theories (described in Chapter 8) are molecular theories.

The molar-molecular classification is sometimes confused with the *field theory* versus *monadic theory* dichotomy (Kaplan, 1964). A field theory explains the phenomena under consideration in terms of relations among certain elements, whereas a monadic theory explains by reference to the elements (or attributes of the elements) which are related. Either type of theory may be either molar or molecular, since the distinction depends upon what propositions say about phenomena rather than upon the range of the theory, that is, upon what the propositions are about.

Levels of Analysis

The question of kind of theory is often confused with the notion of level of analysis, which in turn is used with a variety of meanings. In social psychology, level of analysis often refers to the unit of analysis. For example, Krech and Crutchfield (1948) identified three levels of analysis: the individual level, the level of individual behavior in groups, and the level of group and institutional behavior.

When the level concept is applied to theories, it may also refer to a variety of characteristics. Kaplan (1964) noted at least five different meanings of the term:

1 Level may refer to the *range* of the theory; that is, the degree to which it applies to a specific class of subjects or to persons in general.

2 It may refer to the *scope* of the theory; that is, to the number of different kinds of behaviors that the theory attempts to explain. In general, theories may vary in scope from grandiose schemes that we have labeled "orientations," to Merton's "theories of the middle range," to "minitheories" or promising hypotheses.

3 The level of a theory may refer to its *abstractness*. This aspect involves the length of the reduction chain connecting theoretical terms with observable ones. In psychology this would probably refer to the number of intervening variables in the system.

4 A fourth use of the levels concept refers to the *length of the deductions* in the theory; that is, the steps between its first principles and the laws in which it finds application. Kaplan cited the difference between miniature theories of psychology and the usual sociological theory as an example. (There appears to be a close connection between abstractness and length of the deductions of a theory, although the two aspects are conceptually independent.)

5 Level of a theory may refer to the *radius of its explanatory shell;* the smaller the radius, the higher the level of the theory. Thus molecular theories are said to be of a higher level than molar theories.

When a theory is referred to as being of a higher or lower level, there is often the implication of value. A higher-level theory is somehow regarded as "better" than a lower-level theory. It should be clear from our brief consideration of the various meanings of level that this implication of value is not justified. The level of the theory, by any definition, has nothing to do with its scientific standing. In the next section we consider some of the characteristics of a theory which *are* relevant to its standing.

Characteristics of a Good Theory

The question of what constitutes a "good" theory quickly resolves to the problem of validation. On what bases is a theory acceptable to members of the scientific community? Frank (1957) asserted that a system of propositions is acceptable as a theory if the system is logically correct and its conclusions agree with observable facts. In his view, these two criteria are generally acceptable to scientists. Kaplan (1964), however, suggested that more-extensive criteria should be considered. His criteria for the validation of theories included (1) norms of correspondence, (2) norms of coherence, and (3) pragmatic norms. Norms of correspondence refer to the degree to which a theory fits the facts. A theory is acceptable to the extent that its predictions agree with what is already known and/or can be verified by future observations. Norms of coherence involve several aspects of the theory. First, the theory should fit in with the body of theory that is already established. That is, theories that are wholly self-contained cannot be validated. A second aspect of coherence is that of simplicity, which is internal to the theory itself. Kaplan distinguished between descriptive simplicity and inductive simplicity. Descriptive simplicity refers to the description itself, whereas inductive simplicity refers to the thing being described. Although descriptive simplicity may be an important criterion of acceptability, inductive simplicity is of greater significance since it deals with the manageability of the theory. Finally, norms of coherence may include the esthetic aspect of the theory; some theories provide more intrinsic pleasure from contemplation than others. The pragmatic norm deals with the question of what the theory can do for science. A theory is acceptable to the extent that it serves our scientific purposes.

For our purposes, it is helpful to classify characteristics of a "good" theory into two broad classes: (1) characteristics that are *necessary* if the theory is to be accepted and (2) characteristics that are *desirable* but not essential to acceptance. The first category consists of three criteria, including the two criteria suggested by Frank (logical consistency and agreement with known data) and a third one that seems equally important: testability. The first criterion merely points to the fact that a theory must be internally consistent. The various propositions in the theory must not be inconsistent or contradictory. Incompatible predictions from the same theory are untenable. The second characteristic means that the predictions of the theory agree with known facts and future observations; that is, observations made subsequent to the formulation of the theory. A theory that is supported only by data that were available at the time the theory was promulgated may be said to have low antecedent probability of being true. This conclusion is based upon the fact that the theory itself is designed to fit the data; the fact that the theorist has been successful in this endeavor says little about its predictive power. The third criterion, testability, may seem to be a property that is inherent in the "agreement with known data" requirement; however, it is possible for a theory to fit all known data and yet be untestable. For example, the psychoanalytic notion of repression, in its crudest form at least, is not testable, although it agrees with observations: if a traumatic experience is not recalled, it is repressed; if it is recalled, of course it could not have been repressed! Therefore, both recall and failure to recall agree with the theory; there is no behavior that is *not* in agreement with the theory. For a theory to be testable it must be capable of being refuted. A theory can never be "proved," since this would require observation of all possible instances of the phenomenon, an obviously impossible requirement. Instead, the validity of a theory is more or less probable depending upon the amount of evidence supporting it. On the other hand, a theory can be disproved. One unequivocal negative instance is sufficient to refute a theory, although in practice such an instance seldom occurs. Most commonly, data that do not fit the theory lead the researcher to review his procedures to determine whether the instance is in fact a negative one. Rarely, if ever, does the review indicate clearly that the theory is invalid; instead, it may suggest revision of reserach procedures or revision of the theory. However, several equivocal negative instances may call for rejection of the theory.

In addition to these characteristics necessary to an acceptable theory, there are several other characteristics that are desirable. Each of the following should be qualified by the "other things being equal" caveat.

First, a good theory should be as simple as possible, both in terms of description and deduction. Its propositions, corollaries, and hypotheses should be stated in clearly understandable terms so that it is easily communicable to others in the field. The derivation of predictions should be straightforward and unequivocal. After reading some of the theories described in this book, you may decide that most theories in social psychology do not have this desirable characteristic.

Second, a theory should be economical in that it explains the phenomena in question with as few principles as possible. While Occam's razor and Morgan's canon may be passé, it is still true that a theory that accounts for a given phenomenon with a few propositions is preferable to a theory that requires a greater number.

Third, a good theory should be consistent with related theories that have high probability of being true. The fact that a theory is inconsistent with related acceptable theories does not necessarily mean that it is invalid, but it does reduce the antecedent probability that it is true. Conversely, integration into the body of established theory increases the probability that the theory is a valid explanation of the phenomena under consideration.

Fourth, an acceptable theory should be readily interpretable in the sense that it provides a bridge to something in the real world. A theory that is difficult to relate to observable phenomena is not likely to contribute much to either science or everyday living.

Finally, a good theory should serve a useful purpose, not only in the sense that it explains what it is supposed to explain, but also in relation to the advancement of science. In other words, a good theory provides the basis for research. It stimulates and guides scientists in their efforts to understand their world.

PROBLEMS OF THEORY CONSTRUCTION IN SOCIAL PSYCHOLOGY

If social psychologists have been late comers in the business of theory development, it has been because, at least in part, of problems related to the criteria for acceptance of a theory. The major problems faced by the theorist in social psychology are those related to definitions, reliability of data, scope of the theory, and kind of theory.

Definitions

It is obvious that the terms used in theory construction must be precisely defined; unfortunately, the terms used in social psychological theories often do not meet this requirement. Basically, a definition provides a set of terms which is synonymous with the term defined so that they can be used interchangeably (Kaplan, 1964). The set of terms in the definition must be precise enough so that the meaning of the term is clear; that is, different persons will interpret it in the same way. Some definitions are merely nominal in that one term is substituted for another, as in a notation system; for example, "Let X stand for the individual group member's report of personal satisfaction with the group process." But for the most part, theory requires "real" definitions (Hempel, 1952). These definitions state the essential nature or attributes of some entity or theoretical construct. Precisely this type of definition is least adequate in social psychology.

At some point in theory development the theorist formulates concepts concerning the phenomena under consideration. Some term is needed for labeling each concept so that it can be referred to conveniently. In selecting this label, the theorist may choose a term from ordinary language or coin a new term to fit the specific concept. In either case, there are problems of definition and usage. If a term is chosen from the common language, the definition must not only specify the entity or entities to which the term refers as a scientific concept but must also eliminate the surplus meaning that derives from the common language. If a new term is coined, it gives the impression of being esoteric, requires a special definition, and cannot be as easily remembered and communicated as a more familiar term.

Although this kind of definitional problem may be more common in social psychology than in other disciplines, it is by no means unique to social-psychological theories. One attempt to overcome the vagueness of theoretical terms is the use of operational definitions (Bridgman, 1927). The basic notion is that a concept is synonymous with the operations that are necessary for its measurement and manipulation. For example, an operational definition of "leadership" might be the number of votes cast in an election of a leader. The main difficulty of the operational definition, as applied in social psychology, is that the operations are usually not coextensive with the conceptual definition of the term. That is, the theorist usually has a concept in mind that has a certain meaning for him or her. Operations are then devised that the theorist believes will measure the concept. These operations constitute the definition of the concept. Unfortunately, the theorist may also devise other operations that he or she believes will also measure the concept. Thus, the same concept may have two or more operational definitions and, presumably, two or more meanings. Obviously this can lead to confusion. It may be properly objected that this use of the operational definition is at variance with Bridgman's thesis, but this fact does not improve definitions in theories of social psychology.

To the extent that terms are not unambiguously defined, it is difficult to evaluate a theory in terms of internal consistency, agreement with data, and testability. For example, the theory may be internally consistent if a given term is defined in one way but inconsistent if it has another meaning. Adequate definitions would do much to improve theories in social psychology.

Reliability of Data

The problem of the reliability of data is a critical one for the construction of theory in social psychology. The degree to which the theorist relies upon empirical data in the initial formulation of the theory varies from relative independence to complete dependence. It is obvious that the quality of the theory is directly related to the reliability of the data upon which it is based. Data reliability also enters into the process of theory evaluation. The success achieved in determining the degree to which the theory "fits the facts" and in subsequent testing of the theory is very much dependent upon the reliability of data.

Problems of reliability of data arise in social psychology in several instances. In the first place, there is the problem of measurement. To obtain data at all, it is necessary to measure the stimulus and response variables in the social situation. Unfortunately, measurement in social psychology is not as reliable as physical measurement; the researcher and theorist must rely upon less than completely reliable measuring instruments, at least in many instances. For example, formal techniques for the measurement of attitudes have existed for more than fifty years, but the average reliability of attitude scales is on the order of .75 (Shaw & Wright, 1967). Other measuring instruments in social psychology suffer a similar deficiency in reliability.

Most data relative to social theories derive from experimentation, and there are numerous problems of reliability associated with this source of data. The quality of the data obtained from experimentation is a direct function of the adequacy of the experimental design. The ingenuity of the investigator in designing a study that tests the implications of a theory is thus an important determinant of the reliability of the data. The inexactness of experimental procedures is revealed by the low probability that a given experimental finding can be replicated and by the fact that negative results seldom lead to hypothesis rejection. As we indicated earlier, negative results usually lead first to a reconsideration of experimental procedures; it is generally easy to identify sufficient inadequacies in the experimental design to permit retention of the theory.

Another aspect of experimentation is the problem of experimental control. The control and manipulation of variables is of course basic to experimentation. Social behavior is so complex and influenced by so many variables that the problem of control becomes acute. At best, the experimenter is able to control the major known variables influencing the phenomenon in question; control of other variables hinges upon the adequacy of randomization. Effects of unwanted variables almost inevitably contaminate experimental results from social psychological studies.

One kind of unwanted variable is that of the experimenter himself. Orne (1962) and Rosenthal (1966) have demonstrated bias that is often introduced into the experiment by the investigator. The experimenter apparently communicates some of his or her expectations to the subject, often in subtle, difficult-to-identify ways. Such biases reportedly enter into experimental results even when data are collected by an assistant who is unaware of the purpose of the experiment. Although there is still some question regarding the extent of such effects, it is nevertheless true that experimenter biases sometimes do influence results. This source of error in data certainly creates a problem in the development and testing of theories (Silverman, 1977).

Scope of the Theory

The social psychologist who aspires to theoretical greatness is faced with still another set of problems, those related to the scope of the theory: *comprehensiveness, restrictiveness,* and *generality.* Comprehensiveness refers to the range of phenomena which the theory will account for and/or the range of persons to which it applies. Restrictiveness refers to the qualifications that must be appended to the propositions or hypotheses included in the theory; that is, the limitations of the theoretical principles. Generality refers to the degree to which the theory can be extended to include situations and events not specifically included in the phenomena that the theory is supposed to explain. These aspects of a theory are of course interrelated. In general, the more comprehensive, the less restrictive, and the more general the theory, the more useful the theory is likely to be. However, the theorist must take care that attempts in this direction do not lead to overgenerality. The danger is that the theory will become so all-inclusive that it explains everything and nothing. That is, a theory that is so general that it can explain anything that happens cannot be very predictive and contributes little to our understanding of the phenomena of interest. The theorist's task is to construct the theory in such a way that it includes as much as can be adequately handled by the set of theoretical principles, but restrictive enough that it does not suffer from overgenerality. The theory of cognitive dissonance (Festinger, 1957) is an example of a theory that was overgeneralized in its initial form; one of the major contributions of research and theory over the past several years has been the restriction of this theory to more-limited situations (see Chapter 8).

The Problem of Kind of Theory

The theorist must make a number of initial decisions about the theory before construction can begin. In fact, at some point decisions must be made concerning the set of phenomena that the theory will try to explain (i.e., the scope of the theory) and that the form of explanation will be a theory rather than a model. It will be recalled that a theory purports to say something about the real world. A model, on the other hand, postulates a system that represents the kind of situation that might exist, but it does not necessarily reflect what is "out there." A model describes the phenomena in "as if" terms; therefore, it demonstrates how a particular phenomenon or set of phenomena *could* occur but not necessarily how it *does* occur.

Once the decision has been made to construct a theory, the theorist still must decide what kind of theory: concatenated or hierarchical? molar or molecular? constructive or reductive? constructive or principle? Unfortunately, there is no set of rules or principles to guide this choice. For example, if the constructive type is chosen, the theory can be expected to be clear, complete, and adaptable; if the principle type is chosen, the theory can be expected to have a secure empirical basis and should be logically sound. Of course, it is possible to achieve all these advantages with either type, but the probabilities are different. Similarly, there is no logical basis for preferring either a molar or a molecular type of theory, despite the prevalent tendency to believe that a molecular explanation is somehow more basic than a molar one. In the final analysis, it is largely a matter of personal preference which kind of theory is chosen; however, it is well to keep in mind the different consequences of this choice.

Despite the various problems associated with theory construction in social psychology, a number of useful theories have been formulated. A consideration of some of the more-prominent theories in social psychology is the purpose of this book. Most of the theories selected satisfy at least the minimal criteria for a good theory.

PLAN OF THE BOOK: AN OVERVIEW

The general purpose of this work is to present the major theories of social psychological behavior. The intent is to familiarize the student with general principles and propositions of these theories and with some of the related experimental data relevant to them. Our goal is primarily that of exposition rather than evaluation. We have tried to present and clarify the essential characteristics of each theory so that the student will be able to understand the theoretical framework, the interrelations among hypotheses, and the predictions inherent in each theory. Although evaluation is not a primary goal of the book, we have commented on some of the more-obvious strengths and weaknesses of each theory. The reader will undoubtedly be able to identify other evaluative aspects that we have neglected to mention.

We have approached the task of theory exposition by first presenting a description of the general orientation that provides the basis for the various theories being considered. The presentation of each general orientation is followed by an exposition of the several theories that have been developed within that orientation. In deciding whether a given theory derives from a given general orientation, we recognized that theories vary in the degree to which they are firmly based on the more-general system. Our classification suggests only that the particular theory is more nearly representative of the orientation to which it is assigned than to any other orientation. Despite this flexible approach, some theories could not reasonably be assigned to one of the orientations that we have outlined. These theories were grouped on other bases and presented in separate chapters.

Following this general design, Chapter 2 describes the reinforcement orientation, followed by a presentation of theories based on this orientation in Chapters 3 and 4. Chapter 3 deals with theories of imitation and Chapter 4 describes exchange theories. Chapter 5 presents the principal attributes of the field orientation and examples of the application of the approach. Theories that rely primarily on the field orientation are presented in Chapter 6. The cognitive orientation is outlined in Chapter 7, and Chapters 8 and 9 consider cognitive-consistency theories and theories of attribution, respectively. Chapter 10 is devoted to theories of social influence processes, social comparison, social judgment, impression formation, and perceived freedom. These theories also are more closely related to the cognitive orientation than to other general approaches. Chapter 11 describes the role-theory orientation, followed by a presentation of role-related theories in Chapter 12. Theories that could not reasonably be related to one of the general orientations that we have covered are given in Chapters 13 (Theories of Group Processes) and 14 (Single-Principle Perspectives Relevant to Social Psychology).

In the final chapter we attempt to evaluate the current status of theories in social psychology and to show how theories are related to research. With some trepidation, we also suggest some ways that theories and research could be improved in the future.

Part Two

The Reinforcement
Orientation

Chapter 2

The Reinforcement-Theory Orientation

The study of human and animal learning constitutes a large portion of contemporary psychology—such a large portion, in fact, that any single chapter aimed at presenting a comprehensive view of the principles of learning would be a pretentious one indeed. Therefore, in the present chapter our intent is not to present all there is to present in the area of reinforcement and learning. Many other texts specifically directed at the exposition of learning theory and research have better approached this goal of comprehensiveness (Hilgard, 1956; Kimble, 1961; Hall, 1966; Kimble, 1967; Schwartz, 1978). This chapter is directed toward the exposition of the basic principles and constructs of reinforcement theory so that they may be understood in the subsequent two chapters dealing with reinforcement theory in social psychology. The chapter does not take a unitary approach to the discussion of reinforcement theory, but rather it attempts to present several interpretations of selected reinforcement phenomena. It would be faulty to refer to the language of B. F. Skinner, Clark Hull, Kenneth Spence, or of any other single person as *the* language of reinforcement psychology. Many theorists have contributed to the conceptual framework of the reinforcement orientation.

The chapter consists of three sections. The first section is aimed at presenting a *brief* historical foundation for classical conceptions of learning and reinforcement. The second portion identifies and defines some important constructs considered in this section, such as *stimulus* and *response, drive, response strength, generalization, discrimination, reinforcement,* and *extinction.* Where relevant, several orientations, particularly those of Hull and Skinner, are brought to bear upon the identification of these constructs. The third and last section briefly considers the domains of inquiry to which reinforcement theory has been applied in social psychology.

BRIEF HISTORICAL INTRODUCTION

Observations of the efficacy of reward and punishment in the learning process were probably made quite early in human history. However, the formal beginnings of reinforcement theory occurred at the turn of this century. At that time Edward L. Thorndike (1898) and Ivan P. Pavlov (1902) made independent and similar discoveries concerning the role of reinforcement. Thorndike posited that the basis of learning was the formation of a bond between sensory input and impulses to action. He referred to the organism's propensity to emit a given response to a designated stimulus as a habit or "bond." In his early thinking, Thorndike (1913) saw S-R connections as being strengthened by practice and positive consequences and weakened by disuse and negative consequences. The effect of practice on S-R connections was referred to by Thorndike as the *law of exercise.* This law is probably the earliest formal predecessor of contemporary conceptions of the probability of response occurrence. The law of exercise states that the more frequently a given sensory input is followed by a given response, the greater the probability that the connection will be repeated.

Although Thorndike initially considered the law of exercise to be central to any S-R association, he later revised his thinking to account for the predominant role of reinforcement. His *law of effect* slightly predated Pavlov's *law of reinforcement* and held that any S-R connection gains its major strength from the consequences that follow it. If positive consequences or a satisfying state of affairs occurs as a function of the organism's response to a stimulus configuration, the organism will probably repeat that response in order to gain reward. On the other hand, if a response is followed by negative consequences or an annoying state of affairs, the organism will avoid reestablishing this same S-R bond.

Although Thorndike's system was revised by him on several occasions (1932, 1935, 1949), the substance and salience of his major propositions remained basically intact. Despite the continuing controversy that persists in learning theory concerning the nature and role of reinforcement, contemporary conceptions of reinforcement can readily be traced to Thorndike's law of effect.

While Thorndike was formulating his early principles of association, Pavlov was quite independently arriving at similar propositions. Thorndike's goals differed greatly from those of Pavlov. Thorndike was aiming at the practical application of learning principles to the educational process. Both his research and theorizing were done with this goal in mind. Pavlov, on the other hand, did not initially foresee the implications of his data and theory. He was a physiologist seeking neurological explanations for the digestive process. He was seeking a viable method for the measurement of digestive secretions. To this end, he labored to discover a technique whereby the internal process of digestive secretion might be made directly observable. His early investigations led him to the discovery of the "Pavlov pouch," which isolated digestive secretion from particles of food. Through the use of this pouch (see Kimble, 1967) and the insertion of gastric fistula in the stomach wall, Pavlov was able to measure the extent and quality of the gastric secretions of dogs. This research won him the Nobel Prize in 1904. More significantly for the fate of psychological science, his research on digestion led him to the study of salivation as an interrelated form of digestive secretion. He found that a dog would salivate at the mere sight and anticipation of food. Pavlov considered this salivary reflex to be a "psychic reflex" because of its anticipatory components.

In his 1910 book, *The Work of the Digestive Glands,* Pavlov substituted the term "conditioned reflex" for "psychic reflex" (Kimble, 1967). In this same book he stated his initial principles of conditioned reaction. Kimble (1967, p. 30) summarized these principles in the following manner:

   1   The conditioned reflex based on food can be elicited only when the dog is hungry [drive, deprivation].[1] It is not the animal's desire which is essential, however, but the availability of a strong unconditioned reflex to *reinforce* the conditioned reaction [reinforcement].
   2   Repeated elicitation of the conditioned reaction by the presentation of food led to the disappearance of the conditioned response, especially if the presentations occurred in rapid succession [extinction].
   3   This disappearance was not caused by fatigue, because allowing the animal to eat restored the reflex [spontaneous recovery].
   4   Moreover, the inhibition of one conditioned reflex did not necessarily arrest all conditioned reflexes. The inhibition of a reflex conditioned to food has little or no effect on the strength of a reflex conditioned to acid [specificity of reinforcement, discrimination].
   5   In addition to these "natural" reflexes in which the conditioned stimulus was the sight of the unconditioned stimulus, it was possible to form conditioned responses to neutral stimuli such as a tone presented simultaneously with food ["true" conditioning, secondary reinforcement, stimulus substitution].
   6   Sometimes the elicitation of a strong reflex led to the inhibition of a relatively weak one. For example, a response conditioned to the sight of bread might be completely obliterated by the presence of another dog in the laboratory room [interference].

As one can see quite lucidly, Pavlov sowed the initial seeds that later germinated into some of the major constructs of reinforcement theory. Pavlov, like Thorndike, revised and supplemented his theory in many of his later works,

---

[1]Bracketed comments are the authors'.

but his early thinking and research still stand up as a revered ancestor of current reinforcement theory.

Although Pavlov's classical conditioning model was the most pervasive influence in American learning psychology in the early 1900s, the work and thought of his younger Russian contemporary, Bechterev, were more specifically psychological (Kimble, 1961). Bechterev (1908) was concerned with the establishment of an "objective" as opposed to an "introspectionist" psychology, and, to this end, the subject matter of his research was the overt, observable behavior of humans and animals. Bechterev, like Thorndike, was interested in the practical application of his findings to a wide variety of fields extending from psychiatry to social psychology. Bechterev's unique contributions to reinforcement theory were his experiments on the *instrumentality* of behavior. These included his ingenious paradigms of avoidance and escape learning, in which the organism's reinforcement was his escape from or avoidance of punishment (Bechterev, 1932). To assign Bechterev a "first" in the establishment of instrumental conditioning would indeed be a mistake. Thorndike's early work with cats in puzzle boxes definitely predates that of his Russian contemporary. However, Bechterev's clear and systematic statements on the methods of measuring the associative (conditioned) reflex make his early instrumental focus singularly important in the history of reinforcement theory.

With the establishment of Thorndike's connectionism, Pavlov's physiological orientation, and Bechterev's objectivism, the groundwork was laid for the birth of American behaviorism. At the time of the foundation of behaviorism in American psychology, it was literally a science in search of a method. The analysis of consciousness by introspectionist techniques had become stale and unproductive. John B. Watson (1913), virtually reiterating the statements of Bechterev, wrote that the time was ripe for the establishment of an objective psychology. He vehemently criticized subjective methods as nongeneralizable and thus unscientific. In his search for a scientific methodology Watson went as far as to attempt a refutation of Thorndike's effect principle and to attribute learning phenomena to the mere habitual occurrence of S-R connections (Watson, 1914). Watson later saw reinforcement as that which serves to maintain behavior *learned* by a mere contiguous relationship between stimulus and response and continued exercise of that relationship by the organism.

According to Hilgard (1956), Watson was concerned with eliminating the residual subjectivity of such concepts as "satisfiers" and "annoyers." In addition to capitalizing upon Thorndike's law of exercise, Watson also emulated both the physiological approach of Pavlov and the concern with objectivity that Bechterev voiced. Thus, American behaviorism was born through the coalescence of the three aforementioned basic approaches to conditioning and reinforcement. Watson (1919) seized upon the conditioned reflex as *the* paradigm and prototype of all learning. Since his concern for objectivity was paramount, his units of measurement were generally muscular movements, glandular secretions, and the responses which ensue from them (Hilgard, 1956). Although he did maintain that there was organismic intervention between stimulus and response, he saw these intervening events as miniature, covert, stimulus-response connections. Furthermore, Watson maintained that eventually as more-refined measurement procedures were devised, these internal intervening states would be directly observable and measureable (for example, movement of tongue during thinking) (Hilgard, 1956).

Although Watson's brand of behaviorism was not earthshaking in its originality, it reflected the tenor of the times in American psychology after its unsuccessful introspectionist era. As such, it provided the impetus for the development of various approaches to the study of the functional aspects of behavior, especially learning and reinforcement.

Four major theoretical positions grew out of Watson's "behavioristic revolution." These four positions are represented by the theories of Tolman, Guthrie, Hull, and Skinner. Both Tolman's (1932) and Guthrie's (1935) theories were essentially nonreinforcement approaches to learning. Tolman saw reinforcement as facilitating performance and not learning. He demonstrated this point in his latent-learning experiments (Tolman & Honzik, 1930). The mere exposure of a rat to a stimulus configuration led to its learning the elements of that configuration; the introduction of reinforcement activated this learning into the performance of a specified task. Tolman's theory has been referred to as an S-S theory because he conceived of learning as occurring with the organism's integration of environmentally contiguous stimuli (signs). In addition to serving as a devil's advocate to conventional reinforcement theories, Tolman's theory has served as the intellectual predecessor of current cognitive theory.

Guthrie viewed reinforcement similarly to Watson. He saw it as maintaining behaviors learned under the contiguous association of stimulus and response. Furthermore, Guthrie's position was that learning fully occurs on the basis of one-trial contiguous association. In complex behavior, such as social behavior, Guthrie postulated that each simple contiguous association within the complex net is learned in a single trial, and thus the illusion of incremental learning is created by considering only the beginning and final elements (S-R) of complex sequences.

Although the theories of both Guthrie and Tolman yielded much research and controversy in the area of learning theory during the thirties, forties, and fifties, they exist today only in their amalgamation into two general reinforcement approaches. Most contemporary approaches to the problems of learning and reinforcement may be classified as belonging to one or the other of these two general approaches. The first of these is the operant orientation articulated by B. F. Skinner. The second, the mediational orientation, was first extensively outlined by Clark Hull and subsequently revised by Spence, Miller, Mowrer, and their students.

Skinner's orientation is fundamentally based on the direct observation of the frequency of a designated behavior as a function of the reinforcement which is a consequence of that behavior. He deemphasized the teleological basis for increases and decreases in a given behavior by deemphasizing the role of unobservable, "internal" processes. Hull and the mediationists, on the other hand, constructed an elaborate system of postulates and theorems to explain the organism's internal states that lead to variations in the quality or quantity of respondent or operant behavior.

These two current viewpoints will not be elaborated upon here. Instead, they will be linked to our discussions of constructs and reinforcement applications to social phenomena to be presented in the subsequent sections of this chapter.

TERMS AND CONSTRUCTS

The following discussion of reinforcement constructs is directed at providing the reader with an understanding of contemporary conceptions of some basic principles of learning. We do not pretend to cover all the terms that are in any way relevant to reinforcement theory. Rather, we hope to acquaint the uninitiated reader with those terms that provide an adequate basis for our discussion of the social reinforcement theories presented in Chapters 3 and 4.

Stimulus and Response

Kimble (1961) defines a *stimulus* as an external or internal event that occasions an alteration in the behavior of the organism. The alteration in the behavior of the organism is termed a *response*. The stimulus and response taken together constitute the basic bond of all learning, the reflex.

Advocates of a Skinnerian approach to learning would essentially agree with Kimble's definition of a stimulus with one qualification. This qualification is that whether the event referred to as a stimulus be internal or external, it must in all cases be physical or material. Furthermore, they would maintain that for a stimulus to be relevant to the scientist it must be observable and manipulable. Thus, although Skinnerians might concede that "internal" stimuli exist, they usually do not view them as appropriate to the analysis of behavior.

Keller and Schoenfeld (1950), representing the Skinnerian point of view, see stimuli as serving three functions:

1 *Elicitation:* an eliciting stimulus is a part or change in a part of the environment which elicits a specified (almost built-in) response, generally referred to as an unconditioned response. An example of an eliciting stimulus might be the sight of food; an example of the response it elicits might be salivation.

2 *Discrimination:* a discriminative stimulus is one that does not elicit the conditioned response directly but sets the occasion for its occurrence. When present, a discriminative stimulus signals the organism to respond to the eliciting stimulus.

3 *Reinforcement:* reinforcing stimuli are those stimuli that occur as a positive or negative consequence of a response. Thus, food might serve as a reinforcing stimulus when it is administered to a deprived animal after it performs a designated response.

For the Skinnerian, a response cannot be logically separated from its eliciting stimulus and can simply be defined as an alteration in the behavior of the organism that occurs as a function of the eliciting stimulus being presented.

The mediationist would concur with Keller and Schoenfeld's aforementioned three functions of stimuli; however, because their definition of stimuli is a much broader one, they would tend to attribute additional functions to stimuli. For them, stimuli can be external or internal, environmental or physiological and conceptual. In this context mediationists tend to bifurcate stimuli and responses into external (S, R) and internal (s, r). The internal (physiological and conceptual) stimuli and responses are the essence of mediation. Whereas a Skinnerian might abide by a strict S-R paradigm, the mediationist would probably subscribe to an S-r-s-R paradigm. The first paradigm goes no further than stating that an external environmental object or change results in a given response. The second (mediational) paradigm would hold that an external environmental object or change results in an implicit response (r) to that change, and this r then gives off implicit cues (s) that mediate the resulting external response or environmental alteration. These internal r's may be manifold. They can be drives, concepts, physiological secretions, and the like. All these r's, however, in some way alter the internal state of the organism and as such produce new but internal stimuli (s), which then lead to external responding.

In the discussion above of mediational and nonmediational views of stimuli and responses, the differences in orientation between these two reinforcement approaches become apparent. These differences as well as some relevant similarities will be emphasized in our discussion of other relevant behavioral concepts.

Drive

The first postulate in Hull's (1952) system proposes an underlying biological source for the activation of behavior sequences. Hull maintained that the need of organisms for certain specified goals (for example, food, water, sexual contact) is unlearned and based upon metabolic processes within the organism. Experimentally, one may elicit goal-oriented movement by manipulating the external conditions which serve to activate the underlying need structure. Depending upon the strength of the underlying drive energy, the experimenter may condition the organism to perform various simple and complex tasks to reach its desired goal. The speed, strength, and frequency of the performance of the specified task are utilized as indicators of the strength of drive. Correspondingly, the strength of drive can be manipulated by varying the time and/or amount of deprivation or stimulation. In the Hullian or mediational system, then, drive is a force within the organism that, when it reaches an optimum strength, activates behavior in the direction of reinforcement and hence reduction in the drive. According to the mediationists, drive is a variable which intervenes between various antecedent and consequent conditions. It differs from *need* in that need is the underlying *biological* state of the organism (and thus one of the antecedent conditions), and drive is an energizing principle which directs the organism to the alteration of that need state. Although the strength of drive often corresponds to the underlying need state, this is not always hypothesized to be the case. For example, with extreme amounts of water deprivation the animal approaches death; hence his level of available energy drops and this drop leads to a decrement in drive, but physiological *need* for water remains maximal.

Dollard and Miller (1950) have a view of drive very similar to Hull's. They define drives as strong stimuli that impel action. In their analysis, the strong stimulus is the antecedent condition, the impulse to action (drive) is the intervening condition, and the action and ensuing reinforcement (reduction in drive) the consequent conditions. Dollard and Miller maintain that *any* stimulus, when increased in strength, may result in a drive. However, they divide drive into two basic kinds: (1) primary or innate drives and secondary or learned drives. They note that although any stimulus may become strong enough to act as a drive, *primary* or *innate drives* are special classes of stimuli that are the primary basis for motivation. Examples of these primary drives are hunger, pain, thirst, and sex. The strength of these drives varies with the intensity of deprivation or exposure (in the case of drives to avoid a given noxious stimulus). According to Dollard and Miller, *secondary drives* are derived from socially inhibited primary drives. Examples of secondary drives are drives toward monetary rewards, verbal rewards, specific food objects, etc. These socially learned secondary drives do not directly result from concomitant biological needs but nevertheless play the same role as primary drives in impelling the organism to act in a way to reduce the strength of the drive. Furthermore, secondary drives often become socially acceptable alternatives to tabooed primary drives, and as such they serve to reduce the strength of the inhibited primary drive by mere association.

Mowrer, Spence, Osgood, and other noted mediational theorists have views of drives that do not differ essentially in orientation from Hull's and Dollard and Miller's. In summary, then, the mediationists see drive as having energizing and directive functions. It is biologically based and, depending on its strength, impels the organism to move toward drive-reducing reinforcement. Drive is something within the organism that is experimentally manipulated from without by deprivation or noxious exposure. Furthermore, secondary or learned drives can become impulses toward action through their association with primary biologically based drives. Almost all social motivation is attributed to secondary drives.

Keller and Schoenfeld (1950), as spokesmen for the Skinnerian approach, consistently note that drive is a term (not a state) that can be used to describe the animal's strength of response after certain experimental operations (deprivation or stimulation). The most-meaningful differences between the Skinnerian and mediational definitions of drives can be extracted from Keller and Schoenfeld's statements of what a drive is not. They note the following points:

1 A drive is not a stimulus. They feel that drives have neither the status nor functions of stimuli. "It is not a part or change in a part of the environment; it is not, in itself, either eliciting, reinforcing or discriminative; and it is not correlated with a single response to give us our behavioral unit, a reflex" (p. 276). They maintain that equating a drive with a stimulus is confusing the effect of the stimulus with the stimulus itself.

2 A drive is not a response. Although a drive is established by the operations of deprivation and stimulation, it is not in any sense a response to these operations, for it does not follow the same course of strengthening or weakening that a response like bar pressing might.

3 A drive is not a physiological concept. Keller and Schoenfeld maintained that drive-directed behavior can be observed and defined without referring to underlying physiological states which impel the organism to act. For them, the operations used to establish drive define it, and the response which ensues defines its strength. They feel that the most-glaring disadvantage of treating drive as a physiological state is the tendency it fosters of assuming that something physiological intervenes between the establishing operation and the reflex changes (response).

4 A drive is not pleasure directed:

> Hedonic philosophies do not stick close to the facts of behavior in ascribing an objective existence to pleasure, and stressing the procurement of pleasure *per se* as a motive or the purpose of all motives. We do not deprive an organism of pleasure, but of food; we do not reduce hunger with pleasure, but with food, and the purpose of the organism is irrelevant to either deprivation or starvation (p. 278).

In the statement above, Keller and Schoenfeld indicate that the result of food reward is food reward itself. Furthermore, since one cannot specify what changes go on within the animal because it has been rewarded for a given response, then theorizing about these results is both a blind and unscientific practice.

In summary, the Skinnerians conceive of drive merely as a term to express the relationship between some antecedent operations of the experimenter (deprivation or overstimulation) and the strength of the organism's resulting response. On the basis of this conception of drive, Skinnerians have uniformly held that a separate category for secondary or social drives is irrelevant. They believe that some "drives" which have been labeled as social are not specifiable as drives at all (for example, mastery) because the establishing operations cannot be specified. Those "secondary" or "social" drives for which establishing operations can be specified are in no way different from "primary" drives to the Skinnerian.

Response Strength

Measures of the strength or vigor of responses are as plentiful as the universe of possible responses. General categories of measures that have been frequently used as indicators of strength of response include (1) rate or latency measures, (2) measures of magnitude, and (3) probability measures (Hall, 1966). These measures are generally found to vary as a function of (1) the antecedent conditions (amount of deprivation or stimulation, stimulus-presentation variables, etc.) and (2) former practice with the response under conditions of reinforcement. As with drive, there is overall agreement between mediational and nonmediational theorists on the operations necessary to increase the strength of response and on appropriate measures of response strength. Furthermore, there is general agreement that the antecedent operations and the ensuing strength of response when evaluated conjointly serve as indicators of drive. For example, if 24 hours of water deprivation leads an animal to respond more vigorously to a stimulus configuration than two hours of deprivation, the interpretation would be made that increased deprivation established heightened drive. The strength of the ensuing response indicates the success of this establishing operation. This is a first-order interpretation from the data and, as such, would be accepted by mediationists and nonmediationists alike.

Mediationists, however, would tend to go beyond the observable data and make second- and third-order interpretations. Thus, a complete discussion of response strength would necessitate a discussion of concepts such as "habit strength," "reaction potential," and "incentive motivation." One of Hull's (1952) basic postulates stated that an organism's tendency to react to a stimulus is a function of the multiplicative relationship between strength of habit and strength of drive (Hull, 1952). Operationally, habit strength (associative strength) increases through the continued pairing of a stimulus with a reinforced response. Nevertheless, habit strength, like drive, is postulated to be a phenomenon internal to the organism. In Hull's theory, then, the probability that a response will occur is dependent upon the interaction of two inferred states of the organism (habit and drive).

Although specific explanatory concepts such as "habit strength" are not as crucial to the mediationist approach now as they were in the mid-1950s, the mediational orientation remains basically the same. That is, to explain constructs and measures such as drive and response strength, reference must be made to the internal processes (physiologic or "psychic") of the organism. The organism is at all times seen as a participant in his own learning, and, if, for example, its response is significantly stronger on trial 2 than on trial 1, the assumption is made that as a function of experiencing trial 1, the organism has undergone some qualitative or quantitative internal change prior to trial 2.

Nonmediationists resist this teleological orientation and stick close to their operations in defining measures such as response strength and response probability. For them, the probability that a response will occur is a function of the number of times it has occurred in the past under conditions of reinforcement. The strength of a response in terms of rate, latency, or magnitude measures is considered by Skinnerians to vary as a function of the antecedent establishing operations and not the underlying propensities of the organism.

Generalization

The discovery of the principle of stimulus generalization has generally been attributed to Pavlov (Keller & Schoenfeld, 1950; Hilgard, 1956; Hall, 1966). In brief, generalization is that process whereby a novel stimulus evokes a response which had been previously learned to a separate but similar stimulus. Generalization is an important explanatory concept in learning theory because it makes plausible the proposition that all behavior can be defined and modified on the basis of learning principles. If each S-R bond were to be learned discretely, then it would be illogical to attribute the acquisition of complex repertoires to learning. The rapidity with which a child acquires linguistic responses is a case in point. If each word and structure in language were learned through single S-R connections, it would take an infinite amount of time to learn language and its usage. The child accomplishes the bulk of language learning in three years (age three to five years). Thus, if the learning theorist is to propose an explanation for the child's rapid language growth, he needs an economizing construct, such as generalization, as an explanatory base.

There have been many experimental demonstrations of stimulus generalization with many species (Watson & Rayner, 1920; Anrep, 1923; Bass & Hull, 1934; Hovland, 1937; Guttman & Kalish, 1956; Perkins & Weyant, 1958; Thomas & Lopez, 1962; McAllister & McAllister, 1963). These studies have shown that generalization is a replicable phenomenon with human and animal subjects using verbal, visual, or tactile stimuli and either classical or instrumental paradigms.

According to Hall (1966), a number of points of view have been taken in interpreting stimulus generalization. He notes that the least-controversial point of view is the one taken by Brown, Bilodeau, and Baron (1951). They discuss generalization simply as an empirical phenomenon that is manifested by a transfer of training situation. Thus, a learned response to stimulus A will transfer to a previously neutral stimulus B under certain conditions (for example, similarity of the stimuli, instructional set).

Lashley and Wade (1946) proposed that generalization results from the organism's failure to discriminate between stimuli. Thus, they see generalization not as a process but as the failure of a process (discrimination). Hull, on the other hand, took the position that generalization is an organismic *process* in which the learning of a given response takes place to a "zone" of stimuli. Those stimuli closest to the one (S_1) to which the response (R_1) was conditioned have the strongest tendency to also evoke R_1. Those stimuli outside of the zone cannot evoke R_1. This concept of "stimulus zone" has been more frequently referred to as a *generalization gradient*. Simply stated, a gradient of generalization is based on the similarities in the cue properties of stimuli; the less similar the cue pattern, the less the generalization (Miller & Dollard, 1941). Both Hull (1943) and Miller and Dollard (1941), proceeding from a Darwinian framework, imply that stimulus generalization is functional to the survival of the organism and thus is dependent on *innate* organismic processes. Furthermore, Hullians dispute

Lashley and Wade's proposition that generalization is merely the failure to make discriminations. The studies of Hovland (1937), Bass and Hull (1934), and Brown, Bilodeau, and Baron (1951) indicate that subjects can discriminate accurately between stimuli toward which they have shown a generalized response. Razran (1949) amalgamated the positions of the Hullians and Lashley and Wade by proposing a two-process theory of generalization. The first of these processes was referred to as a pseudogeneralization or, simply, apparent generalization due to the failure to discriminate. The second process Razran termed "true generalization" or the organism's capacity to engage in the active process of generalizing stimuli.

The Skinnerian view of stimulus generalization is much like that of the Hullians, namely, that generalization is a functional and adaptive process that can be defined by the response characteristics of the organism. The Skinnerians construe generalization as the basis for consistency in human behavior and, in doing so, come close to agreeing with the Hullian conception of generalization as the organism's innate capacity to economize and organize its perceptions. Keller and Schoenfeld (1950, p. 116) defined generalization as the process in which "an increase or decrease in the strength of one reflex, through reinforcement or extinction, is accompanied by a similar but smaller increase or decrease in the strength of other reflexes that have stimulus properties in common with the first." They, like the mediationists, define "common stimulus properties" in terms of the similarity and contiguity of the cue components of two or more stimuli.

The question arises whether stimulus generalization can occur with two or more stimuli that do not have common stimulus properties. This question is particularly relevant to verbal and social stimuli where the *physical* cue properties of objects similar on other than physical dimensions are very dissimilar. For example, the words *love* and *affection* have few common physical elements (for example, length of word, constellation of letters, common letters); nevertheless both verbally and socially, they often elicit similar responses. Words such as *love* and *affection* are similar predominantly with regard to meaning, and, as such, a generalized response to both presupposes that "internal reference" is made to their meaning components. This concept of *mediated generalization* is a very important one with regard to verbal or social learning. Mediated generalization occurs to stimuli for which external physical properties differ, but which have meaning equivalence.

Discrimination

Keller and Schoenfeld (1950) have referred to generalization and discrimination as a "natural pair." Just as organisms learn to economize their behaviors by generalizing stimuli, they also learn to respond specifically to separate stimuli. Both processes are highly functional and adaptive for the organism. For both mediationist (Miller & Dollard, 1941) and nonmediationist (Keller & Schoenfeld, 1950) discrimination is established when a previously generalized response is rewarded in the presence of one cue (stimulus) and not rewarded in the presence of a second cue (previously generalized). In this case, the formerly generalized response will become specific to the cue situation that leads to reward and drops out to the cue situation that does not. Thus, if finger withdrawal is conditioned to a tone of 1,000 cycles per second and generalizes under conditions of reinforcement to a zone of stimuli ranging from 750 to 1,250 cycles per second, then discrimination between the 750- and 1,250-cycles-per-second tones can be established by reinforcing finger withdrawal to the 1,250-cycles-per-second tone. In this example, the 1,250-cycles-per-second tone would be referred to as the *discriminative stimulus* or the stimulus which sets the occasion for reinforcement. Discrimination becomes increasingly difficult as stimuli become increasingly similar.

In the arena of everyday living, stimuli can seldom be specified as altogether discriminative or altogether generalized. In this sense the dual learning processes of discrimination and generalization occur in complex nets as a function of social context variables. For example, a child may generalize the "stimuli" mother and aunt as females or perhaps as look-alikes. His response to both of them as females might be generalized; however, the commands of his aunt and mother will probably be discriminated and his response to each specific in its nature, latency, magnitude, and other attributes.

Varieties of Reinforcement

As noted earlier in this chapter, contemporary conceptions of reinforcement can be readily traced to Thorndike's law of effect. Theorists subsequent to Thorndike became concerned with the surplus meaning of concepts such as "satisfiers" and "annoyers," and thus the literature is replete with definitions and redefinitions of reinforcement. Nevertheless, with the exception of the nonreinforcement explanations of learning, Thorndike's description of the manner in which reinforcement functions to maintain behavior has not been substantially contested. The centrality of reinforcement to learning theory is exemplified by the inability of the present authors to discuss the principles of drive, response strength, generalization, and discrimination without making reference to the reinforcement process.

Skinnerians provide the simplest definition of reinforcement, so simple in fact that it has often been referred to as a tautology. They define *positive* reinforcers as those stimuli that serve to strengthen responses when presented (for example, food strengthens bar pressing) and *negative* reinforcers, as those stimuli which strengthen responses when removed (for example, the withdrawal of shock strengthens the avoidance of responses) (Keller & Schoenfeld, 1950). The mediationists concur with this definition of reinforcers, but they go on to explain the whys and wherefores of the response-strengthening process and thus embellish reinforcement with additional meaning. Hull (1952) theorized that reinforcement serves to strengthen responses *because* it reduces drive, satisfies need, and builds up habit tendencies. Thus, according to the mediationist, at the same time that reinforcement is resulting in observable changes in the external responses of the organism, it also functions to enforce unobservable changes in the internal states and expectations of that organism. These internal alterations function to strengthen, weaken, or eliminate the observable occurrence of the specified response on subsequent learning trials. Despite orientation or explanation, reinforcement is seen as that consequence of a response that serves to strengthen and maintain its bond to the eliciting stimulus and increase the probability of future response occurrence.

Reinforcement may take many forms varying from objects necessary for physiological survival (for example, food and water) to elements of social interaction (for example, approving nod or word). The efficacy of physical reinforcements, such as food and water, can be controlled for and predicted from the antecedent manipulations of the experimenter, such as deprivation or overexposure. In most cases, the efficacy of social reinforcements is not under the direct control of the "manipulator" but is said to be dependent upon some vague concept, such as the past social reinforcement history of the organism. Thus, a distinction can be made between reinforcement that is effective because of *controlled* antecedent conditions and reinforcement for which effectiveness is the result of *uncontrolled* antecedent conditions. It might be said that the more social a reinforcer, the less prone it is to antecedent experimental control. Dollard and Miller would probably state (1) that all uncontrolled reinforcement antecedents were established through their former association with controlled antecedents and (2) that most uncontrolled reinforcement antecedents result from secondary rather than primary drive states.

The effectiveness of reinforcement also varies as a function of the schedule of its administration. A frequently replicated finding has been that *partial reinforcement* (reinforcement which does not occur on every trial) leads to slower learning but stronger retention of a response than *total reinforcement* (Jenkins & Stanley, 1950; Grant & Schipper, 1952; Goss, Morgan, & Golin, 1959). Since very few responses receive 100-percent reinforcement in the socioenvironmental situation, most social learning occurs on a partial-reinforcement schedule. This factor is extremely relevant to the observed strong resistance to change of attitudes, values, norms, and the like.

Ferster and Skinner (1957) have articulated four kinds of partial-reinforcement schedules for experimental free-response learning situations:

1 *Fixed interval:* reinforcement is administered at some fixed period of time after a previous reinforcement. Thus, an organism on a 60-second fixed-interval schedule will receive reinforcement for the first response that occurs 60 seconds or more after the previously reinforced response.

2 *Variable interval:* reinforcement is administered at some variable period of time after a previous reinforcement. Thus, an organism on a 60-second variable-interval schedule will receive reinforcement for the first response which follows a randomly selected time interval—the average time of the intervals being 60 seconds.

3 *Fixed ratio:* reinforcement is provided after every n^{th} response. Thus, an organism might receive reinforcement on every tenth response, every twentieth response, etc. . . . in a fixed fashion.

4 *Variable ratio:* reinforcement is provided on an *average* of every n^{th} response. Thus, an organism on a 15:1 variable-interval schedule might receive reinforcement after ten responses, then five responses, then twenty responses, then ten responses, etc., to an average of one reinforcement per fifteen responses.

All the above schedules have been used and comparatively tested in experimental situations. For the purposes of this presentation, however, it is sufficient to say that the effectiveness of any one of these schedules is situationally dependent. They are merely presented here as a display of variable methods of inducing partial reinforcement effects.

Before we leave this brief discussion of reinforcement, it should be noted that reinforcement has been divided on the basis of its *primary* versus its *secondary* nature. *Primary reinforcement* is reinforcement that has been specified by the experimenter as the organism's reward for performing a designated response. Its effectiveness may be and often is controlled by the antecedent operations of the experimenter (for example, deprivation). *Secondary reinforcement* can be defined as a stimulus that has not been previously rewarding but becomes so through its association with a primary reinforcer. Secondary reinforcement has been consistently found to maintain a learned behavior after the cessation of primary reinforcement. For example, if a rat is trained to pass through a runway to reach a white goal box where he is rewarded with a food pellet, then after the removal of food he will continue to run to a white goal box for a longer period of time and at a faster rate than he will to a black goal box. In this case, the color of the goal box becomes secondarily reinforcing through its association with the primary reinforcer and thus able to elicit and maintain the designated response.

In summary then, reinforcement varies in (1) its makeup (for example, physical versus social), (2) the schedule of its administration (for example, partial versus total), and (3) its primacy (primary versus secondary). Despite which variety or combination of varieties of reinforcement is used in any specific case, the range of functions and roles of reinforcement remain the same. Although there is controversy among theorists about where in this range reinforcement rightfully belongs, at minimum reinforcement serves to maintain and strengthen the performance of an S-R connection, and at maximum it is the moving principle of all behavior.

Extinction

Extinction can be defined most simply as the progressive decrement in response tendency under conditions of nonreinforcement. Under continued conditions of extinction, a formerly learned response can drop out entirely. Complete extinction is generally not immediate but, depending upon the prior conditions of learning, will take several trials. The organism's *resistance to extinction* is often utilized as a measure of strength of response (Miller & Dollard, 1941; Keller & Schoenfeld, 1950; Hall, 1966).

The extent of this resistance has been found to be a function of several factors:

1 The amount of prior reinforcement: "Most investigators have found that resistance to extinction is an increasing function of the amount of reward obtained during the acquisition of trials" (Hall, 1966, p. 263).

2 The strength of drive during extinction: where drive level is high during extinction (for example, an animal that has been deprived of food for a long period of time) and previous performance of the task led to the relevant reward, resistance to extinction will be stronger (Perin, 1942).

3 The amount of work (effort) involved in performing the conditioned response: responses requiring much effort to perform will show less resistance to extinction than those requiring less effort (Hall, 1966).

4 The schedule with which reinforcement was administered during the learning period: as has already been stated, partial reinforcement has generally been found to be more efficacious than total reinforcement in maintaining a learned response under conditions of nonreinforcement.

The resistance of humans to the extinction of previously learned responses is an important factor in social behavior. It has important implications for the individual's resistance to attitude change, the extinction of first impressions in person perception, and similar social phenomena. According to learning theorists (Miller & Dollard, 1941; Keller & Schoenfeld, 1950), resistance to extinction in the social situation should follow the same "laws" as resistance to extinction in the experimental learning situation.

Several theoretical explanations have been invoked to explain the occurrence of extinction. The Skinnerians, as they customarily do, choose to define and explain the extinction process only in terms of their operations. Therefore, they propose that extinction occurs because positive reinforcement is removed and the organism's response becomes ineffective in the attainment of reward. Guthrie (1935) deviated somewhat further from the observable data in proposing an *interference* interpretation of extinction. He proposed that extinction occurs because when reward no longer follows the conditioned response, it leads to the organism's performance of extraneous responses that interfere with the recurrence of the conditioned response.

An *inhibition* interpretation of extinction was first proposed by Pavlov (1927) and later expanded by Hull (1943). The concept of inhibition deviates even further from the data base than interference and delves within the organism for an explanation of extinction. Pavlov saw extinction occurring because the singular presentation of the conditioned stimulus without reward leads to a central inhibitory state that prevents the conditioned response from occurring. Thus, he proposed a cortical basis for extinction. Hull, on the other hand, postulated a two-process theory of inhibition. He referred to the first process as *reactive inhibition* and the second as *conditioned inhibition*. Simply stated, reactive inhibition occurs as a negative reaction to having made a response (reinforced or not). A frequently cited reason for this negative reaction (negative drive state) has been fatigue. Conditioned inhibition occurs when enough reactive inhibition accumulates to produce a "drive to rest." When rest (cessation of responding) does occur, it serves as a reinforcer and drive reducer because reactive inhibition dissipates. Therefore, resting (nonresponding) becomes a conditioned response in its own right. In Hull's system, reactive inhibition and conditioned inhibition summate to produce the organism's total inhibitory potential. This total inhibitory potential will preclude the occurrence of the conditioned response when it exceeds the organism's reaction potential. Therefore, with the continued nonreinforcement of a previously acquired response, extinction occurs because inhibitory potential is bound to eventually exceed reaction potential.

Although there have been many studies attempting to test the relative viability of these different interpretations of extinction, the issue is still quite unresolved (Hall, 1966).

REINFORCEMENT THEORY AND SOCIAL PHENOMENA

One might argue quite cogently that the foregoing exposition of learning theory is in fact dated and unresponsive to recent transformations in the study of human and animal learning. It is certainly true that our focus in presenting the reinforcement orientation has been a classical one. We have concentrated upon important historical perspectives and the constructs and terms that issued from these perspectives.

It should be remembered that, for the purposes of describing social psychology's theories, our interest is in the general structure of explanation that is provided by different large-scale orientations in psychology. It is very rarely the case that social psychologists engage in the wholesale adoption of a particular view from within learning theory, for example, in order to explain social phenomena. Instead, the general explanatory structures of large-scale orientations are brought to bear on the explanation of those phenomena of interest to social psychologists. In simpler terms, social psychologists are not generally concerned with learning and response acquisition in their own rights, but have been typically concerned with two rather large domains which derive from the functionally based logic of the reinforcement orientation.

The first of these domains has considered the impact of social stimuli (particularly the stimuli given off by the behavior of others) on the acquisition of both social and nonsocial responses. It is clear that the reinforcement orientation holds to the basic assumption that the bulk of human behavior is *lawfully acquired* through exposure to the environment. If one adopts this basic assumption, then one must be intrigued by the observation that so many aspects of human behavioral repertoires are similar across different enactors of those repertoires. If these observed similarities are not construed to follow largely from genetic or biologic givens, then one must conclude that humans transmit norms for behavior to other humans. While one might easily define a number of methods of transmission which derive from the rather direct application of reinforcement principles (*direct teaching, control over rewards and punishments* which socializers hold over the socialized, similarities in the *instrumental adaptive* goals of humans, *generalization* of responses across contexts, etc.), it is clear that behavioral repertoires of adult humans are much too complex and intricate to be explainable by methods of direct reinforcement control alone.

As such, psychologists turned toward *imitation* as a central process in the interpersonal transmission of responses, since imitation seemed a more suitable process for the description of the wholesale adoption of contextually appropriate behavioral repertoires. Very strong hints concerning the pervasiveness of human tendencies to imitate other humans are provided by quite early thinkers such as Aristotle and systematized by turn-of-the-century social psychologists, such as Tarde (1903) and McDougall (1908). It is with the *how* and *why* of imitation that our social-psychological theories deal. How do humans "select" behaviors to be imitated? What is the role of reinforcement in the selection process? What principles of learning are essential to an understanding of imitative behavior?—these are a sampling of general questions governing the theories of imitation described in Chapter 3. It is hoped that the reader's understanding of the classic thought and ideology of the reinforcement orientation, which was presented in this chapter, will enhance his/her comprehension of the behavioral dynamics of social imitation articulated by the subsequently presented theories.

The second domain of social phenomena, which is a derivative of the reinforcement orientation, relates to the tactics and principles of *interpersonal exchange.* The law of effect and its related principles and constructs were constructed to explain how an acquired behavior, response, or habit continues to occur in an organism. In short, when the consequences of a response are positive or rewarding, the response will tend to recur in proportion to the organism's need and the value the organism puts on the contingent reward. However, when the consequences of a particular emitted response are costly, negative, and/or punishing, the response will tend not to recur. Exchange theory applies this deceptively simple principle to the solution of myriad puzzles in the domain of social behavior. For example, since many of the rewards or reinforcements available to humans are given by or available in other humans, then one might ask whether the law of effect pertains to the effects available from social others. In theory, at least, the "law of exchanged effects" might constitute a useful principle describing how and why relationships form and are maintained or terminated. It might provide us with a viable explanation of such phenomena as why we like different people to different extents, why we marry the people we do, why we stay with or quit a job, how we judge whether the prevailing consequences of a relationship or human encounter are "fair" or "unfair," etc. The molar applications of the molecular law of effect are described in Chapter 4, which exposits theories of social exchange and reciprocal reinforcement. The basis for these theories is decidedly provided by the assumptions of the reinforcement orientation, and these theories constitute pivotal examples of the social applications of the reinforcement framework.

Chapter 3

Theories of Social Learning and Imitation

Two basic contexts within which learning occurs are the *physical* and *social* contexts. The physical context simply refers to the material dimensions of the "field" of behavior. The social context moderating the learning process refers to the actual or implied presence and/or participation of "others" while learning is occurring. Social context variables have been shown to be operative with animals as well as with humans (Miller & Dollard, 1941). However, for the purposes of this presentation, we will predominantly concern ourselves with social context variables in human learning.

Social context factors in human learning are manifold, but most often they can be defined in terms of the roles of the social "others" in the learning situation and the relationship which these others bear to the learner. These social "others" vary in the degree to which they participate in the learning process of the learner. The most direct participation of another in an individual's acquisition of responses occurs in the didactic student-teacher relationship. The least direct participation occurs in the situation in which the mere presence or implied presence of a nonparticipating other results in increments in learning and performance. Allport (1924) has referred to this latter process as *social facilitation*. Between these two extremes there are many degrees of social participation that define social context. In the following two chapters, we will concern ourselves predominantly with two broad cases of social context variation in human learning. These are (1) learning through the *observation* of the behavior and consequences of the behavior of others and (2) learning through the interdependent nature of rewards for the participants. This second contextual variation will be dealt with in the next chapter.

A sizable proportion of human learning occurs through the observation of the behavior of other humans. Despite the admonition, "do as I say, not as I do," individuals and particularly children tend to use the behaviors of others as paradigms for their own behavior. This proposition has been demonstrated repeatedly in experimental situations. The classic experimental prototype of the observational learning situation involves two classes of people—the observer and the "behaver" or *model.* Generally, the model will behave in certain specified ways that do or do not lead to reward; the observer will then be placed in the same field of behavior as the model had been performing in, and measures of the degree of his/her *imitation* of the model will be taken. Two important variables in the observational learning process have been (1) the relationship that exists between the model and the observer and (2) the occurrence, amount, and quality of reinforcement that is contingent on the model's behavior. The former is generally dealt with in terms of *identification.* As this factor becomes more relevant, there is less need for direct reinforcing contingencies for imitation to occur.

Although there have been many hypotheses and paradigms of imitative behavior, only two appear to fit our criteria for theories. These two are the approaches of Miller and Dollard (1941) and of Bandura (Bandura and Walters, 1963; Bandura, 1962, 1966, 1969, 1972, 1977). Although tthe major sections of this chapter will be devoted to these two theories, the less-extensive hypotheses of Mowrer (1960) and Skinner (1953, 1957) will also be dealt with in their relationship to these theories.

A CLASSICAL THEORY OF SOCIAL LEARNING AND IMITATION

Miller and Dollard (1941) articulated a Hullian-based theory of social learning and imitation. Their principal and basic assumption is that human behavior is learned; to comprehend its complexity "one must know the psychological principles involved in its learning and the social conditions under which this learning took place" (p. 1). Although they maintained that social learning could be explained by general-learning principles, particularly those principles stated by Hull, they nevertheless considerably modified the principles of Hullian learning theory to arrive at their own theory of social learning.

By modern standards, the Miller and Dollard approach to imitation contains much surplus theorizing, predicated upon general mediational learning principles. This theory is no longer the subject of direct empirical test, but it does constitute a backdrop against which subsequent theories of imitation can be compared. Many of Miller and Dollard's observations and propositions have been embedded in modern minitheories of imitative responding. In this vein, the reader is advised to consult the careful work of Gewirtz and Stingle (Gewirtz, 1971a, 1971b; Gewirtz & Stingle, 1968) for a straightforward extension of the general propositions laid down in Miller and Dollard's classic contribution to social-learning theory. In fact, almost all the more current empirical and theoretical treatments of imitative learning, which view imitation as a special case of reinforced discrimination learning, can be traced to the seminal notions of Miller and Dollard (c.f., Sears, 1957; Baer & Sherman, 1964; Steinman, 1970). Therefore, for reasons of historic richness, we have chosen to offer a rather full account of the major tenets of Miller and Dollard's broad, original formulation of processes of imitation.

Fundamentals of Learning

The four principles that Miller and Dollard saw as being fundamental to all learning, whether individually or socially based, are *drive, cue, response,* and *reward.* These principles were seen as interrelated by Miller and Dollard. Furthermore, in reading their description of these four factors, one is struck with their interchangeability. Thus, a drive may be a cue, and a cue may become a drive or a reward; a reward may become a cue, and a drive may itself be a response. This interchangeability should be kept in mind as the reader grapples with the definitions and operations of these constructs.

Drive   In Chapter 2, we briefly discussed Miller and Dollard's conception of drive. Here we will deal with it somewhat more extensively.

Drive is defined as any strong stimulus that impels the organism to act. Miller and Dollard viewed some stimuli when aroused as being consistently strong enough to be regarded as drives. These stimuli are those that are essential to the maintenance of the organism. They are *primary* and usually innately biological, and they constitute the primary basis for motivation. Primary-drive stimuli include hunger pangs, fatigue, thirst, pain, and sexual needs. With humans in a civilized society, primary drives seldom reach the heights necessary to impel responding incontrovertibly. Miller and Dollard maintained that social organization tends to obscure the primacy of primary drives. They held that, in Western society, only extreme and purportedly atypical cases of war, famine, and poverty tend to activate biologically based drives. Therefore, proceeding from their Hullian-based assumption that drives are a necessary precedent to responding and the moving principle of behavior, they conceptualized a *secondary* category of drives that assumes the directive functions of socially obscured primary drives.

Although Miller and Dollard propose that secondary drives gain their strength through a contiguous association with primary drives, they implied that socially based acquisitions of drives are more dynamically predicated. They located the source of the evolvement of secondary drives in society's facilitation of the "sublimation" of primary needs in socially acceptable directions. When social conditions inhibit the expression of primary drives, secondary drives assume their function; and according to Miller and Dollard they become a façade behind which primary drives are hidden. Thus hunger (primary drive) may be channeled toward a specific food object (secondary-drive stimulus) and sexual needs (primary drive) toward a particular sexual object (secondary-drive stimulus).

Acquired drives are identified as synonymous to social needs and thereby are rewarded and extinguished by the aspects of the social context within which they are operative. There is no one-to-one relationship between primary and social needs, but more often a social need has several underlying primary drives. For example, money and approval as objects of social needs can stem from several primary drives, such as hunger, pain, and sex.

Miller and Dollard maintained that without either primary or secondary drives there would be no occasion for overt behavior to occur. Therefore, since they observed imitation to be an empirical fact, they found it necessary to conceptualize a *drive to imitate* as its base. Here the assumption is made that as an aspect of socialization, matching the response of others becomes a rewarded response in its own right. The more regular the reward, the more firmly established the drive to imitate becomes. Thus, in the case of imitation, (1) the behavior of another serves as a cue; (2) this cue leads to an internal response; (3) this internal response produces a drive to imitate whose strength is based upon previously rewarded imitation trials; (4) this drive to imitate activates imitative responding; (5) imitative responding leads to a reward that in turn leads to the reduction of drive and an increment in the probability that imitation will occur on succeeding trials. From this paradigm it becomes apparent that internal responses are cue produced, external responses are drive produced, increased probability of response is reward produced, and acquired drives are *response produced* (usually by internal responses). For Miller and Dollard, this holds not only for the operation of the drive to imitate but for the operation of all acquired drives.

Therefore, while the complex chain of relationships that transpire between drive, cue, response, and reward culminate in the occurrence of a given behavior, the direct antecedent for the establishment of a secondary drive is the internal response (r). This conception of acquired drives presents a dilemma with regard to imitation. Since imitation is known to occur and if its occurrence presupposes a drive to imitate and this drive to imitate is based upon an internal response, then for the *initial* occurrence of imitation to be explained it must be assumed that the internal response leading to the drive to imitate is in the repertoire of the subject before imitation ever takes place. Does this elevate the drive to imitate to a primary drive? Miller and Dollard never fully dealt with this problem. This same observation can be made concerning most acquired drives.

In a more recent treatment of a Miller and Dollard–like perspective on imitation, Gewirtz and Stingle (1968) circumvent this conceptual difficulty by directly asserting (a) that all newly imitated responses are indeed already in the repertoire of the observer and can be traced by considering past learning history and (b) that sources of *intrinsic motivation* (e.g., primary drives) are unnecessary for the recurrence of already-learned responses in an imitative context. In short, Gewirtz and Stingle discard the concept of internally based drives as a precursor of imitation. Instead they assert that it is the availability of extrinsic motivators (i.e., reinforcement) that facilitates the recurrence of learned responses in a new imitative context. Gewirtz and Stingle are not alone in their discounting of Miller and Dollard's drive-reduction-based notions. Indeed most of the current reinforcement-based approaches to imitation have taken on an operant-instrumental cast and have discarded drive concepts as a necessary mediational step (e.g., Baer & Sherman, 1964; Skinner, 1957; Waxler & Yarrow, 1970).

Cues   Cues determine when and where a response will occur and what response will be made. In Miller and Dollard's vocabulary, a cue is somewhat synonymous with the definition of discriminative stimulus presented in Chapter 2. The difference between cue stimuli and drive stimuli is a matter of strength and distinctiveness. Any stimulus may acquire drive value when it is made strong enough to impel the organism to act. Any stimulus may acquire cue value in terms of its distinctiveness from other stimuli. A cue is distinctive from another different cue in that it leads to a specific class of responses that occur in a specific locale and at a specific time. Thus, a low-intensity tone may be made to signal the occurrence of a response that is different from that signaled by a high-intensity tone. An extremely high-intensity tone may become a drive stimulus in that it impels the organism to respond in a way to discontinue its noxious effect. Miller and Dollard, then, see cues and drives as two aspects of the same phenomena, stimuli.

One of the most important classes of cues in the social learning situation is the behavior of others, whether that behavior is directed at the subject or merely occurs in his presence. Thus, the extended hand of another in a social situation serves as a cue for the extension of the individual's hand, and the response of shaking hands ensues. In this case the cue given off by the social other is a distinctive one and dictates the nature, occurrence, and timing of the respondent's behavior. In the case of imitative learning, the behavior of a model serves to introduce several cues to the observer. These cues become relevant if they are connected with a subsequently rewarded response. Upon observing the overt behavioral responses of a model to cues that lead to reward and cues that do not, the observer acquires a hierarchy of cue values operative in the behavioral field. If we extrapolate from Miller and Dollard's analysis, two types of cues seem to operate in the observational learning situation. The first type is the *response* of the model; the second, the cue properties of the behavioral field itself. It seems that it would be rather difficult to distinguish the functions of these two categories of cues in the modeling situation.

Cues, like drives, can acquire value. A relatively nondistinctive cue can acquire distinctive cue value if it evokes a response that leads to reward. It can also acquire value if it is generalized to a strong and already distinctive cue. In cases where the relevance of the relationship between observer and model is minimal, the model's behavior must acquire distinctive cue value before it occasions the imitative response of the observer.

Response   Miller and Dollard made the curious but apparently logical statement that before any response to a specific cue can be learned and rewarded, it must first occur. Thus they made the assumption that individuals possess an "innate" repertoire of responses that are not initially linked to cues. Learning occurs when a given response is rewarded in the presence of a distinctive cue. However, what is learned? If the response is already part of the subject's repertoire, it is certainly not the response that is learned but rather the bond between a specific cue and a specific response. Nevertheless, reward can increase the probability of the occurrence of a given response already in the *innate hierarchy,* and a new hierarchy of responses is produced. Miller and Dollard referred to this new hierarchy as a *resultant hierarchy.*

In this functional conception of response, Miller and Dollard attached great importance to the mechanism of trial-and-error learning. In the social context, a participating or observed social other can serve to reduce the frequency of trials and errors in the learning of cue-response connections. Thus, these theorists state that, if an observer has learned to attach appropriate responses to the cues of a model's performance (that is, if he has learned to copy), imitation can limit the occurrence of trial and error, and "correct" performance can occur after simple observation of another. Miller and Dollard ascribed a similar role to direct-teaching methods. That is, the role of a "teacher" is to limit the range of trial-and-error responding in the learner. They cite Ford (1939), who proposed that one important function of culture (society, social groups) is that it provides a storehouse of solutions to recurrent problems. Therefore, the role of society's older members is to induce its younger members to perform responses that will result in reward and avoid extraneous and unrewarding responses.

The proposition that any response emitted by the individual is innately available to him before it is learned to a specific cue pattern seems to limit Miller and Dollard's conception of novel responses. They asserted that novel behaviors result from new combinations of "old" responses. As we shall see later in this chapter, Bandura found this conception to be unsatisfactory.

Finally, it should be noted that Miller and Dollard viewed responses as being both overt and covert. In all paradigmatic cases of mediational learning, covert responding precedes overt responding, and the following paradigm is generated:

$$\text{External}$$
$$\text{Cue} \rightarrow (\text{Internal response} \rightarrow \text{Drive}) \rightarrow \text{response} \rightarrow \text{Reward}$$

This paradigm is generally applicable to all learning situations, including social-learning and imitation situations.

Reward   The mechanism of reward or reinforcement has already been discussed in Chapter 2 and also in relation to the above concepts. Since Miller and Dollard's conception of reward is not essentially different from the general mediational approach to reinforcement previously discussed, we will be brief in our discussion of this concept.

Reward is that mechanism which determines whether or not a response is repeated on successive trials. If a response is unrewarded, the tendency to repeat it to the same constellation of cues is weakened. Individuals will seek to make the cue-response connection that results in reward. When reward occurs, its chief function is to reduce the strength of drive. In fact, Miller and Dollard use the term "reward" synonymously with drive reduction. Rewards, like drives and cues, can acquire value. Since reward is functionally defined as drive reduction, then the nature of the drive dictates the nature of the reward. Primary drives are reduced in their intensity by primary rewards, and secondary or acquired drives are reduced in their intensity by secondary or acquired rewards. Food is a primary reward that serves to reduce the primary drive of hunger; an approving nod is a secondary reward that reduces the acquired drive for social approval. Acquired rewards initially gain their potency as drive reducers through their association with primary rewards. In the social-learning situation most rewards are acquired and secondary and therefore reduce the intensity of social drives, which are also acquired and secondary.

As we had noted earlier in this chapter, those current conceptions of social-learning processes which are reinforcement-based have discounted the role of drive reduction in the definition of reinforcement. For example, since Gewirtz and Stingle (1968) consider *intrinsic* drives as irrelevant constructs in social-learning processes, they therefore regard the reduction in intrinsic drive as irrelevant to the definition of reinforcement. Thus while several modern conceptions of social learning and imitation are derivative from Miller and Dollard's original treatment, the basic paradigm from general-learning theory which governs most current reinforcement-based approaches to social learning is more operant than mediational. In particular, the drive-reduction propositions in Miller and Dollard's reformulation of Hullian learning principles have been discarded in most reinforcement-based accounts of social learning extant in today's literature. While the notion of drive has not been entirely discarded from recent social-learning accounts, its redefinition resembles the construction of Keller and Schoenfeld (1950), discussed in Chapter 2 (see pages 30–31). Therefore, it is the *purposive* or *intrinsic* element of the drive-reduction concept that has been recently questioned in several accounts of social-learning phenomena (e.g., Gewirtz & Stingle, 1968; Baer & Sherman, 1964).

It should be noted that, in the subsequent presentation, the applicability of Miller and Dollard's mechanisms of imitation does not hinge upon their particular notion of intrinsic drive. One could well translate the drive and reinforcement concepts in more operant terms and still adopt the basic matched-dependent and copying paradigms as pattern cases of imitation. In a sense, current extensions of Miller and Dollard's discrimination learning reinforcement-based models of imitation evidence such a strategy.

Mechanisms of Imitation

Miller and Dollard proposed that three processes or mechanisms of imitation could account for most or all imitative behavior. These three mechanisms were referred to as *same behavior, matched-dependent behavior,* and *copying.*

Same Behavior   This first mechanism of imitation was not discussed in detail by the theorists because, in fact, it does not warrant such coverage. Simply, same behavior occurs when two individuals respond to independent stimulation by the same cue, after each has learned to make the appropriate response. Examples of this process are plentiful. Some common ones might be (1) two people taking the same bus because they are going to the same destination and (2) two people waiting in line to purchase tickets at the box office of a theater. Same behavior may result from imitation, but it need not.

Matched-Dependent Behavior   This second process of imitation tends to occur in two-party interactions in which one of the parties is older, smarter, or more skilled than the other. Thus, for example, young children will *match* the behavior of, and be *dependent* upon, older people. If we extrapolate to the imitation situation, the observer who is in some manner in a lower relative position than the model will match the model's behavior and be dependent upon the model for appropriate cues as to when to do so. The theorists offered the following pattern case of matched-dependent behavior.

Two brothers were playing while awaiting the return home of their father. Father usually returned home with candy for each of the children. While playing, the older child heard a footstep on the entry stairway. For him, it served as a cue for the father's return, and he responded to it by running in the direction of the stairway. For the younger child, the father's footstep did not yet serve as a distinctive cue and thus did not rouse him to running. On many occasions, the older brother's running did not lead to running in the younger boy; he might have continued playing or just continued sitting. However, on this occasion the younger boy ran behind his older brother. When both had reached the father, they each received candy. On subsequent similar occasions the younger child would more frequently run at the mere sight of his brother's running. Under continued candy reward the younger boy's behavior stabilized, and he would run at the sight of his brother's running in all situations, even though the time and place stimuli were variable. Thus, he had learned to *imitate* his older brother, but his father's footstep had still not acquired distinctiveness as a cue. This pattern case can be represented by the following set of paradigms:[1]

1.   *Behavior of imitation* (younger brother)

Drive. . . . . Appetite for candy
Cue. . . . . Leg twinkle of older brother
Response . . . . Running
Reward. . . . . Eating candy

2.   *Behavior of leader* (older brother)

Drive. . . . . Appetite for candy
Cue. . . . . Father's footstep

[1]All three paradigms and the ones to follow taken from Miller & Dollard, 1941.

Response . . . . Running
Reward . . . . Eating candy

3. *Complete paradigm of matched-dependent behavior*

	Leader	**Imitator**
Drive	Appetite for candy	Appetite for candy
Cue	Father's footstep →Dependent→	Leg twinkle of leader
Response	Running ←—————→Matched——→	Running
Reward	Eating candy	Eating candy

This case and these paradigms simply illustrate Miller and Dollard's concept of matched-dependent behavior. Throughout the above analysis of matched-dependent behavior, it is quite apparent that the theorists see imitation as an object of instrumental learning and solely explainable by the "laws of instrumental learning." Thus, learning to imitate is akin to learning to peck, press, run, push, and so forth. This implies that Miller and Dollard do not see imitation as a unique type of learning. That is, individuals do not necessarily learn *through* imitation, but rather they learn to imitate. In matched-dependent behavior, the crucial characteristics are the cues exhibited to the imitator by the leader. These cues are utilized by the imitator because they are more stable and distinctive than other environmental cues. However, the cues from the leader's behavior are in no way different in function from any other cues within the broad class of acquired cues. With some modification, other social-influence processes such as conformity and attitude change can be conceived of in a matched-dependent learning model.

In addition to the foregoing pattern case of matched-dependent learning, Miller and Dollard discussed four other illustrative cases. In doing so, they asserted that their purpose in using illustrative cases was not to anecdotally prove their hypotheses but rather to exhibit varying circumstances under which matched-dependent behavior will occur. In this respect, the theorists have attempted to define matched-dependent behavior as a function of varying social contexts. Although we will not extensively detail these cases here, we will briefly specify each general contextual variation.

1 *Common goal but differing responses.* In this case both imitator and leader seek the same general goal; however, the goal for one involves a different set of responses than the goal for the other. In an illustration of the theorists, the common goal was the reduction in the hunger drives of two children. The younger of the two was parentally permitted to reduce hunger drive with a familiar food object (cornflakes) and in a familiar context (late afternoon before the parents dined). The older child was recently placed on an adult menu and thus was being trained to a new secondary goal (for example, meat and potatoes). She now was to eat adult food at adult dinner times. Therefore, although the drive toward the old secondary goal (cornflakes) was in a period of extinction training, it was still aroused when the conditions constituting the formerly relevant context were recreated. Thus the leader's behavior in this case served as a cue for the imitator's anticipation of goal-directed behaviors to eat also. However, since the older child was in extinction training with regard to the eating of cornflakes at a time separate from the adult's eating time, she is punished rather than rewarded for requesting "equal treatment." This common-goal-differing-responses prototype yields the following paradigm:

	Leader		Imitator
Drive	Hunger plus appetite		Hunger plus appetite
Cue	Cornflakes and meal situation	→Dependent —→Brother eating	
Response	Eating	→Same goal —→Request to eat	
Reward	Reduction in hunger and appetite drives		Absent, punishment added

In this case, the conditions of learning the initial set of responses (eating cornflakes together) set up the bases for imitation of the leader by the imitator. The leader's behavior served as a cue and had also acquired secondary-drive value. Thus, the imitator was *dependent* upon the eating of the leader in making her response which, while *not matched* (eating versus request for food), nevertheless was directed at a common goal. Under continued conditions of absence of reward the imitative behavior of the older child would be bound to drop out.

The conclusions drawn from the above case can be summarized in the following hypothesis: *the drive to imitate will be aroused in an individual when he/she is confronted with another's response to a familiar and formerly pleasant cue situation to which his/her own response is blocked.*

It is difficult to view this prototypic case as an instance of imitation since imitative behavior does not in fact occur, except perhaps through simile (eating is like requesting to eat) or through some construct like matching another's overt response with a similar internal response.

2 *Secondary reward.* In this case, the imitator gains secondary reward from hearing or seeing the response of another and he/she therefore matches that response. Once successfully matching the response, he/she also gains secondary reward from his/her own behavior, especially if it meets with the approval of the leader. The imitator is also dependent upon the cues of the leader for the specification of when and what responses will occur. Consider the following paradigm, cited by Miller and Dollard, of a child playing "peek" with his/her mother.

	Leader (parent)		Imitator (child)
Drive	Unknown (but probably secondary)		Secondary—wish for
Cue	Sight of child plus other contextual factors	→Dependent —→ Parent playing "peek"	
Response	"Peek" behavior	→Matched —→Playing "peek"	
Reward	Unknown (again probably secondary)		Relaxation at parental attention

A confusing factor here is that the leader's response serves both as a cue for the imitator's response and a secondary drive-reducer. Furthermore, the response of the imitator serves as a response as well as a secondary reward. Thus, taking a closer look, the behavior of the leader serves as a cue upon which the imitator is dependent; a response, which the imitator matches; and the reward object, which leads to drive reduction in the imitator.

The hypothesis suggested by this case is that an *individual will match and be dependent upon that behavior of another which has secondary reward value for him/her*. Furthermore, through generalization, his/her own behavior will also become secondarily rewarding.

3 *Testing.* In this case the leader serves to test the viability of a given response for the imitator. If the leader's response is successful. the imitator will match it. The leader's "test" response serves as a cue for the imitator's matched response. *Thus, the successful responses of another acquire cue distinctiveness and occasion imitation.*

4 *Secondary drives of imitation and rivalry.* Here, imitation derives from the observation of the rewarded responses of another. Miller and Dollard hypothesized that observing the rewarded responses of a leader occasions a drive to imitate. In this respect, this case of matched-dependent behavior is much like that of testing. However, these theorists proposed that a drive to imitate transmutes into a drive to compete when the imitator has already learned the appropriate response and the conditions of reward are such that only one person at a time can make the response. Here the imitator and the leader will compete to receive the earliest administration of reward. Thus, although the follower is dependent on the cues set up by the leader for the initiation of a response sequence, having already learned the response sequence, he/she may seek to complete it with greater speed than the leader in order to be the first to be rewarded. Thus, *imitation once established will lead to rivalry between leader and imitator when the availability of rewards is limited.*

Despite Miller and Dollard's belief that antecedent drives to imitate must be transformed into drives to compete in the instance of case 4, one might well maintain that the limitation of available rewards alone is sufficient to produce rivalry, and thus the alteration in drive state can be regarded as surplus teleology.

Copying

Miller and Dollard described copying as a more complex form of imitation than matched-dependent behavior. In both copying and matched-dependent behavior, the imitator connects his/her responses to cues derived from the responses of a model. Furthermore, in both, the punishment of nonmatched responses and the reward of matched responses eventually establishes the observer's imitation of the model. The most-important distinction between these two processes of imitation is that in matched-dependent behavior, the imitator responds only to the cues of the model, although in copying he/she also responds to cues of *sameness* and *difference* produced by his/her own and the model's response.

In the copying situation, the model performs behaviors that have cue value to the observer. As the observer approximates the behavior of a model, he/she responds to the sameness or difference between his/her and the model's responses as well as the sameness or difference between his/her responses on the current approximation and on previous approximations. Thus, if an observer is attempting to imitate the voice of a model, he/she will evaluate the similarity between his/her voice production and the model's voice production on the basis of similarity of vocal cues, such as loudness or pitch. He/she will also evaluate the cue relationship between his/her current approximation and a past approximation. If the past approximation was a closer match, for example, he/she will tend to find the differences in his/her response (amount of air expended, width of vocal chords) and use these as cues for future matching responses.

When he/she matches the model's behavior, he/she is rewarded and attends to the cues inherent in the match so that he/she might recreate that match on future trials. The response to cues of sameness and difference is greatly facilitated by the presence of a "critic" who rewards the imitator for matches and punishes him/her for nonmatches. Once the individual becomes an accomplished "copier" of a given response, the cues in his/her attempted match that signal difference will acquire anxiety value and the cues that signal sameness will acquire reward value, and the copier may therefore act as his/her own critic.

In line with their entire analysis of social behavior, Miller and Dollard asserted that, if copying occurs, that is, if individuals "make" their responses the *same* as other individuals' responses, then there must exist a *drive to copy*. They indicated that this copying drive may have components of anxiety, over loss of social approval, and reward, in the form of learning new experiences or skills from others. The theorists attribute social conformity to the drive to copy and equate this drive with such concepts as the "herd instinct" (Trotter, 1917) and "compulsions of a moral order" (Sumner & Keller, 1927). Copying is viewed as the source of uniformity in social behavior.

Once again, the "necessity" of a drive to copy as an antecedent to copying would be regarded by most current reinforcement theorists as unprovable surplus teleology.

Comment and Evaluation

Miller and Dollard's theory of social learning and imitation served a valuable historical role. Despite some prior treatises on the nature of imitation (Tarde, 1903; McDougall, 1908) and some early learning-theory approaches to imitation (Humphrey, 1921; Allport, 1924), it was the first extensive and systematic attempt to apply "the laws of learning" to the pervasive social behavior called "imitation." Furthermore, the theory advanced by Miller and Dollard still has relevance to the interpretation of imitation.

As we have noted throughout this chapter, several current approaches to social imitation and modeling draw from the rich base provided by Miller and Dollard's touchstone treatise. In this sense, Miller and Dollard's thoughts on imitation have had an enduring impact on the study of social learning. Furthermore, this theory provides an account of social learning which is thoroughly anchored by generalized concepts of *reinforcement-based* models of response acquisition.

The empirical evidence which constitutes direct confirmation of the specifics of Miller and Dollard's theory is confined to the theorists' own early research. More-recent research demonstrations predicated upon the general perspective of a reinforcement-based model of imitation, however, are plentiful (cf. Gewirtz & Stingle, 1968; Steinman, 1970; Masters, Gordon, & Clark, 1976; Gewirtz, 1971b; Baer & Sherman, 1964; Brigham & Sherman, 1968). What this representative group of studies and reviews has demonstrated is that external reinforcement of a model's behavior is *at least* a sufficient condition for the generation of imitative behavior in a similarly rewarded observer. Like Miller and Dollard, current theorists and researchers of reinforcement-based social imitation models have proposed and clearly demonstrated that the "motive" to imitate another's response *can* become contingent upon the role of that other's response in signaling the potential availability of extrinsic rewards to the observer. Thus, the basic conceptual foundation of Miller and Dollard's paradigms of matched-dependent learning have been repeatedly demonstrated to be plausible. These demonstrations have encompassed a number of behavioral classes, including simple motor acts, verbal behavior, and social-moral behaviors, such as altruism and aggression. While time has taken its toll on some of Miller and Dollard's notions of drive reduction and the fuzzier surpluses of terminology contained in the original model have fallen by the wayside, the conceptual assumptions of a reinforcement-based account of matched-dependent imitation have taken firm hold in current accounts of imitation. One can only offer a positive evaluation of Miller and Dollard's historical perspective on grounds of the theoretical and empirical developments it continues to foster.

Nevertheless, the centrality and necessity of external reinforcement to imitation and observational learning have been theoretically and empirically questioned by the work of Bandura and his colleagues. While the aforementioned set of Miller and Dollard-like perspectives and demonstrations have indicated that reinforcement is a sufficient condition to bring about imitation, Bandura has argued that extrinsic reward is only a necessary condition for the overt enactment of imitative behavior but is ancillary to the acquisition of learned responses on a conceptual level (whether or not they are overtly imitated). The particulars of Bandura's perspective are taken up in the next section.

A VICARIOUS PROCESS THEORY OF IMITATION

Albert Bandura and his associate (Bandura, 1962; Bandura & Walters, 1963; Bandura, 1966; Bandura, 1969; Bandura, 1971; Bandura, 1977) have articulated a data-based theory of imitation. Their major proposition is that imitation is a form of *associative* learning and can be explained by an S-R contiguity paradigm. Their approach, therefore, limits the role of the reinforcing consequences of both a model's and observer's behavior. Reinforcement is viewed as a facilitator of *performance* but is hypothesized not to affect *acquisition* or *learning*. The vehicle of imitative learning in Bandura's theory is the contiguous relationship between the stimuli in the model's environment and the model's response to them. The object of the observer's learning is this contiguous relationship, regardless of whether or not reinforcement results from it. Thus, the observer can learn merely by observation of a model and need not perform the response under conditions of reinforcement.

Bandura has referred to learning by observation as *vicarious* learning and has distinguished this view of imitation from several other popular views, including those of Skinner (1953, 1957), Mowrer (1960), and Miller and Dollard (1941). By extension, Bandura (1971, 1977) has also distinguished his view of learning through observation from other reinforcement-based discrimination learning viewpoints (cf., Gewirtz & Stingle, 1968; Baer & Sherman, 1964). Before proceeding to a discussion of Bandura's theoretical conceptions, we will briefly consider his criticisms of some of the more traditional approaches to observational learning.

Bandura's Evaluation of Other Theories of Imitation

Bandura viewed Miller and Dollard's conception of matched-dependent learning as a special case of instrumental discrimination-place learning. That is, the model's behavior provides discriminative stimuli for the timing and placement of responses that already exist in the observer's repertoire. Matched-dependent behavior has been demonstrated only in the circumstance where the observer is deprived of necessary environmental cues, and thus it is almost exclusively dependent upon the behavior of the model. Bandura asserted that imitation cannot generally be described as place learning but rather involves *response* learning. That is, observers will combine diverse behavioral elements into *novel* responses simply through the observation of the responses of a model. Further-more, contrary to Miller and Dollard's position, neither the model nor the observer has to receive reinforcement for observational learning to occur. Bandura (1965a) demonstrated this latter point in a study that clearly indicated that observers learn novel repertoires through observation both without making immediate matching responses and without reinforcement. A central proposi-tion of Miller and Dollard's approach is that a response must be present in the repertoire of the subject before he can imitate that same response when emitted by a model under conditions of reinforcement. Bandura maintained that this position runs into difficulty in accounting for the *acquisition* of novel responses and places a severe restriction on what can be learned from models.

Skinner's (1953, 1957) approach is defined as being quite similar to that of Miller and Dollard. In this approach, the model's behavior is seen by the observer as discriminative stimuli for reinforcement. This discriminative-stimulus function is endowed on a model's behavior through the differential reinforcement of the model's various responses to cues in the behavioral field. An observer is initially shaped to emit a matched response through the process of *successive approximation*. That is, the observer is rewarded for each approximation of the model's response. With each response of the observer the requirements for reward become more stringent. Thus, the observer must make closer and closer matches with each response in order to consistently attain rewarding consequences. According to Bandura, Skinner's model, like that of Miller and Dollard, can account for the discriminative and reinforcement control of previously learned matching responses, but it does not in any way deal with the acquisition of novel responses through observation (Bandura, 1966, 1972).

Bandura maintained that a distinction must be made between acquisition and performance for the process of imitation to be clearly articulated. Thus, reinforcement is seen as facilitating performance but *not* inducing learning through observation. This position is not new with Bandura. The reader will recall our brief discussion of Tolman's concept of latent learning in Chapter 2.

There have been numerous studies that have shown that reinforcing consequences serve only to activate behavior learned under conditions of nonreinforced observation (Kanareff & Lanzetta, 1960; Walters & Parke, 1964; Bandura, 1965; Kanfer, 1965; Bandura, Grusec & Menlove, 1966; Rosenthal & Zimmerman, 1977). Bandura cited these findings as providing support for his position that the contiguity between the stimuli in the field and the model's response to them is sufficient to lead to the acquisition of responses by the observer. Reinforcement serves only to activate this learning into performed acts. Thus, the proposition that modeling occurs because imitative responding is *instrumental* in the attainment of reward has been strongly questioned by Bandura.

Mowrer (1960) has articulated a two-process theory of imitation, based upon the concept of proprioceptive feedback. Unlike Miller and Dollard (1941) and Skinner (1957), Mowrer's theory "emphasizes the classical conditioning of positive and negative emotions to matching, response-correlated stimuli" (p. 8). Thus modeling is viewed as being dependent upon the contiguous association of the model's behavior with its reinforcing consequences. Through continued observation of these contiguous events, the observer eventually attaches positive affect to responses that lead to reward and negative affect to responses that lead to punishment.

Simply, Mowrer's two processes differ in terms of the directness of the reinforcing consequences for the observer. The first process involves the direct reinforcement of an observer by a model. This reinforcing consequence is contiguous to the model's performance of a given response. With the continued enforcement of the contiguous association between the model's behavior and the observer's reinforcement, the model's responses take on positive value. Through the process of stimulus generalization the observer can in time closely reproduce the model's responses and thus receive self-rewarded feedback. Mowrer referred to his second process of imitative learning as "empathetic" learning. In this case a model performs responses and is reinforced. It is assumed that the observer vicariously experiences the rewarding consequences of the model's behavior and "intuits his/her discomforts and satisfactions." When placed in the behavioral field, the observer will be capable of reproducing the model's responses because they have gained positively reinforcing value. This latter process is a higher-order form of classical conditioning in which the observer experiences sensory feedback empathically while the model is being rewarded.

Bandura noted that, while Mowrer's conception of "empathetic" learning overcomes his criticism of the position which holds that a response must be performed before it can be learned, it still fails to explain the occurrence of imitative learning when neither model nor observer are rewarded. Furthermore, although Mowrer viewed the feedback from a model's responses that an observer experiences as sensory and peripheral, Bandura hypothesized that this feedback is centrally mediated. Thus, for Mowrer the aggressive responses of a model occasion the same sensory feedback whether expressed toward a peer or toward an authority figure. On the other hand, Bandura saw aggressive responding varying as a function of the target, and the nature of differing expressions of aggression being mediated by central processes of target and context discrimination. This latter proposition has received strong empirical support (Bandura & Walters, 1959; Bandura, 1960; Bandura, 1973).

Bandura's criticism of the reinforcement-oriented theories of Skinner, Dollard and Miller, and Mowrer has also been offered in the case of their more recent derivatives (cf., Bandura, 1977). For example, the operant models of imitative learning proposed by Baer and Sherman (1964) and Gewirtz and Stingle (1968) were similarly criticized by Bandura (1977) because of their central focus upon reinforcement-based acquisition of observationally learned sequences.

An Overview of Bandura's Theory

Bandura refers to his theory of imitation as a mediational-stimulus contiguity theory. According to this approach, "during the period of exposure modeling stimuli elicit in observing subjects configurations and sequences of sensory experiences which, on the basis of past associations, become centrally integrated and structured into perceptual responses" (p. 10). Thus, through contiguous stimulation, an antecedent stimulus can eventually elicit imaginal or symbolic representations of associated stimulus events even though they are no longer present (Bandura, 1966). Bandura proposes that a model's response to cues in a stimulus field leads to "internal" imaginal responses in the observer that can be retrieved when the observer is placed in the behavioral field. Therefore, without responding or being rewarded, the observer integrates cue connections in the model's responses and the behavioral field and thereby becomes able to imitate the model's response.

The observer's ability to attach verbal labels to the model's behavior greatly facilitates this process of symbolization. The representational responses that occur in the observer, whether they are verbal associates or imaginal responses, come to serve as internal cues that mediate the observer's matched external responses in the behavioral field. Thus, the internal representational cues become discriminative stimuli for overt matching patterns of behavior.

The foregoing paragraphs provide the reader with an overview of Bandura's theoretical orientation toward modeling. The remainder of this presentation will be devoted to Bandura's articulation of:

1 The processes involved in observational learning
2 The behavioral and cognitive effects of exposure to modeling influences
3 The relevance of vicarious processes to the modeling process

It should be noted that, throughout these analyses, Bandura's propositions are strongly related to a broad data base. Where relevant, references to this data base will be cited.

Processes of Observational Learning

Bandura's portrayal of the psychological processes involved in an observer's incorporation of a model's actions strongly reflects his central concern with *symbolic acquisition* in observational learning. Bandura's (1966, 1969, 1971, 1977) social-learning analysis of modeling phenomena proposes that a model's behavior is a source of information for the observer. Observers do not simply mimic a model's actions through reinforcement-based principles of stimulus-response association. Instead, observers are viewed as active processors of the information provided by a model's behavior. The processes involved in an observer's encoding of modeled repertoires include symbolic and cognitive organizational functions, as well as the motor enactments and motivational inductions centered upon by instrumental theories of imitation. Figure 3-1 provides Bandura's (1977) schematic presentation of the component processes governing observational learning. In the subsequent paragraphs we will briefly elaborate on each of these four categories of process variables.

Figure 3-1   From Bandura, 1977, p. 23.

	Attentional processes	Retention processes	Motor reproduction processes	Motivational processes	
Modeled events →	Modeling stimuli Distinctiveness Affective valence Complexity Prevalence Functional value Observer characteristics Sensory capacities Arousal level Perceptual set Past reinforcement	Symbolic coding Cognitive organization Symbolic rehearsal Motor rehearsal	Physical capabilities Availability of component responses Self-observation of reproductions Accuracy feedback	External reinforcement Vicarious reinforcement Self-reinforcement	Matching performances →

Attentional Processes   It is a point of rather impeccable logic that the observed behavior of another can only occasion "learning" in the observer if it commands his/her attention. As the reader can discern from consulting Figure 3-1, two broad factors determining observer attention to modeled events are features of the *modeling stimuli* and *characteristics of the observer.* Modeling stimuli can vary in attention-directing strength by both physical and social qualities. Thus observers are more likely to attend to modeled activities if they are distinctive, salient, complex, and/or novel behavioral events than if they are common, simple, and indistinctive. Furthermore, the characteristics of the model as a stimulus (as distinguished from the model's behavior) can also occasion variations in attention. For example, one's friends and loved ones should generate greater attention in an observer than affectively neutral others. In the same vein, similar, powerful, attractive, and/or previously rewarding others should occasion greater attention as models than social others who are indistinctive in interpersonal meaning for the observer.

Observer characteristics which affect attention to modeled events involve observer skill, motivation, and perceptual set. Thus, an observer's sensory capacities with respect to information processing will clearly influence what he/she "sees" in a modeled action. Similarly, attention will vary with a perceiver's needs (e.g., for uncertainty reduction, food, money, etc.) and perceptual readiness to observe a model in a given situation. Finally, some modeling stimuli gain high salience simply because they are so intrinsically rewarding. Bandura (1977) attributes the attention-getting qualities of the symbolic modeling provided by television to this latter factor. In fact, Bandura, Grusec, and Menlove (1966) have found that televised models are so effective in engendering the attention of the viewer that much is learned from television without the necessity for special incentives or reinforcements (Bandura, 1977).

Retention Processes   Given Bandura's insistence on the symbolic mediation of modeling effects, it is quite consistent for him to argue that observers could not be terribly influenced by a model if they fail to store and remember the component actions observed in the modeling setting. As Bandura (1977) notes,

> In order for observers to profit from the behavior of models when they are no longer present to provide direction, the response patterns must be represented in memory in symbolic form. Through the medium of symbols, transitory modeling experiences can be maintained in permanent memory. It is the advanced capacity for symbolization that enables humans to learn much of their behavior by observation (p. 25).

The factors involved in the retention of modeled acts are noted in Figure 3-1. The factors of symbolic coding, cognitive organization, and symbolic and mental rehearsal are seen as relying upon two representational systems—imaginal and verbal (Bandura, 1977). The first of these representational systems allows for repeatedly observed modeling stimuli to eventually result in retrievable *images* of modeled activities. These images can be retrieved in the absence of a live model when a new situation suggests their salience. This imaginally based form of representation is particularly important in the early preverbal stages of development.

The verbal representational system is seen by Bandura (1977) as accounting for the speed with which observed acts are encoded and retained by humans. Since most cognitive processes are verbally mediated, an accurate and efficient symbolic encoding, retention, and later reproduction of observed events can be facilitated by converting sensory information and visual images into verbal form. In short, observational learning is greatly enhanced by symbolic verbal codes because such codes allow for an ease of storage and retrieval of modeled information.

The importance of symbolic retention systems to observational learning has been amply demonstrated in some recent research with both children (Bandura, Grusec, & Menlove, 1966; Coates & Hartup, 1969) and adults (Gerst, 1971; Bandura & Jeffrey, 1973; Bandura, Jeffrey, & Barchicha, 1974). In these studies, observers who were induced to code modeling stimuli into verbal or visual symbols retain the observed behaviors better than uninstructed or otherwise-preoccupied observers.

Finally, Bandura notes that the mental and motor rehearsal of observed behaviors is an important facilitator of the observer's retention of modeled behavioral components. Since it is not always possible or relevant to immediately reproduce the behavior of models, mental rehearsal serves to enforce the observed behaviors in memory. Bandura and Jeffrey (1973) have clearly demonstrated that observers who imagine themselves performing previously observed behaviors retain those behaviors for future enactment better than those observers who engage in no prior rehearsal.

In sum, Bandura has proposed and empirically confirmed that the mediational processes involved in storing and retaining modeled behavior pivotally affect the quality of observational learning.

Motor Reproduction Processes   The attention and retention processes described above are directed at accounting for the observer's encoding and symbolic representation of modeled behaviors. The third set of processes in Bandura's model are involved with the conversion of these symbolic representations into overt action. Bandura breaks the motor reproduction processes into two phases:

1   A response selection phase in which the observed behavioral pattern is parsed into units which are then cognitively organized. The efficiency and quality of response selection will depend upon whether the observer possesses the skill to enact the component responses contained in the modeled sequence. The enactment may involve a novel integration of these already possessed components—but the components must either be present in the observer's repertoire or must be learned by the observer prior to accurate reproduction.

2   Phase 2 of the motor reproduction process is similar to the Skinnerian notion of successive approximation. That is, once observed responses are selected and organized, the observer's initial enactments will likely be discrepant from both the modeled sequence and the symbolized version of that sequence. Accurate observational learning issues from the corrective adjustment of the observer's behavioral repertoire on successive attempts to reproduce modeled sequences.

Reinforcement and Motivational Processes   As we have noted in the above overview of Bandura's theory and in his critique of instrumental theories of imitation, reinforcement is viewed within Bandura's system as having its major impact upon the observer's *performance* (as distinguished from the *learning*) of modeled sequences. Observers can thus theoretically learn and symbolically store more responses than they eventually enact. The critical role of reinforcement processes in the production of matching performances in an observer is that it *motivates* their enactment. If a model, by virtue of his/her responses, has obtained outcomes which the observer values, the observer may experience *vicarious reinforcement* and thereby be "motivated" to overtly reproduce the behavior. Similarly, the observer's expectation that his/her matching responses will produce direct *extrinsic rewards* for self will also motivate the overt matching of observed behavior. What should be noted is that in Bandura's model, the impact of such reinforcements is limited to performance induction alone.

When one takes account of the above-described four processes involved in an observer's movement from the observation of modeled events to matching performances, it should be clear that the failure of matching behavior can result from "not observing the relevant activities, inadequately coding modeled events for memory representation, failing to retain what was learned, physical inability to perform, or experiencing insufficient incentives" (Bandura, 1977, p. 29). However, when these processes operate appropriately, observational learning *and* matching performance should result. The various effects of the successful processing of modeling information are discussed in the subsequent section.

Effects of Exposure to Models

Bandura has noted that successful exposure to models can lead to several general effects in the observer. The primary effects are: (1) modeling effects whereby the observer acquires novel responses through the cognitive integration of contiguous cues, (2) inhibitory and disinhibitory effects through which an existing class of the observer's behavior is modified by his observation of a model's responses, (3) facilitation effects whereby the observations of another's behavior may facilitate the occurrence of previously learned, nonnovel, and noninhibited responses in the observer, (4) abstract-rule-acquisition effects where the "rules" governing the enactment of a model are applied to behavioral circumstances which differ from those surrounding the model's demonstrated enactment, and (5) innovation on both the individual and societal level. This last effect is the most diffuse and general of Bandura's stated effects. It refers to the role that distinctive modeled behavior might have as a prominent example for functionally valuable novel behavioral norms in a single observer or for a large collectivity of observers.

Modeling Effects   Modeling effects occur in that situation in which an observer acquires new response patterns through observing a model perform highly novel responses. As we have noted previously, most novel responses contain elements or segments of behavior that are already established in the observer's learned repertoire. Bandura maintains that the observational-learning situation introduces the observer to novel combinations of contiguous cues which he/she integrates on a central level and through which he/she arrives at a new integrative behavior pattern. Thus, it is the patterning of the components of the model's response and those of the ensuing response of the observer that defines novelty. In addition, novel responses are also identified as occurring when already established behavior patterns come under *new* stimulus control. In this case the learned responses occur to a set of cues to which they had not occurred previous to the specific observational experience involved. The previously described attention, retention, motor, and incentive processes are each critical to the observer's recombinatorial efforts.

Bandura noted that studies have indicated that modeling effects occur with a whole host of responses, including physically expressive aggression (Bandura, 1965b), self-reinforcement (Bandura & Whalen, 1966), self-imposed delay of reward (Bandura & Mischel, 1965), linguistic structuring (Bierman, 1965), and many others (cf., Bandura, 1971, 1977).

In all these cases an observer watched a model utilize a unique pattern of response and subsequently displayed that pattern of response when placed in the same behavioral field or a symbolically similar behavioral context. Hence, we speak of a modeling effect. Since none of the subjects in any of the experiments above had an opportunity to practice an observed response pattern before criterion performance was judged, Bandura reiterates that the combining and chaining of matching responses must have occurred through central symbolic and mediating processes, and thus the behavior was learned in "no-trials." As we had noted in our description of motor reproduction processes, one important aspect of no-trial or observational learning is the subject's ability to engage in *covert rehearsal* of the response to be performed.

Recently the symbolic modeling which is available through the mass media—particularly television—has been viewed as an additional potent source of modeling effects. Novel behavioral styles, attitudes, and emotional behaviors have been found to issue from exposure to models portrayed on visual media (cf.. Bandura, 1973; Liebert, Neale, & Davidson, 1973). The fact that such modeling may have widespread effects upon a mass of observers has rendered the media an extremely potent influence in the cultural transmission of behaviors and norms. This point will be dealt with more completely in our treatment of the innovative effects of modeling.

Bandura noted that although empirical data provide support for his stimulus-contiguity explanation of modeling effects, the finding that a majority of observers fail to reproduce the *complete* pattern of the model's response indicates that the contiguity of sensory stimulation is a necessary but not sufficient condition for imitative learning. The contiguous presentation of sensory stimulation through modeling must be followed and facilitated by the four component processes described above and in Figure 3-1 in order for novel modeling effects to be realized in the matching behaviors of an observer.

Inhibitory and Disinhibitory Effects   "The occurrence of inhibitory effects of exposure to models is indicated when, as a function of observing aversive response consequences to a model, observers exhibit either decrements in the same class of behavior or a general reduction of responsivity" (Bandura, 1966, p. 20). Bandura posits that an opposite or disinhibitory effect might also occur as a function of observation. In this latter case, the observation of a model performing either rewarded or unpunished socially unacceptable responses leads to increments in the same class of behavior or a general increase in socially disapproved behavior. In both these cases, the direct reinforcement or punishment of the observer is not a prerequisite. Rather, the positive, negative, or lack of reinforcement of the model is vicariously experienced by the observer while he is observing. Thus, like modeling effects, inhibitory and disinhibitory effects are said to be learned in no-trials.

Bandura's proposition that there are both inhibitory and disinhibitory effects that occur as a function of observation has received impressive experimental support. Walters, Leat, and Mezei (1963) and Walters and Parke (1964) have shown that when an observer witnesses a peer model undergo punishment for engaging in prohibited play activities, his/her propensity to engage in the same deviant acts is decreased. On the other hand, Bandura, Ross, and Ross (1961, 1963) and many others (Siegel, 1956; Lövaas, 1961; Larder, 1962) have shown that when a peer model engages in aggressive behavior without negative consequence, it increases the probability that an observer will also engage in similar tabooed aggressive behaviors when placed in the same behavioral field. More recently, the disinhibitory effects of observing the nonpunishing consequences of another's behavior have been evidenced in therapeutic derivatives of social learning theory (Rachman, 1972; Bandura, 1976; Bandura, 1977). In these studies it has been found that fearful and defensive orientations toward various stimuli are reduced in observers when they view models performing such activities without adverse effects.

Bandura viewed the source of inhibitory and disinhibitory effects to be the occurrence of *vicarious reinforcement*. That is, if the negative behavior of an observer is inhibited or enhanced by observing a model performing that same behavior followed by rewarding or punishing consequences and this observer is not reinforced for these acts, then the assumption is made that he/she experienced the reinforcements of the model and, when placed in the behavioral field, he will display or inhibit the model's reinforced responses on the first trial. Research has revealed that vicarious reinforcement is as efficacious (Kanfer & Martson, 1963) as direct reinforcement at producing behavioral increments.

Vicarious reinforcement processes have also been shown to be moderated by the same variables (magnitude, percentage, schedule) as direct reinforcement (Bandura, 1966).

In line with the four component processes described earlier, Bandura offers four reasons for the efficacy of vicarious reinforcement in inhibiting or disinhibiting the responses of an observer of modeled acts:

1 It provides the observer with information about the probability of attaining reinforcement through the emission of certain specified responses.

2 It provides the observer with knowledge about the stimuli in the field and helps to direct *attention* to these stimuli.

3 It provides the observer with a display of the incentives which might be received for performing a given act.

4 It provides the observer the opportunity to view the affective reactions of the model to receiving a given reinforcement (that is, it provides pleasure and pain cues to the observer).

This final reason is probably further mediated by correlated feelings of pleasure or pain in the observer as he/she witnesses the model being reinforced. It should be noted that with regard to the socially prohibitive aggressive and deviant responses displayed by a model, lack of negative reinforcement is equally as powerful as positive reinforcement in promoting imitative responses in an observer (Walters & Parke, 1964; Walters, Parke, & Caine, 1965; Bandura, 1965). Bandura has attributed this finding to a contrast-of-reinforcement effect. The contrast spoken of here is the contrast between society's usual negative reinforcements for deviant behavior and the lack of negative reinforcement in the contrived modeling situation.

Response-Facilitating Effects Response-facilitating effects of exposure to models occur in that situation in which the model's responses serve as discriminative stimuli for the observer. This discriminative-stimulus function of a model's responses facilitates the occurrence of similar responses in the observer. These effects differ from both modeling and inhibition-disinhibition effects in that the responses facilitated are not novel but are already firmly ensconced in the repertoire of the subject and are not generally socially prohibited responses. Examples of behaviors that might be susceptible to the facilitating effects of a model's response might be (1) making contributions to a charitable cause, (2) volunteering for a chore, (3) looking at the ceiling, and innumerable others.

Bandura notes that the instrumental theories of imitation (Miller & Dollard, 1941; Skinner, 1957) have been almost exclusively concerned with the discrimination function of social cues. That is, the behavior of a model has a facilitative effect on like behaviors of the observer in that it occasions consequent reinforcement and hence becomes distinctive as a cue.

Abstract-Rule-Transmission Effects Bandura (1977) notes that "In abstract modeling, observers extract the common attributes exemplified in diverse modeled responses and formulate rules for generating behavior with similar structural characteristics. Responses embodying the observationally derived rule resemble the behavior the model would be inclined to exhibit under similar circumstances, even though observers have never seen the model behaving in these new situations" (p. 41).

While the implication of abstract-modeling effects had always been contained in Bandura's early treatments of observational learning, the greater explicitness with which Bandura has described such effects in his work in the last decade greatly increases the scope of social-learning-theory applications to socialization. The notion of abstract modeling enhances the applicability of social-learning theory to the understanding of the roles played by parents, teachers, and other ever-present models for children in the long-term development of language rules, moral attitudes, and social preferences. Abstract-modeling effects constitute one clear mechanism through which symbolic and intrinsic controls replace extrinsic sanctions, demands, and immediately available behavioral exemplars in the socialization process (Bandura, 1977). It is Bandura's increasing focus upon the specifics of the internal cognitive mediators (e.g., attention, retention, and symbolizing functions) that has permitted this theoretical development from the early versions of social-learning theory.

The impact of abstract-rule modeling has been empirically demonstrated in areas of language learning (Brown, 1976), moral thought and behavior (Bandura & McDonald, 1963; Bandura, 1973; Kurtines & Greif, 1974), and in social norm–related behaviors (Bryan & Walbek, 1970).

Innovation and Its Diffusion as Modeling Effects   The notion that innovative and distinctly creative behaviors and rules can result from modeling once again follows for Bandura's expanded treatment of the symbolic and cognitive generalizations that issue from modeled observation. The portrayal of modeling as a source of innovation in a society is based upon the proposal that models can serve as primary exemplars for new ideas, values, and behavioral styles. In Bandura's account of social learning, the observer is an active processer of modeling influences. Modeling vehicles with distinct *attention*-grabbing properties (e.g., television) will trigger enhanced internal processing and *retention* and will thus encourage more pronounced covert and overt rehearsal of the observed behaviors as well as a wide application of the norms represented by such behaviors. Bandura (1977) discusses the potential innovative effects of modeling in the particular circumstance of the mass-media modeling. The one-to-many nature of the model-observer relationship available in television media allows for the broad and diffuse transmission of behaviors and norms within a culture. According to Bandura's theory such impacts will produce different products in different observers. The sum total of such impacts will include myriad rearrangements of norms, behavioral styles, and social values depending upon the particular inclinations, past learning, receptivity, and cognitive processing of individual observers. Thus, the collective effects of the symbolic-modeling influences of the media are characterized by a diffusion of innovation in the society. Recent social-learning applications to the understanding of the effects of television on viewers (cf., Liebert, Neale, & Davidson, 1973) are a currently fertile extension of Bandura's model of observational learning.

Vicarious Classical Conditioning

The classification above of the effects of exposure to models was predominantly based upon investigations of the social transmission of instrumental classes of response (Bandura, 1966). In this section we will deal with Bandura's conception of the processes of vicarious classical conditioning that function in imitative behavior. We have chosen to give a careful exposition of these vicarious processes because they are a distinctive contribution of Bandura's perspective and a particularly important factor in the symbolic mediation of modeling effects.

Vicarious Emotional Arousal   Bandura asserted that social cues that signal the emotional arousal of a model can lead to emotion-provoking properties in the observer through the same classical conditioning process that established the positive or negative value of nonsocial environmental stimuli. Thus, the affective responses of a model to a cue situation may elicit similar affective responses in an observer. With the continued pairing of the model's emotional response with the eliciting social cues, the cues themselves gradually acquire the power to elicit emotional responses from the observer. This process involves much more than just parallel reactions to a naturally emotion-provoking cue (for example, shock, fear object). Rather, the concept of vicarious emotional arousal involves an actual "imitation" of the emotional response of a witnessed model by an observer, whether or not that observer is directly confronted with the arousing cue. As an example, Bandura refers to a study in which Lazarus *et al.* (1962) found that college students exposed to films of primitive subincision puberty rites showed increased autonomic responsivity (said to reflect emotional arous-al). It is Bandura's proposal that gradually the cues that occasioned an expression of pain in the subincised other acquired the power to independently elicit emotional pain reactions in the observer. Thus, the observer does not have to be actually placed in the behavioral field containing the emotionally arousing cues in order to experience emotional arousal. Therefore, Bandura maintained that vicarious emotional arousal might occur merely from the simple observation of another's emotional experience.

Vicarious Classical Conditioning   When vicarious emotional arousal is induced in an observer, vicarious classical conditioning can occur if those stimuli that aroused emotional reactions in the model (and hence vicariously in the observer) are associated with previously neutral stimuli. In this case, the neutral stimuli gain the power to elicit the emotional response in both the model or performer and the observer. This phenomenon has been empirically demon-strated (Barnett & Benedetti, 1960; Berger, 1962). Furthermore, Bandura and Rosenthal (1966) have found that the initial arousal level of the observer prior to vicarious conditioning procedures moderates the intensity of the vicariously conditioned response. Specifically, these investigators found that an inverted U-shaped relationship obtains between the observer's initial level of arousal and the magnitude of his conditioned vicarious response. Therefore, increased levels of initial emotional arousal lead to an increased magnitude of the conditioned response up to an asymptotic point, above which increasing the level of arousal decreases the intensity of the vicariously conditioned emotional response.

Bandura (1966) has explained this finding by proposing that observers under high levels of preconditioning arousal will more frequently invoke "stimulus neutralization strategems," or, more simply, competing responses, to combat the effect of additional arousal. This proposal derives from Bandura and Rosenthal's (1966) postexperimental questionnaire data.

Finally, it should be noted that Bandura proposed that just as an observer's responses may be vicariously conditioned either instrumentally or classically through exposure to a model, they also may be vicariously extinguished through simple observation. Thus, for example, an observer witnessing a model approaching a stimulus which he (the observer) had always avoided would gradually undergo vicarious extinction of the avoidance response if he observed the model experiencing no adverse consequences. Bandura postulated that this latter process should be highly relevant to psychotherapy and behavior change.

COMMENT AND EVALUATION

In the foregoing chapter we have attempted to provide a broad and complete exposition of two major theoretical frameworks for the examination of the phenomena of social imitation. These two frameworks constitute seminal sources for both researchers and theorists of social learning. In this latter sense one might easily construe the models of Miller and Dollard and of Bandura as global orientations rather than theories about specific phenomena. Miller and Dollard's work provides an orientational backdrop for subsequently proposed theories of imitation based upon instrumental learning processes; Bandura, on the other hand, provides a comprehensive account of social imitation from a cognitive-mediational perspective, and his work is a primary source of hypotheses for specific theories within this latter perspective. We have provided such extensive coverage of both of these theories of imitation because any attempt to understand the literature of social learning presumes the knowledge of both of these approaches. Those smaller-scope theories of imitation and modeling which deal with specific behavioral and norm acquisitions, such as altruism, aggression, or moral transgressions, are derivatives of these two general approaches and add little to their *theoretical* structure.

In our commentary on Miller and Dollard's theory, we noted that its primary role in the current empirical and theoretical developments in social-learning theory is a historical one. Bandura's theory, on the other hand, must be regarded as the central model of imitative learning available in today's psychology. As a theory, Bandura's perspective has been powerfully generative of a wide range of empirical studies on all aspects of the modeling process. A perusal of the research cited in this chapter reveals that many of Bandura's proposals concerning modeling and imitation have met with convincing empirical confirmation. The most noteworthy empirical verifications of Bandura's viewpoint are those which demonstrate the importance of such phenomena as vicarious reinforcement, no-trial imitative learning, symbolic modeling, inhibitory and disinhibitory effects of modeling, and the operation of attention and retention processes in modeling. The empirical confirmation of the workings of these processes and constructs renders Bandura's stimulus-contiguity view of social imitation a quite plausible one. Thus, by the theory criteria of testability, research generation, and internal and external consistency, Bandura's theory is an exemplary one.

In a final note, it should be pointed out that in the more than ten years since our first treatment of Bandura's theory (Shaw & Costanzo, 1970), the framework has expanded in scope and has encompassed a wide range of new phenomena. Bandura's very explicit articulation of the underlying cognitive processes promoting symbolic modeling has been of major importance to this expansion in scope. Bandura's model not only accommodates explanations of how behaviors are socially transmitted by models, but also includes theoretical propositions to account for how these modeled components are incorporated by the observer as rules and norms to be used in future contexts. This renders Bandura's current framework a more powerful tool for the developmental analysis of socialization than the early presentations of the theory.

Chapter 4

Social Reinforcement–Exchange Theories

There are three theoretical frameworks presented in this chapter: (1) Homans' (1961, 1974) behavioral-sociological model of social exchange; (2) Thibaut and Kelley's (1959) and Kelley and Thibaut's (1978) theory of interpersonal interdependence; and (3) equity theory as exemplified by the work of Walster, Berscheid, and Walster (1976) and Adams (1963).

All three of these theories are loosely derived from reinforcement-based constructs and principles, and each is elaborated by reference to an economic metaphor. The constructs and principles of traditional reinforcement theory and elementary economics are extended to apply to the circumstances governing the exchange of rewards and punishments that occurs in interpersonal interactive contexts. The basic proposal of these three viewpoints holds that small-group interactions will most probably be sustained, positively evaluated, and positively experienced by the participants when they view them as more rewarding than costly. The nature, antecedents, and consequences of rewarding and costly interchanges differ for each of the three approaches, and it is these phenomena that constitute the central concerns of each of the theories.

All three of the theories also share the general intention of serving as comprehensive models of social behavior which bear universal applicability to all domains of social interaction. The first two theories bear a superficial similarity to one another in their inclination to define interpersonal outcomes in terms of the rewards and costs that arise from the conjoint enaction of behavior on the part of two or more individuals. Equity theory is less concerned with *conjoint* action and mutual fate per se and centers almost exclusively upon the applicability of a socially embedded, universal norm of the equitable distribution of reward to myriad domains of social behavior.

We will begin our exposition of these theories with a consideration of the framework of George C. Homans.

A THEORY OF ELEMENTARY SOCIAL BEHAVIOR

The thought and theory of George C. Homans contrast markedly with the primary thought forms extant in sociological theory. Much of the sociology of human interaction is constructivist in nature. That is, it employs higher-order structural constructs, such as status, power, bureaucracy, role, ideology, and the like, to explain and predict explicit patterns of human interaction. Homans' theory is, in contrast, a reductionist model of group phenomena. Thus, it employs explicit patterns of human interaction to explain the emergence of higher-order structural phenomena, such as power and status. Homans (1961, 1974) sought to apply the elementary "facts" of operant behaviorism to the description of interdependent social behavior.

This is indeed a bold venture, which is reflective of Homans' apparent and important working assumptions: (1) There are laws of behavior which are universal to all organisms. (2) These laws of behavior can be understood on the level of fundamental process and should thus be applicable to a wide variety of specific behavioral and social domains. (3) The fundamental processes involved constitute a functional hedonism in that they reflect that organisms in general and humans in particular seek to maximize rewards, pleasure, and gratification and seek to minimize costs, pain, and punishment. (4) Finally, it is assumed that through an understanding of the particulars of operant behavior exchanges between people, one can generate the processes by which natural human groups award status, love, roles, power, and the like to one or more of their members and that social products, such as norms, conformity, leadership, and bureaucracy, can be traced and understood.

In short, Homans' model of social exchange is a comprehensive perspective on human social behavior in which the ultimate goal is the explication of not only the behavior exchanges of individual social units but also the nature and origins of human social organizations.

Social Behavior: The Form and Unit of Analysis

Homans (1961, 1974) took as his unit of theoretical analysis the elementary face-to-face social interchanges that occur between two persons. The theory describes such interchanges by invoking concepts and principles derived from behavioristic psychology and then elaborating these processes by reference to an economic metaphor. Therefore behavioristic operations characterizing such phenomena as reinforcement frequency and value are thought of in terms of elementary economic notions, such as profit and cost. When two individuals exchange behaviors in an interaction, either might reward or punish the other or satisfy or frustrate the other. The kernel notion in Homans' social dynamic is quite simple and basically holds that, depending upon the relative availability of rewards and costs in an interchange, the individual will either earn a "profit" or incur a "loss." Further, profitable interactions and relationships will be reenacted, while unprofitable ones will fall by the wayside. Thus, the survival of social units as small as the dyad and as large as a complex organization is dependent upon the maintenance of profitable exchange outcomes.

In discriminating social behavior which is elementary, Homans (1974) uses three attributes: (1) Elementary forms of social behavior are defined as fundamental processes of behavior exchange, regardless of the particular content of the behavior and how the behavioral processes combine to maintain complex social units, such as families, organizations, and social structures. (2) Elementary social behavior is also the natural and spontaneous behavior arising from interactions. In Homans' (1974) words, it is "behavior that will appear as if of its own accord among men whether or not they have consciously tried to organize it" (p. 3). (3) Elementary social behavior is also so called because the dyad and small groups from which it emerges are construed by Homans to be the elementary building blocks of larger social units.

In summary, the primary phenomena of Homans' theoretical model are noninstitutionalized face-to-face interactions spontaneously arising between people. The form of analysis of these interactions is fundamentally behavioristic, with the major terms deriving from operant reinforcement theory. The outcome of these elementary interactions is cast in terms of simple economic notions, such as payoff, profit, and loss. From a careful behavioral analysis of such social interchanges, Homans felt confident that one could arrive at an understanding of complex social structures.

In the next two sections we will provide a description of Homans' terminology and the propositions he offered to describe and account for human social exchange.

Human Exchange: Terms

One virtue of Homans' approach to social exchange is that it introduces very few new construct terms to describe social interaction. Since the terminology was directly derived from animal behaviorism, the language of Homans' model is an "objective" observation language. In his 1961 work, Homans defined two classes of terms necessary for the observation of human social behavior: *descriptive terms* and *variables*. The descriptive terms designate the behaviors to be observed in social behavior, and the variables are dimensions on which these observed behaviors might be quantified. While the descriptive terms have a particular application to social behavior, the terms designating variables are derivatives of operant learning theory. In the 1961 statement of Homans' theory, the derivative links between animal behaviorism and human social exchange are directly specified by Homans in the form of restated animal-behavior propositions. In the course of this restatement, he defines terms critical to the understanding of the derivative propositions. In the 1974 revision of his theory text, Homans dispenses with restatement of animal propositions. Never-theless, the terms used in the statement of the propositions of human social exchange warrant careful definition.

Descriptive Terms   These are the terms used to describe the kind of behavior which parties to a social exchange enact. In this category there are three basic terms: (1) activity, (2) sentiment, and (3) interaction. As we have noted earlier, *activity* is Homans' translation of Skinner's *operant*. Thus, activities are any voluntary behaviors emitted by the organism. This definition makes the class of behaviors referred to as activities infinite in scope. In his 1974 revision, Homans distinguishes between activities as gross units of behavior (e.g., fishing) and *acts* or *actions* as the finer units which comprise the general behavior class (e.g., casting, baiting a hook, tying a lure, etc.). Depending upon one's interest, either unit, actions or activities, is observable and quantifiable.

Sentiments constitute a broad class of human activities and actions. They are "the activities that the members of a particular symbolic community say are signs of the attitudes and feelings a man takes toward other men" (Homans, 1961, p. 33). Once again these activities may be coded in terms of gross units (e.g., approval) or in terms of their more specific acts (e.g., smiles, kisses, verbal agreements, etc.). In Homans' system, sentiments are not defined by the internal states of the individual but by his overt behavior or *activities.* They resemble other kinds of human social activities in that they may be *exchanged,* and in this process of exchange they reward and punish the behavior of a social other. Thus, like all behavior, sentiments have an effect on the external environment and the organisms within it. For example, a face-to-face human social exchange might involve person A emitting an activity that directly or indirectly affects person B. Person B might then respond to person A's activity by emitting a discriminable sign of a positive or negative sentiment. Person B's sentiment serves as a reinforcer or punisher of person A's behavior. Sentiments may also be the subject of a transitive exchange. That is, the positive sentiment of one party to an interaction might occasion the return of positive sentiment by the second party to that interaction.

The two situations depicted above would both be classed as *interactions* in Homans' system. *Interactions* are defined as occurring when "an activity (or sentiment) emitted by one man is rewarded (or punished) by an activity (or sentiment) emitted by another man" (Homans, 1961, p. 35). What is clear in this definition is Homans' proposal that the actions of one participant in an interaction are the stimuli for the actions of a second participant (Homans, 1974). Interaction then is a matter of socially *interdependent* exchanges of activities. It is apparent from Homans' definitions of his descriptive terms that these terms are hardly independent of one another. As noted, *sentiments* are a special class of emitted *activities;* the exchange of nonsentiment activities, sentiment activities, or both constitutes an *interaction.*

Terms Defining Variables   The two major variables in Homans' system are *quantity* and *value.* These two variables constitute the quantitative variations of activities, sentiments, and interactions.

Quantity is a frequency variable. With regard to activity, it is "the number of units of activity that the organism in question emits within a given period of time" (Homans, 1961, p. 36). Homans' definition of quantity or frequency was directly derived from operant research with animals. In accord with the operant learning perspective Homans views the quantity or frequency of an activity as a function of the *state* (deprivation or satiation) of the organism and the *rate* at which it has been reinforced or punished. Quantity, being a frequency dimension, is usually measured by a simple counting procedure. However, the units of activity in human exchange are often difficult to count, because in fact they are difficult to specify. For example, we can quite accurately count the number of times a pigeon pecks at a target or the number of times a rat presses a bar in a Skinner box; however, it is more difficult to count the number of positive sentiment activities that are exchanged in a two-party interaction. In the latter situation, criteria are less clearly specified and observations are accordingly less reliable. Homans acknowledged this difficulty, but he indicated that the quantity of human-exchange activity can be assessed by specialized experimental-observational techniques. In these cases, the unit of activity in question would have to be defined by the experimenter, and its definition would in turn determine the behaviors to be counted. In this context he cited the interaction analyses of Bales (1950) and Chapple (1940), as well as sociometric analyses. One quantity measure that Homans depicted as being easily countable is the absolute amount of time a person spends with another person over total time observed. On this basis one can evaluate the relative time, for example, person A is engaged in interactions with persons B and C. Measures of the quantity of behavior emitted by one person toward another are measures of *frequency of elementary social behavior.* In his 1974 work, Homans expanded upon this rather restrictive definition of objective frequency and included the likelihood of the occurrence of a behavior as a type of predictive frequency measure. This alteration will be expanded upon in the presentation of Homans' success proposition presented below.

Value was defined in terms of the degree of positive or negative reinforcement an individual receives from another's unit of activity. The greater the degree of positive reinforcement provided by a unit of activity, the higher the value of that unit; the greater the degree of negative reinforcement from a unit, the lower its value. It should be emphasized that the assessment of value in human exchange must be made on a unit-by-unit basis. For just as the efficacy of reinforcement might change for an animal on each trial in a sequence, so the value of a given activity (as reinforcer) can change from one unit emission to another. For example, person A may become *satiated* with the positive units of activity directed at him by person B, and, as a result, the value of these units of activity will be reduced. According to Homans, the measurement of value presents even greater difficulties than the measurement of quantity. The primary problem in measuring value is the specification of "degree" of reinforcement per unit activity.

Homans suggested that the measurement of value per unit activity can be deduced from the methods of measuring the effects of deprivation states in animals. That is, the longer an animal has been deprived of food, the more "valuable" food becomes for him. The assessment of how "valuable" a reinforcement will be to an animal necessitates the examination of that animal's immediate past history with that reinforcement. If we assume that a given object (food) is inherently valuable to the animal, then an immediate past history of deprivation from that object enhances its value. In the human-interaction situation, the same principles hold. That is, if we assume that social approval is desirable and valuable to person A, then the longer he/she has been deprived of social approval in the past, the more valuable it becomes in the present. Furthermore, person A will emit unit activities that have the greatest probability of being approved by person B. As person B emits various sentiment activities indicating approval, person A may become satiated and, as such, the value of approval will decline for him/her. Homans granted that the assessment of the past history of reinforcement of an animal is more exacting (counting hours of deprivation, weighing it, etc.) than the assessment of the past social-reinforcement history of a person. However, he believed that *value* need not be measured any more precisely than on a "more-or-less" basis in order for human interaction to be explained and its products predicted.

Homans noted that there are two components of value. They are (1) the component that specifies the constant value of an activity regardless of the state of the organism and (2) the component that specifies the value of an activity at a particular point in time and that varies as a function of state of the organism. Thus, each individual has a built-in hierarchy of values with regard to social activities. Therefore, the social approval of another may be more important than the physical help of another for an individual. The second component dictates the value of any object at some point in time. Therefore, although approval might be absolutely more valuable than physical help, the individual at a given point in time might attach a greater value to the physical help of another if he has been deprived of the help of another for a much longer period of time than he has been deprived of another's approval.

Considering both value and quantity of the activity of a social other in an interaction, Homans proposed that an individual should expend a greater *quantity* of time interacting with a social other who emits reciprocal activities that are highly valued than he/she would with an individual who emits activities which are less highly valued. Propositions of this sort are considered in the next section.

Human Exchange: Propositions

As we have noted, Homans' descriptive and quantitative terminology derive from an operant learning perspective. His propositions concerning human behavior exchanges have a similar origin. While the subsequently presented propositions are framed in a functional language (e.g., the frequency of an action is a function of the frequency of past rewards attained for such an action), Homans (1974) is quite clear in asserting that his propositions are best considered as describing crude and approximate relationships rather than exact functions with quantitatively precise form. It is also important to keep firmly in mind the overarching purpose of Homans' propositions. It is Homans' goal to discern the principles governing the exchanges between and among people, and the characteristics of those exchanges that result in the maintenance and salience of human social relationships. In short, Homans does not simply engage in trivial restatement of learning principles, but his propositions are novel and important ones because of their application to human social interaction.

Proposition 1: The Success Proposition   This initial proposition of social exchange is a direct derivative of the "law of effect." Homans (1974) stated this proposition as follows. *"For all actions taken by persons, the more often a particular action of a person is rewarded, the more likely a person is to perform that action"* (p. 16). As we shall see, this initial proposition within Homans' system is qualified by some of the subsequent propositions, but it is rather basic to any model predicated on behavioral psychology. The success proposition is thus a general statement of the functional relationship between frequency of actions and frequency of rewards. Since not all rewards are of equal value and too frequent administration of the same reward decreases the value of that reward, the proposition cannot stand on its own.

There are myriad confirmations of the success proposition or law of effect in the literature of animal and human learning. When applied to human social exchange, one is not speaking of any reward from any source but is instead proposing that the more frequently one person's actions reward the actions of another person, the greater the likelihood that the other's action will recur. Homans (1961) illustrated this proposition in a human social context by noting that the more often one person thanks another person for help, the more often the other person will give help to the first person. Thus, individuals can maintain the actions of others with whom they relate by reciprocating those actions with positive sentiments (or perhaps material rewards).

Proposition 2: The Stimulus Proposition   This proposition states that *"if in the past, the occurrence of a particular stimulus, or set of stimuli, has been the occasion on which a person's action has been rewarded, then the more similar the present stimuli are to the past ones, the more likely the person is to perform the action, or some similar action, now"* (Homans, 1974, p. 23). The stimulus proposition is a rather straightforward restatement of the phenomena of *stimulus generalization* and *secondary reinforcement* in human and animal learning. In the social domain particular persons as well as their physical, psychological, behavioral, and verbal attributes constitute the stimulus dimension. When particular people or their salient attributes have in the past served as *discriminative stimuli* for the reward or punishment of an individual's actions, those actions will be reenacted or avoided in the presence of the same or similar stimuli.

It should be noted that in the case of proposition 2, this reenactment of behavior is not a direct function of past reward but rather a response to the presence of reward-associated stimuli. This is the crucial distinction between propositions 1 and 2. For example, if a child had frequently received pleasing hugs from his/her Aunt Sarah in return for a broad smile, then proposition 1 would propose that the child's smiling behavior would come under the *reinforcement control* of Aunt Sarah's affectionate hugging, while proposition 2 would propose that the child's smiling would come under the *stimulus control* of Aunt Sarah's presence. Further, proposition 2 would also predict that the child's smiles would be more evident in response to others who bear an attribute similarity to Aunt Sarah. Thus, the child might smile more frequently than usual in the presence of blue-eyed, chubby, soft-spoken, matronly women. The more closely others exhibit an Aunt Sarah-like attribute(s), the more likely the occurrence of the child's smiling. One of the overwhelming problems with using proposition 2 predictively inheres in the complexity of human stimuli. Humans vary on so many abstract and concrete dimensions that it would appear that, while proposition 2 provides for a source of *post hoc* explanation of socially mediated behavior, it could only be used predictively in the most general way.

Proposition 3: The Value Proposition   In the success proposition Homans proposed that the *frequency* with which a particular past action has led to reward will partly determine the probability of the action recurring. Another determinant of the reenactment of a behavior is the *value* of the rewards which issue from that behavior. Homans states this relationship in the value proposition: "the more valuable to a person is the result of his action, the more likely he is to perform the action" (Homans, 1974, p. 25).

In the terminology of exchange theory, social exchanges will recur when the participants exact a *profit* from their exchanged actions. That is, when the *rewards* of an action exceed its *costs*, it and its exchange context will recur. The value proposition builds upon this basic notion (which is essentially proposition 1) by adding that the likelihood of reenactment increases with increases in the degree of profit which follows from exchanged social acts. There are many sources of reward value in the social domain. The value of various rewards might be biologically determined (e.g., food, water, shelter, etc.) or acquired through socialization (e.g., needs for affection, money, humor, etc.). Further, the value of particular rewards may be situationally specific (e.g., food may only be valuable when hunger is felt) or situationally pervasive (e.g., a person may have constantly strong needs for approval, thereby rendering social approval a persistently valuable reward). In the domain of social relationships, the value proposition would suggest that those relationships yielding the highest degree of profit or reward value will be more likely to be reenacted than relationships yielding smaller profits or less-valuable rewards.

Proposition 4: The Deprivation-Satiation Proposition   Homans (1974) notes that the value proposition is concerned with how valuable a person finds a particular reward in comparison to alternative rewards. The value proposition would lead to rather straightforward transsituational behavioral predictions for a person if his/her reward values were stable from one occasion to another. However, the value of a given reward is not likely to be the same on each occasion. The deprivation-satiation proposition provides a principle which accounts for some of the variance in reward values across occasions. Homan (1974) stated this proposition as follows: *"The more often in the recent past a person has received a particular reward, the less valuable any further unit of that reward becomes for him"* (p. 29).

Homans noted that the deprivation-satiation proposition describes a crude general tendency and is not terribly precise. Different kinds of rewards have different satiation and deprivation thresholds, and some rewards maintain an almost persistently high value and can thus serve as generalized rewards. In the domain of social exchange, this proposition predicts that men will reenact behaviors to the extent that these behaviors will occasion actions on the part of the other which bring needed rewards. When one individual becomes satiated with the particular rewards available from another, interaction in that relationship will decrease until the need for those particular rewards increases.

Proposition 5: The Aggression-Approval Proposition   The foregoing propositions all deal with the antecedent probability of an individual engaging in a particular social exchange. In a sense they define those circumstances that would lead a person to expect a profit or loss from enacting a particular set of actions toward or with another. Putting it very simply, if an individual, on the basis of the past history of reinforcement and interaction in a relationship, currently expects to gain valued rewards at an acceptable cost, he/she will interact with the other. Proposition 5 deals with the emotional consequences of the failure of such expectancies after the enactment of particular interactive behaviors. This proposition is stated in two parts. The first part describes the emotional consequences of obtained rewards falling short of expectations, while the second part describes the emotional consequences of the attained rewards for a person's actions meeting or exceeding expectations.

Proposition 5a states that, *"when a person's action does not receive the reward he expected, or receives punishment he did not expect, he will be angry; he becomes more likely to perform aggressive behavior, and the results of such behavior become more valuable to him"* (Homans, 1974, p. 37). Proposition 5b states that, *"when a person's action receives reward he expected, especially a greater reward than he expected, or does not receive punishment he expected, he will be pleased; he becomes more likely to perform approving behavior, and the results of such behavior become more valuable to him"* (Homans, 1974, p. 39).

In short, proposition 5 defines a set of conditions for the enactment of positive and negative sentiment activities in a social exchange. It should be noted that the anger or approval expressed by one party to a social exchange serves as feedback for the other party to that exchange. For example, upon receiving the aggressive sentiment actions of another, a person should either increase the rewards offered in subsequent exchanges or cease relating to the other. Approval sentiments should also be short-lived because unusually frequent or valuable rewards will become more usual and expected after their initial enactment.

Proposition 6: The Rationality Proposition This last proposition in Homans' system could be referred to as a choice corollary. Given the complexity of human relationships, individuals are always confronted with choices concerning which action among a large number of potential actions should be exchanged in an interaction with another. The principles stated in the first five propositions would suggest that actions have variable probabilities of reward and occasion contingent rewards of variable value. Homans proposes that, since individuals behave to maximize the expected *utility* of an action, the multiplicative product of the probability and value of the rewards contingent on each action will determine the action chosen. In Homans' (1974) words, *"In choosing between alternative actions, a person will choose that one for which, as perceived by him at the time, the value of the result, multiplied by the probability of getting the result, is the greater"* (p. 43).

This proposition is really a clear deduction from the success and value propositions and serves to remind us that neither parameter of reward functions independently of the other in a social exchange.

The Rule of Distributive Justice

Distributive justice as well as being an illustrative rule of exchange in Homans' theory could also be construed as another proposition in Homans' system. In social relationships, the rule of distributive justice holds that *"a man in an exchange relation with another will expect that the rewards of each man be proportional to his costs—the greater the rewards, the greater the costs—and that the net rewards, or profits, of each man be proportional to his investments—the greater the investments, the greater the profit"* (Homans, 1961, p. 75. Italics ours). When the desired proportionality between rewards and costs, and investments and profits, does not accrue from social exchange, the rule of distributive justice is violated. The probable results of this rule violation are expressed by Homans as follows: *"the more to a man's disadvantage the rule of distributive justice fails of realization, the more likely he is to display the emotional behavior we call anger"* (Homans, 1961, p. 75. Italics ours). A corollary to this proposal holds that if the failure of distributive justice in a social exchange is to the individual's advantage rather than to their disadvantage, they will be likely to experience a level of *guilt* proportional to the extent of their undeserved advantage.

Distributive justice, then, is more than an applied case of social exchange; it is also a rule that is operative in all areas of social behavior.

In any social exchange, distributive justice can be characterized as the process of *fair exchange* of rewards and costs. If we assume, as Homans does, that participation in one activity precludes participation in an alternate activity and, further, that the more valuable the alternate activity the greater the cost the person incurs in engaging in the first activity, then engaging in the first activity when the alternate activity is highly rewarding *should*, if fair exchange applies, lead to proportionately high rewards.

Homans stated that one's evaluation of whether or not he/she is receiving a just return on his/her investments in a social exchange is based upon his/her past experience in other social exchanges. These past experiences set up expectations of "exchange rate" in individuals. In our above example, person A would not experience guilt if he/she did not experience the exchange of rewards as disproportionate to the original investment. That is, if his/her past experience was such as to lead him/her to expect large rewards for small investments, the situation depicted above would be considered "just" by him/her. On the other hand, if person B had been accustomed to small rewards for large costs (if a martyr type, for example), then he/she might not experience anger at the depicted exchange. When there are conflicting and noncomplementary standards between two interacting individuals of what a fair rate of exchange is, it will probably be impossible for the rule of distributive justice to determine the course of interaction. In this case the most likely eventuality would be a discontinuance of the exchange. This concept of individually differing expectations of reciprocal or just rewards is very much like Thibaut and Kelley's (1959) concept of *comparison level*, discussed in a later section of this chapter.

Summary and Comment

Homans' theoretical framework provides for a useful and interesting approach to understanding human social interaction. The primary notion in the system is that the occurrences of interpersonal behaviors, like those of individual behaviors, are mediated by the probability that such behaviors will result in valued reward outcomes. Further, the survival of the relationships within which these behaviors are enacted is dependent upon the "usual" profits and losses incurred by the participants to those relationships. One appealing aspect of Homans' approach is that it introduces very few variables and terms to account for these complex human phenomena. In addition, the variables (i.e., frequency and value of rewards) and the descriptive terms (action, activity, interaction, and sentiment) are derived from other more-general systems of thought and require only simple translation to explain human social behavior. In short, Homans' system has the advantage of terminological simplicity and economy. As a consequence, Homans' ambitious model has the virtue of simply explaining complex human events.

In order to make use of Homans' theory, it is important to be aware of the interdependence of his several propositions. Further, it is important to recognize that his propositions demand that current interactions are predicated on past interactions and are thus dependent upon the individual reinforcement histories of the participants. A simply summary of Homans' propositions would state that individuals in a dyadic social interaction will enact those behaviors which have a high probability of obtaining those reciprocated rewards which are most profitable. The propositions deal with the conditions which would render available rewards as potentially profitable (e.g., the person's current need for the reward, the similarity of the interactant to past rewarding partners, etc.). The principles embodied by Homans' propositions are viewed by him as quite powerful, so powerful, in fact, that, if one enacts actions in a relationship and fails to achieve the expected or deserved rewards, emotional behavior (anger, aggression, approval, guilt) will result. If these conditions prevail, expectations will in time change, and, if one is led to expect less than his/her actions invest in a relationship, then the relationship should discontinue. Propositions like this latter proposition are Homans' beginning points for using his system to describe the determinants of complex social structural phenomena like marriages, work groups, governmental behavior, and the like. It is these latter phenomena which the sociologist Homans aspires to explain by his model.

The general thrust of Homans' propositions has been well supported in both experimental and field studies. In his 1974 book, Homans cites a large array of studies on phenomena, including group leadership, conformity, industrial behavior, justice, etc., which are illustrative of one or another proposition within his model. Chadwick-Jones (1976) also provides an excellent summary of those data compatible with Homans' system. Yet, most of the experimental and field studies supportive of Homans' approach were not explicitly designed to confirm his propositions. Instead, Homans' propositions are used to provide *post hoc* explanations of the findings of studies performed for other reasons. The most notable exception to this general point is the work of Gullahorn and Gullahorn (1963, 1965, 1972), which represents largely successful attempts to develop computer simulations of several of Homans' exchange propositions. In short, while Homans' theory is consistent with research evidence in several areas of human social behavior, it has infrequently generated theory-testing investigations. Most of the research cited as supportive of Homans' approach (cf., Chadwick-Jones, 1976; Homans, 1974; Hamblin & Kunkel, 1977) would be supportive of any exchange-theory vision of social interaction (e.g., Blau, 1964; Thibaut & Kelley, 1959; Kelley & Thibaut, 1978; Foa & Foa, 1975). Many of the particulars which distinguish Homans' theory from other exchange views have not met with independent confirmation.

The most pervasive contribution of Homans' thought has been its impact upon the development of behavioral sociology. Homans' use of a Skinnerian-based model of social interaction has generated substantial theoretical controversy for the study of social structure.

A THEORY OF INTERDEPENDENCE

In 1959 Thibaut and Kelley presented an intriguing and ambitious framework for the analysis of social interdependence in small groups. While their framework bore a family resemblance to social exchange models such as Homans', it was at one and the same time more broadly construed and more narrowly predictive. To be more explicit, Thibaut and Kelley offered a broader version of reinforcement-based phenomena, such as interaction rewards and costs, than that provided by the operant-learning base invoked by Homans. While Homans capitalized on the explicit connections and continuities between animal and human learning, Thibaut and Kelley defined the rewards and costs available in human interaction in distinctly human terms. They derived no formal propositions embodying functional relationships between reward frequency and value, for example. Instead Thibaut and Kelley predicated the determinants of social rewards and costs on the findings and principles of social psychology. For example, another's similarity to a person might be thought of as a reward because a sizable body of social-psychological research had determined that it frequently facilitates attraction and bonding. In short, in Thibaut and Kelley's model both the determinants of social reward value (i.e., similarity, complementarity, and the like) as well as the outcomes of the social exchange of rewards (i.e., social norms, power and status relationships, coalition formation, and the like) are viewed as inherently social in nature.

While the Thibaut and Kelley version of rewards and reward exchanges is predicated on a broader definition of reinforcement phenomena than the Homans version, their theoretical framework was viewed as applying to a narrower range of phenomena than that of Homans. While Homans' hope was to account for both small-group behavior and larger social structural phenomena, Thibaut and Kelley were explicitly interested in the behavior and social products of small groups. Finally, Thibaut and Kelley (1959) offered a useful analytic technique for the analysis of social interactions and exchanges, the outcome matrix. While Homans (1974) came to adopt the general structure of the outcome matrix (which is designed to represent the reward and cost consequences of two or more people's joint behavior enactments) for the finer-grained articulation of his propositions, Thibaut and Kelley's outcome matrix notation became the major device for confirming hypotheses concerning socially interdependent relationship phenomena. In short, the Thibaut and Kelley outcome matrix provided a paradigmatic framework for conducting small-group research.

The major conceptual premises for Thibaut and Kelley's approach appeared in their 1959 book entitled *The Social Psychology of Groups*. In 1978 Kelley and Thibaut published a companion piece for this original work. The latter treatment constitutes a theoretically formal elaboration of the original. The analysis of socially interdependent interactions in the second work is more explicit, exacting, and systematic than in the initial presentation. Yet, the basic framework of *The Social Psychology of Groups* is conserved. The major contribution of Kelley and Thibaut (1978) is their painstaking attention to the particulars involved in the interactive transformations of the outcome matrix. Where relevant to our exposition, occasional references have been made to the 1978 work; however, we have largely confined ourselves to the seminal framework provided in the 1959 work in the subsequent presentation of Thibaut and Kelley's theory of social interdependence.

An Overview of the Theory

Thibaut and Kelley stated that the essence of any interpersonal relationship is *interaction*. In their theorizing they were predominantly concerned with *dyadic* interaction. They defined dyadic interaction as occurring when two people emit behavior in one another's presence. The behavior emitted by each person must at the very least have the possibility of affecting the other person. Every individual has an extensive repertoire of behaviors that may be emitted in an interaction. One might analyze the behavior occurring in an interaction in many different ways. A microscopic analysis would involve considering in its intricacy every single unit of behavior that a person emits. A macroscopic analysis, on the other hand, would involve viewing only the general end products of a total sequence of interactive behavior. Thibaut and Kelley claimed to have taken a middle course between these two extremes. They designated the *behavior sequence* or *set* as their unit of analysis. Each specified interactive unit (behavior sequence) consists of a number of verbal and motor acts that are sequentially organized and directed toward a goal. Some of the responses within this sequence are *instrumental* in that they move the individual toward the goal, and others are *consummatory* in that they engender the individual's enjoyment of the goal state. In all cases the individual responses within the sequence are serially dependent. That is, each single response is dependent upon the one preceding it in the sequence. This sequential organization apparent in behavior sequences indicates that the individual maintains a consistent orientation in reference to the goal throughout the sequence. For this reason, behavior sequences are alternately referred to as *sets*.

In a two-party interaction, each party may produce any given set or behavior sequence that is initially within his repertoire. The production of a given sequence can depend upon his/her own internal need state or the instigation of the other person. The "stream of interaction" between two individuals can be described in terms of the items in their repertoire which each produces in the presence of the other, in response to the other or as stimuli to the other.

Although the outcomes of interactions may be described in many ways, Thibaut and Kelley chose to consider the *rewards* and *costs* that accrue to the individual as a consequence of his/her having participated in an interaction. Rewards are the satisfactions and gratifications that a person receives from having participated in a given interaction with another. Costs are those factors that serve to inhibit the performance of a given behavior sequence. They are the negative consequences of emitting a sequence of behavior in an interactive context. Thus, the outcome of any interaction is considered to be a resultant of the rewards received and the costs incurred.

In an interaction, the rewards gained and the costs incurred may be determined by factors external to that interaction or by factors inherent in that interaction. The first category of *exogenous determinants* includes the individual's own needs, values, and abilities or the situational context of the interaction. Exogenously determined rewards and costs may be alternatively gained or incurred by the individual. That is, one particular interaction is not essential to their attainment. The second category of reward-cost determinants is referred to as *endogenous determinants*. These are inherent in the interaction. Therefore, "the specific values associated with A's repertoire depend upon the particular item in B's repertoire with which, in the course of interaction, it is paired" (Thibaut & Kelley, 1959, p. 16). The items in B's repertoire, then, might either interfere with or facilitate A's attainment of positive outcomes. Endogenously determined rewards or costs could not accrue to an individual except through interaction with at least one other individual.

The major analytic technique used by Thibaut and Kelley is the *outcome matrix*. The outcome matrix is formed by noting all the behaviors that two individuals might jointly perform. Each cell of this matrix contains one item of *each* individual's repertoire. Hypothetically, at least, all items of A's behavior repertoire are represented on the horizontal axis of the matrix, and all items of B's repertoire on the vertical axis. Figure 4-1 below illustrates a hypothetical outcome matrix. The rewards gained and the costs incurred by each person are entered in each cell of the outcome matrix. Therefore, in Figure 4-1 the pairing of behavior sequence a_1 with behavior sequence b_2 will yield a quantity of reward to both A and B (r_A, r_B) and a certain cost to both A and B (C_A, C_B). If rewards and costs are combined into a single measure of goodness of outcome. a simplified matrix such as that presented in Figure 4-2 is generated.

The interpretation of Figure 4-2 is relatively clear. If person A enacts behavior a_1 and person B enacts behavior b_1, person A receives six units of positive outcome (positive outcome refers to the resultant of a reward-cost subtraction) and person B receives two units of positive outcome. On the other hand, if person A enacts behavior a_2 while person B enacts behavior b_2, then person A receives two units of positive outcome and person B receives five units of positive outcome. Thus, the paired enactment of behavioral units by two parties in an interaction yields positive outcomes to both parties. In a cooperative relationship, both parties are likely to attempt to maximize their own positive outcomes by enacting those behaviors that yield the greatest positive outcomes for their partner. In the situation in which the paired sequences of behavior do not yield maximal outcomes to both parties, it is likely that the cooperating parties will alternate the paired behavior sequences that they enact in order that both parties attain maximal positive outcomes some of the time.

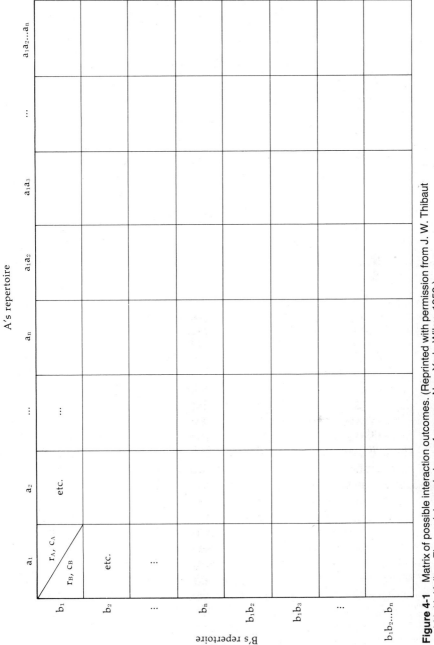

Figure 4-1 Matrix of possible interaction outcomes. (Reprinted with permission from J. W. Thibaut and H. H. Kelley. *The social psychology of groups.* New York: Wiley, 1959.)

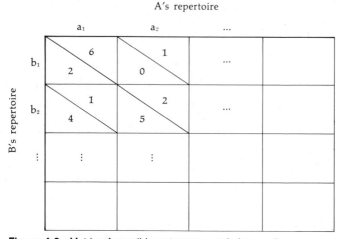

Figure 4-2 Matrix of possible outcomes, scaled according to overall goodness of outcomes. (Reprinted with permission from J. W. Thibaut and H. H. Kelley. *The social psychology of groups.* New York: Wiley, 1959.)

In a competitive relationship, each member of the dyad is likely to enact those behavioral sequences that have the greatest probability of maximal self-reward. However, in interdependent competitive relationships, persons A and B might cooperate for the attainment of maximally positive outcomes.

The outcome matrix, in addition to representing the joint outcomes accruing to the members of a dyad, also aids in "assessing the viability of a group (dyad), the satisfactions and patterns of interdependence of its members, and the processes through which the members influence and control one another" (Thibaut & Kelley, 1959, p. 24). Thibaut and Kelley made several assumptions about the nature of the outcome matrix:

1 All relevant possibilities of rewards and costs for a given interaction are represented in the cells of the matrix.

2 All the possible behaviors of A and B peculiar to the target interaction are represented in the margins of the matrix.

3 The values for rewards, costs, and goodness of outcome vary across time. Thus, interaction does not merely involve the repetition of the most rewarding joint behaviors, but rather consists of successive movements from one cell to another in search of the most-optimal outcome on a given trial. The variation in the reward-cost values of a given cell may be because of many factors. Two prominent ones are satiation and fatigue, both of which tend to increase the cost and lower the reward of emitting a behavior.

4 The matrix is not known to the participants prior to interaction. Instead, the participants continually discover the possible outcome as well as their partner's (opponent's) repertoire as the interaction progresses.

Although the matrix of outcomes was originally devised as a descriptive and analytic tool, Thibaut and Kelley asserted that it might also be used predictively.

When individuals have searched out the contingencies within a matrix, their behavior should stabilize and they should enact those behaviors with the greatest probability of positive outcome. The nature of the matrix in terms of the objectively available outcomes accruing from the joint enactment of two individuals will then determine their most-adaptive behavior sequence. As the matrix changes, the predictions of which behavior sequences of the participants will predominate also change. Furthermore, the pattern of objectively available outcomes can be used to predict the form of interdependent relationship that will develop with interaction. Thus, power and dependence relations may be predicted on the basis of the control one party has over the positive outcomes of the second party.

Since the balance of control can shift back and forth between persons as an interaction progresses, accurate prediction of the course and outcome of a relationship requires a methodology which can characterize such transformations. The major focus of Kelley and Thibaut (1978) is on these transformational processes. In this work, the theorists designate the preinteraction matrix of outcomes as the *given matrix* and distinguish it from the *effective matrix,* or the pattern of outcome possibilities arising from the interaction itself. The specific transformation rules governing the joint behavior enactments of interdependent partners vary depending upon the intent of the participants, the perception of the partner's intent by each participant, and the avowed or experimentally induced purpose of the interaction (e.g., cooperation or competition). Kelley and Thibaut (1978) carefully illustrate the range of possible given→effective matrix transformations in different forms of interaction. In this sense, the Kelley and Thibaut (1978) treatment of the outcome matrix enhances the predictive strength of the original framework and thus allows them to refer more forcibly to their conceptualization of interdependence as a "theory." Those readers with an explicit interest in the elaborated empirical application of Thibaut and Kelley's model would do well to consult their 1978 treatment of matrix transformations.

As noted above, neither participant in a dyad is initially aware of the outcomes that might be attained by interacting with the other. Thus, at the outset of interaction, each member samples the outcomes available to him/her in the target interaction. Members will sustain the interaction after this sampling period only if the experienced or inferred outcomes are sufficient to warrant continued interaction. The adequacy of experienced or inferred outcomes is evaluated on two criteria: (1) the *comparison level* (CL) and (2) the *comparison level for alternatives* (CLalt). The first of these is the standard by which an individual evaluates the attractiveness of a relationship; the second is the standard by which an individual decides whether or not he/she will remain in a relationship. These two criteria are separate ones because, for example, an individual may continue a relationship regarded as unattractive if it is the best available to him/her at the time. The CL is the minimum level of positive outcome which an individual feels he/she deserves from any relationship. If a given relationship yields outcomes which fall above the CL, it should be relatively attractive to the member; if the outcomes fall below the CL, it should be relatively unattractive. There are several determinants of comparison level, and they are discussed in a later section of this chapter.

Thibaut and Kelley defined CLalt as "the lowest level of outcomes a member will accept in the light of available alternative opportunities" (Thibaut & Kelley, 1959, p. 21). The alternative relationship used as a standard to compare a perspective relationship with is generally the member's best available alternative. For a dyad to be formed, the jointly experienced outcomes must exceed each member's CLalt. The CLalt is discussed more fully in a subsequent section of this chapter.

The overview above of Thibaut and Kelley's theory should provide the reader with the necessary understanding of their orientation as well as a sufficient command of their vocabulary to consider the more-specific details of the system. The subsequent sections detail the following considerations: (1) the determinants of reward and cost, (2) the formation and evaluation of relationships, and (3) the products of interaction.

The Determinants of Reward and Costs

The rewards and costs in interactive relationships may be determined by several factors. As we have noted previously, some of these factors are external to the stream of interaction (exogenous factors) and others are dependent upon the stream of interaction (endogenous factors).

Exogenous Determinants   Rewards and costs that do not directly ensue from social interaction and are in fact determined by factors outside the interaction are termed *exogenous*. Exogenous determinants of rewards and costs may include the individual needs and abilities of the participants, the preinteraction similarities or differences in their attitudes or values, and the situational context of their interpersonal contact with one another. In many cases, the exogenous determinants of rewards and costs cited by Thibaut and Kelley are factors which have been found to correlate with sociometric choice (Jennings, 1950; Winch, 1952; Newcomb, 1956). Some of the more-important exogenous determinants discussed by Thibaut and Kelley are ability, similarity, proximity, and complementarity. Let us briefly consider each of these.

Abilities   Persons who are preferred or chosen by others as dyadic partners often have abilities that the nonchosen do not possess. Thus, they possess a greater potentiality for rewarding the other in an interaction. However, depending upon factors such as the person's willingness to participate jointly with the other, his/her own needs that require specific behaviors from the other, etc., the interaction may also involve more or less cost. Nevertheless, a generally positive outcome is more likely in relationships with more-able than in those with less-able individuals. Thus, outcomes are at least partially determined by the abilities of the participants. This is particularly true in interactions in which the goal is problem solution or task completion. Ability has intentionally not been specifically defined here. Depending upon the nature of the interaction engaged in, reward-cost determining abilities may be general (intelligence, for example) or consist of specific skills.

Similarity   There has been much research showing that individuals with similar attitudes and orientations are more prone to select one another as friends, mates, or partners. Thibaut and Kelley have asserted that these findings may be interpreted in a reward-cost framework:

> If we assume that in many value areas an individual is in need of social support for his opinions and attitudes then another person's agreeing with him will constitute a reward for him. . . . Thus two people with similar values may provide rewards for each other simply by expressing their values. This may also be a low-cost operation, since it is easy for a person to express the values he really feels (Thibaut & Kelley, 1959, p. 43).

Thus, preinteraction similarities between participants in a dyad should facilitate the attainment of positive outcomes by both members during the interaction.

Proximity   Citing experimental evidence from several sources (Festinger, Schacter, & Back, 1950; Gullahorn, 1952; Powell, 1952; Newcomb, 1956; Williams, 1956; Priest & Sawyer, 1967), Thibaut and Kelley designated physical proximity as an exogenous determinant of rewards and costs in social relationships. It takes greater effort and therefore involves greater costs to form and maintain physically distant relationships than to form and maintain physically close relationships. Proximity, particularly in natural social settings, might be confounded with similarity, and to this extent these two variables might very well coact in the formation of a relationship. Nevertheless, if one controls for the similarity of the two members of a dyad, those dyads in which the members are in physically close proximity to each other should be more long lasting and should yield a greater opportunity for positive outcomes than the dyads in which the members are spatially separated.

Complementarity   Thibaut and Kelley stated that the formation of a dyad is facilitated by the members being able to reward one another at low cost to themselves. Therefore, complementarity should also be a determinant of outcomes. That is, in a complementary relationship each person can perform activities for the other that the other cannot perform for himself/herself. Thus each can provide something that the other *needs* and cannot procure himself/herself. Dominant persons will have the opportunity to exercise their dominance in relationship with dependent persons; in this same relationship, the dependent persons could receive their dependency gratifications from dominant ones (Winch, 1955). In a complementary relationship, such as the one just cited, the rewards for both participants are high (need gratification) and the costs are low (the emission of behaviors consonant with one's orientation) and thus outcomes are positive for both. Complementarity has indeed been found to be a significant factor in attraction and social bonding (e.g., Jones & Daugherty, 1959: Kerchoff & Davis, 1962; Levinger, Senn, & Jorgensen, 1970).

According to Thibaut and Kelley, the exogenous determinants of rewards and costs function as "boundary conditions" or givens for any interactive relationship. However, the maximum rewards and minimum costs that are potentially available to individuals in an interactive relationship can only be achieved when certain factors endogenous to the relationship are operative. Thus, the exogenous determinants set the limits of achievement of positive outcomes in an interaction setting, and the endogenous factors determine whether or not these outcomes will actually be attained.

Endogenous Determinants The endogenous factors that determine reward-cost contingencies are those factors that arise during and as a consequence of the interaction process. Thus, they are factors internal to a specific dyad or group. Endogenous factors, when optimal, facilitate the maximization of positive outcomes for the participants in an interaction; when they are less than optimal, they attenuate potential positive outcomes.

The endogenous interference with or facilitation of optimal reward-cost possibilities results from the combinations of behavior sequences enacted by the members of a dyad. In a dyad, person A may enact a behavior sequence (a_1) that is incompatible with B's enactment of a behavior sequence (b_1). Insofar as sequence a_1 is incompatible with sequence b_1, it serves as an interference to the performance of b_1 when they occur in combination. Furthermore, if sequence b_1 is incompatible with A's performance of a_1, then these particular sets of the two participants are mutually incompatible and symmetrically interfering.

Consider the following example of a dyadic relationship in which person A and person B are sisters. Person A enacts behavior sequence a_1 involving the playing of some popular records on a phonograph located in the study. Person B, however, is attempting to enact behavior sequence b_1 involving study. It is apparent in this example that behavior sequence a_1 is incompatible with b_1 and thus reduces B's reward probabilities. On the other hand, b_1 is also incompatible with a_1 in that it attenuates A's enjoyment of the records (for example, having to turn down the volume). Thus behavior sequences a_1 and b_1 are symmetrically interfering and thus mutually incompatible. The enactment of the combined a_1b_1 behavior sequences interferes with A and B maximizing their rewards at minimal costs.

To maximize rewards at minimum costs, either person A or person B in the example above might change her behavior sequence. Thus person A might enact behavior sequence a_2, which might involve polishing her shoes in preparation for the next day and thus allowing B to study for a longer period of time. Person B, on the other hand, might switch to behavior sequence b_2 and delay studying in order to listen to some of her favorite records along with person A. Thus, the enactment of either the joint behavior sequences a_2b_1 or a_1b_2 would be mutually facilitating to persons A and B and thus maximize the rewards and minimize the costs of participating in this particular relationship.

Thibaut and Kelley noted that response interference in a dyad may exist at two levels: (1) person A may enact a behavior sequence that interferes with person B's *production* of a given set and (2) person A might enact a behavior sequence that interferes with B's appreciation of the products of the behavior performed by B, or the *consummation* of rewards contingent upon that behavior. In the first case, B's costs are likely to go up although the rewards to B will be only secondarily affected. In the second case, B's rewards will decrease in value and, additionally, the costs to B will also increase as a function of A's production of an interfering sequence.

With regard to A's enactment of a behavior sequence (a_1) which interferes with B's production of behavior sequence b_1, Thibaut and Kelley stated that *"inhibiting or incompatible response tendencies accompanying the production of behavior increase the optimal cost of the behavior, whether in the form of annoyance, embarrassment, anxiety, or the increased effort required to make the appropriate responses"* (Thibaut and Kelley, 1959, p. 53. Italics ours). As we have implied above, interference is often *mutually* produced by the behavior sequence enactments of both parties in a dyad. Thibaut and Kelley invoked a conflict hypothesis to explain the *amount* of cost increase under conditions of set incompatibility. They suggested that the costs induced by interference are proportional to the conflict aroused by the incompatible situation. That is, if a_1 arouses only weak competing tendencies to sequence b_1, then the cost incurred by B will be relatively small. On the other hand, if a_1 arouses strong competing tendencies to b_1, then the cost of B's enactment of b_1 will be high. For example, if a_1 arouses in person B a tendency to enact a behavior sequence with potentially attractive outcomes that at the same time conflicts with sequence b_1, then the cost incurred by B in performing b_1 will increase greatly.

When B's appreciation of the rewards of performing a given behavior sequence is interfered with by A's enactment of a_1, Thibaut and Kelley postulated that there should be a drop in the value of the reward. That is, insofar as a_1 interferes with B's attentive, interpretive, or consummatory responses at the point of reward, then reward value drops, merely because the reward cannot be fully "appreciated."

The formation and maintenance of a relationship is, in part, contingent upon the compatibility of the sets produced by the participants. Thus, for a relationship to survive, the participants must either *synchronize* incompatible sets or, if they cannot, eliminate them. Thibaut and Kelley stated that "behaviors may be synchronized so that only compatible responses are simultaneously performed. Such synchronization may be produced by cues that simultaneously arouse reciprocal or compatible behavior or by the existence of normative prescriptions which co-activate reciprocal role behavior" (Thibaut & Kelley, 1959, p. 63). Thus, if sets a_1 and b_1 are incompatible, they would not be produced simultaneously, but instead the participants would seek our appropriate joint-behavior sequences. Although a_1 is incompatible with b_1, it may be compatible with b_3 and hence paired with b_3 instead of b_1 in future interactions. However, "persistently interfering behaviors may be eliminated from the relationship"

(Thibaut & Kelley, 1959, p. 63). Thus, the behavior sequences of one or both of the participants that consistently instigate low-reward–high-cost outcomes, regardless of the sets with which they are paired, will be eliminated from the relationship. If these sets are not eliminated, the flow of interaction will be inhibited and the relationship will be jeopardized.

The processes by which interfering, nonsynchronous, and maladaptive conjoint behavior sequences are eliminated are a large part of the interactive transformation of given matrixes of outcome into effective matrixes of outcome (Kelley & Thibaut, 1978).

The Formation of the Relationship

Once the initial contact is made between two individuals, the formation and survival of the relationship depend upon the levels of outcomes the individuals experience or expect to experience. Our earlier discussion of the CLalt led to the conclusion that individuals will form and remain in those relationships that promise to yield the best-possible outcomes. In the initial formative phase of a relationship, the participants explore the matrix of possible outcomes in an attempt to evaluate the objective outcome values potentially available in that relationship. Thibaut and Kelley noted that this process of exploring the matrix is accomplished by (1) *experiencing samples of the outcomes* in segments of the matrix and making inferences about the positivity of these outcomes and (2) *forecasting trends* in the outcomes, particularly with regard to their stability.

If the initial contact between two persons results in sample outcomes that fall well below the CLalt, then the relationship will generally proceed no further. That is, if the projected outcomes of forming a particular relationship are not competitive with the outcomes possibly available in other alternative relationships, the individual would gain little and lose much by entering into the interaction on a more permanent basis. If, however, the outcomes sampled on initial contact fall well above the CLalt, the individual will then attempt to forecast trends to determine whether or not these positive outcomes will remain stable across time. If it is likely that the outcome matrix will remain stable, the individual will probably engage in repeated interaction with the target person in order to establish the relationship. When the level of the initially sampled outcomes is only marginally above the CLalt, the individual will attempt to determine if the outcomes will tend to get better or worse in the context of a more permanent relationship.

This process of exploring the matrix of possible outcomes serves to reduce the uncertainty involved in entering into social relationships. This exploration becomes very crucial when permanent relationships, such as marriage, are in their formative stage. Certain broad factors influence the exploration process. These factors were considered from the points of view of the *"production of behavior"* (the stimulus side) and of *"the perception of behavior"* (the response side).

The Production of Behavior   The factors considered under this rubric are those that affect the behaviors that each person selects from his/her repertoire to produce in the formative stages of a relationship. The four factors dealt with by Thibaut and Kelley are strangeness, accessibility and cultural norms, autistic hostility, and autistic friendliness.

Strangeness   The early stages of most relationships are characterized by stereotypic politeness and other stereotyped forms of behavior. Thus, in general, individuals usually restrict the range of behaviors which they are willing to display to new acquaintances. This situation is particularly relevant when the two persons making initial contact are somewhat "strange" or unfamiliar to one another. A pattern case might be the initial meeting between a black who has had predominant social contacts with other blacks and a white who has had predominant social contacts with other whites.

The stranger any two people making initial contact are to each other, the greater difficulty they will have in exploring the matrix of possible outcomes because each individual will display very little of his/her behavioral repertoire. Thus, the perspective participants in the relationship remain relatively uncertain as to whether the interaction in question exceeds their Clalt. In this case, the individuals will have to expend more effort in exploring the matrix before arriving at a decision to form the relationship.

Accessibility and Cultural Norms   As we have already mentioned, in the initial contact between two persons there is generally an air of stereotypic politeness, serving as a "low-cost protection" against the premature formation of intimate relationships. On the other hand, it renders individuals relatively inaccessible on initial contact. Thus, the matrix of possible outcomes can only be minimally sampled. Thibaut and Kelley attributed this situation to cultural norms that proscribe the acceptable degree of intimacy between two individuals in a casual social contact.

Autistic Hostility   Newcomb (1947) proposed that if an initial state of hostility exists between any two individuals, it will tend to preclude the initiation of further communication and render a resolution of the hostility virtually impossible. It is quite apparent that this state of affairs will severely limit the production of behaviors from one's repertoire and thus restrict the items of behavior sampled on first contact.

Autistic Friendliness   In many ways, autistic friendliness is the converse of autistic hostility. If two individuals initially "hit it off," perhaps because they are very similar to each other in needs, values, and attitudes, they will most likely maximize their production of behavior in each other's presence. That is, they will tend to communicate more frequently with each other. The outcomes sampled in this process, however, will be biased because unfavorable outcomes will be underrepresented and favorable outcomes overrepresented. Nevertheless, under conditions of autistic friendliness the individual has a firm basis for forecasting positive trends and will thus probably enter into the relationship on a more permanent basis.

The Perception of Behavior   This step in the formation of a relationship involves the factors which influence one's evaluation and appraisal of another's responses with an eye toward the forecasts that might be made of future outcomes. Four factors which are relevant to this process are the availability of cues, the effect of primacy of cues, the organization of perceptions, and the states of the observer. We will consider each of these briefly.

The Availability of Cues   Thibaut and Kelley noted that the cues available as a basis for the evaluation of another's behavior are at least partially determined by the behaviors that the other emits. At the outset of a relationship the cues available are usually those of external appearances. From these, certain inferences are made about the likely behavior repertoires of the subject. As the interaction progresses, however, but depending upon the other's strangeness and accessibility, more-concrete behavioral cues become available to the person. With this development the individual will have to engage in much less extrapolation to forecast outcomes. Thus, the certainty with which one forecasts outcome trends should be directly proportional to the cues available in the other's behavior productions.

The Primacy Effect   The perceptions of another's behavior and the outcomes that might spring from it are likely to become more differentiated and accurate with increasing interaction. However, data concerning the so-called primacy effect indicate that early information is more influential in molding one's perception of another's behavior than subsequent information. However, Thibaut and Kelley did not note that the primacy effect has been shown to be situationally dependent, and in certain cases recency of information seems to be a more-potent determinant of one's perceptions.

The Organization of Perception   Simply, this factor deals with the manner in which the various behaviors of another unfold before the eyes of the person. That is, the manner (order of presentation of salient elements, the consistency of information, etc.) in which others present themselves to us will determine the way in which we organize our perceptions of them. The primacy effect is a special case of this latter factor.

States of the Observer   The state of the observer (needs, emotions, and anxieties) at the point of initial contact with another will in part color one's perception of that other and hence affect one's interpretation of the outcomes that might be available in a continued interaction with that other.

In their 1978 treatment of a theory of interdependence, Kelley and Thibaut devote an entire chapter to the impact of attribution and self-presentation processes upon the perception and interpretation of interpersonal behavior. Theoretical and empirical developments in the study of attribution and strategic self-presentation over the past decade allow for the detailing of a wide variety of phenomena which might affect the perceptions of a participant-observer to an interaction. These developments allow Kelley and Thibaut to be quite explicit about perceptual and interpretive phenomena impinging upon the transformation of matrices of interaction outcomes in the course of coactive behavior production. The interested reader should consult Kelley and Thibaut (1978, pp. 207–239) for a thorough discussion of these phenomena.

The Evaluation of the Relationship

Earlier in this chapter, we noted that Thibaut and Kelley posited two standards by which dyadic relationships are evaluated. They are the comparison level (CL) and the comparison level for alternatives (CLalt). In this section we deal with the determinants of the attractiveness of relationships; hence, we are predominantly concerned with the comparison level.

The CL can be represented as the neutral point on a continuum ranging from dissatisfaction to satisfaction. If the outcomes of a given relationship exceed this hypothetical neutral point, the relationship will probably be regarded as attractive and satisfactory. If these outcomes fall below this neutral point, the relationship will probably be considered to be unsatisfactory and unattractive. The CL is defined "as being some modal or average value of all the outcomes known to the person (by virtue of personal or vicarious experience), each outcome weighted by its salience (or the degree to which it is instigated for the person at the moment)" (Thibaut & Kelley, 1959, p. 81). It is apparent then that the CL is subject to situational as well as moment-to-moment changes. That is, it should vary as the individual experiences or observes new outcomes which change the hypothetical average or modal value of outcomes. The CL should also change as situational factors alter the salience of certain outcomes. Thus, the major determinants of CL are one's past experience with outcomes in social relationships and the momentary and general salience of certain outcomes. In the following discussion, both of these determinants are considered, as well as individual variation in comparison level.

Experienced Outcomes According to Thibaut and Kelley, one's CL is highly dependent upon the level of outcomes that have been experienced in past relationships and that are being experienced in present relationships. The more superior the outcomes an individual is accustomed to experiencing, the higher the CL will be for future relationships. This follows from the assumption that an individual's comparison level is the average of the positivity of outcomes experienced in past relationships. This formulation makes the implicit assumption that individuals will be attracted only to relationships that exceed this average level, and, therefore, other things being equal, each relationship entered should raise the individual's CL. This proposition should be qualified, however, in that individuals are sometimes forced by circumstance to enter high-cost–low-reward relationships, and these relationships will serve to reduce the CL for the evaluation of future relationships. Thibaut and Kelley compared their conception of CL to Helson's (1948) concept of adaptation level for psychophysical phenomena. For example, an individual who is accustomed to lifting 200-pound packages at work will consider a 50-pound weight rather light, but an individual who customarily lifts nothing over 5 pounds in the course of a day will consider a 50-pound weight heavy. The relevance of this concept to CL seems rather apparent.

Salient Outcomes   Regardless of their positivity, not all outcomes that have been experienced, personally or vicariously, are equally salient. Hence, in the determination of one's CL, more-salient outcomes that have arisen from past relationships will be more heavily weighted than less-salient ones. "Certain outcomes will be highly salient because of the particular circumstances in which the person is asked to make an evaluation of his situation. Others are likely to be salient under almost all circumstances" (Thibaut & Kelley, 1959, p. 84). An example of outcomes that vary in salience as a function of circumstance might be the stereotypic case of an American tourist overseas forming a relationship with another American tourist with whom he or she would not ordinarily form a relationship if at home. In this case, the salience of the outcomes available in the relationship is heightened by several factors, such as language problems, loneliness, unfamiliarity with surroundings, and many others.

Those outcomes that are likely always to be heavily weighted are prone to be highly salient, regardless of whether or not there exist momentary instigations to them. That is, these outcomes are salient across situational variations. With regard to this order of outcome, Thibaut and Kelley proposed the following hypothesis: *"the generally and persistently salient outcomes are those perceived by the individual as instances of variations in rewards and costs for which he himself is primarily responsible—variations over which he has some degree of control"* (Thibaut & Kelley, 1959, p. 85. Italics ours).

As we have noted, the positivity of a person's outcomes is likely to fluctuate with changes in interaction or in the situations in which interaction takes place. The individual, in order to maintain positive outcomes and avoid negative ones, will be prone to alter behavior sequences to fit the interactive situation at hand. The individual can be only partially successful in making these adjustments because only part of the variability between relationships and relationship settings is under the control of the individual. The remaining variability is due to external controls. Attempts to adjust the variability due to external forces is postulated to be nonadaptive and costly. Therefore, the outcomes that are most salient to individuals are those over which they can initiate adjustive control. The outcomes that are susceptible to the individual's control maintain their salience across interactive situations and constitute a stable factor in the determination of CL. These are the outcomes that the individual will seek to attain in nearly all interactions, and they are therefore heavily weighted in the person's CL. Thibaut and Kelley stated that "the outcomes under his (the person's) control will tend to be highly salient under most circumstances; those under the control of others are salient only if they are currently being experienced or if obtrusive cues are present in the immediate situation" (Thibaut & Kelley, 1959, p. 86). Thus, outcomes are weighted in terms of the individual's responsibility over them. This responsibility factor is so determinate that Thibaut and Kelley posited that the CL is roughly approximate to the modal value of those outcomes over which the individual has control.

Certain predictions stem from this proposition concerning the relationship between salience and control. For example, an individual should undergo greater changes in comparison level if the outcomes are achieved than if they are *ascribed.*

Based on some propositions of Festinger (1954), Thibaut and Kelley also posited that individuals will use the amount of control their social peers have over their outcomes as comparison points to evaluate their own control. Thus, the control that relevant social others enact over their outcomes also enters into the person's computation of their CL.

Individual Differences and Comparison Level   The individual difference parameters in CL that Thibaut and Kelley considered are rather broad. That is, they did not generate lists of traits, personality components, or specific social orientations and relate these factors to CL. Instead, they concerned themselves with the differences between individuals in their perception of their own power and effectiveness to attain and control outcomes in future relationships. That is, individuals who are optimistic and therefore see themselves as capable of attaining and controlling presently unattainable outcomes will of course have a higher CL than individuals who are rather pessimistic about their power to attain attractive but presently unattainable outcomes. The former individuals will tend to emphasize the reward components of unattainable outcomes, and the latter will tend to emphasize the cost involved in attaining presently unattainable

Thibaut and Kelley cited experimental evidence (Dickinson & Beam, 1931; Gouldner, 1954; Scott, Banks, Halsy, & Lupton, 1956) which indicates that individuals who perceive themselves as having the power to control outcomes will generally tend to *idealize* unattainable states. They posited that individuals who possess this tendency toward idealization will possess higher CL's than individuals with an opposite "debunking" tendency. Higher CL's in idealizers stem from their tendency to expect more from relationships than debunkers. In brief, then, individuals' CL's will be much affected by their perception of their own power to attain favorable outcomes. Furthermore, Thibaut and Kelley asserted that the CL is generalizable and that persons who have high CL's have constantly high expectations for the satisfaction they are able to gain in social relationships. Thus, the individual, through experiences with outcomes in past relationships, maintains a "general conception of his worth in interpersonal relationships" (Thibaut & Kelley, 1959, p. 97).

Power and Dependence in Dyadic Relationships

The matrix of outcomes indicates that each person in a dyadic interaction has at least the possibility of exercising power over the other. This power is usually manifested by one individual's capability of controlling the reward-cost positions of the other individual: Assuming that the relationship in question yields outcomes that exceed the CLalt for both parties, these outcomes are attractive and desirable. Thus, if person A is *dependent* upon a particular unit of person B's behavior to attain a given positive outcome, then person B wields an amount of power over A which is proportional to the positivity and dispensability of that outcome. The CLalt is all important in the stability of power and dependence relationships in a given dyad. If the average outcomes from a given relationship fall below the average outcomes available in one's best alternative relationship, the bases of power and dependence in that particular dyadic relationship will be weak, and, in time, the dyad will be dissolved. Thus, the CLalt is the crucial evaluative dimension in determining the individual's dependency upon or power within a dyad.

In this section we deal with the types, consequences, and strategies of power that Thibaut and Kelley postulated as arising in dyadic relationship. Throughout this discussion, we make the assumption that the persons in the dyad understand the facts of the outcome matrix; that is, they are aware of the outcomes available to them as a function of various joint behavioral productions.

Through such understanding of the given matrix and the actual behavioral exchanges based upon this initial understanding, effective matrixes of power-dependence relationships should emerge from the interaction (cf., Kelley & Thibaut, 1978).

Types of Power   Thibaut and Kelley defined power in a dyad as a function of "A's ability to affect the quality of outcomes attained by B" (Thibaut & Kelley, 1959, p. 101). The theorists focused on two types of power: (1) A's ability to control B's fate and (2) A's ability to control B's behavior.

Fate Control   If A can alter B's outcomes by varying his/her own behavior, A has fate control over B. The matrix presented in Figure 4-3 is an illustration of fate control. The outcome values in the cells of the matrix represent the units of positive outcome above B's CLalt. Since all values are positive and above zero, it is apparent that the portion of the relationship exhibited in Figure 4-3 is above the CLalt for B.

In the situation depicted in Figure 4-3, A can control the magnitude of B's reward by enacting either behavior sequence a_1 or a_2. From the outcome values presented, it is obvious that B has no control over the level of outcome that will

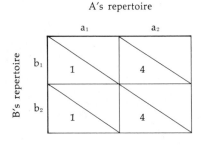

Figure 4-3   Illustration of A's fate control over B. (Reprinted with permission from J. W. Thibaut and H. H. Kelley. *The social psychology of groups*. New York: Wiley, 1959.)

be received. If A enacts a_1, B receives one unit of positive outcome, and if A enacts a_2, B receives four units of positive outcome, regardless of what behavior sequence B selects to enact. Thus, B is completely *dependent* upon A for the level of outcome that will be received, and A wields power over B in terms of the level of outcome A produces for B. The greater the range of outcome values that A can produce for B, the greater A's fate control over B and the greater B's dependence on A. Thus, if the value 9 were substituted for the outcome value 4 in Figure 4-3, A would have even greater fate control over B, and B would be even more dependent upon A for outcomes.

Behavior Control   If A by varying behavior can make it desirable for B to vary behavior, A has behavior control over B. Figure 4-4 represents an illustrative case of A's behavior control over B. In this example, if A varies the behavior sequence from a_1 to a_2, then in order for B to maximize outcomes, B must vary the behavior sequence from b_2 to b_1. The amount of behavior control that A exercises over B is a function of the amount of gain in outcome units that B will experience by adjusting behaviors. Thibaut and Kelley noted that in the behavior control situation, B's outcomes do not vary as a function of either A's behavior or B's behavior, but rather they are contingent upon the joint enactment of a given a, b sequence. Thus, unlike fate control, in behavior control B plays a role in the attainment of outcomes. A's power in this situation stems from the ability to "force" B to emit a specific behavioral sequence to the exclusion of any other behavior sequence in order to gain maximal outcomes. Once again, then, A wields power over B, and B is dependent upon A.

The Conversion of Fate Control to Behavior Control   Thibaut and Kelley noted that fate control may be used to control behavior. Referring again to Figure 4-3, we see that A can control B's behavior by always enacting a_2 when B enacts b_1 and always enacting a_1 when B enacts b_2. Thus, in effect, through fate control A has also initiated behavior control over B. To accomplish this conversion, A must have adequate information about B's choices and, further-more, must follow a set rule when matching behavior choices to B's. Thus, the information A gleans from the interactive situation might be that B has two behavioral sequences available and that B tends to enact these sequences alternately. The rule that might then emerge for person A is that: *on each trial in which I expect B to enact b_1, I will enact a_2, and, on each trial on which I expect B*

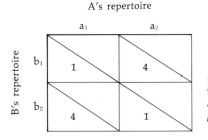

A's repertoire

Figure 4-4   Illustration of A's behavior control over B. (Reprinted with permission from J. W. Thibaut and H. H. Kelley. *The social psychology of groups.* New York: Wiley, 1959.)

to enact b₂, I will enact a₁. This is only one of several matching rules that A might apply. A can just as easily alter the rule and have the a_2b_2 sequence as the maximally rewarding one.

In order for converted fate control to operate, A must communicate the matching rule to B either directly or implicitly by repeated application of the rule. The converted fate-control situation can be an uncomfortable and unpredictable one for B if A does not adequately communicate or misapplies the rules. Thus, the converted fate-control matrix can cause considerable uncertainty and conflict in B.

Mutual fate control may occur if both A and B have fate control over each other. This situation is illustrated in Figure 4-5. This mutual fate-control situation can implicitly be converted to mutual behavior control through the joint application of rules by A and B, once they have sufficient information about each other's repertoires. Through an exploration of the outcome matrix the most mutually satisfactory cell (a_1b_1) will emerge as the one in which interaction will stabilize, according to the theory. Since the joint occurrence of a_1b_1 maximizes rewards for both, each dyad member is both dependent upon and in behavior control of the other member. Hence, just as fate control may be converted to behavior control, mutual fate control can be converted to mutual behavior control.

Patterns of Interdependence   When A has fate control over B, but to exercise this control would affect A's own outcomes in a negative way, then A's power over B is minimally usable. For example, Figure 4-6 presents a situation in which A will affect his/her own outcomes if he/she chooses to exercise fate control over B. In this situation (in contrast to the partial outcome matrix shown in Figure 4-3) A would be rather reluctant to use power over B, because in doing so he/she would reduce his/her own outcomes.

A might also be reluctant to use power over B if B possesses counterpower. This situation is depicted in Figure 4-7. In this case, although A has fate control over B, B has an equal amount of fate control over A. B might also hold counterpower to A's fate control through having behavior control over A, as exhibited in Figure 4-7. Thus, although A has fate control over B, if A wishes to maximize his/her outcomes, A must enact a_2 jointly with B's b_1 or a_1 jointly with b_2 in order to achieve maximal rewards. Thibaut and Kelley noted that this act

A's repertoire

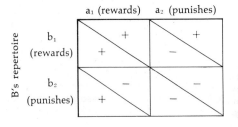

Figure 4-5 An illustration of mutual fate control that gives rise to implicit conversion. (Reprinted with permission from J. W. Thibaut and H. H. Kelley. *The social psychology of groups.* New York: Wiley, 1959.)

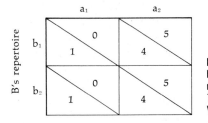

A's repertoire

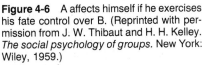

Figure 4-6   A affects himself if he exercises his fate control over B. (Reprinted with permission from J. W. Thibaut and H. H. Kelley. *The social psychology of groups.* New York: Wiley, 1959.)

does not guarantee that B can reduce A's outcomes, but it does give B the opportunity to keep his/her own outcomes high by providing incentives for A's enactment of a_2. One might also conceptualize a matrix in which both dyad members hold behavior control over each other. In the latter three cases, the usable power of each member is limited by the counterpower held by the other member. Thus, the members are *interdependent* upon each other for the maximization of their positive outcomes.

The Consequences of Power   The consequences of power are considered from the standpoint of both the dyad and the individual.

For the Dyad   A dyad in which both parties hold equal and high amounts of power over each other (an ideal but seldom real situation) will consist of members who are more highly interdependent and hence will be a more-cohesive dyad. A general proposition might be that the greater the correspondence and extent of power held by both members of a dyad, the greater the cohesiveness of that dyad. Thibaut and Kelley further noted that the greater power the members have over each other, the greater the convergence and hence similarity in values and attitudes. Thus, interdependence begets further interdependence.

For the Individual   The possession of power or control in the dyadic situation yields the following benefits to the high-power person: (1) The high-power person gains better reward-cost positions. (2) The high-power

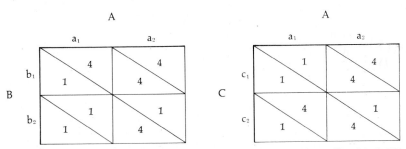

Figure 4-7   B and C have power counter to A's fate control over them. (Reprinted with permission from J. W. Thibaut and H. H. Kelley. *The social psychology of groups.* New York: Wiley, 1959.)

person controls the interaction by dictating the pattern of changes in behavior sequences. This stems from his/her greater certainty in predicting what the outcomes will be under various joint-behavioral enactments. The person with power can *motivate* the other to change behavior at will by manipulating that power. (3) The value and attitude changes occurring in a dyad will generally converge on the attitudes and values of the high-power person. Thus, the high-power person not only has great influence over the other's values and attitudes but also can retain his/her own values and attitudes with little change.

Strategies of Power   Thibaut and Kelley listed seven possible strategies for increasing power in the dyad:

1   Raising one's CLalt so that the dyadic partner can barely keep above it. This has been referred to as "one-upmanship."
2   Reducing the dyadic partner's alternatives, thus preventing the dyadic partner from using strategy 1.
3   Improving one's ability to deliver rewards through a host of techniques, such as better tools and ingratiation. This strategy can also involve increasing the dyadic partner's susceptibility to rewards.
4   Reducing the dyadic partner's skill through interference or some similar technique.
5   Creating a need in the dyadic partner for one's behavioral product.
6   Devaluing the dyadic partner's product.
7   Reducing one's time prespective; that is, one can increase one's power by deferring the attainment of favorable outcomes to some future time. This strategy will serve both to limit the dyadic partner's power and to devalue the rewards.

Comment

In the first edition of this book (Shaw and Costanzo, 1970), we noted that Thibaut and Kelley's theory of interdependence had been a very influential framework in social psychology. Given the small-group research conducted in the past decade, we find no reason to alter that general evaluation. If anything, there has been an upswing in the use of the framework for examining questions concerning negotiation and bargaining, cooperation and competition, power and dependence in dyads, interpersonal trust, as well as more directly relevant issues, such as interactions between marital partners.

The general appeal of Thibaut and Kelley's initially proposed framework is partly a matter of the theoretical appeal of its overarching suppositions (e.g., the proposition of reward maximization at it applies to human interaction), but primarily derives from the empirical usefulness of its major analytic tool—the outcome matrix. This particular device allows for the analoguelike construction of a number of social relationships in an experimental context. Thus, phenomena, such as power, which are typically embedded in the social structure can be structured in the form of simple laboratory simulations. Frequently, these simulations of social relations have taken the form of games and the games have been varied to provide for the study of various types of relationships. Depending upon the matrix of rewards available to the coacting subjects of these game studies, experimenters have manipulated and studied cooperative exchange, competitive exchange, power relations, bargaining situations, and the like. This general methodology, in addition, allows for the examination of the effect of manipulated or preexisting attributes of game participants and/or particular information inductions. For example, the manipulated or actual attractiveness of subjects to one another has been examined as a factor in the time it takes for them to stabilize their game choices in a jointly, maximally rewarding cell of the outcome matrix during cooperative interaction.

The studies conducted within the Thibaut and Kelley framework are much too voluminous to be reviewed here. We suggest that the interested reader consult Kelley and Thibaut (1978), Kelley and Stahelski (1972), Kelley and Thibaut (1969), and McClintock (1972) for extensive reviews of this research literature. It should be noted that the lion's share of the data is largely supportive of both the empirical usefulness of the outcome matrix and of the general hypotheses suggested by the social-interdependence approach. Where qualifications in the major hypotheses occur, they typically involve conditions which differentiate circumstances in which game participants do and do not engage in reward maximization (e.g., Shaw, 1962; Willis & Joseph, 1959). In short, the theoretical framework proposed by Thibaut and Kelley has fared quite well in simulated laboratory explorations of social phenomena.

In their most recent work (Kelley & Thibaut, 1978), these theorists have offered a bold and potentially important advance in their methodology and thought. The newer treatment of interpersonal interdependence, while changing few of the rudiments of the originally proposed theory, provides for methods of matrix transformation which both permit the study of interaction-generated reward-cost shifts across time and allow for firmer predictions concerning the course of particular kinds of interaction. In addition, Kelley & Thibaut's more explicit theoretical and predictive statement allows for the feasible study of three-person as well as dyadic groups. Thus, it has become possible to study the course of coalition formation in social interaction through the use of an outcome-matrix methodology.

While Kelley and Thibaut bring much past data to bear upon the development of their more exacting matrix transformation methodology, the very explicit predictions it permits in forecasting relationship trends now require careful empirical test.

Nevertheless, the importance of the general Thibaut and Kelley framework and analytic strategy does not necessarily rest upon the outcomes of their newest derivation. It has been found to offer a useful construction of social relations which has admirably enhanced the conceptual and empirical understanding of dyadic social interdependence.

EQUITY THEORY

Like the theories of Homans and Thibaut and Kelley, equity theory constitutes a general model for understanding interpersonal relations which is conjointly based upon reinforcement principles and a metaphor from economics. Simply stated, equity prevails in interpersonal transactions when the outcomes an individual derives from a given transaction are equal to the inputs one has invested in that transaction. The reader may have noted that the notion of equity is quite similar to the rule of distributive justice described by Homans (1961, 1974). Indeed, equity theory embodies a principle of interpersonal justice which borders on an implicit social contract. Equity can be viewed as a principle that emerges as a consequence of the conflict between individual tendencies to maximize their own rewards and the needs of social units to appropriately and "fairly" distribute resources. While equity may be imposed by the environment in any given transaction so that individuals do not take unfair advantage of others or exact profits that their efforts do not warrant, one must also presume that equity as a principle governing social interchange is internalized by individuals in the course of socialization. The consequences of an internalized equity norm can be observed in the distress individuals might experience when they have either reaped the benefits of a disproportionate distribution of rewards or suffered the privation of such an unequitable distribution.

While the importance of rules of justice and reciprocity abound in the history of social science and are indeed rooted in antiquity, the first formal proposal of equity theory as a social-psychological paradigm was offered by J. Stacey Adams (1963). The original paradigm, while presaging the more recent empirical and theoretical developments in equity-based phenomena, was more pertinent to problems of readily quantifiable resource exchange than it was to interpersonal exchanges with more implicit psychological inputs and outcomes (such as favor doing, love, having an attractive partner, etc.). As such, Adams' original formulation was of great interest to industrial psychologists studying the psychology of work and employee satisfaction. It is also noteworthy that, during the formative stages of equity theory, there were simultaneous theoretical developments in social psychology which were compatible with the equity framework. In 1959 and 1961 the social-exchange notions of social interdependence were proposed by Thibaut and Kelley and Homans. As we have noted, the equity formulation is quite compatible with these exchange frameworks. Further, the cognitive and cognitive-affective consistency theories discussed in Chapter 8 had "caught on" among social psychologists and were by 1963 witnessing rapid development.

Equity theory embodied a particular consistency rule (i.e., that between a person's inputs and outcomes in an interpersonal exchange) and was therefore concordant with these major theoretical frameworks. One might propose that the receptivity to the equity formulation in social psychology and its use as an interpretive framework was initially a "coattail" phenomenon. That is, its conceptual compatibility with important extant frameworks expedited its adoption into the corpus of social psychology. Currently, given the expansion of equity theory as a general model of social interaction, one might argue that it has become an important framework in its own right.

In keeping with this development of equity-based notions, in 1976 an entire volume of the *Advances in Experimental Social Psychology* series (Berkowitz, 1976) was devoted to the discussion of equity. The lead paper in that volume by Walster, Berscheid, and Walster is the major basis for the exposition of equity theory presented below.[1] Walster, Berscheid, and Walster provide a concise analysis of the formulation, definitions, propositions, and applications of equity-theory notions. Their presentation draws upon the enormous diversity of research which has tested equity theory and expands on the base provided by Adams' seminal proposal.

Equity: Definition of Terms and Theoretical Formulas

At the outset of our summary of equity theory it is most germane to define the term itself. *Equity* is best defined as a state of interactive equilibrium which is achieved when the participants in an interaction or common organization are allocated outcomes proportional to their inputs. Leventhal (1976), in his excellent review of allocation behavior in groups, convincingly notes that equity is only one of a number of reasonable reward-allocation norms that a group might employ to distribute resources. For example, one might propose it equally feasible to offer that rewards be allocated on the basis of need as well as on the basis of useful or effortful inputs. In short, equity is a particular allocational norm which groups and individuals employ to distribute rewards and evaluate the "fairness" of the distribution.

Outcomes (O) are defined in largely the same manner as Homans and Thibaut and Kelley defined them. They are "the positive or negative consequences that a scrutineer (who could be a participant in or observer to a relationship) perceives a participant has incurred as a consequence of his relationship with another" (Walster, Berscheid, and Walster, 1976, p. 3). Following social exchange–based notions, positive outcomes are referred to as rewards, and negative outcomes as costs.

Inputs (I) are "the participant's contributions to the exchange which are seen as entitling him to rewards or costs" (Walster, Berscheid, and Walster, 1976, p. 3). Since an individual might indeed contribute both negatively and positively to dyadic, group, or organizational goals, inputs can have either valence. Positive inputs are referred to as *assets,* negative inputs as *liabilities.* Furthermore, depending upon the setting in which exchange occurs, inputs might consist of material or human resources, such as money and task effort, or they might consist of dispositional, psychological, or physical attributes, such as beauty, politeness, leadership talents, clumsiness, cruelty, and the like.

---

[1]That paper was originally published in *Journal of Personality and Social Psychology,* 1973, *25,* 151–176.

Definitional formulae

From this rather simple, small array of terms the basic model of equity in interaction is derived. As we have stated above, equity prevails in any exchange or reward-allocation situation when individuals' outcomes (rewards, costs) are proportional to their inputs (assets, liabilities). The original Adams (1963) formula merely expressed a balance in two participants' ratios of outcomes to inputs,

$$\frac{O_A}{I_A} = \frac{O_B}{I_B}$$

where O_A and O_B are the outcomes of two interactants A and B, and I_A and I_B are the respective inputs of persons A and B. While this rather simple formula may be appropriate to the work setting, where outcome could be wages and inputs work, it is less applicable to situations (particularly social situations) in which inputs and outcomes might be either positive or negative. Recognizing this, Walster, Berscheid, and Walster (1976) reconstructed the basic equity formula in the following manner:

$$\frac{O_A - I_A}{(|I_A|)^{K_A}} = \frac{O_B - I_B}{(|I_B|)^{K_B}}$$

This formula proposes that equity prevails when the disparity between person A's outcomes and inputs and person B's outcomes and inputs are equivalently proportional to the absolute value of each of their inputs. The exponent K in this formula may be either $+1$ or -1 depending upon the valence of the participants' inputs and gains (outcomes $-$ inputs). Obviously the use of this formula demands that a person's inputs be greater than or less than 0. This calculation device boils down to Adams' original formula with allowances made for the possibility of both negative inputs and negative outcomes (i.e., losses or punishments).

While the actual use of these formulas is not a necessity in most of the equity research, they represent a conceptual symbolization of the equity notion. However, in using such formulas one runs into the same kind of problem encountered in scaling outcomes in the Thibaut and Kelley outcome matrix or in quantifying Homans' notions of quantity and value. That is, while material gains are easily quantified (in terms of dollars, for example) and physical inputs are reasonably quantifiable (e.g., number of products made or number of hours worked), psychological rewards, costs, assets, and liabilities are much more difficult to quantify reliably. In doing so, one must frequently adopt the rankings of the participants themselves. If two participants rank their respective inputs and outcomes in the psychological domain differently, then they will indeed disagree in their beliefs concerning the relative level at which their allocations or relationships deviate from an equitable distribution. While an external "scrutineer" might resolve the issue by ranking each participant's outcomes and inputs on the same scale, it is the case that inequity is experienced by participants on the basis of their own subjective accounting of their relative gains. It is the subjective perception of inequity that is most pivotal in the distressing consequences that we will later discuss as following from it. The outsider's judgment of inequity might be viewed as governing the sanctions and remedies that social agents (such as legal institutions or labor arbitrators) might bring to bear on inequitable distribution.

Equity: Propositions

Walster, Berscheid, and Walster (1976) offer four basic propositions which embody the assumptions and general hypotheses of the equity-theory framework. The first two of these propositions are largely assumptions about human conduct and societal functioning, while the latter two assumptions are primarily data-derived conceptual hypotheses which are concerned with the predicted consequences of inequity.

Proposition 1 *"Individuals will try to maximize their outcomes (where outcomes equal rewards minus costs)"* (p. 2). This proposition should have a familiar ring at this point in this chapter. As well as constituting a prime assumption of equity theory, it is central to the reinforcement-based social exchange notions of Homans and Thibaut and Kelley.

Corollary 1.1 *"So long as individuals perceive that they can maximize their outcomes by behaving equitably, they will do so. Should they perceive that they can maximize their outcomes by behaving inequitably, they will do so"* (p. 5). This corollary basically proposes that selfish, hedonistic motives governing reward maximization are more potent than external and internalized norms governing equity in exchange.

Proposition 2a *"Groups can maximize collective reward by evolving accepted systems for equitably apportioning rewards and costs among members"* (p. 2).

Proposition 2b *"Groups will generally reward members who treat others equitably and generally punish members who treat others inequitably"* (p. 2).

The two components of proposition 2 constitute socially mediated remedies for the prepotent hedonism of men detailed in proposition 1. In short, society and its members and institutions adopt systems for inducing and imploring its members to operate on the basis of equity. The irony is that, once again, reward-maximization tendencies are viewed as so prominent that the major control technique for inducing equity is itself the reward maximization of individual people. Walster, Berscheid, and Walster cite representative evidence demonstrating that society's supposed efforts successfully induce equity norms. It has been demonstrated that individuals will surrender benefits when their partners are deprived of their fair share. Conversely, deprived individuals will indeed demand their fair share of benefits (cf., Leventhal, Allen, & Kemelgor, 1969; Marwell, Ratliffe, & Schmitt, 1969).

Since social agents and institutions are not forever present to induce equity and equity seems to prevail in many human encounters, one must assume that the norm of equity is internalized in the process of socialization. Walster, Berscheid, and Walster argue that, since individuals will encounter sufficiently frequent punishment for behaving inequitably, inequity comes to be associated with punishment during the socialization process. The internalization of the equity norm gives rise to propositions 3 and 4.

Proposition 3 *"When individuals find themselves participating in inequitable relationships, they become distressed. The more inequitable the relationship, the more distress they will feel"* (p. 6). Certainly the kind of distress experienced will depend upon whether one benefits or suffers from inequity. Walster, Berscheid, and Walster cite a number of studies which support both elements of this proposition. It has typically been found that guilt follows from unfair benefit and anger from unfair deprivation of rewards. The reader will notice a good deal of similarity between this proposition and Homans' proposition 5 presented in an earlier section of this chapter.

Since tolerance of distress has its psychological limits, Walster, Berscheid, and Walster propose the fourth and last proposition.

Proposition 4 *"Individuals who discover they are in an inequitable relationship attempt to eliminate their distress by restoring equity. The greater the inequity that exists, the more distress they feel, and the harder they try to restore equity"* (p. 6).

This last proposition constitutes a primary prediction for equity researchers. It ramifies into a motivational dynamic, which is quite kindred to the cognitive dissonance hypothesis discussed in Chapter 8. It also affirms that individuals have so internalized the norm of equity that they will engage in a number of psychological and social actions in order to reestablish it in particular relationships.

The tactics involved in the restoration of equity and bringing about a decrease in inequity-based distress vary widely with the kind of interpersonal or social relationship involved. Speaking generally, there are two broadly descriptive categories of tactics for equity restoration:

1 *Direct tactics.* These involve a participant in reducing inequity distress by the direct alteration of either his own inputs and/or outcomes, or the inputs and outcomes of the other participants. For example, a worker might work less energetically if underpaid and more energetically if overpaid. On the other hand, an employer might reduce or increase monetary compensation to fit worker input. In more socially relevant domains, a harmdoer might psychologically or materially compensate his/her victim for the insult or attack that has been suffered, or, perhaps, the victim might reciprocate with an attack of his/her own. An unselfish act of helping by one participant toward another might create inequity in a relationship and result in an act of repayment by the recipient. In each of these cases the acts involved in restoring equity and reducing inequity distress are designed to directly alter the outcome-input balance in the direction of equity among participants.

2 *Defensive tactics.* A second large category of equity-restoring tactics is an alternative to the direct alteration of the outcomes and inputs of participants. These tactics typically involve the psychological distortion of the perceived outcome-input proportionality among participants. These defensive tactics typically involve phenomena like denial, derogation of the victim or helper in harmdoing or altruistic circumstances, rationalized justification for the inequitable state, ego-enhancing distortions on the part of the benefactors of inequity (e.g., the self-perception of great latent talent might justify inordinately high salary for an inordinately easy job), or distortion of the importance of tolerating inequity (e.g., "I'm terribly underpaid, but the job I do is so important that it warrants my efforts").

Both general kinds of equity-restoring tactics ramify differently in different behavioral and social domains and a major task of researchers of equity phenomena has been and will continue to be determining the particular behaviors that follow from inequitable distributions of outcomes and inputs in specific arenas of social behavior.

Comment

As we noted at the outset of our presentation of equity theory, it has been construed as a general model for the understanding of all forms of social transactions. Indeed, Berkowitz (1976) notes that equity theory was developed "in the hope of providing the glimmerings of the general theory that social psychologists so badly need."

It is certainly the case that equity theory is comprised of a simple set of general and internally consistent propositions that could well be translated into the several domains of social interaction, without inordinately stretching its applicability. Yet, it might be well to note Leventhal's (1976) implied caveat that equity is simply one rule or norm of reward allocation, and several other plausible dynamics governing interpersonal transactions, based on allocative logic, also warrant consideration.

As a model for generating research, the equity-theory framework has been exemplary. In the time between its original introduction in 1963 and the 1976 publication of the *Advances* volume, Adams and Freedman (1976) note that some 170 authors have published studies concerned with equity phenomena. The range of content areas to which it has been applied is quite broad, in keeping with its claim to being a general theory of social behavior. Equity theory has been used as a model for the study of business relationships, children's acquisitions of interactive norms, victimization, justice, romantic love and attraction, helping, exploitative relationships, and the like. The equity-based studies of these phenomena reported upon, in volumes such as the *Advances* and in a recent compendious work by Walster, Berscheid, and Walster entitled *Equity Theory and Research,* have been overwhelmingly supportive of the basic applicability of the equity propositions. The interested reader is directed to these volumes for a comprehensive coverage of the equity literature.

One of the difficulties with the theory is not dissimilar to the difficulties met with Homans and Thibaut and Kelley's approaches, namely, in the psychological and social domain it is quite difficult to quantify the largely metaphoric constructs of cost, reward, outcomes, and inputs. Indeed, Adams and Freedman propose that this should constitute one of the major directions taken by subsequent research on equity. The other useful research directions proposed by Adams and Freedman relate to the greater specification of the nature, uses, and dynamic consequences of inequity distress and its resolution.

Whether equity theory evolves into a general theory of social behavior or not, it has the merits of being simply stated, conceptually evocative, empirically flexible, and generalizable.

Part Three

The Field-Theoretical
Orientation

Chapter 5

Basic Concepts and Constructs of Field Theory

The orientation that came to be known as *field theory* emerged from the conceptualization of behavior formulated by Kurt Lewin and his students (de Rivera, 1976).[1] Lewin was interested in and concerned with almost all aspects of human behavior. Why do people eat what they eat? How do people set goals for their actions and how does such goal setting affect behavior? How can one bring about social change? What factors influence the development of language? knowledge? social interrelationships? emotions? How can the productivity of industrial workers be increased? What effects do cultural backgrounds have on people and their behavior? What conditions lead to marital conflict and how can such conflicts be resolved? What are the important factors in minority relations? Can we reeducate people to improve society? How does the "social atmosphere" influence behavior in groups? Lewin and his associates investigated all these questions and many more.

[1]Lewin's theoretical orientation is not the only one that can properly be called "field theory." The theories of Tolman (1932), Wheeler (1940), Lashley (1929), and Brunswik (1949a), to mention a few, have been called field theories (Marx & Hillix, 1963). Not everyone agrees with these classifications, however, and none of these theories deals specifically with social behavior. For these reasons, we have chosen Lewin's approach as the best representative of the field-theory orientation in social psychology.

During the course of these investigations Lewin became convinced that, in order to understand behavior, it is essential to put it in context; i.e., in the surrounding field. The meaning of behavior depends on the whole of which it is a part. The whole is different from the sum of its parts. In essence, field theory is an attempt to describe the present situation (field) in which a person or persons participate (behave).

Field theory is closely related to gestalt psychology, and many of the principles of field theory are identical with those found in gestalt theories. Because of this close affiliation, it will be helpful to review briefly the major tenets of gestaltism before considering field theory.

Gestalt psychology was founded as a school by Max Wertheimer, Wolfgang Kohler, and Kurt Koffka in Germany near the beginning of the twentieth century. According to Marx and Hillix (1963), it had its beginnings with a 1912 paper on apparent movement by Wertheimer. The founding of this school appeared to be a reaction against the atomistic approaches that were currently popular in Europe and the United States. Its major emphasis was on the part-whole relationship, which was exemplified by perceptual phenomena. Briefly, their position may be stated as follows: parts or elements do not exist in isolation but are organized into units or wholes. For example, when we look at a building, we do not see bricks, lumber, glass, and similar parts; instead we see a house. The integration of the parts is determined by certain principles of organization, which lead the organism to perceive the best gestalt or figure possible under the given conditions. The principles of organization also determine which parts will be incorporated into which whole. The laws of science are thus the laws of systems and are equally applicable to diverse disciplines, such as physics and psychology.

Lewin was a student of the founders of the gestalt movement during its formative years. He was thus thoroughly indoctrinated with the principal viewpoints of the gestalt psychologists. It is not surprising, therefore, that these views should be recognizable in his own theorizing. However, the gestalt school was concerned primarily with perceptual phenomena, whereas Lewin soon became interested in problems of personality and social psychology. He considered the gestalt principles to be inadequate for the task of analyzing these new and different issues. New approaches were therefore necessary. Lewin's version of field theory is thus derived from early gestalt ideas, but his approach proceeds in a different direction and goes well beyond the gestalt school.

The following explication of the field-theory orientation is an attempt to synthesize the conceptualizations presented by Lewin and his students. We have relied heavily on *Field Theory in Social Science* (Lewin, 1951). The expositions by Deutsch (1954), Cartwright (1959a), Marx and Hillix (1963), and de Rivera (1976) have also contributed to our understanding of field theory.

THE PRINCIPAL ATTRIBUTES OF FIELD THEORY

According to Lewin (1942), there are six attributes of field theory that are particularly important:

1 The use of a constructive method
2 A dynamic approach
3 An emphasis upon psychological processes
4 Analysis based upon the situation as a whole
5 A distinction between systematic and historical issues
6 A mathematical representation of psychological situations

An explication of these characteristics is necessary to provide a background for understanding field theory.

The *constructive method* is essentially an attempt to overcome the difficulties inherent in other methods that are designed to develop general concepts and laws of behavior. Lewin argued that once generalities have been abstracted from individual differences, there is no logical way to deal with the individual case. General categories such as "normal person," "average child," etc., are of little value for predictions of individual behavior. And he questioned whether they have any value if they do not permit such predictions. He proposed that psychology must shift from the "classificatory method" to a "constructive" or "genetic" method. In the first method, objects, persons, and events are grouped according to similarities; in the constructive method, they are grouped according to their relationships (that is, the way they can be derived from each other). The classificatory method uses elements of abstraction, whereas the method of construction uses elements of construction. Elements of abstraction are objects of the scientist's experience; elements of construction are his ideas (Cartwright, 1959a). An example drawn from studies of conflict behavior may serve to clarify the differences between these two approaches. Using the classificatory method, the scientist might observe that a given person revealed conflict when faced with a choice between apples and pears, a choice between chops and steaks, a choice between pie and cake, etc. He might then classify all these as *food conflicts*. Similarly, conflicts between various forms of entertainments might be grouped into a type called *entertainment conflicts*. Applying the method of construction to the analysis of conflict, Lewin showed how various types of conflict can be constructed from patterns of psychological forces.

A *conflict* situation is described as one in which the forces acting on the person are opposite in direction and about equal in strength (Lewin, 1946). Conflict situations may involve driving forces, driving and restraining forces, or own forces and various combinations of induced and impersonal forces. Driving forces may result in conflict when (1) the person is located between two positive valences, (2) the person is between two negative valences, or (3) a positive and negative valence are in the same direction with respect to the person. It may be noted that the first two situations correspond to what is usually called choice. Figure 5-1 depicts these three possibilities. For example, *(a)* might represent the situation in which p must choose between going to a concert (G_1+) or attending a play (G_2+). In this example, fG_1 represents the force toward the concert (a positive valence) and fG_2 the force toward the play (also a positive valence). According to the goal gradient hypothesis, when the person p moves toward either G_1 or G_2, the strength of the force toward the chosen goal increases and

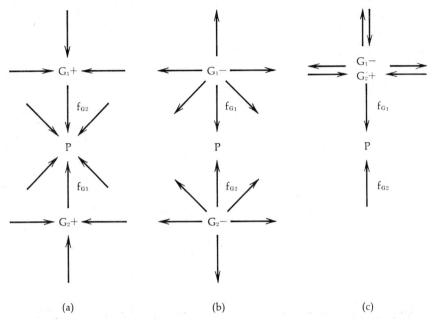

(a)   (b)   (c)

Figure 5-1 (a) A force field corresponding to two positive valences; (b) a force field corresponding to two negative valences; (c) a force field corresponding to a positive and a negative valence in the same direction. (Adapted with permission from K. Lewin. *Field theory in social science.* New York: Harper and Row, 1951.)

the force toward the other decreases. Thus initially, the positive-positive (or approach-approach) (Miller, 1944) conflict is unstable, and any movement toward one goal region determines the direction of conflict resolution. In the second situation *(b)*, an avoidance-avoidance conflict situation is shown. Here, forces are acting to cause p to move away from both G_1 and G_2. If p moves away from G_1, the strength of the force away from G_1 decreases, but the strength of the force away from G_2 increases (since p is moving toward it). When p reaches a position where the two opposing forces are equal in strength, a quasi-state of equilibrium has been achieved, and p tends to remain in that position. Actually, p may overreact and move beyond this position, correct by moving back in the opposite direction, etc., and thus vacillate between the two negative goals. This is called a *stable* conflict situation because the conflict tends to remain unresolved. It should be clear that, in order for this type of conflict situation to occur, there must be barriers or restraining forces that prevent the person from "leaving the field;" that is, moving away from both goal regions.

In the third situation *(c)*, the two goals represent positive and negative valences in the same direction. This approach-avoidance conflict situation tends to be stable also, since movement toward G_1 (and consequently toward G_2) increases both fG_1 and fG_2. The strength of fG_2, which is negative, increases more rapidly than that of fG_1 (which is positive), so the person moves to a quasi-state of equilibrium, as in the avoidance-avoidance situation. Psychologically, the person is in the same position as a person in the avoidance-avoidance situation who is prevented from leaving the field. Experiments by Brown (1942) and Miller (1944) demonstrate these phenomena.

It should be clear from this example that the constructive method considers general laws as statements of empirical relations between constructive elements or certain properties of them. The "constructive elements" are really psychological constructs such as "position," "life space," "boundaries," and similar concepts. A consideration of the major constructs of field theory will be presented later in this chapter.

In applying the constructive method, Lewin maintained that the approach must satisfy several requirements. First, the approach must be *dynamic*. This refers to an interpretation of changes that are the result of psychological forces. He was critical of traditional approaches that emphasize the "static" aspects of behavior. In order to understand behavior in depth, it is necessary to formulate scientific constructs that deal with the underlying forces of behavior. Psychoanalysis is cited as the outstanding example of the dynamic approach, although it has not always met the requirements of scientific method.

In addition to being dynamic, the approach must at all times be *psychological*. Field theory is said to be behavioristic in the sense that concepts are defined operationally. However, field theory breaks with other behavioristic approaches that have "confused" the need for operational definitions with a demand for the elimination of psychological descriptions. Behavior must be described in terms of the psychological field as it exists for the individual at any given time. One might say that the description of the situation must be "subjective" rather than "objective." That is, the situation must be described from the viewpoint of the individual whose behavior is under consideration, rather than from the viewpoint of the observer. Scientific constructs must therefore represent psychological concepts.

In order to use scientific constructs in the dynamic analysis of behavior, field theory holds that the *analysis must begin with the situation as a whole*. Instead of beginning with isolated elements of the situation and later attempting to organize them into an integrated system, field theory begins with a description of the situation as a whole. After the initial characterization of the whole situation, it is then possible to examine it for specific elements and relations among these elements. This approach is presented as being analogous to the approach taken in physics. It presupposes that there are properties in the field that can be seen under certain conditions as a unit. The types of properties that are used (for example, "space of free movement," "social climate") in the analysis of the situation as a whole are seen as being similar to physical concepts (for example, "field of gravity," "electrical field").

Behavior must be analyzed in terms of *the field at the time* the behavior occurs. The approach must be systematic rather than historical in nature. This is one of the major distinctions between theories based upon the gestalt orientation and those derived from other viewpoints. Gestalt-like theories assert that it does not matter how the situation came to be the way it is at the present time; it has the same effect on behavior regardless of its historical antecedents. Lewin pointed out that few psychologists would accept the proposition that behavior can be derived from future events. But, he argued, derivation of behavior from past events is just as unacceptable because past events no longer exist and hence cannot affect behavior in the present. Of course, he recognized that the past can have an indirect effect on behavior via its effect on the psychological field. The past psychological field serves as an origin of the present field, and the present field in turn affects behavior. But in most cases the ways in which the past influences the present are not known in enough detail to be useful in the analysis of behavior. Although field theory may be applied to historical problems in order to understand the developmental process, the analysis of behavior per se should be ahistorical in its approach.

The language of scientific analysis must be logically strict and in line with the dynamic, psychological, constructive method of analysis. This meant, for Lewin, that the language must be *mathematical.* He rejected the common notion that mathematics cannot handle qualitative data. On the contrary, he maintained that certain forms of geometry, especially topology, are exceedingly useful in representing the structure of psychological events. (As we shall see later, topology is the major mathematical tool exploited by field theorists.) Topological and vector concepts are the most powerful and precise conceptual tools available to psychologists. Progress in psychological analysis can be made only if such conceptual tools are employed to represent psychological situations.

In summary, Lewin's formulation of field theory requires a dynamic, psychological application of the "constructive" method to psychological problems. The behavior must be viewed as a function of the situation as a whole as it exists at the moment for the individual. The psychological situation must be represented in the most-precise terms possible, and this task requires a mathematical representation.

With the general orientation of Lewin clearly in mind, we are now ready to examine the major theoretical constructs that he employed in attempting to explain social phenomena. The reader should also keep in mind that Lewin's constructs were introduced in piecemeal fashion, rather than as parts of a unified and integrated theory. That is, the various constructs were formulated as needed to handle the particular social problem of concern at the moment. If the following presentation appears somewhat disjointed, it is because, at least in part, of the fact that Lewin's ideas were presented in a series of papers and were never organized into a single integrated theory.

THE MAJOR CONSTRUCTS OF FIELD THEORY

Science is usually defined as systematized knowledge of any one department of mind or matter, and *scientist* is defined as one who is skilled in science. Thus, the scientist is one who systematizes knowledge. To Lewin this definition meant that the scientist's task consists of the process of conceptualizing; his task is to make appropriate translations from phenomena to concepts (Lewin, 1951). This is no easy job, since a useful scientific concept not only must represent both the qualitative and quantitative aspects of the phenomenon, but also must adequately represent its causal attributes. Furthermore, it should be formulated in such a way that operational definition is easy (or at least possible) and should permit the stating of general laws that may be applied to the individual case. As D. Cartwright pointed out (in foreword to Lewin, 1951), this calls for powerful concepts and a powerful method to generate them. Lewin believed that the method of construction was equal to the task.

To apply the method of construction to psychological phenomena, one must also develop elements of construction and techniques for organizing these elements into a system (Lewin, 1944). In psychology, elements of construction are such things as "life space," "field forces," and "tension systems." Such scientific terms are not to be confused with popular terms, such as "frustration," "hope," "aggression," and "learning." A popular term cannot be considered an element of construction because it lacks conceptual definition through coordination with mathematical concepts and refers to many different settings rather than to one conceptually definable situation. For example, the field-theoretical approach insists that it is impossible to investigate the laws of frustration without investigating at the same time what frustration *is* psychologically.

Lewin suggested that concepts like "learning" and "frustration" are related to easily observable but superficial properties, whereas more-adequate scientific constructs go beyond this level. One evidence of higher-level constructs is the possibility of defining their conceptual type and their conceptual dimension. Again appealing to physics for an example, Lewin indicated that speed and acceleration do not have the same conceptual dimension, since speed is distance over time and acceleration is distance over time squared. Everything that can be expressed as speed has the same conceptual dimension as do all things that can be expressed as force. This distinction is important, since only those things that have the same conceptual dimension can be compared as to magnitude, that is, quantitatively. Unfortunately, he did not develop the idea of conceptual dimensions in detail. He did, however, indicate some psychological concepts that have the same conceptual dimension and some that are different. For example, psychological position has the same conceptual dimension as group belongingness, occupational position, and cognitive structure. Concepts having different conceptual dimensions include such things as locomotion (a relation of positions at different times), force (a tendency to locomotion), and goal (a positive valence).

The foregoing ideas underlie the development of formal constructs in Lewin's theoretical work. In the following pages we will attempt to identify and describe the major constructs proposed by Lewin and show how these were applied to selected social problems. His most fundamental construct is, of course, the field. In psychology, the field that must be considered is the *life space* of the individual.

Life Space

The life space of an individual consists of the person and the psychological environment as it exists for him. It is the totality of all psychological factors that influence the individual at any given moment. In a similar manner, the life space of a group consists of the group and the environment as it exists for the group at the time. Before going into a detailed discussion of the nature of the life space, it will be helpful to consider some of the general characteristics of this construct.

The first important aspect of life space is that it includes all the things that have *existence* and excludes all that do not have existence for the individual or group at the time. For Lewin, a thing exists if it has demonstrable effects. The task of the scientist, therefore, is to determine specifically what things exist for the individual or group and to devise methods of observation and measurement adequate for representing the life space. Adequate representation of the life space will then permit the statement of laws concerning the properties of the life space and the changes of these properties. Lewin devoted much time to the question of what should be included in the life space and what should be excluded. It is relatively easy to decide many things that should be included, such as the needs and goals of the individual, and also many things that should be excluded, such as events occurring in remote parts of the world and unknown to the individual. However, there is a broad zone of ambiguity where the decision is not so easy. For example, there are many economic and political events that affect the individual's behavior, although the events occurred in remote places. These must be included in the individual's life space. Lewin also stated that there are certain unconscious states that can be determined to have effects on behavior and therefore must be included in the life space.

The various elements of the life space are characterized by *interdependence*, although the degree of interdependency may vary. This fact imposes many problems of conceptualization and measurement that were never adequately solved by Lewin. However, his concern with these problems led to many useful insights, as we shall see later.

Finally, it is important to remember that Lewin regarded the properties of the field at any given time as the only determinants of behavior. This *ahistorical orientation* is often seen as a denial of the efficacy of learning, but such a view reflects a misunderstanding of the principle. Lewin recognized that the life space at any given time was partially determined by past events, but his position was that these past events were not directly related to behavior. For example, if a person is thirsty, he or she will drink—and it does not matter whether the thirst was produced by several hours of water deprivation or one hour of hard work. The important thing for behavior is that the need for water is a part of the individual's life space at the time water is available. Similarly, if a person has "learned" that a wire is charged with electricity he or she will respond to it in the same way, regardless of the source of this information, provided, of course, that other parts of the life space remain constant.

We are now ready to examine the nature of the life space: its cognitive structure and dynamic characteristics. We will look first at the life space of an individual and later show how this may be applied to the group. The first thing of significance is that the life space is *differentiated* into *regions*. A region (or life sphere) is any major part of the life space that can be distinguished from other parts of the life space. Examples of life spheres are needs, profession, family, friendships, and the like. These life spheres are further differentiated into smaller units. In practice, the degree to which the differentiated parts of the life space must be considered will depend upon the purposes of the analysis. In some cases it will suffice to identify only life spheres, whereas in others the differentiation of these spheres must be taken into account.

The degree of differentiation of the life space of an individual depends upon a number of variables, such as the age of the person, his or her intelligence, and the experiences that he or she has had. The life space becomes more differentiated as the child grows older; the more-intelligent person has a more highly differentiated life space than the less-intelligent person, and so forth. Figure 5-2 shows the life space of a hypothetical person as a child and as an adult. We can see that the adult's life space is considerably more complex than the child's, and thus the adult's behavior is determined by more variables than the behavior of the child is.

The diagrams in Figure 5-2 also illustrate two additional dimensions of the life space: the *fluidity* of the system and its *reality-irreality* characteristics. The fluidity of the life space refers to the degree to which regions are distinguishable from each other, to the ease of moving from one region to another. The life space of the child is more fluid than the life space of an adult in that the various regions are less clearly defined and different regions are often only vaguely distinguishable. In the case of the newborn, for example, no region called "my own body" exists; only later in life does the infant begin to pay attention to his or her own body and to differentiate it from the environment (Buhler, 1939; Lewin, 1946). The relative fluidity of the various regions of the life space is due to the *rigidity* of the *boundaries* of the regions. This aspect of the life space is shown in Figure 5-2 by the width of the boundaries separating regions. The wider the boundary the more distinguishable the region, the more rigid the boundary, and the less fluid the system. This aspect of the life space will be of further interest in connection with our consideration of tension systems, presented in a later section.

The second aspect of the life space, the reality-irreality dimension, is indicated in Figure 5-2 by the two levels marked "I" (irreality level) and "R" (reality level). The level of irreality involves imagery and fantasy, whereas the level of reality involves more-objective aspects of the life space, such as the toys in a playroom. The level of reality in the psychological future corresponds to what is expected, whereas the level of irreality corresponds to the hopes and fears for the future. Dynamically. the level of irreality is more fluid and more closely related to the central layers of the personality than the level of reality.

To conclude this section, we might note that the structure of the life space

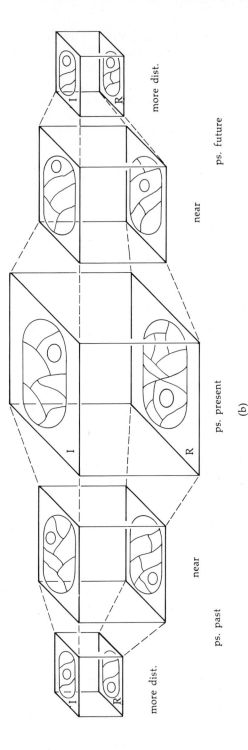

Figure 5-2 The life space at two developmental stages. The upper drawing represents the life space of a younger child. The lower diagram represents the higher degree of differentiation of the life space of the older child in regard to the present situation, the reality-irreality dimension, and the time perspective. (C=child; R=level of reality; I=level of irreality; Ps past=psychological past; Ps present=psychological present; Ps future=psychological future.) (Reprinted with permission from K. Lewin. *Field theory in social science.* New York: Harper and Row, 1951.)

consists of the positional relations of its parts and is expressed by Lewin by the topology of the life space. Changes in structure may occur in a variety of ways:

1   By an increase in differentiation of a region
2   By a combination of two or more regions into one
3   By a decrease in differentiation
4   By breaking up a region into relatively independent regions
5   By restructuring, that is, by a change in pattern but no change in differentiation

Behavior and Locomotion

Behavior means any change in the life space. Behavior is coordinated to the movement of the person in the life space, but not all such movements are behavior. For example, if a man is moved from his office (professional region) to a hospital (health region) while he is unconscious, this would be movement in the life space but would not constitute behavior. On the other hand, if he went to the hospital for a checkup, this movement would be behavior.

Behavior may be regarded as *locomotion* of the person in the life space, since locomotion refers to voluntary movement within the life space. Locomotion is not the only change in the life space, but Lewin states that it is the most important one (Lewin, 1936, p. 47). There are different kinds of locomotions: for example, a person may move about (bodily locomotion), or he or she may approach or avoid certain goals (psychological locomotion). But the person may locomote in only some parts of the life space; that is, only some parts of the life space are open to him or her from his or her present position. This *space of free movement* is usually a multiply connected region, limited by what is forbidden to the person and by what is beyond his or her abilities. Such a *barrier,* defined as a boundary that offers resistance to locomotion, limits the space of free movement when it is impassable or impenetrable.

Locomotion may be produced by a *need,* which corresponds to a tension system of the inner-personal region. The extent to which the need will produce locomotion depends in part on the degree to which the inner-personal region is in *communication* with another region, where two regions are said to be in communication if a change of state in one region produces a change of state in the other region. If two regions are in communication and a need is aroused in one of the two regions, locomotion from that region to the second occurs until a state of equilibrium is reached, that is, until the opposing forces in the two regions are equal in strength.

Force and Force Fields

When an individual moves from one part of his or her psychological field to another, locomotion occurs, but the structure of the life space determines what locomotions are possible at any given time. In handling this problem, Lewin invoked the construct *force.* A force is defined as that which causes change

(Lewin, 1936). Its properties are direction, strength, and point of application. (In Lewin's diagrams, direction and strength are represented by a vector and point of application by an arrow.) Thus, for any given point in the life space, the construct force represents the direction of and tendency to change. A number of forces can act on the same point at any given time, and the combination of these forces is called the *resultant* force. This is the effective force operating to determine behavior. When the resultant force is greater than zero, there is either a locomotion in the direction of that force or a change in the cognitive structure that is equivalent to locomotion. Conversely, if a locomotion or change in structure occurs, resultant forces exist in the direction of that change (Lewin, 1946).

Psychological forces represent or correspond to relations between regions of the life space. This can be illustrated by the situation depicted in Figure 5-3. The force *fg* is acting on the person p in the direction of the goal G. The strength of this force depends upon the state of p and the nature of the region G. For example, if the person is very hungry and the goal region consists of food, the force is relatively strong; if the person is only slightly hungry, the force is relatively weak. In the example shown in Figure 5-3, the goal region is attractive to p and so is said to have a positive *valence* (indicated by the + beside G).

The term "valence," like many other terms in Lewin's system, was adopted from the physical sciences, where it is used to refer to the combining power of an element. Lewin used "valence" to describe a field of forces in the life space. Valences may be either positive or negative, depending upon the attractiveness or repulsiveness of the goal region; that is, forces may produce locomotion either toward or away from the goal region. If only one force exists, as in Figure 5-3, then p will locomote to G. More commonly, however, p is subjected to many forces, some of which are positive and some of which are negative with respect to any given goal region. This happens when the goal region both attracts and repels p or when two or more mutually exclusive goal regions having positive valences are in the individual's life space. In such cases, the resultant force on p is some combination of all the forces acting on him or her.

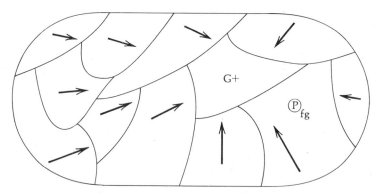

Figure 5-3 An example of a field of forces corresponding to a positive valence. (Adapted with permission from K. Lewin. *Field theory in social science.* New York: Harper and Row, 1951.)

The strength of force toward or away from a goal is a function of the strength of the valence and the psychological distance between the person and the goal. The strength of the valence, as we have indicated before, depends upon how attractive or repulsive the goal region is for p. The effect of psychological distance on force strength is somewhat complicated. In general, the closer p is to the goal, the stronger the force acting on p. However, it is important to remember that Lewin was talking about *psychological* distance, not physical distance. Although psychological and physical distance are correlated, they are not identical, and it is the former that is important. The unattainable young lady may be only 3 feet away. Furthermore, the change in the strength of the force with distance to the goal (called *goal gradient*) is different for positive and negative valences. Force strength increases much faster as p approaches a negative goal than when he or she approaches a positive goal.

Lewin identified several types of forces: driving forces, restraining forces, induced forces, forces corresponding to one's own needs, and impersonal forces. Forces toward a positive or away from a negative valence are called *driving forces* because they lead to locomotion. However, locomotion may be hindered or prevented by physical or social obstacles or barriers. Such obstacles are called *restraining forces*. They do not lead to locomotion but they do exert an influence on the effects of driving forces. For example, if an individual sees a friend (positive valence) on the other side of a high fence (barrier acting as restraining force) and wishes to approach him or her (driving force), locomotion cannot be in a straight line; the individual must detour by way of a gate. Social barriers can be equally effective as restraining forces. A worker may wish to enter the boss's office and demand a raise, but social restraining forces prevent this action.

The kinds of driving forces used in the examples above might also be classified as corresponding to the person's *own needs*. There are forces, however, that do not correspond to the person's own desires but to the wishes of another person. Such *induced forces* are exemplified by the wishes of a mother for her child, of a foreman for his workers, etc. There are also forces that do not correspond to either an individual's own needs or to the wishes of another person but rather to the requirements of the situation. Social norms represent one example of such *impersonal forces*.

Finally, it should be noted that the point of application may be any part of the life space. Most frequently, perhaps, the point of application of a force is the region corresponding to one's own person, but it is sometimes the case that the point of application is a region of the life space of another person. For example, a child may experience that "doll wants to go to bed" (Lewin, 1951).

Tension and Tension Systems

In any life space or field there exist opposing forces, for example, two or more positive forces toward different goals or both positive and negative forces toward the same goal region. As a result, a state of tension exists. As evidence for the existence of tension, Lewin cited studies of the effects of interrupting subjects before they completed an assigned task. The general finding was that interrupted tasks are both recalled (Zeigarnik, 1927) and resumed (Ovsiankina, 1928) more frequently than completed tasks (the so-called Zeigarnik effect). Tension is aroused when the person accepts task completion as a goal. The tension associated with the task region presumably is discharged or reduced to an acceptable level by task completion. When the procedure is interrupted before the task is completed, the tension level remains relatively high and produces the drive toward resumption and the greater recall of incompleted tasks. The fact that resumption and recall rates are greater for incompleted than for completed tasks is therefore taken as proof of the existence of tension. (The reader will recall that for Lewin a thing exists if it can be shown to have effects.)

At this point it is necessary to digress from a consideration of the nature of tension systems and elaborate upon Lewin's idea of tension reduction. First, it is important to notice that he does not mean the same thing by tension reduction as Hull and other S-R theorists. For Lewin, tension reduction means that the tension associated with one region changes in such a way as to achieve equilibrium (or a quasi-state of equilibrium) with neighboring regions. Thus, when the tension level of a given region is the same as that of surrounding regions, tension reduction has occurred. Note that this does not imply a zero level of tension. In fact, the absolute tension level may remain relatively high after tension reduction has occurred. This has important implications for behavior change, as revealed by studies of group decision (Lewin, 1951). Change can be produced either by increasing the tension in the region where the behavior originally took place or by decreasing the tension in the region to which locomotion is desired. In the first instance, the overall tension level is increased and leads to dissatisfaction; in the second case, the overall level is decreased and satisfaction is relatively high.

Tension presumably has both general and specific effects. Lewin was never very clear on this point, but apparently the tension is associated with a particular region in some cases, whereas in other cases it is more pervasive and affects the entire system. The degree to which the tension level in one system can affect the tension level in another depends upon the *permeability* of the boundaries between regions. When the regions are highly differentiated and separated by rigid boundaries, the effects of events in one region on the tension level of another region are minor. However, when the regions are less clearly differentiated and the boundaries less rigid (and therefore more permeable), the interregional effects are great. This interregional exchange of tension reduction is referred to as *substitute satisfaction*.

Lewin suggested that the substitute value of an activity depends upon the degree of similarity of the substitute and the original activity and upon the degree of difficulty of the substitute activity. For example, if an individual is working toward completion of an arithmetic task and is interrupted, he may reduce the tension by completing other (substitute) arithmetic problems. Reduction of tension is greater if the substitute problems are more difficult than the interrupted ones. Lewin (1951) cited a study by Mahler (1933) as evidence. She found that talking could serve as a substitute for task completion when the task was to solve a problem (where talking could lead to solution), but talking was much less effective as a substitute when the task was construction of a material object (where talking could not lead to task completion).

Substitute effectiveness may also depend upon the degree of differentiation of the cognitive structure, as stated above. One might say that the possibility of substitution depends upon permeability of boundaries, but whether substitution is in fact effective depends upon similarity and difficulty. In the Mahler studies, the subjects ranged in age from six to ten years, and their cognitive structure was presumably less highly differentiated and the boundaries more permeable than in older persons (although Lewin reported that little differences are found between children and adults). The greatest differences in permeability of boundaries would be expected between normal and mentally deficient persons. According to Lewin (1935), the mentally deficient person is less highly differentiated than the normal, but the boundaries between regions are more rigid and less permeable than in the normal person. Therefore, the effects of activities in related regions upon tension levels should be less in mentally deficient persons than in normals. Evidence for this expectation has been provided by Shaw and Bensberg (1955), who demonstrated that success and failure on one task had greater effects on the level of aspiration for a different task when subjects were normal than when they were mentally deficient.

The psychological satiation of needs was cited as still further evidence of tension and tension reduction. It is well known that eating large amounts of food will lead to satiation of the hunger drive. Lewin suggested that similar satiation occurs with regard to other activities. He cited a study by Karsten (1928), which showed that repetition of tasks such as writing letters, drawing, and turning a wheel led to measurable evidences of satiation (or tension reduction).

In summary, Lewin proposed that regions of the life space are characterized by tension, and the relations among the various regions constitute tension systems. These systems function as forces toward action. Activities in one region *can* affect the tension in another system to the extent that the boundaries between regions are permeable. The degree to which the activities *do* influence the tension level in other regions is a function of the similarity of the activities and their relative difficulties. Repetition of an activity leads to psychological satiation or tension reduction.

The Relation of Tension and Force

Lewin was never very specific regarding the relation between psychological tension and psychological force. Force was defined as the cause of change and tension as a state of a region relative to surrounding regions. Tension was said to involve forces at the boundary of the region that tend to produce changes such that differences in tension are diminished (Lewin, 1936). This seems to imply that tension is the source of force. However, according to Cartwright (1959a), tension is more appropriately related to inner-personal regions. Thus, when an inner-personal region is in a state of tension, a related environmental region becomes the center of a force field (acquires positive valence). Which environmental region becomes the center of a force field depends upon the qualitative nature of the tension and of the region. If the tension system corresponding to hunger is aroused, the environmental region that acquires a positive valence will be that associated with eating. As Cartwright so aptly stated, the exact manner in which regions are selected has not been worked out in field theory.

APPLICATIONS OF THE THEORY

In the preceding pages we have given, for the most part, only abstract definitions and principles of field theory. The constructs described may become more meaningful if they are exemplified in concrete situations. Therefore, in this section we will give two applications of the field-theoretical orientation to social problems. The first example is an analysis of social power by French (1956) and the second is an analysis of cooperation and competition by Deutsch (1949a).

An Analysis of Social Power

French was concerned with the general question of social power and how group members use their power to influence others in the group. Basically, he attempted to reduce influence to a summation of interpersonal influences involving three patterns of relations: the power relations among group members, the communication patterns in the group, and the relations among opinions within the group.

The Model of Social Influence

The model of opinion change formulated by French was derived from Lewin's (1951) theory of quasi-stationary equilibrium. Changes in opinion are conceptualized in terms of forces operating along a unidimensional continuum. Social influences are analogous to force fields induced by one person with respect to another. Power is coordinated to the strength of these forces; that is, A has power over B in proportion to the strength of the force fields which A can induce on B. This power is potential power that will be effective only if A communicates to B in some manner. For example, when A expresses an opinion or argues with B, then the forces which A can induce on B are activated in the direction of a central position corresponding to A's opinion. In groups larger than dyads, other group members may also have power over B that can be invoked through communication. The actual change in B's opinion will thus be a function of the resultant force from all these member forces and a force corresponding to B's resistance.

To demonstrate how the model can be used to derive the exact amount of influence that each group member will have over every other group member, French assumed a unidimensional continuum of opinion which can be measured by a ratio scale. Suppose two persons, A and B, hold the initial opinions represented in Figure 5-4. In Figure 5-4 the ordinate indicates the strength of the force that A can induce for B and the strength of the resistance that B can

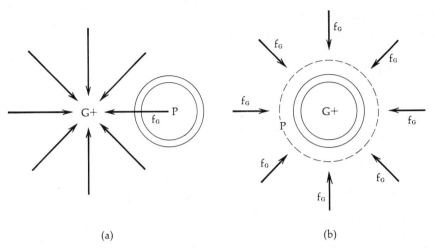

(a) (b)

Figure 5-4 Force fields influencing opinion change by person B. (Adapted with permission from J. R. P. French, Jr. A formal theory of social power. *Psychol. Rev.,* 1956, *63,* 181–194.)

mobilize against A, and the abscissa indicates the opinion continuum. The solid line represents the forces that A can induce with respect to B, and the broken lines indicate the forces of resistance emanating from B against A. Where these two gradients intersect, there is an equilibrium point where the two forces are equal in strength and opposite in direction. At all points to the right of this point of equilibrium A's forces are stronger than B's resistance and B will change his opinion in the direction of A. At all points to the left of the equilibrium point, B's resistance is stronger than A's forces and B will move toward the point of equilibrium (although it is difficult to understand how B could be in such a position). The effects of forces induced by other group members in larger groups can be derived in a similar manner.

Influence in groups is a gradual process that requires time; therefore, French divided the influence process into units. He defined a unit as the time required for all members who are being influenced to change their opinions to the point of equilibrium of all the forces operating at the beginning of that unit. At the end of that unit, a new constellation of forces is in operation to produce a new equilibrium to which all members shift during the next unit. This process will continue until all group members have the same opinion or until the maximum change possible has occurred. (Conditions determining whether uniformity of group opinion can be achieved will be considered in a later section). This analysis assumes that all persons change at the same rate.

French made a distinction between *direct* and *indirect influence.* Direct influence is mediated through direct channels of communication (A communicates directly with B), whereas indirect influence is mediated through other persons. According to the above formulation, direct influence always occurs during the same unit, whereas indirect influence requires two or more units.

The Bases of Social Power

Social power was defined as "the power of A over B (with respect to a given opinion) is equal to the maximum force which A can induce on B minus the maximum resisting force which B can mobilize in the opposite direction" (French, 1956, p. 183). The basis for interpersonal power was defined as a more or less enduring relationship between A and B. Following an earlier analysis (French & Raven, 1959), five bases of power were identified:

Attraction power, which is based on a liking or identification relationship, labeled by French and Raven as "referent power"

Reward power, based on A's ability to mediate rewards for B, that is, A's ability to administer positive valences and remove or decrease negative valences

Coercive power, based on A's ability to mediate punishments for B, that is, A's ability to administer negative valences and remove or decrease positive valences

Legitimate power, based on B's belief that A has a right to prescribe B's behavior

Expert power, based on B's perception that A has greater resources (knowledge or information) within a given area

Reward and coercive power both lead to dependent behavior; that is, their effectiveness depends upon the presence of A. The other three types are less dependent in that the presence of A is irrelevant.

It should be noted that various bases of power are not independent, since a given person's power may have more than one basis. For example, one may believe that it is right that an informed person should have power over him (legitimate *and* expert power). The exercise of one type of power may also increase or decrease the basis for another type of power. For example, if A exercises reward power over B, it may be expected that B's liking for A will increase and thus increase attraction power.

Postulates

French formulated three postulates concerning power relations, opinion relations (discrepancies), and opinion change. The first postulate refers to all of the bases of social power outlined above.

Postulate 1. For any given discrepancy between A and B, the strength of the resultant force which an inducer A can exert on an inducee B, in the direction of agreeing with A's opinion, is proportional to the strength of the bases of power of A over B (French, 1956, p. 184).

Postulate 2. The strength of the force which an inducer A exerts on an inducee B, in the direction of agreeing with A's opinion, is proportional to the size of the discrepancy between their opinions (French, 1956, p. 184).

Postulate 3. In one unit, each person who is being influenced will change his opinion until he reaches the equilibrium point where the resultant force . . . is equal to zero (French, 1956, p. 185).

Postulates 1 and 2 state merely that the strength of the resultant force in situations similar to the one depicted in Figure 5-4 will be proportional to the strength of the bases of power and the discrepancy among opinions in the group. French cited experimental evidence supporting both of these postulates. Postulate 3 is an application of Lewin's assumption that locomotion will take place in the direction of any resultant force that is greater than zero. French stated that this assumption is consistent with empirical studies but cannot be tested directly.

Theorems

French selected certain representative theorems for consideration. We shall discuss those related to the power structure of the group, communication patterns, and patterns of opinions.

Power Structure   In formulating theorems about the effects of the power structure on the influence process, French (1956) represented the power structure in terms of the mathematical theory of directed graphs. A directed graph (or digraph) is a finite set of points and a subset of the directed lines between these points. Points were coordinated to group members and directed lines to power relations. The property of a digraph labeled "degree of connectedness" was used to characterize the power structure of groups. To explicate this property, it is necessary to define *complete digraph* and *directed path*. A digraph is complete if there exists a directed line from each point to every other point. Thus, for a power structure to be complete, each group member must have power over every other member. A directed path is a collection of points (for example, A, B, C,) together with a sequence of directed lines beginning at the first and ending at the last point; that is, there is a directed line from A to B and from B to C, but not directly from A to C.

In an unpublished work, Harary, Norman, and Cartwright defined four degrees of connectedness: strong, unilateral, weak, and disconnected. French adopted their definitions, which may be stated as follows:

1 A digraph is *strongly connected* if, for every pair of distinct points, A and B, there exists a directed path from A to B *and* from B to A.

2 A digraph is *unilaterally connected* if, for every pair of points, A and B, there exists a directed path from A to B *or* from B to A.

3 A digraph is *weakly connected* if it is impossible to separate its points into two classes such that no line of the digraph has one end point in one class and the other end point in another class.

4 A digraph is *disconnected* if its points can be separated into two or more classes of points such that no line goes from one class to another class.

From these definitions it is clear that all complete digraphs are strong, although not all strong digraphs are complete; that all strong digraphs are unilateral and weak; that all unilateral digraphs are weak; and that all weak digraphs are not strong. However, French used each label to mean digraphs that fit only the definition given for that particular degree of connectedness. For example, *strong* refers to a digraph that is strongly connected but is not complete, *unilateral* to a digraph that is unilaterally connected but not strong, etc.

According to the model of opinion change and the postulates given above, French was able to specify the nature of opinion change in each type of power structure. In groups where each member communicates to all other members over whom he or she has direct power during every unit of the influence process, the following theorems may be derived:

Theorem 1. For all possible patterns of initial opinions, in a complete power structure the opinions of all members will reach a common equilibrium level, equal to the arithmetic mean of all initial opinions, in one unit.

Theorem 2. In a strong power structure, all members will reach a final common opinion at the arithmetic mean in an infinite number of units.

Theorem 3. In a unilateral power structure, group members will reach a final common opinion in an infinite number of units.

Theorem 4. In a weak power structure group members will not reach a common opinion except under special conditions in the distribution of initial opinions.

No theorem was stated for a disconnected structure, but French noted that, when the final equilibrium has been reached, there will be at least as many different final opinions as there are classes of members (cliques), because no clique can influence any other. The power structure of each clique will determine the course of opinion change in that clique, in accordance with theorems 1 through 4.

The theorems presented thus far have considered power as an all-or-none relation. Theorem 5 refers to the effects of variations in power, derived primarily from postulates 1 and 3.

Theorem 5. The greater the bases of power of A over B, the more influence A will have on B and subsequently on any other person P for whom there is a directed path from B to P.

Communication Patterns   It is clear that a person may not always communicate with everyone over whom he has power, but French assumed that communications stabilize so that they may be treated as consistent communication patterns. It is also obvious that the strength of the influence attempt can vary continuously, although a communication from A to B must be treated as an all-or-none variable in order to use digraph theory. Finally, in formulating theorems about the effects of communication patterns on opinion change, French considered only complete power structures with variations in degree of connectedness of communication channels. With these restrictions, theorems 1 through 4 also apply to communication patterns.

The model can also be applied to situations in which communication patterns are not stable, provided the interaction pattern is specified for each unit. French illustrated this in theorem 6, specifying the following interaction pattern: A exerts influence in the first unit, B and C in the second unit, A in the third unit, B and C in the fourth unit, and so on.

Theorem 6. In a three-person group in which A has power over B, B has power over C, and C has power over A, and the communication pattern is A, BC, A, BC . . . , the final common opinion reached by the group members equals $(2a + b + 2c)/5$, where *a, b,* and *c* are the opinions initially held by persons A, B, and C, respectively.

The expression, "the communication pattern is A, BC, A, BC, . . . ," in theorem 6 means that person A exerts influence in the first unit, persons B and C exert influence in the second unit, etc. Two main consequences of the communication pattern and the power structure are at once evident: the person who speaks first in the interaction sequence has more influence than those who speak later in the sequence, and the person who has direct power over others has more influence than a person who has only indirect power over others.

Patterns of Opinion   In his consideration of patterns of opinion, French analyzed only the case of a completely connected power structure with completely connected communication channels in which every member communicates to everyone else during each unit. Under these conditions:

Theorem 7. The amount of change of a deviate toward the opinions of the majority is proportional to the sum of the deviations of all other members from the opinion of the deviate.

In general, then, the more members in the group the more they will influence the deviate, and the larger the deviations the more the deviate will change his opinion. The studies by Asch (1952) are cited as an example, although French stated that the conditions of the Asch experiments do not fit the model very well.

The analysis by French shows quite well how the field-theory concepts, such as force fields and equilibrium, can be utilized to explain one important problem in social psychology (i.e., opinion change). Deutsch's (1949a) theoretical analysis of the effects of cooperation and competition provides another example of the application of field-theory concepts to social problems.

An Analysis of Cooperation and Competition

Deutsch was concerned with the effects of cooperation and competition upon behavior. He began his analysis with a definition (or conceptualization) of cooperative and competitive situations. He then considered the implications of the definitions and formulated a set of hypotheses about the relative effects of cooperation and competition upon group process.

Definitions   In the process of defining cooperation and competition, Deutsch examined a number of definitions proposed by others (Maller, 1929; May & Doob, 1937; Mead, 1937; Barnard, 1938; Lewis, 1944) and noted that implicit in all definitions was the notion that the major difference between cooperation and competition was in the nature of goal regions in the two situations. His definitions are based upon this distinction and may be stated briefly as follows: A social situation is *cooperative* if the goal regions for each of the individuals or subunits in the situation are defined so that a goal region can be entered, to some degree, by any given individual or subunit only if all of the individuals or subunits under consideration can enter their respective goal regions, to some degree. (The term *promotively interdependent goals* was used to refer to situations in which individual goals are interrelated in the manner described.)

A social situation is *competitive* if the goal regions for individuals or subunits in the situation are such that, if a goal region is entered by any individual or subunit or by portions thereof, the other individuals or subunits will, to some degree, be unable to reach their respective goals. (The term *contriently interdependent goals* was used to refer to this type of goal interrelatedness.)

Implications It follows from these definitions that persons who are in cooperative groups can achieve their respective goals (locomote to the goal regions) only if everyone "locomotes toward the goal regions." Similarly, persons in competitive situations will come to have contriently interdependent locomotions in the direction of their goals; that is, if one person in a competitive group achieves his goal (locomotes to his or her goal region), other persons in the group do not achieve theirs.

Deutsch pointed to the difficulties involved in going from these statements about objective social space to statements about psychological life space. Nevertheless, he believed that one could use the principles of learning and of perceptual and cognitive organization to make the jump more reasonable. He therefore assumed that all action is directed toward need reduction (that is, reduction or removal of tensions associated with needs) and that the significance of an object is developed during action. From these assumptions, he derived that an individual's perceptions and expectations are likely to be veridical to his or her objective environment, in proportion to the simplicity of his or her environment and to his or her capabilities and experiences. Thus, the perceptions of reasonably normal subjects with average abilities who are placed in reasonably obvious social situations should be veridical. Applying this logic to cooperative and competitive situations, the following hypotheses were proposed. Hypotheses have been restated for convenience, but we believe their meanings remain as intended by Deutsch (1949a).

Hypotheses

1 Individuals in cooperative situations will perceive themselves to be more promotively interdependent, and individuals in competitive situations will perceive themselves to be more contriently interdependent.

2   Substitutability for similarly intended actions will be greater in the cooperative than in the competitive situation. (Substitutability means that the acts of one person in the group can be substituted for the actions of another; two individuals need not perform the same act.)

3   A larger percentage of actions by fellow members will be positively cathected (become attractive or be regarded favorably) by members of cooperative than by members of competitive groups.

3a   A larger percentage of actions by fellow members will be negatively cathected (be regarded unfavorably) by members of competitive groups than by members of cooperative groups.

4   There will be greater positive inducibility (production and channeling of own forces in the direction induced by the inducing agent) with respect to fellow group members in the cooperative than in the competitive situation.

4a   There will be greater self-conflict among members of cooperative than among members of competitive groups.

5   Members of cooperative groups will help each other more than members of competitive groups will help each other.

5a   Members of competitive groups will exhibit more obstructiveness towards each other than will members of cooperative groups.

6   At any given time, there will be greater interrelation of activities (working together) among members of cooperative groups than among members of competitive groups.

6a   Over a period of time, there will be more frequent coordination of efforts in cooperative than in competitive situations.

7   Homogeneity with respect to amount of contributions or participations will be greater in cooperative than in competitive situations.

8   Specialization of function will be greater in cooperative than in competitive situations.

9   Specialization of activities will be greater in cooperative than in competitive groups.

10   Structural stability with respect to functions will be greater in cooperative than in competitive situations.

11   Change of roles to adapt to changing circumstances will be greater in cooperative than in competitive situations.

12   The direction of forces operating on members of cooperative groups will be more similar than the direction of forces operating on members of competitive groups.

13   There will be more achievement pressure in cooperative than in competitive groups.

14   The group force in the direction of the goal will be stronger in cooperative than in competitive situations.

15   Cooperative and competitive groups will not differ in total strength of forces (interest and involvement) operating on members in their respective situations.

16   When the task is such that the production of observable signs (participation) is perceived as a means for locomotion, total signs produced per unit time will be greater in competitive groups than in cooperative groups.

17   When locomotion is possible without the production of signs, total signs produced per unit time will be greater in cooperative than in competitive groups.

18 Attentiveness to the production of signs by others will be less in competitive than in cooperative groups.

19 Communication difficulties will be greater in competitive than in cooperative groups.

20 Communication difficulties will be greater, even when attentiveness is optimal, in competitive than in cooperative groups.

21 There will be more mutual agreements and acceptances of communications by communicators and communicatees in cooperative than in competitive groups.

22 Members of cooperative groups will have more knowledge about their active members than will members of competitive groups.

23 Group orientation will be greater among members of cooperative than among members of competitive groups.

24 Productivity per unit time will be greater for cooperative than for competitive groups.

24a It will require less time for a cooperative group to produce a given amount than for a competitive group to produce that same amount.

25 The qualitative productivity of cooperative groups will be higher than that of competitive groups.

26 Members of cooperative groups will learn more from each other than will members of competitive groups.

27 There will be more friendliness among members of cooperative than among members of competitive groups.

28 Members of cooperative groups will evaluate the products of their group more highly than members of competitive groups will.

29 Percentage of group functions will be higher in cooperative than in competitive situations.

30 Percentage of individual functions will be greater in competitive than in cooperative groups.

31 The perception of attitudes of others toward one's own functioning in the group will be more realistic in cooperative than in competitive groups.

32 The attitudes of each member toward his or her own functioning should be more similar to the attitudes of other group memoers toward their functioning in cooperative than in competitive groups.

33 Members of cooperative groups will perceive themselves as having more favorable effects on fellow members than will members of competitive groups.

34 Incorporation of the attitude of the generalized other will occur to a greater extent in cooperative than in competitive groups. ("Attitude of the generalized other" refers to the internal structure resulting from the introjection of mutually interacting attitudes of those persons with whom one interacts frequently.)

In our brief presentation of Deutsch's hypotheses, we have omitted much of the reasoning that contributed to their formulation and thus have not shown how the various hypotheses are interrelated. However, this analysis of cooperation and competition in terms of goal regions and the forces that they activate provides a good illustration of the way Lewin's concepts can be applied to interpersonal behavior.

In the next chapter we will consider several theories that adopt the basic field-theoretical orientation but do not derive directly from the Lewinian conceptualization.

Chapter 6

Field Theories in Social Psychology

The field-theoretical orientation exemplified by the Lewinian model has been attractive to a number of theoreticians. Its appeal probably derives from the emphasis upon humanistic and phenomenological concepts, without at the same time sacrificing rigor. Some social psychologists object to the dehumanization that they believe to be inherent in reinforcement and similar theories (see Chapters 3 and 4). These psychologists seek a theoretical framework which is methodologically sound, but which gives cognizance to the richness and complexity of the phenomenal world of the individual. Field theory represents one attempt to meet these requirements. Although it has not been entirely successful in this respect, it is one of the few orientations which emphasize both the scientific and humanistic viewpoints.

Field-theoretical analyses have been provided for many specific problems. In addition to the analyses of social power and the effects of cooperation and competition that we reviewed in the preceding chapter, Lewinian concepts have been applied to level-of-aspiration phenomena (Lewin, Dembo, Festinger, & Sears, 1944), learning (Lewin, 1942), regression (Lewin, 1941), social change (Lewin, 1943; Coch & French, 1948), and feeble-mindedness (Lewin, 1935), to mention only a few. Here, we are more interested in theories dealing with broader aspects of social behavior than that represented by the direct application

136

of Lewinian principles to specific behavioral situations. We are concerned with theories which have adopted the basic field-theoretical orientation, but which have modified and adapted its principles to fairly broad social psychological phenomena. We have identified several theories that we believe approximate this objective, including theories of interpersonal relations (Heider, 1958), social penetration (Altman & Taylor, 1973), two theories of crowding (Schopler & Stokols, 1976; Altman, 1975), and a theory of hope (Stotland, 1969). Each of these theories shows moderate-to-strong field-orientation influences, although none is merely a direct application of Lewinian principles. Indeed, many of the conceptualizations employed deviate markedly from those described in Chapter 5.

A THEORY OF INTERPERSONAL RELATIONS

Heider (1958) was concerned primarily with relations among a few persons, usually two. His theory attempted to answer questions such as: How does one person think and feel about another person? How does one person perceive another person's characteristics? actions? How does one person react to the actions of another? What does one person expect another to do or think? Under what conditions does a person feel shame or embarrassment in the presence of others? What induces one person to attribute emotion, intentionality, responsibility, and the like to others? Thus, he was concerned with events that occur in everyday life and are familiar to all of us.

Heider agreed with Lewin that an individual cannot be described as a lone subject in an impersonal environment, but must be viewed as a part of the total situation. In particular, the psychological world of the other person, as viewed by the subject, must be a central part of the analysis of interpersonal relations. Heider also adopted Lewin's "method of construction," but he appealed to "common-sense psychology" as a source of insight into interpersonal behavior and maintained that scientific psychology could learn much from common-sense psychology, which is important in at least two ways. First, common-sense psychology governs our behavior toward others, and hence it is an essential part of interpersonal phenomena. Second, it contains many truths concerning interpersonal relations.

In making use of common-sense psychology, Heider attempted to use the concepts of everyday language by sharpening them and relating them to each other. This process of *explication* (Carnap, 1953) is seen as a necessary stage in the development of scientific language. The reader will encounter many common terms, such as "can," "trying," and "wanting," but should keep clearly in mind that Heider's use of such terms is usually more specific than their use in everyday language. We will try to give his definition each time a new "common-sense scientific" term is introduced.

Following this common-sense approach, Heider considered several aspects of interpersonal behavior, including perceiving the other person, the other person as a perceiver, the analysis of action, the experiences of desire and pleasure, and the roles of environmental variables. We will consider the more-significant aspects of his theory in the following sections.

Perceiving the Other Person

Following Brunswik (1934), Heider assumed that the principles of person perception are essentially the same as the principles that govern the perception of impersonal objects, such as tables and chairs. However, it is not assumed that there are no differences between the perception of persons and things. Persons are seen as having abilities, emotions, intentions, wishes, sentiments, and other qualities that are not ordinarily attributed to physical objects. Other persons can act to benefit or harm us, they can act purposefully, and they can perceive us in turn. To fully understand person perception, then, it is necessary to consider the conditions that determine a person's perceptions of the environment and the people in it, as well as the consequences of the person's awareness that the other person (o) is perceiving the environment, including the person (p).

In dealing with these problems, Heider resorted to phenomenal and causal descriptions. Phenomenal description refers to the nature of the contact between p and the environment as it is experienced by p, whereas causal description refers to the analysis of underlying conditions that give rise to perceptual experience. Phenomenally, p feels that he or she is in direct contact with persons and things in his or her environment. Objects are seen as if they are "out there" and are readily accessible. People are perceived as having shape, size, color, and other spatial and physical characteristics, but they are also seen as having wishes, needs, intentions, and other intangible properties. These intangibles are also seen as being directly given.

Causal analysis, on the other hand, distinguishes a number of steps in the perceptual process. According to Brunswik (1952) the perceptual process can be likened to a perceptual arc involving the object (called the *distal stimulus*) and the percept, that is, the way the object appears to us. The distal stimulus, then, is the thing that is outside and at some distance from p. The distal stimulus is the starting point of perception, but does not directly affect p. Instead, the distal stimulus is mediated by light and sound waves that excite the sense receptors. The stimulus pattern which impinges directly upon the sense organs is called the *proximal stimulus,* since it is the stimulus that is in direct proximity to p.

Causal analysis of person perception also divides the perceptual process into steps. The other person (o) is the distal stimulus, and the perceptual construction within p that leads to an awareness of o is the proximal stimulus. The *mediation* consists of the manifestations of the personality of o that determine the proximal stimulus pattern. For example, p observes that o has a red face, speaks loudly, and makes hostile statements; these manifestations mediate the perception that o is angry. In many instances, the manifestations that serve as the mediation of person perceptions are obvious or, at least, open to p's awareness. In other cases, however, p may not be aware of the cues that lead to the perception. This is especially true when the cues involve the interpretation of expressive features, such as gestures and tone of voice.

Since mediation serves the important function of giving information about the distal stimulus (the environmental contents), it is necessary to consider the principles that govern the coordination of the mediation to the environmental contents. Mediation is seen by Heider as being either *synonymous* or *ambiguous* in its coordination to the distal stimulus. When the mediation is synonymous, each specific manifestation is coordinated to a specific content of the environment. In such instances, it is necessary only for p to learn these specific connections in order to perceive accurately the qualities of o. In the case of ambiguous mediation, a specific manifestation may derive from (be caused by) any one of several contents. For example, a raised eyebrow might indicate that the person is dubious, amused, or does not understand. Figure 6-1 represents instances of synonymous and ambiguous mediations. In the figure, C_a (cause a) is synonymously (or equivalently) mediated by m_1, m_2, and m_3; m_3 is an example of ambiguous mediation since it can be caused by C_a, C_b, or C_c.

It is probable that most distal stimuli are represented by ambiguous mediation, since a given manifestation is rarely connected to a single environmental content. The coordination of mediation and distal stimulus is not a simple process. However, coordination is rendered less difficult when the manifestations of the distal stimulus are *embedded* in the total situation. In this connection, Heider distinguished between *local* and *total stimulus*. Local stimulus refers to the part of the stimulus pattern that is particularly relevant to the percept, whereas the total stimulus includes the surroundings as well. The term *embeddedness* is used to refer to the fact that, in many cases, the appearance of the local stimulus is determined, at least in part, by the stimuli that surround it. For example, a grimace by o would be interpreted differently by p depending upon the presence or absence of other persons in the immediate environment. The surrounding stimuli thus serve to reduce the ambiguity of at least some mediations.

Although Heider did not clearly identify the case of overlapping ambiguous mediations, it seems clear from his analysis that such situations may reduce the ambiguity of mediations. An example of overlapping mediations is shown in Figure 6-2. The mediations m_1 can be caused by either C_a or C_b, whereas m_2 can

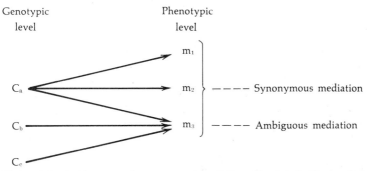

Genotypic level   Phenotypic level

m_1

C_a m_2 — — — Synonymous mediation

C_b m_3 — — — Ambiguous mediation

C_c

Figure 6-1   Ambiguous and synonymous mediation. (Reprinted with permission from F. Heider. *The psychology of interpersonal relations.* New York: Wiley, 1958.)

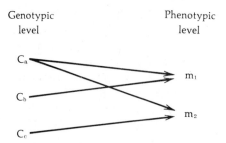

Figure 6-2 Overlapping ambiguous mediations.

be caused by either C_a or C_c. If both m_1 and m_2 occur, the most economical interpretation is that the underlying cause (distal stimulus) is C_a, although, of course, it is possible that these mediations are caused by the simultaneous effects of C_b and C_c.

The Other Person as Perceiver

As we mentioned earlier in this chapter, p is aware that o is also a perceiver and that o's perceptions have effects on o. P's understanding of the way o's perceptions influence o have important effects on p. According to Heider, p is influenced in at least three ways: his or her actions are influenced, his or her expectations are affected, and his or her attributions are determined. For example, if p perceives that the effects of o's perception on o are desirable, p will try to produce those perceptions; if p perceives them as not desirable, p will try to prevent them. Similarly, if p knows that o has perceived something, he or she will expect that o will respond to that perception in appropriate ways; that is, p will expect the consequences of o's perception. Conversely, if p knows that the consequences have occurred, he or she will assume that the necessary perception has also occurred.

Heider gave special attention to selected instances of the common-sense recognition that o's perceptions have certain effects on o which in turn affect p in significant ways. The meaning of "o perceives x" and the way p reacts to this meaning are influenced by the beliefs that p holds concerning the effects on o when o perceives x. Common-sense psychology holds that when o sees x, his or her knowledge of x is improved, and Heider asserts that most of the effects of perception can be interpreted as the effects of this improved knowledge. These effects include the following:

1 Control over the environment
2 Evaluation of x
3 Motivation for further action with regard to x
4 Ability to report about x to others
5 Communion with others

Let us consider the consequences of each of these effects for p.

When o can observe x, o has more control over it and thus more control over the environment, than when o cannot observe x. It follows that o's action possibilities are also increased. Being aware of this, p may try to influence o's perceptions as a means of influencing o's actions. For example, p may try to create conditions such that o perceives p as helpful and thus encourage o to act in a favorable manner toward p. Or p may attempt to conceal his or her thoughts from o in order to avoid control by o.

Evaluation is a common tendency in everyday life. When o observes x, o is likely to judge it as either favorable (positive) or unfavorable (negative). Therefore, p often tries to influence o's perceptions so that evaluation of p by o will be favorable. For instance, p may reveal personal qualities and/or possessions (e.g., that p is intelligent, owns stock in Exxon, etc.) that p believes will cause o to perceive p in a favorable light. Conversely, p may attempt to conceal personal aspects that may lead to unfavorable evaluations by o (e.g., that p is prejudiced toward minority groups). Knowing that o is an evaluating perceiver may also lead to heightened self-consciousness on the part of p that may be manifested by shyness or embarrassment. Therefore, p may try to avoid conditions that give rise to this state, or p may deliberately try to create the conditions that will produce embarrassment in o, if that suits his or her purpose.

The perception of x by o may produce motivation for o to act in a particular manner. Again, p may try to influence o's perceptions in order to arouse motivations toward actions that p wishes o to engage in, or to prevent the arousal of motivations toward actions that are not desired by p. For example, if p acts in ways that are known to arouse anger in o, p will seek to prevent o's learning about those actions.

If o perceives x, he or she can tell other people about x. This simple fact often leads p to try to influence o's perceptions so that o may report to another person if x is favorable to p or so that o cannot report to others if x is unfavorable to p. For example, a workman (p) may try to ensure that another workman (o) observes p's good works if p thinks o will tell p's boss about it. On the other hand, if p has engaged in socially disapproved behavior (e.g., left the job before quitting time), p will try to prevent o's learning about it and thus prevent o from reporting the disapproved behavior to the boss.

Finally, communion is an effect of mutual perception. Heider considers "communion through the eyes" as a unique form of interaction, since the eyes are the only organs that can both send and receive simultaneously. In this, he follows Simmel (1921), who asserted that the direct mutual glance represents the most-perfect reciprocity in the entire field of human relationships. Communion through the eyes is said to create such a deep interpersonal experience that the mutual glance is only maintained when a deep intimacy is desired. Thus, p allows this kind of communion with o when he desires intimacy and avoids it by deflecting his gaze when he does not wish to be intimate. Several interesting experimental studies have been reported concerning the conditions and effects of mutual communion through the eyes. (See Exline, 1963; Gibson & Pick, 1963; Exline, Gray, & Schuette, 1965; Nachshon & Wapner, 1967; Kleinke, 1977: Ellsworth, Friedman, Perlick, & Hoyt, 1978).

Naïve Analysis of Action

Interpersonal relations depend to a large extent upon a person's perceptions (interpretations) of the actions of others. According to Heider (1958), it is an important principle of both scientific and common-sense psychology that man understands reality by referring transient and variable behavior and events to relatively invariant underlying conditions. These relatively unchanging underlying conditions are called *dispositional properties;* that is, properties that "dispose" objects and events to manifest themselves in certain ways under certain conditions. It is these properties that make our world more or less stable, predictable, and controllable. For example, if an individual learns rapidly, solves problems easily, etc., it may be inferred that p is intelligent. The learning and problem-solving behavior are relatively transient events, which become understandable when related to the more-permanent property called intelligence.

When a person observes the actions of another, therefore, he or she seeks to understand the action by referring it to certain dispositional properties. In general, the result of an action is seen as depending upon factors within the person and factors within the environment. The outcome of the action is thus a function of some combination of *effective* personal forces and *effective* environmental forces, where the term *effective* means the totality of forces deriving from the person or the environment. (Presumably, environmental forces can be either positive or negative with respect to personal forces. For example, task difficulty is seen as an environmental force that operates in opposition to the personal force directed toward the completion of that task.)

Effective personal force is analyzed into a power factor and a motivational factor. Power is determined primarily by ability, although other characteristics (for example, temperament) may also affect power. The motivational factor refers to a person's *intention* (what he or she is trying to do) and *exertion* (how hard he or she is trying to do it). Power and trying are related in a multiplicative manner, since effective personal force is zero if either power or trying is zero.

If a person has the power to do something regardless of the effective environmental forces, common-sense psychology perceives that he or she *can* do it. (*Can* is used by Heider to refer to the possibility of a given action being performed by a specific person.) Like "trying," *can* is also seen as a dispositional property—at least under most circumstances. In the naïve analysis of action, *can* and *trying* are said to be the necessary and sufficient conditions for purposive action. Thus, if person p can do x, but does not, he or she is seen as not trying; that is, he or she is not motivated to do x and hence is not exerting himself or herself in that direction. Conversely, if p is seen as being unable to do x, his or her power is not sufficient to overcome the effective environmental forces with respect to x.

The motivational factor (trying) is the factor that propels and guides action; it is the thing that gives action its purposive quality. Heider regarded this factor as the major one that distinguishes personal and impersonal causality, which in turn are major determinants of interpersonal behavior. For this reason, he dealt extensively with the differences between personal and impersonal causality.

Personal and Impersonal Causality

The term *personal causality* was used by Heider to refer to those instances in which p intentionally produces x; that is, situations which he designated as purposive actions. Thus the intentions of the person are central to the attribution of personal causality, and it becomes important for a person to determine whether a given event is the result of an intention on the part of another person. In making such a determination, the person makes use of the causal network in personal and impersonal causality. In the case of personal causality, the actions of the other person are directed toward the production of a single end result, and his or her actions change in response to altered circumstances. In Heider's terms, the means are variable, but the end is invariant (a situation which he labeled equifinality). Figure 6-3a depicts an instance of personal causality and its characteristic of equifinality. When p (a person with intention to produce a given effect e) notes that circumstance c_1 exists, p employs means m_1; if c_2 obtains, p employs m_2; etc., in order to produce e.

Impersonal causality, on the other hand, is characterized by multifinality. In this case, the effects of an impersonal event vary with the circumstances surrounding the event; if the circumstances change, so do the effects produced by the impersonal event. Figure 6-3b depicts an instance of impersonal causality.

As we indicated earlier, Heider stressed the fact that intention is the central factor in personal causality. Thus we hold a person more or less responsible for the outcomes of his or her actions, depending upon whether the act is seen as an indication of his or her motives. In the naïve analysis of action, a given outcome that is produced by p is not always attributed to p, but is sometimes attributed to environmental factors. The concept of responsibility is used differently at different stages of development. As the individual develops (becomes socialized), he or she moves through successive levels of sophistication. At each level of development, he or she takes into account successively more variables or circumstances relevant to the situation. Heider identified five such levels:

Level 1 is the most primitive level, and the concept of responsibility is such that the person is held responsible for any effect that he or she is associated with in any way. At level 2, the person is held responsible for any effect that is caused by actions ascribed to him or her, whether or not he or she could have foreseen

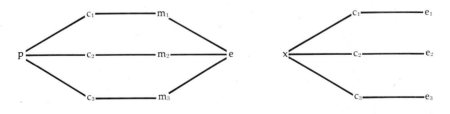

a. Personal causality   b. Impersonal causality

Figure 6-3 Equifinality and multifinality as characteristics of personal and impersonal causality. (Adapted with permission from F. Heider. *The psychology of interpersonal relations.* New York: Wiley, 1958.)

the consequences of his or her actions. This corresponds to Piaget's (1932) objective responsibility stage. At level 3 the person is held responsible for effects resulting from his or her actions that could have been foreseen, except that the person was careless or unconcerned about the possible consequences of his or her actions. At the next level, the person is held responsible only for intentionally produced outcomes. This is what Piaget called subjective responsibility and corresponds to Heider's personal causality structure. Finally, at the most advanced stage (level 5) the person is held less responsible for intended outcomes if the circumstances justify his or her actions; that is, if most other people would have acted as the person did under the conditions that existed at the time. Evidence supporting this analysis has been provided by Shaw and Sulzer (1964).

Desire and Pleasure

In the preceding analysis of trying, intention and exertion were identified as the constituents of trying. The conditions that elicit trying were not specified, although Heider emphasized that people have strong needs to understand the conditions underlying the events that they experience. *Desire* is seen as one of the important conditions of trying; *pleasure,* as the experiential consequence of achieved desire. Heider admitted that desire is conceptually ambiguous, since it refers to motivational states variously labeled as desire, need, wish, want, etc. Desire differs from intention in that it refers to the motive that gives rise to the intention, whereas the intention is identified only by the structure of personal causality. Desire is one answer to the question, why does p intend to produce x?

Desire and action are often coordinated in that desire may arouse the person to action or that desire may be inferred from action. If p is seen as trying to do x, it is often inferred that p desires x. However, desire and action are not invariably coordinated. The person may desire x without engaging in any action directed toward the attainment of x. This event happens when x appears unattainable or when the other effects resulting from the action necessary to attain x are sufficiently undesirable as to negate the desire for x. For example, a man may desire a beautiful woman but take no action because he is convinced that she would rebuff him. Winners of the Miss America contest often report that their social lives suffer because young men are reluctant to ask them for dates. Sometimes, of course, no action is necessary; the desire may or may not be realized quite independently of p's action. Furthermore, a given desire may lead to different actions, depending upon the environmental requirements. Actions are determined not only by desire but also by the way the person sees the causal structure of the environment. Nevertheless, desire has important implications for interpersonal behavior. If another person does something that most people like to do or if he or she appears pleased with a given effect, it will be assumed that he or she desired it. A person's reactions to various possibilities, occurrences, and actions regarding x will also be largely determined by the person's desires about x.

When the desire is fulfilled, common-sense psychology postulates that pleasure invariably follows. This a priori connection between wish fulfillment and the experience of pleasure cannot be contradicted by experience. Suppose p states that he or she desires x and subsequently obtains x, only to find that he or she does not experience the expected pleasure. Instead of concluding that desire fulfillment and pleasure are not invariantly related, the naïve observer concludes that p did not really desire x, that the obtained x was not the one really desired, or that the apparent lack of enjoyment displayed by p is mere pretense—that p really experienced pleasure but wished to conceal this fact for his or her own purposes. The desire-pleasure principle remains unchanged by contrary evidence.

Conceptually, common-sense psychology postulates two relations between the person and the object of his or her desire: *value* and *distance*. The value relation refers to the sentiment and is reflected by statements of the form "p likes x." This implies that there is something about x that is positively valued by p, although it does not necessarily deny the existence of negatively valued characteristics of x. For example, a person may like to smoke, although he or she knows that smoking may have deleterious effects on his or her health.

The distance relation between the person and the object of his or her desire refers to the psychological distance between person and object. It includes relations such as contact and the possibility of wish fulfillment. In the case of desire, the person and the valued object are separated, whereas in pleasure they are in contact, that is, the distance relation is zero. Thus, if p is seen as being in contact with a valued x, it is inferred that p is experiencing pleasure; if p values x but is not in contact with it, it is assumed that p will wish for x. For example, suppose it is known that John places high value on a position of leadership in his organization and has just been named to that position; we would assume that he is pleased by the appointment. But if someone else gets the job, it is "obvious" that John is unhappy. Again, common-sense psychology presumes harmonious relations among desire, liking, contact, and pleasure, and events that appear to be inharmonious are reinterpreted to reestablish the expected harmony.

Particularly significant effects result when a person almost obtains a desired x or almost loses an enjoyable x. A near success is said to lead to heightened frustration, whereas a near loss evokes a sense of relief or feelings of being blessed or warned. According to Heider, the intense negative reaction to a near success is partially because of the possibility of wish fulfillment: the perceived possibility of wish fulfillment increases as the distance to the goal decreases. We might note in passing that the effects of a near success are consistent with the goal-gradient hypothesis discussed in Chapter 5 and the rising-expectations interpretation of black militancy (Abeles, 1976).

Sentiment

Although sentiment plays an important role in Heider's common-sense psychology, he adopted a position more closely related to cognitive theory than to field theory. For this reason, we give only brief attention to his treatment here and defer a more-detailed discussion to Chapter 8.

A sentiment refers to the way a person feels about a person or thing. This feeling may, of course, be either positive or negative, and Heider used the terms *liking* and *disliking* to indicate positive and negative sentiments, respectively. Whether a person likes another person or the other person's products has important implications for interpersonal relations. A liking relation between two persons is likely to increase interaction, determine the quality of the interaction, and cause similar effects.

In his analysis of the effects of sentiments on interpersonal events, Heider employed two major concepts (in addition to liking): *unit formation* and *balanced state*. Unit formation refers to the quality of belongingness. Two or more objects (which may be persons) are in unit formation when they are seen as belonging together. For example, a person and his or her products are seen as forming a unit. When a number of persons and/or objects are considered, there is a strong tendency for the liking and unit formation relations to be such that a state of balance is achieved. A situation is said to be in a balanced state if the unit and sentiment relations can coexist without stress, that is, when there is no pressure toward change. In general, a situation is in a state of balance if the product of the signs of the relations is positive. For example, if p likes o, and p likes o's products, there are three positive relations: the two positive liking relations and the unit relation between o and his products. The product of three positive relations is positive; so the situation is balanced. But if p likes o and dislikes o's possession, there are two positive and one negative relation and a state of imbalance exists. Pressure to change therefore exists and disharmony will result. Balance can be achieved either by changing one of the positive relations to negative or the negative relation to a positive one. (See pages 199–204 for a more-detailed presentation of Heider's balance theory.)

Oughts and Values

In addition to the factors so far considered, the evaluation and determination of behavior and its consequences are also influenced to a great extent by the perceived requirements of the situation. According to common-sense psychology, we often feel that specific consequences should follow certain actions; the bad actor deserves his or her punishment and the doer of good deeds merits praise. Heider uses the term *ought* to refer to this requiredness (Wertheimer, 1935) of the situation.

Oughts are said to derive from perceived demands of the objective order; p feels that he or she ought to do x because of the demands of the environment rather than because of the demands of others. This indicates two important aspects of ought; oughts are impersonal, and they are dispositional in character. Hence, oughts have interpersonal validity: all people should perceive the same ought requirements in a given situation. Obedience or disobedience of ought requirements thus determines whether a person should be praised (or blamed) for his or her actions. This notion of oughts is related to the just-world hypothesis (Lerner, 1965), which suggests that people generally believe that people get what they deserve (cf. Rubin & Peplau, 1975). This minitheory will be discussed in greater detail in Chapter 13.

The concept of *value* also plays an important role in the determination and evaluation of behavior, as pointed out earlier in this chapter. Heider used the term *value* in two different, albeit related, ways. First, it was used to mean the property of an entity; second, it was used to mean a class of entities. In both cases there is the connotation of being objectively positive. Like oughts, values are impersonal and dispositional, and therefore they have interpersonal validity. But ought and value differ with regard to the force field. Ought is said to represent a field of forces, whereas value represents a potential force and thus results in action only under certain conditions. Heider stated the difference succinctly:[1]

> In brief, the ought can be considered a cognized force with objective validity; value can be considered a cognized positive property of something, a relevance with objective validity. These cognized forces and relevances have, of course, a great influence on *p*'s own forces because in most cases there will be a strong tendency to be in harmony with them. (Heider, 1958, p. 226.)

Request and Command

Ought and value were described above as environmental forces that induce action, but action may also be evoked by personal forces. Heider listed five ways in which p may induce action in o:

1 p may change a valence for o, so that an unattractive x becomes attractive to o.
2 p may show o the desirable consequences of x.
3 p may create additional (derived valences) for o by promising him rewards or punishments.
4 p may require o to do x.
5 p may command o to do x.

The latter two instances involving *request* and *command* are based on sentiments and power relations, respectively. When p asks o to do something, p is implying dependence on o's good will; i.e., that o should grant p's wish because o has a favorable attitude (positive sentiment) toward p. On the other hand, when p commands o to do x, it is implied that o must comply with p's wishes. Therefore, the forces on o toward doing x derive from a power relation between p and o. However, the distinction between requesting and commanding is not always clear-cut, since the "request" of a person in a power position often has the force of command.

[1]Here it may be noted that Heider's theory is most directly related to Lewin's field orientation and Heider used the concept of force field in the same sense that Lewin used it. See pp. 121–123 for a discussion of Lewin's treatment of force fields.

The conditions surrounding requests and the reactions to requests involve not only sentiments, but also oughts, can, values, power, and the consequences of the requested action. Ought forces play a role in that o may believe that he or she should comply with p's request. If o can do x and p cannot, o often believes that the objective order requires that o comply with p's request to do x, even when o has no positive sentiment toward p. For example, few adults would refuse to comply with a small child's request for a glass of water, even if they disliked the child. On the other hand, a person is seldom asked to do something that others know the person cannot do. The value of x for p and for o also influences p's willingness to make the request and o's readiness to comply. For example, if a man is seriously ill, he ordinarily will not hesitate to ask a physician for help and the physician is unlikely to deny that request. *Power* relations are involved to the extent that compliance implies the relative superiority or inferiority of o. If compliance to a request implies that o is superior to p, o is likely to accede to p's wishes; if compliance can be viewed as a weakness on the part of o, compliance is unlikely. Finally, the consequences of the action for p and for o influence compliance with the request. Desirable consequences create forces toward compliance, and undesirable consequences create forces against compliance.

Benefit and Harm

When o responds to a request or command by p, o *benefits* p by compliance or obedience, and fails to benefit p or *harms* p by noncompliance. More generally, o benefits p when o produces an x that has positive value for p and harms p when he or she produces an x that has negative value for p. Thus benefit and harm include a causal factor and an evaluative factor. The circumstances surrounding causality and evaluation are of course significant determinants of p's reactions to o's behavior. Heider invoked the concepts of *local* and *total* relevance in analyzing these effects. The local relevance of an event includes only the beneficial or harmful nature of x and the fact that o caused x. The wider implications of the circumstances surrounding the event are referred to as the total relevance of the event. The relative strength of local and total relevance varies with the level of development (maturation and socialization) of the persons involved. Total relevance becomes more salient with increasing maturation. (See Chapter 9 for a review of Heider's five stages or levels of maturation with respect to attribution.)

The perception of and reaction to benefits and harms are also influenced by sentiments, power, and ought forces. If o likes p, he or she may be expected to benefit p; if p likes o, he or she tends to see o's actions as a benefit; the actions of a disliked o are prone to be perceived as a harm; and, if a disliked o benefits p, his or her actions are suspect and p may look for ulterior motives. Similarly, a benefit produced by a powerful o is perceived as the result of o's own forces, whereas a harm by a powerful o may be accepted as the natural order of interpersonal relations. Thus, ought forces play a role in the acceptance or rejection of harm. Ought forces also influence p's feelings of obligation to o for benefits produced by o. If o ought to benefit p, p feels no obligation to o. In like manner, p may reject a benefit that he or she believes is not merited and may resent an undeserved harm.

Reactions to the Experiences of Others

When another person experiences a benefit or harm, there are, according to Heider, four types of reactions that may occur:

1 Sympathetic enjoyment, in which o's positive experience is positive for p
2 Compassion, in which o's negative experience is negative for p
3 Envy, in which o's positive experience is negative for p
4 Malicious joy, in which o's negative experience is positive for p
(Heider did not consider instances in which p is indifferent to the experiences of o.)

The first two types are said to be concordant reactions, and the last two discordant reactions. In common-sense psychology, all these reactions are referred to as feelings or emotions.

Sympathetic enjoyment and compassion are both sympathetic reactions to the experiences of others. Heider pointed out that a number of writers (Becker, 1931; Westermarck, 1932; Asch, 1952; Scheler, 1954) have distinguished between true sympathy and emotional contagion. True sympathy has as its object the feelings of the other person, whereas emotional contagion takes place only in the presence of others. With true sympathy, the point of application is the other person, but with contagion the point of application is one's own person. A person who experiences sympathy will try to make a sad o happy (and try to see that a happy o remains so), whereas a person responding to emotional contagion will join a happy o but will avoid an unhappy o.

The reaction of p to the experience of o is influenced by (1) p's sentiment toward o: p tends to be sympathetic toward a liked o; (2) p's own experience: p's own state provides a background or standard against which o's experiences are evaluated, in accordance with the principles of contrast and assimilation; and (3) p's similarity to o: if p considers himself or herself in the same class as o, his or her reactions to o's experiences are apt to be of the concordant type.

Comment and Evaluation

The preceding presentation is, at best, an abridged account of Heider's views and does not do justice to the richness of his formulation. His appeal to common-sense psychology yielded many insights into the complex realm of interpersonal relations. It is obvious even to the casual reader, however, that his analysis is far from being naïve. His work is clearly a major contribution to social psychological theory, especially with regard to attribution theory and consistency theories.[2] For instance, the attribution theories proposed by Kelley (1967) and by Jones and Davis (1965) derive fairly directly from Heider's analysis of personal and impersonal causality; Festinger's theory of cognitive dissonance (1957), Newcomb's A-B-X theory (1953), and Osgood and Tannenbaum's (1955) congruity theory all have their basis in Heider's analysis of sentiments. (See Chapter 9 for a detailed discussion of attribution theories and Chapter 8 for details of consistency theories.)

The theory meets the minimal criteria for acceptance, but it is, of course, open to certain criticisms. The alert reader will have noted that it is primarily a theory about interpersonal perception and only secondarily a theory about interpersonal relations. It is concerned largely with an analysis of the processes by which one person perceives and interprets the behavior of another person. Although Heider noted the relevance of these perceptions and interpretations for interpersonal behavior, he failed to consider in detail the connections among perceptions, attributions, and interpersonal behavior. It is also easy to get the impression that Heider has considered a series of isolated topics concerning interpersonal perception and behavior. Although he made it clear that the various aspects of interpersonal relations are interrelated, he failed to spell out the nature of these interrelations in explicit detail. Furthermore, the reader is not prepared for the somewhat abrupt shift from attribution to balance theory. The first part of the theory apparently derives from a gestalt-field orientation, whereas the second part adopts a more strictly cognitive position. Both analyses derive from his earlier work on attribution (Heider, 1944) and on balanced structures (Heider, 1946). (It is recognized that gestalt, field, and cognitive orientations have much in common and that Heider's two treatments are not necessarily incompatible. However, there are some important differences that are apparent in the two analyses.) Finally, theoretical propositions are often stated in a form that makes it difficult to test them empirically. The frequent appeal to statements such as "x tends to follow y" illustrates this point. When x does not follow y, the proposition is not invalidated. Nor did Heider specify the conditions under which y is not expected to follow x. In some cases, the consequences that theoretically may follow from a given set of conditions are so numerous and varied that one is led to conclude that "anything can happen."

Nevertheless, many significant and testable hypotheses may be found in or derived from Heider's analysis. Our purpose is not to review exhaustively the research relevant to the theory, but a few examples may be instructive. For instance, it will be recalled that Heider suggested that, when persons can observe the environment (including other persons), they have more control over it. Knowing this, individuals often try to influence others' perceptions of them in order to influence the action possibilities of others and others' evaluations of them. Therefore, a given person's behavior in social interaction is determined, in part, by the kinds of perceptions that he or she wants to stimulate in the other

---

[2]The interested reader is well advised to read the original version of Heider's *The Psychology of Interpersonal Relations.*

person. Research generally supports this aspect of the theory. For example, Gergen and Taylor (1969) found that high-status persons described themselves in ways designed to avoid conformity to the expectations of others when productivity was the assigned goal; when the goal was solidarity, both high- and low-status persons conformed to the expectations of others. Similarly, Shaw and Wagner (1975) allowed male subjects to view either an attractive or an unattractive female through a one-way mirror and then asked them to choose either a high-, medium-, or low-status role to enact while interacting with the female. Role choices were significantly biased in the direction of higher-status roles when the female was attractive but not when the female was unattractive. If we assume that males want to make favorable impressions on attractive females, these data support Heider's analysis. Findings by Schlenker (1975) that under conditions of anonymity self-presentations were favorable and unaffected by expectations of actual performance are also in accord with the theory. Research by Jones, Gergen, and Davis (1962) suggest that such tactics may indeed be effective in influencing others.

In his analysis of action, Heider suggested that ability and motivation are seen as inversely related as naïve explanations of performance. That is, if a person has ability but performs poorly, we attribute low motivation to that person; conversely, if high motivation is attributed to a person who performs poorly, it follows that the person must not have much ability. Williams (1975) suggested that it follows from this analysis that attributed motivation, attributed ability, or both will be employed to account for observed changes in performance over time. He reported data supporting this prediction. A study by Weiner and Kukla (1970) is also supportive of Heider's proposals with regard to the naïve analysis of action.

When we observe a change in a person's behavior or an effect produced by a person's actions, we may attribute it to internal or personal causes (personal causality), to external or environmental causes (impersonal causality), or to some combination of these two sets of factors (Heider, 1958). This general proposition has been tested in a number of ways. Jones, Davis, and Gergen (1961) tested the hypothesis that behavior that is appropriate to a well-defined social role is relatively uninformative about personal characteristics. Subjects were required to listen to an interview in which a person was heard being instructed to respond as if he or she very much wanted to qualify as an astronaut (in two treatments) or as a submariner (in two treatments). The interviewee responded in line either with the specified qualifications for an astronaut (inner-directedness) or with those specified for a submariner (other-directedness). Thus there were four experimental conditions corresponding to in-role behavior regarding the astronaut position and the submariner position and out-of-role behavior with respect to each of these two positions. As predicted, the out-of-role interviewees were perceived to be revealing their true characteristics more than the in-role interviewees.

Two experiments reported by Thibaut and Riecken (1965) also related to the same general hypothesis. The specific hypothesis tested was that the perceived locus of causality for a stimulus person's compliance with an influence attempt will be internal for a high-status person and external for a low-status person. Subjects attempted to influence the behavior of two paid confederates, one who posed as a high-status and the other as a low-status person. Both complied with the influence attempt. Subsequent interview and rating scale data supported the hypothesis.

Another significant part of Heider's theory related to the development of "sophistication" in the attribution of responsibility. Presumably, persons advance through levels during their development (socialization); at each successive level the person considers additional variables (circumstances) in judging whether the person is responsible for the consequences of his actions. The rate of development is theoretically related to age and experience. Several studies have provided evidence on this point. Shaw and Sulzer (1964) devised questionnaires to describe situations representing the minimum variables needed to elicit attribution from an individual at each level of development and were able to demonstrate that children's attributions of responsibility were more "primitive" (showed less differentiations among variables) than the attributions of adults. Studies of cultural differences also support the general theory. For example, subjects from deprived environments develop at a slower rate than subjects from less-deprived environments (Shaw & Schneider, 1967; Garcia-Esteve & Shaw, 1968). Comparisons of subjects from Latin and American cultures also reveal differences in attribution that are consistent with differences in child-rearing practices in the two cultures (Shaw, Briscoe, & Garcia-Esteve, 1968). Several other studies provide general support for Heider's attribution theory (Aronfreed, 1961; Kohlberg, 1963; Sulzer, 1964; Feather, 1969; Feather & Simon, 1971; Reisman & Schopler, 1973; and many more).

People want to be in contact with a desired object or person, and such contact is pleasurable, according to Heider's theory. It was observed many years ago that people who live near each other tend to become friends (Festinger, Schachter, & Back, 1950; Rosow, 1961), but does the converse hold, as Heider's theory proposes? A study by Byrne, Ervin, and Lamberth (1970) suggests an affirmative answer. They staged a "computer dance" and surreptitiously recorded the distance between couples as they stood before the experimenter's desk. They found that the more the partners liked each other, the closer they stood.

Sometimes people believe that they *ought* to do certain things, that such things are required by the objective order (Heider, 1958). Rubin and Peplau (1975) presented a great deal of evidence supporting this hypothesis. To some extent, the degree to which a person responds to a request by another depends upon the requiredness or ought characteristics of the situation. For instance, Heider stated that responding to a request may depend upon the apparent need of the requestor. Data relevant to this expectation was provided in an experiment by Latane and Darley (1970). They asked passersby in New York City for a dime and found that only 34 percent responded to the request. When the request was accompanied by the statement that the requestor needed the dime to make a phone call, 64 percent acceded to the request, and when the requestor stated that he or she had lost his or her wallet, 72 percent gave the dime. Further, Heider proposed that one is more likely to respond to a request from a liked than from a disliked other, a proposition that was found to be consistent with helping behavior in disaster situations. Form and Nosow (1958) found that in a disaster friends were helped first, then neighbors, and finally strangers.

Finally, Heider's theory holds that people are more likely to expect benefits from a liked other and harm from a disliked other. This general proposal was examined in a study by Schlenker, Brown, and Tedeschi (1975). They found that the perception of attitude similarity (which has been shown to induce liking, Byrne, 1971) produces expectations of greater benefits mediated by a similar other person, but that the perception of attitude dissimilarity was not related to expectations of harm. This latter finding, of course, is not in accord with Heider's theory.

In summary, not all of Heider's theoretical proposals have been investigated, but those that have been tested have stood the test quite well. It should be noted, however, that not all of the research cited as being consistent with the theory was based on the theory and some of it was completed before the theory was formulated.

SOCIAL PENETRATION THEORY

Social penetration theory (Altman & Taylor, 1973) is another theory that attempts to develop a broad set of ideas relevant to the growth of interpersonal relationships. The term *social penetration* refers to overt interpersonal behaviors that occur in social interaction as well as internal subjective processes that precede, accompany, and follow overt exchange. Altman and Taylor were concerned with the entire range of interpersonal events occurring during the development of social relationships. Their stated goal was to describe the development and dissolution of such relationships and what happens as individuals form and manage various types of interrelationships. They attempted to answer such questions as: What kinds of things do two people reveal about themselves at different stages of a relationship? Do their activities differ at different points in the history of the relationship? Does emotional involvement vary from early to late periods in the development of a relationship? In dealing with these kinds of questions, they suggested that three general classes of factors play a role in hastening or restraining the growth of interpersonal relationship: (1) personal characteristics of participants, (2) outcomes of exchange, and (3) situational context.

The theory of social penetration consists of three basic divisions or categories of analysis. First, Altman and Taylor outlined their assumptions about the personality structure, which correspond very closely to Lewin's conception of personality. They felt it was necessary to describe their assumptions about personality because the social penetration process involves an overlapping in exploration of the personalities of the persons involved in social relationships. The second broad category of the theory involves a specification of how rewards and costs influence the social penetration process. This part of the theory really specifies the forces underlying the growth of interpersonal relationships; it in effect deals with the dynamics of the social penetration process. The third part of the theory consists of a description of the specific aspects of the social penetration process and is perhaps the most significant and unique part of the theory. We will first present Altman and Taylor's treatment of these three divisions and then try to show how the theory relates to known evidence about interpersonal relationships.

Assumptions About the Personality Structure

Altman and Taylor state that their conception of personality is analogous to Murray's (1938) intraindividual needs, Rokeach's (1960, 1968) belief system, and Lewin's (1935, 1936, 1951) delineation of the self into regions, but it is evident that their conception corresponds most closely to Lewin's view of personality. According to Altman and Taylor's analysis, personality consists of the individual's ideas, feelings, beliefs, and emotions about self, other people, and the world. These items of personality are organized into substantive areas, such as sex and family. There are two general dimensions of personality within the structure: breadth category and breadth frequency. Breadth category refers merely to the number of major topical areas or categories within the personality structure. Breadth frequency refers to the amount of interaction within each area. The major topical areas of personality are seen as varying along a central-peripheral or depth dimension. The outer layers of personality relate to specific superficial things, such as biographical information, but as one proceeds toward the central core the areas become more fundamental characteristics of personality. The important aspect of the depth dimension is that it has important implications for interaction. The key properties of the depth dimension of personality are:

1   Items having to do with peripheral and public characteristics, such as age and sex, are at the peripheral layers of personality and attitudes and opinions are at intermediate layers, whereas such things as fears and self-concepts are in the central layers of personality.

2   The more-central areas have greater impact on the peripheral areas than vice versa and also more linkages to other aspects of personality. That is, as we move from the outer to inner cores of personality, there are more one-to-many relationships among the various aspects of personality. For example, if we know something about the central aspects of personality, it would be possible to derive many peripheral personality characteristics.

3   From the peripheral to central layers of personality, items vary from common to unique and from high to low visibility. For example, preferences for different kinds of clothing or hair styles are easily observable from very limited social interaction, whereas such things as one's self-concept are not so readily observable.

4   The degree of vulnerability of an aspect of personality increases with the depth of the characteristic.

5 The central layers of personality contain the more socially undesirable characteristics.

6 The central aspects of personality are more general than the more peripheral ones. They are more likely to concern the total self than specific situational aspects.

As noted earlier, these assumptions about personality have important implications for social interaction. These implications are represented in Figure 6-4 and may be considered as additional assumptions regarding personality. It can be seen from Figure 6-4 that the innermost layers of personality which are most remote from contact with a social environment include all of those things that contribute to self-perception, such as needs, values, physiological processes, etc. These are presumed to set the stage for responses in a social situation.

The next innermost layer represents a general definition of the situation or a subjective analysis of what is demanded by the situation and a plan for meeting those demands. Proceeding outward, we reach the series of behavioral events that lead to the creation of interpersonal images and initial contact with a social environment. The interpersonal images presumably are created through the use of such things as clothing and static self-markers, nonverbal behaviors, body positions, etc. The outermost layer of the personality is the one in which social interaction actually occurs. Interaction involves continuous verbal behavior, dynamic self-marker behavior, and dynamic/reactive use of the environment.

These assumptions about behavior in relation to personality are important for the social penetration process. The critical concepts are depth and breadth of social penetration. Depth refers to penetration toward the central core of the personality. Depth of penetration increases gradually as the social relationship develops. The breadth dimension refers to the amount of interaction and includes breadth category and breadth frequency. Breadth category refers to the general areas of personality and concerns the number of specific aspects or items included in the personality structure. In describing the growth of an interpersonal relationship or the social penetration process, Altman and Taylor hypothesize that, as a relationship grows, more and more facets of personality are mutually opened and made available. That is to say, each person makes available to the other items from the more central parts of the personality structure.

Breadth frequency refers to the idea that there are specific items or pieces of information within each area of personality. It is hypothesized that as an interpersonal relationship develops, increases in breadth frequency occur first at superficial layers of personality and only later at the more intimate levels of personality.

Breadth time refers to the amount of time that people spend interacting with other people. Altman and Taylor hypothesize that, as the social penetration process proceeds, the facets of personality already made accessible to the other receive an increasing amount of the time devoted to mutual exchange. That is, once an aspect of personality has been made accessible to the other person, more time is spent in interaction that involves that area of personality.

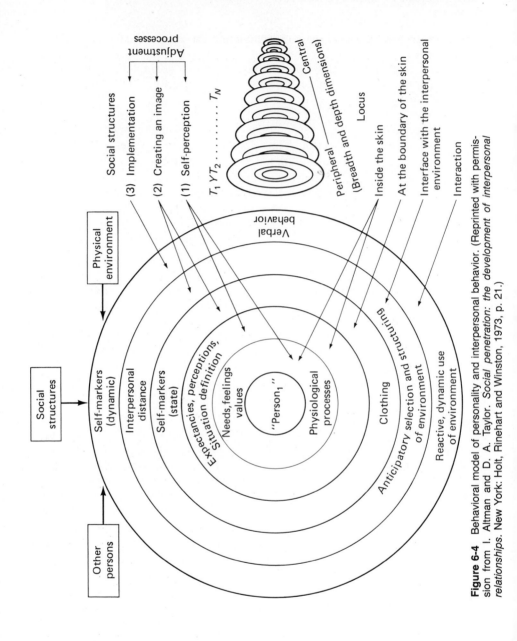

Figure 6-4 Behavioral model of personality and interpersonal behavior. (Reprinted with permission from I. Altman and D. A. Taylor. *Social penetration: the development of interpersonal relationships*. New York: Holt, Rinehart and Winston, 1973, p. 21.)

General Properties of Interpersonal Rewards and Costs

So far, we have been discussing the more descriptive aspects of the social penetration process. However, the social penetration process does not proceed in a haphazard way, but is presumed to be influenced by the nature of the interpersonal rewards and costs incurred in the interaction process. Altman and Taylor draw their concepts of rewards and cost and their effects upon the interaction process primarily from the works of Thibaut and Kelley (1959) and of Homans (1950, 1956, 1961). Their assumptions about the properties of rewards and costs can best be presented by quoting from Altman and Taylor's presentation. They state that these properties are:

> 1 Reward/cost ratios: This refers to the balance of positive and negative experiences in a social relationship (i.e., the relative number of rewards to costs). The greater the ratio of rewards to costs, the more satisfying the relationship.
> 2 Absolute reward and cost properties: These involve the absolute magnitude of positive and negative experiences in a relationship. For example, two social relationships might have the same relative reward/cost ratios but be very different in the absolute amounts of rewards and costs and, consequently, in psychological characteristics.
> 3 Immediately obtained rewards and costs: These refer to the set of rewards and costs that accrue from a finite, temporarily bound, relatively immediate social interaction. The temporal locus is what just happened.
> 4 Forecast rewards and costs: These are projections to future rewards and costs. As indicated later, such forecasts play an important role in propelling relationships forward or in slowing down and even reversing their growth.
> 5 Cumulative rewards and costs: These encompass the cumulation of rewards and costs throughout the history of a dyad. Conceptually, they can be represented as a reservoir or pool of positive and negative experiences up to a given point in time, and extending back to the point of formation of the relationship. (Altman & Taylor, 1973, p. 32–33.)

The process of social penetration is influenced greatly by the rewards and costs resulting from social interaction. When strangers encounter each other for the first time, the initial interaction involves superficial exchanges in the nonintimate layers of the personality. But at the same time evaluations of the interaction and forecasts concerning future interactions are made. For instance, when two persons have engaged in interaction, each person will evaluate the rewards and costs that were obtained during the interaction. The basic question will be whether the immediate rewards are greater than the cost. In general, if the rewards/cost ratio is positive, the relationship will be evaluated favorably; if it is negative, the relationship will be evaluated unfavorably. This evaluation process is of course similar to the concept of comparison level proposed by Thibaut and Kelley (1959).

Based on their evaluations of reward/cost ratios in past interactions, dyad members are then hypothesized to make forecasts about future interactions. This forecasting process is similar to the concept of comparison level for alternatives (Thibaut and Kelley, 1959). If evaluations and forecast judgments are favorable, persons will normally make a decision to continue the relationship, whereas, if the judgments are negative, the relationship will be terminated or the social penetration process will be interfered with.

Altman and Taylor also propose the existence of a central memory repository, which they assume represents a cumulative reservoir of prior reward/cost experiences. According to the theory, as the relationship develops the outcomes of evaluation and forecast are stored in this central memory and contribute to a cumulative history of the relationship. This repository of outcomes permits comparison of any particular social relationship with any other. Once the social penetration process develops to a point where the relationship is clarified, there begins a continuous cycling process: Interaction occurs, outcomes are stored in the central memory, forecasts are made, decisions about future interactions are made, and new interactions are likely to occur.

Specific Aspects of Social Penetration

To this point, the theoretical analysis has considered the general nature of the social penetration process, but has not explained the dynamics of the process. Altman and Taylor attempt to remedy this by considering a number of specific aspects of the process that may be considered hypotheses about the growth of social relationships. These are stated as follows:

"Social penetration processes proceed from superficial to intimate levels of exchange" (p. 39). This suggests that social interactions begin with exchanges in the superficial regions of the personality (persons exchange information about occupation, place of residence, etc.), but do not stop there unless the reward/-cost ratio is highly negative. As the relationship develops, exchange begins to occur in more intimate regions; attitudes, values, and feelings will eventually be revealed. This progress occurs because each person forecasts that the rewards of such exchanges will be greater than the costs. This results in moderate progress toward more intimate interpersonal relationships.

"Interactions continue to occur and expand at the same levels of intimacy of exchange" (p. 39). The point being made here is that once a relationship has developed and rewarding interactions have occurred, the same interactions (exchanges) are likely to continue because it is known that the reward/cost ratio for such exchanges will be positive. At the same time, members of such a relationship are likely to forecast that the reward/cost ratio will be positive if exchanges occur in more intimate areas. Therefore, social relationships involve a blend of interaction in established areas and new areas.

"Continued interaction in already accessible areas is readily accomplished" (p. 40). People who have in the past exchanged information in a given area and found it rewarding find it easy to continue these exchanges.

"Social penetration processes move gradually to adjacent levels of intimacy" (p. 40). This is one of the key hypotheses in social penetration theory.

Altman and Taylor state repeatedly that social penetration processes proceed in a systematic and orderly manner from superficial to intimate areas of exchange and from established to newer areas. The primary reason for this is that forecasts of reward/cost ratios are more certain for adjacent areas of exchange than for more distant ones. A secondary factor is that both rewards and costs are greater in the central regions of the personality than in the peripheral ones. For instance, consider the consequences for a man who tells his wife that he has had sexual relations with another woman, forecasting that she would "understand," only to find that she reacts by demanding a divorce. Assuming that he wants to stay married, the cost of this exchange is far greater than, say, having a friend misunderstand his reasons for predicting that it will rain tomorrow.

"The rate and level of social penetration varies as a function of interpersonal reward/cost characteristics" (p. 42). This hypothesis is really an attempt to explain the common observation that the growth of interpersonal relationships differs both with respect to the rate and terminal level of the relationship. According to Altman and Taylor, both of these effects depend upon the relative balance of rewards and costs as well as their absolute magnitudes. The greater the ratio of rewards to costs, the more rapid the growth of the relationship. Similarly, if equal or nearly equal reward/cost ratios are assumed, the greater the absolute magnitude of rewards and costs, the more rapid the growth of the relationship.

"The rate of development of a relationship varies over time" (p. 44). Altman and Taylor propose that the development of a social relationship proceeds at a faster rate in the early and middle than in the later stages of development. This expected slowdown in social penetration processes is the result of several factors. First, the more central areas of the personality have stronger barriers and hence are less accessible than the more peripheral areas. Second, the prediction of reward/cost ratios is less certain in the central areas; less certainty leads to caution in moving into those areas. Third, there are changes in the central memory reservoir over time such that a given reward or cost probably has a greater impact early than later in the history of the relationship.

The above descriptions assume that the relationship is a relatively pure one with generally positive outcomes (experiences). Not all relationships fit this pattern; relationships may also involve mixed or negative outcomes. Altman and Taylor describe several prototypes of relationships, resulting in various patterns of outcomes. In general, the rate of growth of a relationship depends upon the type of relationship (i.e., its favorability), the rewards and costs stored in the central memory, the predicted (forecast) outcomes, and the assessment of those outcomes. Consider a relationship that has the following characteristics: highly favorable but turning unfavorable, large positive reward/cost ratio stored in the central memory reservoir, positive outcomes forecast, and negative assessment. Altman and Taylor's analysis suggests that the probable outcome will be a gradual slowdown in development. We might note in passing that it is not clear why a relationship that has a large positive reward/cost ratio stored in the central memory and forecasting positive outcomes should turn unfavorable or lead to a negative assessment.

Finally, Altman and Taylor note that the reciprocity of exchange is an important aspect of the social penetration process. This notion derives primarily from Gouldner's (1950) norm of reciprocity and Jourard's (1959) work on self-disclosure. They suggest that liking leads to disclosure, which in turn leads to liking, in a continuous, mutually reciprocal fashion. They also hypothesize that self-disclosure and, more generally, exchange are reciprocal processes that are derived from (a) the dynamics of dyadic encounter, (b) the level of intimacy of topics discussed, (c) situational properties, and (d) participant characteristics. Reciprocity, however, is seen as a set of behavioral events and not necessarily as an explanation of social exchange.

Evaluation of Social Penetration Theory

The classification of social penetration theory as an example of a theory derived from the field orientation is somewhat debatable, since Altman and Taylor have drawn from many sources. For example, the use of rewards and costs to explain the dynamics of the process is consistent with the reinforcement orientation (Chapter 3). Nevertheless, the major parts of the theory appear to be more closely related to the field orientation than any other. The arguments that the social penetration process involves the person in situational context, the description of personality, the use of terms such as "forces" and "barriers," and so forth give the theory the flavor of the field orientation.

The theory integrates a great deal of data concerning the acquaintance or social penetration process, appears to be internally consistent, and does not contradict well-established hypotheses or principles of social behavior. Many interesting, but untested, hypotheses may be derived from the theory. On the other hand, propositions and hypotheses are sometimes stated vaguely or ambiguously, so that predictions cannot be derived with certainty.

Social penetration theory has not generated large amounts of research to date, although Altman and Taylor cite much research conducted before the theory was formulated that is consistent with its hypotheses and predictions. We will not attempt an exhaustive review of all relevant research, but we will mention some of the more closely related work, giving special attention to investigations completed since the theory was published.

One of the central hypotheses of social penetration theory is that the growth of an interpersonal relationship is gradual and proceeds from peripheral to central areas of the personality. Social penetration develops through a process of reciprocity, which declines as the relationship develops. Altman and Taylor cited several studies that they believe supported this aspect of the theory. For example, Newcomb's (1961) extensive study of the acquaintance process revealed that early friendships were based upon superficial things, like proximity and biographical characteristics. However, later in the acquaintance process, attraction was based on similarity in attitudes and values. In Altman and Taylor's terms, "rewards and costs associated with superficial exchange provided the initial basis for interpersonal relationships but, as the relationship progressed, compatibility was based more on exchange outcomes in intimate areas of personality" (Altman and Taylor, 1973, p. 65).

Studies of self-disclosure also generally support the theory. For example, an examination of interaction between members of socially isolated male dyads revealed an increase in breadth and depth of interaction over a ten-day period (Altman and Haythorn, 1965). Frankfurt (1965) observed increases over time in discussion (breadth frequency) of both intimate and nonintimate topics, with greater increases for nonintimate topics. Taylor (1968) studied self-disclosure between college roommates as they interacted over a thirteen-week period. Students reported that they communicated increasingly greater amounts of information and spent increasingly more time on biographical and attitude-value topics.

More recent investigations also provide evidence that is generally in accord with theoretical expectations. For instance, Johnson and Dabbs (1976) found that subjects were reluctant to disclose highly intimate information regardless of interpersonal distance. Davis (1977) examined self-disclosure of same-sex dyads who were either encouraged or not encouraged to discuss how intimate they wanted to be. A monotonic movement toward discussion of more-intimate topics occurred in the no-discussion situation, although dyads varied in rate of social penetration. In the discussion situation, social penetration first accelerated and then leveled off.

The reciprocity process in social penetration was examined in two studies. In one study (Rubin, 1975), an experimenter communicated either high-, medium-, or low-intimate information to subjects by either copying a message or creating a written message. Subjects reciprocated only when the experimenter merely copied the message. When the message was created, subjects disclosed more when the message was of intermediate intimacy. Rubin speculated that highly intimate messages may have aroused suspicion or lack of trust of the experimenter. The second study (Morton, 1978) examined the hypothesis that the acquaintance process is characterized by increasing intimacy and decreasing reciprocity of intimate communications. Spouses and strangers discussed items that they selected from a list of intimate and nonintimate topics. Spouses communicated more private facts, but not more personal feelings or opinions, and reciprocated intimacy less than strangers.

In summary, the evidence to date generally supports propositions that social penetration is characterized by a gradual increase in the intimacy of information shared and this increase operates through a reciprocity process, which declines as the relationship develops. However, the evidence also indicates some exceptions to these propositions that are not predicted by the theory (for example, the finding by Morton that spouses and strangers do not differ in disclosure of personal feelings and opinions).

A second major proposition of social penetration theory is that the growth of an interpersonal relationship is a function of the reward/cost outcomes of

social interaction. The evidence concerning this proposition is somewhat inconsistent. For example, Frankfurt (1965) found that reward/cost variations affected
the social penetration process primarily in intimate areas, whereas a study by
Colson (1968) observed reward/cost effects primarily in nonintimate areas. The
effects of reward/cost outcomes on the pattern of development of social
relationships were examined in two rather similar studies. In the first study
(Taylor, Altman, & Sorrentino. 1969), subjects interacted verbally with a
confederate (ostensibly another subject) by choosing statements from a pool of
items varying in intimacy. After the subject had described himself, the confederate provided a self-description that created one of four reward/cost conditions:
(1) continuous positive (the confederate agreed with the subject and approved
what he said 80 percent of the time), (2) continuous negative (the confederate
was disagreeable and disapproved 80 percent of the time), (3) later positive
(confederate began negatively but ended positively), or (4) later negative
(confederate began positively but ended negatively). Measures of social penetration included average item response time (breadth time), the number of items
chosen from the pool of items (breadth frequency), and the average intimacy
scale value of the selected items (depth). Results showed that the favorable
reward/cost groups (continuous positive and later positive) had greater increases
in talking time and selected more intimate items than the unfavorable re-
ward/cost groups.

In the second study (Taylor & Altman, 1975), a confederate created these
same four reward/cost interaction histories. Again, it was found that reward/cost
patterns influenced self-disclosure as predicted by the theory and the impact of
reward factors occurred primarily in intimate areas.

The results of these two studies are generally supportive of the theory, but a
study by Martens and White (1975) yielded results that appear to contradict the
theory. Subjects engaged in a competitive game with an opponent and won
either 30, 50, 70, or 90 percent of the time. Subjects were better satisfied with an
opponent who won 50 percent of the time or more than with an opponent who
lost to the subject more often.

In general, the theory of social penetration has reasonably good empirical
support, although there is some evidence that does not seem to be altogether
consistent with it. Its strongest point is that it integrates a considerable amount
of knowledge about the development of interpersonal relationships and provides
a framework for further research. Its weakest point is that it is often imprecise.
This imprecision makes it impossible to derive unambiguous hypotheses or make
unequivocal predictions about interpersonal relationships.

THEORIES OF CROWDING

Humans, for a variety of reasons, come together in situations that are often
labeled "crowded." Instances of crowded situations come readily to mind: the
fully occupied elevator, subways and buses at rush hour, Filene's basement, the
registrar's office during student registration, certain urban areas. Generally,

overpeopled situations of this sort are considered to be unpleasant and undesirable, although there are exceptions to this general rule. Crowded situations may be endured to achieve some goal (e.g., riding a crowded bus to get to work) or because people are unable to avoid them (e.g., people in urban slums who have no other place to go). Since crowding is usually viewed as undesirable, the question naturally arises concerning the effects of crowded situations on people in those situations. The relatively recent ecological concerns, such as overpopulation, pollution, and urban problems, have increased the interests of social scientists in crowding behavior, but this interest has existed for at least a century (Schopler and Stokols, 1976).

Current theoretical issues in crowding center around three major themes: the definition of crowding, the variables that determine crowding, and the consequences of crowding. In this section, we depart somewhat from our usual procedure and discuss several theories of crowding. The characteristics of these theories are not always in accord with the field-theory orientation, but all have in common a concern with the total situation and make use of such "fieldlike" concepts as psychological space, barriers, etc. The discerning student will undoubtedly see the influence of other orientations on these theories.[3]

A Setting-Specific Analysis of Crowding

The setting-specific theory was formulated by Schopler and Stokols (1976) after several years of research on crowding (e.g., Schopler and Stockdale, 1977; Stokols, 1972a, 1972b, 1975, 1976; Stokols, Rall, Pinner, & Schopler, 1973). Crowding was defined as the need for more space, resulting from a combination of personal and environmental factors. Thus crowding is a psychological experience in contradistinction to physical density or the amount of space per person in any given setting. In more general terms, they defined crowding as a syndrome of stress, resulting from personal, social, cultural, and spatial factors.

Schopler and Stokols made several assumptions about the nature of human crowding: (a) crowding experiences involve psychological stress; (b) this stress is the consequence of perceived loss of control over the regulation of space (including interpersonal distance); (c) when people experience crowding stress, they initiate coping attempts designed to reduce the stress; and (d) crowding will be most intense and difficult to cope with when a person's need for space is associated with perceived threats to personal security (i.e., physical safety and emotional well-being). The last assumption is very important because it implies

---

[3]We have omitted a number of theoretical discussions of crowding because they do not qualify as theories, at least by our definition of theory. Interesting hypotheses about the experience of crowding include, to mention a few, Freedman's (1975) use of the term "crowding" to refer to population density, Desor's (1972) hypothesis that crowding is the reception of excessive social stimulation, Esser's (1973) proposal that the presence of others leads to an arousal state in the brain and the crowding experience occurs when a person is threatened in his or her selective attention to rational and communicable judgmental processes during this arousal, Wicker's (1973) view that crowding occurs when there are more people than the setting can accommodate (the manning theory), and Worchel and Teddlie's (1976) argument that individuals become aroused by violations of their personal space and attribute this arousal to other people in the environment.

that the more severe the consequences of the person's inability to obtain more space (physical or psychological), the greater will be the stress experienced by that person.

After explication of their definition of crowding, Schopler and Stokols attempt to derive criteria for predicting where and when crowding stress will have its greatest impact on people. They began by making a distinction between primary and secondary environments, following an earlier analysis by Stokols (1976). Environments are seen as varying along three dimensions: (a) the extent of continuity of encounter occurring in the setting; (b) the psychological centrality of the behavioral functions enacted by persons in the setting; and (c) the degree to which relations among persons in the environment occur on a personal versus anonymous level. *Primary environments* are those in which the person spends much of his or her time (i.e., high continuity), engages in a wide range of personally important (i.e., psychologically central) activities, and relates to others in the environment on a personal level. *Secondary environments* involve transitory encounters, inconsequential behaviors, and anonymous relations with others. Residential and work environments are examples of primary environments, whereas barbershops, airport waiting rooms, etc. are secondary environments.

Primary environments, because they involve psychologically central behaviors and more enduring relationships, are expected (by Schopler and Stokols) to produce crowding experiences that are more intensely stressful and more difficult to resolve than secondary environments. This prediction is based upon three interrelated assumptions: (a) owing to the large amount of time spent in primary environments and the importance of activities in these environments, persons in primary environments are assumed to have higher levels of subjective involvement relative to persons in secondary environments; (b) occupants of primary settings will have a greater need to control the environment relative to occupants of secondary settings; and (c) social interference arising from high physical density will be more disruptive and frustrating in primary than in secondary environments. Again, the third assumption is perhaps the most important one. It derives from the expectation that the proximity of others will be more likely to interfere with psychologically important goals and activities in primary than in secondary environments and thus threaten the person's emotional security.

Schopler and Stokols note that the above analysis does not imply that the frequency of crowding experiences will be greater in primary than in secondary environments or that everyone in a particular setting will be equally susceptible to crowding. Differential status and power may negate the effects of physical density, as when a powerful person controls the environment to ensure that his or her goals are not interfered with by others. It is argued, however, that, when crowding experiences do occur, they should be more intense in primary than in secondary environments.

It is further suggested by the theory that primary environments are associated with higher levels of perceived control than are secondary environments. Therefore, occupants of primary environments should be particularly concerned with any condition which might interfere with their ability to control the environment, such as the presence of other people. This expectation led to a consideration of those aspects of environments that limit occupants' ranges of personal control and hence their abilities to cope with crowding when it does occur. Schopler and Stokols identify two dimensions that relate to this question: the open-closed dimension and the neutral versus personal crowding dimension.

The dimension of "openness" refers to the ease of exit from the setting. Open settings are surrounded by weak barriers, and there are many paths for leaving them. Closed settings, on the other hand, are surrounded by strong, impermeable barriers. Shopping centers and playgrounds, for example, are open settings, whereas space ships and submarines are closed settings. In general, primary environments are less open than secondary ones; the greater amount of time spent in primary settings and the importance of the activities and relationships in those settings make it more difficult for occupants to leave those settings than secondary ones. Thus, Schopler and Stokols reasoned that the relative ease of leaving open settings suggests that, when crowding stress occurs, occupants with low crowding thresholds will leave and thus reduce physical density (and presumably crowding stress). Withdrawal is, therefore, seen as the primary response to crowding in open (or secondary) settings. On the other hand, because primary settings are more difficult to leave than secondary ones, the experience of crowding, when it occurs, should be more intense and persistent in primary than in secondary environments. Occupants of primary environments must devise more complex coping mechanisms, and the degree and duration of crowding stress will depend upon the effectiveness of those mechanisms.

The "neutral" or "personal" nature of the crowding experience is a situational dimension that refers to the perceived intentionality of the interferences experienced by people in the setting. In neutral crowding, the need for more space derives from unintentional annoyances, such as limitations of privacy due to the proximity of others or constraints on activities resulting from spatial limitations. When interferences are intentionally imposed by another person or persons, personal crowding results. The degree of loss of control over the environment is greater in personal than in neutral crowding, and, consequently, the negative effects of personal crowding are likely to be more numerous and more intense than of neutral crowding. Further, Schopler and Stokols propose that the probability of personal crowding is greater in primary than in secondary environments.

To summarize, Schopler and Stokols (1976) assume that crowding involves psychological stress, resulting from perceived loss of control over the regulation of space, and that crowding stress will be most intense when the need for space is associated with perceived threats to personal security. Further, it is assumed that, when people experience crowding stress, they initiate coping attempts to reduce the stress. They hypothesize that crowding experiences will be more stressful and more difficult to resolve: (a) in primary environments than in secondary environments, (b) in closed than in open settings, and (c) in personal than in neutral crowding.

Comment

This analysis of crowding provides a framework for attempting to answer a number of questions about crowding, 'but it provides relatively few precise hypotheses for predicting behavior related to crowding. For instance, the theory proposes that people who feel crowded will make coping attempts, designed to reduce the stress associated with crowding, but it gives no hint about the nature of such attempts or when people will make one rather than another coping response. It does, however, offer some hypotheses about the magnitude or intensity of crowding stress and about the relative ease of resolving stress. Despite the fact that the theory is of relatively recent origin, there are some data relevant to these issues.

One of the propositions of the setting-specific theory of crowding is that crowding stress results from perceived loss of control over the environment. A study by Langer and Saegert (1977) supports this proposition. They provided persons in high-density settings with increased cognitive control by giving them information about the effects of crowding and compared their performance and emotional reactions to persons in similar settings who did not have this information. The provision of information (which presumably increased control over the environment) improved performance and ameliorated aversive emotional reactions to density.

Limited evidence is also available concerning the relative intensity of the crowding experience in neutral and personal environments (Baron, Mendel, Adams, and Griffen, 1976). Data were collected from occupants of double and triple dormitory rooms with respect to perceptions of self, roommate, and room properties. Occupants of triples expressed greater feelings of crowding, and more negative feelings about their roommates and the rooms and perceived less control over room activities than occupants of doubles. If one accepts the interpretation that doubles represent neutral crowding in a primary environment, whereas triples represent personal crowding in a primary environment, these findings are in accord with the theory.

Finally, there is limited evidence concerning the interference hypothesis. According to this hypothesis, persons in a crowded situation will experience interference to the extent that behavioral goals conflict with environmental conditions. One group of researchers (McCallum, Rusbult, Hong, Walden, & Schopler, 1979) successfully induced the experiences of crowding and interference by creating scarce resources via the manipulation of group size. Increased experiences of crowding and interference adversely affected performance and increased reported stress—effects that were greater for more important behaviors. Another study (Morasch, Groner, & Keating, 1979) also provided evidence that the experience of crowding is related to the degree to which density interferes with group activities. Thus, the limited research relative to the theory tends to support it.

A Model of Crowding

The model of crowding proposed by Altman (1975) attempts to integrate crowding phenomena with the concepts of privacy, personal space, and territoriality. Briefly, crowding is said to exist when a person's privacy-regulation system does not work effectively, so that there is more social contact than the person desires. The privacy-regulation system consists of boundary control mechanisms and coping behaviors; i.e., verbal, paraverbal, nonverbal, personal space, and territorial behaviors. Crowding results in stress, leading to physical, physiological, and psychological costs. The model will be easier to understand if we begin with a discussion of Altman's conceptions of privacy, personal space, and territoriality.

Privacy, Territoriality, and Personal Space   According to Altman (1975), *privacy* is an interpersonal boundary process that helps a person or group regulate interactions with others. Presumably, each person establishes a "self-boundary" over which he or she exerts selective control. The self-boundary may be made more or less permeable, depending upon the degree of interaction desired by the person. In other words, the person can vary the amount of desired privacy by varying the openness of the self via permeability of self-boundaries.

Territoriality refers to "the personalizing, ownership, and defense of geographic areas" (Altman, 1975, p. 5). Territoriality is one of the mechanisms that people use in the service of privacy. The possession, ownership, and defense of territories are important ways of regulating social interaction.

Altman accepts the common conception of *personal space* as the area immediately surrounding a person's body that is regarded by the person as personal and private (Hall, 1966; Sommer, 1969). Intrusion into this personal space is assumed to lead to discomfort and anxiety. Personal space is considered to be another privacy-regulation mechanism; the person alters the angle of orientation and distance from others in order to maintain the desired level of privacy.

Basic Factors   Altman's model of crowding is shown in Figure 6-5. The model "includes *antecedent factors,* which contribute to desired and achieved levels of privacy, *internal subjective responses,* which help monitor the situation, *overt coping behaviors,* designed to implement a desired level of privacy, and *psychological and physical costs,* which result from operation of the privacy system" (Altman, 1975, p. 154).

Beginning at the left side of Figure 6-5 it can be seen that personal, interpersonal, and situational factors combine to determine the level of privacy desired by a person or a group. Assuming that the desired level of privacy is not already in existence, various coping mechanisms (or boundary regulation mechanisms) are set in motion to establish the desired level of privacy. These mechanisms involve personal space and territorial behaviors, but also include verbal, nonverbal, and paraverbal behaviors. The person may use various

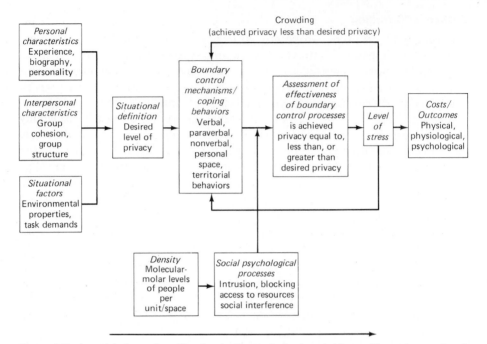

Figure 6-5　A model of crowding. (Reprinted with permission from I. Altman. *The environment and social behavior.* Monterey, Calif.: Brooks/Cole Publishing Co., 1975, p. 155.)

combinations of these mechanisms in the attempt to achieve the desired level of privacy.

Having engaged in these boundary regulation behaviors, the person or group makes an *assessment* of the effectiveness of these behaviors. If it is determined that the goal has been achieved, no further action is needed. But if achieved privacy is less than desired privacy, the person or group feels crowded. Further, Altman hypothesized that *stress* accompanies both overshooting and undershooting the goal. That is, if the person or group fails to achieve the desired level of privacy (there is more interaction than desired), crowding exists and the person experiences stress; or, conversely, if the person or group reduces interaction below that desired level (there is more privacy than desired), stress also results. In either case, the stress motivates the person or group to readjust boundary regulation behaviors in an attempt to achieve just the desired level of privacy. For instance, if too much interaction exists (i.e., crowding exists), a person may express displeasure about being intruded upon, raise his or her voice, slam doors, etc. Thus, a feedback system is proposed that controls the assessment–stress-adjustment process.

The maintenance of an acceptable level of privacy is not without cost. When a person or group has less privacy than desired and thus experiences crowding, the use of boundary regulation mechanisms requires the expenditure of physical, physiological, and psychological energy. For example, physical energy is required to maintain personal space requirements and defend territory; physiological energy in the form of adrenal functioning and cardiovascular activity may be expended as people try to regulate their contact with others; and psychological energy is used in assessing the effectiveness of boundary control processes, in being open to others or tuning them out, and similar processes.

Altman (1975) hypothesized that physical density increases the probability that intrusion, social interference, and blocking of access to resources will occur. Intrusion refers to infringement on a territory or personal space, social interference refers to an ongoing activity that is interrupted or otherwise interfered with, and blocking of access to resources refers to a person or group being prevented from attaining a desired goal. In short, physical density increases the probability of interference with boundary control mechanisms.

Finally, Altman suggests that duration is an important factor in crowding behavior. Stress, coping behaviors, and costs probably are more extensive in long- than in short-term situations.

The model has a few implicit features that Altman considers of some significance. First, he proposed that crowding can exist even if the desired level of privacy is maintained. This happens when boundary regulation processes are successful, but the costs are extremely high. Second, extreme crowding exists when a number of factors occur in combination. For example, a person who does not desire interaction and whose coping behaviors do not work very well or are very costly will experience extreme crowding if he or she is in a socially dense situation for a long period of time. This proposal suggests further that, since various factors may differ in amount, crowding is a matter of degree. Third, it is hypothesized that crowding may occur even if some variables, such as physical density, are not present. For example, a person may feel crowded if an unattractive other imposes on the person's personal space in a large open field and the person cannot "escape."

Comment

Altman's model of crowding provides an interesting integration of several areas of theory and research, with the concept of privacy being the key element. In fact, it is difficult to know whether he intended to present a theory of privacy, with crowding as one aspect, or a theory of crowding with privacy as a central component. The theory is internally consistent and does not appear to contradict known facts or accepted theory.

There are a few troublesome aspects to the theory, however. First, the model is said to apply to both persons and groups. Since the supporting evidence relative to personal space and privacy derive from individual studies, it is unclear how these concepts relate to groups. Altman provides little in the way of transitional propositions. Second, the model is weakened somewhat by one feature said to be implicit in the model. The key proposition in the theory is that crowding exists when achieved privacy is less than desired privacy. But in discussing the related properties of the model, Altman (1975, p. 158) states that crowding can exist even if there is successful maintenance of privacy. If this statement is regarded as part of the theory, internal consistency breaks down.

Altman devoted a major portion of his presentation to showing how the model relates to other theories and that data from past research are consistent with the model. Indeed, the model draws heavily on the theoretical work of Stokols (1972a, 1972b), Desor (1972), Esser (1973), Milgram (1970), and others. The reader will note many similarities between the present conceptualizations and those proposed by Schopler and Stokols (1976) and outlined in the previous section.

Altman's theory of crowding is of relatively recent origin, and there has not been a great deal of research designed specifically to test its predictions. The research that has been conducted, however, generally supports the theory. One study (Greenberg and Firestone, 1977), examined the effects of personal-space intrusion, privacy reduction through surveillance, and restriction of isolation-withdrawal behaviors upon the perception of crowding. The theory predicts that each of these factors, singly and in combination, will increase the feeling of crowdedness. Male subjects participated in a moderately personal interview in one of eight experimental conditions: intrusion or no intrusion, surveillance by unwanted strangers or no surveillance, and corner seat location or center seat location. Both intrusion and surveillance increased reported feelings of crowding stress and the effects were additive. In both conditions, subjects exhibited significantly more withdrawal behaviors. Seating position had no effect on the perception of crowding. Another study (Taylor and Stough, 1978) examined differences between urban and suburban subjects' responses to various settings that were familiar situations in their daily activities. Results confirmed Altman's views concerning the importance of the dimensions of centrality and temporal duration in the experience of crowding.

In brief summary, crowding theories are not yet complete in terms of explaining crowding phenomena and relatively little supporting data are available. The data available appears to be consistent with theoretical propositions.

A THEORY OF HOPE

Hope is a common experience of humans. We *hope* that our goals will be achieved, our communications to a friend will be understood, our affections for certain others will be reciprocated, and our dreams of glory will come true. A person with hope is active, alive, enthusiastic; a person without hope is lifeless, spiritless, and apathetic. Hope thus has important consequences on the individual and his or her behavior. Stotland's (1969) theory of hope is concerned with the conditions leading to hopefulness (or lack of it), the effects of hopefulness for the person, its consequences for action, and similar phenomena.

Hope, of course, is a subjective, common-sense term rather than a scientific one. Consequently, Stotland began by defining hope more precisely in order to make the concept more compatible with experimental psychology. He regarded *hope* as a shorthand term for an expectation about goal achievement, and *degree of hopefulness* as a person's perceived probability of goal attainment. Thus, hope is an expectation greater than zero of achieving a particular goal. In many ways, the theory of hope is a theory of motivation. As such, it is not merely a theory in social psychology but may be applied to nonsocial events as well.[4]

The heart of the theory of hope consists of seven propositions about motivational and cognitive processes. These propositions are then used to derive hypotheses, either in combination or by combining a proposition with a plausible assumption.

Major Propositions

According to Stotland (1969), the first proposition, being merely a formal statement of the truism that hopefulness is a necessary condition for action, is self-evident:

> Proposition I: *An organism's motivation to achieve a goal is, in part, a positive function of its perceived probability of attaining the goal and of the perceived importance of the goal* (Stotland, 1969, p. 7).

As used in this proposition, the term *goal* includes anything that is so perceived or symbolized by the organism (life goals or M & Ms!) and *motivation* refers primarily to action (i.e., doing something). Stotland followed Lewin (1951) in maintaining that this "something" can be either overt or covert, and may involve skeletal, cognitive, or perceptual behavior. Motivation also refers to the directed quality of the action.

> Proposition II: *The higher an organism's perceived probability of attaining a goal and the greater the importance of that goal, the greater will be the positive affect experienced by the organism* (Stotland, 1969, p. 8).

Positive affect is employed in this proposition to include such things as pleasure. satisfaction, joy, and euphoria.

> Proposition III: *The lower an organism's perceived probability of attaining a goal and the greater the importance of that goal, the more will the organism experience anxiety* (Stotland, 1969, p. 9).

Anxiety is defined as a state of physiological arousal accompanied by subjectively negative affect.

> Proposition IV: *Organisms are motivated to escape and avoid anxiety; the greater the anxiety experienced or expected, the greater the motivation* (Stotland, 1969, p. 10).

[4]The theory of hope is included in this volume primarily because hope is an important element in interpersonal behavior and only secondarily because it was formulated by a social psychologist.

Proposition IV merely states the organism's reactions to being anxious and, again, is seen as a truism by Stotland.

> Proposition V: *The organism acquires schemas as a result either* (1) *of his perception of a number of events in which examples of the same concepts are associated; or* (2) *of communication from other people* (Stotland, 1969, p. 11).

The first four propositions concern "the level of expected probability of goal attainment; propositions V, VI, and VII are concerned primarily with *schemas,* which are viewed as the more complex aspects of a person's cognitive structure. According to Stotland, they often take the form of propositions, such as "I can play the banjo," or "All brunettes are sexy." Schemas are composed of concepts. The above propositions, for example, incorporate concepts of self, a musical instrument called a banjo, sexiness, etc. The next proposition concerns the invocation of schemas:

> Proposition VI: *A schema is invoked by the organism's perceiving an event similar to a constituent concept of the schema or by the individual's receiving a communication from another directing him to invoke the schema; the greater the similarity between the event and the constituent concept, or the greater the importance of the person directing him, the more likely is the schema to be aroused* (Stotland, 1969, p. 12).

It may be noted that schemas are likely to be invoked unequally, and they vary in probability of remaining in a state of arousal when the individual perceives events inconsistent with them.

> Proposition VII: *The probability that a schema will be invoked and remain aroused is, in part, a positive function of the number of times that it has been invoked previously; of the number of events previously perceived as consistent with the schema; of the importance to the organism of the person, if any, from whom one acquired the schema* (Stotland, 1969, p. 12).

When Stotland refers to the degree of invocability of a schema, he is referring to both the invocability and the tendency of the schema to remain aroused.

Hope and Action

The theory proposes that motivation is determined by the importance of the goal and the expectation of achieving it. These determinants lead to overt action toward the goal, symbolic action toward the goal, and selective attention to goal-relevant aspects of the environment. Taken together, these considerations lead to the following hypotheses:

Hypothesis 1. The greater the expectation of goal attainment, the more likely it is that the individual will attempt to attain the goal.
Hypothesis 2. The more important the goal, the more likely it is that the individual will attend selectively to goal-relevant aspects of the environment.

Hypothesis 3. The more important the goal, the more overt action directed toward goal attainment.

Hypothesis 4. The more important the goal, the more the individual thinks about how to attain it.

Hypothesis 5. The greater the expectation of goal attainment, the more the individual thinks about how to attain it.

Hypothesis 6. The greater the expectation of goal attainment, the more likely it is that the individual will attend selectively to goal-relevant aspects of the environment.

Stotland cited several experiments demonstrating that the likelihood that a person will act to achieve a goal varies directly with the expectation of attaining it (hypothesis 1). For example, Zipf (1963) gave subjects the task of tapping 3 holes in each of 100 circles. After some experience with the task, they were informed of the probability of working fast enough to earn a $2 reward, with probabilities ranging from 0 to 1.00. Increases in speed were directly proportional to the stated probabilities. Similar findings were reported by Diggory (1966), Diggory, Klein, and Cohen (1964), and Battle (1965).

Reviews of the research relevant to the influence of perception on orientation toward a goal (Easterbrook, 1959; Jones & Gerard, 1967) were cited to support hypothesis 2. Hypotheses 3 and 4 were said to be self-evident, and no research supporting hypotheses 5 and 6 was known to Stotland.

Hope and Anxiety

Propositions III and IV concern the relationship between anxiety and hope. Anxiety is defined as an affective state, involving a subjectively negative state. Stotland proposes that anxiety is a consequence of perceived low probability of attaining important goals. This proposition is consistent with the proposals of other theorists (e.g., Freud, 1936; Goldstein, 1940; Maslow, 1943) and also has empirical support. One study (Kasl & French, 1962) found that, as men moved upward in the status hierarchy, their visits to the infirmary decreased.

It was further derived from proposition III that, if a person's goal is to avoid pain in a given situation and the person has learned an action that will avoid pain, the person will not be anxious. Evidence supporting this prediction was reported from laboratory experiments and from "real life." For example, when subjects were told that they could avoid shock by lifting their fingers from electrodes when a tone sounded, cardiac response to the tone dropped (Bersh, Matterman, & Schoenfeld, 1956). Several examples from natural situations were given (Miller, 1959; Haggard, 1949).

Since the individual is motivated to avoid anxiety (proposition IV), an individual in a state of anxiety might try to escape this state by raising the expectation of goal attainment, lowering the importance of the goal, or both. If the person tries to increase the expectation of goal attainment, the same difficulties that led to low expectations in the first place may prevent this action. If the person devalues the goal, he or she may become depressed and apathetic. Stotland notes that, despite this difficulty, people may lower the importance of the goal in extreme situations (see, e.g.. Bettelheim, 1960). Another possible action is shifting attention to subgoals that are more easily attainable (Lewin, 1951; Freidman, Chodoff, Mason, & Hamberg, 1963).

Hope and Schemas

Schemas were defined by Stotland as associations between concepts in the individual's cognitive structure. They are composed of classes of events or objects, or classes of relationships between and among objects and events. The implication is that people can learn concepts that refer to classes of objects and events or to relationships, an implication well supported by research (e.g., Kohler, 1951; Spence, 1937; Kuenne, 1946). Proposition V indicated that one way of acquiring schemas is via observation of examples of the schema. Thus, by recalling prior occasions of exemplars of given schemas, new schemas can be developed that subsume the given one.

This suggests that higher-level schemas are more likely to be developed if the individual recalls the occasions when the lower-level ones functioned. This expectation is supported by data showing that concepts are easier to develop if individuals have displayed before them positive and negative exemplars of the concept (Cahill & Hovland, 1960; Bourne, Goldstein, & Link, 1964).

Schemas may be in either a latent or arousal state. Change from latency to arousal is termed invocation of a schema. Once aroused, a schema is said to guide a person's perceptions and thoughts, determine perceptual and mental sets, and possibly influence overt behavior. For example, persons may develop schemas about their actions and the outcomes of persistence on particular tasks. According to Stotland, this analysis helps explain why people persist on tasks in the face of difficulties.

Proposition VI asserts that schemas are invoked by the perception that events are similar to the elements of those schemas. Therefore, the more similar a new task is to the tasks from which the schema was developed, the more likely that the schema will be invoked. For instance, if a person has succeeded on tasks of a given type, a schema about the outcome of persistence on such tasks will include success; if the person has failed, the schema will include failure. Stotland reasoned that previous levels of performance determine expected levels of performance on the same or similar types of tasks. Furthermore, the effects of success and failure on schemas are cumulative over time. Research on the level of aspiration (see Chapter 13) was cited to support these proposals (Lewin, 1951; Lewin et al., 1944).

The theory predicts that, in general, people will tend to avoid tasks on which they fail. This prediction was based on proposition IV, presumably on the assumption that failure arouses anxiety. Several studies show that people prefer tasks on which they have succeeded over those on which they have failed (Gebhard, 1948; Gewirtz, 1959; Nowlis, 1941).

Since people's expectations and preferences are influenced by success and failure, Stotland predicts that their performances will also be affected. This prediction is based upon the belief that expectations influence motivations, which in turn influence performances. Thus, by a somewhat circuitous route, we are led to the proposal that hope influences actions. Stotland cited numerous studies to support the effects of a history of success or failure on performance (e.g., Zipf, 1963; Osler, 1954; Rhine, 1957; Feather, 1966).

Comment and Evaluation

The theory of hope includes an intriguing array of propositions, hypotheses, and predictions about the effects of expectations about goal achievement. The theory is internally consistent and agrees quite well with other theoretical positions and with available research data. It also appears to be externally valid in that it fits observations in natural situations. Furthermore, Stotland shows in some detail how the theory can be applied to helping others, understanding psychoses and other mental problems, the therapeutic process, and similar problems.

The theory generates many testable hypotheses and should provide an adequate guide for research. However, to date it does not appear to have generated new research.

Part Four

The Cognitive Orientation

Chapter 7

Basic Concepts of the Cognitive Orientation

The *cognitive orientation* has gained great popularity among social psychologists in recent years. The various balance and consistency theories (Chapter 8) gave the initial impetus to this trend, and the theories of attribution (Chapter 9) continued the theoretical movement toward cognitive explanations. Indeed, some social psychologists believe that social psychology is dominated by cognitive theories (Manis, 1977). The appeal of the cognitive orientation derives from the functions it serves. It provides the techniques for the description of social stimulation and incentives and serves the function of explanation (Zajonc, 1968).

Cognitive theory is a term used to refer to the general theoretical orientation that emphasizes central processes (for example, attitudes, ideas, expectancies) in the explanation of behavior. This orientation may be contrasted with behavioristic approaches that emphasize peripheral factors (that is, stimulus and response variables) as the major explanatory concepts. In fact, proponents of cognitive theory usually express their views in contrast to behavioristic principles. Scheerer (1954) apparently found it necessary to outline behavioristic principles in order to present the cognitive viewpoint. His statement of cognitive theory is largely a polemic against behaviorism in which he described what cognitive theory is *not*. More recent treatments of cognitive theory adopt a similar approach, albeit more limited than Scheerer's (e.g., Neisser, 1976). Ausubel (1965a) stated explicitly that any exposition of cognitive theory must begin with an examination of contrasting views of cognitive and neobehavioristic theorists. He outlined several points of disagreement between neobehaviorism and cognitive theory:

1 Behaviorism deals with operant and classical conditioning and rote, instrumental, and discrimination learning, whereas cognitive theory is more concerned with concept formation, thinking, and the acquisition of knowledge.

2 Behaviorism tends to rely upon observable responses, whereas cognitive theory appeals to so-called mentalistic concepts, such as knowing, meaning, understanding, and similar conscious experiences, as the most significant data of science.

3 Behaviorism tends to assume a basically organismic process underlying psychological or "cognitive" events, whereas cognitive theory tends to "define cognitive events in terms of differentiated states of consciousness—existing in relation to organized systems of images, concepts, and propositions in cognitive structure—and the cognitive processes on which they depend" (Ausubel, 1965a, p. 7).

To this list may be added:

4 Behaviorism tends to adopt a molecular form of analysis, whereas cognitive theory usually assumes a molar approach (Krech & Crutchfield, 1948; Scheerer, 1954).

5 Behaviorism reveals a genetic bias in that genetically early events are regarded as more fundamental than events that occur later, whereas cognitive theory rejects this view (MacLeod, 1947).

6 Behaviorism tends to assume that behavior is activated by specific primary or derived needs and that no learning occurs without the reduction of these needs, whereas cognitive theory holds that learning may occur without need or tension reduction (Allport, 1937).

Of course, not all behaviorists accept all of the beliefs and assumptions attributed to behaviorism in the list above (see Chapter 2), nor do all cognitive theorists reject them or make different assumptions. The cognitive position should become clearer after we consider cognitive explanations of specific psychological phenomena.

The cognitive theoretical orientation is most closely related to gestalt psychology and Lewin's field theory (see Chapter 5). However. there are significant differences in the nature of theoretical explanations offered by representatives of cognitive, gestalt, and field orientations. The major similarities and differences have been stated clearly by Ausubel (1965a, p. 5).

Historically, the cognitive viewpoint is most closely identified with the theoretical position of *Gestalt* psychology insofar as it is nonmechanistic and focuses on organized and differentiated conscious experience such as is involved in perception and thinking. All cognitive theorists, however, do not necessarily endorse the *Gestalt* doctrines of perceptual nativism, psychophysiological isomorphism, the insightful nature of *all* problem solving, and the perceptual dynamics underlying the trace theory of forgetting. And, similarly, although Kurt Lewin was an extremely influential 'cognitive-field' psychologist, not all cognitive theorists necessarily subscribe to his concepts of life-space and psychological tension, to his topological diagrams, and to his insistence on the contemporaneity and invariable purposiveness of behavior.

As implied in Ausubel's statement, there is no set of general principles that is acceptable to all (or even most) cognitive theorists, nor is there general agreement regarding the identification of cognitive theorists. For example, Edward Chace Tolman is sometimes identified as a cognitive theorist (Scheerer, 1954), apparently because his theory makes use of cognitive elements such as "expectancy" and emphasizes the molar rather than the molecular approach (Tolman, 1932). On the other hand, Hilgard (1948) called Tolman's theory behavioristic, and Tolman's most recent statement (1959) is strongly behavioristic in flavor, despite his "mentalistic" concepts. Thus, it is clear that any exposition of cognitive theory must be either very brief or offensive to some who have different views concerning the "basic" principles of cognitive theory.

In the following sections of this chapter, we have attempted to reveal the essential flavor of the cognitive orientation through a discussion of the positions of individuals who are identified, by themselves or others, as cognitive theorists. In this discussion we consider cognitive definitions of some basic concepts in psychological theory and cognitive explanations of significant psychological phenomena. In the final section of the chapter, we present the cognitive principles formulated by Krech and Crutchfield (1948) as an example of the cognitive orientation applied to social psychology. Their formulation remains the most explicit statement of a cognitive theory of social psychology that is presently available.

COGNITIVE DEFINITIONS OF BASIC TERMS

It is always presumptuous to attempt to identify the "basic" concepts used in theories proposed by others. Nevertheless, it is necessary to identify and define concepts and terms that seem to be most central to cognitive theory, at least in the sense that they are used frequently. It is obvious that *cognition* and the related terms *cognitive* and *cognitive structure* are basic to cognitive theory. In addition, it will be helpful to consider cognitive-theory definitions of *stimulus, response,* and *meaning.*

Cognition and Cognitive Structure

Most cognitive theorists use the concept *cognition* without explicitly defining it, perhaps because they believe it is so frequently used as to require no definition (e.g., Anderson, 1976; Carroll & Payne, 1976). However, some writers have attempted to define cognition. For example, Scheerer (1954) referred to cognition as a centrally mediated process representing internal and external events. "It takes the form of phenomenal organization *which is centrally imposed between* the source of stimulation and the behavioral adjustment" (Scheerer, 1954, p. 99). Festinger (1957) identified "cognitive elements" as cognitions, which he defined as the things a person knows about himself, his behavior, and his surroundings. He used the term "knowledges" to refer to these things. Brehm and Cohen (1962) defined cognitions as items of information. Neisser (1967) stated that the term refers to the processes by which any sensory input is transformed, reduced, elaborated, stored, recovered, and used. Thus, cognition seems to be that which is known or knowledge acquired through personal experience.

Cognitive structure, on the other hand, is usually explicitly defined. Zajonc (1960) defined cognitive structure as an organized subset of the attributes an individual uses to identify and discriminate a particular object or event. In a similar vein, Scott (1963) used the term *cognitive structure* to mean those structures whose elements consist of ideas consciously held by the person or as the set of ideas maintained by a person and relatively available to conscious awareness (Scott, 1962). The content of experience is believed to be organized into more-complex structural assemblies, and it is these structures that give meaning to specific elements (for example, particular beliefs, knowledges, values, expectancies). These cognitive structures play a significant role in learning, perception, and similar psychological processes, as we shall see later.

Since cognitive structures are seen as consisting of various attributes and relationships among attributes, it is necessary to identify and describe the properties of these relationships. For purposes of analysis, Zajonc (1968) assumed that objects and events are perceived in terms of psychological dimensions. A *psychological dimension* was defined as the capacity to map consistently a set of responses onto an ordered collection of stimuli. The properties of cognitive structures were identified as *differentiation, complexity, unity, degree of organization, homogeneity, segmentation,* and *valence* (Zajonc, 1968). Differentiation refers to the number of attributes constituting a given cognitive structure, complexity to the degree of interrelatedness of attributes, unity to the degree to which attributes are functionally dependent upon each other, and degree of organization to the extent to which the unity of the total structure is built around a single core. Homogeneity, segmentation, and valence were not explicitly defined.

A similar but somewhat more-detailed analysis of cognitive structure has been made by Scott (1962, 1963). He identified three major structural properties: *differentiation, relatedness,* and *integration.* Differentiation was used to refer to the distinctiveness of elements that contribute to the set of ideas maintained by a person. This usage contrasts with Zajonc's use of the term to refer to *number* of attributes, but it is quite similar to Bieri's (1955) concept of complexity of attributes and to the construct measured by Kelly's (1955) rep test. Scott's formulation is also similar to the definition of differentiation as a heterogeneous state of an organismic system (Witkin, Goodenough, & Oltman, 1979), although the latter definition was proposed in a somewhat different context. Differentiation is necessary before one can consider relations among elements. In a later analysis (Scott, 1969, 1974) it was stated that differentiation depends upon both dimensionality of the cognitive space and articulation of the attributes within the space. *Dimensionality* refers to the space utilized by the attributes, and *articulation* was defined as the number of reliable distinctions that an individual makes with respect to the attribute.

Relatedness refers to two aspects of the cognitive structure. On the one hand, it refers to types of relations, such as similarity, association, proximity, covariance, and so forth; on the other hand, it refers to the phenomenal influence of one element on another. With regard to the latter, when two elements are correlated in this way the question always arises whether elements are causally related but independent or are merely undifferentiated. *Salience* of an attribute may also be regarded as an aspect of relatedness. Scott defined salience of an attribute as the likelihood of the attribute's being aroused by environmental cues. It is represented structurally as the number of concepts with which the attribute is associated in a dependent fashion, and in this sense is similar to Zajonc's concept of unity. When a person's cognitive structure has many attributes with equal salience, there exists a state of dispersion among saliences. [In later work, the term "centrality" was substituted for "relatedness," but appears to be conceptually the same (Scott, 1974)].

Integration refers to the degree of connectedness among parts of the structure and the manner in which images in the domain are related (Scott, 1963, 1969). When the cognitive structure is integrated, the relations among the various attributes are known to the person and can be manipulated. The person can shift from one attribute to another and combine them in various ways in responding to the world. According to more recent analyses (Scott, 1974), there are various modes or kinds of integration. Examples include *centralization* (a primitive mode in which some small number of attributes are treated as central), *affective balance* (in which objects are grouped cognitively in ways that are consistent with their affective relevance for the person), *image comparability* (in which all phenomenal objects are judged on the same set of attributes), and *affective-evaluative consistency* (in which objects are liked or disliked to the extent that they are seen as possessing desirable or undesirable characteristics).

A rather different approach was taken by Abelson (1976). His basic theoretical concept is a *cognitive script*. A cognitive script was defined as a coherent sequence of events expected by an individual, involving the individual either as a participant or as an observer. Scripts are learned through participation in event sequences and observation, including vicarious observation, of events. Since everyone has a different learning history, Abelson proposed that people have different kinds of scripts that vary on such things as length of time frame, number of active characters, and whether or not the separate events in the script are concrete or generic.

The basic ingredient of scripts was called a *vignette*. A vignette is an encoding of an event of short duration. It usually includes both an image and a conceptual representation of the event. Abelson (1976) hypothesized three processes relative to the establishment of vignettes: (1) vignettes may be stored as single experiences; (2) similarity groupings can build up categorical vignettes based on many single experiences in a given type of situation; and (3) an individual may, with enough experience in a given domain, be able to process lists of features instead of single or multiple vignettes. These processes are seen as progressing from the concrete to the abstract and are referred to as *episodic, categorical,* and *hypothetical,* respectively. Scripts, which are merely chains of vignettes, may also be episodic, categorical, or hypothetical. Scripts at all three levels are presumed to be available to an individual in familiar content areas.

Implicit in each of these analyses is the notion of a structure consisting of differentiated parts (ideas, concepts, attributes, vignettes, etc.) that are related to one another in such a way that an integrated organization exists. Indeed, McGuire (1968) argued strongly that people's conceptions are highly interconnected (structured) and a high degree of coherence is maintained within this structure. It is this cognitive structure that enables a person to deal with a complex environment in a meaningful way.

Stimulus and Response

Stimulus and response are complex concepts for the cognitive theorist, and adequate definition requires consideration of the whole perceptual process. According to Scheerer (1954), cognitive theorists have not separated stimulus and response in the traditional manner. In fact, most cognitive theorists appear to avoid the entire question of stimulus and response, except to castigate those who rely on these concepts as central to the explanation of behavior. However, Scheerer examined this question and came to the conclusion that there are at least three definitions of stimulus, roughly corresponding to the three elements in the perceptual process: (1) The stimulus consists of the physical objects which affect the organism through the medium of proximal stimulus relations. (2) The stimulus is the total proximal field distribution which elicits patterns of excitation in the central nervous system. (3) The stimulus is the phenomenal representation of the geographic object.

It is clear that cognitive theorists have used all three definitions of *stimulus,* although in practice (experimentation) the most common one appears to be definition (1). However, the stimulus in this sense is not merely an isolated object in the physical world, but a more-complex molar organization. A stimulus, for most cognitive theorists, would consist not only of the object, such as a table, but also of other elements of the total situation and the relations among them.

Response is viewed by Scheerer as a process of organization. For example, the configurational response to the relations among proximal stimuli is the phenomenal representation of the stimulus. The response is thus relational rather than specific, and its organization depends upon relations among stimulus elements.

An apparently similar view is expressed by Hunt (1962). According to his formulation, the adult person has learned a number of large information processing units. These units are specifically designed for the manipulation of an internally represented environment. This environment is, of course, symbolically coded. Using these learned information processing units, the individual is able to construct an internal model of the environment. This environment can then be used to predict external events. He concluded that these routines could be regarded as responses.

These two views of response agree in that the response is regarded as a complex event that is not clearly separable from the stimulus. Unfortunately, it is not made clear exactly how a response can be identified, if, indeed, this is possible, nor how it can be measured. Without such specification it is difficult to see how the response can be studied.

Meaning

Meaning is a central concept in cognitive theory and plays a role in theoretical explanations of almost all complex psychological processes. Ausubel (1965b) viewed meaning as an "idiosyncratic phenomenological product" of meaningful learning. In the learning process the potential meaning inherent in symbols (or in sets of symbols) is converted into differentiated cognitive content. No underlying organismic process is assumed, except, of course, for the organized system of images, concepts, and propositions (that is, the cognitive structure). It is the relation of new content to this cognitive structure that results in new meanings. Ausubel did not deny that neurophysiological events may underlie meaning as a cognitive phenomenon, but he viewed such events as bearing a substrate relationship to meaning. That is, there is no causal connection between meanings and neurophysiological events.

Bruner (1957a) reflected a similar view in his discussion of perceptual readiness. In his view, the meaning of whatever is perceived derives from the class of percepts with which it is grouped. Meaning is thus a consequence of a categorization process that is basic to perception. This conceptualization will be clarified when the cognitive view of perception is considered.

COGNITIVE EXPLANATIONS OF SELECTED PSYCHOLOGICAL PROCESSES

We will not attempt to present the cognitive view of all significant psychological processes that cognitivists have attempted to explain. Instead we have selected the ones which have been dealt with most extensively and which most clearly reveal the cognitive orientation; namely, *perception, learning,* and *reinforcement.*

Perception

Many cognitive theorists have accepted the gestalt conceptualization of the perceptual process, and all are strongly influenced by the gestalt position. For example, Scheerer (1954) reviewed the gestalt principles of perception, which hold that perception is the phenomenal representation of distal objects, resulting from the organization of the distal stimuli, the medium, and the proximal stimuli, and concluded that this phenomenal organization is a cohesive structured field in which the units represent objects in the geographic environment.

Berlyne (1957) reviewed Piaget's work on perception in relation to thought, identifying several aspects of perception that set the perceptual process apart from thinking:

1   The perceived properties of a stimulus vary according to the pattern of which it is a part.
2   Perceptions are variable from person to person and from time to time.
3   Perception varies with the direction (focus) of the sense organs.
4   Perceptions tend to develop in a particular direction and are largely irreversible. For example, once a concealed object is discovered in a "hidden-figures test," it cannot be ignored.

Krech and Crutchfield (1948) considered the determinants of perception and asserted that perception is determined by two major sets of factors or variables: structural variables and functional variables. The structural variables are those inherent in the physical stimuli and the neural events they produce in the nervous system. Functional factors are those that reside in the perceiver; for example, needs, moods, past experiences of the perceiver, and other individual characteristics.

These views of the perceptual process tell us something about the cognitive theoretical orientation, but they do not delve very deeply into the nature of perception. The analysis offered by Bruner (1957a) considered the problem in greater detail. According to Bruner, perception is a process of categorization. The organism is stimulated by some appropriate input (external object, event, etc.) and responds to it by relating it to a category of objects or events. This relating of input to category is an active process in which the person selects the appropriate category—the one which will provide identity and meaning for the new information. Thus, all perception is generic, since anything that is perceived is placed in and gets its meaning from the class of percepts to which it is related.

In addition to being categorical and inferential in nature, Bruner described perception as varyingly veridical. Historically, it has been assumed that what is perceived is to some extent a representation of the external world. This so-called representative function of perception has been a source of controversy among both philosophers and scientists, but the manner in which this representation is accomplished is still unclear. Most writers agree, however, that the degree to which the percept represents the external world varies with a variety of circumstances; for example, an object in a cloudy sky may be perceived as a plane when it is "really" a bird. It is this variable degree of correspondence between percept and object that Bruner referred to as "varying veridicality" of perception.

Since perception involves inference, Bruner concluded that it rests upon a decision process (see also Brunswik, 1949a; Tanner & Swets, 1954). Even the simplest perceptual event requires a decision; when the object in the cloudy sky stimulates the organism, he or she must decide whether it is a plane or a bird. This decision determines to a large extent the category to which the input will be referred and, consequently, the meaning it has for the person. In many cases, however, there seems to be a sequence of decisions involved in the perceptual process. Having decided that the object in the sky is, indeed, a plane, the person may decide whether it is a commercial plane or a private one, whether it is preparing to land at the airport or fly past, etc. This example is what Bruner called a "bracketing" process in which there is a gradual narrowing of the category in which the object is placed. He identified four stages in the decision sequence:

1 *Primitive categorization* is a "silent" process in which the object or event is isolated and marked by certain spatio-temporal-qualitative characteristics. At this stage, meaning is minimal.

2 *Cue search* is a stage in which the perceiver is scanning the environment for additional information that permits selection of the proper category for object placement. When the event is highly practiced or there is high cue-to-category probability linkage, this second process may also be silent. In other cases the searching is a conscious experience.

3 *Confirmation check* occurs after the object has been tentatively placed in a category. At this stage the perceiver is no longer open to maximum stimulation; instead, the search is limited to additional confirmatory cues. Bruner referred to this as a "selective gating process" that reduces the effectiveness of irrelevant inputs.

4 *Confirmation completion* is the final stage in the process and is characterized by the termination of cue search. Openness to additional cues is greatly reduced and inconsistent cues are either "gated out" or modified to fit the category.

Bruner summarized his considerations about the general properties of perception in a series of propositions. These propositions may be briefly paraphrased as follows:

1 Perception depends upon a decision process.

2 The decision process involves the utilization of discriminatory cues which make it possible to assign inputs to categories.

3 The process of cue utilization involves the operation of inference, which leads to the placement of the object in a category.

4 A category is a set of specifications or rules concerning the kinds of events that will be grouped together.

5 Categories vary in the readiness with which a stimulus input will be identified in terms of the category; that is, in terms of accessibility.

6 A perception is veridical to the extent that the stimulus inputs are referred to the appropriate category.

7   When conditions are less than optimal, perception will be veridical to the degree that accessibility of categories reflects environmental probabilities.

The common thread running through the views expressed by the various cognitive theorists is that perception is not merely the passive reception and automatic interpretation of stimuli, but rather it is an active process in which the incoming data are selectively related to the existing cognitive structure. It is the relationship of the inputs (sensory data) to the organization of cognitive elements (cognitive structure) that determines and gives meaning to the thing perceived. The details of this perceptual process are viewed differently by different theorists, but there seems to be relatively good agreement concerning the general nature of the process.

Learning and Memory

Cognitive theorists usually regard learning and memory as different processes, albeit closely related. The typical cognitive theorist recognizes more than one type of learning and holds that the principles that are adequate for the explanation of one type are not necessarily applicable to other types. Ausubel (1961) identified four types of learning, which he labeled *reception learning, discovery learning, rote learning,* and *meaningful learning.* These types are not independent, since both reception and discovery learning can be either rote or meaningful. The distinction between reception and discovery learning cuts across the rote- versus meaningful-learning classification, and the distinction between rote and meaningful learning cuts across the reception- versus discovery-learning classification.

In reception learning, the learner is required only to "internalize" materials that are available to him, so that they will be functionally reproducible at some time in the future. No discovery is required on the part of the learner, since all of the material is given. In discovery learning, however, the content to be learned must, for the most part, be independently discovered by the learner. Examples include concept formation (in which the thing to be learned is the set of attributes common to a number of diverse items or events), meaningful problem solving (in which the task is to discover the exact nature of a relationship between two events), and similar learning tasks. Discovery learning requires more than the mere internalization of content. Therefore, the learning process is one in which the information is reorganized and integrated into the cognitive structure, followed by further reorganization or transformation of the integrated combination. All of this occurs before internalization; afterward, the discovered content is internalized in the same way as in reception learning.

Ausubel also noted that repeated encounters with the learning materials produces different outcomes in reception and discovery learning. In reception learning repeated encounters primarily increase the degree and duration of retention, whereas in discovery learning repetition gives rise to successive stages in discovery.

The distinction between rote and meaningful learning was said by Ausubel to represent an entirely different dimension from the reception- and discovery-learning distinction. Rote learning refers to the situation in which the learner intends to memorize the learning material verbatim, as a series of arbitrarily related words. Meaningful learning, on the other hand, refers to situations that have at least two characteristics: (1) the material to be learned is potentially meaningful and (2) the learner's set is to relate substantive aspects of new concepts or information to relevant components of existing cognitive structures. Such integration makes possible "the incorporation of derivative, elaborative, descriptive, supportive, qualifying, or representational relationships" (Ausubel, 1961, p. 18). Learning material is potentially meaningful if the relation of concepts to the cognitive structure can be done on a nonarbitrary basis (a property of the material) and related nonarbitrarily to the particular cognitive structure of the particular learner (a property of the learner). It should be clear from the definitions above that reception learning is most likely to be rote, and discovery learning is most likely to be meaningful, although this is not necessarily so. When discovery is involved, rote learning corresponds to trial-and-error learning and meaningful learning to insightful problem solving.

The model of cognitive organization proposed by Ausubel (1963) for meaningful learning assumes that the cognitive structure consists of a hierarchical organization of conceptual *traces,* where the term "trace" is a hypothetical construct used to account for the continuing representation of past experience in the cognitive structure. That is, there exist highly inclusive traces under which less-inclusive traces are subsumed. As new information enters the cognitive field, it interacts with and is subsumed under a relevant and more-inclusive conceptual system. At first, this serves to facilitate learning and retention by anchoring the new information to related materials. At this point, it can be dissociated from the subsuming concept and recalled as an individual entity. Later, however, a stage of obliteration begins. It is easier and more economical to retain a single concept than many specific bits of information; hence, individual items of information become progressively less dissociable from the subsuming system until finally they cannot be reproduced as specific entities. That is, they are forgotten.

The alert reader will have noted the similarity of Ausubel's subsumption theory of learning to Bruner's analysis of the perceptual process. In fact, it is difficult to make a clear distinction between Bruner's view of the perceptual process and his views of the learning process, at least insofar as meaningful learning is concerned. Distinctions among types of learning are implicit in the writings of Bruner and his associates, although he seems to consider meaningful learning and problem solving as the more-significant kinds of learning. For example, he stated that effective learning results when future use of the learned material is no longer bound to the specific situation in which the learning occurred (Bruner, 1959).

Bruner, Wallach, and Galanter (1959) asserted that much of learning and problem solving can be regarded as a task of identifying recurrent regularities in the environment. This task requires a model of regularity. The learner may employ an existing model or, if none exists, construct a new one. In either case, the problem is to identify the recurrent regularities and relate them to the model. Difficulties arise when the recurrent pattern is so complex that it exceeds the individual's cognitive span or when there are sources of interference. Sources of interference may be in the stimulus situation, in the pattern of responding, or in the organism. When interferences exist, learning consists largely in separating recurrent regularities from interferences. When there are no interferences and the memory span is not exceeded, learning is merely a matter of immediate recognition.

The information-processing theory proposed by Newell, Simon, and Shaw (1958) is similar in many respects to the viewpoints outlined above. They postulated an information-processing system with a large storage capacity holding complex programs or strategies. These strategies may be evoked by stimuli which determine which one or ones of the available strategies will be evoked. The content of these strategies is largely determined by previous experience. As a consequence of these storage systems and an active response to stimuli, the system is capable of responding in a highly selective and complex manner. Learning occurs when a response of the system to successive presentations of the same stimulus produces more or less lasting change in the response of the system.

Many cognitive theorists have emphasized memory processes rather than learning; among them J. R. Anderson is perhaps most important (e.g., Anderson & Bower, 1963; Anderson, 1976). Anderson proposed a theory of the mind, called ACT. The core of this theory is a distinction between declarative knowledge and procedural knowledge. Declarative knowledge consists of facts, whereas procedural knowledge includes high-level cognitive processes involved in memory acquisition and retrieval, language acquisition and comprehension, sentence generation, and inference. In short, the distinction between procedural and declarative knowledge is the difference between knowing how and knowing that.

According to Anderson (1976), three features distinguish between declarative and procedural knowledge: (1) declarative knowledge is possessed in an all-or-none manner, whereas procedural knowledge can be partially processed; (2) a person can acquire declarative knowledge suddenly (e.g., by being told), whereas one acquires procedural knowledge gradually by performing the skill; and (3) declarative knowledge can be communicated verbally, whereas procedural knowledge cannot.

In ACT declarative knowledge is represented in a propositional network, i.e., a network of nodes representing concepts and propositions. The nodes in the network are connected by links that are labeled to indicate different relationships among nodes. For instance, a propositional network of family relations might include links labeled "mother-of," "husband-of," "cousin-of," etc. Relationships may also be propositional in nature, such as "John hit Mary." Since each node in a propositional network represents a concept, all the facts that a person knows about the concept are attached to that node. Hence, if a person retrieves a concept's location in memory, all the facts known about the concept become available.

Procedural knowledge is represented as *productions*. A production specifies a condition or set of conditions that must be satisfied for a cognitive process to occur. According to Anderson, "Productions may examine, test, and add to the contents of the propositional network but they may not operate on themselves" (Anderson, 1976, p. 118). Procedural knowledge is therefore specific to the circumstances where it is intended to apply. For example, if a person dials a particular telephone number often enough, he or she often loses the ability to verbalize the number and can retrieve it only by dialing (i.e., through production).

In summary, with respect to learning, the significant aspect of the various proposals by cognitive theorists is that different kinds of learning are recognized. Rote learning, conditioning, and similar types of learning occur, but these are regarded as relatively unimportant forms of learning, at least for complex human behavior. The kind of learning that Ausubel (1961) labeled "meaningful learning" is emphasized as the type of learning that is most useful and most likely to lead to advances in human knowledge and welfare. This sort of complex learning requires active participation on the part of the learner and involves complicated internal processes such as subsumption, identification of recurrent regularities, and evocation of strategies. By comparison, few cognitivists have examined memory processes in as much detail as learning processes. The work of Anderson exemplifies the cognitive approach to memory and is far richer than may be indicated by our very abbreviated description.

Motivation and Reinforcement

The cognitive orientation generally deemphasizes the role of motivation and reinforcement in learning and behavior. A careful reading of their writings, however, reveals that this deemphasis is more apparent than real. At minimum, most cognitive theorists implicitly assume the existence of a need for cognition or cognitive structure. This assumption has been made explicit by Cohen, Stotland, and Wolfe (1955), who defined need for cognition as a need to structure relevant situations in meaningful and integrated ways. The person needs to understand his or her world as it is experienced and to make it reasonable. (Incidentally, it is probably the assumption of such a need that underlies the cognitive consistency hypothesis discussed in Chapter 8.) In order to demonstrate this need, Cohen et al. devised two independent measures of cognitive need that yielded consistent results. The subjects indicating either high or low need for cognition were presented either an ambiguous or a structured situation. The ambiguous situation produced more frustration than the structured one, and this effect was greater for high- than for low-need persons. These findings were taken as evidence of the existence of a need for cognition.

Perhaps what is really being objected to by cognitive theorists is the concept of motivation as tension and the proposition that all reinforcement consists of tension reduction. Scheerer (1954) pointed out that although drive reduction may be satisfying under some circumstances, it is just as often the case that the organism seeks drive intensification. He proposed that capacity fulfillment may be a more important source of gratification than tension reduction. When an individual sets a goal for himself, he is in effect creating a state of tension for himself. Moreover, goal attainment is satisfying (reinforcing) because it leads not so much to tension reduction as to the cognitive enrichment resulting from goal attainment. This cognitive enrichment leads to a changed, differentiated state of the organism, which produces satisfaction.

The most notable examples of the use of reinforcement in cognitive theory are those found in cognitive balance and consistency theories. Heider (1946) proposed that the person's (p's) cognitive structure representing his sentiments toward another person (o) and o's products (x) tend toward a balanced state. If the relations are unbalanced (for example, if p likes o but dislikes x), a state of tension results, and forces to restore balance are generated. A balanced state is preferred and is more pleasant; hence, reduction of imbalance is pleasant and satisfying to the person. Other consistency theories posit a similar mechanism. Newcomb (1953) postulated a strain toward symmetry in interpersonal communication. The principle of congruity advanced by Osgood and Tannenbaum (1955) holds that judgmental frames of reference tend toward maximal simplicity. Festinger's (1957) theory of cognitive dissonance also posits a form of tension reduction. According to his theory, two cognitive elements are dissonant if the obverse of one follows from the other. Such a state of cognitive dissonance is asserted to be psychologically uncomfortable and hence will motivate the person to achieve consonance.

All these cognitive-balance or consistency theories assume, either explicitly or implicitly, that imbalance or inconsistency creates a psychological state that is psychologically unpleasant, and the reduction of imbalance relieves the unpleasant state. This proposition is in no essential way different from the behavioristic principle of tension reduction. The cognitive consistency theories are discussed in greater detail in Chapter 8.

KRECH AND CRUTCHFIELD'S COGNITIVE THEORY

The most ambitious attempt to formulate a cognitive theory of social psychology is that by Krech and Crutchfield (1948). In this attempt, they began with a presentation of the basic principles of cognitive theory, which were then applied to social behavior. Their presentation is also probably the most explicit and precise statement of cognitive theory that is available. For these reasons, it will be instructive to examine their propositions as an example *par excellence* of cognitive theory. These propositions were grouped into those dealing with the dynamics of behavior, the perceptual process, and the reorganization of perceptions. We have followed their organization.

The Dynamics of Behavior

The first set of propositions presented by Krech and Crutchfield (1948) was concerned with the basic principles of motivation. The term "motivation" was used rather broadly to include emotions as well as needs and values. This first set of propositions also included statements concerning methodological questions that were seen as being intimately related to cognitive analysis. For the most part, the propositions are self-explanatory; each one is discussed here, only briefly.

> Proposition I. *The proper unit of motivational analysis is molar behavior, which involves needs and goals* (p. 30).

This proposition clearly reveals the concern for method and reflects the molar bias of cognitive theory. The authors assert that only by considering all the behavior of an individual occurring at a given time can one really understand the complex effects of motivational factors. Molar behavior consists not only of overt actions but also of thoughts, perceptions, needs, etc., and the relations among these units of behavior. Since the person is a unit, these elements are interrelated and cannot be arbitrarily separated.

> Proposition II. *The dynamics of molar behavior result from properties of the immediate psychological field* (p. 33).

Two problems are involved in this proposition: the immediate dynamic problem and the genetic problem. The first problem deals with the needs and goals of a given person in a given situation. The genetic problem deals with the question of how these needs and goals have developed. Krech and Crutchfield emphasized that motivational anaylsis need not look for the causes of behavior in the past; instead, all motives can be treated as contemporaneous.

> Proposition III. *Instabilities in the psychological field produce 'tensions' whose effects on perception, cognition, and action are such as to tend to change the field in the direction of a more stable structure* (p. 40).

At any given moment the organization of the psychological field is likely to involve inconsistencies that give rise to tensions. These tensions produce conscious correlates such as vague feelings of restlessness, feelings of needs, and perceived demands of the environment. Tensions persist until resolved and evoke behaviors that may be actions toward a goal, cognitive reorganization, or a general restructuring of the field.

> Proposition IV. *The frustration of goal achievement and the failure of tension reduction may lead to a variety of adaptive or maladaptive behaviors* (p. 50).

When motives are blocked so that the person cannot achieve the goal, frustration results. Frustration of motives may result from environmental factors (physical or social) or personal factors (biological or psychological). The person may respond with adaptive behaviors (such as intensification of effort to achieve the goal, reorganization of the perceptual field, or substitution of goals) or maladaptive behaviors (such as aggression, withdrawal, rationalization, or autism).

> Proposition V. *Characteristic modes of goal achievement and tension reduction may be learned and fixated by the individual* (p. 66).

Although Krech and Crutchfield assumed that instabilities in the psychological field give rise to tensions that evoke behaviors oriented toward tension equilibrium, they maintained that this process is not static or mechanical. Instead, it is an active process that often leads to successively higher levels of organization.

Perceptual and Cognitive Structure

Krech and Crutchfield maintained that all people's molar behavior is shaped by their private conceptions of the world. Therefore, it is necessary to describe the social world as perceived by the individual and discover the general principles of perception and cognition. The propositions stated in this section are concerned primarily with the second problem, that is, the formulation of the laws of perception and cognition.

> Proposition I. *The perceptual and cognitive field in its natural state is organized and meaningful* (p. 84).

This proposition is illustrated by the tendency of people to form integrated impressions of others, jump to conclusions, and resist changes in attitudes.

> Proposition II. *Perception is functionally selective* (p. 87).

The individual is exposed to a vast array of stimuli that might be perceived, but it is manifestly impossible to attend to all of them. Instead, only certain objects play an important role in perception—those which are functionally significant to the person. In this way, the individual is able to integrate perceptions into the existing cognitive structure with the least threat to stability.

> Proposition III. *The perceptual and cognitive properties of a substructure are determined in large measure by the properties of the structure of which it is a part* (p. 94).

This proposition states merely that any given perception has meaning only in relation to the cognitive structure in which it is embedded. It supposedly says something about the nature of relationships between a given perception and the cognitive structure of that perception. Two reformulations were given to clarify the general proposition.

> 1 *When an individual is apprehended as a member of a group, each of those characteristics of the individual which correspond to the characteristics of the group is*

affected by his group membership, the effect being in the direction either of assimilation or of contrast (p. 96).

2 *Other things being equal, a change introduced into the psychological field will be absorbed in such a way as to produce the smallest effect on a strong structure* (p. 98).

The first of these is exemplified by the effects the tendency to group people according to race, religious beliefs, social class, etc., has on our perceptions of individual persons. The second one points to the fact that the strongest cognitive structures are least susceptible to disruptive influences. For example, a man's strongest beliefs are least subject to change in the face of contradictory evidence.

> Proposition IV. *Objects or events that are close to each other in space or time or resemble each other tend to be apprehended as part of a common structure* (p. 102).

This proposition is clearly based on the gestalt principles of similarity and proximity as determinants of perception. However, Krech and Crutchfield did not accept the gestalt view that these are purely structural variables. Instead, culture and training are significant factors in the determination of what will be seen as "similar" and, hence, in the determination of perceptual organization. Nonstructural aspects of proximity are perhaps not so evident, but Krech and Crutchfield believed that social factors also play a role here. For example, in some primitive cultures the birth of twins and a disastrous earthquake occurring at the same time could be organized into a single event caused by the devil.

Cognitive Reorganization

Cognitive structures are constantly changing in response to the individual's changing experiences. Changes may result from situational changes (learning), from changes in the person's physiological state, or from the effects of dynamic factors involved in retention (forgetting). The propositions discussed in this section deal with cognitive reorganization and include the reorganization involved in learning, thinking, problem solving, forgetting, and physiological change.

> Proposition I. *As long as there is a blockage to the attainment of a goal, cognitive reorganization tends to take place; the nature of the reorganization is such as to reduce the tension induced by the frustrating situation* (p. 112).

This proposition states that the effects of frustration will continue over time until tension is reduced by cognitive reorganization. The nature of the reorganization is determined by several factors, including the strength of needs, characteristic mode of response, and perception of the block to the goal. When the need is very intense or the block to the goal is misperceived, maladaptive reorganizations tend to occur. The person's characteristic mode of response may also be nonadaptive or maladaptive.

Proposition II. *The cognitive reorganization process typically consists of a hierarchically related series of organizations* (p. 117).

This proposition points to the fact that each successive step of the learning process is meaningfully organized. This fact has several important implications regarding the learning experience: (1) repeated situations provide the opportunity for a continued cognitive reorganization rather than a gradual build-up of the final structure; (2) the experiences that influence the reorganization are the perceived experiences of the individual; and (3) consciously directed education is vitally important in shaping the cognitive reorganization. The main point is that the reorganization process is unified and interdependent.

Proposition III. *Cognitive structures, over time, undergo progressive changes in accordance with the principles of organization* (p. 125).

The major point of this proposition is that cognitive reorganization may occur independently of needs; that is, not all cognitive reorganization is because of blocking of the goal and subsequent tension reduction. Some important changes occur during the time between the formation of the structure and the moment it functions again in the person's behavior. Essentially, this proposition asserts that forgetting may occur and usually does.

The specific changes in cognitive structure over time were attributed to the structural and functional properties of the original cognitive organization and to the relation between the properties of the original structure and intervening perceptions.

Proposition IV. *The ease and rapidity of the cognitive reorganization process is a function of the differentiation, isolation, and rigidity of the original cognitive structure* (p. 135).

Krech and Crutchfield took the point of view that the problems of speed of reorganization and of individual differences in ease and rapidity of reorganization can best be handled by an analysis of the biological characteristics of the person. In general, simple and isolated structures are more easily reorganized than differentiated and interdependent structures.

SUMMARY

The major viewpoints of cognitive theory should now be apparent, although the definitions and explanations may not be as clear as we would like them to be. Let us restate briefly the chief cognitive tenets:

1   Complex behavior can be understood only by considering the so-called mentalistic concepts such as percept, idea, image, and expectancy. One must analyze these central processes in order to adequately conceptualize the more complicated and more important forms of human behavior.

2 The proper method of analysis is the holistic, or molar, approach. It is impossible to understand unitary behavior by studying molecular elements.

3 Not only is behavior organization molar but cognition is the most important element in this organization. Thus, perception is seen as a process of relating incoming data to existing cognitive structure and learning as a process of cognitive reorganization.

4 Learning and other behavior may be a consequence of tension and tension reduction, but capacity fulfillment is at least equally important in the determination of behavior.

5 Neurophysiological events may underlie psychological phenomena, but there is no necessary causal relationship between physiological and psychological events.

Perhaps all these can be subsumed under the general proposition that behavior is organized, this organization is molar, and the most important element in this organization is cognition.

Chapter 8

Cognitive Consistency Theories

The term *cognitive consistency theories* refers to a host of proposals based upon the general proposition that inconsistent cognitions arouse an unpleasant psychological state, which leads to behaviors designed to achieve consistency, which is psychologically pleasant. The inconsistent relation among cognitions is referred to variously as cognitive imbalance (Heider, 1946), asymmetry (Newcomb, 1953), incongruence (Osgood & Tannenbaum, 1955), and dissonance (Festinger, 1957). Similarly, these inconsistent relations arouse either tension, strain toward symmetry, pressure toward congruity, or psychological dissonance, respectively. There are wide variations among theories concerning the identification of cognitions that are psychologically inconsistent, the nature of the psychological state resulting from inconsistent cognitions, and the kinds of behavior leading to consistency. Theories also differ in scope of application. Perhaps the most limited theory is the principle of congruity (Osgood & Tannenbaum, 1955), which is concerned only with attitude change. Without question, the most extensive theory is the theory of cognitive dissonance (Festinger, 1957), which deals with behavior in general, both social and nonsocial.

Historically, Heider (1946) appears to have been the first person to use the concept of cognitive inconsistency (imbalance) in a social psychological theory. Later theories are largely variations, modifications, and/or extensions of his formulation. The basic notion that inconsistent cognitions lead to behaviors directed toward the achievement of consistency appears as a central proposition in all theories. All these theories represent the general cognitive orientation (see Chapter 7) in that they appeal to central factors such as attitudes, expectations, knowledges, and beliefs as basic elements in the explanation of behavior.

In this chapter we have chosen to discuss four consistency theories that appear most prominently in social psychology and reflect the major conceptualizations that have grown out of this general theoretical approach. These are Heider's (1946, 1958) p-o-x theory, Newcomb's (1953) A-B-X system, Osgood and Tannenbaum's (1955) principle of congruity, and Festinger's (1957, 1964) theory of cognitive dissonance. Festinger's theory is not, strictly speaking, a social psychological theory, but is included here because it has been highly influential with respect to research in social psychology. In addition, we have included Brehm's (1966, 1972) theory of psychological reactance because, although it is not, strictly speaking, a cognitive consistency theory, it deals with similar phenomena and has been used to complement dissonance theory (Varela, 1971). Related theories that are not reviewed in this book include those proposed by Abelson and Rosenberg (1958), Cartwright and Harary (1956), Pepitone (1958), Bem (1965), Kiesler (1974), and Nuttin (1975).

THE p-o-x THEORY

Sentiments play an important role in interpersonal relations. The feelings that one person has toward another—liking, loving, hating, gratitude, anger, trust, etc.—often exert strong influences on the behavior of that person toward the other. The p-o-x theory (Heider, 1946, 1958) was proposed to bring some order into the diversity of possible situations and events involving sentiments. As originally proposed by Heider (1946), the theory was concerned with the sentiments of a person (p) toward another person (o) and an impersonal object (x) "belonging" to o. The later formulation was expanded to include more-general interpersonal relations; for example, the x element could be not only an impersonal object but also another person who is related to o in some way.

In general, the theory holds that separate entities (for example, p, o, and x) constitute a unit when they are seen as belonging together. When the unit has the same dynamic character in all respects, a balanced state exists and there is no pressure to change. When the various elements cannot coexist without stress, tension is aroused and there is pressure to change the cognitive organization to achieve a balanced state. This general proposition is simple enough, but the identification and description of the elements that result in either a balanced or an imbalanced state and the explication of methods of achieving balance become complicated processes.

Relations Among p, o, and x

Heider proposed two types of relations in the p-o-x system: unit relations and sentiment relations. *Unit relations* are either U or notU; that is, two or more elements are seen either as belonging together (U) or as not belonging together (notU). The concept of unit formation plays a critical role in Heider's theory, since the notion of a balanced state is most relevant when entities are seen as forming a unit. For example, if p likes o and dislikes x, the question of balance is of no great concern so long as o and x are seen as entirely separate entities. Heider considered the U relation as positive and the notU relation as negative, but he recognized that the notU relation is ambiguous.

According to Heider, unit formation is governed largely by the gestalt principles of perceptual organization. The major unit-forming factors are therefore similarity, proximity, common fate, good continuation, set, and past experience. It follows that two or more separate elements (entities) will be seen as belonging together if they are similar in some respect, are together in space and time, experience the same consequences, and so on. For example, two dogs walking along together are more likely to be perceived as belonging together (in unit formation) than a dog and an elephant walking in different directions. In the case of interpersonal relations, a person is often seen as being in unit formation with others of the same nationality, religion, family, and so on. Similarly, people and their actions, properties, and products are seen as belonging together. Prelinger (1959) has demonstrated experimentally that a person sees some things as related to self and others as related to nonself.

The formation of a unit may also depend upon surrounding factors. Whether two things are seen as being in unit formation varies with the properties of other entities in the environment, and an existing perceptual unit may be either strengthened or weakened by the presence of other factors. For example, if two girls are interacting, they are likely to be seen as a unit; if they are joined by a boy of the same age, the unit may be strengthened (e.g., if the girls are seven-year-olds) or weakened (e.g., if the girls are seventeen-year-olds).

Sentiment relation refers to a person's evaluation of something. It includes such relations as liking, admiring, approving, rejecting, disliking, condemning, worshipping, adoring, and similar evaluative reactions. As in the case of unit relations, sentiment relations may be either positive (designated L) or negative (designated DL). It is relatively easy to classify sentiment relations: such relations as liking, approving, and admiring are positive; disliking, disapproving, and rejecting are negative.

With regard to the sign character of relations, Cartwright and Harary (1956) pointed out that it is desirable to distinguish between the opposite of a relation and the complement of a relation. For example, the DL relation has been taken as the opposite of L, whereas the notU relation has been used as the complement of the U relation. They suggested that notU is best conceived as neutral rather than negative, and their analysis supports this view, as we shall see later.

Balanced and Imbalanced States

Heider (1958) defined a balanced state as a situation in which the relations among the entities fit together harmoniously and in which there is no stress to change. His basic assumption was that unit relations and sentiment relations tend toward a balanced state. In general, dyads are balanced when the relations between the two elements are all positive or all negative. Imbalance arises when one relation is positive and the other is negative. Triads are balanced when all three relations are positive or when two of the relations are negative and one is positive. Imbalance results when one relation is negative and two are positive. When all three elements are negative, the situation is ambiguous. (It is important to remember that the situation is always considered from p's viewpoint. Balance and imbalance result from p's cognitions.)

Examples of balanced and imbalanced situations will illustrate these proposals. If p likes x and p owns x, the dyad is balanced since two positive relations are involved; if p owns x but dislikes x, the dyad is imbalanced. Similarly, in the case of triads, if p likes both o and x, and o produced x, there are two L relations and one U relation; so the triad is balanced. If p dislikes both o and x, and o produced x, the situation is also balanced, since there are two negatives (DL's) and one positive (U) relation. If p likes o but dislikes o's product (x), the triad is imbalanced.

Consequences of the Tendency toward Balance

Heider proposed that there are at least three kinds of effects resulting from the tendency toward a balanced state: preference for balanced states, induction of relations, and change of imbalanced to balanced states. Heider's analysis led him to conclude that balanced states are preferred over imbalanced states. When the situation is imbalanced, the cognitions seem to be pulling in different directions and give the person a disturbed feeling. Heider recognized that unbalanced situations may sometimes arouse pleasure, as in the case of certain puzzles, magic tricks, and the like. However, the most common reaction is a preference for balanced states. From this proposition he inferred that balanced states would also be more stable and hence learned more quickly and remembered better than imbalanced states.

Given a particular relation, the tendency toward balance *induces* other relations that result in a balanced state. For example, p tends to dislike a dissimilar o; therefore, p dislikes o induces p dissimilar to o. Likewise, p in contact with o induces p likes o; p likes o induces p in contact with o; p likes o induces o familiar to p; p owns x induces p likes x; and so on. In more common terms, the first example above states that, if a person dislikes another, he or she will tend to see the other person as dissimilar.

Perhaps the major consequence of the tendency toward balanced states is that imbalanced states arouse pressure to change cognitive relations. In general, balance can be achieved by a change in either sentiment relations or unit relations. Consider an unbalanced triad consisting of an L relation, a DL relation, and a U relation. A balanced state can be attained by changing the L relation to DL, the DL relation to L, or the U relation to notU. For example, Joe might see a painting that he admires very much (L relation), but later he learns that the artist (U relation) is a woman he detests (DL relation). He might achieve balance by deciding that the painting is not very good after all, that the artist is really a likeable person, or that the artist did not do the painting and is claiming credit for something she did not do.

In addition, there is one other way that imbalance can be changed to balance: a change in unit relations through differentiation. That is, p can resolve imbalance by differentiating o into parts, some of which are positive and some of which are negative. In our example, Joe might decide that the part of the artist that is in unit formation with the liked painting is acceptable, but her other characteristics are still detestable. This relatively sophisticated method of achieving a balanced state is probably used infrequently.

Strengths and Weaknesses of the p-o-x Theory

The p-o-x theory is logically consistent, simple, and generally testable. It fits known data reasonably well and is not inconsistent with other accepted theories in social psychology. According to the usual criteria, then, the theory is at least minimally acceptable.

Perhaps the strongest point of the theory is that it has provided a basis for the development of other systems and has, directly or indirectly, stimulated a tremendous body of research. Although there are some notable exceptions, the support for the theory has been generally favorable. Related to this support is the fact that it provides a wealth of testable hypotheses; however, this also represents a weakness, since the predictions are not always precise. In fact, Heider stated most of his hypotheses in the form "*x* tends to produce *y*," and he maintained that exceptions do not invalidate the hypothesis of a tendency toward balance. For example, exceptions might result from uncontrolled factors that have nothing to do with the hypothesis. There may also be factors relevant to the hypothesis that have not been considered or fully analyzed. It should be evident, however, that well-designed experiments would not permit the first possibility as an attractive alternative. The second condition is of course an admission of the limitations of the balance hypothesis, at least as formulated by Heider.

The ambiguity of the notU relation has already been referred to, but it remains one of the difficulties with the p-o-x system. It can be treated as a neutral relation, as suggested by Cartwright and Harary (1956); their reanalysis of data reported by Jordon (1953) showed that treating notU as a neutral relation increased the significance of the preferences for balanced triads. Perhaps another alternative would be to limit the theory to situations involving U relations; indeed, treating the notU relation as neutral has this effect in many situations.

Heider also pointed out that the case of all negative relations is ambiguous. For example, if p dislikes o, p dislikes x, and o is not in unit formation with x, it is difficult to see why this should be unharmonious. In fact, it is difficult to see why the three relations should be considered simultaneously. On the other hand, suppose that p dislikes x, p dislikes o, but learns that o also dislikes x. In this case, some disharmony might be expected. Thus two apparently identical situations, in terms of relations, appear to produce different cognitive experiences. Newcomb (1968) suggested that p-o-x structures should be classified as balanced, nonbalanced, or imbalanced. He has shown that this three-category classification gives a better account of data from studies in which structures are rated for pleasantness than Heider's two-category classification.

Finally, it is important to note that the relations proposed by Heider are all-or-none in nature; that is, a given relation is regarded as either positive or negative with no provision for degree of positivity or negativity. Intuitively, it would be expected that the *degree* to which the relation is positive or negative would be an important determinant of balance. The principle of congruity (Osgood & Tannenbaum, 1955), which is discussed in a later section of this chapter, does take degree into account and provides for varying degrees of system balance-imbalance. The Cartwright and Harary (1956) extension of Heider's theory also provides a basis for degree of system balance. Both approaches demonstrate that the p-o-x theory would be improved if degree of positivity and negativity were considered.

The experimental evidence for the p-o-x theory falls into three general categories: preferences for balanced structures, learning and recall of balanced and imbalanced structures, and changes in relations to achieve balance in imbalanced structures. With regard to preferences, Heider cited a study by Jordon (1953) showing that, when subjects were presented with verbal descriptions of balanced and unbalanced triads, they expressed a significant preference for balanced situations. More recent studies also tend to support the theory. Crockett (1974) found that balanced states were rated as more pleasant than imbalanced states, where x was described as either a third person or a controversial political figure. The evidence was less clear when x was described as an acquaintance. In another study, ratings of structural balance correlated significantly with ratings of pleasantness, but not as highly as with ratings of tension (Gutman & Knox, 1972). Balanced triads have also been found to be more attractive than unbalanced triads (Insko & Adewole, 1979). Still another investigation revealed preferences for balanced social structures but also found that these preferences could be reversed by strategic considerations. Thus, the evidence supports the theory but also shows that other factors may be determinants of preferences (Brickman & Horn, 1973).

The p-o-x theory also suggests that balance should influence learning and recall of social structures. The evidence for this prediction is sparse but generally supportive. Two experiments tested this hypothesis directly and found that balanced structures were learned more rapidly than imbalanced ones (Yang & Yang, 1973; Zajonc & Burnstein, 1965). However, in the Yang and Yang study balanced structures were learned more quickly than imbalanced structures only by high-anxious subjects. Cottrell (1975) found that persons were more effective in classifying descriptions of triadic situations when they followed a balance rule than a rote-learning control group. In another study, subjects were asked to recall stories that were either balanced or imbalanced (Picek, Sherman, & Shiffrin, 1975). In general, balanced stories were recalled better than imbalanced ones.

Changes toward balance may involve the production of new relations, modification of sentiment or unit relations, or differentiation. Most experimenters appear to have examined the first of these, the usual method being to present incomplete triads and ask subjects to complete them by inferring the missing links. Several studies report evidence from this paradigm supporting balance theory predictions (e.g., Wyer & Lyon, 1970; Gollob & Fischer, 1973; Wellens & Thistlethwaite, 1971; Fuller, 1974; Insko, Songer, & McGarvey, 1974; deCarufel & Insko, 1979).

Differentiation as a means of achieving balance appears to be used relatively infrequently (Esch, 1950). Subjects were asked to judge what a person would be likely to do in imbalanced situations. About 2 percent thought differentiation would occur, compared with 75 percent who thought a sentiment relation would change and 5 percent who thought the unit relation would be challenged. Eighteen percent failed to resolve the imbalance. A more recent study, however, provides more supportive evidence (Stroebe, Insko, & Reisman, 1970). Subjects were given descriptions in which Dr. M supported or attacked a theory, married or divorced a wife, was an expert or an inexpert scientist, and was a nice or awful person. Dr. M as a scientist was differentiated from Dr. M as a person.

In brief summary, these representative studies generally support balance theory predictions, although there are some qualifications that require further consideration.

THE A-B-X SYSTEM

Individuals engage in a variety of behaviors vis-à-vis each other that are often referred to as "interaction." One person or group of persons may find it easier to influence another person if the group is cohesive than if it is not cohesive. If pressure is brought to bear upon a deviate group member and resisted by that member too long, the member may be rejected. Persons who interact frequently may increase their liking for each other. Newcomb (1953) believed that this general kind of social behavior can be more adequately understood as communicative acts. The A-B-X theory was developed to show how this can be done. Since the initial formulation, the theory has undergone minor modification (Newcomb, 1959, 1961), but its essential features remain unchanged. The original formulation is presented, with reference to later variations at appropriate points in the presentation.

The theory is based upon the general hypothesis that there are lawful relations among beliefs and attitudes held by a given individual, that certain combinations of beliefs and attitudes are psychologically unstable, and that such instability results in events leading to more stable combinations. To this extent, the theory does not differ from the p-o-x theory. However, Newcomb extended this hypothesis to include communications among individuals and relations within groups. His concept of system strain, discussed later, has much in common with field-theory concepts and could be considered as representing that general orientation as readily as the cognitive orientation. We elected to present it here because of its obvious similarities to other consistency theories that are more truly representative of the cognitive approach.

Newcomb (1953) began with the initial assumption that communications perform the necessary function of enabling two persons to maintain simultaneous orientations toward one another and toward objects of communication. He then presented a rationale for this assumption and derived a set of propositions from it. Before considering the system in detail, it is necessary to define certain terms that are basic to the theory.

Basic Definitions

The key concepts in the A-B-X system are communicative act, orientation, coorientation, and system strain. A *communicative act* is a transmission of information from a source to a recipient. Information consists of stimuli that are associated with a thing, state, property, or event and that enable a person to discriminate the thing, state, property, or event from other things. These stimuli were called "discriminative stimuli (see Chapter 2 for a fuller discussion of stimulus and response concepts). According to Newcomb's analysis, the simplest communicative act is the case in which one person (A) transmits information to another person (B) about something (X). He represented this act as AtoBreX.

Orientation was used by Newcomb to refer to individuals' "cognitive and cathectic habits of relating themselves" to others and to the objects around them. This is conceptually identical to the usual definition of attitude as an organization of affective and cognitive processes about some aspect of the individual's world (for example, see Krech & Crutchfield, 1948). However, Newcomb distinguished between orientations toward persons and orientations toward things. An orientation toward another person was called *attraction* and orientation toward an object was called *attitude.*

Orientations were categorized in terms of both cathectic and cognitive aspects. The cathectic aspects refer to approach-avoidance tendencies; hence, orientations vary in sign (direction) and strength. The cognitive aspects of orientations refer to the ordering, or structuring, of attributes of the object of the orientation. Discrepancies among cognitive orientations constitute the system variables of interest.

Coorientation or simultaneous orientation was used to refer to the interdependence of A's orientation toward B and toward X. The definition of coorientation was not stated explicitly, but Newcomb apparently intended it to mean that a given person orients toward another person and an object at the same time and in the same context. For example, when A attributes to B an attitude toward X, and A himself holds an attitude toward X, A is coorienting toward B and X. In this case, an individual A-B-X system exists for A.

System strain or *strain toward symmetry* refers to a state of psychological tension resulting from perceived discrepancy of self-other orientations or from uncertainty as to the other's orientation. This concept is similar to Heider's (1958) notion of tension arising from imbalanced states and resulting in a tendency toward balance. According to Newcomb (1959), the amount of system strain varies with the degree of perceived discrepancy, the sign and degree of attraction, the importance of the object of communication, the certainty of the person's own orientation, and the relevance of the object of orientation. The notion of system strain will become more meaningful when A-B-X systems have been considered in greater detail.

Systems of Orientation

Newcomb was really concerned with two kinds of systems: individual systems that are "within the person" and group systems that involve relations among persons. In both cases, the minimal components of an A-B-X system are (1) A's attitude toward X, (2) A's attraction to B, (3) B's attitude toward X, and (4) B's attraction to A. For convenience, Newcomb identified attitudes as either favorable or unfavorable (measured in terms of both sign and intensity) and attraction as either positive or negative. Thus, A and B may have similar attitudes toward X (both favorable or both unfavorable) or different attitudes toward X (one favorable and the other unfavorable). The same is true with regard to attraction. When the attitudes and/or attractions of A and B are similar, they are symmetrical; when they are dissimilar, they are asymmetrical.

In individual systems, the relations are those perceived by one person. If person A is being considered, the relations are A's orientations toward B and X and A's perceptions of B's orientations. For example, if A has a favorable attitude toward X and is attracted to B, and A perceives that B has an unfavorable attitude toward X, the system relations are asymmetrical, and there exists strain toward symmetry.

The group system was designed to fit two-person communication with several limitations imposed:

1 Communicative acts were treated as verbal acts in face-to-face situations.
2 Initiation of communication was assumed to be intentional.
3 It was assumed that the communicative act is attended to by the recipient.
4 A and B were assumed to be group members in the sense of continued association.

Coorientation was assumed to be essential to human life because orientation of A toward B seldom occurs in an *environmental* vacuum and orientation of any person toward X seldom occurs in a *social* vacuum. That is, persons rarely are able to maintain a relation between themselves without reference to others, and few objects are so private that the person's attitude toward them is uninfluenced by the attitudes of others. Therefore, Newcomb concluded that orientation toward objects and toward other persons oriented toward these same objects is a necessary process. Furthermore, to the extent that A's orientation toward either B or X depends upon B's orientation toward X, A will be motivated to discover B's orientations toward X and/or to influence B's orientation toward X. For example, if A's friend B has an unfavorable attitude toward an X that A is favorable toward, A may try to influence B in the direction of a more favorable attitude toward X.

Values of Symmetry

Symmetrical relations were seen by Newcomb as having several advantages or values to the person. The first advantage is that cognitive symmetry permits an individual to calculate (or predict) the other's behavior. If A and B have similar orientations toward X, there is less need for either of them to translate X in terms of the other's orientation and thus less chance of error. Coorientation thus becomes less difficult.

Second, there is the advantage of consensual validation of attitudes toward X. Coorientation is presumed to be rewarding (e.g., a person is more confident of his or her attitude toward X if others hold the same attitude); hence, the stronger the forces toward A's coorientation with respect to B and X, the greater will be A's strain toward symmetry with B regarding X and the greater the probability that communicative acts will lead to increased symmetry.

This postulate led to the formulation of several hypotheses. First, under conditions in which the orientation toward either B or X demands orientation toward the other, the greater the intensity of the attitude toward X and of attraction toward B, the greater the force toward coorientation. From this, it follows that the greater the intensity of the orientations toward B and X, the greater the likelihood that they will result in symmetry. Second, the likelihood of perceived symmetry increases with attraction and with intensity of attitude. This proposition was based upon the view that judgments of symmetry are influenced by autistic and reality factors, which are a function of attraction and attitude and which lead to increased perceived symmetry. Communication is the strongest reality factor, and the studies cited above reveal that this varies with attraction. Autistic factors presumably lead to distortion of perception, and these factors are stronger the greater the attraction and intensity of attitude. Third, perceived symmetry is hypothesized to be a determinant of symmetry-directed communications.

Consequences of Asymmetry

As we have already noted, asymmetry leads to tension, which activates behaviors directed toward the achievement of symmetry. It is not entirely clear whether the motivation is directed toward tension reduction or toward the advantages resulting from symmetry or both. The amount of strain toward symmetry, however, was postulated to vary with a number of factors (New-comb, 1959):

1   Degree of perceived attitude discrepancy between A and B
2   Sign and degree of attraction between A and B
3   Importance of X (the object of communication)
4   Certainty of own orientation (the degree of commitment of A and B)
5   The relevance of X to the system

These system-strain variables were categorized as accompanying either positive or negative attraction. Since this distinction is of theoretical importance, strain was labeled positive or negative strain in accordance with the sign of the attraction. For example, any time A is positively attracted to B and there is a perceived discrepancy between A's and B's attitude toward a relevant X, the system is in a state of cathectic strain, from A's viewpoint.

Newcomb identified seven ways in which an individual can reduce strain. He may (1) reduce the strength of his attraction to B, (2) reduce the relevance of X, (3) reduce the perceived relevance of X to B, (4) reduce the importance of X, (5) reduce the perceived importance of X to B, (6) change his own attitudes, or (7) change his perception of B's attitude toward X. All these can be accomplished without communication, although the processes may be facilitated through communication. As we have already indicated, A may communicate to B in an attempt to change B's attitude toward X.

At the interpersonal level, Newcomb was concerned with the relationships among orientations, system strain, and communicative behavior. He proposed that several group properties are outcomes of its communicative practices. These include *homogeneity of orientation toward certain objects, homogeneity of perceived consensus,* and *attraction among members.*

Homogeneity of orientation means that group members are in agreement with regard to expectations; for example, each person is expected to assume a particular role but it is not necessarily expected that all members will act alike. The group becomes aware of these expectations through a process of communication (verbal or nonverbal), and communication varies according to the dynamics of the A-B-X system. *Homogeneity of perceived consensus* refers to agreement in judgments concerning homogeneity of orientation. Newcomb proposed that any degree of accuracy of homogeneity of perceived consensus is the result of communication. *Attraction among members* is usually regarded as a necessary state if the group is to continue to exist. Newcomb suggested that interpersonal attraction varies with the degree to which the demands of coorientation are met by communicative acts.

Strengths and Weaknesses of the A-B-X System

In many ways, Newcomb's theory is identical with Heider's p-o-x theory. It also meets the minimal criteria for acceptance as a theory. Its strongest point probably is the extension of the balance principle to relations among persons.

His analysis clarified many aspects of the interpersonal situation and has provided interesting and testable hypotheses concerning interpersonal behavior.

There are two major weaknesses of the theory. The first is a lack of clarity of some definitions and postulates. The conception of strain and the process of strain reduction are not precisely formulated. As we noted earlier, it is not clear whether the motivation derives from a desire to achieve the advantages presumably deriving from symmetry or from the satisfying consequences of tension reduction. In several instances, it is also unclear what prediction would be made from the theory. For example, Newcomb suggested that although system strain leads to change, it does not necessarily do so. There is a strong need for a specification of the circumstances under which strain does and does not lead to system change.

Another problem is related to one of the theory's strengths: the application of balance theory to interpersonal situations. Osgood (1960) criticized Newcomb for sliding too easily from the individual to the group situation. In his explication of the theory, Newcomb did not clearly distinguish between individual and group systems. The reader cannot always tell whether a given principle applies to the individual system, to the group system, or to both. The problem of negative relations raises special difficulties when the elements in a triad are three persons. Price, Harburg, and Newcomb (1966) reported a failure to verify balance theory predictions concerning affective reactions to triads involving two or more negative relations. They proposed the concepts of *uncertainty, ambivalence,* and *engagement* to account for their findings. They suggested that when relations among persons are positive, assumptions of reciprocity can be made with confidence; however, when relations are negative, such assumptions cannot be made dependably. Paralleling this uncertainty is a degree of ambivalence toward disliked others (negative relation). As a consequence of these factors, there is less engagement in situations involving negative relations than in those involving positive relations. That is, in a situation involving negative relations among three persons, A, B, and X, each is unconcerned with the attitudes, beliefs, and feelings of the other two.

The experimental evidence regarding the A-B-X system is not extensive, but it is generally supportive. Newcomb (1961) reported an extensive study of the acquaintance process based upon the A-B-X system. Two sets of 17 male students were provided a rent-free house in return for their services as experimental subjects. In each case, the students were observed, tested, questioned, rated, and so on for several hours per week over an entire semester. The subjects had been selected as total strangers at the beginning of the semester. He found a strong tendency for those who were attracted to one another to agree on the way they perceived themselves, their ideal selves, and their attractions to other group members. Both real and perceived similarities tended to increase over time, in agreement with predictions from the theory. In a later report (Newcomb, 1963), however, he noted that estimates of others' attraction toward oneself did not become more accurate with increasing acquaintance, contrary to theoretical expectations.

Experimental studies by Burdick and Burnes (1958) also yielded results in support of the theory. In one study they found that measures of the galvanic skin response, assumed to be an index of emotional reaction, were significantly different when the subject agreed with a well-liked experimenter than when he disagreed with the same experimenter. The results of a second study showed that subjects who liked the experimenter changed their opinions in the direction of agreement with him and those who disliked the experimenter changed their opinions in the direction of disagreement.

THE PRINCIPLE OF CONGRUITY

Throughout recorded history people have tried to change the attitudes of other people. Politicians try to influence people to view them favorably; men and women in business try to induce favorable attitudes toward their products; all of us try to get others to agree with our cherished beliefs and attitudes. It is not surprising that the study of attitude change has occupied a central position in social psychology.

The congruity theory (Osgood & Tannenbaum, 1955) is a theoretical model that was designed to account for the most significant variables in attitude change. The theory was concerned with prediction of attitude change in a typical experimental situation in which a communication from an identifiable source urges a person (the subject) to adopt a particular attitude toward some object. The variables that were deemed as most important in this situation included the existing attitude toward the attitude object,[1] the existing attitude toward the source of a message about the attitude object, and the evaluative nature of the assertion relating source and attitude object. Osgood and Tannenbaum believed that their model would permit predictions of the directions and amounts of attitude change toward both the source and the attitude object.

Underlying Assumptions

The congruity theory grew out of research concerning the meaning of concepts. The general view emerging from this research was that the connotative meaning of a concept can be defined by its location in space on a number of dimensions (Osgood, 1952). Research yielded three factors, labeled evaluation, activity, and potency. Osgood assumed that the evaluative factor represented the rater's attitude toward the concept being rated. Hence, *attitude* toward an attitude object (concept) is its projection onto the evaluative dimension of semantic space. That is, attitude toward an object is an evaluation of that object.

A second underlying notion was that judgmental frames of reference tend toward maximal simplicity. This notion led to two correlated assumptions: first, it was assumed that extreme all-or-none judgments are simpler than more finely discriminated judgments of degree. If this is true, it suggests that there is

[1]Osgood and Tannenbaum used the term "concept" in referring to the thing toward which persons hold attitudes; we have used "attitude object" because we believe this term is more descriptive than "concept."

continuing pressure toward polarization along the evaluative dimension; that is, there is a tendency for objects to be viewed as either all good or all bad. Second, Osgood and Tannenbaum proposed that the assumption of identity is a simpler process than maintenance of distinction; therefore, there should be a continuing pressure toward the elimination of differences among objects which are evaluated in the same direction. That is, all objects that are viewed as good in any degree should be viewed as the same or at least similar, and all those viewed as bad to some degree should be grouped together.

The set of assumptions regarding judgmental simplicity led to the conclusion that the simplest frame of reference is one that consists of two tight clusters of polarized, undifferentiated concepts that are diametrically opposed on the evaluative dimension. This frame of reference operates to push any new concept toward one or another of the two clusters. The less sophisticated the person, the more likely it is that he or she will adopt this simplistic judgmental frame.

The Congruity Principle

The principle of congruity, as formulated by Osgood and Tannenbaum, states that changes in evaluation always occur in the direction of increased congruence with the person's frame of reference. That is, when two or more attitude objects are linked by an assertion, there is a tendency for the evaluation of one or both of the objects to change so that the evaluations of the two objects are more similar. For example, if Senator Kennedy (positively evaluated) praises (associative assertion) Arafat (negatively evaluated), there is a tendency for Kennedy to be evaluated more negatively and Arafat more positively.

In applying the principle to specific situations, it was necessary to consider (1) situations in which congruity is an issue, (2) the directions of change that lead to congruence, and (3) the amount of stress created by incongruity and its distribution among attitude objects.

The Issue of Congruity   Osgood and Tannenbaum asserted that the issue of congruity arises only when two or more attitude objects are related by an assertion. Although "assertion" was not explicitly defined, it apparently refers to any statement linking two objects. Assertions vary in complexity and in direction. The simplest assertion is a *descriptive statement,* such as "modern art is interesting." This may create some pressure to change if parts of the assertion are different in evaluation; that is, if "modern art" is evaluated negatively and "interesting" is evaluated positively. *Statements of classification,* such as "John is a senator," may arouse stress similar to that produced by descriptive statements. More-complex assertions are those in which a *source makes a statement about an object,* such as "university administration denies tenure to advocate of civil rights." With regard to direction, assertions may be either associative (positive) or disassociative (negative). An associative assertion is a statement such as "John is intelligent," "Tom likes Mary," and the like. Statements such as "John is not intelligent" or "Tom does not like Mary" are disassociative assertions.

Assertions may reflect evaluations of (attitudes toward) an object, and in these cases the issue of congruence arises. Attitudes, according to Osgood and Tannenbaum, can be positive, negative, or neutral. When attitudes toward both the source and the attitude object are polarized, the nature of the assertion determines congruence or incongruence. The general notion propounded by Osgood and Tannenbaum is that sources that we evaluate favorably should support the things that we support, like the things that we like, and so on. Similarly, sources that we dislike should attack the things we support and dislike the things we like. For example, if a university president (positive) supports academic freedom (positive), this would be consistent with the frame of reference of most university professors and hence attitudinally congruent. On the other hand, if the university president (positive) came out in opposition to academic freedom (negative), it would be incongruent.

If the evaluations of both the source and the object are neutral, the issue of congruence between them does not arise. Any change in evaluations will be determined completely by the nature of the assertion. For example, if John praises Tom (neither of whom is known, hence neutral), the evaluation of Tom is likely to increase because the assertion was positive. That is, Tom gains in value through the simple process of "being praised." The effect of the assertion is on the recipient rather than on the source.

The Directions of Change   From these considerations, Osgood and Tannenbaum stated the following principle of congruity:

Whenever one object of judgment is associated with another by an assertion, its congruent position along the evaluative dimension is always equal in degree of polarization (d) to the other object of judgment and in either the same (positive assertion) or opposite (negative assertion) evaluative direction (Osgood & Tannenbaum, 1955, p. 45).

This principle asserts that, if two attitude scores toward two attitude objects AO_1 and AO_2 are assigned a value d representing degree of polarization, the congruent position can be defined as follows: When AO_1 is positively related to AO_2 the congruent position of AO_1 is equal to the polarization of AO_2. When the two attitude objects are negatively related by the assertion, the congruent position of AO_1 is equal to that of AO_2 but in the opposite direction.

Since attitude scores were derived from the semantic differential, they ranged from 1 to 7, with 4 treated as neutral.[2] For convenience, negative scores were assigned values of -1, -2, and -3 and positive scores values of $+1$, $+2$, and $+3$; the midpoint was assigned a value of zero. Thus three degrees of polarization in each direction are possible. When a source and an attitude object are linked by a positive assertion, and the polarization score of the source is $+2$, congruence requires that the polarization score of the attitude object be $+2$. The degree to which the polarization scores depart from the congruent position is a measure of incongruity.

---

[2]The assumption that the midpoint of a rating scale represents a neutral attitude is open to question, as we shall see later.

Amount and Distribution of Pressure   The total amount and distribution of pressure toward congruity may be derived from principle 1, as stated in principle 2:

> *The total available pressure toward congruity (P) for a given object of judgment associated with another by an assertion is equal to the difference, in attitude scale units, between its existing location and its location of maximum congruence along the evaluative dimension; the sign of this pressure is positive (+) when the location of congruence is more favorable than the existing location and negative (−) when the location of congruence is less favorable than the existing location* (Osgood & Tannenbaum, 1955, p. 46).

Principle 2 thus asserts that the total pressure to change an evaluation of either the attitude object or the source is equal to the difference between its polarization and the point of maximum congruence. For example, if source and attitude object are related by a positive assertion, and the initial polarization of the source is +3 and the initial polarization of the attitude object is +1, the total pressure to change the evaluation of the attitude object is +2. That is, there is a pressure of two units to change the attitude in a more favorable direction. The pressure to change the evaluation of the source is of the same magnitude but in the opposite direction, that is, −2.

The third principle was based on the assumption that intense attitudes are more resistant to change than less-intense attitudes:

> *In terms of producing attitude change, the total pressure toward congruity is distributed between the objects of judgment associated by an assertion in inverse proportion to their separate degrees of polarization* (Osgood & Tannenbaum, 1955, p. 46).

Principle 3 may be stated alternatively in the following formula:[3]

$$AC_{ao} = \frac{d_s}{d_{ao} + d_s} P_{ao}$$

where AC_{ao} is change in the evaluation of the attitude object (attitude change), d_s is the degree of polarization of the source with direction ignored, d_{ao} is the degree of polarization of the attitude object without regard to direction, and P_{ao} is the total pressure to change the evaluation of the attitude object. Similarly, the predicted amount of change in evaluation of the *source* is given by the formula:

$$AC_s = \frac{d_{ao}}{d_s + d_{ao}} P_s$$

The formulas above make the implicit assumption that assertions are credible. However, Osgood and Tannenbaum noted that not all assertions are

[3]The symbols have been changed to make them consistent with our terminology, but the formula is essentially the same as that given by Osgood and Tannenbaum.

believable, especially in an experimental situation. For example, a statement such as "Hitler loved Jews" is not likely to be accepted at face value. Principle 4 attempted to take the variable of credulity into account:

> *The amount of incredulity produced when one object of judgment is associated with another by an assertion is a positively accelerated function of the amount of incongruity which exists and operates to decrease attitude change, completely eliminating change when maximal* (Osgood & Tannenbaum, 1955, p. 47).

Incredulity is limited to situations in which incongruity arises; that is, when similarly evaluated objects are associated by a positive assertion. According to principle 4, the amount of incredulity in such situations increases with the total amount of pressure toward congruity. The predicted attitude change (AC) must therefore be corrected for incredulity. The exact nature of the incredulity function was regarded as an empirical question, although the following function was proposed as an approximation:

$$i = \frac{1}{40} (d_s^2 + 1) (d_{ao}^2 + d_{ao})$$

where i refers to incredulity and $\frac{1}{40}$ and 1 are constants; d_s and d_{ao} refer, of course, to degree of polarization of source and attitude object, respectively. In predicting attitude change, the correction for incredulity (i) is always added to predicted negative change and subtracted from predicted positive change; that is, the effect of the correction is always a reduction in the amount of predicted change.

Still another correction was proposed for the prediction of change in attitude toward the attitude object: a correction for the direction of the assertion. It was pointed out that, in the typical case, the assertion is directed toward the attitude object rather than toward the source. If A praises B, the praise applies primarily to B. Similarly, when A denounces B, the denunciation applies chiefly to B. Therefore, Osgood and Tannenbaum proposed an "assertion constant" ($\pm A$) which must be added when predicting attitude change toward the attitude object. The sign of the constant is always the same as that of the assertion. The value of this constant was determined empirically to be approximately $\frac{1}{6}$ of a scale unit.

Corollaries of the Congruity Principle

Five corollaries were derived from the principle of congruity. These may be paraphrased as follows:

1 Changes in evaluation are always in the direction of equalization of polarization of objects associated by an assertion.
2 With a given degree of pressure toward congruity, it is easier to change toward greater than toward lesser polarization.

3 Amount of attitude change is an inverse function of the intensity of the initial attitude toward the object.

4 Attitude change toward an attitude object (or source) in the direction of an assertion is an approximately linear function of degree of favorableness of the initial attitude toward the source with which it is associated.

5 When two differently polarized, nonneutral objects are linked by a congruent assertion, the more-polarized object becomes less so.

Evaluation of the Congruity Principle

Like the two previous theories, the congruity principle is logically consistent and testable. It is moderately simple and is easily understood by anyone who takes the trouble to read its principles carefully. It has served a useful purpose in stimulating research and articulating variables that have been neglected by other theories. However, it agrees with known data only moderately well. The theory appears to predict direction of attitude change, but it is less than adequate in predicting degree of change.

The congruity theory has accomplished at least one very significant advance over previous attempts to predict attitude change: it has provided a method for making precise mathematical predictions of the amount and direction of change. This exact formulation makes explicit the implications of the theory and permits direct testing of predictions. However, there are, as usual, certain criticisms that may be directed toward the theory. We have already mentioned the lack of a precise definition of "assertion" and the problem of treating the midpoint of a rating scale as reflecting a neutral attitude. Although it is clear that an assertion is a statement linking two things (usually a source and an attitude object), the treatment of types of assertions and how these affect pressure toward congruity was not spelled out in detail. The distinction between associative and disassociative assertions is especially vague.

The problem of "neutral attitude" is well known but unsolved. Theorists disagree widely about even the *existence* of a neutral attitude (see Shaw & Wright, 1967, for a discussion of this controversy). However, in connection with the congruity theory, we are more concerned with the meaning of a particular point on a rating scale. To identify any particular score as a neutral point, it is necessary to show, at minimum, that persons who earn such a score do in fact perceive themselves as being neutral toward the object being evaluated. There seems to be no evidence that the midpoint on the semantic differential meets even this minimal requirement (or that it does not).

Several other problems should be considered. First, the precision achieved by considering degree of evaluation was not extended to assertions. It seems intuitively clear that the intensity of the assertion should be a factor in attitude change. Faint praise would not be expected to have as much effect as a highly laudatory commendation.

Second, the importance and relevance of the attitude for the person is ignored. It is possible that an individual may hold an intense attitude toward an object that is of little importance to him and/or is of little relevance to him. The effect of these variables is not clear, but there is some evidence (Kerrick, 1958) that the congruity theory predicts better for relevant than for nonrelevant sources.

Third, the theory may be criticized for limiting the resolution of incongruity to changing evaluations of the source and attitude object (Brown, 1962). This is legitimate criticism, although in a later report that considered other consistency theories as well as the congruity model, Osgood (1960) listed six methods of achieving congruity:

1   The sign or existence of a relationship may be changed.
2   The sign or existence of a cognitive element may be changed.
3   Other cognitive elements that are in a relation of balance with the dissonant elements may be added (bolstering).
4   Other cognitive elements that are in a relation of imbalance with the dissonant elements may be added (undermining).
5   One or more of the dissonant elements may be divided so that one part is in balance with the other cognitions (differentiation).
6   Dissonant elements may be combined into a larger unit which is balanced (transcendence).

These methods, of course, do not apply exclusively to the principle of congruity. The general problem of determining when each of the various modes of resolution will be utilized also remains unsolved. This problem is discussed more fully in a later section of this chapter.

Fourth, polarity and intensity appear to be used interchangeably. Although it is true that more-extreme (highly polarized) attitudes are usually more intense, it is possible to hold an extreme attitude of low intensity, and vice versa. However, the degree of correspondence between polarity and intensity is sufficiently close that failure to distinguish between them probably introduces little error of prediction.

Finally, Insko (1967) objected to the corrections for incredulity and assertions. He correctly noted that these corrections do not follow from the principle of congruity; however, his suggestion that they were introduced to "patch up" the implications of the congruity principle does not seem warranted. There is no reason why more than one principle should not be used in formulating a theory; in fact, it appears that the congruity theory could be much improved by a consideration of still more variables that are known to affect attitude change.

The experimental evidence generally supports the theory. For example, Jones and Kohler (1958) found that subjects with prosegregation attitudes learned plausible prosegregation statements and implausible antisegregation statements more rapidly than implausible prosegregation and plausible antisegregation statements. The opposite was found for subjects holding antisegregation attitudes. This finding supports the notion of incredulity. However, Waly and Cook (1966) failed to replicate the Jones and Kohler results. As noted above, Kerrick (1958) presented evidence supporting the theory when the situation was relevant to the subject. A later study (Kerrick & McMillan, 1961) compared informed and uninformed subjects with respect to attitude change. It reported that attitude change was in the expected direction in all cases in which subjects were uninformed (which, of course, is the situation to which congruity theory applies). Tannenbaum and Gengel (1966) produced changes in experimentally created attitudes in a manner consistent with the congruity principle. Fishbein and his associates (Triandis & Fishbein, 1963; Fishbein & Hunter, 1964; Anderson & Fishbein, 1965) applied the model to evaluations of composite stimuli with varying degrees of success. It is questionable, however, whether the theory was intended to apply to this kind of situation. Although not designed to test congruity theory, research by Eiser and White (1975) and by Trope and Burnstein (1977) yielded results that are generally consistent with the theory.

A THEORY OF COGNITIVE DISSONANCE

The theory of cognitive dissonance grew out of an interest in understanding the general area of communication and social influence (Festinger, 1957). This broad area includes the study of rumors, the effects of mass media, interpersonal communication, attitude change, and similar phenomena. Once formulated, however, the theory was used to attempt to understand and explain an even broader range of phenomena. The theory is like other consistency theories in that the essential principle is a tendency toward consistency or balance. However, the theory differs from other theories in two important respects: (1) it purports to deal with cognitive behavior in general and hence is not primarily a theory of social behavior and (2) its influence on social psychological research has been much more dramatic than that of any other consistency theory. It is probable that this latter effect is because of Festinger's genius in formulating intriguing hypotheses rather than of the characteristics of the theory per se.

The basic core of the theory of cognitive dissonance is deceptively simple: there may exist "nonfitting" relations among cognitive elements that give rise to cognitive dissonance; cognitive dissonance creates pressures to reduce dissonance and to avoid increases in dissonance; the results of such pressures are manifested by changes in cognition, behavior changes, and selective exposure to new information and opinions. However, problems related to the nature of the "nonfitting" relations, the nature of dissonance, and the modes of dissonance reduction are complex problems indeed.

In this presentation, we begin with an outline of the model as originally presented in 1957, followed by a consideration of the more-significant modifications of the theory. An evaluation of the theory is also attempted, although a detailed evaluation that does justice to the mass of experimental data that have accumulated is beyond the scope of this book.

Definition of Dissonance

Believing that "consistency" and "inconsistency" possess unwanted logical connotations, Festinger substituted the terms "consonance" and "dissonance," respectively. Dissonance and consonance were used to refer to relations that exist between pairs of elements. *Elements* were defined as cognitions, where the term *cognition* refers to any knowledge, opinion, belief, or feeling about one's self or one's environment. Elements, then, are knowledges that a person has about his or her psychological world. Festinger raised two questions in connection with the notion of elements of cognition: (1) When is an element of cognition a single element and when is it a group of elements? (2) How are cognitive elements formed and what determines their content? The first question was left unanswered, but Festinger asserted that this lack poses no problem of measurement. In answering the second question, he proposed that the most important determinant of cognitive elements is reality.

Relations were classified as irrelevant, dissonant, or consonant. If two elements have nothing to do with each other, then one cognitive element implies nothing about the other. A relation of irrelevance exists between them. For example, suppose that a person "knows" that it never snows in Hawaii and that jet airliners can fly faster than the speed of sound. The two cognitions have nothing to do with each other; hence, an irrelevant relation exists between them. (Most persons would probably say that there is *no* relation between them.) A relation of irrelevance is similar to Heider's notU relation. On the other hand, there are cognitions that are related in such a way that one implies something about the other. The relation between them is relevant and may be either consonant or dissonant.

Dissonance was defined in the following way: Two elements are in a dissonant relation if, considering the two alone, the obverse[4] of one would follow from the other. For example, if a person is standing in the rain, it would follow that he or she should get wet. Therefore, cognitions of a person standing in the rain and not getting wet would be in a dissonant relation. A *consonant* relation exists when two elements are relevant and not dissonant, that is, when one cognition follows from the other. It is not always easy to determine whether the obverse of one element follows from the other, and in this respect the definitions of dissonance and consonance are ambiguous. To complicate the situation further, Festinger asserted that motivations are desired consequences and may also be factors in the determination of dissonance. For example, he cited the case of a man who continues gambling and losing money in a card game with professional gamblers. Continuing to play is dissonant with cognitions about the other players, but, if the man wanted to lose, continuing to play would be consonant with cognitions about the other players.

The phrase "follows froim" also may take on different meanings, suggesting that dissonance may arise from several sources. Festinger identified four: (1) *logical inconsistency* (e.g., the belief that water freezes at 0 degrees Celsius is inconsistent with the belief that ice will not melt at 30 degrees Celsius); (2)

---

[4]Festinger apparently used the word "obverse" in a highly specialized way. "Obverse" usually refers to an opposite view of the same fact. For example, the obverse of "A is B" would be "not A is not B." Clearly, this is not what Festinger meant when he used the term; instead, he used "obverse" to refer to the negation of a given fact. For example, according to his usage, the obverse of "A is B" would be "A is not B."

cultural mores (what follows from a given cognition in one culture may be just the opposite in another culture); (3) *opinion generality* (dissonance may arise because an opinion is included in a more general opinion, as when a Democrat prefers a Republican candidate); and (4) *past experience* (dissonance will arise if a cognition is inconsistent with past experience).

Magnitude of Dissonance

Since not all dissonant relations are of equal magnitude, Festinger attempted to identify the determinants of the strength of dissonant relations between two elements and between two clusters of elements. His general proposition was that the magnitude of dissonance between two elements is a function of the importance of the elements to the individual. Two elements that are of little consequence are not likely to arouse much dissonance, regardless of how inconsistent they may be. On the other hand, two very important dissonant elements may be expected to arouse considerable dissonance.

The definition of dissonance involves two elements taken alone; however, it is unlikely that the individual ever considers only two elements. Instead, any given element is relevant to many others, and some of these are likely to be consonant and others dissonant. Festinger noted that it is rare for no dissonance at all to exist within a cluster of elements. It is therefore necessary to consider the total amount of dissonance between any given element and other cognitive elements relevant to it. Accordingly, he asserted that the total amount of dissonance between a given element and other cognitions will depend upon the weighted proportion of relevant elements that are dissonant with the one in question. "Weighted proportion" was meant to indicate that each relevant relation should be weighted in proportion to the importance of the elements involved in the relation. Unfortunately, he provided no way of determining relevant relations or degree of importance.

The maximum amount of dissonance possible was said to be equal to the total resistance to change of the least resistant element. When dissonance reaches this level of magnitude, the element will change and dissonance will be reduced. Of course, it is possible that changing the least-resistant element will create greater dissonance in some other system, in which case the element would not be changed.

Consequences of Dissonance

The general consequences of dissonance were indicated by two basic hypotheses. First, dissonance is psychologically uncomfortable and motivates the person to try to reduce dissonance and achieve consonance. For example, suppose a person buys a new car and then learns that friends think it is a "lemon." Dissonance will be aroused and the person will be motivated to reduce it. This can be accomplished by selling the car (changing a behavioral element), convincing friends that the car is in fact a fine machine (changing an environmental cognitive element), or obtaining favorable opinions about the quality of the car from others (adding new cognitive elements).

The second hypothesis states that, when dissonance is present, the person not only tries to reduce it, but also actively avoids situations and information that are likely to increase it. For instance, a person who has just purchased a Mazda probably will not read advertisements for other kinds of cars. Seeking new information is a highly selective process.

Implications of the Theory

According to Festinger, the theory has important implications for many specific situations. He considered implications for decisions, forced compliance, exposure to information, and social support.

Decisions   Festinger asserted that dissonance is an inevitable consequence of decision. This proposition is based upon the notion that an individual must be faced with a conflict situation before a decision can be made; that is, a "decision" between an alternative that is all good and one that is all bad cannot properly be called a decision. Therefore, there may be decisions between two completely negative alternatives, two alternatives having both positive and negative aspects, or among several alternatives. (Festinger did not indicate that a decision may also be between two completely positive alternatives, but it seems apparent that this decision is at least theoretically possible.) In each of these cases, the choice of one alternative results in a dissonant relation between the knowledge that a choice has been made and one or more aspects of the two alternatives. In the typical case, the dissonant elements are the negative aspects of the chosen alternative and the positive aspects of the rejected alternative.

The magnitude of postdecision dissonance, according to Festinger, is determined by the importance of the decision, the relative attractiveness of the unchosen alternative, and the degree of cognitive overlap of the alternatives involved in the decision. The more important the decision and the more attractive the unchosen alternative, the greater the dissonance. The effect of cognitive overlap is perhaps less evident. The consideration here is that many elements may be common to the two alternatives. Such common elements would not be expected to contribute to dissonance; hence, the greater the cognitive overlap, the less the dissonance created by the decision.

Pressure to reduce postdecision dissonance may be manifested by revocation of the decision, altered attractiveness of the alternatives, or the creation of cognitive overlap.

Forced Compliance   The application of dissonance theory to forced-compliance situations is limited to public compliance without an accompanying change of private opinion at that time. Such public compliance is brought about through either threats of punishment or promises of reward. The source of dissonance is the person's awareness of having behaved publicly in a manner that is inconsistent with private opinions. The magnitude of dissonance is a function of the importance of the private opinions and the magnitude of the punishment or reward. The more important the opinions, the greater the dissonance, but the *smaller* the punishment or reward, the greater the dissonance. (Of course, the reward or punishment must be sufficient to elicit the desired compliance.) Dissonance resulting from forced compliance can be reduced by subsequent change of private opinion or by magnification of the reward or punishment.

Exposure to Information   As stated earlier, dissonance results in selective exposure to information: the individual will seek consonance-producing information and avoid dissonance-producing information. Festinger hypothesized that active information seeking is curvilinearly related to the magnitude of dissonance. If there is little or no dissonance, the person will neither seek consonant nor avoid dissonant information. Moderate amounts of dissonance lead to maximum information-seeking/avoidance behavior. With near-maximum dissonance there is again a decrease in selective exposure, and the person may actually seek out dissonance-producing information. This latter is based upon the assumption that the person will try to increase the dissonance to an intolerable level that will bring about a change in some aspect of the situation and, ultimately, dissonance reduction. In cases of involuntary exposure to dissonance-producing information, the person may alternatively set up defensive processes that prevent the cognition from becoming firmly established as part of the person's cognitive system.

Social Support   Cognitive dissonance may be produced by a person who knows that another person holds an opinion that is contrary to his or her own. This aspect of the theory is closely related to Festinger's social comparison theory (Festinger, 1950, 1954; see Chapter 11). The magnitude of dissonance produced by the lack of social support is a function of (1) the extent to which objective, nonsocial cognitive elements that are consonant with the person's opinion exist, (2) the number of persons known to the individual who have the same opinion, (3) the importance of the elements, (4) the relevance of the disagreeing person or group to the opinion, (5) the attractiveness of the disagreeing person or group, and (6) the extent of the disagreement. Such dissonance may be reduced by changing one's own opinion, by influencing those who disagree to change their opinion, or by making those who disagree not comparable to oneself.

Modifications of Dissonance Theory

Research findings have led to several suggested changes in the theory that are primarily restrictive in nature; that is, they suggest that the theory applies only under certain conditions. Early modifications and limitations were suggested by Brehm and Cohen (1962). They emphasized the roles of *commitment* and *volition* in the arousal of dissonance. They maintained that whether one cognition follows from another depends on the degree of commitment. For example, if a person makes a decision but is free to reverse the decision, no dissonance should be aroused, whereas an irreversible decision would be expected to create dissonance and lead to dissonance-reducing processes.

Volition or choice is also important: the individual must believe that he or she has acted *voluntarily* in order for dissonance to occur. More recently, Wicklund and Brehm (1976) conducted an extensive review of the literature dealing with the theory and concluded that the only necessary modification is that the person must feel *responsible* for bringing the inconsistent cognition into the inconsistent relationship. Recent research supports this position (Goethals, Cooper, & Naficy, 1979). It was found that dissonance could be produced by behavior that was performed where no negative consequences were explicitly foreseen, although it is possible that subjects believed they should have foreseen the bad effects of their actions.

Festinger has also made some modifications in the original theory. In the 1957 version, he assumed that prior to a decision the individual is faced with a conflict situation during which information relevant to the decision is sought and evaluated objectively. Only after the decision is made does the person experience dissonance and try to reduce it. Predecision conflict was presumed to increase the magnitude of postdecision dissonance: the greater the prior conflict, the greater the dissonance following a decision. Postdecision dissonance was said to be at maximum immediately after the decision, declining with the passage of time. Later, he modified these views in at least three ways (Festinger, 1964). First, he came to the conclusion that predecision activity probably has some effect on postdecision behavior, although the nature of this effect could not be specified at that time. Second, he accepted the notion of commitment proposed by Brehm and Cohen. However, he proposed that a person is committed to a decision if the decision unequivocally affects subsequent behavior. He rejected the notion that the decision must be irrevocable in order for the person to feel committed to it. Thus, his 1964 version limited dissonance theory (at least as applied to decisions) to the situation in which the individual experiences commitment. Third, he changed his view of the course of dissonance following a decision. His modified view was that there is a period immediately following the decision in which the decision maker experiences regret. This is the period after the decision and before dissonance reduction becomes effective. Although he is not very clear on this point, it appears that he believed dissonance and regret are experienced simultaneously.

Aronson (1968) suggested that dissonance theory had neglected several variables of importance. First, the theory assumes, at least implicitly, that all persons respond in the same way to dissonance and that no one has much tolerance for dissonance. Aronson argued that dissonance may be tolerated and that people differ in degree of tolerance. He suggested that individual differences need to be considered. His major point, however, was that Festinger mislocated the source of dissonance. According to Aronson, what is dissonant is the relation between cognitions and self-concept. People usually regard themselves as sensible persons, and the knowledge that they have behaved in nonsensical ways is inconsistent with their cognitions about themselves. For example, if a woman considers herself to be a good mother and at the same time knows that she abuses her child, she should experience dissonance. Thus, expectancy plays an important role in the production of dissonance: The individual expects to behave in a certain way and behavior that contradicts that expectancy arouses dissonance.

Bramel (1968) took a similar position, although he did not agree with Aronson on all points. He asserted that dissonance arises when (1) the individual encounters information which disconfirms an expectation and/or when (2) he discovers that he has chosen incompetently or immorally. He proposed that dissonance is a feeling of personal unworthiness—a type of anxiety. This feeling probably can be traced to rejection of the person by others either in the present or in the past. He also suggested that the reason dissonance is greatest when a person feels responsible for his behavior is that this corresponds to the situation under which rejection most frequently occurs. The basis for these speculations was the observation that experimental results which most strongly and consistently support dissonance theory predictions have been found in situations in which both disconfirmation of expectation and incompetent or immoral behavior occurred.

The original theory of cognitive dissonance made no provision for individual differences, but later theorizing introduced this factor. For instance, Aronson (1968) proposed three ways that individual differences are relevant to the theory: (1) people differ in their ability to tolerate dissonance, (2) people may differ in their preferred mode of dissonance reduction, and (3) people may differ in the kinds of things that are dissonant or consonant. Individual-difference variables are also considered important by other dissonance theorists (e.g., Wicklund & Brehm, 1976; Sherman & Gorkin, 1980).

Some writers have interpreted Festinger's (1964) statements as implying that successful dissonance reduction tends to be irreversible (Lepper, Zanna, & Abelson, 1970). This particular hypothesis is controversial, with some theorists supporting it (Lepper et al., 1970) and others presenting evidence of reversibility (Wilhelmy, 1974; Wilhelmy & Duncan, 1974; Higgins, Rhodewalt, & Zanna, 1979).

Finally, some persons have maintained that the effects attributed to dissonance arousal and attempted reduction can be explained more plausibly and simply without assuming the existence of dissonance at all. Perhaps the most publicized alternative is self-perception theory (Bem, 1965), which is presented in some detail in Chapter 9. Briefly, self-perception theory holds that people's beliefs and attitudes, and the beliefs and attitudes that others attribute to them are both partial inferences from the same evidence, namely, the public behaviors and accompanying stimulus cues that have been learned through socialization. It is argued that the effects observed in dissonance experiments occur because of the judgmental and self-observational abilities of the subjects, rather than because dissonance has been aroused. In support of this view, Bem has shown that, if such experiments are described to subjects and they are asked to predict results, their predictions agree with actual findings (Bem, 1965, 1972). On the other hand, Wicklund and Brehm (1978) argue that the self-perception experiments cannot precisely replicate the results of dissonance experiments and the self-perception theory cannot adequately explain dissonance phenomena related to clarity of decision consequences, alternative modes of dissonance arousal, resistance to change of cognitive elements, surprise consequences and responsibility, and dissonance as a tension state. We will consider the evidence for and against self-perception theory in Chapter 9.

Impression management theory has also been proposed as an alternative to dissonance theory (Tedeschi, Schlenker, & Bonoma, 1971). They maintained that dissonance phenomena can be more coherently explained by a single hypothesis, namely, that subjects in dissonance experiments are engaged in managing the impressions that the experimenter forms about them. Consistency of words and deeds presumably enhances an individual's credibility and thus enables him or her to be more successful in influencing others. According to their arguments, contradictory cognitions will lead to discomfort (dissonance?) only if the person believes that others perceive that the person is being inconsistent. (See Chapter 12 for an elaboration of impression management theory.)

With respect to the forced-compliance paradigm in dissonance research, Nuttin (1975) proposed a response-contagion theory as an alternative to dissonance theory. According to this view, when people are asked to make two evaluative responses, such as a forced-compliance response and responses to an attitude scale, response contagion occurs to the degree that the two responses are in close temporal proximity and to the degree that the first is subject to *perturbation*. Perturbation results when an individual is subjected to unexpected or undesirable treatments, and is said to generate arousal. This arousal, in turn, energizes whatever response is in progress at the time. Thus, there will be contagion from the first to the second response, resulting in a shift in direction that is consistent with the perturbed response. Aside from the fact that response contagion applies only to forced-compliance situations, evidence relative to the theory is limited. On the other hand, Cooper (1980) suggested the interesting hypothesis that dissonance theory can explain positive changes that result from psychotherapy. For example, he demonstrated that persons who expend much effort in attempting to reduce fears and increase assertiveness changed in the desired direction, but only under conditions of high decision freedom.

In concluding this section, it should be noted that many theorists believe that one or more of the attribution theories presented in Chapter 9 can also explain dissonancelike phenomena.

Evaluation of Dissonance Theory

Of all the consistency theories, the theory of cognitive dissonance has been by far the most popular—and the most unpopular. It has been tested, questioned, applied, modified, vilified, accepted, and rejected. The reasons for this furious reaction to a basically simple theory are not easy to identify. The supporters of the theory are obviously active researchers, and their penchant for predicting nonobvious results undoubtedly contributed to its popularity. Perhaps it has aroused so much negative reaction because it threatened many pet theories. Whatever the reasons, it has stimulated massive research, and for many this research is sufficient justification for greatness.

Dissonance theory is logically consistent, permits the formulation of testable hypotheses, and is basically simple. Some of its predictions are not consistent with widely accepted theories (for example, reinforcement theory), but it is necessary to point out that these other theories are not universally accepted. It is also not always evident just what the theory would predict in certain relevant situations.

The major difficulties inherent in cognitive dissonance theory involve inadequate definitions, the problem of arousal, multiple modes of dissonance reduction, and oversimplification. The major sources of ambiguity with regard to definitions center around the concepts of *elements, inconsistency, relations,* and *relevance.* The theory assumes that there are elements (attitudes, cognitions) that are mutually relevant and that may be related in inconsistent ways. The definition of an element is very broad: an element is a cognition, and a cognition is "knowledge" about the individual's world. Pepitone (1966) noted the problems this imprecise definition has caused in experimentation relative to dissonance theory.

The definition of inconsistency or dissonance is also a problem, and this is of course tied in with the problem of relations. Two elements or cognitions are said to be in a dissonant relation if the opposite of one "follows from" the other. How one is to determine what follows from what is left unexplained. Similarly, there is no clear specification of relevance; there is no way of determining (from the theory) when two cognitive elements are mutually relevant.

It is proposed by the theory that dissonance is a motivational state aroused by the existence of dissonant relations among cognitions. The only way the existence of this motivational state can be identified is indirectly, via predicted outcomes. Furthermore, the exact circumstances required for dissonance arousal, the nature of the motivational state, and the like are not specified by the theory. Only recently have theorists and researchers turned their attention to the analysis of dissonance-arousal variables (e.g., Pallak & Pittman, 1972; Cooper & Scalise, 1974; Zanna, Higgins, & Taves, 1976; Cooper, Fazio, and Rhodewalt, 1978).

Once dissonance has been aroused, the theory predicts that it can be reduced by a variety of methods, but it fails to specify the conditions under which a given method will or will not be employed. Festinger (1957) hinted that the change will occur in the weakest element or relation when he asserted that the maximum possible dissonance is equal to the total resistance to change of the least resistant element; however, he did not elaborate this point. In practice, experimenters have implicitly assumed that inconsistency will be reduced by whatever means is available to the individual. Hence, they have attempted to block all modes of resolution but the one of interest. Change in elements related to this one mode is then measured. This procedure is reminiscent of the attempt to isolate the sense modality employed by white rats in learning to negotiate a maze (Moss, 1946). It will be recalled that one sense modality after another was eliminated, but the animal always successfully negotiated the maze.

What is called for here is a specification of all the ways in which inconsistency can be reduced in a given situation and the examination of behavior relevant to all these methods. It should then be possible to determine whether the individual attempts to resolve inconsistency by *any* method. It is possible that some individuals can tolerate dissonance and make no attempt to reduce it, as suggested by Aronson (1968). Evidence for individual differences in dissonance reduction has been reported by Harvey and Ware (1967) and by Silverman (1971). The procedure described above would also permit specification of the conditions under which given modes of reduction will be adopted. Some progress has been made in this direction. Walster, Berscheid, and Barclay (1967) hypothesized that individuals will choose that mode of reduction that is least likely to be challenged by future events. A somewhat more complex hypothesis (Hardyck & Kardusch, 1968) holds that, when any mode of reducing dissonance is available, "stopping thinking" will be the preferred mode; that is, the person will prefer to passively forget about the dissonance or actively suppress it. If the most preferred mode is blocked, simple change in one of the two cognitions in the dissonant relationship will be the next-preferred mode. Finally, if simple change is not possible, restructuring will be attempted.

The problem of oversimplification is self-evident. By oversimplification is meant the failure to consider the relevant variables in the situation to which the theory is supposed to apply. The neglect of the variables of commitment, volition, self-esteem, and responsibility have already been referred to in the discussion of modifications of dissonance theory (e.g., Brehm & Cohen, 1962; Aronson, 1968; Bramel, 1968; Wicklund & Brehm, 1976). Pepitone (1966) noted that the theory has not been related to theories in general psychology and that findings relevant to dissonance may be explained by other formulations.

Perhaps the best evaluation of cognitive dissonance theory is in terms of its agreement with known data. As noted earlier, a complete review of the research findings is not feasible in this book, but a number of reviews are available for the interested reader (e.g., Brehm & Cohen, 1962; Chapanis & Chapanis, 1964; Freedman & Sears, 1965; Insko, 1967; Wicklund & Brehm, 1976). We will consider only some of the major areas of research and try to indicate the trend of the findings.

Revaluation of Chosen and Unchosen Alternatives   The most common type of research is one in which the individual evalutes two objects, "freely" chooses one of them, and then reevaluates the two objects. Dissonance theory predicts that the evaluation of the chosen object should increase and the unchosen decrease. In spite of difficulties in interpretation due to the usual procedures of discarding subjects who choose the lower-valued object, who are suspicious, and so on, the results are generally in accord with theoretical predictions.

Forced Compliance   Compliance with the wishes of the experimenter can be induced either by promise or reward, threat or punishment, or other justification for the behavior. The theory predicts that the greater the justification for an overt act that is inconsistent with private opinion, the less will be the subsequent attitude change. The results of the research in this area are extremely difficult to evaluate because of the difficulty of inducing compliance without at the same time inducing opinion change, the elimination of subjects, and other problems of design. It is clear, however, that the results are inconsistent and generally inconclusive. These are the findings that led Brehm and Cohen (1962) to conclude that choice or volition is a necessary condition for arousing dissonance through forced compliance. However, it is difficult to show that a person can be forced to comply with the experimenter's wishes and still believe that he or she acted on his or her own volition. The evidence for Brehm and Cohen's contention is limited and inconclusive, leading Insko (1967) to the conclusion that the necessity for volition is still unproven.

Playing a role that is counter to one's own attitude might be considered an example of forced compliance because the subject is behaving overtly in a manner that is contrary to his or her own attitudes. The theory predicts that the role player will subsequently change his or her own opinion to bring it into agreement with the role that he or she has played. Although research is relatively limited in quantity, the results are much more consistent than in other areas and generally support the theory.

Selective Exposure   The general prediction of dissonance theory is that the existence of dissonance will lead the individual to seek consonant information and avoid dissonant information. Freedman and Sears (1965) conducted an extensive review of the research on selective exposure and concluded that the evidence does not support the dissonance theory prediction.

Social Support   Dissonance may be aroused through lack of social support; this dissonance can be reduced by changing one's own view, by seeking to change the views of those who do not support one, or by finding others who do support one's own position. Some research on this point, that dealing with mass proselyting after belief disconfirmation, was reviewed earlier. The two studies cited yielded different results, one supporting the dissonance prediction and one failing to support the theory. Other relevant studies have been just as inconsistent; hence the evidence regarding the effects of lack of social support is ambiguous.

This brief survey is perhaps sufficient to indicate the unsettled state of research relevant to the theory. Generally supportive evidence exists for the revaluation of alternatives following a choice, and certain kinds of justifications in forced-compliance studies. The evidence concerning the effects of punishment and choice in forced-compliance studies is inconclusive, and the evidence regarding selective exposure fails to support the theory. The many failures to find unambiguous support for the theory suggests that it needs modification in several respects. The attempts by Brehm and Cohen (1962), Aronson (1968), Bramel (1968), and Wicklund and Brehm (1976) are indicative of the kinds of revisions that are required.

A THEORY OF PSYCHOLOGICAL REACTANCE

It is a common observation that people often behave in ways that appear perverse to the casual observer. A mother tells a friend that her child does not like carrots, and the child procedes to eat five of them. A husband suggests that he likes his wife's hair long, so she gets a bobbed haircut. A fellow student suggests that a particular course is a "must" for another student; the other student refuses to even consider taking it. Jack Brehm noted this "reverse psychology" and proposed an explanation or theory about the underlying process (Brehm, 1966, 1972). His major thesis was that there is a psychological process that is common to all phenomena of the sort listed above.

The basic aspect of the theory is that people are motivationally aroused any time they think a freedom has been threatened or eliminated. This motivational arousal was called *psychological reactance* (Brehm, 1966). Reactance moves people to try to restore freedom that is threatened. In addition to this major proposition, reactance theory attempts to explain the ways that freedoms can be threatened or eliminated, the determinants of the magnitude of reactance, and the consequences of reactance.

Threats to Freedom

Threats to, or elimination of, freedom can occur in several ways. Obviously, a powerful other person or group may threaten or eliminate freedoms by fiat, as when an autocratic government takes away freedom of speech or the foreman of a work group arbitrarily modifies working conditions. However, there are more subtle ways that freedom may be threatened. For instance, in the examples cited above freedom was threatened by the mere implication that another person was trying to influence one's behavior. Brehm also maintained that the threat to or elimination of freedom arouses reactance whether the origin is social or nonsocial. For example, if an "auto buff" learns that a Jaguar XKE is no longer available, freedom to purchase that car is eliminated and reactance will be activated.

Magnitude of Reactance

The theory of psychological reactance assumes that reactance varies in magnitude, depending on several factors. First, Brehm (1972) notes that it is a given that the person in question believes that he or she possesses a particular freedom. Such a belief may derive from the experience of having exercised the freedom, from formal agreements (e.g., constitutional freedoms), from observing others exercising the freedom, and probably from a variety of other sources.

Thus a person may have more or less *confidence* that he or she has a particular freedom, and the magnitude of reactance to threat or elimination is a direct function of how confident the person was that he or she actually had the freedom in the first place.

Second, the more *important* a freedom is to a person, the greater the reactance when the freedom is threatened or eliminated. The importance of a freedom is said to be determined by the significance of the motives that may be uniquely satisfied by exercising the freedom. When a significant motive can be satisfied in only one way by exercising a freedom, threat to that freedom arouses a high-magnitude reactance. When a freedom provides only one of many ways of satisfying a significant motive or when the motives it can uniquely satisfy are insignificant, threat or elimination of the freedom arouses little reactance.

Third, if a person has more than one freedom, the magnitude of reactance aroused by threat or elimination is a direct function of the *proportion* of freedoms that is threatened or eliminated.

Finally, psychological reactance may be aroused by *implied reduction* of freedoms. If a person believes that one of his or her freedoms has been threatened, that person may infer that other freedoms are also threatened. For example, if the freedom to smoke in a classroom is eliminated, students may suspect that smoking will soon be prohibited in other areas on campus and/or that other similar freedoms may be eliminated. The greater the implied threat to a freedom, the greater the magnitude of psychological reactance.

Consequences of Reactance

According to the theory, psychological reactance is a motivational state that consists of pressures directed toward the reestablishment of the threatened or eliminated freedom. This pressure cannot be measured directly but can be detected by its behavioral manifestations. These manifestations may be direct action, such as exercising the freedom, or indirect evidences, such as physiological tension and modifications of perceptions and judgments. More importantly, reactance is presumed to affect people's psychological processes. The consequences of reactance are of two major kinds: subjective and behavioral. The subjective effects of reactance are observed primarily in verbal reports. For example, if a person is asked to evaluate a particular behavior both before and after a threat to or elimination of a freedom, the evaluation should be more favorable the second time. In general, motivational changes of reactance induce changes in perceptions and judgments that are consistent with them.

Psychological reactance presumably affects behaviors that help to restore the threatened or eliminated freedom. These behaviors may be either direct or indirect. That is, a person may try to restore freedom directly by exercising it or indirectly by attacking the source of the threat or elimination. The latter behavior may be engaged in if there is some hope of getting the agent to withdraw the threat and/or if the person is not concerned about possible retaliation.

Comment

The theory of psychological reactance is logically consistent and requires relatively few assumptions. It generates testable hypotheses about the kinds of psychological processes that are involved in the behaviors it attempts to explain. It does, however, have certain limitations and areas of uncertainty. For instance, the variables determining confidence that a freedom is possessed are not clearly specified, nor are the determinants of implied threats to freedom. Also, there is no specification for the quantification of the magnitude of reactance or the consequences of reactance. That is, all statements are relative, taking the form "more than/less than." In short, the theory lacks precision.

Several investigations have yielded results that are consistent with reactance theory. For instance, the theory predicts that to the extent that a communication forces a person to hold a particular opinion (i.e., threatens the person's freedom to hold a contrary opinion), reactance motivates the person to adopt the opposite position. This effect has been demonstrated in a number of studies (e.g., Sensenig & Brehm, 1968: Wicklund & Brehm, 1968; Heller, Pallak, & Picek, 1973). Similar effects have been observed in other situations. Mazis (1975) found that housewives deprived of the freedom to use laundry detergents containing phosphates expressed more favorable attitudes toward those detergents than nondeprived controls. Evidence is also available to support the hypothesis that reactance is greater when more important freedoms are threatened or eliminated. It is generally assumed that group members conform to group standards more when the group is attractive than when it is not. One study (Brehm & Mann, 1975) showed the usual relationship between conformity and attraction when conformity threatened a relatively unimportant freedom, but the opposite effect occurred when the freedom was relatively important.

Reactance theory also suggests that the effects of a forewarning of a persuasive intent will affect the way a subsequent communication will be processed. The results of at least one study showed that forewarning reduced persuasion, increased counterargumentation, and reduced favorable thoughts to a greater extent under high- than under low-involvement conditions (Petty & Cacioppo, 1979). These findings were interpreted as being consistent with reactance theory.

However, there is some evidence that reactance may not be as simple as proposed by the theory. In one study, subjects were given choice or no-choice options either from their coworker (interpersonal condition) or by random assignment from an unknown agent (noninterpersonal condtion) (Heilman & Toffler, 1976). As predicted by reactance theory, threats produced greater compliance when a choice was offered than when it was not offered in the interpersonal as compared with the noninterpersonal conditions. The authors suggested that the social nature of experimental settings may provide the impetus for freedom-affirming behaviors. Similarly, Snyder and Wicklund (1976) found that a communication attempting to persuade persons to adopt a particular position had lesser reactance effects the more the subjects were initially in disagreement with the communicator. In a different setting, preference for a forbidden toy was found to be greater than for an easily attainable toy, as predicted by reactance theory, but only for two-year-old boys (Brehm & Weinraub, 1977). The fact that the effect was observed in two-year-old boys suggests that reactance does not depend on cognitive development, but failure to observe the effect among two-year-old girls raises questions about the role of cultural factors in the process.

Finally, the traditional effectance motivation aspect of reactance theory has been challenged by some writers. For instance, impression management theory (see Chapter 12) suggests that people are less concerned about the actual loss of freedom than they are about the outward appearance of being free. In support of this alternative interpretation, it has been shown that verbal threats to freedom produced attitude change only when persons expressed their postcommunication attitudes publicly (Baer, Hinkle, Smith, & Fenton, 1980).

Chapter 9

Attribution Theory in Social Psychology

Based upon the sheer volume of empirical research, the attribution-theory perspective can be regarded as the primary paradigm in contemporary social psychology. If the reader wishes to verify this rather sweeping generalization, she/he need only peruse the current contents of social psychology's major research journals or consult recently published reference volumes in the field. Perhaps the growing appeal of the attribution framework derives from the wide array of social interaction phenomena to which it might be applied.

Put most broadly, *attributional processes* are those processes governing a perceiver's attention to, thought about, and apprehension of perceived "events." The events which serve as objects of perception might consist of the actions of social others, one's own actions, and/or environmentally produced effects. Attribution theory is typically concerned with the processes and schema invoked by the perceiver in assigning *causes* to these events. Through such causal analyses the perceiver arrives at inferences about the dispositions of other persons and himself/herself, as well as inferences about the stability of environmental entities. Presumably such inferences can mediate a wide variety of consequent interpersonal and intrapersonal phenomena. Such phenomena include liking, loving, achievement striving, group behavior, occupational decisions, moral judgments, legal decisions, political preferences, consumer product preferences, among many others. In fact, one could plausibly defend the proposition that all human social behavior follows upon some form of mediating causal analysis. Since attribution theory represents an attempt to specify the nature of these causal analytic processes, it is not surprising that many social psychologists concerned with vastly divergent social-behavioral phenomena have become intrigued by attribution theory as an orienting framework.

While the proliferation of empirical inquiries and theoretical analyses based upon attribution theory per se is a development of the past decade, attribution theory has its origins in a touchstone paper on "phenomenal causality" published by Fritz Heider over 35 years ago (Heider, 1944). In this paper Heider was particularly concerned with similarities and differences in the perception of the causes of personal and impersonal events. His analysis derived largely from principles first articulated by gestalt psychology (cf. Wertheimer, 1923) to describe regularities in object perception. Like the gestalt psychology of the twenties, Heider addressed his analysis to understanding the manner in which perceivers make sense out of what they see in the environment. However, in addition to appealing to the constructivist analysis of perceived events evident in gestalt psychology (which employed constructs such as expectancy or set, proximity of objects, etc., to derive principles of object perception), Heider (1944, 1958) introduced the "naïve" analysis of actions and causes. By adopting the stance of a "naïve" perceiver of personal events, Heider extended gestalt-like notions of object perception to the domain of social perception. The reader is referred to Chapter 6 for an elaborated description of Heider's (1958) treatise detailing the components of this naïve analysis. For purposes of the exposition of current attribution theories in this chapter, it is important to review two prescient general propositions contained in Heider's analysis of interpersonal perception.

1   Heider proposed that interpersonal relations are primarily a function of people's interpretations of the actions of others in the social field. This proposal has been implicitly adopted by current social psychologists and constitutes an article of faith, which propels the field's burgeoning interest in attributional phenomena.

2   He claimed that the motivations underlying attributional processes inhere in people's strong needs to seek understanding of the transient events that they observe by attributing them to enduring dispositional properties of the actor and/or to stable and invariant properties of the environment giving rise to the events. The adaptive significance of the individual's search for invariance in both social others and environmental entities is that such invariance allows for both the understanding of current events and people *and* the prediction of future events and personal actions.

The two major theoretical frameworks presented in this chapter are complementary derivatives of Heider's seminal analysis. The *Theory of Correspondent Inference* (Jones & Davis, 1965; Jones & McGillis, 1976) examines the cognitive processes involved in the attribution of dispositional invariance to personal entities. The *Theory of External Attribution* (Kelley, 1967, 1971, 1972) seeks to detail the causal analytic processes which lead people to attribute events to environmental entities. Each theory provides a more precise specification of the processes involved in its domain of attribution than Heider's original work. Furthermore, both Jones and Kelley all but abandon Heider's field theory-like phenomenalism in favor of rather thoroughgoing cognitive analyses of attribution processes.

The third theory of attribution presented in this chapter might have been derived from Heiderian principles—but it was not. Daryl Bem's *Self-Perception Theory* is particularly concerned with the process by which people "discover" or label dispositions in themselves. As we shall note in the coverage of this theory, Bem's original presentation of self-perception phenomena was constructed from a Skinnerian functional analysis of attitude-behavior relationships. Its original intent was to provide for a parsimonious explanation of the effects found in cognitive dissonance research. At the end of its tenure as the provocateur of an epistemologically unresolvable controversy between dissonance theory adherents and Bem himself, it was recognized as a framework that was quite compatible with attribution theories, particularly Kelley's.

This chapter will first present the original formulations of correspondent inference theory (Jones & Davis, 1965) and the theory of external attribution (Kelley, 1967). After each presentation the revisions and addenda to these theoretical frameworks are detailed (i.e., Jones & McGillis, 1976, and Kelley, 1971, 1972, respectively). After both of these frameworks are exposited, the general features of the research supporting the theories will be presented. The exposition of self-perception theory follows and is based primarily upon Bem's 1972 chapter in Berkowitz's *Advances in Experimental Social Psychology* series. Finally our evaluation of this theoretical framework will be embedded in a section detailing various promising developments and future directions in attribution theory.

A THEORY OF CORRESPONDENT INFERENCES

The theory of inference developed by Jones and Davis (1965) attempts to explain a perceiver's inferences about what another person is trying to do by performing a given action. In engaging this phenomenon, the theorists rely heavily on Heider's (1958) general framework (see Chapter 6) but focus with greater specificity on the characteristics of an action which allow the observer to confidently attribute either an underlying intention or disposition to the actor.

From Heider's analysis, Jones and Davis formulated the following description of the process of inferring personal characteristics (dispositions) from behavior. It is assumed that the perceiver begins with the observation of an overt action of another person. He or she then makes certain decisions about the person's knowledge and ability, which in turn permit inferences about the person's intentions to be made. For example, if the person had no knowledge of (could not foresee) the consequences of the actions, the inference of intention could not be made. Similarly, if the effect produced by the actions required a level of skill (ability) greater than that believed to be possessed by the person, intention would not be inferred. Knowledge and ability are thus preconditions for the attribution of intention. If both knowledge of consequences and ability to produce them are in evidence, intentions are inferred and then used to infer stable personal attributes (called *dispositions* by Jones and Davis).

The theory of correspondent inferences attempts to account for the attribution of specific intentions and dispositions on the basis of particular actions and, to this extent, represents an extension of Heider's analysis. The general thesis is that the intentional significance of an action derives from a consideration of the alternatives open to the actor. That is, the perceiver can understand the motives (intentions) underlying an action only by relating it to other possible actions and effects. For example, Jones and Davis cited an instance in which A and B are working together. It is observed that A gives orders and monitors and criticizes B's work. If the situation is entirely free, one might infer that A is domineering. But if it is known that A has been ordered to play a directive leadership role, there would be less likelihood that A's behavior would be viewed as evidence of a personal quality of dominance. In Jones and Davis' terms, inferences about dominance from actions would be less *correspondent*.

The Concept of Correspondence

The term *correspondence* was used by Jones and Davis to refer to the extent to which the act and the underlying attribute are similarly described by the inference. In the preceding example, the most correspondent inference is the one which holds that the domineering behavior is a direct reflection of the intention to dominate and, hence, of a disposition to be dominant. In short, correspondence of inference varies inversely with the degree to which the action appears to be constrained by the situation in which it occurs.

The formal definition of correspondence can now be stated: *"Given an attribute-effect linkage which is offered to explain why an act occurred, correspondence increases as the judged value of the attribute departs from the judge's conception of the average person's standing on that attribute"* (Jones & Davis, 1965, p. 224). Thus the attribution of an attribute or trait on the basis of a given action implies that the action departs from normative expectations. It is worth noting here that Jones and McGillis (1976) revised this definition by adding that correspondence would also be expected to increase when the judged value of an attribute departs from "the judge's prior conception of where the actor stood on that attribute" (p. 391).

Jones and Davis defined *act* rather broadly as a molar response that reflects choice on the part of the actor and has one or more effects on the environment or actor. The choice of the actor may be only between action and inaction, although it is usually between alternative actions. *Effects* were defined as discriminable changes produced by actions.

The act of concern to the theory is the terminal act in an action sequence. For example, if a person rises, crosses the room, and closes the door, the act of interest is "closing the door." The act may have only one effect or it may have several effects. When multiple effects are produced, inference becomes more difficult. However, it is usually the case that certain effects are common to both the chosen and unchosen alternatives. The theory assumes that these common effects could not have been helpful to the actor in the choice of action and hence do not give information about intentions. But there may be (and often are) multiple noncommon effects; that is, the action may produce several effects which would not have occurred if the actor had chosen any other alternative action. Jones and Davis asserted that the perceiver usually assumes that some effects are more desirable to the actor than others and therefore more indicative of the actor's intentions. In general, effects that are seen as desired by most people are seen as being desired by the actor.

In most cases, a chosen action will produce both positive (desirable) and negative (undesirable) effects. The perceiver usually assumes that the actor acted in that particular way in spite of the negative consequences of the action. Jones and Davis went further and stated that the importance of nonnegative effects increases in direct proportion to the negativity of other effects produced by the action. Therefore, the probability of inferring intention from desired effects increases to the degree that negative outcomes are also involved.

But Jones and Davis found a problem: to know that a person chooses a universally desired effect tells little about the person's unique characteristics. The theory holds that an inference must characterize the person as deviating from the norm if it is to be considered as correspondent. The authors concluded, therefore, that actions whose effects are no more universally desired than those of other possible actions provide the greatest amount of information regarding intentions and dispositions. This latter point is quite important in the reformulation of Jones and McGillis (1976) since their revised portrayal of correspondent inference subsumed the variability in inference due to desirability phenomena within the more general category of factors which provide the perceiver with varying amounts of *information gain*. This issue will be taken up explicitly in a subsequent section.

Two aspects of the inference process were identified by Jones and Davis. When an observed action leads to multiple effects, the perceiver first assumes that certain effects are more likely to be the goal than others. If all effects are negative except one, the perceived probability that this one positive effect was the actor's goal is 1.00. In other cases, the probability of any given effect being the actor's goal varies directly with the assumed desirability of the effect and inversely with the number of other positive effects produced by the action. The attribution of intention reflects some combination of assumed desirability and number of noncommon effects.

The second part of the inference process is the attachment of personal significance to the effect(s) identified as the actor's goal. According to the definition of correspondence, relative extremity of the action is the crucial variable. As noted earlier, assumed desirability positively affects the judgment of relative extremity. Therefore, an inference from an action to a disposition is an inverse function of the number of noncommon effects of the action and the perceived desirability of these effects. It follows that the most correspondent situation is one in which both the number of noncommon effects and the assumed desirability of these effects are low. Hence, it is important to consider the factors influencing the assumed desirability and the assessment of commonality of effects.

Factors Determining Assumed Desirability

Jones and Davis asserted that there are a number of conditions that might influence the perceiver's assumption that the actor desires the same effects as people in general. They suggested that these factors might include such things as the actor's appearance, the perceiver's stereotypes about identifiable groups, and/or shared perspectives relative to the situation in which the action occurs. While Jones and Davis (1965) did not analyze these factors in any detail, Jones and McGillis spend a good portion of their reformulated analysis of correspondent inference on those characteristics of the actor and/or the situation which give rise to differential assumed desirability. While Jones and McGillis' analysis is elaborated in a subsequent section, it is worth noting here that two primary classes of expectancy affect the assumptions the observer might make about the desirability of observed effects for the actor. The first of these classes was referred to as *category-based expectancies,* or expectancies concerning the actor's behavior which are derived from the observer's recognition of the category membership(s) of the actor. For example, such expectancies might derive from the actor's race or sex. The second category was referred to as *target-based expectancies,* or expectancies derived from the observer's prior conceptions of a particular actor. Two sets of problems concerning the calculation of the commonality of effects were considered. The first set was concerned with the identification of effects and the determination of commonality of effects, and the second, with the task of sorting out the noncommon effects of the action from all others. Jones and Davis concluded that the first set of problems could be resolved only through research; hence, they did not deal with them in their analysis.

The process of sorting out noncommon effects after common and noncommon effects have been identified was seen as consisting of three stages. The first stage constitutes identifying the different action alternatives that are likely to be noted by the perceiver. The next step is to pool all the effects supposedly produced by the unchosen actions and compare them with the effects of the chosen action. In the final stage, the noncommon effects of the unchosen alternatives are considered as effects that the actor wishes to avoid. These are then treated in the same manner as positive effects produced by the chosen alternative action. The negative noncommon effects of the unchosen alternatives plus the positive effects of the chosen action provide the basis for inferring correspondence.

Jones and Davis presented this analysis as a guide for research and did not suggest that the perceiver proceeds in this manner, although presumably the results of the perceiver's responses to the situation should correspond to the results produced by the researcher's analysis.

A complicating factor in calculating the noncommon effects of an action is the fact that the actor has made choices among action alternatives prior to the action choice under consideration. For example, a person who chooses to attend law school A rather than law school B has already chosen a field, whereas a person who chooses to attend law school rather than medical school has not. The former is therefore at a later stage of the total choice process than the latter. Knowledge of preceding choices may provide information basic to the inference process.

Correspondence and Personal Involvement

In addition to the factors discussed to this point, there are certain variables associated with the perceiver's involvement which affect the attributions of dispositions. Jones and Davis distinguished two levels of involvement, *hedonic relevance* and *personalism*. An action has hedonic relevance for a perceiver if it either promotes or interferes with the perceiver's goal, that is, if the action is either gratifying or disappointing to the perceiver. An action is personalistic if the perceiver believes that he is the intended target of the action, that is, if the perceiver believes that the action was intended either to gratify or to spite him. Thus an action can be either relevant or irrelevant to the perceiver; if it is relevant, it may be either personally relevant or impersonally relevant.

The theory holds that correspondence generally increases with increasing relevance, and hence relevance is a determinant of the attribution of dispositions. Jones and Davis went a step further and asserted that evaluation of the actor by the perceiver will also be a joint function of relevance and correspondence. If the effects of an action are positive, the perceiver's favorable impression of the actor will increase with increasing correspondence; if the effects are negative, the converse will be true.

Under conditions of personal relevance, the effects of correspondence and relevance on evaluation are enhanced. Jones and Davis believed that a condition of personalism and positive relevance would guarantee a positive evaluation of the actor because this set of circumstances would ensure a correspondent inference of focused benevolence. Similarly, personalism and negative relevance should ensure a negative evaluation of the actor.

A Reformulation of Correspondent Inference Theory

The Jones and McGillis (1976) reformulation of correspondent inference theory does not drastically alter the general form and substance of the theory reviewed in the above paragraphs. Instead, their revision of the correspondent inference framework was undertaken with two purposes in mind:

1 To facilitate the further development of a systematic deductive theory of attributional processes. To this end, Jones and McGillis set out to be more specific about the definition and determinants of such concepts as "correspondence" and "assumed desirability." The voluminous body of attribution research which had emerged in the decade between the original publication of the Jones and Davis (1965) theory and the Jones and McGillis reformulation certainly facilitated the theorists in this definitional goal.

2   To expand the scope of correspondent inference theory. As noted above, as originally designed correspondent inference theory was addressed to the task of understanding the processes engaged in by a perceiver in assigning dispositions and causes to other persons. The Jones and McGillis reformulation allows for the application of the idealized calculus of correspondent inference to environmental attribution and self-attribution, as well as attributions to others. In this sense, Jones and McGillis brought correspondent inference theory in line with Kelley's analysis of attribution, discussed later on in this chapter.

Based upon these two reappraisal purposes, the Jones and McGillis revision of correspondent inference theory has two major theoretical contributions to make to the original formulation: First of all, they revised the definition of *correspondence*. Secondly, they articulated more clearly the particular determinants of *assumed desirability* which give rise to the "calculation" of correspondence.

A Revised Definition of Correspondence

The reader will recall that the formal definition of correspondence offered by Jones and Davis noted that the perceiver's inference of correspondence between an observed behavioral effect and an underlying attribute increases in strength *"as the judged value of the attribute departs from the judge's conception of the average person's standing on that attribute."*

Jones and McGillis observed that such a definition limits the range of phenomena explained by correspondent inference theory to those concerned with the attribution of intentions or dispositions to others. They proposed, however, that correspondent inference theory is not only concerned with dispositional inference, but is more generally addressed to the *information gain* which accrues to the perceiver as a function of behavioral observation. Presumably such information gain can aid the perceiver in his/her understanding of both the actor and the environment in which the action occurred. In keeping with this focus upon information gain, Jones and McGillis redefine correspondence in the following way:

> Given an attribute-effect linkage which is offered to explain why an act occurred, correspondence refers to the degree of information gained regarding the probability or strength of the attribute (p. 391).

The theorists go on to note that:

> When correspondence is defined as information gain, it is obvious that we need to consider more than just whether behavioral effects are noncommon. We also have to consider whether and to what extent they fit the judge's prior expectations concerning people in general or this particular actor. This determinant was originally described by Jones and Davis in terms of effects assumed to be desired in the culture. But the more generic case concerns the prior probability that the particular actor would desire a particular effect. This might be based on assumptions about cultural desirability, or it might be based on prior knowledge about the actor.

Whichever may be the case, it seems useful to conceive of a valence attached to each effect having a possible range from -1 to $+1$. A maximally undesirable effect would have a valence of -1, indicating the highest probability that the individual concerned would seek to avoid that effect. A $+1$ valence, on the other hand, would signify the highest probability of effect desirability. From the point of view of information gain, pursuit of a low valence effect should lead to greater correspondence of inference, other things equal, than pursuit of a high valence effect (Jones & McGillis, 1976, pp. 391–392).

Expected Effect Valence

A second alteration which Jones and McGillis offered in their reanalysis of correspondent inference theory is suggested by the above-reviewed information-gain proposal. The original definition of correspondence provided a rather global and undifferentiated source for increasing correspondence. That is, the perceiver's judgment of correspondence was proposed to increase as the judged value of the attribute in question departed from the *judge's conception of the average person's standing on the attribute.* In a sense, Jones and Davis were proposing that the perceiver's expectancies of observing a particular behavior varied with the general cultural desirability of the behavior. The more deviant from expectancy, the more likely the observer would be to make a correspondent inference. However, Jones and Davis were not particularly clear about the sources of a perceiver's inferences of assumed desirability.

With the more precise formulation of an information-gain analysis of correspondent inference described above, firmer bases for perceiver assessments of desirability as a component of *expected valence* were necessary. To this end Jones and McGillis proposed two kinds of base rate expectancies which could provide for a better calculation of assumed desirability or, more appropriately, *assumed expected valence.*

The first of these expectancies was referred to as a *category-based expectancy.* The category-based expectancy was seen as deriving from the observer's prior knowledge that the actor is a member of a particular class, category, or reference group. For example, a perceiver can readily observe a particular actor's race, sex, and age. Further, the perceiver might have information which informs him of the actor's occupation, social class, marital status, and the like. Depending upon the actor's category membership, particular behaviors will be seen as more or less likely and/or more or less desirable. If an actor is a member of overlapping categories (which is highly likely, of course), each category of membership contributes to the refinement of expectancies, against which observed behavior is judged.

The second class of expectancy described by Jones and McGillis was referred to as *target-based expectancies.* Such expectancies issue from the perceiver's prior information about a particular actor. As the theorists note, "the perceiver's task is to extrapolate from one set of judged dispositional attributes (traits, motives, attitudes) that set of attributes relevant to the behavior observed." Using an example offered by the theorists, if we are aware that a particular actor opposes abortion, we might infer that the actor also favors restrictive control of massage parlors. If we have the opportunity to observe the actor's positive attitude toward a bill restricting massage parlor trade, we will have confirmed a target-based expectancy about that particular actor. In many ways, target-based expectancies operate in terms of the "implicit personality theory " of the observer.

While the articulation of both category- and target-based expectancies enhances the specificity of the information-gain definition of correspondence, it is the notion of target-based expectancy which allows for the easy application of correspondent inference theory to the case of self-attribution. We do not only hold target-based expectancies for particular others, but we also have such expectancies for ourselves. Our "implicit personality theory" about self provides for a set of expectancies which allows us to make correspondent inferences about our own observed behavior. Since a more limited but meaningful contribution to self-attribution is also made by the expectancies generated by our recognition of our own category memberships, the laudable specificity of the determinants of assumed expected valence provided for by Jones and McGillis serves to enhance the scope of correspondent inference theory. It should be noted that both category- and target-based expectancies are probabilistic rather than absolute expectancies.

A Summary of the Reformulated Correspondent Inference Process

In the attributional sequence designated by correspondent inference theory, the observer gains information about an actor's dispositions most readily when the actor is assumed to have knowledge, ability, and free choice and when the actor's choice of behavior was made among alternatives with a low number of noncommon effects which in turn are not expected by the observer to be desirable to the actor. The later modifications of correspondent inference theory differ from the original formulation in the more extensive treatment of the nature of the observer's expectancies; the clearer application of the model to ongoing person perception, including self-perception; and the conception of correspondence as the reflection of "changes in the subjective probability of inferring a disposition given an observed behavior" (Jones & McGillis, 1976).

A THEORY OF EXTERNAL ATTRIBUTION

As noted earlier, the analysis of the attribution process proposed by Kelley (1967, 1971, 1972, 1973) is related to the theory of correspondent inference in that both derive from Heider's work. However, unlike correspondent inference theory, which is primarily concerned with the circumstances under which causes and dispositions are attributed to actors, Kelley's theory focuses upon those conditions which lead a perceiver to attribute cause to an environmental entity with which an actor or group of actors interacts. Therefore, Kelley's analysis considered the problem of ruling out personal causes rather than identifying and accounting for them. The initial statements of each theory (Jones & Davis, 1965; Kelley, 1967) clearly reflected this complementarity in focus. However, because of the added flexibility afforded the correspondent inference model by the Jones and McGillis revision, both theories can be employed to account for similar attributional phenomena.

Kelley's theory is alternatively referred to as the ANOVA cube model of attribution because of his use of a statistical analogy to describe the attributional processes used by perceivers in inferring environmental causality.

The Attribution Process

Kelley (1967) defined *attribution* as the process of perceiving the dispositional properties of entities in the environment. He accepted Heider's analysis of the perceptual process and especially his view that attribution may be either to the person or to the environment. In the perception of dispositional properties, then, there is a choice between external attribution (to the environment) or internal attribution (to the self). For example, if a person enjoys a television program, the person may attribute this enjoyment to the intrinsic nature of the program (external attribution) or to his or her idiosyncratic tastes (internal attribution). The variables determining this choice are the ones Kelley attempted to identify.

In his analysis, Kelley adopted John Stuart Mill's method of differences as his basic analytic tool: the effect is attributed to that which is present when the effect occurs and absent when the effect does not occur. This basic notion of covariation was used to examine variations in effects with respect to entities, persons, time, and modalities of interaction with the entity. The general hypothesis is that attribution to the environment rather than to the self requires that the actor respond *differentially* to the thing (entity) and *consistently* over time and over modalities and that the response be in *agreement* with other persons' responses to the entity. For example, enjoyment of a television program (entity) is attributed to the environment (the program) if the person does not enjoy all programs (differential response), if the person enjoys it a second time (consistency over time), if the person enjoys it not only at home but also at the home of friends, in the bar, and/or in black and white as well as in color (consistency over modalities), and if others also enjoy it (consensual agreement). To the degree that these conditions are not met, the enjoyment will be attributed to the self.

Informational Dependence and Influence

The four criteria for external validity mentioned above may now be defined more precisely:

Distinctiveness: an effect is attributed to the external environment (the entity) if it uniquely occurs when the entity is present and does not occur when the entity is absent.

Consistency over time: an effect is attributed to the entity if the effect is the same or nearly so each time the entity is present.

Consistency over modalities: an effect is attributed to the entity if it occurs even when the mode of interaction with the entity varies.

Consensus: an effect is attributed to the entity if the entity is experienced the same way by all observers; that is, if the entity produces the same effect on everyone.

According to Kelley, the degrees to which people's attributions fulfill these four criteria determine how confident they feel that they have a valid picture of their external world. If their attributions meet all of these criteria, they feel confident, make judgments quickly, and take action with vigor; if their attributions do not satisfy these criteria, they are unsure and hesitant to take action. Thus, these criteria provide an index of a person's state of information regarding the world. The index is based primarily on differentiation and stability. The information level is high if an individual can make highly stable but differentiated (distinctive) attributions.

Information level provided Kelley with a basis for the analysis of information dependence. His general view was that person A is informationally dependent on another person B if B can raise A's level of information to a higher level than A can attain from other sources. (This is analogous to Thibaut and Kelley's analysis of outcome dependence. See Chapter 4.) Information dependence may be defined in terms of actual or potential effects or in terms of anticipated or experienced effects. Anticipated and potential effects refer to the future, whereas actual and experienced effects refer to the present or past. When future reference is involved, A may seek information from B in order to raise his/her information level. In general, individuals may be expected to seek information when their information level drops below the level that they expect to be able to attain. These information-seeking activities lead to increased interaction with other persons upon whom the individual is informationally dependent.

The Analysis-of-Variance Cube

Kelley (1967) effectively uses the statistical technique of analysis of variance to analogize about the manner in which distinctiveness, consistency over time and modality, and consensus combine in the reasoning of the observer in the course of attributional inference. In this ANOVA cube model the criterion of distinctiveness is treated as the numerator or between-conditions term of an F-ratio. The greater the between-entity response variation, the more any response to a single entity is determined by that entity. The degrees of inconsistency and lack of consensus are relegated to the denominator as within-conditions error terms. These two variables index the stability or instability of the distinct entity effects. The size of the resulting mythical F-ratio is directly proportional to the degree of perceived entity causation in attribution. This analogy to analysis of variance highlights the fact that Kelley's model is quite simply a direct application of fundamental statistical methodology to naïve observation and inference. In keeping with this, Jones and McGillis (1976) refer to Kelley's theory as a "lay version of experimental design and analysis." Thus Kelley's theory views human attributors as distinctly rational, inferential thinkers who (at least by analogy) engage in careful processes of data sorting to arrive at their impressions of the environment.

Revisions in Kelley's Original Framework

In the first edition of this book we noted that Kelley's (1967) treatment of the attribution process, while logically consistent and informative, was perhaps an implausible model for real-world attributions. An experience with another person may occur only once, in only one setting, and with no evidence regarding the reactions of others to the person. Nevertheless, confident and speedy attributions are often made to the person or the environment in which the person has acted. The 1967 version of Kelley's theory provided no way of explaining this type of attributional circumstance.

A second problem with Kelley's (1967) original analysis of attribution, and one not noted in our earlier (1970) treatment of Kelley's framework, is that, while each of the criterial cues (distinctiveness, consensus, and consistency over time and modalities) constitutes a necessary base for an attributive inference, none of them *taken alone* is theoretically sufficient. While an ANOVA analysis does not *formally* require that all cells of the ANOVA matrix be filled, it does not clearly specify how missing and theoretically necessary data are dealt with by the attributor. Further, the full-blown analysis does not clearly detail those reasoning devices for comparatively weighting multiply present cues.

In the later elaborations of his attributional model, Kelley (1971, 1972) considered each of these problems with the original full-blown attributional calculus.

Unlike the Jones and McGillis revision of correspondent inference, Kelley's revisions of his original model did not involve an alternation of either the definitions of primary terms or the criteria giving rise to the perceiver's attributional analysis. Instead, Kelley's (1967) original model *stands* as a kind of elaborated analysis of attributional processes. His theoretical writings subsequent to the original proposal are primarily directed at solving the two problems noted above. He engaged this task by proposing shorthand calculational devices and principles which a perceiver might use to solve the problems of either insufficient or mutually ambiguous attributional data. There are two primary devices which Kelley proposed to handle the above problems: *causal schemata* and *causal principles*. These two addenda to Kelley's theory are taken up in the subsequent paragraphs.

Causal Schemata

Kelley (1972, 1973) has basically retreated from the position that a perceiver requires a wealth of "experiment-like" information and criteria prior to arriving at an attribution.

> It would be foolish to suggest that anything like a large data matrix is filled out before a causal inference is made. . . . Beyond that, it is obvious that the individual

is often lacking in the time and motivation necessary to make multiple observations. . . . In these circumstances he may make a causal inference on the basis of a *single observation* of the effect (1973, p. 113).

Since the individual, in the course of life experience, acquires a repertoire of ideas concerning the relationships among causal factors, these internalized structures provide him/her with solutions to the need for rapid attributional analysis in natural environmental contexts (Kelley, 1972). Kelley refers to these causal conceptions or structures as *causal schemata.* These schemata can thus be regarded as general frameworks of behavioral inference, within which bits of relevant information can be inserted to allow the perceiver to arrive at "good causal inferences" in spite of limited data availability (Kelley, 1972).

Kelley proposes that a causal schema functions as an *"assumed pattern of data in a complete analysis of variance framework"* (Kelley, 1972, p. 2). This proposed assumption has the virtue of allowing for the maintenance of a link between the analysis of causal schemata and the full-blown network of inference implied by the larger model described earlier. In addition, since schemata are seen as cognitive paradigms emergent from experience, it is reasonable to assume that they derive from the "explicit external organization that [a perceiver] imposes upon complex and complete sets of data in order to interpret them" (Kelley, 1972).

Given the potential multiplicity of limited data arrays that might confront perceivers in natural contexts, the array of heuristic schemata that might be proposed to accommodate a partial causal analysis is potentially quite large. Kelley (1972) considers several schemata that might be more prominent in resolving limited-data decision ambiguities. We will describe two of the more prominent of these for illustrative purposes.

1 *Multiple Sufficient Causal (MSC) Schemata.* There are many instances, both in the natural environment and within certain of social psychology's experimental paradigms, in which a perceiver is confronted with knowledge of an effect produced by an actor (e.g., attitude advocacy) which could derive from more than one causal source. If the causal sources from which the effect derives (e.g., external compliance pressure *or* a held attitude congruent with the advocacy) would be *equally sufficient* sources for the effect, the perceiver of that effect is confronted with a relatively ambiguous circumstance. However, since either cause *alone* would be sufficient to produce the effect, the additional information that one of the causes is present *reduces* the plausibility that the other cause is operative or a strong determinant of the actor's behavior. If, however, there are two plausible causes for a behavior and the perceiver *knows* that one is absent, the probability that the other has caused the observed effect is increased. Thus, if we are aware that our attitude advocator has not been pressured or induced to express an overt attitude, we will infer that his *internal* attitude has caused the observed effect.

In a sense then, the *multiple-sufficient-cause schema* suggests that when there are two or more causes for a particular observed effect, knowledge of the presence of one of the causes reduces the plausibility that the other cause(s) is also present. Conversely, the absence of one of the plausible and sufficient causes for an observed effect increases the probability that the other cause(s) has led to the effect. While there are qualifiers on such a scheme which derive from the fact that there is differential ambiguity in the "presence" and "absence" circumstances, this statement connotes the general tenor of the multiple-sufficient-cause schema.

As can be seen by the above illustration, the particular inference scheme described obviates the necessity for having all criterial data available prior to engaging in an attributional process. The above schema can be employed when only *one* instance of a behavior is observed and, in fact, when only an effect and one of its causes are known. The second inference schema we will describe has similar heuristic value.

2 *Multiple Necessary Causal (MNC) Schemata.* There are a number of attribution-like problems in the real world and in laboratory settings which are characterized by a structure in which there are two or more necessary causes for an effect but none of the causes taken alone is sufficient to produce the effect. In this instance, the multiple necessary causal schema allows for the inference that *both* causes are operative (Kelley, 1972). As distinguished from the multiple sufficient schema then, the presence of one cause does *not* imply the absence of another plausible cause. When the effect is present, the use of this scheme is quite straightforward. For example, if a perceiver observes that an actor who is successful on a difficult achievement task is highly motivated, she/he, by using the MNC schema, would still infer that ability is a plausible cause of the effect. The issue, however, is both more ambiguous and more complex when the positive effect is observed to be absent (i.e., the actor fails on a difficult achievement task). In this instance, lack of effort (for example, the person doesn't even attend to the task) may become a reasonably sufficient cause for the observed failure effect. In short, the MNC schema does not appear to apply equally well to cases where effects are present versus where they are absent (Kelley, 1972). Nevertheless, the two schemata appear to be reasonable heuristic devices which perceivers might well invoke in limited-information, single-observation circumstances.

"Shorthand" Causal Principles

Kelley's (1971) proposal of causal principles was made once again to accommodate to the fact that it is quite likely that perceivers will offer speedy and confident attributions in the face of limited data arrays. However, the principles appear to be directed at a slightly different problem with the original analyses than were the proposed schemata. As we have noted, Kelley's full-blown ANOVA model implies that, for a *complete* attributional analysis to be made, information about distinctiveness, consensus, and consistency is required. This further presumes that none of these criteria taken alone, without the others, constitutes a *sufficient* cause for making a clear attributional inference. A further implication of this state of affairs is that, if *more* than one of the criteria is available and the perceiver is required to decide about the particular strength of *only* one of the criteria, she/he is in an ambiguous circumstance at best. In order to address this problem, Kelley (1971) proposed a few causal principles which might allow perceivers to "sort" between causes for the most plausible one. In general the shorthand causal principles allow perceivers to consider conjointly occurring causes for an effect in one-time observations or in multiple-time but limited observational contexts. We will briefly describe three causal principles below.

1   *The Covariation Principle.* This particular principle was quite evident in Kelley's (1967) proposal of the larger theory. In fact "covariation" itself is at the heart of Kelley's attributional analysis. The covariation principle provides that *"an effect is attributed to the one of its possible causes with which, over time, it covaries"* (Kelley, 1971, p. 3). Thus, when there are two or more plausible causes for an effect, the one that the effect is *consistently* contingent with across time will be seen as the stronger cause. Certainly this causal principle is directly related to the general criterion of consistency over time, but, as a principle, it allows for making an attribution in the absence of the other criteria. Thus, it is a shorthand principle of attributional analysis.

2   *The Discounting Principle.* This particular principle is implied by the multiple sufficient causal schema described above. It states that, *"the role of a given cause in producing a given effect is discounted if other plausible causes are also present"* (Kelley, 1971, p. 8). While certainly an implication of the MSC schema, it does relate to a slightly different circumstance. The discounting principle is likely to be employed when an effect is observed and *more than one* sufficient cause for that effect is *known* to the perceiver. In this instance, the less plausible (although sufficient) cause is discounted in favor of the more plausible cause. The reader will note the similarity between the discounting principle and Jones and Davis' account of noncommon-effects analyses (see pp. 235–236).

3   *The Augmentation Principle.* This principle stipulates that, "if for a given effect, both a plausible inhibitory and a plausible facilitative cause are present, the role of the facilitative cause will be judged greater than if it alone were presented as a plausible cause of the effect" (Kelley, 1971, p. 12). For example, if a person of high ability (facilitating cause) succeeds (effect) on a task, ability would be thought to be greater if this person were unpracticed at the task (inhibitory cause) than if he or she had practiced.

Both the principles and schemata described above increase the breadth of application of Kelley's attributional perspective. They allow for the logical processing of attributional information in limited-information contexts and/or depict perceivers as possessing mechanisms for deciding on the differential plausibility of different causes when more than one cause is present in the observational circumstance.

With these addenda to the original (1967) model and the Jones and McGillis alteration of the correspondent inference framework, each theory is now capable of addressing the very same phenomena. The comparatively higher appeal of the Jones and Davis model to the "one-time" circumstance of attributional observation is reduced by Kelley's addenda. Conversely, the advantage in logical consistency and "data-processing" comprehensiveness of the original Kelley model over that of Jones and Davis is reduced by the Jones and McGillis framework. Finally, the original complementarity of the two derivatives of Heider's thought is now not quite so evident. The theories are not only highly compatible with one another, but are equally capable of explaining the very same phenomena.

Together they represent alternative models of contemporary social psychology's major theoretical orientation.

Research Support for the Kelley and Jones Perspectives

At this point in social psychology, it is clear that both the correspondent inference theory and ANOVA cube models of attributional process serve well the criterion of research generation. In the past decade, each of these theories has either directly or indirectly generated a voluminous body of research applications. Many of the studies, while founded on these seminal attribution perspectives, had not been designed to test directly the "truth" value of the theories. Rather, much of the research invoking the attributional notions of Jones and Kelley is involved with testing the applicability of these models to one or another traditional problem domain in social psychology (e.g., attraction, sex-role perceptions, achievement, attitude change, and the like).

It is also the case, however, that a considerable body of research has been directed at attempting to discern whether the principles of logical inference suggested by the two theories are paradigms of social thinking employed by "real people" as well as thoughtful theorists. While a comprehensive review of the research which supports and/or amplifies the proposals of these attributional frameworks is well beyond the scope of the current text, the consideration of some of the research which has been pivotal to the frameworks is in order.

Some of the primary evidence in support of correspondent inference theory has been derived from the study of attitude attribution. Two of the better-known studies exemplary of this work are reported by Jones and Harris (1967) and Jones, Worchel, Goethals, and Grumet (1971). In these experiments, observer subjects are presented with attitude statements (i.e., a speech or essay) of a target person and asked to estimate the target person's "true" attitude. The target person, in addition, is represented as having either *chosen* or been assigned the position advocated in his/her essay or speech. Furthermore, the position advocated by the attitude statement either confirms or disconfirms the observer's expectancy. The manipulation of choice in these studies serves a twofold theoretical purpose: (1) according to the theory, choice is a necessary condition for the attribution of personal disposition and (2) this manipulation serves to vary the number of noncommon effects since there are more reasons for making the attitude statement in the assigned than in the choice conditions.

The expectancy manipulations in these studies have been accomplished in different ways. In the Jones and Harris (1967) experiments, expectancies were associated with normative considerations (i.e., they were roughly *category-based*), while, in the Jones et al. (1971) studies, expectancies were based upon prior information provided the observer concerning related attitudes of the actor (i.e., they were *target-based* expectancies). The findings from these studies are reasonably consistent with the suppositions of the theory; that is, attributed attitudes are more in line with behavior when the target has choice than when the target has no choice. Furthermore, these choice/no-choice differences are larger when a prior expectancy is disconfirmed than when it is confirmed.

Thus, the major propositions of correspondent inference theory stand up well to the tests provided by these attitude attribution studies. The attribution of personal dispositions is indeed enhanced when the actor has choice in his/her behavior, when there is a low number of noncommon effects, and when the behavior disconfirms the observer's expectancy.

Nevertheless, there are some apparent qualifications on how observers use information concerning choice and expectancy which derive from these and related studies: (1) While choice indeed leads to stronger attributions to disposition, it is also the case that attitudes are attributed in line with behavior even in the no-choice conditions of the above studies. This phenomenon has been associated with what has been referred to by Ross (1978) as the *fundamental attribution error* and had been earlier referred to by Heider (1958) as "behavior engulfing the field." That is, there is a pervasive tendency in perceivers to "overattribute" behavior to the personal dispositions of actors. These kinds of unexpected findings impose some qualifications on the thorough-going logic of the correspondent inference framework and have led some investigators to designate the sources of *bias* in the attribution process as a prime area of study (cf. Ross, 1978). (2) A *contrast effect* of expectancy found in the Jones et al. (1971) study is apparently not replicable (cf. Jones & McGillis, 1976; Jones & Berglas, 1978). That is, the proposition that the more "dramatically a clear expectancy is disconfirmed by a clear behavior, the more will attitude attributions reflect that behavior" (Jones et al., 1971, p. 4) has not been consistently found to be stable. Instead, expectancy disconfirmation appears to be best regarded as a moderator of the number of noncommon effects and thus as a moderator of information gain (i.e., correspondence).

The most noteworthy and comprehensive study of Kelley's full-blown ANOVA model is embodied in the work of McArthur (1972). Her study was a questionnaire-based inquiry in which she presented subjects with items which reported responses (emotions, opinions, achievements, or actions) of another person. In order to test Kelley's notions, she manipulated information connoting the distinctiveness, consensus, and consistency factors accompanying the actor's responses. Subjects were asked to assign causality to four causal sources—the person, the stimulus, the circumstance, or a combination of the three. While this complicated array yielded complex results, they are reasonably consistent with Kelley's major propositions. We summarize the findings: (1) attribution of cause to the person was most pronounced in the low-distinctiveness, low-consensus, and high-consistency conditions; (2) attribution to the stimulus was found in high-distinctiveness, high-consensus, and high-consistency conditions; (3) attribution of cause to the circumstance was largely evident in low-consistency conditions; and (4) distinctiveness information was found to be a stronger source of both person and stimulus causal attribution than consensus information.

While neither the attitude-attribution studies nor the McArthur study of Kelley's comprehensive model come close to an exhaustive description of the research probing the Kelley and Jones attribution frameworks, both are exemplary of the research in support of the theory.

In the cases of both Jones's and Kelley's viewpoints, it seems that two current research directions are evident: (*a*) With regard to correspondent inference theory, there is now a concerted attempt to examine "overattribution" and other biases evident in people's applications of attributional calculi. (*b*) With regard to the ANOVA cube, the partial information schemata, heuristics, and principles are now being explored and found plausible in their own right, and it is not likely that multifactorial investigations of the comprehensive model beyond McArthur's work will be the major foci of subsequent research.

As an overarching comment on the purposes to which research might be put in exploring attributional calculi, it is probably important to note that it is not likely to be "critical-test" research. As Jones and McGillis (1976) note, "The theory *cannot be invalidated* by experimental research any more than game theory can be invalidated by the choices of players in a prisoner's dilemma game. Of course, it may turn out that the theory is not very useful in stimulating research, and it might, of course, prove vulnerable to logical criticism as well" (p. 404).

This quote is as applicable to the ANOVA model as it is to correspondent inference theory. In short, these models are being construed as rational baselines in which the a priori logic is impeccable. Since logic per se is only confirmable by its structural consistency, data on how it is employed are not terribly informative about whether it is "correct." Instead, the rational baseline principles proposed by Kelley and Jones might serve their most useful functions as "straw-men" (Jones & McGillis, 1976, p. 405) against which the perceptions of real people are compared. However, if this is the case, the calculational attributional theories described above are no longer "testable" in the sense that theories typically are. Combining Kelley's and Jones's compatible perspectives, one would have to designate them as a framework for promoting inquiry into social understanding rather than theories possessed of determinable predictive power.

SELF-PERCEPTION THEORY

In the face of the rather comprehensive attribution frameworks just discussed, Bem's theory of self-perception can be regarded as a quite limited-scope theory detailing one specific kind of attribution covered implicitly and explicitly by the larger models. Put most broadly, the phenomena of concern to self-perception theory are the individual's understanding of his/her own attributes and predilections and the processes that account for such self-knowledge.

While it is certainly the case that both Jones and Kelley provide us with ready calculi for inferring such self-knowledge and it will become clear that

Bem's more-limited model could well be derived from the broader attribution frameworks, it is indeed a theory whose origin is independent of attribution theory per se. Bem's initial purpose in pursuing an understanding of self-perception processes was to provide a logically consistent, parsimonious alternative to cognitive dissonance theory's motivational suppositions concerning the nature of "changes" in self-perception.

In its initial form, Bem's theory could hardly be seen as having the cognitive cast so evident in attribution theory. Quite to the contrary, it is probably the case that Bem would have originally eschewed the mentalistic calculi of attribution theory with the same vigor that he opposed the elusive motivational proposals of dissonance theory. Indeed, the primary model upon which Bem built his conception of self-perception processes was the functional analysis evident in Skinnerian reinforcement theory. In fact, in the first edition of this book, Bem's theory was assigned the auspicious role of providing a clear exemplar of the application of Skinnerian concepts to a socially relevant domain. In its original form (Bem, 1964), it is still the case that Bem's model is a quite evocative and thoroughgoing exercise in "Skinnerian social psychology," and the reader is referred to that work if she/he is interested in pursuing such an application of basic learning principles.

The major point in Bem's original reanalysis of cognitive dissonance phenomena attending on self-attribution was that newly acquired self-knowledge is not necessarily a motivational or cognitive derivative of "old" self-knowledge. Instead, he proposed that individuals come to know their attitudes, beliefs, and attributes through the simple observation of their immediate behavior in the field in relationship to the "demand" properties in that field. In short, they engage in a functional analysis of their own behavior in order to arrive at a self-perception. If the self-observed behavior is perceived to be free and thus unfettered by environmental inducements or constraints, the behavior is seen as reflecting a self-relevant attribute. Conversely, if the behavior is constrained, then it will not be seen by the actor as a reflection of internal state, trait, or attitude. The comparability of this portrayal and the later works of Jones on attitude attributions to others or Kelley on multiple sufficient causal schemata in the reasoning about others is now—in retrospect—compelling. At the time of the original proposal, however, the major theoretical perspective with which it was compared was cognitive dissonance.

It will be remembered that cognitive dissonance theory (see Chapter 8) broadly proposed that an individual will *adjust* his/her self-perceived attitude to be congruent with his/her recent behavior when that behavior contradicts the individual's prebehavioral attitude in a clear and unambiguous way. Further, the moving force in such adjustments of self-perception was constituted by a motivationally based consistency principle. This principle proposed that, since people desire consistency in their self-cognitions, they will respond aversively when their cognitions about their behavior contradict their cognitions about their stable, important beliefs. Given the noxiousness of such aversive arousal, individuals will seek to restore belief-behavior consistency by altering their attitudes in the direction of their behaviors *if* the behaviors are freely chosen and *if* there is no compelling environmental explanation for them.

Bem's proposal differed from the dissonance theory approach in two extremely critical and related ways: (1) Bem argued that individuals at the time of action do not recollect or regard as salient their initial attitudes and (2) therefore, they could not possibly be motivationally aroused by their behavior, and, in fact, in their own "phenomenology" they would not regard attitudes resulting from their behavior as representing a "change."

In short, Bem was proposing that, rather than regarding newly-arrived-at attitude self-perceptions following free behavior as representing a "change" in a contrary initial attitude, one should regard them as simply novel self-perceptions of the moment. Such novel self-perceptions can be intuited by people by simply considering the nature of their behaviors and the degrees to which they were constrained. If unconstrained, they will be seen as evidence of internal attitudes. This then is the pivotal functional analysis of attitude self-perception offered by Bem. Bem went on to assert that such an analysis is much more parsimonious than a dissonance theory analysis, does not require "proof" of aversive arousal—a proof not clearly discovered by dissonance theory, and brings self-perception in line with the perception of others and thereby increases the generality of such processes.

Partly because of the stridency and logical simplicity of Bem's presentation and partly because of the centrality that dissonance theory held in social-psychological research in the 1960s, Bem's proposal hardly fell on deaf ears. Instead it generated great foment and a full-scale controversy over which was the more valid approach to the understanding of self-relevant attitude phenomena. Bem's research in support of his framework employed what he referred to as "interpersonal replications" or "simulations" of cognitive dissonance's live paradigms. That is, he explored the viability of the proposal by describing to observer subjects the constraint and/or choice conditions that live subjects are exposed to in cognitive dissonance lab studies. He told the observer subjects of the typical behaviors of the live subjects and invited their inferences about the presumed final attitudes of the live subjects. Since he found his observer subjects in the simulations able to replicate the findings of the live subjects in the original studies, Bem assumed that the functional analysis pertinent to other-perception (simulation) applies to self-perception (live study) and thus the supposed interior motivations and prior attitudes of live subjects were irrelevant to the self-perception of attitude. Dissonance researchers, on the other hand, attempted to discern those conditions in the interpersonal simulations that would establish Bem's effects either as "confounds" of some other process or as referring to different phenomena. In fact, not very much in the way of resolution came out of this adversary research process, and the conflict itself was epistemologically unrevealing.

Nevertheless, Bem's model of the self-perception process provided a compelling alternative to dissonance theory at a time when social psychologists were apparently becoming skeptical about the use of the dissonance approach to describe a wide array of social behavior. As noted earlier, it was not until several years after its original proposal that self-perception processes as described by Bem were recognized as being subsumed by the major attribution frameworks of the day (i.e., correspondent inference theory and the ANOVA cube model). Nevertheless, Bem's work contributed greatly to what might be called a "paradigm shift" in social psychology. The counterintuitive motivational-consistency models, so evident in the 1960s, were slowly declining in influence, and the highly intuitive attribution models were taking their place as primary frameworks for the study of social behavior. If we may strike a perhaps ingenuous analogy, while the comprehensive calculi of Jones and Kelley provided the spiffy V-8 engine for this transformation, Bem's contentious self-perception model was the petrol that propelled the shift.

With this brief detour into the historical origins and original formulation of Bem's self-perception framework, we can proceed to describe the basic postulates of the approach and some of its qualifications. Our presentation of the theory will indeed be brief since self-perception is basically a simple paradigm with only two major postulates. Further, as previously noted several times, its postulates and predictions are easily derivable from the major attributional models, described in the earlier sections of this chapter.

Self-Perception: The Postulates

The two rather clear-cut postulates proposed by Bem to account for the processes by which individuals come to "know" their self-attributes have basically been stated in the above quasi-historical account of the model. As noted earlier, the current abbreviated account of the theory is taken from Bem's (1972) chapter in Berkowitz's *Advances in Social Psychology*.

> *Postulate 1: "Individuals come to know their own attitudes, emotions and other internal states partially by inferring them from observations of their own overt behavior and/or the circumstances in which this behavior occurs"* (Bem, 1972, p. 225).

> *Postulate 2: "To the extent that internal cues are weak, ambiguous, or uninterpretable, the individual is functionally in the same position as an outside observer, an observer who must necessarily rely upon those same external cues to infer the individual's inner states."*

One can see quite clearly in these two postulates the "radical behaviorist" cast of Bemian self-perception theory. Knowing what is inside oneself in the way of traits, attitudes, values, emotions, and the like is a matter of considering the functional relationship between one's own overt behavior and the circumstances which give rise to it. For Bem's purposes, the most important "circumstances" for engaging in self-perceptual analysis are those which suggest the degree to which the environment (e.g., objects, constraints, and other people) *control* the expression of the person's overt behavior. Very simply, if the controlling circumstances are strong, the person regards his/her overt behavior as not particularly reflective of internal states or traits. On the other hand, if the overt behavior is apparently freely engaged in without environmental urging, it will be seen by the individual as a "true" reflection of the inside attributes of self.

What is further evident from this portrayal of self-perception processes is that the functional analysis leading to an inference of self-attributes is similar, if not identical, to the functional analysis that a naïve perceiver might engage in when intuiting the traits, states, and attitudes of another. This latter point is the basic hypothesis communicated in postulate 2. Indeed, as we have noted earlier, correspondent inference theory proposes a quite compatible functional information-processing analysis in the case of attitude attributions to others. A rather controversial aspect of postulate 2 is the notion that, in the absence of immediate behavioral and environmental data, our inward perceptions of self-attributes, attitudes, or affect are indefinite and ambiguous at best. While controversial in the face of the motivationally guided cognitive dissonance theory, the proposals embodied in postulates 1 and 2 were certainly compatible with the external stimulus-guided theories of emotion proposed by Schachter (1964, see Chapter 14) and Valins (1966), and reasonably consistent with the implications of the then-emerging attribution analyses of Jones and Kelley.

Some Qualifications on Self-Other Comparabilities in Attributional Inference

While the postulates reflect the radical behaviorist ideology of Bem's original model, in the 1972 chapter Bem relented a bit on the implication that there are no differences between self-perception and interpersonal perception. Partly because of developments in research and partly because the advocacy of "strict no-difference" had already served its adversarial role in the Bem/dissonance controversy, Bem proposed the following four qualifications on the comparability of self- and other-perception:

   1 *The Insider-Outsider Difference.* Bem proposed that all of us have access to internal stimuli and knowledge to which an uninformed observer cannot gain access. In noting this, he is clear that a Skinnerian analysis of self-attribution need not argue "that we make *no* discriminations among internal stimuli, but only that we are far more severely limited than we suppose in this regard because the verbal community is limited in how extensively it can train us to make such discriminations" (Bem, 1972, p. 260). For an example of possible "inside" knowledge that an observer might not be privy to but that constitutes a pivotal stimulus in an actor's self-attribution, he cites the actor's awareness of the mental effort she/he might be putting into problem solutions. The insider can infer that she/he is trying hard and thus can further assign high difficulty to the problem. The "outsider," with an absence of overt evidence for such mental efforts, might view the actor as lazy or incompetent and the problem as easy.
   2 *Intimate versus Stranger Difference.* This particular source of difference between self- and other-perception simply refers to the fact that people have

both clear knowledge about their past behavior in various domains and probably have formed stable attributions about self in some of those domains. For example, if a person has a long history of positive academic achievements, she/he might be more prone to attribute a particular failure to the difficulty of a task, while an outside observer of "one-time" achievement behavior might be more likely to make a dispositional inference of low ability. This perspective is quite congruent with Kelley's ANOVA model with respect to the time dimension and Jones and McGillis's notion of the applicability of target-based expectancies to self-perception.

3   *The Self versus Other Difference.* In this instance, Bem is addressing such motivational and defensive mechanisms as esteem maintenance and ego enhancement as bases for self-other disparities in attribution. These motivational bases for qualifying postulate 2 are regarded with mild skepticism by Bem. While acknowledging the possibility of motivational distortions in self-perception, Bem notes that many such distortions are likely accounted for by the intimate/stranger distinction which bears upon a differential knowledge of past history between the self and other. Certainly the work of Miller and Ross (1975), which cites expectancy differences as the primary bases for most supposed motivational distortions of attribution, is compatible with Bem's skepticism on this issue.

4   *The Actor versus Observer.* In the case of this self-/other-perception disparity, Bem is referring to a difference in *perspective* between self-perceivers and other-perceivers. Following the hypothesis and preliminary research of Jones and Nisbett (1972), Bem notes that there may be a pervasive tendency for actors to attribute their behavior to external causes and observers to attribute the actor's behavior to his/her disposition. From the Jones and Nisbett proposal it is clear that the basis for such perspective disparities inheres in the adaptive difference in the salience of external versus dispositional information for actors and observers. In short, actors are more vigilant about the controlling circumstances of their behavior, while observers who are keyed to understand an actor are more vigilant about their internal predilections. While there is some evidence to support this actor-observer bias (cf. Jones & Nisbett, 1972), the sources of the perspective differences found are not yet clear from such research.

Within the limits of these four qualifications on Bem's second postulate, the major propositions of self-perception theory are viewed by Bem as an adequate and parsimonious description of the self-perception process. The consistency of this framework with the attributional perspective is a compelling factor in its favor, and the research supporting this relatively simple model is also reasonably compatible with its two postulates.

Research Supporting Self-Perception Theory

A number of research enterprises might be cited as supporting the basic proposals of the self-perception framework. As already noted, some of this work was performed by Bem himself in confronting the theoretical divergence between his perspective and that of cognitive dissonance theory. In addition, there are bodies of research which lend support to the basic notions characterizing self-perception theory, although the research was performed to answer other questions. In his 1972 account of self-perception theory, Bem considers each of these sources of research support for the theory.

With regard to the interpersonal simulation studies discussed earlier (Bem, 1965, 1967a, 1967b, 1968; Bem & McConnell, 1970; Kiesler, Zanna, & Nisbett, 1969; and others), it seems clear from the results that the self-perception-like effects suggested by the two postulates of the theory had been found by researchers using the forced-compliance, free-choice, forbidden-toy, and decisional paradigms from the dissonance research armamentarium of methods. In each instance, the simple description of the live conditions of one or another dissonance study to uninvolved subjects had resulted in those subjects "correctly" describing the attitudes and attributes of the live subjects. Since these studies typically communicate only information about the live subjects' behaviors and the strengths of the constraints governing those behaviors, the reasonable conclusion is that those observers engage in the functional analysis suggested by Bem's first postulate. Since they reproduce the patterns of response that live subjects evidence, Bem assumes that his second postulate is also, in fact, confirmed. Dissonance theory actually provides no compelling alternative to the self-perception notion, even though research on its behalf has demonstrated qualifications on its applicability (e.g., Jones, Linder, Kiesler, Zanna, & Brehm, 1968). In summary then, whether or not self-perception is a "better" alternative to understanding attitude phenomena than dissonance theory, its simulation experiments help establish its viability as a model of self-attribution—particularly with respect to postulate 2.

In other areas of inquiry the research bearing on the viability of the self-perception framework is also quite supportive. Studies of the misattribution of emotion (cf. Schachter & Singer, 1962; Valins & Ray, 1967; Ross, Rodin, & Zimbardo, 1969; Storms & Nisbett, 1970; Nisbett & Valins, 1971) all indicate that, if individuals are either induced to generalized arousal or led to believe that they are atypically aroused (e.g., through false heart-rate feedback), they use the external cues available in the environment to label the nature and causes for the "arousal" they feel. Again, as predicted by self-perception theory, one's knowledge of internal states is fuzzy and ambiguous and the external environment provides cues to make our states of arousal unambiguous and supply us with a label for these self-states. (See the account of Schachter's two-factor theory of emotion in Chapter 14 for an expanded view of self-labeling of internal states.)

In addition to these domains of research, studies of intrinsic-interest inductions in achievement contexts (cf. Lepper, Greene, & Nisbett, 1973) also support self-perception theory. These studies demonstrate that individuals will exhibit (as evidenced by their approach behaviors) intrinsic interest in a particular achievement task when the inducements to engage in that task are low or subtle, but less intrinsic interest in the same task when inducements are high. This kind of finding is clearly compatible with the self-perception framework.

While this cursory review of research support does not do justice to the wide array of phenomena to which self-perception theory has been applied, the sampling does give reasonable evidence for its empirical viability.

Taken together with its simplicity, flexibility, internal consistency, and consistency with other attributional frameworks, this research support indicates that, as a theory, Bem's self-perception model, while limited, is quite exemplary.

A POSTSCRIPT AND PROSPECTIVE ON ATTRIBUTION THEORY

The foregoing chapter has presented what must be considered as the major orienting frameworks for the study of attributional processes in social psychology. As the reader might have noted, a hallmark of these theories is the premium the theorists appear to place on the logical consistency of the propositions. Not only are these theories possessed of logical integrity on the structural level, but they also presume that the primary domain of study for attribution theory consists of the logical properties of the social perceiver as the object of study. In short, attribution theory is an exercise in logical analysis—both in its form and in its substance.

Viewing social perception processes through the calculating eyes of the lay scientist is an analytic convenience which has borne considerable empirical and theoretical fruit during the past decade in social psychology. The foibles of the human information processor in mundane reality are conceived of as deviations from a *model of baseline rationality*—a model that Jones and McGillis (1976) convincingly defend as irrefutable by empirical data.

While these authors have no quibble with the important and burgeoning advances that this model of convenience has brought to the study of social perception, we can only look back with nostalgia at the intriguing questions that originally impelled Heider's thought. It is a considerable distance from the naïve phenomenological perspective of Heider to the naïve science of current attributional frameworks. Much has been gained and much has been lost in this theoretical journey.

If the notion that normal science is naturalistically subject to shifting paradigms and pendulum swings is valid, social psychology may yet find itself tracing its steps back to Heider's phenomenology. Indeed, it appears that the full-scale baseline models of Jones and Kelley are no longer the primary objects of study for attribution researchers. Much of the current-day research and theory in attribution appears to focus upon the perceptual, attentional, and judgmental distortions of logic engaged in by the naïve perceiver. Ross's "fundamental attribution error" (1978), Snyder, Stephan & Rosenfield's work on the impact of egotism in person perception (1978), research on expectancy-based distortions in social perception (Miller & Ross, 1975), Nisbett and Wilson's (1977) exploration of self-report inaccuracies and cognitive "insufficiencies" in perceivers, and Langer's (1978) concepts describing "mindlessness" in naïve social perception are each tracking one or another deviation from baseline processes. For most of this work, the dominant paradigm of attribution theory stands as the model from which these deviations spring. Such phenomena are viewed as the products of disconfirmed expectancies, or liabilities of the use of schemas aiding in processing partial information arrays. In a sense these nonlinear processing deviations are being currently viewed as interrupt mechanisms in the logical chain of social reasoning. It may turn out that such a portrayal of these problems is most appropriate. On the other hand, it is also entirely possible that the pursuit of these issues of logical deviation signals a renewed interest in the phenomenology of social perception (as distinguished from its logic). If such is the case, one might predict an impending moderation of the attribution paradigm in the 1980s. Perhaps our naïve scientist of a social perceiver will be rejoined with his/her naïve humanist counterpart. It may well be that the counterintuitive side of social perception is on the rebound in social psychology. Nevertheless, one should neither expect nor desire a dramatic decline of the highly important models of attribution so dominant in the field at this point in time. There certainly exists an a priori rational baseline of social thought that warrants understanding. However, we would conjecture that in the next decade, social psychologists will be more willing to venture into both the "fair" territory of logic and the counterintuitive "foul" territory of phenomenology, which lie on opposite sides of this firmly drawn baseline.

Chapter 10

Theories of Social Comparison, Judgment, and Perception

Individuals everywhere engage in social comparison processes, make judgments about other people and themselves, perceive that they do or do not have freedom of action, and form impressions of others. Opinions are formed and modified, abilities are appraised and evaluated, and attempts are made to influence the opinions and behaviors of others. These kinds of social behaviors have intrigued social psychologists for many years and many theories have been advanced to "explain" them. Since opinions, judgments, and the like are essentially cognitive concepts, it is not surprising that many of these theories reflect the cognitive orientation. Indeed, the cognitive consistency theories discussed in Chapter 8 and the attribution theories presented in Chapter 9 also attempt to explain many of these same phenomena. In this chapter we have chosen to present six somewhat loosely related theories dealing with social influence processes, social comparison, social judgment, impression formation, and perceived freedom.

SOCIAL COMPARISON THEORY

Social comparison theory was formulated by Festinger (1950, 1954). Development of the theory began with a consideration of the effects of social communication on opinion change in social groups (Festinger, 1950) and was later extended to include the appraisal of abilities as well as the evaluation of opinions. Basically, the theory holds that social influence processes and certain kinds of competitive behavior stem directly from a need for self-evaluation and the necessity for this evaluation to be based on comparisons with other persons. Although the process is essentially the same for both opinion evaluation and ability appraisal, there are some important differences between the two processes. First, there is a unidirectional upward push in the case of abilities that is lacking with regard to opinions. Second, opinion change is relatively easy when compared with performance or ability change.

The major principles of the theory of social comparison processes were presented by Festinger (1954) in the form of hypotheses, corollaries, and derivations. These statements concerned the need to evaluate, sources of evaluation, the choice of persons for comparison, factors influencing change, the cessation of comparison, and pressures toward uniformity.

The Drive to Evaluate Opinions and Abilities

The basic assumption underlying the theory of social comparison is that *there exists a drive to evalute one's opinions and abilities* (hypothesis 1 in Festinger, 1954). That is, people need to determine whether or not their opinions are correct and to obtain an accurate appraisal of their abilities. The individual's opinions and beliefs, as well as his or her evaluation of his or her abilities, are important determinants of his or her behavior. Correct opinions and accurate appraisals of ability are likely to lead to satisfying or rewarding behavior; incorrect beliefs and/or inaccurate appraisals of ability lead to unpleasant consequences (punishment).

Festinger (1954) made a distinction between situations in which evaluations of ability function like opinions and situations in which they do not. Since abilities are reflected in performance, their manifestation varies in clarity. For example, a person's weight-lifting ability can be appraised directly in "objective reality," but, in evaluating ability as an abstract artist, one must rely on the opinions of others (that is, on "social reality"). In the latter instance, evaluations of ability are really opinions about ability; however, in the first instance the appraisal depends more on a comparison of one's performance with that of others than on the opinions of others. Festinger was concerned with relatively unambiguous ability appraisal.

The existence of a drive to evaluate opinions and abilities implies that people will behave in ways designed to satisfy this need; that is, in ways which enable them to accurately evaluate their opinions and abilities. How people attempt to do this becomes an important question.

Sources of Evaluation

Festinger asserted that, in general, a person will use objective reality as a basis for evaluation when this means is available, but will rely on the opinions of others (social reality) when objective reality is not available. Thus, hypothesis 2 stated that *people evaluate their opinions and abilities by comparison with the opinions and abilities of others, respectively, to the extent that nonsocial means are unavailable.* For example, people cannot readily test by objective means their beliefs that democracy is the best form of government in existence, because there is no known way of doing so; hence, they rely on the opinions of others. Similarly, one might measure the time required to solve a particular problem, but this would reveal little about one's problem-solving ability unless one knew something about the time required for others to solve the same problem.

As a corollary of hypothesis 2, Festinger proposed that *subjective evaluations of opinions and abilities are unstable when there is neither a physical nor a social basis for comparison* (corollary 2A). Evidence for this proposition was drawn from studies of level of aspiration which show that judgments of the quality of performance are stable when there is a comparison standard (Gardner, 1939; Gould, 1939), but they are unstable when such a standard is absent (unpublished study by J. W. Brehm).

It was also proposed that *evaluations of opinions will not be based upon comparisons with others when an objective basis is available* (corollary 2B). Festinger cited the study by Hochbaum (1953) as evidence for this corollary. This study showed that subjects who were persuaded that their abilities to judge ths issue under consideration were very good did not change their opinions very often when others in the group disagreed with them, whereas those subjects who were persuaded that their abilities were poor changed their opinions frequently when others disagreed with them. The results of this study seem to support Festinger's proposition; however, it may be noted that the conformity studies by Asch (1951) yielded results that appear to be somewhat inconsistent with the corollary. Subjects exposed to a unanimous majority who made obviously incorrect judgments of length of lines agreed with the majority about 30 percent of the time.[1]

Choice of Persons for Comparison

Given that there is no objective basis for comparison, then people will seek to evaluate their opinions and abilities by comparison with others. But there are usually many others that might be chosen for comparison. Festinger hypothesized that *the tendency to compare oneself with another decreases as the discrepancy between one's own opinion or ability and that of the other person increases* (hypothesis 3). The point here is that people will choose to evaluate

---

[1]Tversky and Kahneman (1973, 1974) report that persons faced with a difficult task of judging frequency or probability of events employed a limited number of "heuristics," which reduce these judgments to simpler ones. Commonly used heuristics are representativeness (an event is judged as probable to the extent that it represents the essential features of its population), availability (the ease with which relevant instances come to mind), and adjustment from an anchor (judges begin with judgments based on an initial value and then adjust to yield a final value). These findings may appear to be inconsistent with corollary 2B; however, subjects in these studies were not given the option of comparing their judgments with the judgments of others.

their opinions and abilities by comparing them with their peers or near peers. For example, a college student will choose other college students for comparison rather than prison inmates; teenagers will choose other teenagers rather than adults. Corollaries 3A and 3B follow: *Given a choice, a person will choose someone close to his or her own opinion or ability for comparison* (3A). *If only a divergent comparison is available, the person will not be able to make a precise evaluation of his or her opinion or ability* (3B).

Evidence for this set of hypotheses comes from a study by Whittemore (1925) which showed that in group-task situations subjects almost always reported the selection of someone whose performance was close to their own as a competitor.

Using hypotheses 1, 2, and 3, Festinger was able to derive a number of further predictions. Derivation A held that evaluations are stable when others close to one's own opinion or ability are available for comparison. Derivation B stated the other side of the coin: evaluations will tend to change when the available comparison group has opinions and abilities which differ from one's own opinions or abilities. Data from the level of aspiration studies cited above also tend to support these propositions.

Derivation C states that an individual will be less attracted to situations in which others have different opinions and abilities than to one in which others have opinions and abilities similar to the individual's own. This suggests that persons will be attracted to groups or persons who provide the most acceptable basis for comparison. Thus derivation C follows directly from hypothesis 1 and corollaries 3A and 3B. This proposal is consistent with the similarity-attraction theories (e.g., Byrne, 1971; Newcomb, 1956) described in Chapter 3.

Derivation D asserts that a discrepancy in a group with respect to abilities or opinions will lead to action designed to reduce this discrepancy. This follows from hypotheses 1, 2, and 3. Since there is a drive to evaluate opinions and abilities, it should produce behavior directed toward producing a state in which an acceptable evaluation can be made. This is a situation in which discrepancies are small or absent. Therefore, the behavior should be directed toward reducing discrepancies in the group.

Factors Influencing Change

There are two major factors that influence change of abilities as compared with opinions: the unidirectional upward pressure with respect to abilities and the relatively greater ease of changing opinions. Thus Festinger's hypothesis 4 states that *there is a unidirectional drive upward in the case of abilities which does not exist in the case of opinions*. At least in the American culture, high-performance scores are valued; therefore, there is pressure to continually improve performance. In the case of opinions, however, there is no inherent basis for comparison and hence no general pressure to change in any particular direction.

The second factor is considered in hypothesis 5, which states that *there are nonsocial factors which make it difficult or impossible to change one's abilities, but such factors are largely absent for opinions.* A woman might believe that she should be able to lift a heavy weight but be physically unable to do so. No amount of effort can enable her to lift the weight. On the other hand, if this same woman decides that her opinion about a particular issue is incorrect, she ordinarily can change her opinion without too much difficulty.

Reconsidering derivation D, it is now clear that the behavior toward reducing intermember discrepancies in opinions is a simple pressure toward uniformity. The action with regard to abilities, however, is more complicated, since the pressure to reduce discrepancies interacts with the unidirectional upward push toward better performance. The net result of these forces is pressure toward uniformity up to a point where the individual is just slightly better than others—at which point the pressure toward uniformity ceases to operate. Thus, when a discrepancy exists with respect to opinions or abilities there will be tendencies to change one's own opinion or ability in the direction of others (derivation D_1) and to change others in the group to bring them closer to oneself (derivation D_2). Festinger suggested that, when opinions are involved, the expressed action will be primarily social; that is, persons will try to influence each other. In the case of abilities, the action will be primarily toward the environmental restraints. For example, people who have little weight-lifting ability in comparison with others may practice weight lifting in order to improve their performance. Festinger cited data from three experimental studies to support these two derivations (Back, 1951; Festinger & Thibaut, 1951; Gerard, 1953).

Cessation of Comparison

Under certain conditions an individual will cease to make comparisons with particular others; that is, comparability can be achieved by changing the composition of the comparison group. Derivation D_3 postulated that there will be tendencies to cease comparing oneself with persons in the group whose opinions or abilities are greatly discrepant from one's own.

Festinger believed that the consequences of cessation of comparison would be different for opinions and abilities. This was based upon the fact that opinion discrepancy implies that one's opinions are incorrect, whereas no such negative implications necessarily accompany ability discrepancy. This general view is stated as hypothesis 6: *To the extent that continued comparison with others implies unpleasant consequences, the cessation of comparison will be accompanied by hostility or derogation.* Corollary 6A states that *cessation of comparison will be accompanied by hostility or derogation in the case of opinions but not in the case of abilities.*

Festinger cited evidence from studies by Festinger, Schachter, and Back (1950) and by Schachter (1951) to support the prediction regarding opinions. These studies revealed a tendency of the group to reject group members who had very divergent opinions. The data relative to the abilities prediction came from a study by Hoffman, Festinger, and Lawrence (1954). One of three subjects was made to score higher than the other two on an intelligence test. When the situation permitted, the two low scorers competed with each other but ceased to compete with the high-scoring subject.

Pressures toward Uniformity

In several of the preceding propositions it was indicated that the drive to evaluate abilities and opinions gives rise to pressures toward uniformity. The strength of these pressures is determined by a number of factors. From hypotheses 1, 2, and 3, Festinger derived that any factor that increases the drive to evaluate an opinion or ability will also increase pressures toward uniformity with respect to that opinion or ability (derivation E). Similarly, hypothesis 7 states that *any factor which increases the importance of a group as a comparison group for an opinion or ability will increase pressure toward uniformity with respect to that opinion or ability.*

Several corollaries to the above two propositions were formulated to specify some of the factors determining strength of pressures toward uniformity. Corollary to derivation E asserts that *pressures toward uniformity will increase with an increase in the importance of an opinion or ability, or with an increase in the relevance of an opinion or ability to immediate behavior.* The position here is that an opinion or ability that is regarded by the person as of little importance will arouse little or no drive toward evaluation and that the greater the relevance of the opinion or ability to behavior, the greater will be the drive to evaluate the opinion or ability.

Corollary 7A states that *the pressure toward uniformity with respect to opinions and abilities will vary with the strength of attraction to the group.* The more attractive the group is to a person, the more important it will be as a comparison group. Therefore, the pressures to reduce discrepancies between one's self and the group will be stronger. These pressures should be manifested as (1) a tendency to change one's own position, (2) an increased effort to change others, and (3) a greater tendency to make others noncomparable. Back (1951) showed that members who were highly attracted to a group made more influence attempts; Festinger, Gerard, Hymovitch, Kelley, and Raven (1952) found that members of highly cohesive groups changed their opinions more than members of low-cohesive groups; and Festinger, Torrey, and Willerman (1954) found that feelings of inadequacy regarding task performance were greater in low-attractive than in high-attractive groups. Corollary 7A thus appears to be in agreement with the experimental evidence available at the time it was formulated.

Corollary 7B holds that *pressure toward uniformity varies with the relevance of the opinion or ability to the group.* Despite some lack of clarity of the concept "relevance," Schachter (1951) was able to create differences in perceived relevance and to demonstrate that rejection of deviates was greater in high-relevance than in low-relevance conditions.

In addition to factors that influence the three forms of pressure manifestation, there are some factors that affect these manifestations differently. Thus, Festinger hypothesized that the tendency to narrow the range of comparability becomes stronger when persons whose opinions or abilities are divergent from one's own are perceived as also being different on attributes consistent with the opinion or ability divergence (hypothesis 8). Evidence supporting this hypothesis was taken from studies by Gerard (1953) and by Festinger and Thibaut (1951). In both studies group members were led to believe that the group held either homogeneous or heterogeneous opinions on a given issue. Actually, there was considerable variation in opinions held by group members in both conditions. During discussion there was less communication directed toward deviates in the heterogeneous than in the homogeneous groups. Festinger interpreted these results as showing that the perception of heterogeneity enabled subjects to narrow the range of comparability.

Hypothesis 9 is rather long and involved, so perhaps it is best cited verbatim:

> When there is a range of opinion or ability in a group, the relative strength of the three manifestations of pressure toward uniformity will be different for those who are close to the mode of the group than for those who are distant from the mode. Specifically, those close to the mode of the group will have stronger tendencies to change the positions of others, relatively weaker tendencies to narrow the range of comparison and much weaker tendencies to change their own position compared to those who are distant from the mode of the group (Festinger, 1954, pp. 134–135).

Festinger cited little direct evidence for this hypothesis, although the results from the Festinger et al. (1952) experiment are consistent with it. In comparison with conformers, deviates were found to change their opinions more frequently, to show less tendency to influence others, and to show a greater tendency to redefine group boundaries to exclude those with divergent opinions.

Implications for Group Formation

The preceding sections have dealt primarily with the effects of the drive for evaluation on behavior in groups. However, the drive for self-evaluation also has important implications for group formation and the changing of group memberships. In the first place, since comparison can be accomplished only in groups, the drive for self-evaluation should cause the person to belong to groups and to associate with others. Secondly, the groups that provide the greatest promise of satisfaction are those which hold opinions near the person's own. Therefore, individuals will be more attracted to groups holding similar opinions and will tend to move out of groups that hold different opinions. This move will more or less guarantee that extant groups will be composed of persons whose opinions and abilities are similar. Festinger suggested that the segmentation into groups that are similar with respect to abilities gives rise to status in a society.

Consequences of Preventing Incomparability

We stated earlier that individuals will tend to redefine groups to render incomparable those whose opinions and abilities are too divergent from their own opinions and abilities. Festinger identified two kinds of situations in which this may not occur; that is, in which comparability is forced. The first situation is one in which the attraction to the group is so strong that the person continues to remain in the group in spite of divergencies of opinions and abilities. In this case, the power of the group over the individual is strong and differences in opinion will probably be eliminated. There will also be strong pressures on individuals to improve their performances. Since people cannot be expected to change their abilities, they would be expected to experience feelings of inadequacy and failure.

The other situation in which incomparability is not possible is one in which the individual is constrained from leaving the group. For example, people in prison cannot leave their group. Of course, there are also social restraints that may be equally effective in preventing the person from leaving the group. If a man must work in order to support his family, he may continue in a group (work group or family group) he dislikes. In such cases, the group would have little power over the individual and uniformity would be expected only when coercion was used. This should lead to public compliance but private resistance.

Current Status of the Theory

The social comparison theory is internally consistent and the hypotheses are stated in a form readily amenable to empirical evaluation. The theoretical propositions agree reasonably well with data available at the time the theory was formulated. Data from more recent research have provided additional support but have also raised questions about some aspects of the theory. Research relevant to social comparison theory falls into five general categories: (1) the hypothesis that there exists a drive to evaluate opinions and abilities, (2) the role of similarity in the choice of a comparison person or group, (3) the effects of social comparisons on the attractiveness of persons or groups, (4) the assumption of a universal drive upward in the case of abilities, and (5) modification and extension of the theory.

Drive to Evaluate Opinions and Abilities   The drive to evaluate has been examined by several investigators with generally positive results. Gordon (1966) and Hakmiller (1966b) found that the desire to affiliate for social comparison purposes increased as opinion discrepancy decreased and that the desire was greater when the group had been shown to be correct than when it had been incorrect. Darley and Aronson (1966) reported that subjects threatened with electric shock preferred to be with persons who reported being slightly more nervous than themselves. Latané and Wheeler (1966) found results from a field study of an airplane crash that were inconsistent with the Darley and Aronson results, but this could have been because of the lack of control over relevant variables in the field study. The evidence thus generally supports the assumption of a drive toward self-evaluation. Currently, investigators appear to assume the existence of a drive to evaluate opinions and abilities and concentrate their efforts toward establishing the variables determining its manifestation.

Similarity and Choice of a Comparison Other Festinger's hypothesis 3 holds that the tendency for persons to compare themselves with others decreases as the discrepancy between their own and others' opinions or abilities increases. Corollary 3A asserts that, if a person has a choice, someone with similar opinions or abilities will be chosen for comparison. Several studies have attempted to test this prediction, with mixed results. Similar others are chosen for comparison when the characteristic to be judged is positively valued (Wheeler, 1966; Gruder, 1971) and when the person is uncertain of his or her own ability (Gordon, 1966; Hakmiller, 1966b; Gruder, 1971; Fazio, 1979; Zanna, Goethals, & Hill, 1975). Jones and Regan (1974) found that the tendency to choose a similar other is strongest when those others are experienced in using the ability in decision-relevant situations.

Similar others are not chosen more frequently than dissimilar others when negative characteristics are being evaluated (Hakmiller, 1966a) or when relatively unfamiliar characteristics are being judged (Thornton & Arrowood, 1966). In the latter instance, it appears that a person who is a positive example of the attribute being judged will provide a more accurate evaluation than a similar other (Arrowood & Friend, 1969).

Corollary 3B and derivations A and B state that social comparison can yield accurate and stable self-evaluation only when comparison is with a similar other. In testing this hypothesis, Radloff (1966) demonstrated that subjects judged their performance on a pursuit rotor task more accurately when similar comparison scores were provided. In the absence of similar comparison persons, self-evaluation was found to be inaccurate and unstable. In a further test, Wilson (1973) found that persons exposed to a similar ability evaluation score felt more certain about their ability evaluation and found this information more helpful in evaluating their own performance than did persons given dissimilar evaluation scores. The limited evidence supports the hypothesis.

Social Comparison and Attractiveness Derivation C suggests that, since similarity of abilities enables people to accurately assess their abilities, similar others should be more attractive than dissimilar others. This relationship has been demonstrated in an extensive series of investigations (Byrne, 1971), although these studies were not stimulated by Festinger's theory. The similarity-attraction relationship, however, is a complex one. Some investigators report a tendency to dislike superior others more than similar others (e.g., Senn, 1971; Mettee & Wilkins, 1972), whereas others find that when "psychological distance" between a superior other and an observer or teammate is reduced, superior-ability others are liked better than similar-ability others (e.g., Aronson, Willerman, & Floyd, 1965; Mettee & Wilkins, 1972). Similarly, Mettee and Riskind (1974) found that promotion of a decisively victorious competitor to an "incomparably superior ability level" made the decisive winner more likeable than a similar-ability competitor who only marginally defeated the person. Conversely, Miller (1977) found that attraction to a group increased preferences for social comparison. Finally, Santee (1976) found that only those kinds of similarity that inform people about reinforcement generate attraction. Overall, the evidence for derivation C is not convincing and emphasizes the need for more detailed consideration of the interrelationship between social comparison processes and attraction.

Unidirectional Drive Upward for Abilities   The assumption of a unidirectional drive upward in the case of abilities was said to be a determinant of the choice of a comparison person (Festinger, 1954), but just how the choice is affected was not clearly stated. As Latané (1966) noted, it is not clear whether Festinger believed that the person would choose for comparison another person who had higher ability or one who had less ability than the person himself. Wheeler (1966) found that, given a choice, subjects elected to compare themselves with persons of slightly higher rank. Since this upward comparison correlated with assumed similarity to someone higher in the rank order, Wheeler interpreted his results in terms of motivation leading to assumed similarity, which in turn led to comparison choices that were expected to confirm this assumption of similarity. He viewed his findings and interpretations as supporting Festinger's theory.

In another attempt to test the unidirectional-upward-drive hypothesis, Samuel (1973) gave subjects false feedback, indicating they would score either superior, average, or inferior on an ambiguous test of mental functioning. Subjects then compared their score and test forms with those of another person. Comparison others available to them were described as being either superior, average, inferior, or similar to the subject (with no other evaluative information being given). Overall, the expressed desire to see another's data was ranked in the order superior-average-inferior-similar other. Samuel interpreted this finding as supporting the unidirectional-drive-upward hypothesis, but he also noted the need for a more precise definition of similarity. Gastorf and Suls (1978) found that performance similarity with respect to comparison others had no effect on evaluation certainty, but subjects were more certain about their performance evaluations after comparison with others who were similar with respect to college classification (college versus graduate student).

Modification and Extension of the Theory   The results of the several studies attempting to test the social comparison hypothesis reveal that social comparison is a more complex phenomenon than indicated by Festinger's theory. The fact that the definition of similarity is ambiguous has been noted frequently, and some attempts have been made to clarify the meaning of similarity. For instance, Samuel (1973) pointed out that persons may be similar on a variety of characteristics and presented data showing that, in the case of abilities, people choose comparison others who are similar on task-irrelevant characteristics (geographical location, activities). The perception of similarity may also be influenced by other variables. For example, Schwartz and Smith (1976) found that persons who were inferior in performance were more reluctant to admit that there was an ability difference than those with relatively superior performances.

A more serious problem for social comparison theory is the evidence that comparison processes are influenced by needs for self-enhancement and self-esteem. For instance, Hakmiller (1966a) proposed that comparison with someone worse off than oneself can lead to self-enhancement, especially when the person feels threatened about the characteristic in question. His findings indicated significantly greater downward comparison among highly threatened subjects than among mildly threatened subjects. However, Thornton and Arrowood (1966) found that comparisons were upward when the characteristic being evaluated was positive, whereas there was no directional preference when the characteristic involved was negative. In another investigation (Wilson & Benner, 1971) it was shown that, for males, persons with high self-esteem were more likely to choose persons with high ability for comparison, whereas those with low self-esteem were more likely to choose someone lower in ability. The effect of self-esteem was greatest when the person was certain about his standing in the group. The authors concluded that social comparison motives will be affected by the situation, nature of the available information, and alternatives available for obtaining additional information. They also suggested that pure ability evaluation may be interfered with by such other motives as defensiveness and self-presentation. Self-esteem effects were also demonstrated in competitive situations (Conolley, Gerard, & Kline, 1978). Higher levels of uncertainty about one's own ability led to higher levels of competition, but only under conditions that minimized threat to self-esteem.

In conclusion, the results of several studies cited above provide considerable support for social comparison theory, but at the same time point out its deficiencies. The major need is for a more precise definition of similarity, a clearer specification of the conditions under which proposed relationships do and do not hold, and an analysis of other variables (motives) influencing social comparison processes. Unlike Festinger's theory of cognitive dissonance (Chapter 8), his theory of social comparison has not shown a meteoric rise in popularity; instead, it has had a modest but enduring influence on research in social psychology. For instance, several recent and interesting studies based on social comparison theory are reported in a volume edited by Suls and Miller (1977). In addition, the basic tenets of the theory have been applied to such diverse processes as the influence of a model's success on an observer's perseverance on a task (Berger, 1971) and the risky shift phenomenon (Baron & Roper, 1976; Goethals & Zanna, 1979).

SOCIAL JUDGMENT THEORY

Social judgment theory (Sherif & Hovland, 1961; Sherif, Sherif, & Nebergall, 1965) derives directly from the general approach originally espoused by Sherif (1935, 1936). Sherif's approach could be considered as an orientation rather than as a theory, since it embodies a conceptual framework that he has applied to such diverse situations as norm formation, attitude change, and intergroup conflict. Nevertheless, it appears to be generally cognitive in nature, although it involves some field-theory constructs and "borrows selectively" from other theoretical orientations (Sherif, 1967).

From the beginning, Sherif was concerned with an attempt to bring together data from the work of psychologists on judgment, perception, learning, and memory, as well as data from the work of anthropologists and sociologists. The basic proposition underlying all his work is that men and women structure situations that are important to them. This structure includes both internal (attitudes, emotions, motives, the effects of past experiences, etc.) and external factors (objects, persons, etc., in the physical surround) that are operative in the situation at any given time. The interaction of these internal and external factors constitutes the "frame of reference" of any given behavior or act, which can only be understood within this frame of reference. However, Sherif stressed the fact that there is no such thing as a frame of reference in the abstract (Sherif & Sherif, 1956). Instead, he insisted that one should consider only the frame of reference of behavior at a given time. The frame of reference at a given time includes all those factors, internal and external, that influence behavior at that time. Sherif argued that behavior is not directly determined by internal and external factors; rather, behavior follows a central patterning of these factors.

Sherif emphasized that internal and external factors are not additive in their influences upon the patterning process. Their relative influence depends upon the degree of stimulus structure and the intensity of the motive state. In general, the greater the stimulus ambiguity and the more intense the motive state, the greater will be the influence of internal factors. Conversely, the more structured the stimulus and the less intense the motive, the greater will be the relative influence of external factors.

Although behavior can be understood only within the total frame of reference, there are reference points or anchors within the total frame of reference that may be more influential than other parts. Much of Sherif's work has been concerned with the identification and analysis of the main anchors which individuals use in making judgments. This work led to the social judgment theory that concerns us here.

Social judgment theory is concerned primarily with the psychological processes underlying the expression of attitudes and the change of attitudes through communication. A basic assumption underlying the theory is that the principles governing basic judgmental processes in general also apply to attitude expression and change. Therefore, Sherif et al. began with a consideration of the principles derived from psychophysical studies of judgment. These principles were then related to attitudinal processes and additional principles derived from studies designed specifically to study attitudes.

The basic assumption of judgment theory is that it involves discrimination and categorization of stimuli, whether these be neutral or attitudinal in nature. Discrimination and categorization involve comparison between alternatives. One of these alternatives may be (and often is) an internal frame of reference or standard of judgment. The formation and use of such standards depend upon the range of experiences that the person has had with the universe of stimuli, anchoring effects, degree of ego involvement, the person's own categories (latitudes of acceptance, rejection, and noncommitment), and assimilation and contrast effects. The social judgment theory consists of a set of interrelated hypotheses or propositions concerning the effects of these variables on the judgment of social events.

Judgment Scales

When an individual is faced with the necessity of making a judgment concerning a particular stimulus (for example, whether to accept or reject an attitude item), he or she can do so only by comparing the stimulus (item) with *something*. This "something" may be another stimulus, a frame of reference, or other judgment scale. Judgment thus requires discrimination or choice between two or more alternatives, which involves a comparison between these alternatives (Sherif, Sherif, & Nebergall, 1965). For example, when a person chooses to attend one school rather than another, a process of judgment is involved. This judgment is based not only on the merits of the two schools, but also on the person's own interests, values, and goals.

Sherif and Hovland (1961) suggested that judgment could be studied either in order to determine the discriminative capacity of a particular sense modality or to analyze the placement or categorization of particular stimuli in a series. Their analysis was concerned primarily with the process of placement. Since they were interested in attitude formation and change, their analysis dealt with the person's placement of attitude items such as those used in attitude measurement (for examples, see Thurstone & Chave, 1929; Likert, 1932; Shaw & Wright, 1967).

The major principles concerning the development of judgment scales derive from experimental studies using neutral stimuli, such as weights, tones, and lines. The general conclusion drawn from such studies is that an individual who is confronted with a series of stimuli from a given universe of stimuli tends to form a psychological scale of judgment. In a typical experiment the subject is presented with a series of stimuli (for example, weights), one at a time, and asked to make a judgment (for example, whether the weight is heavy or light). Under such conditions, subjects quickly develop a subjective standard or judgment scale which is near the center of the range of stimuli being judged. Those stimuli above the subjective standard are judged heavy and those below light. Similarly, if the subject is asked to place the stimuli into more than two categories, category thresholds are established; that is, the judgment scale consists of several subjective standards which delineate categories and determine the placement of specific items. These effects have been demonstrated in a number of experiments (Wever & Zener, 1928; Fernberger, 1931; Volkmann, 1951). These same effects have been shown to occur even when the stimulus series is not well graded by objective standards. For example, McGarvey (1943) demonstrated that all the effects found with physical stimuli could be reproduced with social stimuli (that is, social acts such as "lying to mother," "spitting on the crucifix," and "committing murder").

The particular nature of a judgment scale is largely determined by the conditions under which it is formed. When the scale is established on the basis of an unambiguous stimulus series with well-graded stimulus differences and with explicit anchors provided within the series, stimulus values and scale values correspond closely. For example, if the stimulus series consists of weights ranging from 5 to 100 grams and an anchor weighing 50 grams is provided, the psychological scale and the objective scale correspond closely and the reference scale is relatively stable (Bressler, 1933; Long, 1937). To the extent that the stimulus series lacks an explicit anchor or standard, the psychological judgment scale is less stable than when an anchor is provided. Furthermore, the placement of items located in the middle portion of the series is less accurate than those near the ends of the series (Needham, 1935; Volkmann, 1951). Therefore, it appears that the end points of a judged series of stimuli serve as anchors in the formation of judgment scales.

When the series of stimuli to be judged lacks both unambiguous graded differences and an explicit standard, the effects of internal factors and social influences on the formation of the judgment scale are increased. Evidence for this proposition comes from a number of studies in which autokinetic movement was used as the stimulus situation. When a stationary pinpoint of light is presented in a completely dark room, it appears to move. When the light is presented several times, judgments of the amount of movement become more or less stabilized within a particular range (Sherif, 1935). However, when subjects are asked to make their judgments in a group, judgments tend to converge to a common range and standard (Sherif, 1935; Bovard, 1948). This factor plays an important role in the Sherif and Hovland approach, as will be seen later.

Assimilation and Contrast Effects

It was noted in the preceding section that the judgment scale is more stable and scale values correspond more closely to objective values when an anchor is available than when it is not. It was also shown that the end points of the stimulus range serve as anchors (Volkmann, 1951). When there are no well-defined end points to the stimulus range, the first and last category labels used in the instructions serve as anchors (Eriksen & Hake, 1957).

The effects of anchors discussed thus far are those produced by an anchor within the stimulus range. But in natural situations the anchoring stimulus often lies outside the stimulus range being judged. The effects of anchors outside the stimulus range depend upon the remoteness of the anchor. An anchor placed slightly above or slightly below the ends of the series will lead to a shift in item placement *toward* the anchor, whereas an anchor placed considerably above or below the stimulus range will produce a judgment shift *away* from the anchor (Rogers, 1941; Postman & Miller, 1945; Heintz, 1950). Sherif and Hovland (1961) labeled the shift toward the anchor *assimilation;* presumably, the anchor is assimilated into the stimuli being judged. It is as if the stimulus range is extended to include the anchor. The shift away from the anchor in the case of remote anchors was referred to as a *contrast* effect. These effects have also been demonstrated when the anchor is internal (Hunt, 1941; Hovland & Sherif, 1952; Sherif & Hovland, 1953).

Latitudes of Acceptance, Rejection, and Noncommitment

According to Sherif and Hovland, these same judgmental processes operate when the individual is required to indicate whether he or she agrees or disagrees with a statement, as in the case of attitude measurement. There are, however, two features in addition to those operating in psychophysical judgment. First, if the person has an attitude toward an object or class of objects, he or she brings to any particular situation a set of established evaluative categories. Therefore, the question of acceptability or unacceptability of the attitude object becomes a factor in judgment. Second, social judgments vary from individual to individual, whereas in the case of psychophysical judgments there is little interindividual variability.

Individuals also differ in their acceptance or tolerance of positions other than their own and in the range of positions they regard as objectionable. Furthermore, they differ with respect to the importance of a given issue in their own psychological organization. The observation of these differences led to the concepts of latitudes of acceptance, rejection, and noncommitment. *Latitude of acceptance* refers to the range of positions that an individual is willing to accept or, at least, to tolerate. It includes not only the position that is most acceptable to the person but also other tolerable positions. *Latitude of rejection* refers to all those positions that are unacceptable or objectionable to the individual. It includes the most objectionable position and all other unacceptable positions. *Latitude of noncommitment* includes all those positions that are not included in either the latitude of acceptance or the latitude of rejection; that is, all positions that are neither acceptable nor objectionable. Thus a person's judgment of a particular statement will depend upon its relation to these latitudes. If it reflects a position that falls within the latitude of acceptance, the person will agree with it: if it falls within the latitude of rejection, he or she will disagree with it.

In attempting to measure latitudes of acceptance, rejection, and noncommitment, Sherif, Sherif, and Nebergall (1965) made several assumptions: (1) There are at least two positions that may be taken toward the attitude object, and these are known to the subjects. These positions need to be defined as clearly as possible. (2) The alternatives within the domain are ranked in the same order by all subjects when the dimension for ranking is degree of favorability. This applies only to unequivocal statements; no assumption was made regarding equality of intervals. (3) People are free to determine for themselves the number of positions they are willing to accept, reject, or remain neutral toward.

Based on several experimental studies (Hovland & Sherif, 1952; Sherif & Hovland, 1961), it was concluded that strong commitment to a position involves a lowered threshold of rejection. This led to several hypotheses about the relationship between extremity of position and size of the various latitudes: (1) With regard to controversial issues, the latitude of rejection of those taking an extreme position will be greater than those taking a moderate position. (2) For extreme subjects, the latitude of rejection will be greater than their latitude of acceptance. (3) The latitude of noncommitment will vary inversely with extremity of position. A study of the 1960 presidential campaign yielded results consistent with these hypotheses (Sherif et al., 1965).

Patterns of Acceptance and Rejection

Sherif and his associates have conducted numerous studies of the distinctive patterning of acceptance, rejection, and displacement in social judgment. Based on these studies, several propositions were formulated (Sherif et al., 1965):

1 If individuals have an attitude toward a class of items, they will have a set of well-established categories for judging it, including ranges of acceptance and rejection. Any specific item will be judged in relation to these categories.

2 To the extent that people are involved with respect to the class of items, the position that they accept as their own serves as an anchor for the placement of other items in the same class.

3 To the extent that individuals' own positions become the most salient anchor, their placements of an item will reflect their evaluations of it. This proposition will be true even if people are instructed to disregard their own feelings.

4 When people's own positions serve as anchors and when the item lacks, in some degree, objective properties that cannot be ignored, items will be assimilated or contrasted in proportion to their proximities or discrepancies from people's own positions. That is, the items will be displaced toward a person's own position when they are near his or her position and displaced away from a person's own position when they are remote from it.

These propositions may be conceptualized as follows: When people use their own positions as anchors, they become involved and hence selective about those items they are willing to accept. Only those items that are close to their own positions are assimilated into the latitude of acceptance. The threshold of acceptance is high, and the range of items that will be assimilated is inversely proportional to degree of involvement. Conversely, the threshold of rejection is lowered, and the range of unacceptable items increases in proportion to degree of involvement.

These effects were said to be accentuated when subjects are permitted to use whatever number of categories seems appropriate to them. On the basis of this assumption, the following additional propositions concerning categorization were formulated:

1 The number of categories that a person chooses to use varies inversely with the person's degree of involvement. Persons who are strongly committed to positions use fewer categories than less-involved persons.

2 Highly involved persons place large numbers of items in the unacceptable category, put a few into the acceptable category, and tend to ignore the noncommital category. Uninvolved persons do not reveal this systematic bias in use of category widths.

3 These variations in distribution of items are the result of assimilation-contrast effects relative to the person's own position.

4 The degree of favorableness of the items does not affect these distributions.

Social Judgment and Attitude Change

Sherif and Hovland (1961) pointed out that studies of the effects of communications on attitude change have yielded inconclusive and sometimes contradictory results. For example, Remmers (1938) reported positive shifts in attitude scores following communications, whereas Manske (1937) and Russell and Robertson (1947) found shifts in the direction opposite to that advocated by a communication. Both positive and negative changes have been reported as a function of the subject's initial position (Wilke, 1934; Knower, 1935). Sherif and Hovland suggested that these contrasting effects were on account of the size of the discrepancy between the person's own position and that advocated by the communication. When the discrepancy is small, the communication is assimilated and hence produces positive attitude change; when it is very large, contrast effects occur and the attitude changes away from the position advocated by the communication.

This general interpretation was elaborated by Sherif et al. (1965), who suggested that placement or evaluation of a communication is relative to the individual's reference scale, which includes latitudes of acceptance, rejection, and noncommitment. Whether or not people experience a discrepancy between their own positions and the communications (and hence whether they experience stress) depends upon the positions of the communications relative to latitudes of acceptance, rejection, and noncommitment. The degree to which these latitudes serve as this type of anchor depends upon the extent to which the individual is personally involved with the issue. The degree of involvement can be determined by comparing the number of positions in each of the three latitudes. The greater the personal involvement with the issue, the greater will be the latitude of rejection in relation to the latitude of acceptance and the more nearly will the latitude of noncommitment approach zero.

It therefore follows that, when an individual is involved with an issue, his or her own latitude of acceptance becomes an anchoring point for the evaluation of communications concerning the issue. When the communication does not diverge greatly from the latitude of acceptance, it will be assimilated and will be judged as "fair," "unbiased," and probably "true." The person's own position is shifted in the direction of the communication. On the other hand, if the communication advocates a position that is too far removed from the person's latitude of acceptance so that it falls within his or her latitude of rejection, contrast effects occur and the communication is judged as "unfair," "biased," and probably "false." In such cases the attitude is likely to shift away from the position advocated by the communication (the so-called boomerang effect). Studies by Hovland, Harvey, and Sherif (1957) demonstrated that such effects do indeed occur when subjects varying in attitude toward prohibition are asked to judge a moderately "wet" communication.

Comments and Evaluation

Sherif and his colleagues have formulated an interesting set of propositions concerning the judgment process that fit very well the experimental data from which they were derived. The theory is internally consistent, makes relatively few assumptions, and permits the derivation of precise and testable hypotheses about the judgmental process. Like social comparison theory, its popularity has been modest but enduring; it continues to stimulate research in such diverse areas as the formation of judgment scales, assimilation and contrast effects, patterns of acceptance and rejection, and attitude change.

In addition to the experimental evidence cited by Sherif et al. (1965), several recent investigations provide evidence relevant to social judgment theory. For instance, the theory proposes that, if an anchor (a known point on the stimulus continuum) is available, a person's judgment of any other position or stimulus will be displaced *toward* the anchor when it is within or near the ends of the stimulus range to be judged (assimilation), but will be displaced *away* from the anchor when it is outside and distant from the stimulus range to be judged (contrast). These effects have been demonstrated in the categorization of attitude items (Eiser & White, 1975), judgments of moral character in criminal cases (Pepitone & DiNubile, 1976), judgments of the importance of a social issue (Sherman, Ahlm, & Berman, 1978), and judgments of the positions of candidates on political issues (Granberg & Brent, 1974). At least one study suggests that contrast effects are due to accentuation phenomena; i.e., judges make more polarized pro-anti judgments if they perceive attitude positions as also differing on the agree/disagree dimension (Judd & Harackiewicz, 1980).

The theory also holds that the relationships among latitudes of acceptance, rejection, and noncommitment vary with degree of ego-involvement. Carolyn Sherif and her associates (Sherif, 1973; Sherif, Kelley, Rogers, Sarup, & Tittler, 1973) present evidence from several studies showing that degree of involvement is inversely related to fineness of discrimination in judging one's beliefs about one's own reference group and attitude change in response to short communications, directly related to selectivity in attributing credibility to communicators and to the probability of action and positive response to social pressure, and "associated" with the priority of values in one's reference group.

Another major hypothesis of the theory is that, if a persuasive message is judged to be within the latitude of acceptance, attitude change in the direction advocated by the message occurs, but, if the message is judged to be within the latitude of rejection, either no attitude change occurs or the change will be away from the position advocated by the message. Some general support for this hypothesis derives from attitude change studies (e.g., Atkins, Deaux, & Bieri, 1967; Peterson & Koulack, 1969), but at least one investigation yielded results that are inconsistent with this hypothesis. Eagly and Telaak (1972) gave subjects a message on birth control that was either mildly, moderately, or strongly discrepant from their own positions. For all levels of discrepancy, subjects with wide latitudes of acceptance showed more attitude change than subjects with medium or narrow latitudes of acceptance. Since the mildly discrepant message was within the latitude of acceptance for even those subjects with a narrow latitude of acceptance, the authors argued that the degree of attitude change in response to this message should have been the same for all subjects (if the hypothesis is correct). Another study suggested that contrast effects on ratings are response-based rather than perceptual in nature, but that salient ratings may influence later behavior and attitudes (Sherman, Ahlm, Berman, & Lynn, 1977).

Although the available evidence, for the most part, is in accord with predictions derived from social judgment theory, it is not beyond criticism. One difficulty is a practical one concerning the determination of the various latitudes and degree of involvement. According to the theory, the nature of the latitudes of acceptance, rejection, and noncommitment are so closely related to the degree of commitment that it is difficult to separate them.

Social judgment theory may also be criticized on theoretical grounds. According to the theory, assimilation and contrast effects are the result of altered psychological quantities; that is, the position advocated by a persuasive communication is perceptually distorted so that people exposed to different messages are, in effect, judging different stimuli. Upshaw (1969, 1975, 1978) has pointed out that these effects may also be explained in terms of reference scale phenomena; that is, the phenomena of assimilation and contrast may be merely a shift in reference scale origin toward or away from an experimental anchor. He presented evidence that he believed supports this latter interpretation. Whatever the outcome of this controversy, the theory deals with an important set of social issues that have relevance to most forms of social interaction. The theory will probably continue to stimulate research and undergo modification as new evidence accumulates.

A THEORY OF CHOICE

Philosophers have debated extensively the question of free will, or the freedom of persons to make choices about the things that affect their lives. Behavioral scientists usually take the position that freedom of choice to behave in one way or another is a myth; behavior is determined by needs, personality characteristics, and other variables that constrain the person to behave in this way and not in that way. The philosophers' controversy has not been resolved nor can the behavioral scientist prove that determinism is a valid principle. However, the arguments and beliefs of academicians have little consequence for the average person; people "know" that they have freedom of choice and action—and behave accordingly. Even behavioral scientists often act as if determinism applies only to others. Thus, it is the *perception* of freedom of choice that is important for behavior.

The theory of choice (Steiner, 1979) is concerned with the variables that determine the perception of choice and the consequences of such perceptions for a variety of psychological processes and behaviors. The basic formulations of the theory were first presented in a paper on "perceived freedom" (Steiner, 1970) and elaborated later under the heading "A Theory of Choice" (Steiner, 1979). The theory presented here is the one outlined in the later work.

Definition of Choice

Before defining choice, Steiner distinguished between decision control and outcome control. *Decision control* refers to the process of selecting actions or choosing among options; *outcome control* refers to control over the eventual outcomes of the selected option. Obviously, a person may be able to choose an option without being able to control the consequences of that option. It is decision control that gives a person the feeling of having a *choice*. Thus choice is conceptually the same as decision freedom (Steiner, 1970).

The theory of choice is concerned with decision control; that is, with people's judgments of their own or others' control over the selection of options. However, outcome control is not ignored, since perceived control over an option's outcome may make the option more attractive than perceived lack of control over the outcome.

Expected Utility of Options

The attractiveness or desirability of an option is a function of its utility—the degree to which its positive benefits outweigh its negative aspects. Steiner thinks of desired outcomes as payoffs and undesired ones as costs. The utility of an outcome is expressed by the following formula (Steiner, 1980, p. 7):

$$\text{Expected utility} = \sum_{1}^{n} (\text{valence of payoff} \times \text{probability of payoff})$$

$$- \sum_{1}^{n} (\text{valence of cost} \times \text{probability of cost})$$

where n = the number of payoffs or costs to which the individual attends
    valence = the desirability of the outcome (payoff or costs)
probability = the perceived likelihood of the occurrence of the outcome

According to this formula, the net gain (positive or negative) that the person believes will result from the selection of an option is the expected utility of that option. Therefore, an option is desirable to the extent that expected payoffs exceed expected costs. However, the theory does not assume that people always behave rationally in evaluating payoffs and costs. Instead, people often have some goal in mind and discontinue the analysis of expected payoffs and costs when an acceptable alternative is found. Steiner noted that these formulations are in agreement with the views of many other theorists (e.g., Edwards, 1954; Fishbein, 1965; Luce, 1959; Restle, 1961; Rotter, 1954; Tversky, 1972; March & Simon, 1958; Tolman, 1959; Vroom, 1964).

Comparison and Choice

Steiner apparently distinguishes between the *desirability* and *attractiveness* of an option. He argued that an option's potential to satisfy (desirability?) depends on its expected utility but its attractiveness depends in part on the expected utilities of other alternatives with which it is compared. Available options are compared with one another and/or with other options that constitute a salient comparison set. Options that are not currently available may constitute a salient comparison set either because they have been available in the past, are believed to be available to members of the individual's reference group, or have somehow been identified as appropriate options for comparison.

The attractiveness of any given option was hypothesized to depend on its expected utility relative to that of other appropriate options and on its expected utility relative to that of other available options. According to the theory, comparison with appropriate options precedes comparison with other available options, although the latter may sometimes have a greater effect on feelings of choice.

The theory further proposes that there are at least three reasons why people may feel they have choice. People feel that they have *evaluative choice* if the utility of one or more of their options is at least as high as that of appropriate alternatives that serve as a comparison set. People may experience a feeling of having *discriminative choice* if the best available alternative exceeds the second best. Discriminative choice is therefore based upon comparisons among acceptable available alternatives. People are said to experience *autonomous choice* when, through a comparison of options having approximately equal utilities, they feel that decisions reflect their own judgments and personal preferences. In summary, evaluative choice is a function of the discrepancy between expected utilities of one or more available options and a standard (appropriate comparison set), whereas both discriminative and autonomous choice are functions of the discrepancy between the expected utilities of available options. Discriminative choice presumably results from large discrepancies, whereas autonomous choice presumably results from small discrepancies.

These considerations permit the following hypotheses:

1 Evaluative choice is most likely to be experienced when at least one option is somewhat more attractive than other available options and when the goal is to find an option that is "good enough."

2 Discriminative choice is most likely to be experienced when the discrepancy between the utilities of available alternatives is large.

3 The more nearly equal the utilities of available options, the more attention is directed toward specific aspects of the options and the more likely that autonomous choice will be experienced.

4 High autonomous choice should be associated with slow and difficult decisions.

5 High autonomous choice should be associated with low confidence that the best selection has been made.

6   When the individual feels that evaluative choice is low, discriminative and autonomous choice will also be low; if evaluative choice is high, discriminative and/or autonomous choice may be either high or low.

Multiple Options and Selections

Whether people feel that they do or do not have a choice may depend upon the number of available options and the number of permitted selections. In general, the more alternatives available, the greater the amount of cognitive-evaluative work that is necessary to identify the best and next-best options. For instance, it is known that reaction time increases with increases in the number of alternatives (Berlyne, 1960: Garner, 1962). Furthermore, when the options are of about equal expected utility and/or are complex, individuals may settle for an alternative that is just "good enough" and make a quick decision (Hendrick, Mills, & Kiesler, 1968; Kiesler, 1966; Pollay, 1970). Consequently, the effects of the number of alternatives (set size) on the experience of choice depend upon whether the individual persists in making comparisons or discontinues comparison as soon as an acceptable option is identified. In the former case, evaluative and autonomous choice should increase and discriminative choice should decrease as a function of set size. In the latter case, residual uncertainty about the identity and utility of best and second-best options should lead people to feel that they have no choice or relatively little choice. Therefore, Steiner concluded that evaluative and autonomous choice should be curvilinear functions of set size, whereas discriminative choice should be negatively related to set size.

In some situations a person may choose only one alternative from available ones (e.g., selecting a wife), whereas in other cases more than one alternative may be chosen (e.g., selecting books to be read). The first case is said to be disjunctive because using one option precludes the use of other options; the second case is additive because the utilities of selected options are cumulative. The theory holds that the privilege of selecting more than one disjunctive option should increase the feeling of autonomous choice; the privilege of selecting more than one additive option should decrease the importance of making maximizing decisions. Thus evaluative choice should be positively correlated and discriminative choice negatively correlated with the number of permitted additive selections.

Effects of Commitment

In addition to comparison of expected utilities, the decision-making process involves a survey of probable consequences of alternatives and estimates of the probabilities of occurrences. In "real life," the two processes occur simultaneously and may affect each other. Thus comparisons that are made early are likely to favor judgments that influence later information search and assessment. These considerations suggest that commitment may have an important effect on the feeling that one has a choice.

Commitment means that, to some degree, a person is prevented from reversing a decision. Feelings of commitment are generated by publicly mani-fested decisions (Bennett, 1955; Cohen, Brehm, & Fleming, 1958), concern that one will appear inconsistent with one's self (Tedeschi, Schlenker, & Bonoma, 1971), or even compulsory investments of time and resources (Steiner, Doyen, & Talaber, 1975).

According to the theory, initial comparison of options with widely discrep-ant utilities should lead to early commitment, but, when discrepancies are moderate, commitment will be delayed until alternatives are evaluated more carefully. Moderate initial discrepancies in expected utilities are hypothesized to become smaller as the time for commitment approaches. Such a decrease in discrepancies implies an increase in autonomous choice and a decrease in discriminative choice. Evaluative choice should be unaffected.

Once a person is committed, the processes that delayed selection of an option arouse concern about the wisdom of the selection. This threat can be minimized by behaving in a way that inhibits further comparison, augmenting the expected utility of the chosen alternative, and/or diminishing the expected utility of rejected options. The theory proposes that augmenting the selected alternative will be the most effective because it increases both evaluative and discriminative choice.

Attribution of Choice to Others

People often attribute choice to others despite the fact that ordinarily they cannot know the expected utilities of others. Steiner proposes that such attributions are based on inferred expected utilities of others. In the case of precommitment attributions, a person may infer the other's evaluation of an option by assuming similarity to self or invoking a stereotype. When people know about the other's decision-making behaviors and/or have learned which option was selected, attributions are more likely to be based on probabilistic "base-rate information" provided by stereotypes or on tentative generalizations based on assumed similarity. People will infer expected utilities that are adequate to account for the other's behaviors.

The time required to reach a decision may also influence attributions to others. For instance, it has been shown that observers attributed more autono-mous choice to persons who took longer than average times to reach decisions than those who reached decisions quickly (Harvey & Johnson, 1973). Converse-ly, more discriminative choice is attributed when decision times are short (Kruglanski & Cohen, 1974). But extremely long or short decision times may lead to perceptions of unwillingness or inability to make a choice, in which case no attributions of choice will be made (Jellison & Harvey, 1973). Thus Steiner concluded that, within the moderate range, people interpret decision times as an inverse indicator of preference for the selected option.

Comment and Evaluation

The theory of choice is an interesting set of hypotheses about an important psychological process. The theory appears to be internally consistent, does not conflict with established principles of other theories, and fits reasonably well the research data from which many of the hypotheses were derived. However, there are some problems with the theory. Many of the hypotheses are stated rather loosely and do not permit precise predictions. In fact, it is sometimes difficult to determine whether Steiner is proposing a theoretical proposition or merely summarizing the data from past research. There is also some confusion in the terminology. For example, it is not clear whether desirability and attractiveness are the same thing or conceptually different, nor is it clear whether perceived freedom (Steiner, 1970) is the same as choice (Steiner, 1979).

The theory of choice was presented so recently that there appears to be no research derived directly from it. However, despite the question of the relationship between perceived freedom and choice, the research based on Steiner's earlier work is relevant to the theory of choice. That is, many of the hypotheses in the two analyses are essentially the same. This research has been concerned almost exclusively with the perception or attribution of choice or freedom. For instance, Jellison and Harvey (1973) reported data showing that perceived choice was greater when the discrepancy in attractiveness between two alternatives was small than when it was large and when uncertainty about the attractiveness of the alternatives was low rather than high. These findings were interpreted as supporting the theory of perceived freedom. Several studies have been conducted to test hypotheses about the attribution of freedom to others. Kruglanski and Cohen (1973) reported evidence that greater freedom is attributed to an actor when the act is consistent with the actor's predispositions. Similar evidence was reported by Trope (1978). On the other hand, a series of three studies failed to reveal evidence of a positive relationship between perceived freedom and nearness of equality of the behavior probability (Trope & Burnstein, 1977). The researchers concluded that their results could not be interpreted in terms of perceived decision freedom. Finally, Upshaw (1979) has shown that the attitude toward the reasons for an action is a determinant of the perception of freedom.

In summary, the data relative to the theory of choice are indirect and very limited. In general, the data fit the predictions of the theory moderately well, but the validation of the theory must await the outcome of future research.

INTEGRATION THEORY

All of us are exposed to a plethora of information about almost all aspects of our world. This information must be processed in some organized way if it is to be useful in responding to a complex environment. Many diverse bits of information must be integrated to form a unified response to the object or event to which the information is relevant. For example, in forming a judgment about another person, one must take into account such diverse information as opinions of others, written records about the person, outcomes of interactions with the person, and direct observation of physical and other characteristics of the person. Integration theory is concerned with the process by which information is integrated or combined to permit a unified judgment or response (Anderson, 1968, 1970, 1973, 1974). Although most of the experimental work has been done in the area of social perception, the theory is regarded as a unified general theory of information integration.

Basic Operations

The two basic operations assumed in integration theory are valuation and integration. *Valuation* refers to the processes that determine the stimulus parameters, whereas *integration* refers to the processes whereby the stimuli (information) are combined to determine the overall response. These two operations are the basic concerns of integration theory.

The theory further assumes that each bit of information (stimulus item) can be represented by two parameters, labeled s and w. The first parameter, s, represents the value of the item along the dimension of judgment and w represents the weight or importance of the item with respect to the overall judgment. Determination of these two parameters is necessary and represents a major problem for the theory. Scale values are hypothesized to vary with both item and dimension of judgment. For instance, the s-value of "forgetful" may be near zero for a college professor, but highly negative for an attorney (Anderson, 1968). The w-value of an item depends even more strongly on task variables, such as the reliability of the information. One way of viewing weight is in terms of the amount of information; i.e., weight is, in general, the amount of information in a stimulus, although other factors also influence weight in some situations. For instance, an extreme stimulus will tend to be more diagnostic than a less extreme one.

The foregoing statements should make it clear that Anderson is dealing with subjective metrics, which require a theory of measurement. He asserts that integration theory also includes a theory of measurement. In his functional measurement approach, the algebraic model of integration provides the scaling frame. It is assumed that agreement between actual judgmental data and theory (or model) predictions simultaneously validates the measurement procedure *and* verifies the theory.

Averaging Model

Several different algebraic models of integration have been proposed (e.g., additive, distance-proportional averaging, constant-weight averaging), but Anderson devotes most attention to the following averaging model (reprinted with permission from Anderson, 1968, p. 239):

$$R = C + \sum_{i=0}^{N} w_i s_i \Big/ \sum_{i=0}^{N} w_i + e$$

where R = the overall response
  C = an additive constant which allows for an arbitrary zero in the response scale

N = the number of stimuli in the set
s_i = the scale value of item i
w_i = the weight or importance of item i
e = an additive random variable with zero mean that represents
     response variability (error)

It is important to note that weights in the above formula are effective or *relative* weights that sum to one. Relative weights vary with context, and adding new relevant stimuli to the set causes a decrease in the relative weight of stimuli in the original set.

The formula presented above applies to a set of stimuli available at a given time, but it can easily be extended to stimuli presented sequentially by allowing the weight parameter to depend on serial position (Anderson, 1974). In extending the model, Anderson assumed that all stimuli at a given position would have the same natural weight and that weights would follow the usual serial position curve. That is, both early and late stimuli should have greater effect on the response than intermediate stimuli. Early stimuli might be more important in crystalizing the impression, whereas later ones might be fresher in memory.

Comment and Evaluation

Integration theory is primarily descriptive in nature. It attempts to show how information might be integrated to permit a unitary response, but it does not assert that it explains how integration actually does occur. It requires only that the person act *as if* the process were the one described by the model. In this sense, it is not quite as much a theory as it is a model—a representation of a possible integration process.

As Anderson has noted, many others have proposed similar models in other situations (for example, Garner, 1962, using statistical information theory; Edwards, 1968, using Bayesian theory; Brunswik, 1956, using multiple regression analysis). The proposed model is generally consistent with these related approaches.

The usual experimental test of integration theory is a comparison of the overall response with that predicted by the model. Evidence supporting the theory derives from numerous studies in such diverse areas as impression formation (Kaplan, 1971; Himmelfarb, 1973; Anderson, 1962, 1965; and many more); group attractiveness (Anderson, Lindner, & Lopes, 1973); performance, motivation, and ability (Anderson & Butzin, 1974); attitude change in group decisions (Anderson & Graesser, 1976); and jury decisions (Kaplan, 1977). Kaplan (1971) also found the predicted effects of set size and context on responses. These citations are representative rather than exhaustive.

In general, then, integration theory has good support and appears to serve its descriptive function well. Problems concerning set size and context effects, however, still require further analysis.

A THEORY OF ATTITUDES AND BEHAVIORAL INTENTIONS

Attitude has been a central concept in social psychology throughout its history (Allport, 1935; Newcomb, 1950). An attitude is one of many constructs that psychologists have invoked to help explain observed consistencies in behavior and, perhaps more importantly, variations in behavior under similar situational conditions. For instance, if person A responds favorably toward a particular national group and person B responds unfavorably toward that same group, the differences in behaviors can be "explained" by attributing different attitudes to the two persons. Despite the controversy concerning the actual relationship between attitudes and behavior (e.g., Wicker, 1969; Calder & Ross, 1963; Ajzen & Fishbein, 1973), there is continued interest in the nature and formation of attitudes and their influence on behavior. The theory outlined in this section is concerned with these issues.

The theory that we have labeled "A Theory of Attitudes and Behavioral Intentions" was formulated by Fishbein and his associates (Fishbein, 1967; Ajzen & Fishbein, 1970, 1972, 1973). We have taken some liberty in presenting their formulations as a single theory, since, to our knowledge, they have not combined their various proposals into a unified theoretical statement. However, they apparently do view their models of attitudes and behavioral intentions as merely parts of a larger theoretical framework (Fishbein & Ajzen, 1976).

The theory may be said to consist of two parts, one concerned with the nature and formation of attitudes and the other with a model for predicting behavioral intentions.

The Nature of Attitudes

An *attitude* is characterized as a learned implicit response that varies in intensity and tends to guide (mediate) an individual's overt responses to an object (Fishbein, 1967). Attitude refers only to the evaluation of a concept and there is a mediating evaluative response to every stimulus. Consequently, according to Fishbein, people have attitudes toward all objects, which may be positive, negative, or neutral.

A *belief* was defined as the probability that there is a particular relationship between the object of the belief and some other object. A belief may take the form, "Obese people are jolly," which means only that there exists a probability greater than zero that there exists a relationship between obesity and jollity. Beliefs are presumed to be ordered hierarchically in terms of relationship probability; those having higher probabilities are more likely to be elicited by the object of belief.

Attitudes are learned as a part of the concept formation process, according to secondary generalization principles.[2] All stimuli are said to have evaluative

[2]This aspect of Fishbein's approach is obviously derived from behavior theory (see Chapter 2); it is cognitive only in that attitude and belief are cognitive concepts.

responses associated with them so that any time a new concept is learned, an attitude is automatically acquired. Thus, attitude acquisition is an automatic process that occurs in conjunction with concept formation.

According to the theory, an individual's attitude toward any given object is a function of the strength of his or her beliefs about the object and the evaluation of the response to the object (the evaluative aspect of the beliefs). These proposals are shown by the formula (Fishbein, 1967, p. 394, reprinted with permission):

$$A_0 = \sum_{1}^{N} B_i a_i$$

where A_0 = the attitude toward object o

B_i = the strength of belief i about o

a_i = the evaluative aspect of B_i

N = the number of beliefs about o

Fishbein noted that this predictive model is very similar to formulas derived from more cognitive theories (e.g., Rosenberg, 1956; Zajonc, 1960) and that the hypothesis that attitudes are a function of beliefs about an object and the evaluative aspects of those beliefs is consistent with most standard attitude-measurement instruments.

Although all beliefs about an object serve as indicants of an individual's attitude toward that object, only *salient* beliefs serve as *determinants* of attitude (Fishbein, 1967). A salient belief is one that appears in the person's hierarchy, that is, is above some response threshold. The theory holds that probably only 6 to 11 beliefs can be salient at any one time and thus serve as attitude determinants. This proposition is based upon the observation that most people can only perceive and attend to 6 to 11 objects at the same time (Woodworth & Schlossberg, 1954; Miller, 1956).

The Prediction of Behavioral Intentions

The original attitude model was extended later (Ajzen & Fishbein, 1970) to the prediction of behavioral intentions, which are, in turn, presumed to mediate overt behavior. According to the extended model, the two major components in predicting behavioral intentions are the person's attitude toward performing the act and beliefs about what is expected in the situation, that is, the person's normative beliefs. Normative beliefs are multiplied by the person's motivation to comply with the norms, and both major components are weighted for importance. These ideas can be expressed algebraically as follows (Ajzen & Fishbein, 1970, p. 467, reprinted with permission):

$$B \sim BI = [A\text{-act}]\ w_0 + [NB(Mc)]\ w_1$$

where B = overt behavior
                 BI = behavioral intention
              A-act = attitude toward performing the act in a given situation
                 NB = normative beliefs
                 Mc = motivation to comply with norms
w_0 and w_1 = empirically determined weights

Fishbein noted that inclusion of the Mc component is not always crucial; it is often omitted when testing the model. When this is done, behavioral intentions are presumed to be a function of attitudes toward the performance of the behavior, normative beliefs, and the weights of these predictors. It should be noted that the A-act component can be predicted from the attitude model described in the preceding section.

It is important to note that, although behavioral intentions are viewed as the immediate determinant of overt behavior, the formula predicts only intentions. Ajzen and Fishbein are careful to note that many factors can influence the relationship between the predicted behavioral intention and the behavior itself (e.g., Ajzen & Fishbein, 1970, 1973, 1974; Fishbein & Ajzen, 1975, 1976). For example, the relationship is influenced by the specificity at which intentions and behaviors are measured, stability of the intention, and degree of volitional control of the behavior.

Comment and Evaluation

The theoretical framework concerning attitudes, beliefs, and behavioral intentions is internally consistent and in accord with the established principles of other theories. We have already noted the similarity of the attitude formulation to that in other theories. It may also be noted that the behavioral intention model corresponds quite closely to other theories, such as Rotter's (1954) social-learning theory and Edwards' (1954, 1961) behavioral decision theory.

One bothersome aspect of the theory is that weights are empirically derived and vary from situation to situation. Some intentions are said to be determined primarily by attitude components, some primarily by the normative component, and some by both. According to the theory, weights are expected to vary with the behavior being predicted, conditions under which the person must act, and personal characteristics of the actor, but the particular effects of these factors are not specified. At least one study has shown that committed subjects placed most weight on attitudinal components, whereas uncommitted subjects placed most weight on norm considerations when making behavioral decisions (Gabrenya & Arkin, 1979). This is the kind of specification the theory needs.

In general, research findings support the theory. For example, Fishbein and associates have reported unusually high correlations between predicted and measured attitudes ($r = .80$, Fishbein, 1967; r's ranging from .47 to .67, Jaccard & Fishbein, 1975). Predictions based on the model of behavioral intentions have also been verified by a number of studies (e.g., Ajzen & Fishbein, 1972, 1973; Ajzen, 1971; Hornik, 1970; Jaccard, Knox, & Brinberg, 1979). However, at least one study found results that were interpreted as questioning the generality of the model (Songer-Nocks, 1976). She measured the relationship between actual and predicted behavior and found that certain situational factors were capable of altering the model significantly. She concluded that the association between attitude and behavior depends upon prior experience with the behavior. Fishbein & Ajzen (1976) argued persuasively that the model was not intended to be a direct predictor of overt behavior and relative weights of components in the model are expected to vary with conditions.

In brief summary, the theory is internally consistent, consistent with other accepted theories, and has reasonable support from empirical data. There are some ambiguities and questions that remain to be clarified, but the theory shows promise as a guide for research and further theory development.

INOCULATION THEORY

People in the American society are bombarded daily with attempts to change their opinions, beliefs, and attitudes about almost all aspects of their lives. Politicians try to convince their constituency that they are the best candidates available; marketing managers in industry try to convince their customers that they have the best products; crusaders try to convince everybody that their ideas are morally correct; and educators try to instill their "knowledge" in their students. McGuire (1964) was concerned with inducing resistance to the many influence attempts. He noted that in our society people who are autonomous, make their own decisions, and resist social influence are admired, whereas the persons who succumb to influence attempts are held in low esteem. Consequently, he believed that one must look for ways of inducing "healthy" processes if one is to increase resistance to change. This reasoning led him to formulate a theory by analogy to the medical immunization procedure.

Underlying Assumptions

The biological analogy suggested that, in order to produce "healthy" resistance to persuasion, it may be necessary to do some "unhealthy" things, just as inoculation against smallpox may make the person temporarily ill. The problem, then, was to identify the kinds of pretreatments that, although they might induce some initial doubt about the truth of an opinion or belief, would eventually enable the person to resist attacks on those opinions or beliefs. Inoculation theory assumes that people are susceptible to persuasion attempts with respect to many beliefs for two reasons: (1) the believer is unpracticed in defending his or her belief and (2) the believer is unmotivated to undertake the necessary practice. These reasons are especially important for truisms. The person is unpracticed because the belief has never been questioned and unmotivated to practice defense because the belief seems unassailable.

It follows from these assumptions that an effective immunization process must motivate the person to develop defenses against attacks on a belief that the person considers invulnerable. This can be done by making the person aware that the assumption of invulnerability is invalid. Thus, if the believer is exposed to a weakened form of threatening arguments, he or she should become aware that the belief is vulnerable to attack and become motivated to develop defenses against attack. However, motivation alone may not be sufficient for effective defense. Lacking practice, the believer may not be able to develop defensive material without help or over a long period of time. This means that the believer must be given guidance or other assistance in developing defenses.

Defensive Variables

Inoculation theory postulates three variables that affect the effectiveness of immunization. The first one is the amount of threat contained in the defense. The two basic types of defense that vary in amount of threat are called supportive and refutational. *Supportive* defenses are nonthreatening and provide the believer with arguments in support of the truism. *Refutational* defenses are more threatening and contain arguments threatening the truism, followed by refutations of those arguments. Refutational arguments can either mention and refute the same arguments against the truism (refutational-same) or mention and refute different arguments against the truism (refutational-different). According to inoculation theory, threatening arguments should arouse greater motivation to develop defenses than nonthreatening attacks; therefore, refutational defenses should induce greater resistance to persuasive arguments than supportive defenses. Furthermore, inoculation theory states that resistance to persuasion derives from the generalized motivational effect of threats; therefore, both refutational-same and refutational-different defenses should induce resistance to persuasion.

A second variable presumed to affect degree of resistance to persuasion is the amount of unguided, active participation in the defense required by the believer. This variable can, of course, range from complete passivity (e.g., reading or listening to defensive materials) to highly active participation (e.g., producing arguments and refutations unaided). This variable is presumed to be relevant to both lack of practice and motivation, but in a very complex way. Since the believer has little prior practice, active defense is hypothesized to be less effective than passive defense: the believer's practice deficit, which imposes more demands to provide bolstering material from an inadequate cognitive repertory, leads to poor task performance in the active defense condition. When the believer is supplied with well-prepared defensive materials, lack of practice should be no great handicap. On the other hand, active defense should have a greater effect on motivation than passive defense: the poor performance of the believer in the active defense situation should be sufficient to shake his or her confidence in the truism.

A third important variable is the interval between the defense and subsequent persuasive attacks on the truism. Building up immunity may require time and acquired immunity may decay over time. McGuire assumes that the threatening aspect of defense, which provides the motivation to develop defense, will persist for some time and the believer will continue to accumulate bolstering defensive materials. After a time, however, motivation begins to decrease and the person ceases to accumulate belief-bolstering materials. Therefore, induced resistance deriving from the motivational mechanism should first increase, then decrease following an attack on the truism. The second resistance-conferring mechanism, the actual communication of the belief-bolstering material, is hypothesized to show a much simpler temporal sequence. Resistance resulting from this mechanism is dependent upon retention of the material; therefore, it should decrease over time as a simple function of forgetting. Decay should follow the ordinary forgetting curve.

Comment and Evaluation

Like many other theories we have presented, inoculation theory is internally consistent and does not conflict with accepted principles of behavior. It makes use of certain motivational and learning principles that are well established in general psychology. The major bases for evaluation, therefore, are the degree to which it has generated research and the degree to which researh findings support the theory. The first is moderately favorable to the theory: it has generated a modest amount of research activity.

The research relative to the theory relates primarily to supportive versus refutational defenses, active versus passive defenses, the effect of forewarning, and sequential effects. It will be recalled that inoculation theory predicts that refutational defenses will induce greater resistance to persuasion than support-ive defenses, and refutational-same and refutational-different defenses should be equally effective. The greater effectiveness of refutational defenses has been demonstrated in a number of studies by McGuire and his associates (McGuire & Papageorgis, 1961, 1962; Anderson & McGuire, 1965). The equal effectiveness of refutational-same and refutational-different defenses was also observed in these investigations.

Inoculation theory predicts that passive defenses will be more effective than active defenses; however, the greater superiority of passive over active defenses will be greater with refutational-same than with supportive defenses, which will be greater than with refutational-different defenses. An investigation conducted by McGuire (1962a) supported all of these expectations, whereas a study by McGuire and Papageorgis (1961) supported the prediction of overall greater effectiveness of passive defenses but only marginally supported the prediction that passive defenses will be relatively more effective with refutational-same than with supportive defenses.

According to the theory, forewarning an individual that an attack on his or her belief may occur should motivate that person to develop bolstering materials and counterarguments and, therefore, increase resistance to change. McGuire and Papageorgis (1962) reported data supporting this expectation, a finding verified in at least two more recent experiments (Dean, Austin, & Watts, 1971; Petty & Cacioppo, 1977). However, in one of the two experiments reported by Dean et al., it was found that forewarning increased attitude change for females, contrary to inoculation theory predictions.

The temporal and sequential effects predicted by inoculation theory are complex, and data are not extensive. However, McGuire, employing supportive, refutational-same, and refutational-different defenses, (1962b) tested his hypotheses concerning the persistence of resistance induced by passive defenses. As predicted, mean belief decreased significantly over time with supportive defenses and more slowly with refutational-same defenses and showed a nonmonotonic trend with refutational-different defenses. In another study (McGuire, 1964), it was found that resistance increased over time with all three types of active defense, as predicted by inoculation theory. The predicted combined effects of defenses have also been supported by research data (e.g., McGuire, 1961a,b), but the predicted sequential effects were not found. The theory also predicts that the effects of actual communication of belief-bolstering material will decrease over time, a result that also has been verified by research (Watts & Holt, 1979).

In summary, the evidence provides surprisingly good support for inoculation theory, despite some negative findings. The major lack of support has to do with sequential effects. The theory has been criticized because it sometimes fails to adhere to the biological analogy upon which it is based (Insko, 1967), but this does not appear to be a serious problem. More importantly, perhaps, is the possibility that the theory is incomplete in that it fails to consider other possible defenses that might be effective in conferring resistance to persuasion.

Part Five

The Role-Theory
Orientation

Chapter 11

Role Theory

Role theory is a body of knowledge and principles that at one and the same time constitutes an orientation, a group of theories, loosely linked networks of hypotheses, isolated constructs about human functioning in a social context, and a language system which pervades nearly every social scientist's vocabulary. It, more than any of the foregoing approaches, eludes the grasp of our classification system. Roles as the basic data within this "theoretical system" have been considered from many viewpoints: learning, cognitive, field-theoretical, sociocultural, and dynamic points of view. As such, role theory seems to be more of a subject matter than a theoretical framework. Indeed, it has occupied this standing in several basic social psychology texts (Sargent & Williamson, 1958; Secord & Backman, 1964; Brown, 1965; Newcomb, Turner, & Converse, 1965; McDavid & Harari, 1968).

Although specific theories of role and role processes have been proposed from various orientations and disciplines in the social and behavioral sciences, we have not chosen to exposit these specific theories. Instead, this chapter presents the language of role theory peculiar to most of these orientations. Because of the proliferation of concepts that have been classified under the role-theory rubric, we do not pretend to present every phrase, concept, or construct relevant to roles. Instead, we have drawn heavily upon the classification system proposed by Biddle and Thomas (1966) in an attempt to present the most important and relevant constructs and processes.

Before we embark on a discussion of the language of role theory, several introductory considerations about roles should be noted:

1   Historically, the concept of role has been borrowed from dramatic and theatrical circles. Beginning with the early Greek and Roman theaters, a role referred to the characterization that an actor was called upon to enact in the context of a given dramatic presentation.

2   From these roots the concept of role migrated into the language of the social sciences. In this migration, the definition of role changed very little. *It refers to the functions a person performs when occupying a particular characterization (position) within a particular social context.*

3   Just as one actor's role is partially defined by the roles that other actors take in the same performance, so one person's role is partially dependent upon the roles of related others in the social context. Neither a dramatic presentation nor a social structure could long survive if the roles of its various "actors" were not linked to one another.

4   The evolution of the concept of role in the social sciences has been truly a transdisciplinary evolution. Most of the contributions to role theory have come from the fields of anthropology, sociology, and psychology.

5   The early precursors of modern role-theoretical constructs uniformly alluded to the concept of role while pursuing the study of other aspects of their respective disciplines. For example, James (1890) and Baldwin (1897) were psychologists studying the "self"; Sumner (1906), Ross (1908), and Durkheim (1893) were sociologists concerned with the mores, norms, and structure of society; yet each of these contributed greatly to role theory. Some other significant works which contributed to the foundation of role theory were those of Dewey (1899), Cooley (1902), Moreno (1919), and Simmel (1920).

6   This cross-fertilization of ideas from various social science disciplines led to the emergence of a system of linguistic and conceptual referents within role theory that defies classification as psychological, sociological, or anthropological.

THE LANGUAGE OF ROLE THEORY

Biddle and Thomas (1966) have written and edited a significant text in the area of role theory. In addressing themselves to this task, they utilized a framework or classficatory universe within which the many constructs of role theory were reduced to comparatively few basic constructs. In short, they have devised a scheme for classifying the most frequently recurrent terms from the role theory framework. In the subsequent paragraphs of this section, we use this schematic superstructure in articulating the language of role theory. It consists of four terminological classes: (1) terms for partitioning persons, (2) terms for partitioning behaviors, (3) terms for partitioning sets of persons and behaviors, and (4) terms for relating sets of persons and behaviors. Two or more descriptive terms fall within each of these general classes.

Terms for Partitioning Persons

Terms for partitioning persons break down into two basic categories. First, the *actor* is the person who is currently behaving in a given role. Secondly, the *target* or *other* is an individual who bears a relationship to the actor and his role. Either the actor or the other may be an individual or an aggregate of individuals. Thus, the "actor" might be the aggregate choir performing a singing-and-entertainment role in relation to the audience as the aggregate-other. In the language of role theory, the actor has been alternately referred to as the *person,* the *ego,* and the *self;* and the other has been alternately referred to as the *alter ego* (or merely *alter*), the *target,* and the *nonself* (Biddle & Thomas, 1966).

This classification of individuals or aggregates into actors or persons and others is not peculiar to role theory. The reader will recall similar classifications in Heider's theory of interpersonal relationships (Chapter 6), Heider's p-o-x theory (Chapter 8), Newcomb's A-B-X theory (Chapter 8), and Jones and Davis' theory of correspondent inferences (Chapter 9). Although these theories are not role theories in the strict sense of the term, their hypotheses and propositions concerning interpersonal relationships, interpersonal attribution, or interpersonal perception can be interpreted in a role-theoretical framework. As a matter of fact, nearly every structured two-party or multiple-party relationship, in which person-other classifications are possible, can be subjected to role-theoretical analysis. The basic situation within which roles can be studied is one which involves an *actor* behaving (in its broadest sense) in the presence of, toward, or in reference to an *other,* where the actor and the other have roles which are linked by factors such as similarity, complementarity, friendship, and the like.

Cooley (1902) and Mead (1934) were two of the first theorists to be concerned with the importance of person-other relationships as they predispose the person to a course of role-appropriate behavior or thought. Both these men viewed the "other" as a generalized entity which the person utilizes as a reference point for his own behavior. As such, they were not particularly concerned with the actual component interactions between a particularized person and a particularized other. Both Mead and Cooley concluded that the person, ego, or self is given its identity by the generalized other. According to Mead, the person takes the attitude of the generalized other toward himself, but Cooley maintained that the person uses the generalized other as a mirror that reflects the characteristics and effects of the person's behavior and feeling. These early views of the referential function of the other and the generalized other were later expanded by Merton and Kitt (1950), Kelley (1952), and several other theorists. Referential functions are dealt with more extensively in the subsequent section on the partitioning of behaviors.

Finally, it should be noted that Secord and Backman (1964), following the lead of Bredemeier and Stevenson (1962), have designated the *person* as the individual occupying the *focal position* in an observed relationship and the *other* as the individual occupying a *counterposition.* Thus, they viewed the other as a *role partner* to the person. This position-counterposition view of the person and his/her related other can be most lucidly illustrated by noting some structured role relationships, such as mother-child, boss-employee, and husband-wife. From these examples, it can be seen easily that role partners are in a reciprocal relationship with one another. Subsequent sections of this chapter will go into greater detail on the concepts of position and role partner.

Terms for Partitioning Behaviors

Biddle and Thomas (1966) cited five terms that depict role-related behaviors. They are *expectation* and *norm, performance* and *evaluation,* and *sanction.*

Role Expectations and Norms   Role expectations are simply expectations held by particularized or generalized *others* for the appropriate behavior (again in its broadest sense) that *ought* to be exhibited by the *person* or persons holding a given role. Thus, for example, the society at large, individual patients, patients from different socioeconomic classes, and similar groups have expectations concerning how a person should function in the role of physician. Some expectations are generally held, some are only held by "pockets" of others, and some are idiosyncratic and characteristic of specific person-other relationships.

There seems to be an interchangeability of the terms "norm" and "expectation" in role-theory literature. Expectations are generally viewed as shared or individual norms of how persons occupying a given position-role should function in that role. However, Secord and Backman (1964) noted that norms are only one of two categories of expectations. They bifurcate role expectations on the basis of (1) their anticipatory nature and (2) their normative nature. McDavid and Harari (1968) made a similar distinction between *predicted role expectations* and *prescribed role expectations.* Expectations that are anticipatory or predictive in nature are generally not based on norms in the strict sense. Rather, they are used by a given individual to anticipate or predict the manner in which another will respond to them or to a particular situation. Thus, the statement, "I know my husband well, and, when I tell him that I've purchased a $60 hat, he will hit the ceiling," is a predictive or anticipatory expectation. It is not strictly normative because "hitting the ceiling" or losing one's temper is not a usual prescription characteristic of the role of husband (that is, it is not necessarily what a husband *ought* to do or *ought not* do in order to fulfill the husband's role either in the eyes of the society at large or probably even in his wife's eyes).

Secord and Backman (1964) noted that the anticipatory quality of expectations is a guiding force in interaction. Anticipations and predictions are usually made on the basis of experiences with individual person, classes of persons, specific situations, or generalized situations. Although continuing experience in interaction may facilitate the acquisition of internal standards about the behavior of others or the reactions of others, they cannot be strictly classified as norms because these anticipations do not have obligatory qualities. That is, the fact that sound experience leads an individual to predict certain contingencies in interaction does not *obligate* another party in that interaction to live up to those predictions.

The normative or prescribed quality of role expectations represents the "oughts" and "shoulds" of a given role. Normative role expectations are the overt or covert rights and obligations that accompany the occupation of a given role position. The degree to which an individual lives up to the obligations or normative expectations of a role which he holds is a measure of his fulfillment of that role (at least insofar as social standards are concerned). The larger society and specific subgroups within it hold standards which they use to organize and evaluate the role behavior of others.

Biddle and Thomas (1966) have divided role prescriptions (the "oughts" and "shoulds" of roles) into those that are covertly held and those that are overtly expressed. They reserved the term *norm* for the former category and referred to overtly expressed prescriptions as *role demands*. Many parental prescriptions for their children are couched in the form of demands. Thus, a child may be overtly admonished to use his/her utensils when eating at the table, to thank others for favors, to adhere to particular authority rules, and so forth. Role demands are by no means limited to parent-child or superior-underling relationships, but they are probably most salient in these forms of relationship. Biddle and Thomas pointed out that in the course of socialization many role demands are internalized by the person and become covertly held norms. Most of the important prescriptions which govern adult role behavior and the evaluation of adult role behavior are based upon internalized norms which correspond to given roles.

Role Performance Role performance consists of the behaviors displayed by an actor which are relevant to the particular role which he/she is currently playing. In contrast to normative expectations, which are the "oughts" or the behavioral requirements of a given role, role performance is the actual behavior exhibited by an actor in a role. There may be considerable variation in the manner in which different actors enact the same role or in the manner in which the same actor enacts the same role on different occasions. Any number of different role behaviors may fulfill the expectations of the same role. Hence, if we assume that disciplining children is one of the expected functions of the father role, a particular father may enact this function by physical punishment, psychological deprivation, dependency manipulations, and so forth. In all cases, the father is responding to at least one of the expectations of the father role. Although any single form of role enactment may be considered to be the most adequate, the enactment of alternative acceptable modes of role behavior is not precluded. In short, role theory does account for the infinite variety of behavior that an individual may exhibit. Even though role theory tends to classify people into categories of actors (for example, father, boss), and attribute relatively uniform expectations to a given category, it does not propose that these uniform expectations are met by all relevant actors with the same expressed behavior.

Indeed, the theater, which has been cited as the originator of the concept of role, yields the most paradigmatic examples of how different individuals playing the same role may exhibit different role behaviors. No two actors characterizing

Hamlet, Macbeth, Othello, or Willie Loman enact exactly the same behaviors. The dialogue may be the same, but the gestures or vocal intonations are usually different. In the real world, the goals of the various functions associated with roles (for example, disciplining children) may be the same, but the paths to the goal may differ widely.

For these reasons, role theory tends to classify role performance not in terms of the specific behaviors performed in the enactment of a role, but rather in terms of the generic quality of the behavior and the goals or motives of that behavior (Biddle & Thomas, 1966). Thus, role behavior might be classified as "work performance," "school performance," "athletic performance," etc., or it might be classified in terms of the goals of the enacted behavior, such as "the disciplining of a child," "the earning of a living wage," "the maintenance of order," and the like. Role performance, then, is generally classified in terms of its nature and ends rather than its means. This characteristic of role theory, however, does not preclude the fact that certain means of enacting a given role function may be sanctioned by the group. For example, a father might be fulfilling a role function in disciplining his misbehaving son by hanging him upside down by his toes. Nevertheless, this behavior would most probably be negatively sanctioned in Western culture. In general, the means of achieving a role function or living up to a specific requirement of a given role, usually becomes important in role theory only when that means comes into conflict with other aspects of the total role. Thus, the father who disciplines his son by hanging him by his toes violates some of the expectations of the father role, such as affection toward the child, justice toward the child, and so forth. Therefore, the actor is free to vary in his/her expression of a role function within the limits imposed by related role functions and expectations.

Two of the more prominent role theorists concerned with role performance have been Sarbin (1966) and Goffman (1959). In defining some dimensions of role enactment, both have been concerned with the relationship between the self and the role that the self is called upon to play. Sarbin classified role enactment in terms of the intensity of the enactment. He defined intensity along a dimension of self-role differentiatedness. He proposed that there are seven levels of role enactment varying in terms of their intensity. His levels range from the lowest level of enactment, which involves a rather mechanical implementation of a role function and where self and role are clearly differentiated, to a level of enactment which involves the complete integration of self and role. In this highest level of enactment, the self and the role it is taking are undifferentiated, and hence the enactment is highly intensified. In short, Sarbin proposed that a very salient dimension of variation in role performance is represented by the individual's involvement in the role being enacted.

Goffman (1959) was concerned with the proposition that an actor performing in a role is attempting to convey, overtly or covertly, to the other that part of himself/herself that he/she wishes to be known. As such, Goffman became concerned with the expressive characteristics of role performance. He termed these expressive characteristics a "front," which the actor constructs in order to impress the other with the fact that he/she is living up to the idealized aspects of a given role. For example, if one of the perceived expectations of a college professor is that he/she be scholarly in his/her interests and pursuits, the professor might publicly convey to the other that he/she is living up to this expectation by shelving scholarly periodicals in full display on his/her living-room bookshelves. However, he/she may conceal his/her private penchant for comic books by stacking them in a less-accessible portion of the house. Thus, Goffman implies that the public role performance of the actor in an actor-other context at least partially constitutes the construction of a role-consistent "front." The actor, then, might impress the other with his/her fulfillment of role expectations through the selective expression of limited facets of himself/herself.

It should be noted that many theorists have articulated many different dimensions of role performance. That we have not covered these many views here is not intended to be an indictment of their relevance. Instead, the necessary limitation in this chapter's scope precludes their coverage. The interested reader is strongly urged to refer to Biddle and Thomas' (1966) text and readings for further discussion of and reference to the concept of role performance.

Role Evaluation and Sanction   It is rather difficult to separate the behaviors of evaluation and sanction as they apply to role. Biddle and Thomas (1966) distinguished the two in that they defined evaluation as the expression of approval or disapproval toward the role behavior of oneself or another. They reserved the term *sanction* to apply to the behavior of oneself or another that attempts to achieve either constancy in or change of a given role behavior. Therefore, evaluation involves the making of "positive" or "negative" *judgments* about a particular role behavior, and sanctioning is a procedure engaged in either to maintain positively evaluated role behaviors or to change negatively evaluated ones.

Both evaluations and sanctions are based upon normative expectations. Thus, a role behavior will most probably be positively evaluated and sanctioned when it conforms to the normative expectations for the role in question and negatively evaluated and sanctioned when it does not. Evaluations and sanctions can be either external or internal. Secord and Backman (1964) noted that with external sanctions the source of positive or negative reward is the behavior of others. For example, a boss may negatively sanction workers for not living up to standards of production by firing them, or may positively sanction their adequate role performance by giving them a salary bonus. On the other hand, the source of internal sanctions is the actor himself/herself. Thus, an individual may be dissatisfied with himself/herself when he/she does not live up to the normative expectations of a role which he/she holds. Furthermore, Secord and Backman noted that, in the socialized adult, internal sanctions are usually most salient with important norms and external sanctions most salient with norms of little importance.

Biddle and Thomas (1966) made a similar distinction between the *overt* and *covert* natures of evaluations and sanctions. They referred to overt evaluations as *assessments* and covert evaluations as *values*. The former class is most frequently used by others to evaluate the role behavior of the actor, and the latter is usually used by the actor to evaluate his/her own behavior. Values might be conceptualized as the internalized assessments of others that are held by the actor. Thus, the values of the actor are based upon the communication of normative expectations by others through predominantly overt means. A mother's socialization of her child generally involves the communication of normative expectations through external assessments and sanctions to the point where the child accepts and internalizes those norms as governors of his/her own behavior. With the internal acceptance of other-based norms, the individual forms a system of internal values through which he/she self-regulates his/her own behaviors. Socialization is a process which occurs throughout the individual's lifetime. Each time he/she enters a new social situation or assumes a different role he/she must to some extent rely on the external assessments of others in order to derive a set of role-relevant internalized values.

Although the evaluation and sanction of the actor by others is an important aspect of role theory, the actors' evaluation of their own role behavior is even more important. We have already alluded to the proposition that the external evaluations of "others" are the source of the internalized values which the actor utilizes to evaluate his/her own role performance. This proposition has been repeatedly articulated by psychologists and sociologists alike. Merton and Kitt (1950) dealt extensively with the concept of *reference group* in attempting to define the source of value formation in the actor. The reference group is a group that the actor is a member of or one in which he/she desires membership. In either case, it serves as a *reference point* that the individual uses to derive standards that he/she might utilize to evaluate his/her own performance and to obtain or maintain membership in the group. Kelley (1952) stated two functions of reference groups. He referred to the first of these as the *normative function*. The normative function of reference groups entails the role which they play in enforcing the standards (objectively correct or not) for action and belief in the person. To perform this function, the person must have face-to-face contact with the group or its representative, and the group must have the power to sanction the person for deviation. The person is motivated to abide by normative pressure because of his/her desire to secure or maintain membership in the group. If the individual internalizes the standards induced by the group's normative pressure, they become his/her individual *values* for action. Insofar as the norms and standards enforced by the reference group deal with aspects of the actor's role behavior, the process of normative group pressure is a very important one for role-theoretical analysis.

The second function of reference groups that Kelley defined is the *comparative function*. This function involves the person's use of the group as a comparative index of the "objective correctness" of his/her attitudes, opinions, and behaviors. The comparative function can operate without interaction and without concerns about group membership. Here, the group usually does not exert the pressure of sanction, and the individual uses the group only for informational purposes. The comparative function of reference groups is not as relevant to self-role evaluation as the normative function.

Several other dichotomous classifications of the self-group relationships and processes involved in arriving at a self-evaluation are very similar to Kelley's descriptions. Deutsch and Gerard's (1955) concepts of normative and informational social influence, Thibaut and Strickland's (1956) group set (normative) and task set (comparative), and Jones and Gerard's (1967) reflected appraisal (normative) and comparative appraisal are some of the more-important ones. Furthermore, Festinger's social comparison theory discussed in Chapter 10 is also relevant to the self-evaluation process.

Last, it should be noted that Biddle and Thomas discussed a further term for partitioning behaviors relevant to roles. They referred to the process whereby an individual simply articulates the components of a given role as *role description*. Role description differs from role evaluation and sanction in that it does not involve affective or evaluative factors. The mere description of roles, then, is free of value judgments. A covertly held description of a role was referred to as a *role conception,* and an overtly expressed description was called a *role statement* (Biddle & Thomas, 1966). Both the individual's *cognitions* and *perceptions* of what a role consists of, in terms of functions, obligations, position, and rights, are involved in role description.

Terms for Partitioning Sets of Persons and Behaviors

Certain terms in the vocabulary of role theory refer to the combination of a behavioral partition with a person partition. For example, role evaluation may occur with actors or with others. The behavioral partitions and person partitions come together in the general concepts of *position* and *role*. Thus, a given role behavior is often evaluated as a function of what category the actor falls within. A position in the social structure and a role associated with that position define both the actor and the course of action he is obligated to take.

Position   Secord and Backman defined position as a category of persons (actors) who occupy a specified place in a social structure. Biddle and Thomas (1966) gave a similar definition to position but secondarily added that a position consists of a set of persons sharing common attributes or who are similarly perceived by others. Thus, they define position as *"a collectively recognized category of persons for whom the basis for such differentiation is their common attribute, their common behavior, or the common reactions of others toward them"* (Biddle & Thomas, 1966, p. 29. Italics ours). According to this definition, Biddle and Thomas have posited three bases for the assignment of persons into a position category. The first involves the assignment of persons on the basis of a common attribute or several common attributes. The examples they noted for this basis are classification by age, sex, or race. Thus, an individual might be classified in the category of teenager or female or black or all three of these categories. As more attributes go into the making up of single categories, the category becomes narrower and more exclusive. Hence, only certain blacks are females, and even fewer blacks are both females and teenagers.

The second basis for position categorization that Biddle and Thomas noted is common behavior. Some examples of this basis might be criminals, athletes, leaders, and so forth. Individuals might be classified into such categories on the basis of the similarity in their behavior, at least on one dimension. Position categories based upon behavioral characteristics may cut across categories based on common attributes. Thus criminals, athletes, or leaders may be white or black, old or young, male or female and so forth. One may arrive at narrower classifications of categories by subdividing a large category into some representative components on the basis of even more precise similarity in behavior. Hence, a criminal can belong to several smaller subcategories, such as thief, murderer, kidnaper, rapist, and so forth. More-exclusive categories of position might also be derived by combining common attributes with behavioral similarities. Thus, for example, one might speak of teenage criminals (or juvenile delinquents), black leaders, or woman athletes.

The third basis for positional categorization is the similarity in the behavior of others toward the persons in question. A prime example of this type of categorization as noted by Biddle and Thomas is the category of scapegoats. Scapegoats are classified together regardless of their varying attributes or behaviors because of the similarities in the manner that people treat them. As with common behavioral determinants of position, this third basis of position may be further subdivided into smaller component categories. For example, a specific category of scapegoats could be political scapegoats and this category might be distinguished from social scapegoats.

The proposition that there are at least three underlying bases for positional categorization could well be the source of various disagreements on how position should be defined. The generalized classification of bases of positional categorization proposed by Biddle and Thomas is an organizational schema that can be used to unify the several conceptualizations of the term "position." A minimally acceptable definition of position is its designation as a "unit of social structure" (Newcomb, 1950; Gross, Mason, & McEachern, 1957). Specifying the "acceptable" bases for the formation of social structure units further differentiates and articulates the concept of position.

Role Biddle and Thomas noted that although role is the central concept in role-theoretical analysis, it is probably the most controversial concept used by role analysts. Many definitions of role have been offered from many schools of thought. Together, Nieman and Hughes (1951) and Rommetveit (1954) reviewed 100 or more role definitions. Biddle and Thomas (1966) pointed out that a review of these many definitions indicates that the most common definition of role is that it is a set of prescriptions that define the desired behavior of a position occupant. Almost all definitions of role universally acknowledge that it pertains to the behaviors of particularized persons. Although many definitions of role confine the person-behavior relationship to behaviors associated with collective positions, Biddle and Thomas believed this to be too limiting a definition. Instead, they proposed a matrix of person-behavior relationships which they saw as giving the necessary broadness to a concept as pervasive as role.

The Biddle and Thomas person-behavior matrix consists of a set of behaviors that is ordered by both a set of subjects (persons) and a set of behavioral classes. Figure 11-1 is a prototype of the proposed matrix.

In this figure the horizontal dimension labeled P_1-P_m is the set of subjects and consists of all relevant partitions of persons. Usually, the subject set should be limited to person-units within a single larger social unit. Hence the total subject set may be the family, P_1 the father, P_2 the mother, P_3 the son, and so forth. The vertical dimension labeled from C_1-C_n consists of all relevant classes of behavior. Each class of behavior is a category that includes specific individual behavioral partitions. Hence, C_1 might consist of a group of prescriptions, C_2 a category of evaluation, C_3 a category of actions or perhaps sanctions, and so forth. The cell entries (B_{11}, B_{12}, etc.) are the behaviors enacted by individual units of the subject set. Thus, if P_1 were father and C_1 normative expectations, then B_{11} might be a specific expectation which father holds about his own role or the role of another person in the subject set.

Essential portions of the matrix presented in Figure 11-1 are the areas that are sectioned off both horizontally and vertically. The vertical section was referred to by Biddle and Thomas as the *person segment* and is made up of all the behaviors displayed by a single person or a subset of persons, regardless of the

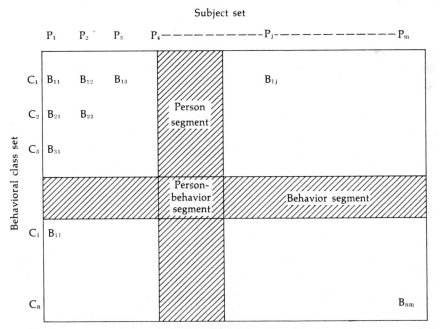

Figure 11-1   The person-behavior matrix and its segments. (Reprinted with permission from E. J. Thomas and B. J. Biddle. Basic concepts for classifying the phenomena of role. In B. J. Biddle and E. J. Thomas (Eds.), *Role theory: Concepts and research.* New York: Wiley, 1966. Pp. 23–45.)

behavioral classes from which they originate. Thus, the person segment may consist of all the prescriptions, evaluations, sanctions, actions, and descriptions taken together that are characteristic of father's behavior or both mother's and father's behavior (that is, the subset parents), or sons' and daughters' behavior (that is, the subset children), and so forth. The vertical column representing the *person segment* can vary in width with the number of persons or aggregates falling into the subject subset under investigation. Biddle and Thomas noted that the person segment of the proposed matrix can serve as a singular device to encompass the many particularized descriptions of person-roles which have been proposed in the literature. Hence, the person segment can represent:

1 *Individual roles,* or all the behaviors characteristic of a particular individual
2 *Aggregate roles,* or all the behaviors of an aggregate of individuals
3 *Behavior roles,* or all the behavior of the actor(s) in a role partnership or role complex
4 *Target roles,* or all the behavior of the "other(s)" in a role partnership or role complex.

Person segments can also be devised to represent the behavior of the many particularized roles that have been proliferated in role-theory literature (for example, mother role, male role, leader role).

The horizontal axis that consists of selected behavioral classes is referred to as the *behavior segment.* The behavior segment constitutes the behaviors of all persons taken together that can be placed in a single behavioral class or a set of behavioral classes. Thus, Biddle and Thomas noted that the behavior segment is made up of behaviors that are person-general and behavioral-class specific. The roles that emerge from a consideration of the behavior segment of the person-behavior matrix are the following:

1 *Overt role,* or public role
2 *Covert role,* or private role
3 *Prescriptive role,* or normative properties of roles in a selected social system
4 *Descriptive role,* or the role conceptions within a social unit
5 *Evaluative role,* or the norms for evaluating roles in a social unit
6 *Active role,* or the varying role performances of all actors in a social unit
7 *Sanctioning role,* or the sanctions which are applied to norm violation in the selected social unit.

The intersect of the person segment and the behavior segment was referred to by Biddle and Thomas as the *person-behavior* segment. In this segment of the matrix an individual's or aggregate's behaviors become classified into a specific behavioral class or into a selected set of behavioral classes. Thus, one may speak of the combination of any person segment or segments with any behavioral segment or segments. For example, person-behavior segments may consist of individual-prescriptive roles, aggregate-evaluative roles, overt-prescriptive roles, and so forth. In family systems, a classification of the father-prescriptive role would include all the prescriptions which are held by father. The examples that might be generated by a consideration of the person-behavior segment are endless, particularly if one considers the infinite variety of person roles and behavior roles that are possible within any social unit.

Biddle and Thomas's person-behavior matrix does not add any new concepts to the definition of role. Rather, it provides a descriptive schema for classifying the endless varieties of roles described in the literature into manageable categories. Furthermore, it provides a superstructure within which all roles, regardless of their description, can be classified along the same dimensions. Lastly, the person-behavior matrix provides a necessary basis for a broad definition of the role concept. It does not limit role to prescriptions of given position occupants or behaviors of role holders, but it instead envisions role as the combination of any person segment (individual or aggregate) with any behavioral segment (action, prescription, evaluation, sanction, or description).

Terms for Relating Sets of Persons and Behaviors

Although the analytical distinctions separating behaviors from other behaviors, and persons from behaviors are necessary for an understanding of role theory, to conceptualize a *role* fully these behavioral and personal elements must be merged into an integrated picture. For example, single normative prescriptions are often *related* to other normative prescriptions, or they may be related to actions or evaluation. Similarly, behavioral partitions, such as norms, actions, and evaluations are often intricately related to particular persons (for example, the specialist concept).

Biddle and Thomas (1966) proposed three criteria for inferring the existence and strength of the relationships among any set of behavioral partitions or between any person partition(s) and behavioral partition(s). (They did not consider concepts depicting the relationship between person partitions, because very few of these concepts are available in the literature of role theory.) These three criteria are (1) the degree of *similarity* or dissimilarity between or among partitions, (2) the degree of *codetermination* or interdependence for any two or more partitions, and (3) the jointly operating criteria of similarity and determination.

In the following paragraphs we give a brief resumé of Biddle and Thomas's discussion of the concepts pertaining to each of these relationship criteria.

The Criterion of Similarity Any two behavioral partitions or person-behavior partitions may be related to one another on the basis of their similarity or lack of it. The role concepts for which the criterion of partition-interrelationship is similarity are *differentiation, consensus, uniformity, specialization,* and *consistency*.

Differentiation is a term reserved for the relationship between behavioral partitions. For two or more behavioral partitions to be differentiated from one another, there must be discernible differences between them. For example, the norms which a social group holds for its members may be discernibly different from the norms it holds for nonmembers. In this case, the two sets of norms are differentiated and distinguished from one another. Therefore, the relationship between them is one of dissimilarity.

Consensus is defined by Biddle and Thomas as the amount of agreement on a specific topic. As with differentiation, consensus deals with the relationship between behavioral partitions. That is, people as an undifferentiated class must agree about *something* in order to reach consensus. The objects of agreement that were cited as most relevant are prescriptions, evaluations, descriptions, and sanctions. The consensus on any one of these classes of behavioral partitions may be either overt or covert. The covert consensus among individuals on prescriptions was referred to as norm consensus, while the overt prescription consensus was referred to demand consensus. Similarly, covert consensus on evaluation was referred to as value consensus, and overt consensus as assessment consensus. Relationships of consensus are based upon the *similarity* between several individuals' prescriptions, evaluations, descriptions, or sanctions for specified roles. Biddle and Thomas characterized two forms of lack of consensus on these partitions. The first, *nonpolarized dissensus,* involves several disagreeing opinions on the behavioral partitions. That is, the opinions on what the appropriate prescriptions for a role are might fall into quite a few categories of opinion. The second, *polarized dissensus* or *conflict,* involves disagreements on partitions which are prone to fall into two opposing camps. This latter form of dissensus is the basis for role conflict.

Role conflict is a specific form of polarized dissensus, which has been given much attention by social psychologists and sociologists alike. For this reason, we have decided to devote considerable space to a discussion of this form of dissensus. A very detailed discussion of role conflict and strain may be found in Secord and Backman's (1964) text. Here, however, we concentrate upon several basic aspects of role conflict.

Role conflict results when the expectations associated with several positions that an actor might hold are incompatible with one another (inter-role conflict) or when the expectations associated with a single position an actor holds are incompatible (intra-role conflict). Inter-role conflict occurs partly because it is highly improbable that any individual will hold only one role in the social system. Further, it is improbable that the set of roles that an individual holds (his/her *role set*) will consist of individual roles that do not have expectations conflicting with those of other individual roles that he/she holds. Thus, a father's role in his family may consist of some expectations in direct conflict with those pertaining to his occupational role. Intra-role conflict results from a lack of clarity or consensus concerning the expectations belonging to a single role held by the actor. Thus, two expectations ascribed to the role father may conflict with one another resulting in a level of strain that hinders adequate role performance.

The source of the conflicting expectations for either inter-role or intra-role conflict may be the actor himself, his/her role partners, society at large, or any combination of these agencies. Regardless of the source, a general proposition about role conflict is that, when it inculcates enough strain in the actor to preclude his adequate role performance, he/she seeks to resolve it. Several theories of and hypotheses concerning role-conflict resolution have been proposed from several theoretical orientations (Parsons, 1951; Getzels & Guba, 1954; Merton, 1957; Gross, Mason, & McEachern, 1957; Goode, 1960; Turner, 1962). The theory of conflict resolution proposed by Gross, Mason, and McEachern (1957) is presented as an example.

Gross, Mason, and McEachern's theory of role-conflict resolution is applicable to both intra-role and inter-role conflict. Essentially, they proposed that three factors that enter into the resolution of the conflict between any two expectations are (1) the relative legitimacy of the two expectations, (2) the sanctions incumbent upon the nonfulfillment of each of the expectations, and (3) the moral orientation of the actor. Expectations are classified as legitimate if the actor perceives that his/her role partners have the right to hold them and illegitimate if he/she perceives that they do not have a right to hold them. Considering this determinant of resolution independently, the actor would most probably decide to gear his/her role performance to the most legitimate expectations. However, additional problems arise when two conflicting expectations are equally legitimate or illegitimate or when the actor might be sanctioned for not responding to a less-legitimate or illegitimate expectation. In such cases, sanctions and/or moral orientations serve as bases of resolution.

Sanctions have already been discussed and refer to the positive or negative reinforcement which an actor might receive for not fulfilling role expectations. Gross, Mason, and McEachern defined positive sanctions as the gratification of the actor's needs by a role partner, which is contingent upon the fulfillment of expectations. Negative sanctions involve the frustration of the actor's needs by the role partner. If this basis of resolution is considered independently, it is reasonable that the actor would fulfill expectations that are positively sanctioned when they conflict with negatively sanctioned actions. However, when legitimacy and sanction are combined, the resolution becomes much more complex than this. That is, legitimate or illegitimate expectations may either be sanctioned positively or negatively. Therefore, what does an actor do when he/she is experiencing a role conflict between a legitimate expectation that prescribes a negatively sanctioned behavior and an illegitimate expectation that prescribes a positively sanctioned behavior? To deal with contingencies such as these, the theorists proposed that the moral orientation of the actor will interact with both legitimacy and sanction to determine resolution strategy.

They proposed three differing model orientations of actors: (1) the moral orientation, (2) the expedient orientation, and (3) the moral-expedient orientation. In considering all combinations of legitimate and illegitimate expectations and positive and negative sanctions that might be met in the conflict between any two expectations, they made 16 separate predictions for *each* form of actor orientation. Their predictions may be summarized in the following statements: (1) The morally oriented actor will emphasize legitimacy over sanction. Thus, if the conflict is between any two legitimate expectations, he or she will take a compromise course of role behavior regardless of sanction. If role conflict is between any two illegitimate sanctions, he or she will choose neither and avoid acting regardless of sanction. Finally, if the choice is between an illegitimate and a legitimate sanction, he or she will respond to the legitimate one regardless of sanction. (2) The expediently oriented actor will emphasize sanction over legitimacy. Thus, he or she will compromise between any two positively sanctioned and conflicting role behaviors regardless of legitimacy. Where the choice is between a positively and negatively sanctioned role behavior, he or she will always respond to the positively sanctioned one regardless of legitimacy. He or she will respond only to legitimacy when the choice is between legitimate and illegitimate expectations that are both negatively sanctioned. He or she will avoid resolving the conflict when the choice is between two illegitimate expectations where the resulting behaviors are both negatively sanctioned. (3) The morally and expediently oriented actor will consider both legitimacy and sanction. He or she will always select the legitimate expectation over the illegitimate when the sanctions are positive or negative for both. Where both conflicting expectations are either legitimate or illegitimate, he or she will always select the positively sanctioned one or will compromise if they are both positively sanctioned. Furthermore, he or she will compromise in the case of an illegitimate-positive and legitimate-negative conflict. Like the other two actor orientations, he or she will avoid deciding between two illegitimate expectations that are both negatively sanctioned.

Gross, Mason, and McEachern (1957) present experimental findings that provide impressive support for their theory of role-conflict resolution. However, independent replications are necessary before their propositions can be accepted as substantiated.

Uniformity is the communality in the role performance of two or more individuals holding a similar role. Thus, the role performance of a given person is *related* to the role performance of another person on the basis of the similarity between their performances.

Specialization involves the distinction between persons that are based upon their differentiation in a given domain of behavior. For example, medical practitioners may be grouped into a large undifferentiated role category. Within the category, however, one might distinguish subcategories of roles that differentiate between the generalist and the specialist and between various types of specialists. Although there exists both uniformity and consensus with regard to the role of physician in general, there are specific prescriptions, descriptions, evaluations, sanctions, and actions characteristic of the subroles or specialties within the general category. Divisions of larger role categories into specialist categories are based upon both the absolute amount of behavior engaged in by a group of persons and the number of differentiated behaviors they engage in. Hence, a part-time occupation is not as specialized as a full-time occupation; whether part-time or full-time, a given occupation may be more specialized because a fewer number of behaviors are engaged in. Thus, a full-time teacher is more a specialist than a part-time teacher, and a music teacher is more a specialist than a teacher who instructs in several subjects.

Classifications of specialists, then, are based upon the criterion of dissimilarity of the prescriptions, evaluations, descriptions, actions, or sanctions peculiar to particularized persons. As Biddle and Thomas noted, specialization presupposes a lack of consensus or uniformity.

Consistency exists when any two or more behavioral partitions are related in such a way that one of them implies or follows from the other(s) or when any two partitions logically belong together. Thus, relationships between behavioral partitions are based upon the similarity between the implications of those partitions. Inconsistency may be of two types, *logical* or *cognitive*. Logical inconsistency involves the exhibition of two dissimilar partitions. Thus, Biddle and Thomas noted that the prescription of the commandment, "Thou shalt not kill," is logically inconsistent with the prescription advocating wartime killings. Cognitive inconsistency (see Chapter 8) involves the occurrence of nonfitting partitions in the same person. For example, it is cognitively inconsistent for an individual holding Christian Science norms to be a surgeon at the same time. Thus, inconsistency is one basis for the relationships of differentiation between behavioral partitions.

The Criterion of Determination or Interdependence Interdependence involves a causal or determinative relationship between the behaviors or behavioral partitions of two persons. Individuals in role relationships (for example, mother-child, doctor-patient) are in certain respects dependent upon one another for norms, sanctions, behavioral goals, and so forth. The behavioral partitions of two persons may be dependent upon one another in that they facilitate or hinder one another's performances or in that they determine the rewards and costs of one another's performances.

Facilitation and hindrance might characterize the behavioral partitions of two persons A and B. There are several types of facilitation and several types of hindrance characteristic of structured relationships. Briefly, person A's performance may facilitate or hinder person B's performance; person A's and person B's performances might be mutually facilitative or hindering; or person A's and person B's performances may be independent of one another. Thus, there may exist persons who are dependent upon other persons for the fulfillment of a role, persons who are dependent upon one another for the fulfillment of both of their roles, and persons whose roles are totally independent of one another.

Reward and *cost* as conceptual terms have been dealt with extensively by Thibaut and Kelley (see Chapter 4). Biddle and Thomas's discussion of the reward-cost determinants of the relationships among role partitions is derived from their theory. In many role-interdependent relationships, facilitation and hindrance are directly related to interdependencies of rewards or costs. Simply, the behavioral partitions of any two parties may be dependent, interdependent, or independent with respect to rewards and costs. That is, one person's role behaviors may determine another's rewards or costs, both persons' role behaviors may determine one another's rewards or costs, or neither person's role behavior may be a determinant of the other's rewards or costs.

The Combined Criteria of Similarity and Determination   Some concepts dealing with the relationship between role partitions are jointly based on the criteria of similarity and determination; three such concepts are *conformity, adjustment,* and *accuracy.*

Conformity is the correspondence between an individual's performance and the other's performance or between his/her performance and the prescriptions for his/her performance. It is important to note that the conformity process is based upon both the similarity between the prescription or norm and the resultant behavior, and the degree to which the prescription determines the conforming performance. Conformity behavior in response to the normative prescriptions that one holds for himself/herself or the prescriptions that another holds for him/her constitutes a very important functional concept in role theory. Thus, conformity or the lack of it is implied by the degree of correspondence between the role expectations for and role performance of a given role occupant.

Adjustment involves a determinative relationship between prescriptions and behavior that is the converse of that for conformity. It occurs when the role performance determines the prescriptions appropriate to the role. That is, adjustments occur whenever prescriptions are brought in line (or made similar to) the observed behavior of a role occupant. Biddle and Thomas cited the situation in which a mother of a mentally retarded child sets her prescriptions at a level commensurate with the child's observed performance as an example of adjustment.

Accuracy is said to characterize the relationships among role partitions when role descriptions are similar to and determined by role performance and role expectations. Role descriptions are inaccurate when they misrepresent the expectations and performance characteristic of a given role.

Contemporary Applications of the Role-Theoretical Orientation: The Functional Components of Social Structural Analysis

The foregoing exposition of the conceptual language of role theory is largely unchanged from the exposition provided in the first edition of this book. This lack of change should not be taken as either a mark of the authors' laziness or as a measure of the stagnant quality of the field. Instead, it should be noted that role concepts provide for a primarily *structural* perspective on social relationships. The particular terms used to exposit this structural perspective have a constancy of use in the changing fabric of interactional theories of social behavior. In short, role theory provides a model for thinking about the structure of social relationships.

The major theoretical developments which have issued from a role-theoretical perspective over the past 10 years have dealt with the phenomena of role enactment. The primary theoretical focus of these recent viewpoints is self-presentation and its derivatives. Since the role-theory orientation provides a terminology for describing the largely *conscious* structure of social relationships, it is no surprise that such aspects of the social structure are naïvely perceivable and knowable by ordinary folks, as well as social scientists. For example, parents, students, teachers, physicians, lovers, workers, etc., are aware of their positions in the immediate social structure as well as the expectations and demands that accompany those positions. Similarly, each of us has an idea of how we should appear in order to be thought of as a nice person, attractive sexual partner, smart person, altruistic person, etc. Furthermore, each of us, in our various roles and self-characterizations, becomes aware of the sanctions (implicit and explicit) for not meeting our role expectations as well as the rewards for exemplifying positive role behavior. Given these sanctions and the paucity of circumstances for which *self* and *role* are utterly congruent (Sarbin, 1966; Goffman, 1959), each of us engages in a variety of tactics to convince other participants to an interaction as well as self that we have met or exemplified the requirements of the role in question. The products of such self and social engineering can range from achieving the liking and respect of a role partner to being viewed as competent or nondeviant.

The four theories presented in the subsequent chapter attempt to account for one or another dynamic property of self-presentation. Ingratiation theory (Jones, 1965; Jones & Wortman, 1973) details a set of psychologically minded tactics which an interactant uses to achieve the liking and respect of a high-status other. Impression management theory (Schlenker, 1980) examines the processes involved in the social projection of images of the self. Snyder's (1972) self-monitoring hypothesis examines individual differences in people's capacities to enact role-consistent, socially laudatory or acceptable behaviors, which may indeed be contrary to the "true attributes" or current affective states of the enactors. In a slightly different vein, Duval and Wicklund (1972) examine the intrinsic motivational process that is triggered by the self-recognition of deviation from role and self ideals. They label the state accompanying such recognition as objective self-awareness, and it resembles in many respects Mead's (1939) seminal ideas concerning role behavior. In addition to these role-related theories, Horner's (1968) perspective on the sex-role limitations upon female achievement is presented in Chapter 14. While it examines a rather specific phenomenon, it is nevertheless an example of the untoward consequences of self-presentational concerns. At the heart of Horner's argument is the notion that the exemplification of achievement and competence in many domains is *inconsistent* with the socially defined female role. For the less-talented or less-achievement-inclined woman, the solution to the dilemma is to self-present as a "nonachiever;" however, for the more-talented and/or more-achievement-inclined woman, the consequence is performance-disruptive anxiety.

In summary, the theories exposited in the next chapter, along with Horner's viewpoint, describe the functional and motivational consequences of enacting roles and provide examples of how the ancient role-theory perspective has been embedded in modern social-psychological theorizing.

Chapter 12

Role-Related Theories in Social Psychology

The historical durability of the role-theory perspective in the social sciences is a manifestation of the flexibility with which this system of thought might be applied to an understanding of diverse domains of social behavior. In fact nearly all, if not all, of the theories presented in this book could profitably be reconstructed in role-theoretical terms. A person's attitudes, values, social preferences, inferences about the social environment, social judgments, and interpersonal affects are describable by reference to the normative language of role theory. Yet, in the first edition of this book we defined no specific theory as primarily based upon a role-theory perspective.

At that time, role theory primarily served as a system for providing alternative *descriptions* of the social phenomena examined by other theoretical frameworks. In the past decade, however, social psychology has evidenced some alterations in perspective which have led to the emergence of self-contained theories of role-related phenomena. A number of influences contributed to this shift in focus:

1 The decreasing centrality of social theories focused upon shared motivational processes (e.g., the cognitive dissonance and cognitive consistency notions) signaled a shift from functional-dynamic theorizing to more structurally based thinking.

2 The time-paralleled advance of theoretical frameworks based upon structural definitions of persons and situations (i.e., the advance of attribution theory, labeling theory, and their concomitants).

3 The development of the symbolic interactionist perspective in sociology (cf. Hewitt, 1979) led to the reemergence of such theorists as Mead (1934) and Goffman (1959) as pivotal reference points for theorizing about social phenomena.

4 The concern for "relevance," which was so pervasive during the late 1960s and early 1970s, resulted in the emergence of theory and research which attempted to explain broad social phenomena as they affected and were affected by social system variables (e.g., the study of sex and race biases, race relations, interpersonal transactions in "real" groups or dyads, etc.).

5 As part of the same move toward relevance, the social science establishment picked up on examining questions concerned with self-identity, authenticity in interaction, and the formation of positive relationships, which had formerly been the domain of a primarily nonempirical humanistic psychology.

Out of all of these influences there emerged developing concerns with such phenomena as social system biases, self-realization, and manipulative "inauthentic" social interaction. Along with the emergence of these concerns came a renewed interest in social-structural models, such as role theory. While the theories to be exposited in this chapter could fall under other theoretical rubrics and, indeed, might be classified in alternative ways by the theorists themselves, it is our view that each of these theories have at their core person/target, self/role, or self-expectancy/social system–expectancy structural dichotomies, and these fit most appropriately into the domain of role theory.

As noted in the previous chapter, four theories will be discussed in this chapter. Ingratiation theory (Jones, 1965; Jones & Wortman, 1973), the collected hypotheses of self-monitoring theory (Snyder, 1979), and impression management theory (Schlenker, 1980) each deal with separate aspects of manipulative self-presentation. Self-awareness theory (Wicklund, 1975) attempts to account for the consequences of objective self-recognition in terms of the deviation of self from role or personal ideals. An additional theory relevant to role-related phenomena will be taken up in Chapter 14. This latter theory details Horner's fear-of-success proposal, which examines the concomitants of social system–mediated role conflict as it pertains to gender roles.

INGRATIATION THEORY

The theory of ingratiation first proposed by Jones (1965) and reformulated by Jones and Wortman (1973) was constructed to examine the interpersonal strategies which individuals invoke to impress others with their positive qualities. In keeping with this purpose Jones and Wortman (1973) proposed the following working definition of ingratiation:

a class of strategic behaviors illicitly designed to influence a particular other person concerning the attractiveness of one's personal qualities (p. 2).

Several elements of the above definition are critical. First of all, ingratiation is defined as *strategic* or *tactical* behavior because the actor's behavior is *preconstructed* to bring about effects in the target. The strategies are *illicit* because (when they are well constructed) the purposes of ingratiating communications are neither stated nor evident from implicit social contracts underlying typical interactions. The *desired effects* of these illicit strategic behaviors typically involve successfully impressing the target of one's ingratiating efforts with one's own positive attributes and attractive qualities.

In order to appropriately describe the processes involved in ingratiation, we must elaborate several theoretical phenomena articulated by Jones (1964) and Jones and Wortman (1973). In particular, in the subsequent paragraphs, we will concern ourselves with the determinants, tactics, and effects of ingratiation.

The Determinants of Ingratiation

Jones and Wortman (1973) describe three cognitive and/or motivational factors that are likely to determine the use of ingratiating behaviors, or behaviors designed to elicit the attraction of another. These three determinants are (1) incentive-based reasons, (2) the subjective probability of successful ingratiation, and (3) the perceived legitimacy of tactical behavior.

Incentive Bases   The rewards that result from successfully ingratiating oneself with a high-status other can constitute an inducement to ingratiation. Such rewards may take the form of the increased feelings of self-worth that might derive from currying the favor of a high-status other or might be more instrumental in quality (i.e., a job promotion, pay raise, etc.). In either case, Jones and Wortman define two variables that are likely to determine the incentive value of ingratiation: (1) the *importance* of the goal to the ingratiator and (2) the perceived *uniqueness* of the target person as a source of reward.

With regard to goal importance, the incentives for engaging in ingratiating behavior are stronger when the potential ingratiator possesses a *need* for the rewards available from the target. This need may inhere in the potential ingratiator's dispositions (e.g., a strong and chronic need for approval or chronic acquisitive needs with regard to money or status) or the need may be situationally induced. For example, an individual who has suffered an encounter with his/her own incompetence or an individual who experiences a lack of financial resources should be more motivated to ingratiate himself/herself with an appropriate target to alleviate such lacks than an individual who has experienced neither recent assaults on his/her worthiness nor recent financial privations.

Even in instances in which goal importance is high, the probability of ingratiating behavior will at least partly depend upon the availability of a target who has unique attributes which allow for the satisfaction of the ingratiator's needs. Jones and Wortman offer as a testable proposition that "the strength of the motive to be ingratiating to a particular person varies inversely with the number and saliency of other persons who can also produce the benefit that the ingratiator desires" (Jones & Worman, 1973, p. 39). Approval- and status-seeking behaviors are thus likely to be directed at those individuals who possess the power or position to afford approval or rewards to the ingratiator that have meaning for his/her worthiness or instrumental gain.

In summary, then, the incentive determinants of ingratiating behavior are conjointly based upon the *value* of the desired goal (i.e., incentive magnitude) and the availability of a target who has unique attributes that might mediate the ingratiator's achievement of the goal.

Subjective Probability of Successful Ingratiation   Jones and Wortman note that incentive-based determinants of ingratiation are necessary but insufficient conditions for evoking ingratiating tactics. Since ingratiation consists of a set of illicit and manipulative interaction tactics, the social costs of unsuccessful ingratiation are likely to be high (e.g., rejection by the target, embarrassment, resulting feelings of inauthenticity, etc.). As a consequence, potential ingratiators (even when they confront an appropriately unique target who controls resources of high incentive value) will likely assess the probability of successful ingratiation prior to invoking manipulative social tactics. Jones and Wortman propose several factors which are likely to affect the potential ingratiator's assessment of probable success. Most of these factors inhere in qualities, states, and attributes of the target person. Thus, the probability of successful ingratiation is viewed as a function of the ingratiator's assessment of:

1 *The target person's liking for the particular tactical behavior.* In other words, targets who view favor doing, opinion conformity, and/or flattery (tactics to be discussed in the next section) as positive social acts are more likely to be viewed as manipulable than targets who view one or more of these social tactics negatively.

2 *The target person's momentary need for the benefit provided by the ingratiator.* Thus, the higher the level of the target's current need for approval or belief support, for example, then the higher the potential ingratiator's estimate of successful ingratiation.

3 *The personality characteristics of the target.* Some targets are likely to be viewed as dispositionally more susceptible to ingratiating overtures than others. In line with this, Kaufman and Steiner (1968) have demonstrated that individuals portrayed as high in authoritarianism are less likely to be ingratiated than those portrayed as low in authoritarianism, and Schneider and Eustis (1972) found that self-enhancing tactical behaviors were more likely to be invoked with high-disclosing than with low-disclosing targets. In short, some "personality types" are likely to be judged as more vulnerable ingratiating targets than others.

4 *The salience of the benefit sought in the response hierarchy of the target.* Thus, "if a person (the potential ingratiator) knows that the benefit she/he desires is not likely to be present in the target person's response hierarchy, then she/he should be less likely to engage in ingratiating overtures" (Jones &

Wortman, p. 41). Even if the ingratiator might make a generally favorable impression on the target, ingratiation will not be successfully predicted unless the target is viewed as able to endow the ingratiator with the specific benefit desired.

5   *The control the ingratiator possesses over the circumstances (e.g., time, place, and context) of his/her interaction with the target.* In short, because ingratiating behaviors are inherently manipulative and illicit, the ingratiator must possess the wherewithal to engineer the social circumstances in order to both "disguise" (i.e., make less salient) the manipulative quality of the behavior and ensure the receptivity of the target. For example, an employee seeking a job promotion might more effectively invoke ingratiation tactics toward his/her boss in the informal atmosphere of a coffee lounge, cocktail bar, or office party than during a formally appointed meeting initiated by the boss. Under the latter circumstances, the employee's behavior is likely to be situationally constrained and offhanded flattery of his/her boss, for example, is likely to be more discernible.

6   *The suspiciousness of the target person concerning the intent of the ingratiator's overtures.* This particular determinant of the ingratiator's assessment of the probability of successful ingratiation is implied by most of the previously cited determinants. In fact, it is likely that ingratiation attempts will backfire when the ingratiator's motives are transparent to the target.

It should be noted that the several factors leading a potential ingratiator to assess a reasonable probability of successful ingratiation are embedded in his/her perceptual skills, social guile, and role knowledge. A "good" ingratiator is one whose ingratiating overtures are based upon effective and correct assessments of success probability.

Perceived Legitimacy   A third determinant of a person's attempt to employ ingratiating tactics toward a target person is the degree to which the person perceives such actions to be legitimate. It must be remembered that, since ingratiation is defined as an *illicit* attempt to gain another's favor, then the decision to tactically manipulate another's impression has ethical ramifications. Since open dishonesty and self-seeking inauthenticity are not easily incorporated without undue cost to one's self-perceptions, the illegitimacy of such tactics require at least cognitive mollification before they are employed. Jones and Wortman point out that the ethics of ingratiation are, at best, ambiguous. Whether the benefits which an ingratiator mediates for a target (i.e., good feelings about self, belief, support, favors, etc.) are cheapened by the self-interest inherent in the ingratiator's ends constitutes the ethical dilemma that a potential ingratiator confronts. Ingratiation is partly determined by the manner in which this dilemma is resolved. Jones and Wortman note a number of primarily attributional resolutions to this dilemma.

1   *The ingratiator can convince himself/herself that the statements made to a target are true.* Thus, if the ingratiator resolves that the target deserves his/her compliments or favors, then ingratiation will be perceived as legitimate and will be more likely to occur.

2   *The ingratiator can admit that his/her tactical behavior does not reflect his/her true feelings, but attributes his/her duplicity to benign rather than self-seeking motives.* For example, the ingratiator could view his/her ingenuine behavior as an instance of legitimately "being nice" to or saving the feelings of a vulnerable target rather than in its self-seeking terms.

3   *The ingratiator can admit that his/her tactical behavior was illicit but focus upon circumstances that would morally justify duplicity.* Several examples of this type of legitimacy enhancement may be given. (*a*) The potential ingratiator might seek consensual validation or social comparison information. In this sense, Jones and Wortman describe the manner in which a suitor might justify his/her flattery of a potential lover by noting the pervasiveness of such "sweet-talking" tactics in male-female relationships. (*b*) Ingratiation might be viewed as morally justifiable when the target is cast as an enemy who does not deserve equitable treatment. (*c*) If the ingratiator finds him-/herself in a relationship of involuntary "servitude" to the target, then ingratiation might be morally justified as a survival tactic. For example, army draftees typically feel that the ingratiation of superior officers is a legitimate means of improving their position or warding off negative treatment. (*d*) If a potential ingratiator finds him-/herself bereft of resources through no fault of his/her own, he/she might rationalize ingratiation as a tactic for relieving privation. Thus a financially impoverished person is likely to feel that ingratiation with a well-heeled target for purposes of monetary enhancement is a legitimate course to take.

4   *The ingratiator might possess attributes, traits, or values which lead him/her to perceive ingratiation tactics as legitimate social behaviors.* Therefore, certain individual differences in personality might render the supposed ethical dilemma created by tactical self-presentation as less of a dilemma regardless of the circumstances. Individuals with so-called Machiavellian tendencies (cf. Christie & Geis, 1970) or cynical values concerning human relationships may have little conflict about the legitimacy of ingratiation. It should be noted that such individuals are still likely to base their decision to engage in ingratiation upon the aforementioned two determinants: incentive magnitude and potential success of the behavior.

While Jones and Wortman elegantly describe three important classes of factors which might serve to determine the occurrence of ingratiation, they readily admit that there is little basis for proposing combinatorial principles which comparatively weight the importance of these determinants to the occurrence of an ingratiation attempt. To quote the theorists:

> How these three factors [incentive value, probability of success, and perceived legitimacy] combine is, unfortunately, far from clear. It might be argued that the combination is multiplicative since if any factor is zero, ingratiation will presumably not occur. Intuitively, it may turn out that perceived legitimacy is more a dichotomous variable than either incentive value or subjective probability. Moral decisions tend to have an either-or quality about them. This would suggest that incentive value and subjective probability combine multiplicatively to produce a

strong or weak tendency to ingratiate. Legitimacy then plays a role as a threshold factor, providing a go or stop signal for the behavior once the tendency to ingratiate reaches a certain strength. Thus a person may flatter or ingratiate even though he knows this behavior is illegitimate, once the importance and the likelihood of obtaining a benefit reach a certain combined value (Jones & Wortman, p. 44).

In light of the difficulty in establishing a priori the relative importance of each of the determinants of ingratiation detailed by Jones and Wortman, it would seem that research which examines the relative prominence of ingratiating overtures when manifestations of each of the three proposed determining factors are simultaneously varied would appear warranted. At present, much of the research examining the ingratiation-generating properties of each of the afore-mentioned determinants consists of piecemeal inquiries into the effects of a single determining condition (e.g., incentive magnitude or target need or ingratiator personality). Some of these inquiries were not designed with the purpose of examining ingratiation theory per se, but of demonstrating the viability of related but independently generated hypotheses. For the most part, the research supports the importance of the proposed determinants to forms of strategic behavior. This work will be briefly discussed in a subsequent section pertaining to research on the processes of ingratiation.

In the next section we will describe the primary tactics used by ingratiators to curry favor or acquire instrumental gain from a target person. The employ-ment of these tactics is presumed to be dependent upon the adequate determina-tion of appropriateness on the part of the ingratiator. In short, in the next section we will consider the tactics which Jones and Wortman propose will follow upon the combined determination of the person's strong need for a valuable benefit from a target, the subjective assessment of successful attainment of the benefit through strategic interaction, and the perceived legitimacy of such self-seeking tactical behavior.

Proposed Tactics of Ingratiation

In describing tactical variations in ingratiation, Jones and Wortman allude to a wide variety of popular accounts of successful tactics for winning over and influencing people (e.g., Dale Carnegie's popular works), as well as a bevy of empirical studies which qualify the success of various approaches to interperson-al manipulation. In this section we will confine ourselves to the definition of the four primary strategies of ingratiation noted by Jones and Wortman and briefly describe limiting and facilitating factors which affect the success of such tactics. The four tactics of ingratiation proposed by Jones and Wortman are: *other enhancement* or flattery, *opinion conformity, favor doing,* and *manipulative self-presentation.*

Other Enhancement   Other enhancement refers to those ingratiating be-haviors by which an ingratiator seeks the positive evaluation of another by giving that other compliments which enhance other's esteem. In bolder and naïve psychological terms, other enhancement refers to *flattery*. Through other enhancement "the ingratiator finds ways to express a positive evaluation of the target person and emphasizes the latter's various strengths and virtues" (Jones & Wortman, p. 4). This class of tactics need not be entirely duplicitous in quality. In fact the compliments one affords another in the process of ingratiation are probably most effective when they express actual qualities of the other in exaggerated form, but perhaps fail to include certain perceived negative attributes of the other. This class of tactics is particularly "designed to convey the impression that the ingratiator thinks highly of the target person" (Jones & Wortman, p. 4).

The theorists note that the effectiveness of other enhancement in currying the favor of the target person seems to derive from the premise that liking is likely to be reciprocated in relationships. Nevertheless in order for flattery to serve the ingratiator's ends, the target person must attribute a motive to the ingratiator which is correspondent with the flattering behavior (i.e., "he expresses liking toward me because he really believes that I possess the positive qualities he has mentioned"). Of course, a number of alternative attributions less likely to render the ingratiator's behavior effective are also possible. For example, the complimenter's manipulative motives might be perceived, or the complimenter might be seen as a compulsively nice person who simply offers positive evaluations to everyone.

Given Jones and Wortman's focus upon an attributional model of ingratiation, a critical mediating step in the effectiveness of ingratiating behavior inheres in the attributions the target makes in order to assess the *credibility* of the ingratiator and the *uniqueness* of his/her feedback to the target. We will see that these credibility and uniqueness factors are quite relevant for all four classes of tactical behavior to be described in this section.

Jones and Wortman discuss a number of factors that are particularly relevant to the success of other-enhancement and the reader is directed to their monograph for a more elaborated discussion of such factors. One particularly important factor in the success of other enhancement has to do with the ingratiator's selection of the attributes of the target to enhance. Their discussion of this issue suggests that (*a*) the more certain and confident a target is that he possesses the attribute enhanced by the ingratiator, the less effective the ingratiating attempt and (*b*) the more certain and confident a target is that he/she does *not* possess the attribute enhanced by the ingratiator, the less credible the ingratiator, the more transparent his/her ingratiating motives become and the less effective the ingratiating attempt. In short, other enhancement is viewed as a most effective strategy when the ingratiator succeeds in flattering the target on dimensions the target values but is *uncertain* of possessing.

Opinion Conformity   A second class of tactical behaviors available to an ingratiator is opinion conformity. *This class of behaviors is predicated upon the assumption that people like others whose attitudes and beliefs are similar to their* *own.* The ingratiator capitalizes upon this "fact" by expressing agreement with beliefs and attitudes he/she presumes or knows the target possesses. The form that this agreement might take could vary widely from simple assent to complex forms of behavioral imitation. As with other enhancement, the ingratiator behaviorally invoking opinion conformity should be particularly cognizant of the need to impress the target with the *authenticity* or credibility of his/her agreeing stance as well as with the uniqueness of his agreement to the particular attitude of the target person at hand. Of course, if the target person attributes the ingratiator's agreement to illicit motivations or views it as a product of the ingratiator's pervasive tendency to agree with everyone, opinion conformity will fail to produce the desired effects of the ingratiator. As with other enhancement, the skilled opinion conformer is most effective when he/she expresses agreement with attitudes or beliefs about which the target person is a bit uncertain. Further, the ingratiator will probably further enhance the credibility of his or her agreement on a particular issue by tactically expressing occasional disagreement on other issues.

In short, according to Jones and Wortman, the skilled opinion conformer, like the skilled flatterer, must successfully manipulate the attributions of the target such that:

1   His/her ingratiating motives are not perceivable.
2   The authenticity and credibility of the agreement is made salient.
3   The behavior is perceived by the target as a unique expression to him/her rather than as an indiscriminant act of the ingratiator.

Rendering Favors   A third tactic of ingratiation discussed by Jones and Wortman is the giving of favors to a target person. "Like compliments, favors may convey to a target person that we like and respect him and suggest that his welfare is important to us. They may also convey that the favor-doer is a kind and thoughtful person." (Jones & Wortman, p. 19) Once again however, there are clear qualifications on the effectiveness of favor doing as an ingratiation strategy. As with the other strategies discussed, the ingratiator must be cognizant of the need to "engineer" the attributions of the target person such that he/she fails to perceive the manipulative nature of the act, while correspondingly linking the ingratiator's behavior to the ingratiator's uniquely high opinion of him/her.

Self-Presentation   This fourth tactic of ingratiation involves the direct manifestation or description of one's positive attributes to a target in order to increase one's attractiveness to that target. Self-presentation can refer to either the direct verbal expression of one's traits and attributes (e.g., "I am a charitable person.") or might involve exhibiting behavior which implies the possession of the trait in question (e.g., telling another that you donate one-third of your salary to charity each month).

According to Jones and Wortman, self-presentations based upon one of two kinds of information are likely to be effective: (1) The ingratiator might present himself/herself in terms of the idiosyncratic preferences of the target person. (E.g., if the target appreciates and values seriousness, one can describe oneself as intense and somber or, indeed, behave that way.) (2) The ingratiator might present himself/herself as possessing traits that are generally valued in the culture. The first of these requires good intuitive skills; the second requires accurate social knowledge.

As with the other strategies, self-presentations as ingratiating tactics will require that the ingratiator manipulate the attributional context presented to the target in order to ensure that the manipulative intent of the behavior goes undetected. As a consequence, obvious self-presentational tactics (e.g., boorish boasting) are quite likely to be ineffective or even counterproductive. Indeed, indirect and behavioral methods of presenting one's positive traits to a target are likely to be most effective because of their subtlety.

In discussing self-presentation, we have focused upon the presentation of positive self-attributes to a target. It should also be noted that *modesty* and *self-deprecation* might also be invoked as self-presentational strategies. Such tactics gain their effectiveness in ingratiating with another by serving as an acknowledgement of the person's dependence on and noncompetitive relationships to the target. Nevertheless, the ingratiator should exert care to self-deprecate on unimportant rather than important traits and attributes or on the ingratiator's assets that are already known to the target.

General Considerations in Employing Tactical Behaviors

In presenting Jones & Wortman's account of tactical behaviors, we have frequently referred to several factors limiting the effectiveness of interpersonally manipulative acts. What Jones and Wortman point out is that tactical behavior in the service of impression management engages the aspiring ingratiator in the process of "attribution management" as well. What must be recalled is that ingratiation is *illicit* social behavior, typically directed at targets who have high status or control important and needed resources for the ingratiator. In other words, the ingratiator is *dependent* upon the target's positive evaluation of him/her or dependent upon the positive effects that the target might mediate for him/her. Such dependency is likely to render the target wary of unsolicited compliments, favors, and belief supports and make self-aggrandizement less credible.

In short, the ingratiator is confronted with the dilemma of favorably impressing a somewhat wary target person without arousing the target person's awareness that he/she is being ingratiated.

The distinction between "good" and "bad" versions of each of the four tactics described turns on the ingratiator convincing the target of the *credibility* and *uniqueness* of his/her tactical behavior. In order to be most effective, flattery, agreement, favor doing, and self-aggrandizement must all be seen as deriving from the genuinely positive attributes of the ingratiator. At the same time, the targets should be led to infer that the ingratiating behavior is directed toward them because they have unique attributes which warrant enhancement, generate favors, compel agreements, or evoke disclosures on the part of others.

In a sense then, the ingratiator must engage in his/her duplicitous behavior in ways that manipulate the targets' attributions of causality for such behaviors. In all instances of tactical behavior the successful ingratiator implicitly directs the target away from attributions which increase his/her awareness of the ingratiator's desire to impress him/her or win his/her favor. Jones and Wortman, then, offer the clear generalization "that if it is clear to the target person that the ingratiator has something to gain by impressing him, then all of these ingratiation tactics are less likely to be effective" (p. 25).

In formalizing a theoretical principle expressing the ingratiator's dilemma, Jones and Wortman offer that *"the extremity or obviousness of ingratiation overtures interacts with the degree of apparent social dependence to determine whether or not attraction will be gained"* (p. 25). This relationship is expressed in Figure 12-1. As this figure shows, the target's attraction toward the ingratiator will increase with increases in the extent of tactical behavior. However, at levels of extreme tactical use, the target's attraction to the ingratiator will diminish. The degree of decreased attraction is directly related to the obviousness of the ingratiator's dependence upon the target.

Therefore, as we have already noted the ingratiator must be a credible communicator. In order to gain the attraction of the target, his/her compliments, favors, agreements, and self-presentations must not imply his/her ulterior motives. The above family of curves defines two situational parameters which are predicted to effect ingratiator credibility—the extent of tactic use and the degree of ingratiator dependence on the target.

The Effects of Ingratiation

Aside from the intended effects that the ingratiator might have upon a target person, there are several other proposed consequences of ingratiating overtures

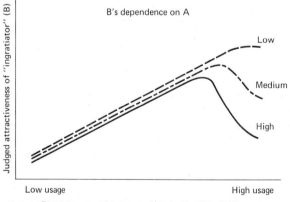

Figure 12-1 Theoretical relationship between use of ingratiation tactics and judged attractiveness of the ingratiator. (From Jones and Wortman, 1973.)

noted by Jones and Wortman. Ingratiation may have effects upon both the ingratiator and the target, as well as on the quality of relationships.

Effects on the Target of Ingratiation

Having positive status-enhancing behaviors directed toward oneself is likely to generate some quite salient effects on the target. The nature of these effects is likely to be a joint consequence of the attributions of motivation the target makes concerning the ingratiating behavior and the degree to which the ingratiator bases his/her tactical behavior on factual states and factual information.

1 Ingratiating behavior, like most behavior communicating feedback to an individual, will affect the recipient's view of reality and his/her relationship to that reality. *If the ingratiator's enhancements, favors, and agreements have some basis in fact, they are likely to facilitate the target's accurate conception of reality and allow him/her to behave with more certainty and self-assuredness in response to that reality.*

2 *If the ingratiator's tactical behavior is in the primary service of furthering his/her own image and thereby unduly distorts his/her true evaluation of the target, it will threaten the target's valid appraisal of reality and lead the target to make inaccurate inferences about himself/herself.*

3 *A target person in a position of power and status* (a highly likely occurrence) *may develop mistrust of the loyalty, flattery, and compliance of those dependent upon him/her.* The more pervasive the target's power, influence, or control of resources, the more ambiguous is the complicity of others and the more likely that others will ingratiate him/her. In short, individuals who, because of their status and role, are likely targets of ingratiation are prone to become less trusting of the positive behaviors of others toward them. Strickland (1958) has demonstrated an effect of this kind in his research on work supervision. He found that initial performance monitoring of workers leads to continued monitoring because the work supervisor fails to trust that the basis for work compliance is somehow intrinsic to the worker.

Effects on the Ingratiator

There are three general effects of ingratiation behavior on the ingratiator which are noted by Jones and Wortman.

1 *The ingratiator may change his/her self-view as a function of positive self-presentation.*

2 *The ingratiator may come to view the target more positively as a function of his/her enhancement of the target, favor doing, or complicity toward the target.*

3 *The ingratiator's private opinions and beliefs might be altered by his/her expression of opinion conformity to the target.*

Jones and Wortman provide a lengthy discussion on the vicissitudes of each of these effects, and the interested reader is directed to their monograph for this account. For our purposes it is important to note that there are a few general

factors which should theoretically govern whether or not an ingratiator incorporates the content of his/her tactical behavior into his/her self-perceptions,
perceptions of the target, opinions, or attitudes. In a general sense, the more the
ingratiator's behavior is viewed by him/her as deriving from *true* and accurate
internal sources, the greater the probability that it will be viewed as credible.
This latter proposition is derivable from the theories of cognitive dissonance and
self-perception, described previously. In summary, a set of limiting factors
which might inhibit the ingratiator from "trusting" his/her own tactical presentations are listed.

1 The more salient the ingratiator's motive to achieve the desired benefit
from the target is than the expression of true belief, for example, the less likely
the ingratiator will be to incorporate the implications of the ingratiating behavior
into his/her self-picture or view of the target. Thus, under conditions where the
incentive value of ingratiation is high and the ingratiator is led to view tactical
behavior as legitimate, he/she will likely attribute his/her behavior to these
sources and be less inclined to "believe" the positive self-statements, other
enhancements, or agreements as expressing "truth."
2 In a related vein, the greater the status and power of the target, the
more salient the manipulative aspects of ingratiating tactics and the less likely
that their content will be incorporated by the ingratiator.
3 The more effort an ingratiator invests in impressing a target and the less
spontaneous his/her positive self- and other enhancement, the less credible
the positive feedback received from the target and the less likely that it will be
taken as a "true" appraisal. In short, the more energy that goes into
successful ingratiation, the less meaningful its success to the ingratiator's self-
perceptions.

Each of the above three functional statements have been previously alluded
to in other parts of the chapter. Once again, the credibility of an ingratiator's
tactical behavior to both himself/herself and the target is a joint function of
the extent of the ingratiator's dependence on the target and the degree of the
ingratiator's usage of tactical behavior. These two factors are important from the
perspective not only of the target but also of the ingratiator.

Effects on Relationships

In this discussion of effects, Jones and Wortman concern themselves with the
larger sociocultural implications of the widespread use of ingratiation for human
social relationships. They note that ingratiation pervades social systems in which
people are dependent upon other people because of an inequitable distribution
of material, social, and personal resources. Since such inequity seems to be more
or less present in all social systems, one would expect ingratiation to be a
frequently invoked class of social behavior. As such, what are its larger
sociocultural effects? Jones and Wortman imply that ingratiation fits into the
social fabric and can help lead to adaptive social relationships. While our implicit
knowledge that ingratiation pervades interaction might lead us to view interpersonal feedback, the expression of positive sentiment, modesty, agreement, and

the like as ambiguous social acts, the alternative of complete candor in social interaction is not always appropriate nor adaptive. To quote the theorists,

> We are essentially proposing that effective group functioning requires a delicate balance between valid social information and constructive social support. A group that leans too far in the direction of ruthless candor is likely to require various reparative processes to smooth over the frictions of disagreement or hostility. But a group so wrapped up in social support activities that little valid information gets through has obvious problems of another sort (p. 52).

Comments on Ingratiation Theory

Ingratiation theory constitutes a thoughtful and internally consistent framework examining the structure and dynamics of interpersonal tactical behavior. While it had its origins in a provocative 1964 book by Edward E. Jones, the analysis of ingratiating behaviors, their determinants, and their social outcomes have been conceptually extended in the above reviewed monograph by Jones and Camille Wortman (1973). The major conceptual extension provided by the more recent work overtly represents ingratiation as a more complex set of processes than the original treatment. The ingratiator can be characterized as not only engaging in impression management, but, if one is to be a successful ingratiator, also having to be concerned with *"attributional management."* While the original theoretical piece certainly alludes to this prerequisite, the more recent treatment formalizes a set of hypothetical considerations which would allow for testing the attributional management notion. The attributional implications of tactical behavior were in no small measure discerned by the theorists partly as a function of the growing predominance of the attributional perspective in social psychology over the past decade—a development which was strongly influenced by the Heiderian-derived attribution theory perspective of Jones (see Chapter 9).

Insofar as the adequacy of ingratiation theory qua theory, the evidence is not yet sufficiently rich to allow for a careful assessment of its empirical status. It is indeed internally consistent in its several propositions and meshes well with attributional, dynamic, and role-enactment viewpoints in social psychology. In addition, it offers clear and testable hypotheses concerning (*a*) the conditions that should give rise to ingratiation, (*b*) the characteristics of the target, ingratiator, relationship, and behavior that should give rise to successful ingratiation, and (*c*) the likely attributional consequences of particular variations in ingratiation strategies. As such, several propositions of the theory are certainly open to test. While the Jones and Wortman monograph sometimes makes hypothesis discernment difficult because it frequently adopts the expository ploy of offering advice to a potential ingratiator, the "advice" consistently specifies the important variables governing the success of ingratiation attempts. We hope the above condensation of their work renders the hypothetical structure of the theory clear to the reader.

By noting that the empirical status of the theory is indefinite, we do *not* mean to imply that research on ingratiation processes and several propositions of the theory has been absent. For example:

1   The notion that the incentive value of ingratiation should increase as a function of recent experiences with incompetence is indirectly supported by experiments by Walster (1965); Jacobs, Berscheid, and Walster (1971); and Schneider (1969). Jones and Wortman describe Schneider's work in some detail. He found that subjects who failed a test and subsequently were asked to provide a questionnaire self-description to an interviewer, who would presumably give them feedback on their social sensitivity, were significantly more positive in their self-descriptions than failing subjects who had no anticipation of interviewer feedback.

2   With regard to the subjective probability of success determinant of ingratiation, Jones, Gergen, Gumpert, and Thibaut (1965) found that conformity toward a target person only occurred if the subject was led to believe that the target would be appreciative of such a tactic.

3   The work of Kaufman and Steiner (1968) and Schneider and Eustis (1972), briefly discussed previously, indicates that ingratiation is indeed more likely if the target exhibited particular personality characteristics. More specifically, the first study found that tactical conformity was more likely toward a low- than high-authoritarian target. The latter study found greater self-enhancement in the face of a previously high-disclosing than in the face of a low-disclosing target.

4   Jones, Gergen, and Davis (1962) and Upshaw and Yates (1968) have found that successful ingratiators are likely to come to view their self-enhancing statements as accurate self-descriptions. These latter findings relate to previously discussed strategies for enhancing the perceived legitimacy of ingratiation.

5   In addition, Jones and Wortman cite a sizable number of studies which have examined the conditional success of one or another ingratiation strategy in producing the desired attraction effect (e.g., Stires & Jones, 1969; Jones, Gergen, & Jones, 1963; Jones & Gordon, 1972; Jones & Jones, 1964). In the main these studies are quite consistent with the theoretical suppositions of the ingratiation framework.

While the spate of studies in support of the hypotheses concerning the effectiveness of various ingratiation strategies provides ample evidence for the validity of ingratiation phenomena, the critical attributional mediations described by Jones and Wortman require further empirical elaborations. In other words, ingratiation theory, while quite generative of research in its classic (Jones, 1964) form, now requires confirmation of its newer attributional implications.

IMPRESSION MANAGEMENT THEORY

Impression management theory is an emerging theory that has its historical roots in a variety of approaches to interpersonal relations. Aspects of the theory can be seen in such diverse approaches as symbolic interactionism (e.g., Dewey, 1922; Cooley, 1902; Mead, 1934), self-presentation (Goffman, 1959), constructive alternativism (Kelly, 1955), Heider's (1958) theory of interpersonal relations, and, to a lesser extent, script theory (Abelson, 1976). Consequently, it would probably be inaccurate to attribute impression management theory to any single person. However, in order to present an integrated, consistent approach, we have chosen to base our presentation on the formulation proposed by Schlenker in his recent treatise *Impression Management: The Self-Concept, Social Identity, and Interpersonal Relations* (Schlenker, 1980). In its present stage of development, the theory consists of a set of assumptions concerning the self-concept and motivations to establish and maintain social identity, a set of propositions and hypotheses concerning impression management as a means of protecting the self, and some less-well-formulated proposals concerning management tactics. Before discussing these aspects of theory, it may be helpful to state Schlenker's definition of impression management:

> Impression management is the conscious or unconscious attempt to control images that are projected in real or imagined social interactions (Schlenker, 1980, p. 6).

The Self and Social Identity

The self-concept and social identity are two important elements in the theory of impression management. According to Schlenker, the self-concept is a theory that a person constructs about himself/herself, whereas social identity refers to the ways people are defined and regarded in social interactions. The self-concept is presumed to emerge from the social interaction process. During the socialization process people categorize themselves on various dimensions that they regard as relevant for them. Examples of these construct categories are such things as friendly-unfriendly, competent-incompetent, conforming-independent, and dominant-submissive. The person's view of his or her proper category derives from the person's interactions with others, including the person's perceptions of the impressions others form about him or her (called reflected appraisals by symbolic interactionists). In other words, people's self-concepts develop as they see themselves reflected in the actions of significant others.

The self-concept is said to serve several important functions for the individual. First of all, it can be regarded as a mechanism that enables the individual to maximize pleasure and minimize pain during his or her lifetime. People who have an accurate conception of their own capabilities and potential accomplishments can utilize this knowledge to increase positive outcomes from life. Second, the self-concept provides a framework within which the person's experiences can be organized and interpreted. It serves as a guide for processing self-related information and thus helps the person respond appropriately to a diverse and complex world. Finally, the self-concept is presumed to facilitate the maintenance of self-esteem. Impression management theory assumes that everyone is motivated to create and maintain the highest self-esteem possible, as we shall see. Therefore, this function of the self-concept has important implications for impression management theory.

In contrast to the self-concept, which is a private construct that is accessible only to the individual, social identity is the self as known to others and is therefore largely external to the person. Social identity concerns the way persons are viewed by other persons. Social identity, like the self-concept, emerges through interactions with others. When two persons interact for the first time, each is trying to learn as much as possible about the other, and each is trying to create or project a particular image to the other. Thus, interactants are simultaneously trying to determine what each other is "really like" and to influence the other's perceptions of their selves. Social identity is a consequence of many such interactions, and through this identity a person becomes part of the social relationships among people.

Schlenker (1980) suggests that social identity is our perceptions of either our own identity or the identities of other people. Presumably, this means only that people have concepts concerning how other people perceive them, as well as perceptions of what other persons are like. In this sense, perceptions of one's own identity are a part of one's overall self-concept. In order to maintain or enhance their self-concepts, people attempt to influence the identities they project to others through impression management tactics. Thus, if a person sees himself or herself as competent and independent, he or she is likely to behave in ways that convey the impression of competence and independence. Similarly, if a person perceives another person as competent and independent, he or she will likely behave in ways that imply that the other has those characteristics. The attempt to cast another into a particular identity is called alter-casting and represents an indirect attempt to influence the other person's identity in the relationship.

It is possible to distinguish between *situated identities* and *composite identities*. Situated identities are specific to particular interactions with particular others, whereas composite identities are general and subsume a variety of social interactions with different people. Thus, a person may have many situated identities but only one composite identity. It follows that a person may attempt to monitor and control one identity in the presence of another person. This does not imply that people have complete control over their identities or that they always make a conscious choice of identities to attempt to monitor and control.

Finally, there are individual differences in the ways that people attempt to project social identities. Some persons are more publicly self-conscious than others (self-awareness), some are more sensitive to the social situation and the impressions they are creating (self-monitors), some have greater need for social approval, and some are more manipulative then others (Machiavellians).

Constructing Personal Realities

As noted earlier, the need for self-esteem occupies a central position in impression management theory. The observation that people behave in ways that maximize their positive characteristics and minimize their negative ones is so pervasive that the proposition scarcely requires documentation. *Why* people behave in such egotistical and self-serving ways, however, is controversial. According to Schlenker, the most common answer is that people have a need to maintain or enhance their self-esteem. He does not rule out the possibility that the need for self-esteem is innate, but he proposed that self-serving actions and perceptions might have their basis in the social interaction process. The most relevant aspects of the social interaction process are identified as controlling identities, public descriptions of attributes, management of the self-image, and claiming images. These processes are obviously not independent, but are interrelated events that contribute to the maintenance and/or enhancement of the self.

Controlling identities is viewed as necessary if one wishes to function effectively in social interactions. One *must* influence the attitudes and behaviors of others and attempt to guide them to desirable courses of action, because the identities that people establish affect the ways they believe they should behave in the presence of others, the ways they are treated by others, and the outcomes that they receive from social interactions.

One of the most obvious ways of attempting to control impressions (and therefore social identity) is through public descriptions of one's own attributes, behaviors, and events. The public descriptions may or may not correspond to the private perceptions of the person.

Managing the self-image is presumed to be learned through the socialization process. People learn the rules of society and also establish personal standards that permit them to evaluate their own actions even when no one else is present. The association between what is good and rewards received is established early in life, and a person may feel good about an action even if no one is watching. In this sense, people may be concerned about managing their own impressions of themselves as well as managing the impressions that others have of them.

Claiming images may be the most common way of establishing and maintaining social identity. This is a complex process that involves much more than the relative attractiveness of images. Although one might desire to project the most attractive image possible, reality imposes constraints that limit the effectiveness of such an attempt. People are expected to be what they claim to be, and recognition that a person has violated this expectation leads to negative sanctions. There are several aspects of the process of claiming images that merit further consideration.

A *claim* to a particular image is said to occur when people try to associate themselves with that image. When a claim is made, there exists the *requirement* that the claim be legitimate; i.e., that the person have those characteristics involved in the claim, that the person be able to perform as claimed, etc. Questions may arise about the legitimacy of one's claim to an image and lead to *challenges*. Challenges may come from either other persons or facts. When challenged, the person must either abandon the image or satisfy the audience that the challenge is invalid. Images are *successfully claimed* when either they are not challenged or the person can demonstrate that the challenge has no merit.

When a claim to an image is successful, benefits accrue to the person who makes the claim, but if the claim is repudiated, all benefits are forfeited. Worse still, the person making the repudiated claim may suffer from shame, guilt, or embarrassment; may be ridiculed or ostracized; or may even be perceived as a liar or out of touch with reality. Thus, sanctions may be either internal or external. These considerations led Schlenker to distinguish between the *expected value of an image* and the *expected value of a personal claim to an image*. The expected value of an image is the presumed worth of a successfully claimed image, whereas the expected value of a personal claim to an image is the expected worth of what the person thinks would happen if he or she claimed the image. The former is an ideal image—the way a person would like to be—but it is the latter expectation that is most likely to influence impression management attempts. The expected value of a personal claim to an image depends upon the expected value of the image, the perceived probability that a claim to it would be successful, and the expected value of sanctions resulting from an unsuccessful claim to the image. Thus, the theory hypothesizes that it is the expected value of claims to images that allows the prediction of people's public and private relevant behaviors.

It is also proposed that people want to associate themselves with desirable images and dissociate themselves from undesirable images. For instance, when people associate themselves with admirable people and events, their identities are enhanced through reflected glory; by dissociating themselves from despicable others, they avoid or diminish negative outcomes that may threaten their own identity or self-concept.

Protecting the Self

If a person has successfully constructed the desired social identity, he or she is often faced with events that threaten this identity. People cannot always anticipate the consequences of their own actions, they cannot control events that may affect their identities, and unexpected events may occur that affect their identities. Any event that threatens the person's identity creates a predicament. When a person finds himself or herself in a predicament, attempts are made to eliminate or reduce the negative consequences for the person's identity. Propositions and hypotheses concerning the use of impression management in predicaments constitute a major part of Schlenker's theory.

Predicaments are defined as "situations in which events have undesirable implications for the identity-relevant images actors have claimed or desire to claim in front of real or imagined audiences" (Schlenker, 1980, p. 125). Predicaments vary greatly in severity, ranging from minor embarrassing incidents to calamities that may completely destroy one's carefully constructed identity. The theory proposes that the severity of a predicament is determined by the undesirability of the event that precipitated the predicament and the degree to which the person is perceived to be responsible for the event: the more undesirable the event and the more responsible the person appears to be for it, the more severe the predicament. Presumably, the more severe the predicament, the greater the threat to the person's identity. Since the consequences of predicaments are negative, people attempt to avoid them whenever possible and conceal them when avoidance is not possible. Failing either to avoid or to conceal a predicament, the person ordinarily engages in remedial behavior.

Remedial Behavior   When people find themselves in predicaments that cannot be avoided or concealed, they will engage in behaviors designed to reduce the potential negative consequences and maximize their expected reward/cost ratios, and, the more severe the predicament, the greater is the motivation for such remedial behavior. In general, there are two tactics that people may adopt: retreat or remedial action. Retreat may be the most normal reaction to a predicament or, at least, the most immediate impulse. The person wants to run away and hide until the worst repercussions of the predicament are over. Flight may or may not be advantageous. The theory proposes that the flight response will be advantageous to the person when the expected consequences are severe, the person's expectations of successfully dealing with the predicament are low, and there is a reasonable probability of being able to escape. Escape may be temporary and thus permit one to become better prepared to handle the predicament, or it may be permanent. On the other hand, flight sometimes turns a bad situation into a worse one. For example, if a person who is accused of a transgression flees, he or she may appear to be more guilty, and later attempts to handle the predicament may become more difficult.

Remedial tactics are much more complex behaviors that are designed to deal with the predicament. In general, these are activities that provide the audience with an explanation or apology so that the audience can see the person and/or event in a different perspective. Thus there are two general classes of remedial tactics: accounts and apologies. *Accounts* are explanations of the event that created the predicament and are designed to minimize the severity of the predicament. Schlenker suggests that there are three basic forms of accounts: defenses of innocence, excuses, and justifications. *Defenses of innocence* are attempts by people to show that they are not associated with the event that caused the predicament. They may suggest that the event did not occur or, if it did occur, that they had nothing to do with it. Thus, defenses of innocence may take the form of defense of nonoccurrence or defense of noncausation.

Excuses are attempts to avoid responsibility for the predicament-creating event. In attempting to provide excuses, the person may say that the undesirable consequences could not have been foreseen (or they were not foreseen by the person), there were extenuating circumstances, or other people were also responsible for the event (diffusion of responsibility).

Justifications are attempts to reduce the undesirable nature of the predicament-creating event. Justifications may be direct attempts to minimize the negativity of the consequences (for example, a student may argue that the test he or she has failed is invalid) or indirect attempts through social comparison or higher goals. For instance, people may try to justify their actions by noting that others have behaved as badly or worse or by embedding the undesirable event in a larger set of values that are desirable.

The use of accounting tactics to remedy predicaments may be summarized by the following hypotheses:

1   The more severe the predicament, the more likely that people will employ an accounting tactic.
2   The more severe the predicament, the more likely that actors will use accounting tactics in an extreme way.
3   The accounting tactics selected will be those that people believe will maximize their expected reward/cost ratios.
4   The accounts chosen will be those that people believe are fitted to the situation as it appears to be known by the audience.

Apologies, the second major class of remedial tactics, are designed to convince the audience that the undesirable event should not be regarded as a fair representation of what the actor is really like as a person. A full-fledged apology is said to contain five elements: (1) an expression of guilt, embarrassment, regret, etc.; (2) a statement that one recognizes what the appropriate behavior should have been and an acceptance of the application of negative sanctions for rule violation; (3) a rejection of the inappropriate behavior and a disparagement of the part of self that misbehaved; (4) approval of the appropriate behavior and a promise of more desirable conduct in the future; and (5) performance of penance and an offer of compensation.[1]

When the violation is minor, the use of apologies is perfunctory. The infraction is so inconsequential that no one is very concerned about it. But as predicaments increase in severity, apologies are taken more seriously by both the actors and the audience. In such cases, the actor is, at best, forgiven, but everyone knows that he or she is guilty. If the actor expects to eliminate all negative consequences of the predicament, an apology is not the best tactic. These considerations suggest that apologies are most likely to be used when people do not mind admitting guilt, because either the predicament is trivial or they believe it is unlikely that they can escape being adjudged guilty.

Although apologies and accounts represent distinct classes of remedial tactics, they overlap and are often used together. People combine tactics in whatever ways they believe will maximize their expected reward/cost ratio.

Acclaiming

Remedial behavior deals with undesirable situations and the ways people try to minimize the negative consequences of these situations for their selves and social identities. But there is a positive side. When a desirable event occurs, the consequences are positively evaluated, and association with the event has positive effects on the self and social identity. It follows that people should try to take advantage of such events to help establish, maintain, and/or enhance their self-concepts and social identities. Schlenker calls such behavior *acclaiming.* Acclaiming tactics are attempts to explain a desirable event in ways that maximize the desirable implications for the actor. Again, there are two classes of tactics: *entitlings* and *enhancements.* These are the counterparts of excuses and

---

[1]Schlenker adopted this analysis from Goffman (1971).

justifications, respectively. That is, entitlings are attempts to claim responsibility for the positive event, and enhancements are attempts to increase the desirable nature of the event.

Comment and Evaluation

Impression management theory as presented by Schlenker is internally consistent, does not contradict well-established hypotheses or known facts, and integrates a considerable amount of data concerning the ways people try to establish and maintain their social identities in interactions with others. Furthermore, it generates testable predictions that should be of heuristic value for social psychology. The theory also does not contradict what is "known" from everyday experience; that is, the theory deals with phenomena that are familiar to all or most people, and no one is likely to reject the theory because it does not agree with their own casual observations.

The particular form of the theory that we have described was published very recently and consequently has not generated much research (other than the research by Schlenker and his associates). However, considerable research has been stimulated by closely related theories, such as Goffman's (1959) self-presentation theory, Heider's (1958) theory of interpersonal relations, and earlier formulations by Schlenker. In addition, Schlenker (1980) cited a substantial body of other research in support of most major propositions and hypotheses. Although it will not be our purpose to review all of the research cited by Schlenker to support his proposals, it will be helpful to mention some of these to show the kind of evidence believed to support impression management theory.

First, it may be noted that propositions concerning the self-concept, need for self-esteem, construction of social identities, and motivation to maximize reward/cost ratios are accepted almost as givens. Consequently, the research cited in support of these notions is indirect and often theoretical rather than experimental in nature. Nevertheless, Schlenker builds a convincing nomothetic network to bolster the several assumptions of the theory.

The proposition that the severity of a predicament is a function of the undesirability of the predicament-creating event and the actor's responsibility for it is supported primarily by research on the attribution of responsibility. This research generally shows that people react more negatively when an actor is responsible for an undesirable event and when the event involves severe negative outcomes (Shaw & Reitan, 1969; Shaw & Tremble, 1971).

The strongest experimental evidence that Schlenker reports is in support of the hypothesis that, the more severe the predicament, the more likely it is that people will use accounting tactics. For example, Modigliani (1971) asked subjects to take a test on which they failed in front of the experimenter and several other subjects. He found that the more embarrassed the subjects were (and presumably the more severe they perceived the predicament they were in), the more accounting they did later when interacting with an audience. In another study, Mynatt and Sherman (1975) had subjects serve as advisors to another person, either alone or with two other advisors. The advisee was a confederate who took the subject's advice on 80 percent of the trials and performed either very well or very poorly. Presumably, giving advice that is accepted and leads to a poor performance should create a predicament for the advisor. Under these conditions, subjects accounted for the advisee's poor performance both when alone and when in a group. When in a group, they admitted that they had influenced the advisee and the advisee had done poorly, but they denied personal responsibility for this outcome. When alone, they did not deny responsibility, but they provided indirect excuses for the advisee's failure. For instance, they reported that the advisee took their advice only 56 percent (not the actual 80 percent) of the time and also suggested that the advisee's performance was not really so bad after all. Several other studies were cited by Schlenker showing similar effects (e.g., Calder, Ross, & Insko, 1973; Cialdini, Kenrick, & Hoerig, 1976; Collins & Hoyt, 1972; Davis & Jones, 1960; Gaes, Kalle, & Tedeschi, 1978; Glass, 1964; Schlenker et al., 1980).

Schlenker cited the work of Brock and Buss (1962) to support the hypothesis that, the more severe the predicament, the more people should use accounting tactics in an extreme way. College students were given the task of teaching another person a series of problems by delivering an electric shock for each mistake. The "learner" was a confederate who made a predetermined number of mistakes on the learning task. Subjects who were given high choice in deciding whether to deliver shocks minimized reports of how painful the shocks were and underestimated the degree to which they harmed the other person. In contrast, subjects who were given low choice increased their reports of how painful the shocks were.

Proposals concerning the use of apologies derive some support from unpublished research by Schlenker and his associates.[2] For example, when students are asked to role-play the part of a central character in a predicament-creating situation, they said they would use a minimal apology, such as saying, "Pardon me." When the outcome was more severe, they more frequently used complete apologies. Two additional studies indicated that apologies reduce the negative consequences of the predicament. Other research provides indirect evidence concerning the use of apologies. For instance there is evidence that the enactment of repentant acts reduces negative sanctions (Austin, Walster, & Utne, 1976; Bramel, Taub, & Blum, 1968) and that juries show more leniency toward defendants who show repentance (Austin et al., 1976; Kalven & Zeisel, 1966; Walster et al., 1978).

Proposals concerning acclaiming are supported primarily by research conducted by Schlenker and his associates (Goldman & Schlenker, 1977; Schlenker & Riess, 1979; Schlenker & Schlenker, 1975). The results of these studies show that people do use acclaiming tactics when circumstances appear to deprive them of credit for desirable events.

There are some aspects of impression management theory that are open to criticism. We have already mentioned that the theory concerns events that are

[2]Personal communication.

familiar to everyone and the hypotheses of the theory are consistent with everyday experiences. One might ask, therefore, what new contributions the theory makes to our understanding of interpersonal behavior? Apparently anticipating questions of this sort, Schlenker devoted the final chapter of his treatise to specifying hoped-for contributions of his analysis. From our point of view, the theory provides a systematic framework for impression management processes, encourages controlled investigations of these processes, and makes it easier to demonstrate processes that are familiar to most of us. Therefore, this criticism of impression management theory may be more apparent than real.

It is also regrettable that Schlenker elected to define some terms in accordance with the usage of philosophers and microsociologists. Thus some terms are given meanings that are inconsistent with similar terms that have well-established usage in other social-psychological contexts. For example, the term "excuses" is used in a way that is very similar to Heider's (1958) use of "justification," and Schlenker's "justification" is given a meaning more in accord with attempts to modify perceived outcome.

Finally, an attempt has been made to encompass a wide variety of social phenomena under the umbrella of impression management theory. In doing so, it is often necessary to make numerous assumptions, many of which are not adequately demonstrated by data. A more-limited application of the theory may be preferable.

A THEORY OF SELF-MONITORING

Mark Snyder first proposed his intriguing perspective on self-monitoring processes in a 1972 Stanford University dissertation. In many respects, self-monitoring theory bears a kinship relationship to both the ingratiation-theory and impression-management-theory perspectives just presented. Like these theories it concerns itself with the controls persons exert to manipulate the images and impressions that others form about them in the course of social interaction. As noted at the outset of this chapter, the authors consider all of these perspectives to be derivatives of role-related processes. In particular, one of the classic issues in role theory has to do with the congruities between a person's self and the roles he/she enacts in his/her various social interactions and relationships.

Snyder's theory is particularly concerned with the process implications of stable individual differences between social styles characterized by enactors who evidence comfortable self-role distance and enactors who more or less "behave as they are."

In the subsequent treatment of self-monitoring processes we have relied heavily on Snyder's (1979) *Advances in Experimental Social Psychology* paper. In expositing the propositions of self-monitoring theory, we will largely follow Snyder's organization. In successive sections we will present the definition of the construct of self-monitoring; a description of its assessment; and a detailing of the processes, consequences, and strategies involved in self-monitoring behavior.

The Construct of Self-Monitoring

The central concerns of the self-monitoring orientation are expressed in the following two questions: (1) "To what extent do individuals actively attempt to control the images and impressions that others form of them during social interaction?" and (2) "Of what consequence is the adoption of such a strategic and pragmatic orientation to interpersonal relationships?" (Snyder, 1979, p. 86).

The core assumptions of self-monitoring theory embody the answers to these two questions. Snyder begins by assuming that it is propositional that individuals have both the ability and inclination to exercise control over their expressive behaviors, self-presentations, and affective displays. Further he assumes as propositional that such controls have profound influence upon social behavior, social interactions, and ideological perspectives. In buttressing these assumptions, Snyder cites a number of prior perspectives (e.g., James, 1890; Goffman, 1959; Jones, 1964) which establish that impression management and expressive control is a stable social phenomenon with meaningful implications for social relationships.

What is unique to Snyder's formulation is the notion that while impression management and self-monitoring processes may be pervasive and indeed employed by all of us at one time or another, such processes are differentially evident in different persons. In short, Snyder asserts that there are important and measurable individual differences in the extents to which people can and/or do manage their self-presentations. In fact, Snyder conveys the defining characteristics of self-monitoring through prototypic descriptions of individuals high and low in such tendencies.

The high–self-monitoring individual has concerns about the situational and interpersonal appropriateness of his/her behavior, as a consequence is sensitive to cues to the social appropriateness of behavior, and uses these cues to regulate or control (i.e., monitor) his/her verbal and nonverbal self-presentations. In contrast, the expressive behavior of the *low–self-monitoring individual is controlled by his/her internal affective states and stable attitudes rather than being self-consciously constructed to fit the social situation.*

The construct definition of self-monitoring is expressed in the individual-difference dichotomy embodied in the above prototypes. The theory proceeds from this dichotomy to consider both the interpersonal consequences of these stylistic individual differences in expressive behavior orientation and the interpersonal processes which underlie this personality distinction. Before we move to these theoretical and empirical considerations, we will take up Snyder's method for assessing a person's level of self-monitoring.

Measurement of the Self-Monitoring Construct

In order to assess the consequences of the above proposed dichotomy in expressive styles, Snyder constructed and validated an instrument designed to discriminate individuals high and low in self-monitoring skill. This instrument consists of 25 self-report, true-false items which probe 5 components of self-monitoring:

1 "Concern with the social appropriateness of one's self-presentation (e.g., At parties and social gatherings I do not attempt to do or say things that others will like)" (p. 89)
2 "Attention to social comparison information as cues to situationally appropriate expressive self-presentation (e.g., When I am uncertain of how to act in social situations, I look to the behavior of others for cues)" (p. 89)
3 "The ability to control and modify one's self-presentation and expressive behavior (e.g., I can look anyone in the eye and tell a lie—if for a right end)" (p. 89)
4 "The use of this ability in particular situations (e.g., I may deceive people by being friendly when I really dislike them)" (p. 90)
5 "The extent to which one's expressive behavior and self-presentation are molded to fit particular situations (e.g., In different situations, with different people, I often act like very different persons)" (p. 90)

It might be implied that it is Snyder's contention that the complex elements comprising the different self-monitoring styles are validly assessed with a rather simple self-report instrument. In fact, it does appear that this contention is well supported. Snyder reports on a wide range of studies which provide evidence for the construct validity of the self-monitoring scale. For example, researchers have found that:

1 Individuals scoring high on the self-monitoring scale are rated by their peers as responsive to cues of social appropriateness, having good control over their expressive behavior, and effective in managing others' impressions (Snyder, 1974).
2 Criterion groups that should score higher in self-monitoring skills, such as actors, indeed do so (Snyder, 1974).
3 High scorers on the self-monitoring scale are better able to intentionally express various affects and portray themselves as possessing particular traits than are low scorers on the scale (cf. Snyder, 1974; Lippa, 1976).
4 High self-monitors are more attentive to information concerning the self-presentations of their peers than low self-monitors (Snyder, 1974) and more likely to recall such information than low self-monitors (Berscheid, Graziano, Monson, & Derner, 1976).

In sum, it appears that Snyder has not only conceptually identified an important component of individual differences in expressive behavior, but he has also derived a simple assessment methodology for indexing individual differences in expressive orientation. Snyder also claims that self-monitoring can be reliably discriminated from other personality constructs which portray variants of one or another strategic interpersonal stance (i.e., his studies on the discriminant validity of the self-monitoring scale reveal that it indexes different attributes than scales designed to assess Machiavellianism, need for social approval, and introversion). Nevertheless, further independent evidence for the construct validity and reliability of the self-monitoring scale appears warranted.

The remainder of Snyder's theoretical account of self-monitoring processes addresses itself to the consequences and processes of strategic expressive control. It should be kept in mind that, while some of Snyder's propositions concerning expressive control are constructive in nature (i.e., they follow from the definition of the construct), others are empirical in their derivation.

The Consequences of Self-Monitoring

Given the prototypic descriptions of the high and low self-monitor, several theoretical propositions are evident. An overarching principle is expressed in the following general statement: *Individuals differing in self-monitoring should exhibit differences in the degree to which they rely on either situational or interpersonal specifications of appropriate social action versus the degree to which they rely on internal states, personal dispositions, and subjective attitudes to impel their social behavior.* The former focus is descriptive of the high self-monitor; the latter is descriptive of the low self-monitor.

The ramifications of this overarching proposition are:

1 High self-monitors are proposed to have both the requisite skills and inclinations to mold their self-presentation to the social situation at hand.

2 In order to do so, high self-monitors, as compared with their low–self-monitoring counterparts, should be more attentive to the actions of others and more desirous of social comparison information.

3 Finally, high self-monitors not only attend to information signaling appropriate situational behavior but are capable of flexibly expressing the verbal and nonverbal gestures which translate such information into situationally appropriate action.

4 Low self-monitors, on the other hand, derive their action tendencies from the state of their viscera at the moment and the consistent intrinsic orientations they take toward objects, people, and circumstances.

Two related hypotheses fall out of these differences in information focus and expressive manipulation:

Hypothesis 1: High self-monitors should evidence behavior in social situations which is specifically relevant to those situations, while low self-monitors should evidence behavior in situations which is derivative of their own states and traits (i.e., their behavior should not reflect situational specificity to the extent that the behavior of high self-monitors does).

Hypothesis 1a: Because of the propensity of high self-monitors to tailor their behavior to the situation, high self-monitors should show greater cross-situational variability in behavior than low self-monitors.

Snyder reports two related studies which tend to confirm each of these hypotheses. Snyder and Monson (1975) found that the tendency of high self-monitors to conform to the opinions of peers was dependent upon the manipulated normative appropriateness of conformity, while the conformity of low self-monitors was unaffected by experimenter-induced situational variations in the normative appropriateness of conformity. In other words, the conformity behavior of high self-monitors was situationally specific, while that of low self-monitors was cross-situationally consistent in conforming tendency.

In a related vein these same authors (Snyder & Monson, 1975) asked high- and low–self-monitoring subjects what behaviors they would display in nine variations of situations calling for either generosity, honesty, or hostility. For each variation, subjects estimated the likelihood that they would engage in the relevant behavior. The variance of each subject's behavior across each of the situations constituted the index of that subject's cross-situational variability in generosity, honesty, and hostility. In accordance with the above-stated hypotheses, high–self-monitoring individuals reported greater cross-situational variability in behavior than low self-monitors in all three domains of behavior.

A Consistency Corollary for High Self-Monitors

While the construct of self-monitoring seems to appropriately predict that high self-monitors will evidence greater situational specificity and cross-situational variability than low self-monitors, such a tendency may not be pervasive. Snyder maintains that the self-monitoring construct suggests a range of situations for which the self-expressions of high self-monitors should be *more* consistent than their low–self-monitoring counterparts. Specifically, because of the control that high self-monitors are purported to possess over their expressive behavior, their manifest behavior should be less subject than that of low self-monitors to interior shifts in mood state. In short, self-monitors should be more capable and more inclined to present a socially desirable "affective front" than their low–self-monitoring counterparts. This leads us to derive another hypothesis which embodies a consequence of self-monitoring strategies.

Hypothesis 2: Because of the expressive control that high self-monitors possess, they should be more skilled at and more inclined toward presenting themselves as consistently manifesting socially desirable *expressive background traits* than low self-monitors. Low self-monitors, on the other hand, because of their reduced inclination and ability to control expressive behavior, should be more variable in the *expressive background traits* which they present to others.

Lippa (1976, 1978) has indeed found that high self-monitors tend to be perceived as consistently more friendly, outgoing, and extroverted, and less worried, anxious, and nervous than their low–self-monitoring counterparts. In short, high self-monitors are successful at conveying a background picture of stability and friendliness to social others.

Behavior-Attitude Congruence: An Attribute of the Low Self-Monitor?

Because the high self-monitor tailors his/her behavior to the specific situation at hand, it is likely that he/she will evidence minimal consistency between his/her interior attitude and his/her overt behavior. On the other hand, low self-monitors should evidence considerable correspondence between their interior attitudes and overt behaviors. This proposition details another consequence of self-monitoring orientation and can be viewed as *Hypothesis 3* within Snyder's system of thought. It should be noted that social psychologists have long puzzled about the surprising level of inconsistency between people's attitudes and behaviors. While some (cf. Mischel, 1968) have argued that such inconsistency defines the "true" nature of the attitude-behavior relationship, others (Calder & Ross, 1973; Ajzen & Fishbein, 1977) have attributed the found inconsistencies to procedural and/or conceptual flaws in attitude-behavior consistency studies.

It is Snyder's argument that, for some individuals (i.e., high self-monitors), there is no reason to expect attitude-behavior congruence since their behaviors are in the service of social-expression rather than self-expression. However, for other individuals (i.e., low self-monitors) behavior seems to be in the service of self-consistent expression and thus high attitude-behavior congruence is expected. Studies by Snyder and Swann (1976) and Snyder and Tanke (1976) tend to confirm the implications of this dichotomous portrayal.

Thus, it appears that hypothesis 3 also meets with empirical confirmation. Nevertheless, there are limits to the applicability of the attitude-behavior congruence differences between high– and low–self-monitoring individuals. Once again, because low self-monitors are more likely to express alterations in interior mood state there are instances (when fatigued, angry, impatient, upset, etc.) in which their behavioral expressions may not conform to their true feelings and attitudes. On the other hand, if the high self-monitor's capable expressive control is taken as given, such fluctuating mood states would be less likely to affect their portrayal of background attitudes. Ickes, Layden, and Barnes (1978) have provided reasonable evidence for the plausibility of this corollary to the hypothesized differences in attitude-behavior congruity between high– and low–self-monitoring individuals.

The Consequences of Self-Monitoring Differences for Social Interaction

Snyder discusses two broad consequences of self-monitoring in the interpersonal domain. First of all, since the vicissitudes of the high self-monitor's social orientation in any given situation are dependent upon the particular array of social stimuli confronting him/her, he/she should be more motivated to have a clear and orderly view of such stimuli for purposes of effective action. As a consequence of this presumed motivation of high self-monitors, they should be likely to construe others in terms of traits and dispositions. Such a stance should serve to facilitate the individual's ability to both predict and influence the behaviors of others in social contexts. In keeping with this perspective we may derive *Hypothesis 4: High self-monitors are more likely than low self-monitors to perceive the behavior of others in dispositional terms and use these perceptions as cues to monitoring their expressive behavior toward those individuals* (Snyder, 1976).

In support of this hypothesis, Berscheid, Graziano, Monson, and Dermer

(1976) found that high self-monitors who observed another person with the anticipation of social dating were more likely than low self-monitors to notice and remember information about the observed other, make inferences about his or her traits, and express liking for their prospective dates. Snyder concludes that "the prospect of social interaction may initiate perceptual and cognitive processes that predictably channel the [high self-monitor's] search for potentially relevant information, the interpretation of that information, and the form and substance of the images constructed of those with whom they anticipate further social contact" (Snyder, 1979, p. 99).

A second interpersonal realm which is likely to differ as a consequence of high– and low–self-monitoring styles is the development of interpersonal relationships. While the construct of self-monitoring does not immediately suggest predictions of individual differences in the process of developing social contacts, some recent research by Ickes and Barnes (1977) and Pilkonis (1977) suggests that high self-monitors are more likely than low self-monitors to initiate, lead, and otherwise take an active role in social encounters. Snyder (1979) speculates that the high self-monitor's regulatory orientation disposes him/her to a leadership role in group interactions.

Processes Underlying Self-monitoring

At this point in the development of self-monitoring theory, the presumed differential consequences of the dichotomous orientations are much more cogently hypothesized about than the underlying processes which eventuate in these differential consequences. Snyder's (1979, pp. 100–111) recent theoretical account of self-monitoring process differences takes a rather speculative cast. Nevertheless, he solidly locates the origin of the different situational orientations and interpersonal inclinations of high and low self-monitors in the differential focus of their respective self-conceptions. Put simply, high self-monitors tend to conceive of self in terms of the characteristics of the situations in which they find themselves (Sampson, 1978). They tend to attribute their behavior to situational factors (Snyder, 1976) and they base their self-conceptions on their involvements with other people. In contrast, low self-monitors prefer dispositional explanations for their actions (Snyder, 1976), claim congruity between their values and actions, and construe their self-identities in terms of enduring attributes (Sampson, 1978). In summary, the high–self-monitoring individual possesses a flexible self-concept (or many self-concepts) to accommodate his/her variations in myriad situations, while the low self-monitor is attached to a rooted and relatively inflexible self-identity.

From this point of origin in differential self-conception, Snyder adopts the descriptive device of "person-in-situation scenarios" to play out the individual's transitions from self-conception to expressive action. To quote the theorist:

> High self-monitoring individuals and low self-monitoring individuals are thought to differ in the identity of the person who is the central character in their cognitive scenarios. High self-monitoring individuals are thought to construct their person-in-

situation scenarios by reading the character of each situation that confronts them to identify a prototype of the ideal person (either a specific prototypic example of a generalized ideal image) called for by situations of that type. Low self-monitoring individuals also construct their person-in-situation scenarios by first reading the character of the situation, but then using stored information about those enduring self-conceptions relevant to that type of situation to create an image of a person acting in accord with their characteristic natures. These person-in-situation scenarios, whether they involve images of prototypic others or characteristic selves, then may provide the operating guidelines for constructing and enacting patterns of social behavior (Snyder, 1979, p. 104).

The remainder of Snyder's treatment of the differential underlying cognitive processing propensities of high and low self-monitors predominately centers upon general descriptions of the kinds of knowledge and skill required in reading the characters of situations. While this analysis is pertinent to the self-monitoring construct, its connections to the individual differences themselves are primarily speculative.

Comments on Self-Monitoring Theory

Self-monitoring theory constitutes an account of self-presentation strategies in social interaction which has an individual difference variable at its theoretical core. The theory offers a testable and well-tested set of hypotheses and propositions concerning the differential *consequences* of each self-monitoring style. In addition, the theorist has provided a promising tool for assessing the two expressive styles. Thus, one might expect that further research investigating the differential social strategies of individuals varying in self-monitoring will be forthcoming.

In its current form, the theory is somewhat incomplete. The process connections between self-monitoring propensities and the consequences which issue from them are not yet firmly established nor clearly hypothesized about by the theorist. Snyder's interesting account of the differential "person-in-situation scenarios" of high– and low–self-monitoring individuals constitutes a beginning approach to the examination of differential process. But, much remains to be articulated in the process domain. In the absence of the clear development and empirical confirmation of process distinctions in the social orientations of high and low self-monitors, this theory, like several other theories of social behavior based on individual difference variables (e.g., Rotter's locus-of-control theory), is potentially endangered by the spector of reification.

In a final note, with regard to the inclusion of an apparent "theory of personality" in this book on social theories, we are inclined to adopt Snyder's interesting perspective from the latter portions of his *Advances* chapter (1979). That is, our understanding of social behavior is likely to be advanced by a careful consideration of individual behavior variations as they relate to social contextual effects. Presumably each of us engages in self-monitoring in at least some situations and self-consistency expressions in others. By understanding the behavior, motives, and cognitive processes of individuals whose personal styles are weighted in a particular direction, we may come to understand also the character of situations which consistently evoke behavior in that particular direction. As such, the understanding of stylistic variations in social action might indeed be one path to the understanding of universal consistencies in human social behavior.

A THEORY OF OBJECTIVE SELF-AWARENESS

In 1972 Duval and Wicklund first published an intriguing theoretical account of the vicissitudes of a state that they labeled *objective self-awareness*. The theory postulated that when an individual's conscious attention is directed at self-as-object, the typical consequence is aversive motivational arousal. This arousal was viewed as stemming from the individual's necessary confrontation with the discrepancy between what one *sees* of self and what one idealizes self to be. The theory goes on to specify the consequent reactions to the arousal of salient self-ideal discrepancies during self-awareness and a set of "tactics" or adaptations designed to relieve the aversive motivational press of objective self-focus.

We have categorized this theory as role-related because of its core focus upon the subjective self–objective self dichotomy. In this sense, it bears comparison with the theoretical ideas of George Herbert Mead (1934). In keeping with this connection to Mead, the individual in an objective state of self-focus can be viewed as taking the role of the generalized other toward self (i.e., seeing self as one is seen by others). The proposed motivational consequences of objective self-focus are more comfortably conjoined with the cognitive dynamic contentions of theories such as Festinger's dissonance theory and Brehm's theory of reactance. In this vein, the supposed inconsistency giving rise to aversive motivational arousal is constituted by the perceived- versus ideal-self manifestation rather than attitudes and behavior, for example.

In the subsequent account of the theory of objective self-awareness, we have relied heavily on Wicklund's (1975) chapter in *Advances in Experimental Social Psychology* and his 1978 addendum to that chapter published in *Cognitive Theories of Social Psychology* (Berkowitz, 1978). We will present this theory in a brief propositional form, beginning with its major assumption concerning attention focus and proceeding through the description of a series of propositions detailing the sequelae of self-focused attentional states. Finally, we will consider an overview of the research performed on the bases of the theory.

Two States of Consciousness: The Major Assumption of the Theory

The major assumption of the theory of objective self-awareness is that *conscious attention is a dichotomous phenomena.* It can either be directed toward self or toward the environment. While individuals are viewed as capable of vacillating between these two conscious foci, it is viewed as implausible for a self-focus and environmental-focus in consciousness to be simultaneous. The particular direction of one's conscious attention is determined by external stimuli which either evoke self-reflection or pull attention outward. To quote Wicklund (1978):

> Stimuli that remind a person of his objective status will increase objective self-awareness, while all other stimuli will tend to draw attention outward (p. 466).

Stimuli evocative of attentional self-focus can vary widely and include images or symbols of self (such as reflections in a mirror or tape recordings of one's own voice) as well as the studied attention of others toward the self (such as might occur when an individual is observed by an audience).

The stability and persistence of self-focused attention is portrayed as a rather tenuous phenomenon. The intrusion of any salient external stimulus or distraction serves to turn our attentions outward and, momentarily at least, dissipates objective self-focus. As we shall see later on in this exposition, the ready availability of distracting, outwardly focusing stimuli can be a countervailing force, which might serve to reduce the motivational arousal occasioned by objective self-awareness.

Theoretical Propositions of Objective Self-Awareness Theory

Following upon the statement of the above-described dichotomous consciousness assumption, Duval and Wicklund (1972) and Wicklund (1975) proceed to a theoretical account of the consequences of self-focused attentional states. We will condense their account into a series of related propositions—each of which is subject or has been subjected to direct or indirect test.

Proposition 1: The Arousal Proposition

When an individual is induced to adopt an objective, inward self-focus of attention, the predominant consequence consists of the arousal of an aversive motivational state. The negative affect stems from the individual's recognition of particular discrepancies between the image or symbol of self focused upon and the ideal image of self. The amount of negative affect experienced is proposed to be a joint function of the proportion of time spent in an objective focus and the size of the self-ideal discrepancy.

Proposition 2: A Positive-Affect Corollary

In the original statement of self-awareness theory, the motivational state evoked by objective self-focus was presumed to be an exclusively negative or aversive one, as expressed in the first proposition. In a later account of the theory, Wicklund (1975) depicted one exception to the negative arousal consequence. It was noted that, in the case where objective self-focus is preceded by a recent potent success experience, the arousal state experienced would be a positive one. In this instance, since the individual's recent crowning success might be construed as portraying self as having exceeded or matched one's ideal, the discrepancy between self and ideal is more likely to be a positive (i.e., self-favoring) one, and self-focused attention is then likely to constitute a positive experience. As with the negative affect, contingent upon one's attention to negative discrepancies, the extent of positive affect experienced during the perception of positive discrepancies is presumed to vary directly with the size of the discrepancy.

Despite the recent theoretical addition of the positive affective consequences of self-focused attention, it is Wicklund's (1975) contention and assumption that virtually all *naturally occurring* discrepancies are negative. Thus, we will largely confine our subsequent presentation to negative-discrepancy phenomena.

Proposition 3: Self-Evaluative Reactions

The immediate consequence of one's focus of attention turning toward a salient negative self-ideal discrepancy is a self-evaluation. In the more typical negative-discrepancy case this self-evaluation will take the form of self-criticism, self-blame, or lowered self-esteem. In the positive-discrepancy case the self-evaluation may involve self-aggrandizement and raised self-esteem.

Proposition 4: Avoidance—The First Line Defense

The initial consequence of negative-discrepancy salience, self-evaluation, will persist for as long as the individual remains in a self-focused state of consciousness. Conversely, if the individual can distract himself/herself or be distracted from self-focused attention, self-critical reactions will cease and the negative affect generated by objective self-awareness will dissipate. As a consequence, it is proposed that individuals confronted with negative discrepancies will adopt one or more strategies to avoid the self-conscious state. Wicklund (1975) describes three routes to such avoidance:

1   The individual might simply physically avoid self-awareness–provoking stimuli, such as mirrors and cameras.
2   The individual might attempt to create distractions for himself or herself, such as watching television or listening to music.
3   The individual might engage in overt motor activities which demand that attention be directed outward.

Proposition 5: The Last Resort—Discrepancy Reduction

When avoidance strategies which distract the individual from an objective self-focus fail or are impossible, the aversive consequences of negative discrepancies and their self-evaluative sequelae will persist in fueling the individual's aversive motivational experience, and the individual will be impelled to reduce the negative self-ideal discrepancy. In most instances the attempts at discrepancy reduction are typically in the direction of a "specifiable personal standard of correctness." Hence, it has been found that self-awareness–induced individuals will give more veridical self-reports.

In many respects, discrepancy reduction might resemble dissonance reduction (see Chapter 8). Therefore an individual might engage in changes in expressed attitude as a method of discrepancy reduction. Another form of discrepancy reduction might involve altering elements of one's behavior toward others. Research has indicated, for example, that self-aware individuals will inhibit the level of aggression directed at others by restricting the intensity of shock administered during a bogus experiment.

Comments and Evaluation of Objective Self-Awareness Theory

While our propositional account of self-awareness theory may not do justice to the intricacies involved in its formulation, it does present the basic premises and principles of the framework. We have chosen a propositional presentation, because, at base, the theory is a simple one with very few constructs and processes involved. Thus on cursory observation one would suppose that confirmation of the theory's primary predictions would also be rather straight-forward. This has not been the case. Self-awareness theory has generated considerable foment and controversy, primarily because of the difficulty of empirically assessing its pivotal proposition, i.e., the proposal of a negative arousal state occasioned by self-focused attention.

Nevertheless, a great deal of research has been generated by the theory. In particular:

1   The notion that self-evaluative activity follows upon the inducement of objective self-awareness seems plausible. For example, Ickes, Wicklund, and Farris (1973) found that subjects exposed to tape recordings of their own voices showed significantly greater self-ideal discrepancies on an adjective checklist instrument than non-self-aware subjects. Similar negative self-evaluative phe-nomena were reported by Duval and Wicklund (1973) and Wicklund and Duval (1972).

2   The notion that self-aware subjects will either seek out or benefit from distraction in the avoidance of aversive motivational arousal has been supported by a number of investigations (Duval, Wicklund, & Fine, 1972; Davis & Brock, 1974; Liebling, Silver, & Shaver, 1974).

3   Finally, various tactics of discrepancy reduction have been found to alter successfully the arousal state occasioned by self-awareness. For example, Pryor, Wicklund, and Gibbons have found increases in self-report validity in response to a mirror manipulation of self-awareness. Scheier, Fenigstein, and Buss (1974) found that self-aware subjects inhibit the intensity of shock delivered to experimental confederates. A more extended review of the research in support of the self-awareness framework is provided by Wicklund (1975). At this point it seems warranted to conclude that self-awareness theory has been quite genera-tive of research in support of its propositions.

The major problem with self-awareness theory is similar to the problems encountered with dissonance theory. It is quite difficult to assess the viability of the "aversive motivational state" proposition except through its predicted effects. This circularity remains a problem for the viability of the framework. In addition, naïve consideration suggests that univocal avoidance of self-awareness–generating stimuli is unlikely to be plausible. People view themselves in mirrors daily, enjoy being photographed, and at times go out of their way to pose before TV cameras. While this latter observation in and of itself is not devastating for the theory, such considerations pose a logical bound on the everyday applicability and external validity of the model. Self-awareness theory may need to be *more* explicit about both the particular set of conditions that trigger states of negative arousal and the manner in which such arousal might be assessed.

Part Six

Specialized Theories

Chapter 13

Theories of Group Processes

In the preceding chapters we have outlined some of the more general theoretical orientations and presented theories that appear to have been derived more or less directly from those general orientations. However, there are several important theories that are not clearly related to any particular one of the major theoretical systems that we have discussed. Some of these theories make use of elements of two or more general orientations, whereas others appear to have adopted an independent orientation. For lack of a better label, we have called such theories "transorientational approaches."

This chapter is devoted to theories that are concerned with various aspects of group process. We have already discussed a number of related theories that derive from the general reinforcement orientation (see Chapter 4), and the interested reader may wish to compare those theories with the ones presented in this chapter. The theories that we will discuss include a theory that considers levels of intimacy among interactants (Argyle & Dean, 1965), a theory concerned with the process and effects of removing group members and adding new ones (Zander, 1976), a theory of group compatibility (Schutz, 1955, 1958), a theory of motives and goals in groups (Zander, 1971), a theory of group process and productivity (Steiner, 1972), and a contingency theory of leadership (Fiedler, 1964, 1967).

AFFILIATIVE CONFLICT THEORY

When people engage in social interaction, they frequently look at each other. Eye contact is usually of short duration, but plays a significant role in the interaction process. Simmel (1921) asserted that the union and interaction of persons is based upon mutual glances, and Heider (1958) stated that communion through the eyes creates an intense interpersonal experience. Looking the other person in the eye is commonly supposed to reflect honesty and forthrightness, and prolonged mutual eye contact between a man and woman is often seen as an indication of intimacy and sexual interest. Despite these common conceptions of the meaning and functions of gaze behavior, relatively little is known about the psychological functions of eye contact. These were the kinds of considerations that stimulated the formulation of affiliative conflict theory (Argyle & Dean, 1965). Basically, the theory attempts to relate eye contact to the need for affiliation.

Basic Propositions

Argyle and Dean noted that many writers have pointed out the functions that eye contact can serve, such as feedback about the reactions of others, indicating when speaker and listener should switch roles, establishing and recognizing particular social relationships, and the like. Their theory, however, was concerned with the function eye contact serves in the affiliation process. The heart of the theory is contained in the following propositions:

1 Eye contact is influenced by both approach and avoidance forces. Approach forces include such things as need for feedback and need for affiliation, whereas avoidance forces include such things as fear of being seen, fear of revealing inner feelings, and fear of being rejected.

2 Since there are both approach and avoidance forces acting on eye contact, the same conflict behaviors should occur as in other kinds of behavior. Thus, the conflict analysis proposed by Miller (1944) is seen as applicable to eye contact. According to this analysis, there should be an equilibrium level for eye contact for an individual coming into social contact with another individual; eye contact above the equilibrium will be anxiety-arousing.

3 Approach-avoidance forces and the equilibrium process also apply to other types of behavior that are associated with affiliative motivation. Therefore, there will be an equilibrium level for physical closeness (interpersonal distance), intimacy of conversation, and amount of smiling. In general, the more these behaviors occur, the more the affiliative motive is satisfied, but extreme amounts arouse anxiety. (Although not specifically stated, Argyle and Dean apparently believed that this process involves a variety of nonverbal behaviors other than those mentioned, such as body orientation, body lean, nodding, gestures, etc.)

4 An equilibrium develops for "intimacy" which is a joint function of eye contact, physical proximity, intimacy of topic, smiling, and other nonverbal behaviors. For any given pair of individuals, equilibrium would be at a certain level of intimacy. A basic deduction is that, if one of the components of intimacy is changed, one or more of the others will shift in the opposite direction in order to maintain the established equilibrium. For example, if amount of smiling is

reduced and intimacy of topic and physical proximity do not vary, eye contact would be expected to increase sufficiently to restore the equilibrium level of intimacy.

5 If attempts to restore equilibrium fail, either because the person is unable to change components or the deviation is too extreme, the person will feel uncomfortable. If equilibirum is shifted in the direction of too much intimacy, avoidance forces will predominate, and anxiety about revealing inner states or rejection will result. If the disturbance is in the direction of too little intimacy, the person will feel deprived of affiliative satisfaction.

Comment and Evaluation

Affiliative conflict theory is a "minitheory" that is relevant to a restricted aspect of social interaction, albeit an important one. It is internally consistent and agrees quite well with general conflict theory (see Miller, 1944). It permits the derivation of many interesting, testable hypotheses and has generated an acceptable amount of research. The major shortcomings of the theory include the failure to specify all the types of nonverbal behaviors that are relevant to the equilibrium level of intimacy and how each behavior is expected to relate to the equilibrium level. In addition, data concerning sex differences do not fit into the theory in its present form. The theory would also be strengthened by some provision for quantifying the components of intimacy.

Argyle and Dean (1965) presented evidence that they interpreted as supporting affiliative conflict theory. For example, persons placed at a distance of 2 feet from others tried to increase the interperson distance, those at 10 feet tried to reduce it, and those at 6 feet did not attempt to alter interperson distance. They also found that eye contact varied with interperson distance in expected ways.

Subsequent research has also been generally supportive of affiliation conflict theory. Physical proximity has been shown to correlate negatively with directness of body orientation (Watson & Graves, 1966) and with angle away from frontal approach (Clore, 1969; Pellegrini & Empey, 1970; Patterson, 1973). Eye contact was found to correlate negatively with directness of body orientation for American subjects (Patterson, 1973; Watson, & Graves, 1966), but not for Arab subjects (Watson & Graves, 1966). In an experimental situation, persons approached more closely exhibited more blocking behavior and leaning away than persons approached less closely (Patterson, Mullens, & Romano, 1971). Similarly, persons orient less directly and engage in less eye contact when approached closely (Patterson & Sechrest, 1970). Still another study (Aiello, 1972) revealed that eye contact increased linearly with increasing distance for males, but not for females.

At least two studies found results that are at least partially inconsistent with affiliative conflict theory. In one study, head nods were found to be more frequent at an interperson distance of 4 than of 10 feet (Kleck, 1970), whereas the theory would predict the opposite effect. In the other study (Coutts & Schneider, 1976), friends engaged in more individual and mutual gaze and spent more time smiling than did strangers, as predicted by the theory; however, reduction in the gazing of one member of a dyad did not elicit a compensatory increase in the immediacy behaviors of the other member, as the theory would predict.

A THEORY OF REMOVING AND RECRUITING GROUP MEMBERS

The theory of affiliative conflict discussed in the previous section considers some of the processes affecting satisfaction of the motive to affiliate, or form relationships with others. The focus was upon the motives and desires of the participant regarding affiliation with others. In groups, however, it is often the case that collective decisions must be made about affiliation. Members of a group, or some subgroup, must make the decision to admit new members or remove certain persons from the group. These are critical processes for the group's continued existence. Consider a department of psychology in a large university that is faced with a "problem" faculty member. This faculty member, a man 52 years of age, has been a member of the department for more than 20 years. Until the last few years, he has served honorably and well, but now he appears to have unofficially retired. Students report that he often fails to show up for scheduled classes; he no longer attends faculty meetings, has ceased professional research and writing altogether, maintains no office hours, and in general fails to meet the obligations expected by other faculty members. For the good of the departmental group, he should be removed, but no action is taken.

This is not an atypical example; similar situations may be observed in any large organization. As Zander (1976) notes, removing an undesirable group member is a severe source of strain not only for the person removed, but also for the group as a whole. Recruiting new members may be just as painful. Potential members must be identified, screened, sorted, and decisions made as to which shall be interviewed or otherwise considered further. Pressures may arise from both within and without the group as individual members, subgroups, or others try to assure that the person they like gets chosen and/or the ones they dislike get rejected. Whatever happens, some group members will be unhappy.

The present theory is concerned with the processes of enrolling and disenrolling group members. Unlike most writings about this topic which emphasize the feelings of the target person, the theory is group centered. The processes of removing and recruiting group members are considered to be performed by the group for the good of the group (Zander, 1976). The theory consists of a set of propositions about removal/recruitment of group members and a set of hypotheses about things that increase or inhibit the rate of removal or influence the admission of new members.

Removing Group Members

The propositions that Zander formulated are based upon his experience with organizations and groups and his knowledge of related research. He tried to state them in a form that permits them to be easily related to concepts that have commonly been used in the study of groups. These propositions may be paraphrased as follows:

Proposition 1A. The members of the group decide what conditions must not be allowed to develop in the group as a consequence of the actions of group members.

In order for a group to exist and function satisfactorily, relationships among members, parts, and activities must be organized. These regularizing conditions are often referred to as norms or social standards. The significant thing about proposition 1A is the emphasis upon negativity. According to Zander, once group members have agreed upon appropriate conditions in the group, these agreements are stated as negative injunctions. The reason for this is said to be because a restriction is a more precise criterion than an affirmative injunction. It is simply easier to specify what should *not* be done than what should be done. Unwanted conditions typically include such things as embarrassment over the group's poor performance, inappropriate group size, insufficient number of qualified people, inadequate cooperation or excessive conflict among group members, inadequate task-related procedures, and unfavorable relations with interfering agents.

Proposition 2A. The unattractiveness of a group member is a function of the negative value of the member's recent actions and the perceived probability that those actions will be repeated in the future.

The negative value of actions by group members is determined by the significance of those actions and the degree to which they are prohibited by group injunctions. For example, Zander cited studies showing that group members have been ousted for quarrelsome dispositions, immaturity, and unacceptable political beliefs (Caplow & McGee, 1958) and from membership in the American Medical Association for violating ethical standards, such as using drugs improperly or performing an illegal abortion (Derbyshire, 1974).

The severity of any negative action is judged in terms of the perceived probability that it will be repeated, how often, and to what degree. Perceived probability will be greater if the person has been engaging in the activity for some time, is perceived to be unable to stop, is aware that the action is bad to the group but persists anyway, or engages in many rather than few unpleasant actions. Distortion or misperception of these characteristics causes inaccurate appraisals of the person's acceptability.

Proposition 3A. The more unattractive a group member is to his or her fellow members, the more willing they are to remove the member from the group.

Since a group member depends upon the group for desired outcomes, such as affiliation, social power, protection, and the like, the membership of a group can remove a member by arranging things so that these desired outcomes cannot be attained through the group. For instance, a group member may be denied group benefits by not being given a pay check, invited to meetings, provided a workplace, etc.

Proposition 4A. Rejection of unattractive group members may be strengthened or weakened by conditions other than those that initially caused their unattractiveness.

The most obvious "other conditions" are forms of discrimination, such as discrimination against blacks, women, and other minority group members. For instance, in a large university, blacks and women were discharged from noninstructional jobs more frequently than whites or men, and assistant professors were released more frequently than higher-ranking faculty (Caplow & McGee, 1958). There are also inhibiting factors. Derbyshire (1974) reported that physicians seldom report unethical conduct of another physician, even when such information might lead to removal from the medical society. The unreliability of performance appraisals may also inhibit removal, since superiors do not often give unfavorable evaluations of subordinates (Zander & Gyr, 1955).

Removal from the group means that the group is being protected against the consequences of having undesirable members, whereas failure to remove unattractive members means that they are being protected against the group. These considerations led Zander to propose the following hypotheses about things that increase or inhibit the rate of removals from a group:

Hypothesis a. The more cohesive the group, the stronger the tendency to remove an unattractive member.

Early work by Festinger, Schachter, and Back (1950) and by Schachter (1951, 1954) was cited to support this hypothesis.

Hypothesis b. The less just the reason for removal, the weaker is the tendency to remove an unattractive member.

The idea implicit in this hypothesis is that some persons (members of the group or outsiders) may object if the member is being unfairly judged. The amount of weight placed on justice in any given group depends upon such things as tradition, law, and standards and goals set by related organizations that require fair treatment of members.

Hypothesis c. The greater the harm to an unattractive member caused by removal, the weaker the tendency to remove that member.

The major point here is that group members are likely to have compassion for a member, even if that member is unattractive. No research was cited to provide direct support for this hypothesis.

Hypothesis d. The more harmful to the group is the removal of an unattractive member, the weaker the tendency to remove that member.

Removal of an undesirable member often has adverse effects for the group, such as causing the group to look bad or generating conflict among group members. Such factors inhibit removal.

Hypothesis e. If the removal of an unattractive member decreases the valued contribution to the group, the tendency to remove is weaker.

Undesirable aspects of a group member may be discounted if the member makes contributions to the group that outweigh the disliked characteristics. This notion is said to be consistent with Hollander's (1960) concept of idiosyncrasy credit.

Hypothesis f. The greater the probability of retaliation by the rejectee or supporters, the weaker the tendency to remove an unattractive member.

When the group fears retaliation, the unattractive member may be allowed to resign, especially if the member is prestigeful. Similarly, labor union members are not dismissed unless reasons for doing so are compelling.

Recruiting Members

In many ways, Zander's hypotheses and propositions about recruiting new members are "mirror images" of those concerning removal of unattractive members. These propositions and hypotheses are paraphrased below without comment.

Proposition 1B. The members of a group decide what conditions should be developed in the group through the actions of group members.

Proposition 2B. The attractiveness of an individual to members of a group is a function of the value of that person's actions and attributes and the perceived probability that those actions and attributes will be revealed in the future.

Proposition 3B. The more attractive an individual to group members, the more likely the individual will be invited to become a member.

Proposition 4B. Acceptance of an attractive person as a group member may be strengthened or weakened by conditions that did not cause the person to be attractive.

Some of the reasons that the most attractive individuals are or are not actually recruited are expressed in the following hypotheses:

Hypothesis g. The more cohesive the group, the stronger is the tendency of members to prefer attractive recruits.

Hypothesis h. Individuals perceived as more able to benefit from group membership are more likely to be asked to join the group.

Hypothesis i. Relative to a successful group, a failing group is more likely to seek and accept new members.

Hypothesis j. The greater the weight group members place on the importance of objective procedures, the more likely they are to choose a recruit on the basis of merit rather than other attributes.

Hypothesis k. The more cohesive the group, the more members will follow objective procedures in recruiting new members.

Comment and Evaluation

The theory of removing and recruiting group members attempts to organize, integrate, and expand what is known about these important processes. For this reason alone, it makes a significant contribution to the understanding of group process. The theory is internally consistent in that the various parts of the theory are not contradictory; however, the hypotheses do not always derive from the propositions, as would be expected in a "good" theory. Instead, several of the hypotheses appear to be generalizations derived from general knowledge about groups and the behavior of group members. On the other hand, the hypotheses are stated in testable form and should provide a guide for further research. Also, the propositions permit the derivation of additional testable hypotheses.

The content of the theory agrees very well with other theoretical proposals and with research findings available at the time the theory was formulated. No research designed specifically to test the theory could be found in the literature. This is not regarded as a criticism; the theory was formulated so recently that its impact on the research community cannot yet be evaluated.

FIRO: A THREE-DIMENSIONAL THEORY OF INTERPERSONAL RELATIONS

The preceding theories, affiliative conflict theory and the theory of removing and recruiting group members, were concerned with processes that influence group membership. Once members of a group are enrolled, the particular composition of the group will determine, to some degree, the effectiveness of the group. FIRO (Schutz, 1955, 1958) attempts to explain how the characteristics of each group member relative to the characteristics of each other group member influence group effectiveness. FIRO is an abbreviation for "Fundamental Interpersonal Relations Orientation," a phrase reflecting the basic concern of the theory; that is, the theory attempts to explain interpersonal behavior in terms of the orientations of individuals to others.

The theory may be summarized briefly as follows: The patterns of interaction of individuals can be explained largely in terms of three interpersonal needs: inclusion, control, and affection. These needs are developed during childhood through interaction with adults (usually parents). In adulthood, the need for inclusion depends upon the degree to which the child was integrated into the family group; the need for control depends upon whether the parent-child relation stressed guidance, freedom, or control; and the need for affection varies according to the degree to which the child was emotionally approved or rejected. To the degree that these needs are not satisfied during childhood, the individual feels, respectively, insignificant, incompetent, and unlovable. In order to cope with these feelings, he or she develops defense mechanisms which are manifested in characteristic behavior patterns that can be observed in interpersonal interaction. When two people enter into an interpersonal relation, their characteristic behavior patterns may be either compatible or incompatible. That is, their behaviors may be such that the two persons work well together, or they may be such that the two persons cannot work well together. Of course, dyads may vary in degree of compatibility anywhere between the two extremes. Thus, Schutz specified that interpersonal compatibility is a property of a relation between two or more persons; it refers to the degree to which they can work together harmoniously and mutually satisfy their interpersonal needs. In groups, the group atmosphere and the effectiveness of group action are determined in large part by the degree to which the behavior patterns of various group members are compatible or incompatible.

These ideas were formalized in four postulates and related theorems. The first postulate concerns interpersonal needs, the second postulate considers the role of early childhood experiences in the development of these needs, and postulates 3 and 4 deal with the consequences of interpersonal needs for group compatibility and group development. The postulates and related principles are stated in the following section. Later sections describe the implications of the postulates for the development of needs, the associated behavior relative to others, and the effects of this behavior on group processes.

The Postulates

Postulate 1. The Postulate of Interpersonal Needs.
(*a*) Every individual has three interpersonal needs: inclusion, control, and affection.
(*b*) Inclusion, control, and affection constitute a sufficient set of areas of interpersonal behavior for the prediction and explanation of interpersonal phenomena (Schutz, 1958, p. 13).
Postulate 2. The Postulate of Relational Continuity. An individual's expressed interpersonal behavior will be similar to the behavior experienced in his earliest interpersonal relations, usually with parents, in the following way: *Principle of Constancy:* When the individual perceives his adult position in an interpersonal situation to be similar to that in his parent-child relation, the individual's adult behavior positively covaries with his childhood behavior toward his parents (or significant others).
Principles of Identification: When the individual perceives his adult position in an interpersonal situation to be similar to his parent's position in his parent-child relation, adult behavior positively covaries with the behavior of his parents (or significant others) toward him when he was a child (Schutz, 1958, p. 81).
Postulate 3. The Postulate of Compatibility. If the compatibility of one group, *h,* is greater than that of another group, *m,* then the goal achievement of *h* will exceed that of *m* (Schutz, 1958, p. 105).
Postulate 4. The Postulate of Group Development. The formation and development of two or more people into an interpersonal relation (that is, a group) always follows the same sequence.
Principle of Group Integration. For the time period starting with the group's beginning until three intervals before the group's termination, the predominant area of interaction begins with inclusion, is followed by control, and finally by affection. This cycle may recur.
Principle of Group Resolution. The last three intervals prior to a group's anticipated termination follow the opposite sequence in that the predominant area of interpersonal behavior is first affection, then control, and finally inclusion (Schutz, 1958, p. 168).

The Three Interpersonal Needs

Postulate 1 states merely that there are three interpersonal needs and that the areas of behavior related to these needs are sufficient to predict and explain interpersonal phenomena, namely, inclusion, control, and affection. Need deprivation in childhood (that is, either too little or too much gratification) causes the person to develop characteristic patterns of adapting to this lack of complete gratification. The characteristic behavior patterns formed in childhood persist into adulthood and determine the characteristic adult pattern of orientation to others. Let us examine this process relative to inclusion, control, and affection.

Inclusion was defined by Schutz as related to belongingness in a group situation, and the associated need was defined as the need to establish and maintain a satisfactory interactive relation with others. Inclusion behavior may range from intensive interaction to complete withdrawal and detachment. Parent-child relations may be either positive (the child has much contact and interaction with the parents) or negative (the parent ignores the child and there is a minimum contact). The child's anxiety concerns being a worthwhile person and existing as a person. The need is to be taken into account by the group and not go unnoticed by others. If the child is adequately integrated into the family group, no anxiety occurs. If there is inadequate inclusion, the child may try to cope with anxiety by either withdrawing into a shell or making intensive efforts to achieve integration into the group.

Control refers to the decision-making aspect of interpersonal relations. The interpersonal need for control was defined by Schutz as the need to establish and maintain satisfactory relations with others with respect to authority and power. The expression of control behavior may range from too much discipline and control to too much freedom and lack of discipline. Extremes of the parent-child relation range from constraining actions (parents maintain complete control over the child, make all decisions) to licensing actions (parents allow the child to make all decisions, provide no guidance). The associated anxiety concerns not knowing what is expected in a power hierarchy and fear of not being capable of handling problems and therefore not being a responsible person. Either too much or too little control leads to defensive behaviors; the person may follow rules closely and try to dominate others, or withdraw and refuse to control or be controlled by others.

Affection is based on the building of emotional ties with others; hence Schutz defined the associated need as the need to be liked and loved. The expression of affection may be either positive (ranging from attraction to love) or negative (ranging from mild disapproval to hate and revulsion). Consequently, parent-child relations may involve either positive affection (characterized by warmth, approval, love, etc.) or negative affection (characterized by coldness, reserve, rejection, etc.). The anxiety associated with this relation is that the individual will be disliked and rejected. If the child has inadequate emotional acceptance, coping behaviors may be withdrawal (that is, avoidance of close interpersonal relationships), superficially friendly behavior, overly friendly or deferent behavior, or overly possessive behavior.

Types of Interpersonal Behavior

The parent-child relations within each interpersonal need area can involve either an ideal amount, too much, or too little need satisfaction. Schutz described three types of interpersonal behavior within each area; corresponding to the degree of need satisfaction experienced in the parent-child relation. He also described pathological behavior within each area.

Types of Inclusion Behavior   If the child fails to experience an adequate amount of inclusion satisfaction (either insufficient integration into the family or too much inclusion in family affairs), he or she is prone to either *undersocial* or *oversocial* behavior in interpersonal relations.[1] The undersocial type tends toward introversion and withdrawal, avoids associating with others, refuses to join groups, and generally maintains distance between self and others. This behavior may take the form of nonparticipation and noninvolvement, or it may be expressed subtly by being late for meetings, missing meetings altogether, falling asleep during discussions, and so on.

The oversocial type tends to be an extrovert, constantly seeks out others and wants them to reciprocate. The resulting behavior may be exhibitionistic (speaking loudly, demanding attention, forcing one's self on others, and the like) or subtle (making excessive show of skills, name-dropping, asking startling questions, and the like).

Adequate integration into the family during childhood produces the ideal type, the *social*. The social type has no problems relative to interaction and can be happy alone or with people, participating much or little, and committed to the group or not, as the situation calls for.

Types of Control Behavior   Control behavior refers to the decision-making process between people. Three characteristic types of control behavior were labeled "the abdicrat," the "autocrat," and "the democrat" (Schutz, 1958). The abdicrat tends to be submissive and abdicates power and responsibility in dealing with others. This type person prefers a subordinate role, wants others to assume responsibility, and never makes a decision that can be avoided. The autocrat tends to dominate others and prefers the top position in a power hierarchy. Such a person wants to make all decisions, not only for him- or herself but for everyone else as well. The democrat is, of course, ideal. This type has successfully resolved problems associated with interpersonal relations in the control area and can give or take orders, depending upon the demands of the situation.

Control pathology develops when the individual refuses to accept control of any kind. Schutz proposed that this describes the typical psychopath who refuses to respect the rights of others or obey social norms. The obsessive obedience to norms may also reflect control pathology.

Types of Affection Behavior   Affection refers to close emotional feelings between two people (Schutz, 1967). Again, three characteristic types of behavior may result from childhood experiences. Inadequate parent-child relations in the affection area can result in either *underpersonal* or *overpersonal* behavior, whereas the ideal parent-child relation produces *personal* behavior. The under-

---

[1]Schutz originally related too much inclusion, control, and affection on the part of parents to oversocial, autocratic, and overpersonal behavior, respectively; too little inclusion, control, and affection to undersocial, abdicrat, and underpersonal behavior, respectively (Schutz, 1958, p. 89, Table 5–1). Later (Schutz, 1967, and in personal communication), he asserted that either type of behavior could result from either too much or too little gratification of the associated need during childhood. We have followed his later formulation in this respect.

personal type tends to avoid close personal relations, maintains emotional distance, and prefers that others do the same, although superficial friendliness may be displayed. The overpersonal type desires very close emotional relations and attempts to create them. This goal may be approached directly by being extremely personal and intimate or subtly by devouring friends and trying to punish them for establishing other friendships. The personal type has successfully resolved problems associated with affection relations with others and can function adequately and comfortably in either close or distant emotional relations.

Relational Continuity   The postulate of relational continuity asserts that the behaviors that develop in childhood persist in adulthood in specified ways. In the preceding section we have described the characteristic ways that adults are expected to behave as a consequence of their childhood experiences. The principles of constancy and of identification attempt to specify when childhood behavior persists into adulthood and when the adult will imitate parental behavior. Generally, the postulates state that adult behavior will correspond to behavior in childhood when the person's position is perceived to be similar to the childhood position. On the other hand, when the adult perceives the position as being similar to his or her parents' roles, the adult behavior will correspond to the parents' behaviors. Unfortunately, Schutz did not indicate what circumstances lead to the perception of one's own position as "childlike" or "parentlike."

Compatibility

Postulate 3 states that compatible groups will be more effective in achieving group goals than incompatible groups. *Compatibility,* as used by Schutz, refers to a relation between two or more persons. Two persons were said to be compatible if they could work together in harmony. Thus, his definition of compatibility corresponds with the usual dictionary definition of the term.

However, in order to test the implications of postulate 3, it was necessary to identify types of compatibility and specify ways of measuring them. The identification of compatibility types was based upon expressed behavior and behavior wanted from others in each of the three areas. These elements were measured by a set of six Guttman scales (FIRO-B), designed to reveal expressed and wanted behavior in each of the three interpersonal need areas. Compatibility scores reflecting each type of compatibility were then computed by means of formulas developed for this purpose.

Types of Compatibility   Schutz (1958) identified three types of compatibility in each of the three need areas: interchange compatibility, originator compatibility, and reciprocal compatibility. *Interchange compatibility* refers to the mutual expression of affection, control, or inclusion. Maximum interchange compatibility between two persons occurs when the amount of expressed and wanted behavior by one person is the same as that of the other person; the two persons are incompatible to the extent that they differ with respect to amount of expressed and wanted behavior in the area in question.

Originator compatibility is based on the originate-receive dimension of interaction. Originator compatibility occurs in the affection area when those who wish to express affection interact with those who want to receive affection. In the control area, originator compatibility exists when those who wish to dominate others interact with those who wish to be controlled. Originator compatibility in the inclusion area occurs when those who initiate group activities interact with persons who desire to be included in these activities. Incompatibility arises to the extent that group composition deviates from the ideal situation in each area.

Reciprocal compatibility refers to the degree to which each person's expression of inclusion, control, or affection meets the desires of others with respect to each need area. For example, two persons are compatible in the affection area if the amount of affection expressed by each person is consistent with the amount of affection wanted by the other. The greater the discrepancy between the behavior expressed by one person and the amount wanted by the other, the more incompatible the dyad will be. In contrast, interchange incompatibility increases with the discrepancy between the amount of behavior expressed and wanted by one person and the amount of behavior expressed and wanted by the other person in the same area.

Schutz further suggested that overall originator, interchange, and reciprocal compatibilities could be computed by summing across areas. Similarly, overall compatibility within each need area might be determined by summing across types of compatibility. Finally, a total compatibility score might be obtained by summing across both need areas and types of compatibility. Thus, using the FIRO-B scales and the compatibility formulas, Schutz derived 16 compatibility indices.

Compatibility Theorems   Schutz proposed nine theorems relative to the postulate of compatibility. He presented evidence for three of the theorems (1, 2, and 9) and partial support for three others (3, 7, and 8). The theorems may be summarized as follows. (Some of the theorems were formulated with respect to specific experimental situations; we have restated these so that they are understandable without reference to the particular study.)

1   If two dyads differ in compatibility, the members of the more-compatible dyad are more likely to prefer each other for continued personal contact.
2   If two groups differ in compatibility, the productivity goal achievement of the more-compatible group will exceed that of the less-compatible one.
3   If two groups differ in compatibility, the more-compatible group will be more cohesive than the less-compatible one.
4   If a group consists of two or more incompatible subgroups, each member should prefer to work with a member of his or her own subgroup more than with any member of an antagonistic subgroup or with a neutral member.

5 In incompatible groups, members of overpersonal subgroups will tend to like each other more than members of underpersonal subgroups will.

6 In incompatible groups, overpersonal subgroup members will tend to overestimate the competence of the person they like best, whereas underpersonal subgroup members will not have this tendency.

7 In compatible groups, persons predicted to be focal persons (key members) and those predicted to be main supporting members should rank each other high on the relation "work well with."

8 Focal persons (key members) will be chosen as leaders by group members in all groups.

9 The effect of compatibility on productivity varies as a function of the degree of interchange in the three need areas required by the task.

Group Development

Postulate 4 asserts that every interpersonal relation follows the same course of development and resolution, namely, that development begins with a concern for inclusion needs, followed by a concern with control and finally by a concern for affection. Resolution follows the reverse order.

As soon as a group is formed, the inclusion phase begins. When people are confronted with one another, they become concerned about being in or out of the group. Decisions must be made concerning whether to become a member, which involve questions about one's place in the group, the importance of the group, one's personal identity, how much commitment to make to the group, and so on. This phase of group development is often characterized by much discussion of issues of little interest to anyone. According to Schutz, such discussions are inevitable and serve the important function of working through problems related to inclusion needs.

After problems of inclusion have been sufficiently resolved, control problems become the center of concern. At this point, the issue of decision making arises. This involves a variety of problems concerning the distribution of responsibility, power, and control. Each person in the group is attempting to structure the situation to achieve just the right amount of responsibility in the group.

Assuming that the control problems are resolved successfully, the group moves to the affection phase. At this point, the group has been formed, and problems of responsibility and power distribution have been worked out; all that remains is the problem of emotional integration. At this stage of development expressions of hostility, anger, and the like are common. Each member is attempting to establish for himself the most comfortable position possible with regard to affectional interchange.

The three phases are not discrete; all types of behavior occur in all phases. However, the phases represent periods in the group's history in which particular problem areas are emphasized. The various phases may also be repeated so that a given group may go through the inclusion, control, affection sequence several times. When the group approaches dissolution, the concern is first with affection, followed by control and inclusion (or perhaps one should say exclusion!).

Schutz used the analysis of group development to derive certain theorems concerning compatibility at various stages in the life history of the group. In general, he proposed that the members of a given group would be most compatible when the group is in the stage corresponding to greatest overall compatibility; that is, if the group is high on inclusion compatibility and low on control and affection compatibility, the members will be most compatible during the inclusion phase; if they are high on control compatibility and low on the other two, they will be most compatible in the control phase; and so on. Evidence for this was largely inferential.

Comments and Evaluation

The theory proposed by Schutz is an interesting set of hypotheses concerning interpersonal behavior. The theory is internally consistent, its predictions are amenable to test, and it agrees reasonably well with available evidence concerning interpersonal behavior.

The theory actually concerns three somewhat different aspects of interpersonal behavior: (1) the existence of three needs and the development of patterns of interpersonal behavior relative to these needs (postulates 1 and 2), (2) the consequences of these patterns of behavior for group compatibility and its effects on group effectiveness (postulate 3), and (3) the relation of the three interpersonal needs to group development and resolution (postulate 4). The portion dealing with the existence of needs and related behavior patterns is not really necessary for predicting behavior in groups. The patterns of behavior could have been determined without reference to past experience, and the predictions about adult behavior would be unchanged. The first part of the theory is therefore useful for "explaining" why the person exemplifies a particular behavioral pattern, but it cannot be readily used as a predictor of interpersonal behavior.

Schutz relied upon two kinds of evidence to support his theory: the writings of other theorists and experimental data. The first kind of evidence was used to establish the "plausibility" of the postulates. Observational studies of parent-child relations (Champney, 1941; Baldwin, Kallhorn, & Breese, 1945; Sewell, Mussen, & Harris, 1955) and theoretical statements by psychoanalysts (Horney, 1945; Fromm, 1947; Freud, 1950) were cited as evidence of the plausibility of postulates 1 and 2. Some of his own empirical studies were also reported in partial support of postulate 2. Postulate 3 was evaluated primarily in terms of experimental data from his own studies (Schutz, 1955, 1958). In the first study, he was able to demonstrate that compatible groups are more effective on certain kinds of tasks than incompatible groups, but as we noted above, only three of nine theorems were unequivocally supported by later investigations. The final postulate concerning group development and resolution was supported by the data from Bennis and Shepard (1956), which was based upon observations of groups undergoing sensitivity training, as indicated earlier in this chapter.

Since the original formulation of the theory, several studies have reported results that are in general agreement with the theory. Schutz (1961) reported a study in which five 14-person groups were formed on the basis of their responses to questionnaires designed to measure behavior relative to the three interpersonal needs (FIRO-B questionnaire). After six meetings, three of the five groups were able to identify their own group descriptions significantly better than chance, one was partially accurate, and one failed to do better than chance. Behavioral differences were also in agreement with theoretical expectations. Yalom and Rand (1966) examined the relationship between compatibility and cohesiveness in outpatient therapy groups. They found that high-compatibility groups, as measured by the FIRO-B questionnaire, were significantly more cohesive and better satisfied than low-compatibility groups.

Two recent studies of interpersonal needs in T-groups yielded conflicting results. In one study, it was found that participants in T-groups were most comfortable and most satisfied when the trainer has the same kind of interpersonal orientation that they themselves possessed, that is, in groups having high interchange compatibility (Lundgren, 1975). In a second study, no evidence was found that compatibility of interpersonal needs between members and trainers has an important effect on members' evaluative attitudes toward the trainer or toward the group as a whole (Lundgren & Knight, 1977).

An attempt to test FIRO predictions in adolescent dyads also yielded nonsignificant results (Armstrong & Roback, 1977). However, inclusion and affect were measured by the Ohio Social Acceptance Scale (Lorber, 1970) and control was manipulated via the prisoner's dilemma situation. It is not clear to what extent Armstrong and Roback were measuring the same needs as those measured by the FIRO-B questionnaire. Nevertheless, these data can scarcely be accepted as support for the theory.

Finally, it should be noted that Schutz has applied the theory to problems of "expanding human awareness" (Schutz, 1967). He pointed out that the problems of group development occur in everyday life and failure to resolve problems associated with the three interpersonal needs often leads to unhappiness and dissatisfaction in day-to-day interpersonal relations. In an interesting application of the theory, he shows how the individual who may have difficulty in the three interpersonal need areas can develop techniques for dealing with these more adequately.

A THEORY OF MOTIVES AND GOALS IN GROUPS

It is a common observation that groups form and continue to exist for some purpose, that is, to achieve some goal or goals. Groups that have clearly established goals are usually organized, effective, and satisfying to their members, whereas groups that do not have such goals often engage in aimless activity, are ineffective, and provide little satisfaction for their members. Despite the fact that the importance of group goals for group functioning is recognized by most students of group behavior, relatively little is known about them. The theory of motives and goals in groups (Zander, 1971) provides a theoretical framework for the investigation of these and other questions about group goals.

Zander adopted level-of-aspiration theory (Lewin, Dembo, Festinger, & Sears, 1944) and achievement motivation theory (Atkinson & Feather, 1966) from individual psychology as bases for analyzing group-oriented motives and goals. The derived theory is a systematic analysis of group and individual goal-setting behavior, effects of external pressures on group aspirations, individual desires for group achievement, relations between person-oriented and group-oriented motives, beliefs of group members as indicators of purposive group behavior, processes of evaluation of personal and group performance, effects of goals and group-oriented motives on group behavior, and the relation of the group's aspirations for a member to the member's own aspirations.

Sources and Functions of Group Aspiration Level

Aspiration level is usually defined as the level of difficulty of that task chosen as the goal for the next action (Lewin et al., 1944). Typically, an individual is asked to perform some task, receives feedback about the level of performance, and is asked to state the level of performance expected on the next trial. The expected level of performance on the next trial is the level of aspiration. It has been shown that groups establish group levels of aspiration and react to them in much the same way as individuals do (Zander & Medow, 1963). According to Zander (1971), a *group performance goal* is an end toward which the joint efforts of group members are directed, whereas a group's *aspiration for the group* is a joint decision about the level of performance expected in the future. Thus group level of aspiration and group goal are not the same thing, although they have much in common. Zander believed that the level of aspiration could be used to study group goals. The theory consists of a number of assumptions and hypotheses which may ɔe paraphrased as follows:

Assumption 1. When group members jointly perform an activity on several occasions and the group's performance varies along a scale of difficulty, they become aware that the probability of attaining some performance levels (scores) is higher than the probability of attaining other performance scores.

Each group member is assumed to have a *subjective probability of success by the group* (Pgs) and a *subjective probability of failure by the group* (Pgf). Pgs varies inversely with difficulty and Pgf varies directly with difficulty of the task. When these estimates are available, group members are either satisfied or dissatisfied with later performances. Thus:

Assumption 2. Satisfaction with attainment of a given score is inversely related to the perceived probability of success; dissatisfaction with failure to attain a given score is inversely related to the perceived probability of failure.

This assumption implies that satisfaction is greater with completion of a difficult task, whereas failure to successfully complete an easy task leads to greater dissatisfaction. The choice of a level of aspiration is the one that best resolves the conflicts among the attractiveness of success, repulsiveness of failure, and perceived probabilities of success and failure.

Assumption 3. A member's aspiration for the group is the one with the highest value, based on the following formula:

Member's aspiration for the group = (greatest perceived probability of success × incentive value of success) − (perceived probability of failure × the repulsiveness of that failure).

A member's aspiration either maximizes expected satisfaction from success or minimizes expected dissatisfaction from failure.

At this point, the similarities and differences of goals and aspirations become important. A goal is often determined by the same conditions that determine aspirations, but this is not necessarily so. For instance, a goal may be so vaguely stated that its location is unknown or the goal may be imposed by forces outside the group. Also, a goal may be influenced by things other than feelings about the group's achievement level.

Assumption 4. Determinants of a group's performance goal may be quite similar to or quite different from the determinants of the group's level of aspiration. The more similar these determinants, the more congruent the location and function of goals and aspirations.

These assumptions led to a series of hypotheses about the placement of the level of aspiration and the evaluation of group performance.

Hypothesis 1. Over trials, a group's mean aspiration level exceeds its mean performance level.

Hypothesis 2. A group's aspiration level is higher when it receives information about its score on a series of trials than when it does not have this information.

Hypothesis 3. Given the same information about the score obtained by a group, observers of a group set the same levels of aspiration as group members.

Hypothesis 4.[2] Members evaluate a performance more highly when it exceeds the group's mean level of aspiration and less highly when it falls below the mean aspiration level.

Hypothesis 5. Members evaluate the group's performance more favorably when they have no information about their score than when they have full information.

Hypothesis 6. Given approximately equal successes on a series of trials, members evaluate performance more favorably if the task is difficult than if it is easy.

[2]Numbers here do not correspond to those used by Zander. We have numbered them sequentially throughout, whereas Zander numbered them sequentially within categories.

Hypothesis 7. Group members recall a successful score fairly accurately but err in a direction favorable to the group after a failing trial.

Zander reported several studies supporting these hypotheses.

Effects of Group Success and Failure

Zander assumed that a group success increases the desirability of success for its members and a group failure increases the repulsiveness of failure. Hence, the more difficult the task, the greater the perceived attractiveness of success and the less the perceived repulsiveness of failure. Thus:

Assumption 5. Group success strengthens a member's expectation of future success and group failure strengthens an expectation of future failure.

The following hypotheses about placement of level of aspiration, motivated beliefs, and evaluation of performance were derived:

Hypothesis 8. During a series of trials, a group's level of aspiration is raised following success and lowered following failure.

Hypothesis 9. The tendency to raise the group's level of aspiration following success is stronger than the tendency to lower the level of aspiration following failure.

Hypothesis 10. The amount of shift in the group's level of aspiration is greater following success than following failure.

Hypothesis 11. The discrepancy between a subsequent level of aspiration and a preceding group performance score is greater after failure than after success.

Hypothesis 12. With increasing failure, the discrepancy between aspiration level and performance becomes larger, whereas with increasing success this discrepancy becomes smaller.

Hypothesis 13. Observers of a performing group, during a series of trials, raise their predicted scores for the group after success and lower them after failure.

In connection with motivated beliefs of group members, Zander stated what he called "general hypotheses," which were formulated in broader terms than his other hypotheses. We follow his terminology.

General Hypothesis 1. After working on a series of objectively more difficult tasks, members describe themselves and other group members as interested in the activity and motivated to do well, but, when the task is easier, they reveal a desire to withdraw and little interest in doing well on the task.

Hypothesis 14. Members of a group that fails more than it succeeds express less confidence that they can attain a future level of aspiration than do members of a group that succeeds more than it fails.

Hypothesis 15. Members of a consistently failing group are more willing to have the group stop setting a goal for each trial than are members of consistently successful groups.

General Hypothesis 2. After a series of trials on which success is more frequent than failure, members report interest in the activity and desire for the group to do well; when the group has failed more frequently than it has succeeded, members say they wish to avoid the group's activity and seek to evade the negative outcomes of failure.

General Hypothesis 3. Motivated beliefs and actions in a successful group are more likely to enhance the ability of the group to succeed in the future, but beliefs and actions of members in an unsuccessful group are more likely to reduce the ability of the group to succeed in the future.

Hypothesis 16. During a series of trials, group failures are likely to exceed group successes.

This hypothesis requires further comment. Since the tendency to raise aspirations following success is stronger than the tendency to lower aspirations following failure (hypothesis 9) and the amount of shift is greater after success than after failure (hypothesis 10), the relative aspiration level should be high and the probability of the performance level equaling or exceeding it should be low. Hence, failures should exceed successes.

Hypothesis 17. Following a series of trials, members' evaluations of a group are more likely to be unfavorable than favorable.

Reactions to Social Pressures Arising Outside the Group

As noted earlier, information and other external pressures may affect the group's aspiration level, whether or not such effects are intended.

Assumption 6. Social pressures that originate externally and that are directed toward either harder or easier group performances, cause members to choose either harder or easier levels of aspiration, respectively, than they would have chosen in the absence of external pressures.

Hypothesis 18. The discrepancy between members' levels of aspiration and prior performances is larger if members learn that their group's performance is worse than the performance of similar groups and smaller if they learn the mean performance of similar groups is worse than their own group's performance.

Hypothesis 19. The discrepancy between a group's aspiration level and prior performance is smaller when observers predict that the group's performance will worsen than when they predict that it will improve.

Hypothesis 20. In groups that perform better than similar groups, the aspiration level is influenced by the awareness of this relatively favorable social comparison and is set below the group's typical level of performance in early trials more often than in later trials.

Hypothesis 21. The availability of a comparison group, awareness of need in the organization to which the group belongs, and pressures to raise the group's goal apparently operate independently and produce additive effects upon increasing the discrepancy between the group's level of aspiration and the group's prior performance.

Hypothesis 22. When the direction of external pressure is unexpected on the basis of prior success or failure, members are less influenced by the external pressure and pay more attention to the views of group members when selecting an aspiration level, and thus the shift in aspiration level after a success or failure is held constant.

Hypothesis 23. When members of a group are offered a reward for performing at a higher level than the group has been attaining, the attractiveness of the reward and the attractiveness of success apparently summate to produce a stronger tendency to select a more difficult level of aspiration than either working alone.

Group-Oriented Motives

Zander postulated the existence of two group-oriented motives that relate to aspiration level and group performance. The *desire for group success* (Dgs) is defined as a disposition on the part of a group member to experience pride and satisfaction with the group if it successfully completes a difficult group task. The *desire to avoid group failure* (Dgaf) is defined as a disposition on the part of a participant to experience embarrassment or dissatisfaction with the group if it fails on a challenging task. Thus:

Assumption 7. Experiencing satisfaction in group success and dissatisfaction in group failure eventually generates desires for success (Dgs) and to avoid failure (Dgaf), respectively.

These group-oriented motives are not impulses for action, but may influence relevant actions. Zander proposes that there are two related impulses to action, called tendencies. The *tendency for group success* (Tgs) is an inclination to have the group interested in the task and intending to perform it well. The *tendency to avoid failure* (Tgaf) is defined as an inclination to have the group resist performing an activity that is expected to lead to failure. Assumption 8 indicates the determinants of Tgs and Tgaf.

Assumption 8. Tgs and Tgaf are multiplicative functions of the desire for group success or failure, the probability of group success or failure, and the satisfaction with group success or dissatisfaction with group failure, respectively. The resultant tendency for action is equal to Tgs minus Tgaf.

Assumption 9. Preference for group scores perceived to be in the intermediate range of difficulty increases with increasing Dgs and preference for group scores perceived to be away from the intermediate range increases with increasing Dgaf, when selecting a group level of aspiration.

This assumption has important implications for task selection. For those persons for whom Dgs is stronger than Dgaf, the resultant tendency to undertake a task is strongest when the perceived Pgs is .50 because that is the point where their expected value of success is maximal. For persons having Dgaf stronger than Dgs, the resultant tendency to avoid engaging in an activity is strongest when Pgs is .50, and they should *least* prefer to undertake such tasks. That is, such persons should prefer tasks that have either high or low probability of success. If the task is very difficult (low Pgs), failure to complete the task can be easily excused (and hence avoid the feeling of failure); if the task is easy (high Pgs), by definition, the feeling of failure is likely to be avoided. Several reasonable hypotheses follow.

Hypothesis 24. Members of strong groups are more likely to select a group aspiration in the intermediate range of difficulty than are members of weak groups.

A strong group is one of high unity and cohesiveness; a weak group has low unity and cohesiveness. Zander assumed that Dgs is stronger in a strong group than in a weak group.

Hypothesis 25. A member in a central position in a group is more likely to choose aspirations in the intermediate range of difficulty than members in peripheral positions.

Hypothesis 26. Members are more likely to select a group aspiration in the intermediate range of difficulty in a reward than in a cost condition (during a series of trials).

This hypothesis assumes that reward arouses Dgs, whereas cost arouses Dgaf.

Hypothesis 27. Following a series of trials, members who prefer a group aspiration that is higher than that selected by the group reveal a greater desire to withdraw from the activity than those who consistently prefer a group aspiration that is closer to the group's selection.

Presumably, the person who prefers an aspiration higher than the group has a stronger Dgaf and thus wishes to withdraw to avoid the experience of failure if the group does not achieve the aspiration level. This is consistent with other parts of the theory when the group aspiration is in or above the intermediate range of difficulty, but is inconsistent with the general thrust of the theory when the group aspiration is *below* the intermediate range of difficulty.

General Hypothesis 4. Groups having stronger Dgs perform better than groups having weaker Dgs.

General Hypothesis 5. Group performance improves with increasing discrepancies between aspiration level and prior performance up to some maximal discrepancy, beyond which performance deteriorates.

The implication here is that a goal closer to the perceived intermediate range of difficulty is more motivating than one that is unreasonably distant from that range.

Person-Oriented Motives and Group Aspirations

Just as a group member has desires relative to group success and failure, they bring to the group individual desires and motives. The *motive to achieve success* (Ms) is defined as the person's capacity to experience satisfaction with successful completion of challenging tasks, and the *motive to avoid failure* (Maf) is defined as the capacity to experience dissatisfaction with potential failure. These motives are stimulated by the performance of challenging tasks, and the person's personal tendency to achieve success or avoid failure through the group depends upon perceived probabilities and incentive values.

Assumption 10. A member's tendency to achieve success through the group is a multiplicative function of motive to achieve success (Ms), probability of group success (Pgs), and satisfaction with group success; a member's tendency to avoid failure through the group is a multiplicative function of the motive to avoid failure (Maf), probability of group failure (Pgf), and dissatisfaction with group failure.

Assumption 11. Motives to achieve success or avoid failure are independent from desires for group success or to avoid group failure. This independence implies that person-oriented and group-oriented motives may supplement one another in an additive manner or may act in contrasting directions and thus either strengthen or weaken the total tendency to approach or avoid.

Hypothesis 28. During a series of trials, groups composed entirely of persons having stronger Ms than Maf more often select aspirations for the group in the intermediate difficulty range than do groups composed entirely of persons having stronger Maf than Ms.

General Hypothesis 6. Group members in whom Ms exceeds Maf more often prefer intermediate aspirations when the desire for group is strong than when it is weak; members having stronger motives to avoid failure than to achieve success less often prefer intermediate group aspirations when the desire to avoid group failure is weak than when this desire is strong.

Hypothesis 29. After a series of trials, persons having person-oriented motives that are dissonant with group-oriented motives become more tense than members having consonant motives.

Hypothesis 30. During a series of trials, coercion by other group members elicits more avoiding behavior, whereas opportunity to refer one's own behavior to that of other group members elicits more approaching behavior.

Hypothesis 31. Members in groups composed of persons whose motives to succeed are stronger than their motives to avoid failure evaluate the group's performance more accurately than members of groups composed of persons with stronger motives to avoid failure than to achieve success.

Hypothesis 32. Members occupying central group positions are more likely to evaluate their own performances in accord with the group outcome than are members in peripheral positions.

The primary basis for this hypothesis is that members in peripheral positions tend to rate their own performances favorably even if the group performs poorly.

Hypothesis 33. Members evaluate their personal performances more favorably when their group has a history of success than when it has a history of failure.

Hypothesis 34. Group members appraise their personal performances in accord with the quality of the group's performance when the group has a history of success, but evaluate their own performances higher than that of the group when it has a history of failure.

Hypothesis 35. Members evaluate their group more favorably as the strength of Ms increases, regardless of the group's history of success or failure.

Group's Aspiration for a Member

The following assumption and hypotheses consider the determinants of congruence between a member's own aspirations and the ones other group members prefer him or her to have.

Assumption 12. The more aware a member is that his or her actions are instrumental to group achievement, the greater the congruence between the member's aspiration level and the one provided by the group.

Hypothesis 36. The more attractive the group, the greater the congruence between a member's level of aspiration and the one the member perceives that other members desire.

Hypothesis 37. If a member perceives an aspiration to be more important to others, the congruence between his or her own and the group-provided aspiration is greater.

Hypothesis 38. A member's desire to do as well as the group expects is greater if the member's personal activity is more relevant to the group's work.

Hypothesis 39. Congruence between personal and group-proposed aspiration is greater when other group members express a stronger desire for the member to achieve a given level of performance.

Hypothesis 40. The amount of congruence between personal and group-proposed aspiration level is greater if the proposed increase is moderately difficult than if it is extremely difficult.

Zander noted that a person may have both internal and overt levels of aspiration. The *overt* level is the one publicly expressed and the *internal* one is the level privately used as a standard for judging whether a particular performance is a success or failure. Overt and internal levels may be the same or different. In general, it is hypothesized by the theory that overt and internal levels will be more similar and both will be more congruent with levels arising in an external source when the proposed level derives from the group than when it is supported by coercive power.

Hypothesis 41. The congruence between a member's internal level of aspiration and that perceived to be expected by other group members is greater if there exists a referent relationship with them than if there exists a coercive relationship.

Hypothesis 42. On a task assigned by a higher-status person, members more readily encourage one another to avoid the unfavorable consequences of their personal performance when the higher-status person is absent than when he or she is present.

Comment and Evaluation

Of necessity, we have presented the theory of motives and goals in groups in skeletal form. Much of the reasoning that led to the formulation of assumptions and hypotheses is therefore missing from this presentation. In some ways, this represents a disservice to the theory, but we believe most of the hypotheses and propositions are self-explanatory. Missing also is the mass of experimental evidence presented in support of the theory.

The theory represents a major analysis of individual and group motives and goals and the interrelations among them. The theory is internally consistent in that propositions and hypotheses do not contradict one another. However, the various hypotheses do not derive directly from the assumptions and other proposals, and in some cases one or more hypotheses appear to be variations of earlier hypotheses. One also gets the impression that the theory is derived from specific research data that are less than optimally integrated. That is, the various assumptions and hypotheses are not interrelated as completely as one might expect them to be.

Perhaps the greatest problem with the theory is the lack of correspondence between the conceptualization of aspirations and goals. Although Zander makes a clear distinction between them when initially discussing these concepts, there is some confusion when the terms are used in hypotheses. If level of aspiration is neither a goal, a motive, nor a task, one might question the extensive use of the concept in formulating a theory of motives and goals in groups.

The large body of experimental evidence cited to support the theory is impressive and largely supportive of the theory. This may not be surprising, since data from the research were used in developing the theory. What is needed is independent evidence from research designed specifically to test the theory. To date, such research appears to be lacking, although several studies provide data consistent with assumptions about individual motivations and task preferences (e.g., Kukla, 1975; Trope, 1975, 1980; Trope & Brickman, 1975).

In summary, the theory is a reasonably consistent set of hypotheses about important group processes. It agrees quite well with the research conducted by Zander (1971), from which the theory was primarily derived. It should serve as a useful guide for future research, which may be expected to lead to necessary modifications and clarifications of the theory.

A THEORY OF GROUP PRODUCTIVITY

Groups form and continue to exist because they serve some purpose. Social groups form to satisfy needs for affiliation, business persons engage in collective actions to further business interests, work groups are established to complete some task or tasks, and so on. Thus, groups appear to be essential for the satisfaction of human needs. Perhaps it is not surprising, therefore, that there has been a continuing concern for the nature of groups: their social structures, their procedures for achieving goals, the rules that they establish for group members, and other aspects of group process. The theory proposed by Steiner (1972) attempts to explicate the processes that influence the productivity of relatively small, task-oriented groups.

Determinants of Productivity

Steiner states that group performance depends upon three classes of variables: task demands, resources, and process. *Task demands* include the requirements imposed upon the group by the task itself or by the rules governing task performance. For example, task demands are analogous to a set of building plans that describe the structure, the materials, the tools, the steps to be followed in construction, and the way the total process is to be managed. Task demands determine what resources are needed, how much of each for optimal performance, and how resources are to be combined to optimize outcomes.

Resources include all the relevant abilities, skills, tools, and the like that are possessed by persons attempting to perform the task. The distribution of resources in the group is also an important determinant of group productivity. For instance, relevant knowledge may be possessed by one group member or different parts of the required knowledge may be possessed by different members.

The use of resources to meet task demands may take many forms; that is, the procedures that are followed, the steps that are taken, and the like, vary from group to group. The term *process* refers to the steps actually taken by a group when attempting a task. Process includes all those interpersonal and intrapersonal actions that group members engage in, nonproductive as well as productive actions. This is a complex process, including intellectual and communicative activities, actions resulting from personal as well as group motivations, competitive actions, evaluations of others' behaviors and abilities, and a variety of other processes.

Task demands reveal the kinds of resources that are needed, resources possessed by the group determine the group's potential productivity, and process determines the degree to which this potential is realized. (It should be noted that Steiner asserted that these three classes of variables also determine individual productivity, although process is less complex in the case of individual task performance.) According to the theory, actual group productivity is equal to potential productivity minus losses due to faulty process; there is no reference to the possibility that appropriate group processes may increase productivity.

Types of Tasks

In order to identify task demands and use them to predict or explain group productivity, some classification of tasks is necessary. Steiner (1972) provided a "partial typology of tasks" in which tasks are viewed as specifications of the goals and procedures for achieving them.

According to the theory, tasks may be categorized along at least three major dimensions: unitary versus divisible tasks, maximizing versus optimizing tasks, and permitted versus prescribed process. *Unitary* tasks are those in which work assignments make mutual assistance or division of labor impracticable, whereas *divisible* tasks are tasks that can be readily divided into subtasks so that a division of labor is practicable. Tasks that have the goal of achieving as much as possible of something or doing it as quickly as possible are called *maximizing* tasks; those that have the goal of achieving some predetermined best or correct outcome are called *optimizing* tasks. Tasks may also be classified according to permitted and prescribed process, although this is not a dimension of tasks in the usual sense. However, job assignments (tasks) may specify the kinds of processes that are *permitted* (but not required) and also the kinds of processes that are *prescribed*: those that are necessary if maximum success is to be achieved. In theory, a given task may fall into any category or combination of categories; that is, a task may be divisible, maximizing, and vary in permitted/-prescribed process, or divisible, optimizing, and involve only prescribed process.

The most important classification for group productivity appears to be the unitary versus divisible dichotomy. Unitary tasks vary with respect to the ways group members can combine individual products. *Disjunctive* tasks require an either-or decision; that is, the group must choose one alternative from those available and reject all others. *Conjunctive* tasks require that everyone in the group achieve the goal for task completion. *Additive* tasks permit the addition of individual efforts so that the outcome is the result of a combination of individual contributions. *Discretionary* tasks permit the group to choose its own process. Disjunctive, conjunctive, and additive tasks may be either maximizing or optimizing, but discretionary tasks are optimizing tasks.

Group Performance of Unitary Tasks

The group's productivity on unitary tasks depends upon task demands, group member resources, and group process. Part of task demands involves permitted and prescribed processes; hence, productivity will vary with the type of task as well as with the resources of group members and the kinds of processes the group employs. Steiner assumed, first, that group resources could be determined by identifying individual resources and, second, that group process is usually faulty. These assumptions led to the following conclusions about group performances of unitary tasks of various types.

According to the theory, disjunctive-task performance depends upon the most competent group member; if one person in the group can complete the task, the group can complete it. Therefore, potential group productivity is a function of the most competent group member. Consequently, if one knows the proportion of persons in the population that can complete the task and the number of persons in the group, one can predict the percentage of groups that can complete the task by the following formula:

$$\text{Percentage of successful groups} = 100 \, (1 - Q^n)$$

where Q = the proportion of the population who *cannot* complete the task and n = the number of persons in the group (cf., Taylor, 1954; Lorge & Solomon, 1955). As noted earlier, however, actual group performance is expected to be lower than potential performance, due to faulty group processes. Steiner utilized data from experiments comparing individual and group performance to test these ideas (Shaw, 1932; Marquart, 1955). Actual productivity corresponded closely to potential productivity; the experiments revealed little evidence of losses due to faulty group processes.

In contrast, group productivity on conjunctive tasks depends upon the performance of the least competent group member; the task is not complete until everyone in the group has achieved the goal. Therefore, potential group productivity on conjunctive tasks can be estimated from a knowledge of population ability and size of group: the percentage of the group that can complete the task is equal to $100 \, (1 - P^n)$, where P = the proportion of persons in the population that can complete the task and n = the number of persons in the group. Steiner cited a study by Steiner and Rajaratnam (1961) in which the data reported by McCurdy and Lambert (1952) were used to examine theoretical expectations, with results that are consistent with the theory.

Additive tasks permit individual contributions to be summed; therefore, potential group performance should equal the sum of individual group members' productivities. Steiner cited an unpublished study by Ringelmann involving individual and group performances on a rope-pulling task. Either one, two, three, or eight persons pulled on a rope and the forces exerted were determined by a weight-measuring scale. As expected, productivity increased with increasing group size, although increments were less than expected on the basis of average individual output. Presumably some potential was not realized, due to faulty group processes such as poor coordination of individual efforts.

Discretionary tasks permit the group to choose whatever combinatorial rule they wish; hence, the potential productivity of the group is hypothesized to depend upon the processes the group actually employs. The prescribed process depends upon the criterion of success adopted by the group and the distribution of individual resources. Productivity reflects the degree to which group process corresponds to prescribed process.

Group Performance of Divisible Tasks

Divisible tasks are more complex than unitary tasks, and the hypotheses concerning group productivity on such tasks are correspondingly less precise. When a task can be subdivided into subtasks, each of which may be performed by a different person or subgroup, division can usually be accomplished in a variety of ways. Often, however, social and environmental factors make only one division acceptable. Thus, a particular division may be specified or the group may be permitted to choose its own division. In either case, individuals or subgroups must be matched with subtasks. The adequacy of this matching is an important determinant of group productivity, as well as the kind of division that is specified or selected.

If individuals are matched with subtasks, the overall task is usually additive in that the final group product derives from some combination of individual outputs, in which case the predictions concerning group productivity are the same as for unitary additive tasks. Of course, it is possible for the task to require that all subtasks be completed correctly in order for the overall task to be completed. For such tasks, predictions would be the same as for conjunctive unitary tasks.

When subgroups of group members are matched with subtasks, the procedures may be such that the task is either disjunctive, conjunctive, additive, or discretionary. That is, subtasks and the way subtask outcomes are combined to a single group product may involve any of these four activities. However, Steiner suggested that in most cases the combinatory process is disjunctive: if one member can integrate subtask outcomes, the group can do so.

When division and matching are specified, potential productivity depends upon the appropriateness of the imposed role structure and the resources of the particular members assigned to particular roles. Thus, actual productivity will be lower than potential productivity to the degree that members do not enact their assigned roles as effectively as their resources permit. When division or matching is unspecified, potential productivity depends upon organizational decisions and role performance. Theoretically, potential productivity can be perfect if the best decisions are made about division and matching and if members enact assigned roles to the best of their ability. If any one of these processes is less than optimum, group productivity will fall below this potentially perfect level.

Effects of Group Size

According to the theory, the effects of group size on group productivity can be predicted with precision if one knows how the relevant resources are distributed in the population from which group members are drawn and the type of task the group is attempting. For instance, if random selection of group members and a disjunctive task are assumed, it follows from the theory that potential group productivity (and hence actual productivity) will tend to increase at a decelerating rate with increases in group size. A study by Ziller (1957) was cited to support this expectation. When the task is conjunctive, productivity is predicted to decrease at a decelerating rate as group size increases. If the task is additive, the relationship between productivity and group size is expected to be positive and linear. The Ringelmann study cited earlier supports this prediction.

When tasks are divisible, predictions regarding the effects of group size on productivity are more complex and more difficult to infer. Steiner states that the relationship should typically be positive and curvilinear.

Group Composition and Group Productivity

It is obvious that groups may be composed of persons with differing resources, but it is also important to note that group composition may be heterogeneous or homogeneous with respect to resources. Heterogeneity with respect to task-relevant resources tends to generate high levels of potential productivity when the task is disjunctive and low levels when the task is conjunctive and is irrelevant when the task is additive.

Heterogeneity with respect to dispositional qualities is more difficult to relate to potential productivity. According to the theory, the effects of this kind of heterogeneity should depend upon task demands. When no role system is available, heterogeneity may facilitate its development. It may also facilitate or inhibit matching persons and subtasks when the task is divisible.

Motivation and Group Productivity

Steiner noted that productivity may be influenced by the motivations of group members. He gave special attention to the effects of the presence of other people. He cited numerous studies on the effects of social facilitation (Allport, 1924; Zajonc, 1966), cooperation and competition (e.g., Deutsch, 1949; Hammond & Goldman, 1961), and cohesiveness (Thibaut & Kelley, 1959; March & Simon, 1958) on group productivity. He concluded, however, that research data do not permit unequivocal conclusions about the effects of these variables on group productivity.

Comment and Evaluation

The theory of group productivity provides a coherent set of propositions and hypotheses about the way task characteristics interact with other variables to determine potential group productivity. These proposals generate many testable hypotheses and provide an excellent guide to research. The theory appears to be both internally and externally consistent and agrees well with data available at the time the theory was formulated. On the other hand, the treatments of the effects of group composition and motivation are weak, and one gets the impression that they are included because they "ought" to be. The theory provides few precise predictions about the effects of these variables on group productivity.

One questionable aspect of the theory is the failure to recognize that group interaction may increase actual productivity relative to the potential predicted from individual productivity and task characteristics. It is possible that such an "assembly effect bonus" (Collins & Guetzkow, 1964) can occur, and research data demonstrate that it sometimes does occur (e.g., Yuker, 1955; Shaw & Ashton, 1976).

The theory apparently has not yet generated much research, perhaps because it is relatively new. In addition to the Shaw and Ashton study cited above, only one article could be located that was derived more or less directly from Steiner's theory. This article reported two experiments employing the Ringelmann rope-pulling task (Ingham, Levinger, Graves, & Peckham, 1974). The first experiment, using individuals and groups ranging in size from two to six persons, attempted to replicate the Ringelmann study. Performance dropped significantly as size increased up to three persons, but the addition of a fourth, fifth, or sixth group member produced insignificant decrements. That is, the relationship was curvilinear rather than linear as predicted by the theory. The second experiment attempted to eliminate coordination effects; the same curvilinear effect was found. Thus, research based upon the theory provide only partial support for it.

A CONTINGENCY MODEL OF LEADERSHIP EFFECTIVENESS

The group member who occupies a central position in the group's social structure exerts a strong influence on group process and productivity. The occupant of the most central position in the group is usually called the group leader. Consequently, the study of leaders and leadership behavior has been an important concern of social psychologists for many years. The contingency model of leadership effectiveness (Fiedler, 1964, 1967) represents an attempt to specify the determinants of effective leadership and the relationships among them. It was an outgrowth of many years of experimentation on leadership and group effectiveness. The program of research was directed largely toward the identification of the personal characteristics that distinguish the effective leader from other leaders. The general approach adopted by Fiedler was based on the assumption that the leader's perceptions of coworkers reflect task-relevant attitudes that influence group interaction and performance. Measures of interpersonal perception were first developed for research on psychotherapeutic relations (Fiedler, 1951) and later adapted to the study of leadership. Studies of the relationship between measures of interpersonal perception and group effectiveness yielded apparently contradictory results; the contingency model represents an attempt to reconcile these data. The general theoretical model assumes that the type of leader that will be most effective depends upon the favorability of the situation to the leader, which in turn depends upon affective leader-group relations, task structure, and the leader's position power.

Definition of Terms

The key terms used in Fiedler's (1964) analysis include *group, leader,* and *effectiveness.* Specific definitions of these key terms were presented to clarify the discussion of the theory.

Group The definition of group was based upon Campbell's (1958) criteria for determining whether an aggregate constitutes an entity. Thus a group was defined as any set of individuals who are similar, who are in proximity, and who share a common fate on task-relevant events. The intent was to include those groups in which members perceive themselves as interdependent in achieving a common goal and to exclude those groups in which members work individually on a task (coacting groups).

Leader The leader was defined as the group member who directs and coordinates task-relevant group activities. Fiedler recognized that leadership functions are shared, but he was concerned only with the one person who performs the traditional leadership role. To be considered a leader, the individual must either be appointed by an agent of a larger organization of which the group is a part, be elected by the group, or be identified as the most influential member on task-relevant questions on a sociometric questionnaire.

Effectiveness The leader's effectiveness was defined in terms of his or her group's performance in achieving group goals. Implicit in this statement is the assumption that the more nearly the group achieves its goal, the more effective is the leader. It is assumed further that task-relevant abilities and skills of members of different groups are similar.

Styles of Leadership and Group Effectiveness

A considerable amount of evidence has accumulated showing that leadership style is related to group process. The early study by Lewin and his associates (Lewin, Lippitt, & White, 1939) revealed dramatic differences in behavioral and emotional aspects of group process as a consequence of autocratic, democratic, or laissez-faire styles of leadership. Since that time, two major types of leadership behavior have been studied, variously labeled as autocratic versus democratic, authoritarian versus nonauthoritarian (Shaw, 1955), supervisory versus participatory (Preston & Heintz, 1949), task-oriented versus human relations–oriented (Katz & Kahn, 1952), directive versus nondirective (Shaw & Blum, 1966), initiation of structure versus consideration (Halpin, 1955), and distant, controlling, managing versus psychologically close, permissive (Fiedler, 1964). Experimental findings concerning the effects of these two styles of leadership have been inconsistent. Some investigators reported autocratic, directive, controlling leaders to be more effective, but the opposite was sometimes found, and often no statistically significant differences were observed.

Since Fiedler's assumption was that interpersonal perception reflects attitudes which influence effectiveness, leadership styles were inferred from measures of interpersonal perception. Initially, this measure was the difference between ratings of most and least preferred coworkers, labeled "assumed similarity of opposites" (ASo); later, it was discovered that ASo scores correlated so highly with the rating of least-preferred coworker (LPC) that it could be used alone as a measure of interpersonal orientations.

The LPC Measure   The LPC scale consists of a set of eight-point, bipolar items of the semantic differential type (Osgood, Suci, & Tannenbaum, 1957). The ends of the rating items are anchored by bipolar adjectives, such as pleasant-unpleasant, friendly-unfriendly, rejecting-accepting, cooperative-uncooperative, distant-close, and similar adjective pairs. The respondent is asked to think of all the people with whom he or she has ever worked. Then the respondent is asked to describe the one person considered to be the least desirable, using the LPC adjective pairs. The LPC score is the mean rating of the selected coworker. The high-LPC person perceives the least-preferred coworker in a relatively favorable manner and derives major satisfaction from successful interpersonal relationships, whereas the low-LPC person perceives the least-preferred coworker in very unfavorable terms and derives major satisfaction from task performance (Fiedler, 1967).

According to the theory, high-LPC leaders are concerned with establishing good interpersonal relations and thereby gaining prominence and self-esteem. Low-LPC leaders are primarily concerned with achieving success on assigned tasks, even if this means poor interpersonal relations with other group members. Differences in the behaviors of high- and low-LPC leaders become most evident when satisfaction of their respective primary needs are threatened. Under conditions of threat, the high-LPC leader will increase interpersonal interaction in an attempt to improve relations with other group members; the low-LPC leader will interact in order to complete the task successfully. Both kinds of leaders will be concerned with the task and also with interpersonal relations, but they do so for different reasons. When leaders have their primary needs satisfied (i.e., there is no threat to primary-need satisfaction), the high-LPC leader will devote relatively more time to task completion and the low-LPC leader will be relatively more concerned with interpersonal relations.

The LPC scores of leaders were related to measures of leadership effectiveness in numerous studies, with inconsistent results. Correlations ranged from $-.69$ (Fiedler, 1954) to $+.60$ (Fiedler, 1955). In the latter study, however, it was found that the direction of the relationship depended upon the leader's affective relations with key group members. Other studies (Gerard, 1957; Anderson & Fiedler, 1964) revealed that leaders in powerful positions behaved differently from those in less powerful positions. This complex set of data provided the stimulus for the development of the contingency model.

Task-Situation Dimensions

The development of the contingency model involved two steps: a description of task-situation dimensions and the specification of the relation between these dimensions and leadership effectiveness. In attempting to identify the significant dimensions of the task situation, Fiedler assumed that the crucial factors would be those that determine whether the situation is favorable or unfavorable to the leader. A favorable situation was described as one in which the group environment makes it easy for the leader to influence the members of the group; an unfavorable situation makes it difficult for the leader to influence group members.

Three situational components were postulated as the critical factors determining the favorability of the situation to the leader: the leader's affective relations with group members, the power provided by the position, and the degree of structure of the group task. *Affective leader-group relations* were assumed to have the greatest effect on situation favorability. The leader who is liked and respected can obtain the compliance of the group without exercising power and can act more decisively and with more confidence than the leader who is disliked and rejected by the members of the group. This dimension was operationally defined by bipolar rating scales.

Task structure was asserted to be the second-most-important determinant of favorability. The task may be highly structured in the sense that the goal is clearly specified and procedures for goal achievement are unambiguous. On the other hand, the task may be highly unstructured in that the goal is unclear and there are many paths to the goal. The theory postulates that the more structured the task, the more favorable the situation for the leader. This dimension was operationally defined by ratings of four task dimensions proposed by Shaw (1963). These are *decision verifiability* (the degree to which the correctness of the decision can be demonstrated either logically or by appeal to authority), *goal clarity* (the degree to which the requirements of the task are known to the group), *goal-path multiplicity* (the degree to which the task can be accomplished by a variety of procedures), and *solution multiplicity* (the degree to which there is more than one "correct" solution).

The *power position* of the leader was the third and least-important determinant of favorability. This refers to the leader's control over rewards and sanctions, authority over group members, and degree to which he or she is supported by the organization of which the group is a part. The powerful leader may be able to influence the group even if the affective leader-group relations are poor. The more powerful the leader's position, the more favorable the situation is for the leader. This dimension was defined operationally by a checklist of items such as "leader can recommend punishments and rewards."

The Favorability Continuum

Fiedler assumed that any particular group situation could be ordered along a favorability continuum, ranging from those that are highly favorable to the leader to those that are highly unfavorable to the leader. This continuum derives from the three task-situation dimensions discussed above. The relation of the three dimensions to the favorability continuum was based on the assumption that affective leader-group relations are most important, task structure next-most important, and leader power position least important as a determinant of favorability. Therefore, the most favorable situation is one in which the affective leader-member relations are good, the task is highly structured, and the leader power position is strong. The most unfavorable situation is one in which the leader-member relations are poor, the task is unstructured, and the leader power position is weak. (Fiedler suggested that an even more unfavorable situation might exist if leader-member relations are *very* poor, the task structured, and the power position strong.)

Leadership Style and Favorability

In order to determine the relationship between leadership style and effectiveness as a function of the favorability of the situation for the leader, Fiedler classified the group situations in a great many experiments that he had conducted. He then plotted the correlations between leader LPC scores and measures of group effectiveness as a function of situational favorability. The results are shown in Figure 13-1. On the basis of these data, he concluded that the style of leadership that is most effective is contingent upon the favorableness of the group-task situation. Managing, controlling, task-oriented leaders are more effective when the group-task situation is either very favorable or very unfavorable for the leader; permissive, considerate, relationship-oriented leaders are more effective when the group-task situation is of intermediate favorability.

According to Fiedler (1967), this "contingency model" generally fits our everyday experiences. When the leader has power, is on good terms with followers, and the task is clearly structured, the group is ready to be directed and willing to be told what to do. Similarly, when the situation is highly unfavorable, permissive leadership may lead to disintegration of the group. Only moderately favorable or moderately unfavorable situations call for considerate, relation-oriented leadership. In this case, the members must be free to offer new ideas and suggestions, and the leader typically cannot force group members to comply with his wishes.

Strengths and Weaknesses of the Theory

Perhaps the major strength of the contingency model is that is specifies conditions under which different leadership behaviors may be expected to be

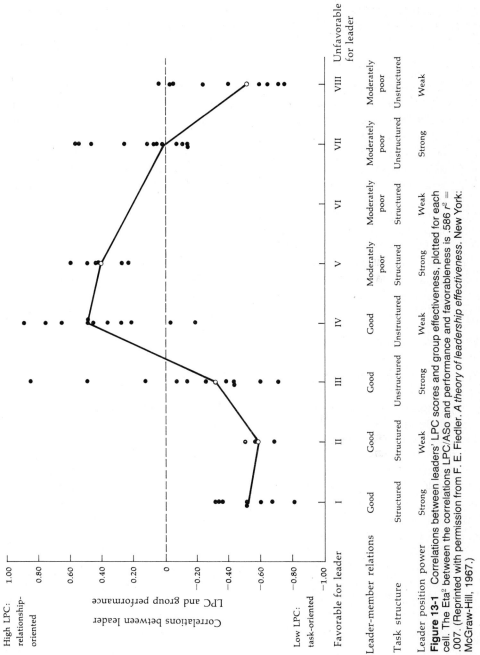

Figure 13-1 Correlations between leaders' LPC scores and group effectiveness, plotted for each cell. The Eta[2] between the correlations LPC/ASo and performance and favorableness is .586 r^2 = .007. (Reprinted with permission from F. E. Fiedler. *A theory of leadership effectiveness*. New York: McGraw-Hill, 1967.)

effective. Previous theoretical analyses have suggested that leadership is a complex phenomenon that is influenced by variables such as personal attributes and situational factors, but relations among variables were not clearly indicated. The contingency theory begins to specify *how* these factors are interrelated in their influence on leadership effectiveness. The theory is logically consistent and agrees with available data concerning leadership behavior.

A second strong point is that it yields testable hypotheses. Since the theory was first conceived in 1962, Fiedler and his associates have conducted several experiments designed to test the theory; they have had generally supportive results. For example, the predicted relationship between leader LPC score and group performance as a function of favorability was found in studies of the following samples: Belgian naval personnel (Fiedler, 1966), American graduate students (Anderson, 1964), Army and Navy ROTC cadets (Meuwese & Fiedler, 1965), members of the ROTC Special Forces Company and the Arab Student Association at the University of Illinois (Chemers, Fiedler, Lekhyananda, & Stolurow, 1966), and members of industrial and business organizations (Hunt, 1967). A study by Shaw and Blum (1966) demonstrated that the theory is not limited to leader characteristics measured by LPC scores. They found that leaders instructed to play a directive role were more effective when the task was highly structured, whereas leaders instructed to play a nondirective role were more effective when the task was less structured (presumably a moderately favorable condition for the leader). Several relatively recent studies also yielded data supporting the theory (Hardy, 1971; Chemers & Skrzypek, 1972; Chemers, Rice, Sundstrom, & Butler, 1975; Jurma, 1978).

The major weakness of the theory is the definition of the favorability continuum. Although the experimental evidence generally supports the theory, there are wide differences between groups classified alike with regard to their favorability for the leader, suggesting that the three group-task dimensions are imperfectly measured or there are other variables which are relevant to the favorability continuum. Both of these are probably true, but the latter is of more serious consequence for the theory. (Of course, the theory itself may be incorrect, but the evidence is sufficiently strong to make this interpretation unattractive.)

Fiedler (1967) pointed to one limitation that is related to the classification of groups. He suggested that situations in which the leader-member affective relations are extremely poor are probably very unfavorable to the leader even when the task is structured and the leader's power position is strong. The description of the favorability continuum does not provide for this possibility. Furthermore, such group situations rarely occur naturally, probably because such groups disintegrate; therefore, there is little evidence on this point.

In general, the theory has good support from experimental work and is probably the best theory of leadership proposed to date. Extensions of the theory to problems of leadership training are promising (Fiedler, 1972; Chemers et al., 1975) and merit further consideration.

certain restrictions on coverage are rather necessary liabilities of textbook writing, it is our opinion that the theories represented in this text exemplify the primary models of thought in social psychology.

We would like to begin our consideration of what we are referring to as "single-principle" theories by noting that the frameworks to be presented here are not to be regarded as either leftover misfits or theories of lesser importance to social psychologists than those already presented. Indeed, at least two of the perspectives to be presented have been quite pivotal frameworks for researching phenomena in social psychology (i.e., Schachter's two-factor theory of emotion and Byrne's attitude-attraction paradigm). Further, the designation of these perspectives as ones constituted upon a single principle should not be regarded in a pejorative sense, as a reflection on either the scope or the importance of the theories. Nevertheless, given the disparity of content and focus of these theories, the fact that *each proceeds from a single overarching principle* to hypotheses that are derivatives of that principle allows for at least one cogent organizational basis for collecting them in a single chapter.

Five theories will be presented in this chapter. However, several frameworks related to or alternative to these theories will also be *briefly* considered when appropriate. The five theories are:

1 A theory of fear of success
2 A two-factor theory of emotion
3 A perspective on obesity-prone behavior
4 An achievement attribution viewpoint
5 The attitude similarity–attraction paradigm

These theories will be described in a rather systematic schematized form. Each will be discussed in four sections. These are: (*a*) purpose of the theory; (*b*) the guiding principle; (*c*) the hypotheses or postulates derived from the principle; and (*d*) a general evaluation of the framework, including a selective evaluation of research evidence, and brief consideration of related perspectives (when appropriate). The first two of these theories will be presented in a comparatively expanded form since they bear upon phenomena of broad significance to social-psychological analysis (i.e., sex-role–constrained achievement strivings and the experience and self-perception of emotion). The latter three theories will be given much briefer coverage. One deals with a limited range of phenomena (i.e., Schachter's obesity framework). Another constitutes a specific application of a more general and already presented framework (i.e., Weiner's achievement attribution model). The third of these is based on an extremely simple principle of social relationships that has been frequently articulated by psychologists, philosophers, and social thinkers (Byrne's attitude-attraction paradigm). It should be made clear to the reader that the length of our resulting presentations should not be taken as an index of either the value or the adequacy of the theory. Clearly all three of the theories subject to our abbreviated analysis have been frequently cited and researched by social psychologists.

A THEORY OF FEAR OF SUCCESS

Purpose

Matina Horner's (1968, 1972, 1974) model of fear of success derived from her observation that highly competent females, when confronted with standard achievement tasks or when on the threshold of culturally desirable attainments, appear to evidence both anxiety and a decrement in performance. Horner developed the construct of fear of success in an attempt to account for this and related phenomena. She reasoned that a theory of achievement motivation particular to women was required since the primary expectancy-value models of achievement offered by personologists (e.g., the McClelland-Atkinson theory) could not adequately explain the "success anxieties" of women. A second purpose of the model was perhaps a more implicit and politically relevant one. That is, if the simultaneous negative operation of system constraints and self-produced anxieties on the attainment of talented females was taken as given, it was likely that female individuals possessed of high ability would typically be lost resources to the culture. Given this latter assumption, Horner proceeded to endeavor to understand the achievement motivation of women through her fear-of-success model.

The Guiding Principle

Horner proposed that there exists a fundamental difference between males and females in the structure of their achievement motives. She argued that the achievement behavior of women was not comprehensible when examined from the purview of typical models of achievement behavior. These models, she proposed, were descriptive of only male achievement strivings. Before presenting the principle guiding her reconstruction of an expectancy-value achievement model to accommodate female achievement behavior, it is important to briefly review the general structure of the Atkinson-McClelland model of achievement to which her revised principle was added.

The so-called Atkinson-McClelland model of achievement motivation (cf. Atkinson & Litwin, 1960) proposed that in the course of socialization people acquire two achievement-related motives—each of which might be regarded as a stable personality trait. The first of these motives, *the motive to achieve success* (Ms), refers to the tendency in each of us to seek success and its positive affective consequences (e.g., self-satisfaction and pride). The second of these motives, *the motive to avoid failure* (Maf), refers to our tendencies to avoid the negative affective consequences of achievement failure (e.g., shame, rejection, and humiliation). Each individual is presumed to possess different levels of each of these motive characteristics. Since these motives have somewhat independent origins, it is theoretically possible that a person might be either high or low on both motives simultaneously. However the theorists (cf. Atkinson & Litwin, 1960) were primarily interested in the achievement behavior consequences of two kinds of individuals. One kind of individual was labeled as *high in need achievement* and was characterized by high Ms and low Maf. The second kind of individual of interest to the theorists was labeled as *low in need achievement* and was characterized by high Maf and low Ms. The pivotal distinction between these two types of individuals is that the first (Ms > Maf) strives to maximize the potential gains of successful achievement, while the second (Maf > Ms) strives to minimize the noxious consequences of failure. What will become noteworthy when we consider Horner's addendum to the Atkinson-McClelland motive types is that the traditional achievement motivation perspective attributes univalent affective consequences to success (i.e., pleasure and pride) and to failure (i.e., shame, guilt, and humiliation).

The primary goal of the motive-based achievement model is to understand and predict achievement behavior. In the interest of this goal, this perspective, through both constructive and mathematical modeling, attempts to account for the disparate achievement behaviors and choices that might differentiate failure-avoiders from success-approachers. A direct and overarching prediction of the model is that people high in need achievement will tend to engage in tasks which "test" their abilities, while people low in need for achievement tend to avoid tasks that test their abilities. This prediction gives rise to two situation-specific variables which coact with motive type to produce achievement behavior—*expectancy* and *value*. In this model, expectancy is defined in terms of the individual's perception of the subjective probabilities of success (Ps) and failure (Pf) on achievement tasks. Value is defined as the incentive value or attractiveness of success (Is) or unattractiveness of failure (If). These two situation-specific properties are not construed to be independent, but instead the positive incentive value of a task is viewed as an inverse function of the probability of success on a task. In short, the less probable success, the more "valuable" it is to the actor.

In combining these variables, Atkinson maintained that "the strength of the motivation to perform some task is assumed to be a multiplicative function of the strength of the motive, the expectancy that the act will have as its consequence the attainment of an incentive and the value of the incentive" (Atkinson & Feather, 1966; see Zander in Chapter 13 for a related perspective). The sum of approach (Ms × Ps × Is) and avoidant (Maf × Pf × If) tendencies was assumed to determine achievement behavior in any particular achievement situation. One of the primary predictions to fall out of this theoretical perspective is that tasks of moderate difficulty (where Ps and Pf are close to .50) will be most likely to arouse the dominant achievement motive of the individual. Those individuals dominated by success approach (Ms) will prefer and seek out tasks of moderate difficulty, while those dominated by failure avoidance (Maf) will prefer tasks of either very high or very low difficulty and avoid tasks of moderate difficulty. Put more simply, individuals motivated to maximize the pleasure of success will prefer "true" achievement tests to sure bets or tasks in which luck or task difficulty alone are likely to determine outcome. Individuals who are seeking to avoid the noxious consequence of failure are likely to wish to avoid tasks that are "true tests of ability."

While this research framework has many more twists and mathematical functions in it, the above adequately describes the theory for purposes of considering Horner's gender-based reformulated principle. Before doing so, it is important to note that the expectancy-value achievement motivation viewpoint has received reasonably consistent experimental support for its major predictions for male subjects. It has been found, for example, that Ms > Maf males are more likely to choose to engage in *achievement* tasks when confronted with a free choice of activities, more likely to prefer tasks of moderate difficulty to easy or very hard tasks, and more likely to persist at such tasks in the face of repetitive failure than are Maf > Ms males (cf. Weiner, Frieze, Kukla, Reed, Rest, & Rosenbaum, 1971). While there has been some controversy about the meaning and stability of these findings, it is not relevant to our current presentation. What is relevant is that the achievement motivation effects which are reasonably well predicted by the model for males, are not clearly evident in the research employing female subjects.

It was this latter observation, along with Horner's more anecdotal perceptions and inferences about the difficulties competent females encounter in achievement circumstances, that led to the proposal of her major theoretical principle. Horner argued that there is a basic and enduring difference between the sexes in their orientation to success. *Whereas males univalently value success (as suggested by the Atkinson-McClelland model) females are ambivalent about achieving successful outcomes.* This led her to further propose that the understanding of female achievement behavior requires the assumption of a third motive, one not discerned in the original expectancy-value model. *Along with possessing motives to approach success (Ms) and avoid failure (Maf), females also possess a motive to avoid success (fear of success, Fs).* She noted that this motive is unconscious and issues from a female-specific socialization process which leads them to anticipate a "loss of femininity" contingent upon traditional success in the culture. This anticipation leads females to become anxious when they approach success, expect a loss of social self-esteem, and presume consequent social rejection.

Since Horner viewed this female-specific fear-of-success motive as originating from a sex-role-specific socialization process, it can be viewed as an instance of anxiety or strain generated by role conflict. That is, the demands imposed by an achieving competitive society on its competent members conflict for competent women with implicit sex-role demands that direct them to be compliant, noncompetitive, and nurturant. As a consequence, achievement circumstances, particularly competitive ones, have the potential for activating both success-approaching and success-avoiding tendencies in women. Horner argues that, in order to understand female achievement behavior, it is necessary to consider both of these orientations toward success. Parenthetically, it is rather easy to classify Horner's theory as a paradigmatic example of social system–mediated *role conflict* (see Chapter 11). In fact it might be easily regarded as a role-related theory, in spite of its embeddedness in the personologic traditions of achievement motivation theory and psychodynamic theory.

Derivative Hypotheses

From this basic principle, which proposed a fear-of-success motive specific to females, Horner derived four hypotheses:

1 The first hypothesis is already stated in the principle itself. That is, *fear of success should be more common among women than among men.* Since the attainment of success is quite congruent in men with male sex-role socialization, there would be no reason to expect an enduring tendency in men to simultaneously seek *and* avoid success.

2 *Fear of success will be greatest in circumstances which amplify the negative consequences of success.* Therefore success should be most threatening to females in *competitive* achievement circumstances in which the *task is male-oriented* and/or in which the *adversary is a male.*

3 *The more competent and able the woman, the stronger the resultant fear-of-success motive.* The reasoning behind this hypothesis is clear. In order for success to be "feared," there must be a reasonable likelihood of attaining it. The irony of this prediction is its implication that the most competent females will be most greatly hampered by fear of success.

4 This hypothesis summarizes the predicted consequences of the arousal of fear-of-success motives in women. *The arousal of the fear-of-success motive occasions the experience of success anxiety in competent women. The result of such success anxiety is to disrupt achievement striving and lead competent females to perform below their ability level on competitive achievement tasks.*

This last hypothesis embodies Horner's prediction about the major dysfunctional consequence of fear of success. This consequence can be considered in the instance of two differentially broad contexts. In the context of the experimental laboratory, success-fearing competent females should perform significantly better in noncompetitive than in competitive circumstances (particularly where the competitor is a male). In the larger societal context, particularly in an achievement-competitive society, very talented females would be expected to fail to live up to their capabilities because of the intrusion of success anxiety. The cultural resources lost and the potential personal anguish derivative of this latter phenomenon lead Horner to attach great importance to the search for the factors mediating and inhibiting female achievement.

General Evaluation of the Fear-of-Success Theory

The fear-of-success theory imposes a potentially important limitation upon the general applicability of expectancy-value achievement motivation models. Its primary proposition creates some difficulty for the researcher interested in studying female achievement behavior because of the assertion that fear of success is an *unconscious* and latent personality trait. While this may indeed characterize the phenomenon of fear of success, it renders its assessment a quite difficult matter. Horner has relied upon the use of a TAT-like projective device for purposes of evaluating the level of the Fs trait in her own subjects. Such projective methodologies, however, are open to concerns about both reliability and validity. While the theory is internally consistent and can be viewed as compatible with the general achievement motivation perspective of Atkinson (Atkinson & Litwin, 1960) in its operative principle, there is at least one logical inconsistency with the theory. As Tresemer (1974) has noted, if fear of success has its major negative impact on high-achieving women of *proven* competence (i.e., Horner's subjects were typically Radcliffe undergraduates—including honors students), then how debilitating could the motive be? That is, the women that had constituted Horner's targeted sample in her research had already attained considerable success in competitive achievement contexts in spite of their apparent propensity to fear success. In fairness to Horner, it may well be that the issue becomes more complex in the arena of occupational attainment than in academic attainment circumstances.

The research literature supporting and/or qualifying Horner's perspective derives from two sources. First of all there is a considerable body of research which examines the competitive behavior of males and females in same-sex and mixed-sex, mixed-motive games (e.g., the prisoner's dilemma game). The consistent general finding of this research is that females tend to experience poorer outcomes and poorer performances at these games when competing against males than when competing against other females. Further, the performance of females in these game circumstances tends to be more affected than that of males by "irrelevant" social factors (e.g., sex of the experimenter, attractiveness of the opponent). These studies (cf. Bedell & Sistrunk, 1973; Benton, 1973; Hottes & Kahn, 1974; Kahn, Hottes, & Davis, 1971; Morgan & Mausner, 1973), while supporting Horner's contention that females tend to experience lowered performance in competitive circumstances with males, give little evidence to suggest that an unconscious fear-of-success motive accounts for such performance decrements. In fact, most of the researchers pursuing these game simulation studies have proposed that lowered female performance in the face of male competition is a primarily conscious, strategic behavior. We will take this issue up briefly when considering perspectives related to Horner's.

A second source of research providing evidence pertinent to Horner's model was initiated by the theorist herself (Horner, 1972). The initial study directly exploring fear of success consisted of two assessments. In the first assessment, male and female subjects were asked to complete a story following the presentation of a verbal lead which described a same-sex individual achieving success in a traditionally male-dominated, competitive endeavor (i.e., medical school). The story completions of the subjects were scored for fear-of-success imagery and subjects were classified as either high or low on the Fs measure. In the second assessment, a subgroup of females from the original sample were given a number of achievement tasks in both a mixed-sex competitive circumstance and a noncompetitive context. Horner reported on two findings relevant to the theory: (1) The incidence of fear-of-success imagery was dramatically higher among females (62 percent) than among males (9 percent). Moreover, fear-of-success imagery tended to be more prevalent among female honor students than among females not enrolled in the honors program. (2) Horner reported that the incidence of performance decrement in the mixed-sex competitive circumstance, when compared to the noncompetitive circumstance, was greater for high- than low-fear-of success females.

While on first consideration it would appear that these findings would tend to support strongly Horner's notions, two factors militate against such a conclusion. First, attempted replications of the story-completion assessment (cf. Tresemer, 1974; Zuckerman & Wheeler, 1975) fail to report either a high incidence of fear of success in women or a sex difference in fear-of-success imagery. Secondly, careful reanalysis of Horner's original data set (cf. Zuckerman & Wheeler, 1975) reveals that her conclusions were a bit premature and not sustained when conceptual problems were accounted for. In addition, studies employing a methodology similar to Horner's tend to support the finding that females in general fare more poorly in mixed-sex competitive performance circumstances than in either same-sex circumstances or noncompetitive situations (e.g., Morgan & Mausner, 1973). However, most of these studies find no relationship between this tendency and premeasured fear of success.

In summary, the empirical support for Horner's model is not particularly strong. However, it is clear that in the process of proposing the model, Horner has helped make prominent an apparently pervasive and reliable tendency for females to perform below their ability levels in competitive achievement circumstances. Because of both the intriguing theoretical ramifications of this pattern of achievement and its importance as a social problem, the theory can be viewed as serving a useful conceptual purpose.

Indeed, several theorists have pursued the question of disrupted female achievement patterns from somewhat different perspectives than Horner. Interested readers are referred to these works if they wish an elaboration of perspectives on female achievement. For purposes of the current presentation we will briefly make note of these related perspectives:

1 *A conscious conflict-impression management perspective.* This perspective largely derives from the mixed-motive competitive game simulations described above. While the predictions made concerning female decrements in mixed-sex competitive circumstances are similar to those of Horner, the bases for these phenomena are viewed differently. Specifically, the notion that "unconscious" success anxiety mediates performance disruptions in women is eschewed, and these disruptions are instead viewed as issuing from the conscious conflicts that women encounter in achievement circumstances. Most particularly these accounts typically propose that females are more responsive than males to the social aspects of competitive situations. As a consequence, they consciously consider both the achievement and social demands (which might conflict) in the course of performance. Frequently, females will strategically and consciously depress performance to achieve satisfactory interaction outcomes and/or manage the impression of their opponent (cf. Kahn, et al., 1971; Bedell & Sistrunk, 1973; Morgan & Mausner, 1973). It is likely that these researchers would argue that female achievement motivation is intruded upon by the same factor of "social interest." Whether one adopts the more psychodynamic view of Horner or the strategic performance depression view of small-group research, one is still attributing causes for female achievement difficulties to the consequences of sex-role socialization.

2 *Gender-nonspecific fear of success.* Canavan-Gumpert, Garner, and

Gumpert (1978) proposed a theory to attempt to account for the phenomenon of fear of success. Like Horner, they viewed this achievement-disruptive phenomenon as unconsciously determined and related to the individual's socialization history. However, unlike Horner, they considered the "success-fearing personality" to be a cross-sexed phenomenon—both men and women might in fact be subject to the untoward motivational effects of fear of success. While such a model does not clearly help to differentially explain the achievement behavior of men and women, it does suggest that achievement motivation theory requires a thorough overhaul. The book which presents their theoretical orientation provides both an interesting and comprehensive review of the research and theory on the motivational dynamics accompanying achievement behavior.

  3 *Expectancy, attribution, and achievement in women.* Deaux (1976) ascribes sex differences in achievement behavior to the differences between men and women in their prebehavioral expectancies for success. Her theoretical model suggests the following sequential pattern: (*a*) Females, because of their socialization in achievement domains, approach achievement tasks with lower levels of confidence in eventual success than males. (*b*) As a consequence, when they succeed, they tend to attribute this success to unstable causes (i.e., luck or effort), whereas males tend to attribute their success to stable causes (i.e., ability). (*c*) Because of the instability of their success attributions, females approach subsequent tasks with continuing low expectancies in spite of prior success. (*d*) Hence the sequence recapitulates, and females sustain their low levels of confidence in their own potentials for positive achievement.

  Presumably such low expectancies will act as self-fulfilling prophecies and therefore intrude upon performance and cause the kinds of performance disruptions alluded to in our coverage of Horner's approach. Deaux's (1976) presentation of this attributional model of achievement disruption in women is quite elaborated and buttressed by an ample consideration of the achievement attribution research literature. This perspective constitutes a very promising application of attribution theory to the understanding of sex differences in achievement behavior.

A TWO-FACTOR THEORY OF EMOTION

Purpose

Stanley Schachter's (1964) theory of emotion was proposed to account for the processes by which the individual proceeds from a generalized state of physiological arousal to a cognition about the nature or cause of that arousal. In other terms, it is a theory which endeavors to understand the self-perception of emotional state.

  As Schachter noted, interest in the individual's recognition of the nature of his/her affective arousal is quite longstanding in psychology. Schachter begins the presentation of his theory with a review of the thought of William James (1890) on the relationship between visceral arousal and the perception of emotional state. James proposed that "the bodily changes follow directly the perception of the exciting fact and that our feelings of the same changes as they occur *is* the emotion" (see Schachter, 1964). A reasonable derivative of this position is that different emotions, for example anger and love, must be accompanied by perceptibly different states of bodily arousal. Schachter, citing some of the data and substance comprising Cannon's (1927, 1929) opposition to the James position, concludes that it is implausible to offer a completely visceral theory of emotion and hew to the proposition that *different* emotions are directly perceivable by the person in terms of different physiological arousal states. For one thing it had been found that complete separation of the viscera from the central nervous system fails to alter emotional behavior. Therefore the kind of link between thought and behavior suggested by the James approach is rendered less plausible. Additionally the viscera consist of slow-reacting and insensitive structures which evidence similar changes when the individual is presumed to be in very different states of emotion (for example, heart-rate might similarly increase in a person when confronted with either a violent physical threat from another or with the erotic approach of a romantic partner).

In short the kind of visceral theory of emotion and our phenomenal experience of it proposed by James is not likely to provide a satisfactory answer to the theoretical questions raised by Schachter. As a consequence Schachter set out to devise a better theory explaining the link between visceral arousal and emotional self-labeling.

It should be noted that Schachter's approach to theorizing about emotion, like his approach to his theories of obesity proneness (reported in the next section of this chapter) and affiliation, is elegant in its simplicity and broad in its implications. In its formulation it is not technically a theory about phenomena that are particular to social psychology—it is indeed a theory in general psychology. Yet, it has stimulated considerable research on labeling and mislabeling processes in social psychology and is compatible with some recent frameworks in attribution theory (particularly Bem's self-perception theory, see Chapter 9, and Festinger's social comparison theory, see Chapter 10).

The Guiding Principle

Schachter proposes as a primary guiding principle of his framework that visceral sympathetic nervous-system arousal is labeled by the individual on the basis of both the characteristics of the precipitating situation and his/her past experience. This principle suggests that, while actual visceral arousal is a necessary precondition for the perception of one's emotional state, it is insufficient to provide the individual with a satisfactory understanding of the specific state of arousal he/she is experiencing. Rather the cognitions which arise from the immediate situation and are interpreted on the basis of past knowledge concerning the "meaning" of different situations guide the individual in understanding his/her specific emotional state.

Derivative Theoretical Hypotheses

From the basic principle of emotional self-labeling described above, Schachter offered 3 derivative hypotheses:

> **1** *To the extent that cognitive factors are potent determiners of emotional states, it could be anticipated that precisely the same state of physiological arousal could be labeled "joy" or "fury" or any of a great diversity of emotional labels, depending upon the cognitive aspects of the situation* (Schachter, 1964).

This proposition highlights the nonspecificity of peripheral arousal and indicates the preeminent role of the individual's cognitive appraisal of the situation in his/her experience of emotional state. While one might argue that such a proposal renders emotional self-perceptions as quite arbitrary, it is important to remember that in most (but certainly not all) instances, the situation provides reasonably veridical cues about the instigators of our bodily feelings.

> **2** If the individual can explain his/her state of physiological arousal by a satisfactory and complete explanation (e.g., I am aroused because I have been given a shot of adrenaline), his/her need to evalute the arousal state is low and a cognitive appraisal of the immediate situation is unlikely to occur.

This proposition presumes that penetrating states of arousal require an evaluative appraisal by the individual. It is this need to evaluate initially poorly understood arousal states that promotes the kind of cognitive appraisal of the immediate situation which gives rise to emotional self-labeling. However, if an explanation is readily available which is sufficient to account for arousal without situational appraisal, the need to evaluate the situation will be vitiated.

> **3** The experience of the state of physiological arousal is a necessary condition giving rise to emotional self-labeling. As Schachter noted, *"given the same cognitive circumstances, the individual will react emotionally or describe his feelings as emotions only to the extent that he experiences a state of physiological arousal."*

General Evaluation of Schachter's Framework on Emotion

As we have noted, Schachter's theory is best regarded as a general framework in psychology which attempts to explain the dynamics of the relationship between visceral physiological arousal and the experience of emotion. Nevertheless, while it preceded the current upswing in attributional theorizing and research, it could also be viewed as a special application of attribution principles to the self-perception of emotion. One could easily reframe Schachter's major propositions in the general context of either correspondent inference theory or the ANOVA cube model (see Chapter 9). Indeed, one critical source which Bem (1972) cited for his reformulation of self-perception theory in attributional terms was Schachter's two-factor theory and the research which followed from it. More recently, Zillman (1976) has reconstructed Schachter's theory of emotion in explicitly attributional terms.

It should now be clear to the reader that the "two factors" spoken of in the designation of the theory are: (1) the fact of physiological arousal and (2) the resulting process of cognitive appraisal leading to emotional self-labeling.

Schachter's concise model comprises an internally consistent theoretical account of the relationship between these two factors. At the time of its proposal more than 15 years ago it was the most extensive consideration of the arousal–self-labeling link attempted since the classic works of James (1890) and Cannon (1929). Currently, it is probably not a serious contender as a theory of emotional process. Recent advances in biological psychology have directed theorizing about emotion toward the understanding of processes of neurochemical transmission at the central-nervous-system level. Nevertheless, the theory remains a useful organizing framework for the study of the self-perception of emotions and it has spawned some interesting derivative approaches (Valins, 1966; Zillman, 1976). In addition, Schachter's peripheral theory of emotion is still generative of research-based controversy (cf. Maslach, 1979; Zimbardo & Marshall, 1979; Schachter & Singer, 1979).

The research testing this theory's major propositions is intriguing and evocative, but not entirely supportive. An excellent review of this work and a thoughtful analysis of the Schachterian theory of emotion is provided by Zillman (1976). The reader interested in exploring further the ramifications of the two-factor model and related perspectives is heartily directed to Zillman's paper.

For purposes of this presentation a brief account of the Schachter and Singer (1962) study should illustrate the typical experimental paradigm invoked to test the two-factor model. In this study, three variables were manipulated. First of all subjects were administered a subcutaneous dose of either epinephrine (a drug inducing peripheral arousal) or a placebo saline solution. Secondly those subjects administered epinephrine were *either* told that they would experience arousing side effects *or* they were uninformed of the drug's effects *or* they were misinformed about the drug's effects (i.e., they were told that they would experience symptoms which are not typically induced by epinephrine). Those subjects administered the placebo were given the same information treatment as the epinephrine uninformed subjects. Finally, for the third manipulation a confederate of the experimenter who had presumably been administered the same drug as the subject was ushered into a waiting room with the subject. This confederate either acted elated and euphoric *or* angry. It is clear that the epinephrine induction manipulated the *arousal state* of the subject (a test of proposition 3 from the theory). The information given concerning the action of the drug either provided the subject with a sufficient explanation for his arousal state or not (to test proposition 2 of the theory). The confederate's behavior constituted the situational cue to be employed by the subject in assessing his own emotional state when an alternative explanation was not clearly provided (thereby testing proposition 1 in the theory).

The results of the study provided reasonable support for all three propositions. Proposition 1 was supported by the finding that, following an injection of epinephrine, uninformed subjects (having no explanation for the arousal state) reported feeling elated when exposed to the "euphoric" confederate and angry when exposed to the "angry" confederate. Proposition 2 was supported by the finding that epinephrine-injected subjects informed about the source of their arousal were rather unresponsive to the cognitive manipulations of affect portrayed by the confederate. However, this latter effect was primarily evident for "anger" and not for "euphoria." Proposition 3 was given qualified support. for, while placebo subjects did evidence some response to the confederate manipulation, it was not as strong as that of epinephrine induced subjects. Further, Schachter convincingly assigned the unexpected emotional reactions of placebo subjects to the effects of artifactual "self-arousal" processes.

A number of related studies invoking similarly manipulative research paradigms (e.g., Schachter and Wheeler, 1962; Nisbett and Schachter, 1966) have demonstrated that our self-perceived emotional states and our emotional behaviors following arousal are not likely to be derivative of *specific* somatic states for each specific emotion or class of emotion. Further these studies have demonstrated that it is plausible to suppose that the individual does indeed rely on environmental cues in arriving at such self-perceived emotions and in engaging in emotion-specific behaviors. In addition to the research directly exploring Schachter's two-factor theory, there are a number of studies of interesting derivative principles. The most noteworthy of these have examined the phenomenon of misattribution of emotion and its potential "therapeutic" consequences (cf. Ross, Rodin, & Zimbardo, 1969). The proposition governing such studies is that, if it is the case that aroused subjects, unaware of the true source of arousal, are susceptible to environmental cues signaling the specific nature of that arousal, then it follows that the bogus manipulation of environmental cues could cause them to misattribute their arousal to sources which had not actually given rise to it (e.g., a subject might attribute subtly manipulated fear to anger if anger elevating stimuli are simulated by experimental or therapeutic operations). The results of the investigations predicated on this derived proposal have tended to lend it reasonable support.

Despite both the theoretical appeal of Schachter's framework and the data in its support, both Leventhal (1974) and Zillman (1976) have forcefully argued the implausibility and low empirical likelihood of one of the theory's major propositions. Specifically, Schachter's portrayal of the aroused individual as unclear about the source of arousal and, thus, in a posture impelling cognitive appraisal and epistemic search for explanation, has been seriously questioned.

Leventhal's (1974) criticism is focused upon a conceptual reevaluation of the experimental manipulations characteristic of the research in support of the two-factor theory. In brief, he has argued that the "lack of information" and "misinformation" manipulations in the Schachter and Singer study as well as in related studies (e.g., Ross, Rodin, & Zimbardo) had *themselves* aroused affects in the subjects by rendering them uncertain and thus making them vulnerable to suggestion. The uncertainty experienced by the subject inheres in the unexpectedness of the bodily arousal. As Zillman (1976) concisely reports, "Leventhal notes that in the Schachter-Singer experiment the aroused, bewildered, and suggestible subject at first simply followed his inclination to *imitate* the stooge's behavior, then *expressed* similar feelings, and finally came to *experience* the feelings he expressed" (p. 349). This reinterpretation of the Schachter-Singer conditions is a compelling alternative to the interpretation suggested by the two-factor theory itself.

Zillman (1976) offers a similar caution about Schachter's theory, noting that the evidence is weak for the "epistemic" search suggested by Schachter in the case of nonspecific emotional arousal. As well as founding this perspective on the questionable empirical support for Schachter's notion, Zillman went on to provide a compelling and related conceptual critique of the embattled epistemic search proposition. In brief, Zillman argued that, in many instances of arousal, responses are immediate, unlearned, and unlikely therefore to be guided by a mediating cognitive appraisal. In keeping to this final criticism, Zillman proposed an alternative "three-factor" model of emotion. Zillman's third factor, labeled a *dispositional factor,* was appended to reconstructed versions of Schachter's two factors. The dispositional factor is described in terms of the motor aspects of emotion-aroused behavior that are either reflexive (e.g., startle reactions) or learned (e.g., phobias). These responses were viewed as unmediated and were incorporated into an elaborated model of emotion, subsuming Schachter's portrayal as a particular instance of emotion reactions. The reader is directed to Zillman's (1976) proposal of this model of emotion attribution for a comprehensive account.

In a final note, one additional framework on emotion, closely aligned to Schachter's, has generated research interest among social psychologists. Valins (1966) and Nisbett and Valins (1972) proposed that *actual* physiological arousal preceding emotional self-labeling, described by Schachter, may be a sufficient but unnecessary condition for the self-labeling process. They noted that a physiologically unaroused subject who is led to *think* she/he is aroused (e.g., by giving false heart-rate feedback) is equally susceptible to the kinds of effects noted by Schachter's model. While this proposal has received empirical support, it suffers from the same limitations that Zillman and Leventhal have located in Schachter's model.

A PERSPECTIVE ON OBESITY-PRONE BEHAVIOR

Purpose

The initial suggestion of Schachter's concern with the phenomenon of obesity-prone behavior appeared in the final paragraphs of his presentation of the two-factor theory of emotion (Schachter, 1964).

He observed that "if it is plausible that the labels attached to feeling states are cognitively, situationally, or socially determined, it becomes a distinct possibility that an uncommon and inappropriate label can be attached to a feeling state" (Schachter, 1964). The reader will notice that this proposal of Schachter's is nearly identical to the "misattribution" derivative of his theory, briefly described earlier. Indeed, Schachter's earliest proposal about obesity implied that overeating in obese individuals is likely to result from their tendency to misattribute a wide array of emotional arousal experiences to the state of "hunger." A similar point was more extensively treated by Hilde Bruch (1973).

From this initial point of origin, Schachter (1971; Schachter & Rodin, 1974) went on to propose a theory exploring the sources of differential general behavior and eating behavior in obese individuals. The purpose of his theory was to discern whether or not the obese could be described in terms of their arousal in the face of eating-eliciting cues differently than normal-weight individuals. In articulating this theory, he departed a bit from his above proposition, derived from the theory of emotion. This then renders the theory as a contribution that offers more than a simple application of Schachter's emotional-labeling theory.

In the subsequent several paragraphs we will provide a *brief* account of this theory. We begin by considering the closely aligned principles and hypotheses of the framework.

Principles and/or Hypotheses

The primary principles in Schachter's (1971; Schachter & Rodin, 1974) theory of obesity are embodied in the first two hypotheses guiding the approach.

1 Obese persons have more limited access to, and are therefore less influenced in their eating behavior by, internal physiological-visceral cues, such as gastric motility and blood sugar–level indicators. Another way of stating the hypothesis is that, for the obese, eating is not as likely as for normal-weight individuals to be determined by an internal hunger state.

The second hypothesis can be viewed as complementary to but somewhat independent of the first:

2 The eating behavior of the obese is more likely than that of normals to be determined by a range of *external* cues associated with eating. Examples of such cues include the taste quality, accessibility, and visual attractiveness of food, the time of day, and the like.

These two hypotheses taken together constitute Schachter's primary explanation for why the obese are obese. That is, obese people overeat because their hyperreactivity to food cues in a food-rich world is unlikely to be moderated by internal, biological cues to satiation.

By conjoining the implications of these two hypotheses, Schachter derived a distinct stylistic quality which he attributed to the obese and labeled *obese externality*. The third hypothesis of the framework is a later derivative and extends this obese-external style to explain the obese individual's responsiveness to stimuli other than food.

3 He proposed that the hypersensitivity to food cues in the obese is a particular derivative of a *general response disposition* (of presumably early origin), which is pertinent to a wide range of cognitive and perceptual cues.

4 Finally in a somewhat related but independent proposition about the determinants of obese externality, Schachter and Rodin (1974) likened the obese person's behavior to that of rats who were inflicted with surgically induced midbrain lesions. It would not be appropriate to refer to this last proposition as a hypothesis, but Schachter and Rodin, early on, suspected that it was plausible that the hyperresponsivity of the obese might be derivative of similar midbrain dysfunctions. Indeed, in some of their research they had found that obese humans and lesioned rats behave somewhat similarly in response to food. It is worth noting here that medical researchers (e.g., Silverstone, 1974; Greenwood & Johnson, 1973) view this last proposition as rather implausible.

General Evaluation

Two of Schachter's three major hypotheses have met with reasonable confirmation in the research literature. Specifically, it has been found that obese individuals are indeed more likely to be responsive to external cues such as food-taste quality, food accessibility, and food prominence (cf. Schachter & Friedman, 1974; McArthur & Burstein, 1975; Schachter & Rodin, 1974; Costanzo & Woody, 1979; Schachter, Friedman, & Handler, 1974; Nisbett & Kanouse, 1969; etc.). Further, it has also been found that non-food-related response phenomena of the obese, such as recognition threshold (Rodin, Herman & Schachter, 1974), time estimation (Pliner, 1973), distraction (Rodin, 1970), and cognitive processing (Pliner, 1973), are more manipulable by variations in external cue properties than are similar response phenomena in normals.

Other studies have examined whether or not the link between food-related externality and nonfood externality in the obese could be established. This research is in the service of determining whether Schachter's proposal of a generalized response style in the obese is a plausible one. The literature here is supportive for college-age subjects (cf. McArthur & Burstein) but not for children (cf. Costanzo & Woody, 1979; Woody & Costanzo, 1981). The finding that food-cue and other forms of externality are apparently not linked in the responses of obese children casts some doubt on the notion that generalized externality is an *antecedent* of overeating, which in turn is an antecedent of obesity. If already overweight children do not evidence such a link, it would be difficult to locate the origin of obesity in a *general* style.

Finally, the one hypothesis from Schachter's models that appears to have been seriously questioned by research data is that internal cues play less of a role in controlling eating in obese than in normal-weight persons. Despite some evidence which has supported the hypothesis (cf. Pliner, 1973b), there is more compelling evidence rejecting it (Wooley, 1972; Wooley, Wooley & Dunham, 1972). It appears from these data that internal biological cues are very weak determinants of episodic eating for all of us, obese or normal. Schachter's theory of obese externality must therefore rest upon the determination of differences in *degree* of externality between normal-weight and obese people.

Given the nature of the pattern of findings just referred to, the notion that obese externality describes an attribute of obese adults in both food- and non-food-related domains has been fairly well accepted in the literature. Yet, Schachter's explanations of the "whys" of these phenomena have not met with equivalent acceptance. In fact a number of alternative perspectives have been offered to account for obese externality. The most noteworthy of these have been proposed by Singh (1973), Nisbett (1972), and Herman (Herman & Mack, 1975).

1 Singh performed a series of studies which suggested that obese externality is not really a "deficit" on the stimulus side, but a result of the difficulty that the obese have in terminating a response once it occurs. That is, the obese eat more because they have difficulty breaking response set and thus changing their eating behavior in the face of changing situational demands. In short the obese are proposed to have a problem at the terminus point of an eating response rather than at the point of initial elicitation (as would be suggested by obese-externality theory). Singh's viewpoint accounts for apparent obese externality by citing such response habits.

2 Nisbett proposed a biogenic source for obese externality. He proposed that obesity probably results from developmentally early overfeeding, which has the consequence of incrementing an individual's gross number of fat cells. It was presumed that fat-cell number is a determinant of optimal weight or "set-point." When individuals fall below set-point (which is likely in our dieting culture), they are by this proposal "starving" their fat cells. Indeed, it seems from the research that obese dieters show many of the visceral physiological phenomena of starving organisms. Nisbett further proposes the rather straightforward notion that the obese overeat in response to external cues because their starvation level (when below set-point) renders them more vigilant about the accessibility and attractiveness of food.

3 Herman's viewpoint is really a corollary to Nisbett's. He and his colleagues presume that, if Nisbett is correct and society is as strident as it seems to be about negatively sanctioning overweight, then many people who are not apparently obese should evidence "below set-point" induced externality symptoms. He refers to these phenotypically nonobese but biologically obese individuals as high-restrainers and claims further that it is high restraint in opposition to biological demand that produces the phenomenon of obese externality.

In summary then, it appears that Schachter's predictions about the differential hyperresponsiveness of obese versus normal-weight people to external cues is rather well accepted. However, the conjectures as to *why* this phenomena prevails are congenially embattled ones and Schachter's particular explanation is not now unambiguously accepted.

For comprehensive reviews of this research literature and perspectives on obese externality consult Leon and Roth (1977) and Woody and Costanzo (1981).

AN ACHIEVEMENT ATTRIBUTION VIEWPOINT

Purpose

Bernard Weiner and his colleagues (Weiner, Frieze, Kukla, Reed, Rest, & Rosenbaum, 1972; Weiner, Russell, & Lerman, 1976; Weiner, 1974) proposed a theory with the purpose of understanding the relationships between a person's causal ascriptions for present achievement outcomes and his/her subsequent achievement behavior and/or achievement motivation. Weiner et al. (1972) traced this interesting problem to the seminal attribution framework of Heider (see Chapters 6 and 9) in that it, like Heider's perspective, begins from the assumption that our behaviors in the world are determined by our causal ascriptions to our selves or the environment in which the behavior occurs. The model of the nature and effect of causal ascriptions about achievement to be briefly presented here is not only traceable to Heider but is probably rather easily derivable from general attributional frameworks, particularly Kelley's (see Chapter 9). It should also be noted that a secondary purpose of Weiner's model was to provide for an attributional alternative to both explanations of achievement derived from Rotter's locus-of-control framework (1959) and the Atkinson-McClelland expectancy-value model (described earlier in this chapter).

The Guiding Principles

The major overarching principle guiding Weiner's theorizing has already been alluded to in our description of his purpose. Weiner and his colleagues proposed that an individual's causal ascriptions for achievement indeed mediate a variety of subsequent achievement behaviors and motivations. In particular such ascriptions affect the individual's future achievement expectancies, his/her persistence at subsequent tasks of similar structure to that for which a causal ascription has been made, and the individual's pride or shame following success or failure.

Hypotheses

Weiner and his colleagues propose two general hypotheses defining the manner in which causal ascriptions for achievement outcomes are related to subsequent achievement. *The first hypothesis* specifies that there are three causal dimensions that individuals use in accounting for achievement outcomes.

Weiner noted that the causes of achievement outcome (i.e., success or failure) are "subsumed within a three-dimension taxonomy" (Weiner, Russell, & Lerman, 1976). He proposed that the first causal dimension involved the *internal versus external* description of causes. That is, one global source to which individuals attribute achievement outcomes is constituted by the self-environment polarity. A second dimension which characterizes the individual's causal ascriptions is their *stability versus instability*. That is, the individual, in deciding upon the sources of his/her achievement, considers whether the cause is a variant one (e.g., effort) or a stable one (e.g., ability). The third and final dimension for causal ascriptions about achievement is comprised of an *intentionality* dimension. That is, the individual arrives at a causal perspective on his/her own achievement partly by deciding whether his/her achievement outcomes are a matter of conscious choice or not. This last dimension was primarily related by Weiner et al. (1976) to the individual's experience of affective intensity subsequent to success or failure. The more individuals view their achievement behavior as a matter of conscious choice, the more they will experience pride following success and shame, humiliation, or anger following failure.

Weiner combined the first two dimensions of causal ascriptions into a fourfold classification. He noted that an individual might attribute cause for an achievement outcome to *internal-stable* (e.g., ability); *internal-unstable* (e.g., effort); *external-stable* (e.g., task difficulty); and *external-unstable* (luck) dimensions.

The second general hypothesis proposed by Weiner concerning causal ascriptions for achievement pertained to the *consequence* of achievement attributions. He offered that three phenomena serve as consequences of our causal ascriptions—*expectancy* of future performance, *affective* or emotional consequences of success, and actual subsequent *performance*. From this general hypothesis, Weiner et al. went on to propose several derivative hypotheses:

1   As the individual's attribution of achievement outcome to a *stable* factor increases, the *expectancy* of success after success, or failure after failure also increase.
2   If individuals attribute achievement outcome to *unstable* causes, there will be little evidence that the attained success or failure is predictive of future successes and failures, respectively.
3   The experiences of pride after success and shame after failure are maximized when achievement outcomes are ascribed internally and minimized when they are ascribed externally.
4   The expectancy levels and affects that derive from causal ascription for achievement outcome influence the subsequent speed, quality, and persistence evident in our performance behavior.

In summary, it appears reasonable to note that Weiner sees our expectancies for future performance deriving from stable causal inferences, achievement-related affect deriving from internal-external causal inferences, and future performance from both.

General Evaluation of the Theory

While an elaborated evaluation of the research supporting this theory is beyond the scope of this abbreviated presentation, it is, nevertheless, important to note that this model of achievement attribution has generated much directly supportive research. In addition, recent work has effectively questioned the viability of Weiner's causal model of achievement attribution (cf. Falbo & Beck, 1979; Passer, 1977; Meyer, 1980). All in all, it does appear as if individuals, if asked, can easily code their explanations for their achievement behavior into the four primary causal categories described by Weiner (i.e., ability, effort, task difficulty, or luck). Further, there is ample evidence, at this point, to support the hypotheses which hold that expectancy for future success, task persistence, and level of performance are reliably and expectedly affected by the dimensions of causal ascription designated in the hypotheses (see Weiner, Russell, and Lerman for a review of this perspective and the research in its support).

Weiner's theory certainly does not stand alone as a current causal attribution model which is directed at explaining achievement behavior subsequent to causal ascriptions. Dweck (Dweck & Goetz, 1978) has proposed and demonstrated that it is possible to remediate the lowered performance level and motivation of children with a repeated history of failure by inducing them to make effort attributions for successful attainment. Lepper and his colleagues (cf. Lepper, Greene, & Nisbett, 1973) have proposed and confirmed the notion that a child's performance and subsequent free interest in an achievement task is enhanced by subtly inducing him/her to make internal attributions for successful performance. In addition to these two related frameworks the interesting perspective offered by Deaux and reviewed briefly earlier in this chapter is a rather direct application of Weiner-like principles to the understanding of sex-role disruptions in achievement.

Finally, it should be noted that the model can be employed equally well in the understanding of one's own *or* another's achievement outcomes. The actor-observer disparity in attribution, that results from direct self-other attributional comparisons, contributes to the understanding of self-enhancement and other biases in achievement attribution. In addition, the earlier reported sex-based difference in the use of Weiner's causal categories (cf. Deaux, 1976), along with the actor-observer divergency studies, demonstrates that the Weiner model might be effectively used as a "natural-baseline" model to which meaningful biases in achievement attribution might be compared and possibly understood.

THE ATTITUDE SIMILARITY–ATTRACTION PARADIGM

While Byrne's attitude similarity–attraction paradigm has both been generated from and has generated a voluminous amount of research, it will be presented in a very abbreviated fashion in this text. The theory (or more appropriately the paradigm) is a very simple and concise one, based upon one large overarching principle, many times confirmed in the literature on attraction, and another principle which details the basis for the operation of the overarching principle.

Byrne's (1969, 1971) viewpoint is directed at understanding "the effect of the expression of attitude statements on subsequent affective responses directed toward the source of such statements" (Byrne, 1969, p. 36). The presumed relationship of importance to Byrne's model is derived and justified through a consideration of a variety of age-old and current common-sense perspectives and current and past research and theory concerning the determinants of attraction.

The overarching principle derived from all of these materials can be stated as follows: *The effect of the expression of attitude statements on subsequent affective responses directed toward the source of such statements will be positive to the extent that such attitude statements are similar to the attitudes and beliefs of the target of such statements. They will be negative to the extent that such expressions of attitude statements differ from the attitudes of the target of those statements.*

In simpler terms, this proposition might be restated: *The attraction between two or more individuals will be a positive function of the degree of attitude similarity between (among) them.*

Byrne's Theoretical Explanation for the Similarity-Attraction Relationships

The particular merit of Byrne's viewpoint is not in its proposal of the attitude similarity–attraction link, since this link had been noted by thinkers and researchers for many years (see particularly Newcomb's A-B-X theory in Chapter 8). Instead, Byrne's contribution is that he provides a quite parsimonious and easily testable explanation for why such a relationship is likely to prevail.

In an early paper on the theoretical determinants of attraction, Byrne (1961) proposed that an underlying assumption of all the research on attraction up to that time was that *"attraction toward X (another person) is a function of the relative number of rewards and punishments associated with X"* (Byrne, 1969, p. 67). Byrne and Nelson (1965) formalized this assumption into a *law of attraction* which was stated quite similarly: *"Attraction toward X is a positive linear function of the proportion of positive reinforcements received from X"* (Byrne, 1969, p. 67).

From the vantage point of the reinforcement-based law of attraction, Byrne accounted for the attitude similarity–attraction relationship by concluding that it was a *special case of reward and punishment*. It was proposed that attitude statements arouse affect for which "the motive involved is the learned drive to be logical and interpret correctly one's stimulus world." Therefore individuals whose attitudes are similar to our own attitudes reward us by providing us with information about the veridicality of our beliefs. Byrne interprets this motive as an effectance motive and asserts that such a motive constitutes an intervening state in the similarity-attraction paradigm. To quote the theorist:

> We continually strive to make sense out of our physical and social world. Especially difficult is the social world of attitudes, beliefs, opinions, and values concerning politics, religion, race relations, and the like. About such topics there is simply no way to determine whether we are correct in making sense out of the stimulus data. When another person agrees with us and hence offers consensual validation concerning the correctness of our position, our "correctness" is supported. Frustration of this motive to be logical and correct takes place when others disagree with our views, when they offer consensual invalidation. Therefore, the finding that the expression of attitudes congruent with those of a subject elicits a positive response while discrepant attitudes elicit a negative response may be interpreted on a reward and punishment basis (Byrne, 1966, pp. 47–48).

In a sense then, Byrne's accounting of the frequently asserted relationship between attitude similarity and attraction is closely akin to a reinforcement–social-exchange theory (see Chapter 4) construction of the nature of social interaction. From this account, we become attracted to others who share our beliefs, attitudes, and values because in that circumstance we can achieve a high level of reward at low "cost." We avoid individuals whose attitudes are dissimilar from our own because in such relationships our potential costs are higher than our potential rewards. Thibaut and Kelley (1959) make much the same point in defining "similarity" as one of the extrinsic determinants of reward/cost ratios in social interaction.

A General Evaluation of the Theory

Byrne's attitude similarity–attraction paradigm proposes a parsimonious explanation of a rather frequently noted "relationship rule" in social psychology. The viewpoint is simple in its formulation and several of its implied propositions (e.g., attitude statements are affect-arousing, needs for effectance mediate the similarity-attraction relationship, and the like) are clearly open to test. In fact Byrne and his collaborators have been quite active researchers and have endeavored to confirm the functional relationship between attitude similarity and rewarding outcomes in dyads in which the individuals are familiar with one another (i.e., married couples) as well as in dyads comprised of strangers. Similarity in various attitude objects, ranging from beliefs about sexuality to political beliefs, have been found to be sufficient provocateurs of attraction in relationships. Byrne (1969, 1971) provides a comprehensive account of the research performed in support of the similarity-attraction perspective. The weight of the evidence is highly supportive of the perspective and the interested reader is directed to the theorists' reviews of this work.

It is hard to fault Byrne's theory on the claim that it is "too simple" a framework to describe real-life relationship bonding, since simplicity and testability were two of the goals that Byrne appeared interested in realizing in his theoretical analysis. Nevertheless alternative theorists who have appealed to the similarity-attraction relationship as a principle of social bonding (e.g., see Newcomb's A-B-X theory in Chapter 8) would identify the principle as one that is mediated by both different and more complicated cognitive and affective dynamics than Byrne's theory suggests.

Part Seven

Conclusion

Chapter 15

Epilogue

Our selective review of theories in social psychology includes some 50 theoretical orientations, theories, minitheories, and "promising hypotheses." This is an impressive number, especially when it is remembered that our selective biases resulted in the exclusion of many theories that others might have included. How adequate are these theories? How much have they contributed to the development of a science of social psychology? What are the characteristics of these theories? What effects have they had on research? These and many other questions seem worthy of consideration. This chapter is devoted to an examination of the current status of theories in social psychology, the relationship of theories to current research, and some thoughts about future directions.

CURRENT STATUS OF THEORIES

The current status of theories in social psychology may be viewed from several perspectives. We will consider them from the following perspectives: form and content, levels of analysis, functions served, general quality, and trends in theory development.

Form and Content

It was noted in Chapter 1 that theories differ in a variety of ways and that several classification systems have been proposed. These classifications are based on either form (e.g., constructive versus principle theories, concatenated versus hierarchical theories) or content (e.g., molar versus molecular theories, field versus monadic theories). With regard to form, theorists in social psychology today reveal a definite preference for principle theories. That is, the starting point of most current theories in social psychology is empirical data rather than hypothetically constructed elements. In many cases theories are no more than attempts to explain experimental results or, less frequently, observations of events in natural situations. In this respect, current theories are disappointing because so little attention is given to the formulation of general propositions that transcend the specific situation that stimulated development of the particular theory.

With regard to content, there is an equally clear preference for molecular theories. This preference is reflected in the many cognitively oriented theories that appeal to intraperson constructs for explanation. For example, the many theories of attribution are basically molecular in content.

Levels of Analysis

The levels-of-analysis concept has been used to refer to several different aspects of theories, the more usual ones being range, scope, and abstractness. *Range* is the degree to which a theory applies to a specific group or class of persons or to people in general. Current theories in social psychology generally apply to all persons, although increasing attention is being given to individual differences (e.g., locus of control, personal needs, cognitive complexity).

Scope refers to the number of different kinds of behavior the theory attempts to explain. The scope of a theory may be all-encompassing and purport to explain all human behavior; or it may be limited to the explanation of a single behavioral phenomenon. It can be stated with confidence that no "grand theory" has appeared in social psychology. The scope of existing social-psychological theories range from Merton's (1949) "theories of the middle range" to minitheories. In recent years, minitheories are definitely in the majority. In fact, many explanations that are called theories are really no more than single hypotheses about some aspect of social behavior. This level of analysis is reflected most strongly in the proposals reviewed in Chapter 14.

Abstractness refers to variations in the length of the reduction chain, or number of intervening variables, connecting theoretical terms with observable ones. Most of the theories that we have reviewed are relatively concrete in that theoretical concepts are tied rather closely to the behavior that the theory attempts to explain. Most reduction chains consist of only three links: the observed stimulus situation, the observed behavior, and the intervening variable that is assumed to link the stimulus situation with the behavior. Of course, both the stimulus situation and the behavior may be complex, and a given theory may involve more than one intervening variable.

Functions of Current Theories

In Chapter 1 we observed that theories organize experience, reveal implications beyond known data, and provide stimuli and guidance for further empirical investigations. The theories that we have presented in this book serve these functions moderately well. All the theories organize the known data about the phenomena that the theory attempts to explain, and most permit inferences beyond the data given. However, theories differ greatly in the degree to which the latter is true—and consequently with regard to the extent to which they serve as guides for research. More will be said about this aspect of current theories in a later part of this chapter.

Quality of Current Theories

Throughout the text we have offered evaluative comments about the theories that we outlined for the reader. It is not our purpose here to repeat those comments or evaluate the quality of specific theories. Instead, we will draw some general conclusions that we believe apply to most of the theories in this volume.

According to the characteristics that an acceptable theory must have (logical consistency, agreement with known data, and testability), current theories in social psychology are moderately good theories. Most, and perhaps all, are logically consistent; that is, propositions or hypotheses in one part of the theory do not contradict propositions or hypotheses in other parts of the theory. However, in some cases, the various propositions are not as interrelated and integrated as might be desirable. All are testable in the sense that predictions can be derived from the theory that are amenable to empirical examination. From the viewpoint of necessary characteristics, their weakest point is agreement with known data. All theories agreed quite well with data available at the time the theory was formulated, but subsequent data generally contain some findings that are inconsistent with the predictions of relevant theories. In some instances, apparently inconsistent data may derive from faulty research, but in many other cases inconsistent data cannot be so easily explained away and theory revision may be necessary. As we discussed in Chapter 1, this theory development–empirical testing–theory revision sequence represents the normal, orderly process of science.

In addition to the essential characteristics, a good theory should, ideally, be simple, economical, consistent with related theories that have a high probability of being true, readily interpretable, and serve a useful purpose (see Chapter 1). With respect to the first of these desirable characteristics, the theories we have reviewed often do not fare overly well. In too many instances the terminology is unnecessarily abstruse and propositions, corollaries, and hypotheses are not stated in unambiguous form.

With regard to economy, the theories in this book would surely be judged to have high quality: most of them try to explain a wide array of behaviors with very few principles. Many theories attempt to explain many diverse behaviors with a single principle, e.g., cognitive dissonance, reactance, impression management, and the like. It is probably not unfair to say that most current theories greatly oversimplify in their attempt to explain basically complex social behavior. The notion that a theory should explain phenomena with as few principles as possible was not intended to mean economy at the expense of adequacy of theoretical explication.

The third desirable characteristic of a good theory, that it should be consistent with related theories that have a high probability of being true, is difficult to evaluate because there are few current theories in social psychology that have a high probability of being true in all details. However, most of the theories that we have examined are consistent with other theories that have moderately strong empirical support.

Are the theories readily interpretable, or do they provide a bridge to events in the "real world"? No general answer can be given to this question, although all theories purport to deal with social behavior that occurs in natural situations. But theories in social psychology vary greatly in ease of application to naturally occurring events. For example, it is very easy to use the theory of cognitive dissonance to interpret (explain?) happenings in everyday life, whereas it is not so clear how integration theory can be so interpreted.

The final desirable characteristic is that a good theory should serve a useful purpose, not only in explaining what it is supposed to explain, but also in the advancement of science. This probably is one of the most important functions that a theory may serve, but, unfortunately, the one least adequately met by current theories. Theories in social psychology have generally been highly successful in generating research, but there is little evidence that the furious research activity has contributed greatly to the advancement of a science of social psychology. It is unclear whether this is a consequence of the characteristics of the theories or the kind of research conducted to test the theories. This question will be examined in greater detail in the next section of this chapter.

Trends in Theory Development

In reviewing the theories presented in this book, the reader will undoubtedly have observed some common aspects or trends in theory development. These trends become even more evident when one examines the empirical research relevant to the theories. We have already noted that most theory development in social psychology begins with empirical data. Furthermore, much of the data derives from current events. A classic example of this is the Kitty Genovese affair that was reported in the *New York Times,* May, 1964. The reader will recall that Miss Genovese was brutally attacked and finally murdered while onlookers made no move to help. This happening stimulated numerous laboratory and field studies on helping behavior and much theorizing about altruism and helping. Although theory and research being derived from current events is not necessarily bad, one cannot but wonder if the science of social psychology might not have been more greatly advanced by a more constructive approach to theory development (see Chapter 1).

A second obvious trend in theory development may be partly a consequence of the first, namely a trend toward faddism. Social psychology appears to move from one theoretical fad to another. For example, in the 1960s cognitive consistency theories dominated social psychology. As noted in Chapter 8, formulation of this general class of theories began as early as 1946 with the appearance of Heider's balance theory. During the next several years, numerous theories of this type were proposed and became the prevailing theoretical approach in social psychology (at least in frequency of invocation). At the present time, attribution theories are in vogue and are most frequently employed as explanations of behavior. (Would the reader care to predict the next fad in social-psychological theorizing?)

Finally, there is an obvious trend toward ahistorical theorizing. Theories typically begin with the assumption that certain intrapersonal characteristics, interpersonal relations, psychological processes, and the like exist, with no consideration of how those elements came to be. This is not the kind of ahistoricity espoused by Lewin (see Chapter 6). Lewin maintained that the present situation is the important thing for understanding social behavior and that the way the present situation came to exist is not important for an explanation of current behavior. However, he did not ignore developmental processes in his overall theoretical system. Too often, current theories give no attention to developmental processes. Perhaps such concern may safely be left to developmental psychologists, but social theories appear incomplete without at least some reference to this aspect. This point becomes particularly salient when it is remembered that many developmental processes are social in nature.

THEORIES AND RESEARCH

One of the basic functions of theory is to provide a stimulus and a guide for research. Consequently, theory-based research has the highest probability of advancing science. It is surprising to note that so much research in social psychology appears to be atheoretical. In reviewing the literature one cannot but be struck by the large number of research articles that begin with statements of the following form: "John Doe (1900) found that condition A produced greater effects than condition B. He maintained that this effect was due to X, but it can be more logically explained by Y. The purpose of this research is to test this expectation." In such instances, no theoretical framework is employed to guide the research, unless one accepts a hunch or an educated guess as a theory. If social psychology is to advance as a science, more theory-based research is mandatory.

In the first edition of this text it was suggested that a move in the direction of more comparative testing of theories would be desirable. Comparative testing of theories not only reveals something about the relative validity of different theories, but also results in expansion and refinement of the theories. Regrettably, we find little evidence that this desirable trend is developing in social-psychological research. If there has been a change in recent years, it is toward less rather than more comparative testing of theories.

Still another regrettable trend is demonstrative research rather than theory development research. By *demonstrative* research we mean research designed to demonstrate that a particular hypothesized relationship exists or that effects like those assumed by a theory occur. This kind of research is epitomized by the plethora of research designed to demonstrate dissonancelike effects. Such research contributes little to theory development. *Theory development* research, on the other hand, attempts to extend the theory to new aspects of behavior, refine theoretical conceptions, and modify the propositional structure of the theory. This kind of research is most likely to lead to important advances in the science of social psychology. Theory development research is illustrated by the dissonance-theory research on the roles of commitment and responsibility in producing dissonancelike effects, but this research represents only a small fraction of the total amount of research generated by the theory of cognitive dissonance.

It is not obvious why research in social psychology so often fails to satisfy these basic requirements of research designed to advance the science of social behavior, but one may derive some clues from an analysis of the research literature and from comments by observers. For instance, Michael Argyle, a British social psychologist, is quoted as commenting on American social-psychological research as follows: "If someone invents a good idea then 500 other people do it again, without asking whether this is a useful paradigm for explaining social behavior" (Evans, 1978, p. 7). This comment reflects the faddish aspect of social psychology that we mentioned earlier in this chapter. When researchers feverishly "jump on the band wagon" and slavishly replicate the currently popular research paradigm (with the required minor variation, of course), one cannot expect the research to involve profound thought about possible scientific contributions.

A second aspect of both theory and research that may lower quality is the tendency to employ current events as stimuli and guides for research and theory construction. Commenting on social theory and research, Gergen (1973) argued that theories of social behavior are primarily reflections of contemporary history. He maintained that dissemination of psychological knowledge modifies the patterns of behavior on which the knowledge is based. Furthermore, he contended that theoretical premises are based on acquired dispositions that change as the culture changes, thus invalidating the premises. Gergen's view of social psychology has been ably contested by Schlenker (1974), who asserted that Gergen's contentions demonstrate a narrow focus on particulars and a misconception of the nature of science. Our consideration of theories in social psychology suggests that Gergen is correct in saying that much of social-psychological theory and research in the past several years reflects history, but we believe he is incorrect in maintaining, at least by implication, that it is impossible for social psychology to be anything but an historical inquiry. For example, the current concern for sex differences and the influence of "sex roles" in our society derives from current social issues. So long as theoretical premises interpret data in terms of differences between men and women, they do indeed reflect history. But such interpretation is inappropriate for scientific theorizing. For instance, a common finding is that on tasks that are more familiar to males than to females, women conform more to majority opinion than men. A possible theoretical premise based on this finding might be: "Females conform more than males." With changing social patterns, this premise could easily be invalidated. But suppose the derived premise is: "Persons who have been subjected to a pattern of socialization that emphasizes dependence will conform more than persons subjected to a socialization pattern that emphasizes independence."

This premise probably would not be invalidated by changing social patterns. As the socializations of females and males become similar, differences in conformity behavior would probably disappear, but, instead of invalidating the premise, such a change would provide further supporting evidence for the premise.

The important point in the above discussion is that social psychologists are currently focusing research and theoretical analyses on current events, whereas efforts should be directed toward the formulation of general principles or "laws" of social behavior that transcend the particular social behaviors that permitted the derivation of the principles. This latter process is characteristic of science and must be adhered to if social psychology is to be more than history.

A final point should be made. Current theories in social psychology often do not permit unambiguous predictions about the social behavior they attempt to explain. In such cases, it is impossible to conduct adequate tests of the theory. This state of affairs may explain, in part, the tendency toward demonstrative research.

A LOOK TO THE FUTURE

In the first edition of this text we were so rash as to make some predictions about future trends in social psychology. We expected that theories would continue to play an important role in social psychology, theory building would become more sophisticated, more attention would be given to formulating general "laws" of social behavior, there would be more comparative testing of theories, etc. Unfortunately, we think, most of our expectations have not been realized. Theories have indeed continued to play an important role in social psychology, but theories do not appear to be more sophisticated nor has there been an increase in the formulation of general principles. In fact, the trend seems to be toward more specific theoretical propositions. We have already noted the disappointing lack of comparative testing of theories.

Despite predictive failure, we continue to believe that the current trends are temporary aberrations that reflect present societal concerns. Concentration on current social issues may be expected to continue for the next several years, but a return to more enduring theoretical concerns seems inevitable. In the first edition we posed the following question: "Will the field of social psychology eventually fall into an epistemological morass in which theories proliferate to the extent that a single postulate is needed for each possible condition in the human social environment?" To date, an affirmative answer is suggested by recent theorizing in social psychology. The failure of current approaches to advance the science of social psychology should be apparent even now, and moves toward more productive theories should be forthcoming in the not too distant future. Toward this end, we have attempted to exposit theories of social psychology in a clear and understandable fashion in the hope that the reader will be stimulated to make conceptual comparisons among theories and attempt to improve them. Again, we idealistically hope that this book may help in some way to stimulate theoretical advances in the field of social psychology.

REFERENCES

Abeles, R. P. Relative deprivation, rising expectations, and black militancy. *Journal of Social Issues,* 1976, *32,* 119–137.

Abelson, R. P. Script processing in attitude formation and decision making. In J. S. Carroll and J. W. Payne (eds.), *Cognition and Social Behavior.* Hillsdale, N. J.: Lawrence Erlbaum, 1976. Pp. 33–45.

Abelson, R. P., and M. J. Rosenberg. Symbolic psycho-logic: A model of attitudinal cognition. *Behavioral Science,* 1958, *3,* 1–13.

Adams, J. S. Toward an understanding of inequity. *Journal of Abnormal and Social Psychology,* 1963, *67,* 422–436.

———, and S. Freedman. Equity theory revisited. In L. Berkowitz (ed.), *Advances in experimental social psychology,* 1976, *Vol. 9,* 43–90.

Aiello, J. R. A test of equilibrium theory: Visual interaction in relation to orientation, distance and sex of interactants. *Psychonomic Science,* 1972, *27,* 335–336.

Ajzen, I. Attitudinal vs. normative messages: An investigation of the differential effects of persuasive communications on behavior. *Sociometry,* 1971, *34,* 263–280.

———, and M. Fishbein. The prediction of behavior from attitudinal and normative variables. *Journal of Experimental Social Psychology,* 1970, *6,* 466–487.

———, and ———. Attitudes and normative beliefs as factors influencing behavioral intentions. *Journal of Personality and Social Psychology,* 1972, *21,* 1–9.

———, and ———. Attitudinal and normative variables as predictors of specific behaviors. *Journal of Personality and Social Psychology,* 1973, *27,* 41–57.

———, and ———. Factors influencing intentions and the intention-behavior relation. *Human Relations,* 1974, *27,* 1–15.

———, and ———. Attitude-behavior relations: A theoretical analysis and review of empirical research. *Psychological Bulletin,* 1977, *84,* 888–918.

Allport, F. H. *Social psychology.* Cambridge, Mass.: Houghton Mifflin, 1924.

Allport, G. W. *Personality: A psychological interpretation.* New York: Holt, Rinehart and Winston, 1937.

———. Attitudes. In C. M. Murchison (ed.), *Handbook of social psychology.* Worchester, Mass.: Clark University Press, 1935. Pp. 798–844.

Altman, I. *The environment and social behavior.* Monterey, Calif.: Brooks Cole, 1975.

———, and W. W. Haythorn. Interpersonal exchange in isolation. *Sociometry,* 1965, *23,* 411–426.

———, and D. A. Taylor. *Social penetration: The development of interpersonal relationships.* New York: Holt, Rinehart and Winston, 1973.

Anderson, J. R. *Language, memory, and thought.* Hillsdale, N. J.: Lawrence Erlbaum, 1976.

———, and G. H. Bower. *Human associative memory.* Washington, D. C.: Winston, 1973.

Anderson, L., and W. McGuire. Prior reassurance of group consensus as a factor in producing resistance to persuasion. *Sociometry,* 1965, *28,* 44–56.

Anderson, L. R. *Some effects of leadership training on intercultural discussion groups.* Unpublished doctoral dissertation, University of Illinois, 1964.

———, and F. E. Fiedler. The effect of participatory and supervisory leadership on group creativity. *Journal of Applied Psychology,* 1964, *48,* 227–236.

———, and M. Fishbein. Prediction of attitude from number, strength, and evaluative aspect of beliefs about the attitude object: A comparison of summation and congruity theories. *Journal of Personality and Social Psychology,* 1965, *2,* 437–443.

Anderson, N. H. Application of an additive model to impression formation. *Science,* 1962, *138,* 817–818.

———. Adding versus averaging as a stimulus combination rule in impression formation. *Journal of Experimental Psychology,* 1965, *70,* 394–400.

———. A simple model for information integration. In R. P. Abelson, E. Aronson, W. J. McGuire, T. M. Newcomb, M. J. Rosenberg, and P. H. Tannenbaum (eds.), *Theories of cognitive consistency: A sourcebook.* Chicago: Rand McNally, 1968. Pp. 731–743.

———. Functional measurement and psychophysical judgment. *Psychological Review,* 1970, *77,* 153–170.

———. Algebraic models in perception. In E. C. Carterette and M. P. Friedman (eds.), *Handbook of perception,* New York: Academic Press, 1974, (Vol. 2) Pp. 215–291.

———. Information integration theory: A brief survey. In D. H. Krantz, R. C. Atkinson, R. D. Luce, and P. Suppes (eds.), *Contemporary developments in mathematical psychology: Measurement, psychophysics, and neural information processing.* San Francisco: Freeman, 1974. *Vol. 2,* Pp. 236–305.

———, and C. A. Butzin. Performance = motivation × ability: An integration-theoretical analysis. *Journal of Personality and Social Psychology,* 1974, *30,* 598–604.

———, and C. G. Graesser. An information integration analysis of attitude change in group discussion. *Journal of Personality and Social Psychology,* 1976, *34,* 210–222.

———, R. Lindner, and L. L. Lopes. Integration theory applied to judgments of groups. *Journal of Personality and Social Psychology,* 1973, *26,* 400–408.

Anrep, G. V. Pitch discrimination in the dog. *Journal of Physiology,* 1920, *53,* 367–385.

Argyle, M., and J. Dean. Eye-contact, distance and affiliation. *Sociometry,* 1965, *28,* 289–304.

Armstrong, S., and H. Roback. An empirical test of Schutz' three-dimensional theory of group process in adolescent dyads. *Small Group Behavior,* 1977, *8,* 443–456.

Aronfreed, J. The nature, variety, and social patterning of moral responses to transgression. *Journal of Abnormal and Social Psychology,* 1961, *63,* 223–241.

Aronson, E. Dissonance theory: Progress and problems. In R. P. Abelson, E. Aronson, T. M. Newcomb, W. J. McGuire, M. J. Rosenberg, and P. H. Tannenbaum (eds.), *Source book on cognitive consistency.* New York: Rand McNally, 1968. Pp. 5–27.

———, B. Willerman, and J. Floyd. The effect of a pratfall on increasing attractiveness. *Psychonomic Science,* 1966, *4,* 227–228.

Arrowood, A. J., and R. Friend. Other factors determining the choice of a comparison other. *Journal of Experimental Social Psychology,* 1969, *5,* 233–239.

Asch, S. E. Effects of group pressure upon the modification and distortion of judgment. In H. Guetzkow (ed.), *Groups, leadership, and men.* Pittsburgh: Carnegie Press, 1951. Pp. 177–190.

———. *Social psychology.* New York: Prentice-Hall, 1952.

Atkins, A. L., K. K. Deaux, and J. Bieri. Latitude of acceptance and attitude change: Empirical evidence for a reformulation. *Journal of Personality and Social Psychology,* 1967, *6,* 47–54.

Atkinson, J. W., and N. J. Feather, (eds.) *A theory of achievement motivation.* New York: Wiley, 1966.

————, and G. H. Litwin. Achievement motive and test anxiety as motives to approach success and avoid failure. *Journal of Abnormal and Social Psychology,* 1960, *60,* 52–63.

Austin, W., E. Walster, and M. K. Utne. Equity and the law: The effects of a harmdoer's 'suffering in the act' on liking and punishment. In L. Berkowitz and E. Walster (eds.), *Advances in experimental social psychology.* New York: Academic Press, 1976. *(Vol. 9)* Pp. 163–190.

Ausubel, D. P. In defense of verbal learning. *Educational Theory,* 1961, *11,* 15–25.

————. Cognitive structure and the facilitation of meaningful verbal learning. *Journal of Teacher Education,* 1963, *14,* 217–221.

Back, K. W. Influence through social communication. *Journal of Abnormal and Social Psychology,* 1951, *46,* 9–23.

Baer, D. M., and J. A. Sherman. Reinforcement control of generalized initiation in young children. *Journal of Experimental Child Psychology,* 1964, *1,* 37–49.

Baer, R., S. Hinkle, K. Smith, and M. Fenton. Reactance as a function of actual versus projected autonomy. *Journal of Personality and Social Psychology,* 1980, *38,* 416–422.

Baldwin, A. L., J. Kallhorn, and F. H. Breese. Patterns of parent behavior. *Psychological Monographs: General and Applied,* 1945, *58,* No. 3 (Whole No. 268).

Baldwin, J. M. *Le développement mental chez l'enfant et dans la race.* London: Macmillan, 1897.

Bales, R. F. A set of categories for the analysis of small group interaction. *American Sociological Review,* 1950, *15,* 146–159.

Bandura, A. *Relationship of family patterns to child disorders.* Progress Report, Project No. M-1734, U.S.P.H.S., Stanford, California, 1960.

————. Social learning through imitation. In M. R. Jones (ed.), *Nebraska symposium on motivation: 1962.* Lincoln: University of Nebraska Press, 1962. Pp. 211–269.

————. Influence of models' reinforcement contingencies on the acquisition of imitative responses. *Journal of Personality and Social Psychology,* 1965a, *1,* 589–595.

————. Behavioral modification through modeling procedures. In L. Krasner and L. P. Ullman (eds.), *Research in Behavior modification.* New York: Holt, Rinehart and Winston, 1965b. Pp. 310–340.

————. Vicarious processes: A case of no-trial learning. In L. Berkowitz (ed.), *Advances in experimental social psychology.* New York: Academic Press, 1966. *Vol. 2.* Pp. 1–55.

————. *Principles of behavior modification.* New York: Holt, Rinehart and Winston, 1969.

————. Social learning theory of identificatory processes. In D. A. Goslin (ed.), *Handbook of socialization theory and research.* Chicago: Rand McNally, 1969.

————. Analysis of modeling processes. In A. Bandura (ed.), *Psychological modeling.* Chicago: Aldino-Atherton, 1971.

————. Modeling theory: Some traditions, trends and disputes. In R. D. Parke (ed.), *Recent trends in social learning theory.* New York: Academic Press, 1972.

————. *Aggression: A social learning analysis.* Englewood Cliffs, N. J.: Prentice-Hall, 1973.

————. Effecting change through participant modeling. In J. D. Krumboltz and C. E. Thoresen (eds.), *Counseling methods.* New York: Holt, Rinehart and Winston, 1976.

——. *Social learning theory.* Englewood Cliffs, N. J.: Prentice-Hall, 1977.

——, J. E. Grusec, and F. L. Menlove. Observational learning as a function of symbolization and incentive set. *Child Development,* 1966, *37,* 499–506.

——, and R. W. Jeffery. The role of symbolic coding and rehearsal processes in observational learning. *Journal of Personality and Social Psychology,* 1973, *26,* 122–130.

——, R. Jeffery, and D. L. Bachisha. Analysis of memory codes and cumulative rehearsal in observational learning. *Journal of Research in Personality,* 1974, *7,* 295–305.

——, and F. J. McDonald. The influence of social reinforcement and the behavior of models in shaping children's moral adjustments. *Journal of Abnormal and Social Psychology,* 1963, *67,* 274–281.

——, and W. Mischel. Modification of self-imposed delay of reward through exposure to live and symbolic models. *Journal of Personality and Social Psychology,* 1965, *2,* 698–705.

——, and T. L. Rosenthal. Vicarious classical conditioning as a function of arousal level. *Journal of Personality and Social Psychology,* 1966, *3,* 54–62.

——, D. Ross, and S. Ross. Transmission of aggression through imitation of aggressive models. *Journal of Abnormal and Social Psychology,* 1961, *63,* 575–582.

——, ——, and ——. Imitation of film-mediated aggressive models. *Journal of Abnormal and Social Psychology,* 1963, *66,* 3–11.

——, and R. H. Walters. *Adolescent aggression.* New York: Ronald Press, 1959.

——, and ——. *Social learning and personality development.* New York: Holt, Rinehart and Winston, 1963.

——, and C. K. Whalen. The influence of antecedent reinforcement and divergent modeling cues on patterns of self-reward. *Journal of Personality and Social Psychology,* 1966, *3,* 373–382.

Barnard, C. I. *The functions of the executive.* Cambridge, Mass.: Harvard University Press, 1938.

Barnett, P. E., and D. T. Benedetti. *A study in vicarious conditioning.* Paper read at Rocky Mountain Psychological Association Convention, Glenwood Spring, Colorado, 1960.

Baron, R. M., D. R. Mandel, C. A. Adams, and L. M. Griffen. Effects of social density in university residential environments. *Journal of Personality and Social Psychology,* 1976, *34,* 434–446.

Baron, R. S., and G. Roper. Reaffirmation of social comparison views of choice shifts: Averaging and extremity effects in an autokinetic situation. *Journal of Personality and Social Psychology,* 1976, *33,* 521–530.

Bass, M. J., and C. L. Hull. The irradiation of a tactile conditioned reflex in man. *Journal of Comparative Psychology,* 1934, *17,* 47–65.

Battle, E. S. Motivational determinants of academic competence. *Journal of Personality and Social Psychology,* 1966, *4,* 634–642.

Bechterev, V. M. *General principles of human reflexology.* New York: International, 1932.

Becker, H. Some forms of sympathy: A phenomenological analysis. *Journal of Abnormal and Social Psychology,* 1931, *26,* 58–68.

Bedell, J., and F. Sistrunk. Power, opportunity costs, and sex in a mixed motive game. *Journal of Personality and Social Psychology,* 1973, *25,* 219–226.

Bem, D. J. *An experimental analysis of beliefs and attitudes.* Unpublished Doctoral Dissertation, University of Michigan, 1964.

———. An experimental analysis of self-persuasion. *Journal of Experimental Social Psychology,* 1965, *1,* 199–218.

———. Self-perception: An alternative interpretation of cognitive dissonance phenomena. *Psychological Review,* 1967a, *74,* 183–200.

———. Reply to Judson Mills. *Psychological Review,* 1967b. *74,* 536–537.

———. The epistemological status of interpersonal simulations: A reply to Jones, Linder, Kiesler, Zanna, and Brehm. *Journal of Experimental Social Psychology,* 1968, *4,* 270–274.

———. Self-perception theory. In L. Berkowitz (ed.), *Advances in experimental social psychology.* New York: Academic Press, 1972, *Vol. 6,* 1–62.

———, and H. K. McConnell. Testing the self-perception explanation of dissonance phenomena: On the salience of premanipulation attitudes. *Journal of Personality and Social Psychology,* 1970, *14,* 23–31.

Bennett, E. B. Discussion, decision, commitment, and consensus in "group decision." *Human Relations,* 1955, *8,* 251–273.

Benton, A. Reactions to demands to win from an opposite sex opponent. *Journal of Personality,* 1973, *41,* 430–442.

Berger, S. M. Observer perseverance as related to a model's success: A social comparison analysis. *Journal of Personality and Social Psychology,* 1971, *19,* 341–350.

Berger, S. M. Conditioning through vicarious instigation. *Psychological Review,* 1962, *69,* 450–466.

Berlyne, D. E. Recent developments in Piaget's work. *British Journal of Educational Psychology,* 1957, *27,* 1–12.

———. *Conflict, arousal, and curiosity.* New York: McGraw-Hill, 1960.

Berscheid, E., W. Graziano, T. Monson, and M. Dermer. Outcome dependency: Attention attribution and attraction. *Journal of Personality and Social Psychology,* 1976, *34,* 978–989.

Bersh, P. J., J. M. Matterman, and W. M. Schoenfeld. Extinction of a human cardiac-response during avoidance conditioning. *American Journal of Psychology,* 1956, *69,* 244–251.

Bettelheim, B. *The informed heart.* Glencoe, Ill.: Free Press, 1960.

Biddle, B. J., and E. J. Thomas (eds.) *Role theory: Concepts and research.* New York: Wiley, 1966.

Bieri, J. Cognitive complexity-simplicity and predictive behavior. *Journal of Abnormal and Social Psychology,* 1955, *51,* 263–268.

Bierman, M. *The use of modeling, reinforcement, and problem solving set in altering children's syntactic style.* Unpublished manuscript, Stanford University, 1965.

Blau, P. M. *Exchange and power in social life.* New York: Wiley, 1964.

Bourne, L., S. Goldstein, and W. E. Link. Concept learning as a function of availability of previously presented information. *Journal of Experimental Psychology,* 1964, *67,* 439–448.

Bovard, E. W. Social norms and the individual. *Journal of Abnormal and Social Psychology,* 1948, *43,* 62–69.

Bramel, B., B. Taub, and B. Blum. An observer's reaction to the suffering of his enemy. *Journal of Personality and Social Psychology,* 1968, *8,* 384–392.

Bramel, D. Dissonance, expectation, and the self. In R. P. Abelson, E. Aronson, T. M. Newcomb, W. J. McGuire, M. J. Rosenberg, and P. H. Tannenbaum (eds.), *Source book on cognitive consistency.* New York: Rand McNally, 1968. Pp. 355–365.

Bredmeier, H. C., and R. M. Stephenson. *The analysis of social systems.* New York: Holt, Rinehart and Winston, 1962.

Brehm, J. W. *A theory of psychological reactance.* New York: Academic Press, 1966.

———. Response to loss of freedom: A theory of psychological reactance. Morristown, N. J.: General Learning Press, 1972.

———, and A. R. Cohen. *Explorations in cognitive dissonance.* New York: Wiley, 1962.

———, and M. Mann. Effect of importance of freedom and attraction to group members on influence produced by group pressure. *Journal of Personality and Social Psychology,* 1975, *31,* 816–824.

Brehm, S. S., and M. Weinraub. Physical barriers and psychological reactance: 2-year-olds' response to threats to freedom. *Journal of Personality and Social Psychology,* 1977, *35,* 830–836.

Bressler, J. Judgments in absolute units as a psychophysical method. *Archives of Psychology,* 1933, *No. 152.*

Brickman, P., and C. Horn. Balance theory and interpersonal coping in triads. *Journal of Personality and Social Psychology,* 1973, *26,* 347–355.

Bridgman, P. W. *The logic of modern physics.* New York: Macmillan, 1927.

Brown, I. Modeling processes and language acquisition: The role of referents. *Journal of Experimental Child Psychology,* 1976, *22,* 185–199.

Brown, J. S. Factors determining conflict reactions in difficult discriminations. *Journal of Experimental Psychology,* 1942, *31,* 272–292.

———, E. A. Bilodeau, and M. R. Baron. Bidirectional gradients in the strength of a generalized voluntary response to stimuli on a visual-spatial dimension. *Journal of Experimental Psychology,* 1951, *41,* 52–61.

Brown, R. Models of attitude change. In R. Brown, E. Galanter, E. Hess, and G. Mandler (eds.), *New directions in psychology.* New York: Holt, Rinehart and Winston, 1962. Pp. 1–85.

———. *Social psychology.* New York: The Free Press, 1965.

Bruch, H. *Eating disorders: Obesity, anorexia nervosa, and the person within.* New York: Basic Books, 1973.

Bruner, J. S. On perceptual readiness. *Psychological Review,* 1957, *64,* 123–152.

———. Learning and thinking. *Harvard Educational Review,* 1959, *29,* 184–192.

———, M. A. Wallach, and E. H. Galanter. The identification of recurrent regularity. *American Journal of Psychology,* 1959, *72,* 200–209.

Brunswik, E. *Wahrnehmung and Gegenstandswelt.* Leipzig and Wien: Deuticke, 1934.

———. Discussion: Remarks on functionalism in perception. *Journal of Personality,* 1949, *18,* 56–65.

———. The conceptual framework of psychology. In *International Encyclopedia of Unified Science, Vol. 1, No. 10.* Chicago: University of Chicago Press, 1952.

———. *Perception and the representative design of psychological experiments.* Berkeley: University of California Press, 1956.

Bryan, J. H., and N. H. Walbek. Preaching and practicing generosity: Some determinants of sharing in children. *Child Development,* 1970, *41,* 329–354.

Buhler, C. *The child and his family.* New York: Harper & Row, 1939.

Burdick, H. A., and A. J. Burnes. A test of "strain toward symmetry" theories. *Journal of Abnormal and Social Psychology,* 1958, *57,* 367–369.

Byrne, D. *An introduction to personality: A research approach.* Englewood Cliffs, N. J.: Prentice-Hall, 1966.

———. Attitudes and attraction. In L. Berkowitz (ed.), *Advances in experimental social psychology, Vol. 4,* 1969, 35–89.

———. *The attraction paradigm.* New York: Academic Press, 1971.

———, C. Ervin, and J. Lamberth. Continuity between the experimental study of attraction and real-life computer dating. *Journal of Personality and Social Psychology.* 1970, *16,* 157–165.

———, and D. Nelson. Attraction as a linear function of proportion of positive reinforcements. *Journal of Personality and Social Psychology,* 1965, *1,* 659–663.

Cahill, H. E., and C. I. Hovland. The role of memory in the acquisition of concepts. *Journal of Experimental Psychology,* 1960, *59,* 137–144.

Calder, B. J., and M. Ross. *Attitudes and behavior.* New York: General Learning Press, 1973.

———, M. Ross, and C. A. Insko. Attitude change and attitude attribution: Effects of incentive, choice, and consequences. *Journal of Personality and Social Psychology,* 1973, *25,* 84–99.

Campbell, D. T. Common fate, similarity, and other indices of aggregates of persons as social entities. *Behavioral Science,* 1958, *3,* 14–25.

Campbell, N. R. *What is science?* London: Methuen, 1921.

Canavan-Gumpert, D., K. Garner, and P. Gumpert. *The success-fearing personality, theory and research with implications for the social psychology of achievement.* Lexington, Mass.: Lexington Books, 1978.

Cannon, W. B. Emotion. *American Journal of Psychology,* 1927, *39,* 106–124.

———. *Bodily changes in pain, hunger, fear, and rage.* New York: Appleton-Century-Crofts, 1929.

Caplow, T., and R. J. McGee. *The academic marketplace.* New York: Basic Books, 1958.

Carnap, R. The two concepts of probability. In H. Feigl and M. Brodbeck (eds.), *Readings in the philosophy of science.* New York: Appleton-Century-Crofts, 1953.

Carroll, J. S., and J. W. Payne. *Cognition and social behavior.* Hillsdale, N. J.: Lawrence Erlbaum, 1976.

Cartwright, D. Lewinian theory as a contemporary systematic framework. In S. Koch (ed.), *Psychology: A study of a science.* New York: McGraw-Hill, 1959. Pp. 7–91.

———, and F. Harary. Structural balance: A generalization of Heider's theory. *Psychological Review,* 1956, *63,* 277–293.

Chadwick-Jones, J. K. *Social exchange theory.* London: Academic Press, 1976.

Champney, H. The variables of parent behavior. *Journal of Abnormal and Social Psychology,* 1941, *36,* 525–542.

Chapanis, N. P., and A. Chapanis. Cognitive dissonance: Five years later. *Psychological Bulletin,* 1964, *61,* 1–22.

Chapple, E. D., and C. M. Arensberg. Measuring human relations: An introduction to the study of the interactions of individuals. *Genetic Psychology Monographs,* 1941, *22,* 3–147.

Chemers, M., R. W. Rice, E. Sundstrom, and W. M. Butler. Leader esteem for the least preferred co-worker score, training, and effectiveness: An experimental examination. *Journal of Personality and Social Psychology,* 1975, *31,* 401–409.

———, and G. J. Skrzypek. Experimental test of the contingency model of leadership effectiveness. *Journal of Personality and Social Psychology,* 1972, *24,* 172–177.

Chemers, M. W., F. E. Fiedler, D. Lekhyananda, and L. M. Stolurow. Some effects of cultural training on leadership in heterocultural task groups. *International Journal of Psychology,* 1966, *1,* 301–314.

Christie, R., and F. L. Geis. *Studies in Machiavellianism.* New York: Academic Press, 1970.

Cialdini, R. B., D. T. Kenrick, and J. J. Hoerig. Victim derogation in the Lerner paradigm: Just world or just justification: *Journal of Personality and Social Psychology,* 1976, *33,* 719–724.

Clore, G. L. Attraction and interpersonal behavior. Paper presented at the meeting of the Southwestern Psychological Association, Austin, Texas, 1969.

Coates, B., and W. W. Hartup. Age and verbalization in observational learning. *Developmental Psychology,* 1969, *1,* 556–562.

Coch, L., and J. R. P. French, Jr. Overcoming resistance to change. *Human Relations,* 1948, *1,* 512–532.

Cohen, A. R., J. W. Brehm, and W. H. Fleming. Attitude change and justification for compliance. *Journal of Abnormal and Social Psychology,* 1958, *56,* 276–278.

——, E. Stotland, and D. M. Wolfe. An experimental investigation of need for cognition. *Journal of Abnormal and Social Psychology,* 1955, *51,* 291–294.

Collins, B. E., and M. F. Hoyt. Personal Responsibility-for-consequences: An integration and extension of the "forced compliance" literature. *Journal of Experimental Social Psychology,* 1972, *8,* 558–593.

Collins, E. B., and H. Guetzkow. *A social psychology of group processes for decision-making.* New York: Wiley, 1964.

Colson, W. N. Self-disclosure as a function of social approval. Unpublished Master's thesis, Howard University, Washington, D. C., 1968.

Conant, J. B. *Modern science and modern man.* Garden City, N. Y.: Doubleday, 1953.

Conolley, E. S., H. B. Gerard, and T. Kline. Competitive behavior: A manifestation of motivation for ability comparison. *Journal of Experimental Social Psychology,* 1978, *14,* 123–131.

Cooley, C. H. *Human nature and the social order.* New York: Scribner, 1902.

Cooper, J. Reducing fears and increasing assertiveness: The role of dissonance reduction. *Journal of Experimental Psychology,* 1980, *16,* 199–213.

——, R. H. Fazio, and F. Rhodewalt. Dissonance and humor: Evidence for the undifferentiated nature of dissonance arousal. *Journal of Personality and Social Psychology,* 1978, *36,* 280–285.

——, and C. J. Scalise. Dissonance produced by deviations from life styles: The interaction on Jungian typology and conformity. *Journal of Personality and Social Psychology,* 1974, *29,* 566–571.

Costanzo, P. R., and E. Z. Woody. Externality as a function of obesity in children: Pervasive style or eating-specific attribute? *Journal of Personality and Social Psychology,* 1979, *37,* 2286–2296.

Cottrell, N. B. Heider's structural balance principle as a conceptual rule. *Journal of Personality and Social Psychology,* 1975, *31,* 713–720.

Coutts, L. M., and F. W. Schniedet. Affiliative conflict theory: An investigation of the intimacy equilibrium and compensation hypothesis. *Journal of Personality and Social Psychology,* 1976, *34,* 1135–1142.

Crockett, W. H. Balance, agreement, and subjective evaluations of the P-O-X triads. *Journal of Personality and Social Psychology,* 1974, *29,* 102–110.

Darley, J. M., and E. Aronson. Self-evaluation vs. direct anxiety reduction as determinants of the fear-affiliation relationship. *Journal of Experimental and Social Psychology,* Supplement 1, 1966, 66–79.

Davis, D., and T. C. Brock. Use of first person pronouns as a function of increased objective self-awareness and prior feedback. *Journal of Experimental Social Psychology,* 1975, *11,* 381–388.

Davis, J. D. Effects of communication about interpersonal process on the evolution of self-disclosure in dyads. *Journal of Personality and Social Psychology,* 1977, *35,* 31–37.

Davis, K. E., and E. E. Jones. Changes in interpersonal perception as a means of reducing cognitive dissonance. *Journal of Abnormal and Social Psychology,* 1960, *61,* 402–410.

Dean, R. B., J. A. Austin, and W. A. Watts. Forewarning effects in persuasion: Field and classroom experiments. *Journal of Personality and Social Psychology,* 1971, *18,* 210–221.

Deaux, K. Sex and the attribution process. In J. H. Harvey, W. Ickes, and R. F. Kidd (eds.), *New directions in attribution research, Vol. 1,* New York: Wiley, 1976.

de Carufel, A. C., and C. A. Insko. Balance and social comparison processes in the attribution of attraction. *Journal of Personality,* 1979, *47,* 432–448.

Derbyshire, R. C. Medical ethics and discipline. *Journal of American Medical Association,* 1974, *228,* 59–62.

De Rivera, J. *Field theory as human science: Contributions of Lewin's Berlin group.* New York: Gardner Press, 1976.

Desor, J. Toward a psychological theory of crowding. *Journal of Personality and Social Psychology,* 1972, *21,* 79–83.

Deutsch, M. A theory of co-operation and competition. *Human Relations,* 1949a, *2,* 129–152.

———. An experimental study of the effects of co-operation and competition upon group process. *Human Relations,* 1949b, *2,* 199–232.

———. Field theory in social psychology. In G. Lindzey (ed.), *Handbook of social psychology.* Reading, Mass.: Addison-Wesley, 1954. Pp. 181–222.

———, and H. B. Gerard. A study of normative and informational social influences upon individual judgment. *Journal of Abnormal and Social Psychology,* 1955, *51,* 629–636.

Dewey, J. *The school and society.* Chicago: University of Chicago Press, 1899.

———. *Human nature and conduct.* New York: Modern Library, 1922.

Dewey, R., and W. J. Humber. *An introduction to social psychology.* New York: Macmillan, 1966.

Dickinson, R. L., and Beam, L. *A thousand marriages.* Baltimore: Williams and Wilkins, 1931.

Diggory, J. C. *Self-evaluation: Concepts and studies.* New York: Wiley, 1966.

———, S. J. Klein, and Cohen, M. Muscle action potentials and estimated probability of success. *Journal of Experimental Psychology,* 1964, *68,* 449–455.

Dollard, J. C., and N. E. Miller. *Personality and psychotherapy.* New York: McGraw-Hill, 1950.

Dreben, E. K., S. T. Fiske, and R. Hastie. The independence of evaluative and item information: Impression and recall order effects in behavior-based impression formation. *Journal of Personality and Social Psychology,* 1979, *37,* 1758–1768.

Durkheim, E. *De la division du travail social.* Paris: Alcan, 1893.

Duval, S., and R. A. Wicklund. *A theory of objective self-awareness*. New York: Academic Press, 1972.

——, and R. A. Wicklund. Effects of objective self-awareness on attributions of causality. *Journal of Experimental Social Psychology*, 1973, *9*, 17–31.

——, ——, and R. L. Fine. Avoidance of objective self-awareness under conditions of high and low intra-self discrepancy. In S. Duval and R. A. Wicklund, *A theory of objective self-awareness*. New York: Academic Press, 1972.

Dweck, C. S., and T. E. Goetz. Attributions and learned helplessness. In J. H. Harvey, W. Ickes, and R. F. Kidd (eds.), *New directions in attribution research, Vol. 2*. Hillsdale, N. J.: Lawrence Erlbaum, 1978.

Eagly, A. H., and K. Telaak. Width of the latitude of acceptance as a determinant of attitude change. *Journal of Personality and Social Psychology*, 1972, *23*, 388–397.

Easterbrook, J. A. The effect of emotion on cue utilization and the organization of behavior. *Psychological Review*, 1959, *66*, 183–201.

Edwards, W. A theory of decision making. *Psychological Bulletin*, 1954, *51*, 380–417.

——. Behavioral decision theory. *Annual Review of Psychology*, 1961, *12*, 473–498.

——. Conservatism in human information processing. In B. Klienmuntz (ed.) *Formal representation of human judgment*. New York: Wiley, 1968.

Eiser, J. R., and C. J. M. White. Categorization and congruity in attitudinal judgment. *Journal of Personality and Social Psychology*, 1975, *31*, 769–775.

Ellsworth, P. C., H. S. Friedman, D. Perlick, and M. E. Hoyt. Some effects of gaze on subjects motivated to seek or avoid social comparison. *Journal of Experimental Psychology*, 1978, *14*, 69–87.

Eriksen, C. W., and H. W. Hake. Anchor effects in absolute judgments. *Journal of Experimental Psychology*, 1957, *53*, 132–138.

Esch, J. A study of judgments of social situations. Unpublished term paper, University of Kansas, 1950. Cited in F. Heider, *The psychology of interpersonal relations*. New York: Wiley, 1958.

Esser, A. H. Experiences of crowding: Illustration of a paradigm for man-environment relations. *Representative Research in Social Psychology*, 1973, *4*, 207–218.

Evans, P. A visit with Michael Argyle. *APA Monitor*, 1978, *9*, (No. 8), 6–7.

Exline, R. V. Explorations in the process of person perception: Visual interaction in relation to competition, sex, and need for affiliation. *Journal of Personality*, 1963, *31*, 1–20.

——, D. Gray, and D. Schuette. Visual behavior in a dyad as affected by interview content and sex of respondent. *Journal of Personality and Social Psychology*, 1965, *1*, 201–209.

Falbo, T., and R. C. Beck. Naive psychology and the attributional model of achievement. *Journal of Personality*, 1979, *47*, 185–195.

Fazio, R. H. Motives for social comparison: The construction-validation distinction. *Journal of Personality and Social Psychology*, 1979, *37*, 1683–1698.

Feather, N. T. The effects of prior success and failure on expectations of success and subsequent performance. *Journal of Personality and Social Psychology*, 1966, *3*, 287–298.

——. Attribution of responsibility and valence of success and failure in relation to initial confidence and task performance. *Journal of Personality and Social Psychology*, 1969, *13*, 129–144.

——, and J. G. Simon. Attribution of responsibility and valence of outcome in relation to initial confidence and success and failure of self and other. *Journal of Personality and Social Psychology,* 1971, *18,* 173–188.

Fernberger, S. W. On absolute and relative judgments in lifted weight experiments. *American Journal of Psychology,* 1931, *43,* 560–578.

Ferster, C. B., and B. F. Skinner. *Schedules of reinforcement.* New York: Appleton-Century-Crofts, 1957.

Festinger, L. Informal social communication. *Psychological Review,* 1950, *57,* 271–282.

———. A theory of social comparison processes. *Human Relations,* 1954, *7,* 117–140.

———. *A theory of cognitive dissonance.* Stanford: Stanford University Press, 1957.

———. *Conflict, decision and dissonance.* Stanford: Stanford University Press, 1964.

———, H. B. Gerard, B. Hymovitch, H. H. Kelley, and B. Raven. The influence process in the presence of extreme deviates. *Human Relations,* 1952, *5,* 327–346.

———, S. Schachter, and K. Back. *Social pressures in informal groups.* New York: Harper & Row, 1950.

———, and J. W. Thibaut. Interpersonal communications in small groups. *Journal of Abnormal and Social Psychology,* 1951, *46,* 92–99.

———, J. Torrey, and B. Willerman. Self-evaluation as a function of attraction to the group. *Human Relations,* 1954, *7,* 161–174.

Fiedler, F. E. A method of objective quantification of certain countertransference attitudes. *Journal of Clinical Psychology,* 1951, *7,* 101–107.

———. Assumed similarity measures as predictors of team effectiveness. *Journal of Abnormal and Social Psychology,* 1954, *49,* 381–388.

———. The influence of leader-keyman relations on combat crew effectiveness. *Journal of Abnormal and Social Psychology,* 1955, *51,* 227–235.

———. A contingency model of leadership effectiveness. In L. Berkowitz (ed.), *Advances in experimental social psychology. Vol. 1.* New York: Academic Press, 1964. Pp. 149–190.

———. The effect of leadership and cultural heterogeneity on group performance: A test of the contingency model. *Journal of Experimental and Social Psychology,* 1966, *2,* 237–264.

———. *A theory of leadership effectiveness.* New York: McGraw-Hill, 1967.

———. The effects of leadership training and experience: A contingency model interpretation. *Administrative Science Quarterly,* 1972, *17,* 453–470.

Fishbein, M. A consideration of beliefs, attitudes and their relationships. In I. D. Steiner and M. Fishbein (eds.), *Current studies in social psychology.* New York: Holt, Rinehart and Winston, 1965. Pp. 107–120.

———. A behavior theory approach to the relation between beliefs about an object and the attitude toward the object. In M. Fishbein (ed.), *Readings in attitude theory and measurement.* New York: Wiley, 1967, Pp. 389–400.

———, and I. Ajzen. *Belief, attitude, intention, and behavior.* Reading, Mass.: Addison-Wesley, 1975.

———, and I. Ajzen. Misconceptions about the Fishbein model: Reflections on a study by Songer-Nocks. *Journal of Experimental Social Psychology,* 1976, *12,* 579–584.

———, and R. Hunter. Summation versus balance in attitude organization and change. *Journal of Abnormal and Social Psychology,* 1964, *69,* 505–510.

Foa, U. G., and E. B. Foa. *Resource theory of social exchange.* Morristown, N. J.: General Learning Press, 1975.

Ford, C. S. Society, culture, and the human organism. *Journal of General Psychology,* 1939, *20,* 135–179.

Form, W. H., and S. Nosow. *Community in disaster.* New York: Harper & Row, 1958.

Frank, P. *Philosophy of science.* Englewood Cliffs, N. J.: Prentice-Hall, 1957.

Frankfurt, L. P. The role of some individual and interpersonal factors in the acquaintance process. Unpublished doctoral dissertation, The American University, Washington, D. C., 1965.

Freedman, J. L. *Crowding and behavior.* New York: Viking, 1975.

————, and D. O. Sears. Selective exposure. In L. Berkowitz (ed.), *Advances in experimental social psychology. Vol. 2.* New York: Academic Press, 1965. Pp. 58–97.

Freidman, S., P. Chodoff, J. W. Mason, and D. A. Hamberg. Behavioral observations of parents anticipating the death of a child. *Pediatrics,* 1963, *32,* 616–625.

French, J. R. P., Jr. A formal theory of social power. *Psychological Review,* 1956, *63,* 181–194.

Freud, S. *The problem of anxiety.* New York: Norton, 1936.

————. Libidinal types. *Collected papers.* London: Hogarth, 1950. Pp. 247–251.

Fromm, E. *Man for himself.* New York: Holt, Rinehart and Winston, 1947.

Fuller, C. H. Comparison of two experimental paradigms of tests of Heider's balance theory. *Journal of Personality and Social Psychology,* 1974, *30,* 802–806.

Gabrenya, W. K., Jr., and R. M. Arkin. The effect of commitment on expectancy value and expectancy weight in social decision making. *Personality and Social Psychology Bulletin,* 1979, *5,* 86–90.

Gaes, G. G., R. J. Kalle, and J. T. Tedeschi. Impression management in the forced compliance situation. Two studies using the bogus pipeline. *Journal of Experimental Social Psychology,* 1978, *14,* 493–510.

Garcia-Esteve, J., and M. E. Shaw. Rural and urban patterns of responsibility attribution in Puerto Rico. *Journal of Social Psychology,* 1968, *74,* 143–149.

Gardner, J. W. Level of aspiration in response to a prearranged sequence of scores. *Journal of Experimental Psychology,* 1939, *25,* 601–621.

Garner, W. R. *Uncertainty and structure as psychological concepts.* New York: Wiley, 1962.

Gastorf, J. W., and J. Suls. Performance evaluation via social comparison: Performance versus related-attribute similarity. *Social Psychology,* 1978, *41,* 297–305.

Gebhard, M. E. The effect of success and failure upon the attractiveness of activities as a function of experience, expectation, and need. *Journal of Experimental Psychology,* 1948, *38,* 371–388.

Gerard, H. The effects of different dimensions of disagreement on the communication process in small groups. *Human Relations,* 1953, *6,* 249–272.

Gerard, H. B. Some effects of status, role clarity, and group goal clarity upon the individual's relations to group process. *Journal of Personality,* 1957, *25,* 475–488.

Gergen, K. J. Social psychology as history. *Journal of Personality and Social Psychology,* 1973, *26,* 309–320.

Gergen, K., and M. Taylor. Social expectancy and self-presentation in a status hierarchy. *Journal of Experimental Social Psychology,* 1969, *5,* 79–92.

Gerst, M. S. Symbolic coding processes in observational learning. *Journal of Personality and Social Psychology,* 1971, *19,* 7–17.

Getzels, J. W., and E. G. Guba. Role, role conflict, and effectiveness: An empirical study. *American Sociological Review,* 1954, *19,* 164–175.

Gewirtz, H. B. Generalization of children's performance as a function of reinforcement and task similarity. *Journal of Abnormal and Social Psychology,* 1959, *58,* 111–118.

Gewirtz, J. L. Conditional responding as a model for observational, imitative learning, and vicarious reinforcement. In H. W. Reese (ed.), *Advances in child development and behavior,* Vol. 6. New York: Academic Press, 1971a.

———. The roles of overt responding and extrinsic reinforcement in "self-" and "vicarious-reinforcement" phenomena and in "observational learning" and imitation. In R. Glaser (ed.), *The nature of reinforcement.* New York: Academic Press, 1971b.

———, and K. G. Stingle. The learning of generalized imitation as a basis for identification. *Psychological Review,* 1968, *75,* 374–397.

Gibson, J. J., and A. D. Pick. Perception of another person's looking behavior, *American Journal of Psychology,* 1963, *76,* 86–94.

Glass, D. C. Changes in liking as a means of reducing cognitive discrepancies between self-esteem and aggression. *Journal of Personality,* 1964, *32,* 520–549.

Goethals, G. R., J. Cooper, and A. Naficy. Role of foreseen, foreseeable, and unforeseeable behavioral consequences in the arousal of cognitive dissonance. *Journal of Personality and Social Psychology,* 1979, *37,* 1179–1185.

———, and M. P. Zanna. The role of social comparison in choice shifts. *Journal of Personality and Social Psychology,* 1979, *37,* 1469–1476.

Goffman, E. *The presentation of self in everyday life.* New York: Doubleday, 1959.

———. *Relations in public.* New York: Basic Books, 1971.

Goldman, H., and B. R. Schlenker. Proattitudinal behavior, impression management, and attitude change. Paper presented at the 85th Annual Meeting of the American Psychological Association, San Francisco, 1977.

Goldstein, K. *Human nature in the light of psychopathology.* Cambridge, Mass.: Harvard University Press, 1940.

Gollob, H. F., and G. W. Fischer. Some relationships between social inference, cognitive balance, and change in impression. *Journal of Personality and Social Psychology,* 1973, *26,* 16–22.

Goode, W. J. A theory of role strain. *American Sociological Review,* 1960, *25,* 483–496.

Gordon, B. F. Influence and social comparison as motives for affiliation. *Journal of Experimental and Social Psychology,* Supplement 1, 1966, 55–65.

Goss, N. E., C. H. Morgan, and S. J. Golin. Paired-associates learning as a function of percentage occurrence of response members (reinforcement). *Journal of Experimental Psychology,* 1959, *57,* 96–104.

Gould, R. An experimental analysis of "level of aspiration." *Genetic Psychology Monographs,* 1939, *21,* 1–116.

Gouldner, A. W. *Patterns of industrial bureaucracy.* Glencoe, Ill.: The Free Press, 1954.

———. The norm of reciprocity: A preliminary statement. *American Sociological Review,* 1960, *25,* 161–178.

Granberg, D., and E. E. Brent. Dove-hawk placements in the 1968 election: Application of social judgment and balance theories. *Journal of Personality and Social Psychology,* 1974, *29,* 687–695.

Grant, D. A. and L. M. Schipper. The acquisition and extinction of conditioned eyelid responses as a function of the percentage of fixed ratio random reinforcement. *Journal of Experimental Psychology,* 1952, *43,* 313–320.

Greenberg, C. I., and I. J. Firestone. Compensatory responses to crowding: Effects of personal space intrusion and privacy reduction. *Journal of Personality and Social Psychology,* 1977, *35,* 637–644.

Gross, N., W. S. Mason, and A. W. McEachern. *Explorations in role analysis: Studies of the school superintendency role.* New York: Wiley, 1957.

Gruder, C. L. Determinants of social comparison choices. *Journal of Experimental Social Psychology,* 1971, *7,* 473–489.

Gullahorn, J. Distance and friendship as factors in the gross interaction matrix. *Sociometry,* 1952, *15,* 123–134.

Gullahorn, J. T., and J. E. Gullahorn. A computer model of elementary social behaviour. In E. Feigenbaum and J. Feldman (eds.), *Computers and thought.* New York: McGraw-Hill, 1963.

——, and ——. Computer simulation of human interaction in small groups. *Simulation,* 1965, *4,* 50–61.

——, and ——. A non-random walk in the Odyssey of a computer model. In M. Anbar and C. S. Stoll (eds.), *Simulation and gaming in social science.* New York: The Free Press, 1972.

Guthrie, E. R. *The psychology of learning.* New York: Harper & Row, 1935.

Gutman, G. M., and R. E. Knox. Balance, agreement, and attraction in pleasantness, tension, and consistency ratings of hypothetical social situations. *Journal of Personality and Social Psychology,* 1972, *24,* 351–357.

Guttman, N., and H. I. Kalish. Discriminability and stimulus generalization. *Journal of Experimental Psychology,* 1956, *51,* 79–88.

Haggard, E. A. Psychological causes and results of stress. In *Human Factors in undersea warfare.* Washington: National Research Council, 1949.

Hakmiller, K. L. Threat as a determinant of downward comparison. *Journal of Experimental and Social Psychology,* Supplement 1, 1966a, 32–39.

——. Need for self-evaluation, perceived similarity and comparison choice. *Journal of Experimental and Social Psychology,* Supplement 1, 1966b, 49–54.

Hall, E. T. *The hidden dimension.* New York: Doubleday, 1966.

Hall, J. F. *The psychology of learning.* Philadelphia: Lippincott, 1966.

Hamblin, R. L., and J. H. Kunkel. *Behavioral theory in sociology.* New Brunswick, N. J.: Transaction Books, 1977.

Hammond, L. K., and M. Goldman. Competition and non-competition and its relationship to individual and group productivity. *Sociometry,* 1961, *24,* 46–60.

Hardy, R. C. Effect of leadership style on the performance of small classroom groups: A test of the contingency model. *Journal of Personality and Social Psychology,* 1971, *19,* 367–374.

Hardyck, J. A., and M. Kardush. A modest modish model for dissonance reduction. In R. P. Abelson, E. Aronson, W. J. McGuire, T. M. Newcomb, M. J. Rosenberg, and P. H. Tannenbaum (eds), *Theories of cognitive consistency: A sourcebook.* Chicago: Rand McNally, 1968. Pp. 684–692.

Harvey, J. H., and S. Johnston. Determinants of the perception of choice. *Journal of Experimental Social Psychology,* 1973, *9,* 164–179.

Harvey, O. J., and R. Ware. Personality differences in dissonance resolution. *Journal of Personality and Social Psychology,* 1967, *7,* 227–230.

Heider, F. Social perception and phenomenal causality. *Psychological Review,* 1944, *51,* 358–374.

——. Attitudes and cognitive organization. *Journal of Psychology,* 1946, *21,* 107–112.

——. The psychology of interpersonal relations. New York: Wiley, 1958.

Heilman, M. E. and B. L. Toffler. Reacting to reactance: An interpersonal interpretation of the need for freedom. *Journal of Experimental Social Psychology,* 1976, *12,* 519–529.

Heintz, R. K. The effect of remote anchoring points upon the judgment of lifted weights. *Journal of Experimental Psychology,* 1950, *40,* 584–591.

Heller, J. F., M. S. Pallak, and J. M. Picek. The interactive effects of intent and threat on boomerang attitude change. *Journal of Personality and Social Psychology*, 1973, *26*, 273–279.

Hempel, C. G. Fundamentals of concept formation in empirical science. *International Encyclopedia of Unified Science, vol. 2, no. 7*. Chicago: University of Chicago Press, 1952.

Hendrick, C., J. Mills, and C. A. Kiesler. Decision time as a function of the number and complexity of equally attractive alternatives. *Journal of Personality and Social Psychology*, 1968, *8*, 313–318.

Herman, C. P., and D. Mack. Restrained and unrestrained eating. *Journal of Personality*, 1975, *43*, 647–660.

Higgins, E. T., F. Rhodewalt, and M. P. Zanna. Dissonance motivation: Its nature, persistence, and reinstatement. *Journal of Experimental Social Psychology*, 1979, *15*, 16–34.

Hilgard, E. R. *Theories of learning*. 2nd ed. New York: Appleton-Century-Crofts, 1956.

Himmelfarb, S. General test of a differential weighted averaging model of impression formation. *Journal of Experimental Social Psychology*, 1973, *9*, 379–390.

Hochbaum, G. M. *Certain personality aspects and pressures to uniformity in social group*. Doctoral dissertation, Minneapolis, University of Minnesota, 1953.

Hoffman, P. J., L. Festinger, and D. H. Lawrence. Tendencies toward group comparability in competitive bargaining. *Human Relations*, 1954, *7*, 141–159.

Hollander, E. P. Competence and conformity in the acceptance of influence. *Journal of Abnormal and Social Psychology*, 1960, *61*, 365–370.

———. *Principles and methods of social psychology*. New York: Oxford University Press, 1967.

———. *Principles and methods of social psychology*. 3d ed. New York: Oxford University Press, 1976.

Homans, G. C. Social behavior as exchange. *American Journal of Sociology*, 1956, *63*, 597–606.

———. *Social behavior: Its elementary forms*. New York: Harcourt, Brace, Jovanovich, 1961.

———. *Social behavior: Its elementary forms*. New York: Harcourt, Brace, Jovanovich, 1974 (2nd edition).

Horner, M. S. *Sex differences in achievement motivation and performance in competitive and non-competitive situations*. Unpublished doctoral dissertation, University of Michigan, Ann Arbor, 1968.

———. Toward an understanding of achievement-related conflicts in women. *Journal of Social Issues*, 1972, *28*, 157–175.

———. The measurement and behavioral implications of fear of success in women. In J. W. Atkinson and J. O. Raynor (eds.), *Motivation and achievement*. Washington, D. C.: Winston, 1974.

Horney, K. *Our inner conflicts*. New York: Norton, 1945.

Hornik, J. A. Two approaches to individual differences in cooperative behavior in an expanded Prisoner's Dilemma game. Unpbl. Master's level paper, University of Illinois, 1970.

Hottes, J., and A. Kahn. Sex differences in a mixed motive conflict situation. *Journal of Personality*, 1974, *42*, 260–275.

Hovland, C. I. The generalization of conditioned responses. II. The sensory generalization of conditioned responses with varying intensities of tone. *Journal of Genetic Psychology*, 1937, *17*, 125–148.

————, O. J. Harvey, and M. Sherif. Assimilation and contrast effects in reaction to communication and attitude change. *Journal of Abnormal and Social Psychology,* 1957, *55,* 244–252.

————, and Sherif, M. Judgmental phenomena and scales of attitude measurement: Item displacement in Thurstone scales. *Journal of Abnormal and Social Psychology,* 1952, *47,* 822–832.

Hull, C. L. *Principles of behavior.* New York: Appleton-Century-Crofts, 1943.

————. *A behavior system.* New Haven: Yale University Press, 1952.

Humphrey, G. Imitation and the conditioned reflex. *Pedagogical Seminary,* 1921, *28,* 1–21.

Hunt, E. B. *Concept learning: An information processing problem.* New York: Wiley, 1962.

Hunt, J. G. *A test of the leadership contingency model in three organizations.* Technical Report No. 47 (67-3), ONR Contract NR 177-472, Nonr- 1834(36), University of Illinois, 1967.

Hunt, W. A. Anchoring effects in judgment. *American Journal of Psychology,* 1941, *54,* 395–403.

Ickes, W., and R. D. Barnes. The role of sex and self-monitoring in unstructured dyadic interaction. *Journal of Personality and Social Psychology,* 1977, *35,* 315–330.

Ickes, W. J., M. A. Layden, and R. D. Barnes. Objective self-awareness and individuation: An empirical link. *Journal of Personality,* 1978, *46,* 146–161.

Ickes, W. J., R. A. Wicklund, and C. B. Ferris. Objective self-awareness and self-esteem. *Journal of Experimental Social Psychology,* 1973, *9,* 202–219.

Ingham, A. G., G. Levinger, J. Graves, and V. Peckham. The Ringelmann effect: Studies of group size and performance. *Journal of Experimental Social Psychology,* 1974, *10,* 371–384.

Insko, C. A. *Theories of attitude change.* New York: Appleton-Century-Crofts, 1967.

————, and A. Adewole. The role of assumed similarity in the production of attraction and agreement effects in p-o-x triads. *Journal of Personality and Social Psychology,* 1979, *37,* 790–808.

————, E. Songer, and W. McGarvey. Balance, positivity, and agreement in the Jordan paradigm: A defense of balance theory. *Journal of Experimental Social Psychology,* 1974, *10,* 53–83.

Jaccard, J. J., and M. Fishbein. Inferential beliefs and order effects in personality impression formation. *Journal of Personality and Social Psychology,* 1975, *31,* 1031–1040.

————, R. Knox, and D. Brinberg. Prediction of behavior from beliefs: An extension and test of a subjective probability model. *Journal of Personality and Social Psychology,* 1979, *37,* 1239–1248.

Jacobs, L., E. Berscheid, and E. Walster. Self-esteem and attraction. *Journal of Personality and Social Psychology,* 1971, *17,* 84–91.

James, W. *The principles of psychology.* New York: Holt, Rinehart and Winston, 1890.

Jellison, J. M., and J. H. Harvey. Determinants of perceived choice and the relationship between perceived choice and perceived competence. *Journal of Personality and Social Psychology,* 1973, *28,* 376–382.

Jenkins, W. D., and J. C. Stanley. Partial reinforcement: A review and critique. *Psychological Bulletin,* 1950, *47,* 193–234.

Jennings, H. *Leadership and isolation.* New York: Longmans Green, 1950.

Johnson, C. F., and J. M. Dabbs, Jr. Self-disclosure in dyads as a function of distance and subject-experimenter relationship. *Sociometry,* 1976, *39,* 257–263.

Jones, E. E. *Ingratiation.* New York: Appleton-Century-Crofts, 1964.

———, and S. Berglas. Control of attributions about the self through self-handicapping strategies: The appeal of alcohol and the role of underachievement. *Personality and Social Psychology Bulletin,* 1978, *4,* 200–206.

———, and B. N. Daughtery. Political orientation and the perceptual effects of an anticipated interaction. *Journal of Abnormal and Social Psychology,* 1959, *59,* 340–349.

———, and K. E. Davis. From acts to dispositions: The attribution process in person perception. In L. Berkowitz (ed.), *Advances in experimental social psychology. Vol. 2.* New York: Academic Press, 1965. Pp. 219–266.

———, and H. B. Gerard. *Foundations of social psychology.* New York: Wiley, 1967.

———, K. J. Gergen, and K. E. Davis. Some determinants of reactions to being approved or disapproved as a person. *Psychological Monographs,* 1962, *76* (Whole No. 521).

———, ———, P. Gumpert, and J. W. Thibaut. Some conditions affecting the use of ingratiation to influence performance evaluation. *Journal of Personality and Social Psychology,* 1965, *1,* 613–625.

———, ———, and R. G. Jones. Tactics of ingratiation among leaders and subordinates in a status hierarchy. *Psychological Monographs,* 1963, *77,* No. 3 (Whole No. 566).

———, and E. M. Gordon. Timing of self-disclosure and its effects on personal attraction. *Journal of Personality and Social Psychology,* 1972, *24,* 358–365.

———, and V. A. Harris. The attribution of attitudes. *Journal of Experimental Social Psychology,* 1967, *3,* 1–24.

———, and R. Kohler. The effects of plausibility on the learning of controversial statements. *Journal of Abnormal and Social Psychology,* 1958, *57,* 315–320.

———, and D. McGillis. Correspondent inference and the attribution cube: A comparative appraisal. In J. Harvey, W. Ickes, and R. Kidd (eds.), *New directions in attribution research, Vol. 1.* Hillsdale, N. J.: Lawrence Erlbaum, 1976.

———, and R. E. Nisbett. *The actor and the observer: Divergent perceptions of the causes of behavior.* Morristown, N. J.: General Learning Press, 1971.

———, S. Worchel, G. R. Goethals, and J. F. Grumet. Prior expectancy and behavioral extremity as determinants of attitude attribution. *Journal of Experimental Social Psychology,* 1971, *7,* 59–80.

———, and C. B. Wortman. *Ingratiation: An attributional approach.* Morristown, N. J.: General Learning Press, 1973.

Jones, R. A., D. E. Linder, C. A. Kiesler, M. P. Zanna, and J. W. Brehm. Internal states or external stimuli: Observers' attitude judgments and the dissonance theory–self perception controversy. *Journal of Experimental Social Psychology,* 1968, *4,* 247–269.

R. G. Jones, and E. E. Jones. Optimum conformity as an ingratiation tactic. *Journal of Personality,* 1964, *32,* 436–458.

Jones, S. C., and D. T. Regan. Ability evaluation through social comparison. *Journal of Experimental Social Psychology,* 1974, *10,* 133–146.

Jordan, N. Behavioral forces that are a function of attitudes and of cognitive organization. *Human Relations,* 1953, *6,* 273–287.

Jourard, S. M. Self-disclosure and other cathexis. *Journal of Abnormal and Social Psychology,* 1959, *59,* 428–443.

Judd, C. M., and J. M. Harackiewicz. Contrast effects in attitude judgment: An examination of the accentuation hypothesis. *Journal of Personality and Social Psychology,* 1980, *38,* 390–398.

Jurma, W. E. Leadership structuring style, task ambiguity, and group member satisfaction. *Small Group Behavior,* 1978, *9,* 124–134.

Kahn, A., J. Hottes, and H. L. Davis. Cooperation and optimal responding in the prisoner's dilemma game: Effects of sex and physical attractiveness. *Journal of Personality and Social Psychology,* 1971, *17,* 267–279.

Kalven, J., Jr., and H. Zeisel. *The American jury.* Boston: Little, Brown, 1966.

Kanareff, V., and J. T. Lanzetta. Effects of task definition and probability of reinforcement upon the acquisition and extinction of imitative responses. *Journal of Experimental Psychology,* 1960, *60,* 340–348.

Kanfer, F. H. Vicarious human reinforcement: A glimpse into the back of the box. In L. Krasner and L. P. Ullman (eds.), *Research in behavior modification.* New York: Holt, Rinehart and Winston, 1965. Pp. 244–267.

———, and A. R. Marston. Human reinforcement: Vicarious and direct. *Journal of Experimental Psychology,* 1963, *65,* 292–296.

Kaplan, A. *The conduct of inquiry: Methodology for behavioral science.* San Francisco: Chandler, 1964.

Kaplan, M. F. Contexts effects in impression formation: The weighted average versus the meaning-change formulation. *Journal of Personality and Social Psychology,* 1971, *19,* 92–99.

———. Discussion of polarization effects in a modified jury decision paradigm: Informational influences. *Sociometry,* 1977, *40,* 262–271.

Karsten, A. Psychische Sattigung. *Psychol. Forsch.,* 1928, *10,* 142–154.

Kasl, S., and J. R. P. French. The effects of occupational status on physical and mental health. *Journal of Social Issues,* 1962, *18,* 65–89.

Katz, D., and R. L. Kahn. Some recent findings in human relations research in industry. In G. E. Swanson, T. M. Newcomb, and E. L. Hartley (eds.), *Readings in social psychology.* Rev. ed. New York: Holt, Rinehart and Winston, 1952.

Kaufman, D. R., and I. D. Steiner. Some variables affecting the use of conformity as an ingratiation technique. *Journal of Experimental Social Psychology,* 1968, *4,* 400–411.

Keller, F. S., and W. N. Schoenfeld. *Principles of psychology.* New York: Appleton-Century-Crofts, 1950.

Kelley, H. H. Two functions of reference groups. In G. E. Swanson, T. M. Newcomb, and E. L. Hartley (eds.), *Readings in social psychology.* Rev. ed. New York: Holt, Rinehart and Winston, 1952. Pp. 410–414.

———. Attribution theory in social psychology. In D. Levine (ed.), *Nebraska symposium on motivation,* 1967. Lincoln: University of Nebraska Press, 1967. Pp. 192–238.

———. *Attribution in social interaction.* Morristown, N. J.: General Learning Press, 1971.

———. *Causal schemata and the attribution process.* Morristown, N. J.: General Learning Press, 1972.

———. The processes of causal attribution. *American Psychologist,* 1973, *28,* 107–128.

———, and A. J. Stahelski. Social interaction basis of cooperators' and competitors' beliefs about others. *Journal of Personality and Social Psychology,* 1970, *16,* 66–91.

———, and J. W. Thibaut. Group problem solving. In G. Lindzey and E. Aronson (eds.), *The handbook of social psychology.* Reading, Mass.: Addison-Wesley, 1969, *Vol. 4,* 1–101.

———, and ———. *Interpersonal relations: A theory of interdependence.* New York: Wiley, 1978.

Kelly, G. A. *The psychology of personal constructs.* New York: Norton, 1955.

Kerckhoff, A. C., and K. E. Davis. Value consensus and need complementarity in mate selection. *American Sociological Review,* 1962, *27,* 295–303.

Kerrick, J. The effect of relevant and non-relevant sources on attitude change. *Journal of Social Psychology,* 1958, *47,* 15–20.

———, and D. A. McMillan, III. The effect of instructional set on the measurement of attitude change through communications. *Journal of Social Psychology,* 1961, *53,* 113–120.

Kiesler, C. A. Conflict and the number of choice alternatives. *Psychological Reports,* 1966, *18,* 603–610.

———. A motivational theory of stimulus incongruity, with applications for such phenomena as dissonance and self-attribution. Paper presented at the annual meeting of the Midwestern Psychological Association, Chicago, Illinois, 1974.

———, R. E. Nisbett, and M. P. Zanna. On inferring one's beliefs from one's behavior. *Journal of Personality and Social Psychology,* 1969, *11,* 321–327.

Kimble, G. A. *Hilgard and Marquis' conditioning and learning.* New York: Appleton-Century-Crofts, 1961.

———. *Foundations of conditioning and learning.* New York: Appleton-Century-Crofts, 1967.

Kleck, R. E. Interaction distance and non-verbal agreeing responses. *British Journal of Social and Clinical Psychology,* 1970, *9,* 180–182.

Kleinke, C. L. Compliance to requests made by gazing and touching experimenters in field settings. *Journal of Experimental Social Psychology,* 1977, *13,* 218–223.

Knower, F. H. Experimental studies of change in attitudes: I. A study of the effect of oral argument on change of attitude. *Journal of Social Psychology,* 1935, *6,* 315–347.

Kohlberg, L. The development of children's orientations toward a moral order. I. Sequence in the development of moral thought. *Vita Humana,* 1963, *6,* 11–33.

Kohler, W. Relational determination in perception. In L. A. Jeffress (ed.), *Cerebral mechanisms in behavior.* New York: Wiley, 1951.

Krech, D., and R. S. Crutchfield. *Theory and problems of social psychology.* New York: McGraw-Hill, 1948.

Kruglanski, A. W., and M. Cohen. Attributed freedom and personal causation. *Journal of Personality and Social Psychology,* 1973, *26,* 245–250.

———, and ———. Attributing freedom in the decision context: Effects of choice alternatives, degree of commitment and predecision uncertainty. *Journal of Personality and Social Psychology,* 1974, *30,* 178–187.

Kuenne, M. R. Experimental investigation of the relation of language to transposition behavior in young children. *Journal of Experimental Psychology,* 1946, *36,* 471–490.

Kuhn, T. S. *The structure of scientific revolutions.* Second edition. Chicago: University of Chicago Press, 1970.

———. Second thoughts on paradigms. In F. Suppe (ed.), *The structure of scientific theories.* Urbana, Ill.: University of Illinois Press, 1974. Pp. 459–482.

Kukla, A. Preferences among impossibly difficult and trivially easy tasks: A revision of Atkinson's theory of choice. *Journal of Personality and Social Psychology,* 1975, *32,* 338–345.

Kurtines, W., and E. B. Greif. The development of moral thought: Review and evaluation of Kohlberg's approach. *Psychological Bulletin,* 1974, *8,* 453–470.

Langer, E. J. Rethinking the role of thought in social interaction. In J. H. Harvey, W. J.

Ickes, and R. F. Kidd (eds.), *New directions in attribution research (Vol. 2)*. Hillsdale, N. J.: Lawrence Erlbaum, 1978.

————, and S. Saegert. Crowding and cognitive control. *Journal of Personality and Social Psychology*, 1977, *35*, 175–182.

Larder, D. L. Effect of aggressive story content on nonverbal play behavior. *Psychological Reports*, 1962, *11*, 14–15.

Lashley, K. S. *Brain mechanisms and intelligence*. Chicago: University of Chicago Press, 1929.

————, and M. Wade. The Pavlovian theory of generalization. *Psychological Review*, 1946, *53*, 72–87.

Latané, B. Studies in social comparison: Introduction and overview. *Journal of Experimental and Social Psychology*, Supplement 1, 1966, 1–5.

————, and J. Darley. *The unresponsive bystander: Why doesn't he help?* New York: Appleton-Century-Crofts, 1970.

Lazarus, R. S., J. C. Speisman, A. M. Mordkoff, and L. A. Davison. A Laboratory study of psychological stress produced by a motion picture. *Psychological Monographs*, 1962, *76*, No. 34 (Whole No. 553).

Leon, G. R., and L. Roth. Obesity: Psychological causes, correlations and speculations. *Psychological Bulletin*, 1977, *84*, 117–139.

Lepper, M. R., D. Greene, and R. E. Nisbett. Undermining children's intrinsic interest with extrinsic reward: A test of the overjustification hypothesis. *Journal of Personality and Social Psychology*, 1973, *28*, 129–137.

————, M. P. Zanna, and R. P. Abelson. Cognitive irreversibility in a dissonance-reduction situation. *Journal of Personality and Social Psychology*, 1970, *16*, 191–198.

Lerner, M. J. Evaluation of performance as a function of performer's reward and attractiveness. *Journal of Personality and Social Psychology*, 1965, *1*, 355–360.

Leventhal, G. S. The distribution of rewards and resources in groups and organizations. In L. Berkowitz (ed.), *Advances in experimental social psychology* (Vol. 9). New York: Academic Press, 1976.

————, J. Allen, and B. Kemelgor. Reducing inequity by reallocating rewards. *Psychonomic Science*, 1969, *14*, 295–296.

Leventhal, H. Emotions: A basic problem for social psychology. In C. Nemeth (ed.), *Social psychology: Classic and contemporary integrations*. Chicago: Rand-McNally, 1974.

Levinger, G., D. J. Senn, and B. W. Jorgensen. Progress toward permanence in courtship: A test of the Kerckhoff-Davis hypothesis. *Sociometry*, 1970, *33*, 427–443.

Lewin, K. *A dynamic theory of personality*. New York: McGraw-Hill, 1935.

————. *Principles of topological psychology*. New York: McGraw-Hill, 1936.

————. Regression, retrogression, and development. In R. Barker, T. Dembo, and K. Lewin (eds.), *Frustration and regression. University of Iowa Studies in Child Welfare*, 1941, *18*, No. 1, 1–43.

————. Field theory and learning. *Yearbook of the National Society for the Study of Education*, 1942, *41*, part II, 215–242.

————. Defining the "field at a given time." *Psychological Review*, 1943, *50*, 292–310.

————. Constructs in psychology and psychological ecology. *University of Iowa Studies in Child Welfare*, 1944, *20*, 1–29.

————. Behavior and development as a function of the total situation. In L. Carmichael (ed.), *Manual of child psychology*. New York: Wiley, 1946, Pp. 791–844.

————. *Field theory in social science*. New York: Harper & Row, 1951.

———, T. Dembo, L. Festinger, and P. S. Sears. Level of aspiration. In J. McV. Hunt (ed.), *Personality and the behavior disorders.* New York: Ronald Press, 1944. Pp. 333–378.

———, R. Lippitt, and R. K. White. Patterns of aggressive behavior in experimentally created "social climates." *Journal of Social Psychology,* 1939, *10,* 271–299.

Liebert, R. M., J. M. Neale, and E. S. Davidson. *The early window: Effects of television on children and youth.* New York: Pergamon Press, 1973.

Liebling, B. A., M. Seiler, and P. Shaver. Self-awareness and cigarette-smoking behavior. *Journal of Experimental Social Psychology,* 1974, *10,* 325–332.

Likert, R. A technique for the measurement of attitudes. *Archives of Psychology,* 1932, No. 140. Pp. 1–55.

Lippa, R. Expressive control and the leakage of dispositional introversion-extraversion during role-played teaching. *Journal of Personality,* 1976, *44,* 541–559.

———. The effect of expressive control on expressive consistency and on the relationship between expressive behavior and personality. *Journal of Personality,* 1978, *46,* 438–461.

Long, L. A study of the effect of preceding stimuli upon judgment of auditory intensities. *Archives of Psychology,* 1937, No. 209.

Lorber, N. The Ohio social acceptance scale. *Educational Research,* 1970, *12,* 240–243.

Lorge, I., and H. Solomon. Two models of group behavior in the solution of eureka-type problems. *Psychometrika,* 1955, *20,* 139–148.

Lövaas, O. I. Effect of exposure to symbolic aggression on aggressive behavior. *Child Development,* 1961, *32,* 37–44.

Luce, R. D. *Individual choice behavior.* New York: Wiley, 1959.

Lundgren, D. C. Interpersonal needs and member attitudes toward trainer and group. *Small Group Behavior,* 1975, *6,* 371–388.

———, and D. J. Knight. Trainer style and member attitudes toward trainer and group in T-groups. *Small Group Behavior,* 1977, *8,* 47–64.

McAllister, W. R., and D. E. McAllister. Increase over time in the stimulus generalization of acquired fear. *Journal of Experimental Psychology,* 1963, *65,* 576–582.

McArthur, L. A. The how and what of why: Some determinants and consequences of causal attribution. *Journal of Personality and Social Psychology,* 1972, *22,* 171–193.

McArthur, L. Z., and B. Burstein. Field dependent eating and perception as a function of weight and sex. *Journal of Personality,* 1975, *43,* 402–420.

McCallum, R., C. E. Rusbult, G. K. Hong, T. A. Walden, and J. Schopler. Effects of resource availability and importance of behavior on the experience of crowding. *Journal of Personality and Social Psychology,* 1979, *37,* 1304–1313.

McClintock, C. G. Game behavior and social motivation in interpersonal settings. In C. G. McClintock (ed.), *Experimental social psychology.* New York: Holt, Rinehart and Winston, 1972.

McCurdy, H. G., and W. E. Lambert. The efficiency of small human groups in the solution of problems requiring genuine cooperation. *Journal of Personality,* 1952, *20,* 478–494.

McDavid, J. W., and H. Harari. *Social psychology: Individuals, groups, societies.* New York: Harper & Row, 1968.

McDougall, W. *Introduction to social psychology.* London: Methuen, 1908.

———. *The group mind.* New York: Putnam, 1920.

McGarvey, H. R. Anchoring effects in the absolute judgment of verbal materials. *Archives of Psychology,* 1943, No. 281.

McGuire, W. Resistance to persuasion conferred by active and passive prior refutation of the same and alternative counterarguments. *Journal of Abnormal and Social Psychology,* 1961a, *63,* 326–332.

———. The effectiveness of supportive and refutational defenses in immunizing and restoring beliefs against persuasion. *Sociometry,* 1961b, *24,* 184–197.

———. Immunization against persuasion. Unpublished report, 1962a.

———. Persistence of the resistence to persuasion induced by various types of prior belief defenses. *Journal of Abnormal and Social Psychology,* 1962b, *64,* 241–248.

———. Inducing resistance to persuasion. In L. Berkowitz (ed.), *Advances in experimental social psychology.* Vol. 1. New York: Academic Press, 1964. Pp. 191–229.

———, and D. Papageorgis. The relative efficacy of various types of prior belief-defense in producing immunity against persuasion. *Journal of Abnormal and Social Psychology,* 1961, *62,* 327–337.

———, and ———. Effectiveness of forewarning in developing resistance to persuasion. *Public Opinion Quarterly,* 1962, *26,* 24–34.

McGuire, W. J. Theory of the structure of human thought. In R. P. Abelson, E. Aronson, W. J. McGuire, T. M. Newcomb, M. J. Rosenberg, and P. H. Tannenbaum (eds.), *Theories of cognitive consistency: A sourcebook.* Chicago: Rand McNally, 1968, Pp. 140–162.

MacLeod, R. B. The phenomenological approach to social psychology. *Psychological Review,* 1947, *54,* 193–210.

Mahler, V. Ersatzhandlungen verschiedenen Realitatsgrades. *Psychologische Forschung,* 1933, *18,* 26–89.

Maller, J. B. Co-operation and competition: An experimental study in motivation. New York: *Teachers' College, Contribution to Education,* No. 384, 1929.

Mandler, G., and W. Kessen. *The language of psychology.* New York: Wiley, 1959.

Manis, M. Cognitive social psychology. *Personality and Social Psychology Bulletin,* 1977, *3,* 550–566.

Manske, A. J. The reflection of teachers' attitudes in the attitudes of their pupils. In G. Murphy, L. B. Murphy, and T. M. Newcomb, *Experimental social psychology.* New York: Harper & Row, 1937.

March, J. G., and H. A. Simon. *Organizations.* New York: Wiley, 1958.

Marquart, D. I. Group problem solving. *Journal of Social Psychology,* 1955, *41,* 103–113.

Marshall, G. D., and P. G. Zimbardo. Affective consequences of inadequately explained physiological arousal. *Journal of Personality and Social Psychology,* 1979, *37,* 970–988.

Martens, R., and V. White. Influence of win-loss ratio on performance, satisfaction and preference for opponents. *Journal of Experimental Social Psychology,* 1975, *11,* 343–362.

Marwell, G., K. Ratcliff, and D. R. Schmitt. Minimizing differences in a maximizing differences game. *Journal of Personality and Social Psychology,* 1969, *12,* 158–163.

Marx, M. H. The general nature of theory construction. In M. H. Marx (ed.), *Psychological theory.* New York: Macmillan, 1951. Pp. 4–19.

———, and W. A. Hillix. *Systems and theories in psychology.* New York: McGraw-Hill, 1963.

Maslach, C. Negative emotional biasing of unexplained arousal. *Journal of Personality and Social Psychology,* 1979, *37,* 953–969.

Maslow, A. H. Conflict, frustration, and the theory of threat. *Journal of Abnormal and Social Psychology,* 1943, *38,* 81–86.

Masters, J. C., F. R. Gordon, and L. V. Clark. Effects of self-dispensed and externally dispensed model consequences on acquisition, spontaneous and oppositional imitation, and long-term retention. *Journal of Personality and Social Psychology,* 1976, *33,* 421–430.

May, M. A., and L. W. Doob. Co-operation and competition. *Social Science Research Council, Bulletin No. 25,* 1937.

Mazis, M. B. Antipollution measures and psychological reactance theory: A field experiment. *Journal of Personality and Social Psychology,* 1975, *31,* 654–660.

Mead, G. H. *Mind, self and society from the standpoint of a social behaviorist.* (Edited and with an introduction by C. W. Morris.) Chicago: University of Chicago Press, 1934.

Mead, M. *Co-operation and competition among primitive peoples.* New York: McGraw-Hill, 1937.

Merton, R. K. *Social theory and social structure.* Glencoe, Ill.: The Free Press, 1949.

———. The role set. *British Journal of Sociology,* 1957, *8,* 106–120.

———, and A. S. Kitt. Contributions to the theory of reference group behavior. In R. K. Merton and P. F. Lazarsfeld (eds.), *Continuities in social research: Studies in the scope and method of "The American Soldier."* Glencoe, Ill.: The Free Press, 1950. Pp. 40–105.

Mettee, D. R., and J. Riskind. Size of defeat and liking for superior and similar ability competitors. *Journal of Experimental Social Psychology,* 1974, *10,* 333–351.

Mettee, D. R., and P. C. Wilkins. When similarity "hurts": Effects of perceived ability and a humorous blunder upon interpersonal attractiveness. *Journal of Personality and Social Psychology,* 1972, *22,* 246–258.

Meuwese, W., and F. E. Fiedler. *Leadership and group creativity under varying conditions of stress.* Technical Report No. 22, ONR Contract NR 177-472, Nonr-1834(36), University of Illinois, 1965.

Meyer, J. P. Causal attribution for success and failure: A multivariate investigation of dimensionality, formation, and consequences. *Journal of Personality and Social Psychology,* 1980, *38,* 704–718.

Milgram, S. The experience of living in cities. *Science,* 1970, *167,* 1461–1468.

Miller, C. E. Using hypothetical P-O-X situations in studies of balance: The problem of "misconstrual." *Personality and Social Psychology Bulletin,* 1979, *5,* 303–306.

Miller, D. T., and M. Ross. Self-serving biases in the attribution of causality: Fact or fiction? *Psychological Bulletin,* 1975, *82,* 213–225.

Miller, G. A. The magical number seven, plus or minus two: Some limits on our capacity for processing information. *Psychological Review,* 1956, *62,* 81–97.

Miller, N. E. Experimental studies of conflict. In J. McV. Hunt (ed.), *Personality and the behavior disorders. Vol. 1.* New York: Ronald Press, 1944, Pp. 431–465.

———. Liberalization of basic S-R concepts: Extensions to conflict behavior, motivation, and social learning. In S. Koch (ed.), *Psychology: A study of a science, Vol. 2.* New York: McGraw-Hill, 1959.

———, and J. Dollard. *Social learning and imitation.* New Haven: Yale University Press, 1941.

Miller, R. L. Preferences for social vs. non-social comparison as a means of self-evaluation. *Journal of Personality,* 1977, *45,* 343–355.

Mischel, W. *Personality and assessment.* New York: Wiley, 1968.

Modigliani, A. Embarrassment, facework, and eye contact: Testing a theory of embarrassment. *Journal of Personality and Social Psychology,* 1971, *17,* 15–24.

Morasch, B., N. Groner, and J. P. Keating. Type of activity and failure of mediators of perceived crowding. *Personality and Social Psychology Bulletin,* 1979, *5,* 223–226.

Moreno, J. L. *Die Gottheit als Komoediant.* Vienna: Der Neue Daimon, 1919.

Morgan, S. W., and B. Mausner. Behavioral and fantasied indications of fear of success in men and women. *Journal of Personality,* 1973, *41,* 457–470.

Morton, T. L. Intimacy and reciprocity of exchange: A comparison of spouses and strangers. *Journal of Personality and Social Psychology,* 1978, *36,* 72–81.

Moss, F. A. (ed.) *Comparative psychology.* Rev. ed. New York: Prentice-Hall, 1946.

Mowrer, O. H. *Learning theory and the symbolic processes.* New York: Wiley, 1960.

Murray, H. A. *Explorations in personality.* New York: Oxford, 1938.

Mynatt, C., and S. J. Sherman. Responsibility attribution in groups and individuals: A direct test of the diffusion of responsibility hypothesis. *Journal of Personality and Social Psychology,* 1975, *32,* 1111–1118.

Nachshon, I., and S. Wapner. Effect of eye contact and physiognomy on perceived location of the other person. *Journal of Personality and Social Psychology,* 1967, *7,* 82–89.

Needham, J. G. Rate of presentation in the method of single stimuli. *American Journal of Psychology,* 1935, *47,* 275–284.

Neiman, L. J. and J. W. Hughes. The problem of the concept of role: A resurvey of the literature. *Social Forces,* 1951, *30,* 141–149.

Neisser, U. *Cognitive psychology.* New York: Appleton-Century-Crofts, 1967.

———. Cognition and reality: *Principles and implications of cognitive psychology.* San Francisco: Freeman, 1976.

Newcomb, T. M. *Social psychology.* New York: Holt, Rinehart and Winston, 1950.

———. An approach to the study of communicative acts. *Psychological Review,* 1953, *60,* 393–404.

———. The prediction of interpersonal attraction. *American Psychologist,* 1956, *11,* 575–586.

———. Individual systems of orientation. In S. Koch (ed.), *Psychology: A study of a science. Vol. 3.* New York: McGraw-Hill, 1959, Pp. 384–422.

———. Interpersonal balance. In R. P. Abelson, *et al.,* (eds.), *Theories of cognitive consistency: A sourcebook.* Chicago: Rand McNally, 1968. Pp. 28–51.

———. *The acquaintance process.* New York: Holt, Rinehart and Winston, 1961.

———, R. H. Turner, and P. E. Converse. *Social psychology: The study of human interaction.* New York: Holt, Rinehart and Winston, 1965.

Newell, A., H. A. Simon, and J. C. Shaw. Elements of a theory of human problem solving. *Psychological Review,* 1958, *65,* 151–166.

Nisbett, R. E. Hunger, obesity and the ventromedial hypothalamus. *Psychological Review,* 1972, *79,* 433–453.

———, and D. E. Kanouse. Obesity, food deprivation, and supermarket shopping behavior. *Journal of Personality and Social Psychology,* 1969, *12,* 289–294.

———, and S. Schachter. Cognitive manipulation of pain. *Journal of Experiental Social Psychology,* 1966, *2,* 227–236.

———, and S. Valins. Perceiving the causes of one's own behavior. In E. E. Jones, D. E. Kanouse, H. H. Kelley, R. E. Nisbett, S. Valins, and B. Weiner (eds.), *Attribution: Perceiving the causes of behavior.* New York: General Learning Press, 1972.

———, and T. D. Wilson. Telling more than we can know: Verbal reports on mental processes. *Psychological Review,* 1977, *84,* 231–259.

Nowlis, H. M. The influence of success and failure on the resumption of an interrupted task. *Journal of Experimental Psychology,* 1941, *28,* 304–325.

Nuttin, J. M., Jr. *The illusion of attitude change: Towards a response contagion theory of persuasion.* London: Academic Press, 1975.

Orne, M. T. On the social psychology of the psychological experiment. With particular reference to demand characteristics and their implications. *American Psychologist,* 1962, *17,* 776–783.

Osgood, C. E. The nature and measurement of meaning. *Psychological Bulletin,* 1952, *49,* 197–237.

———. Cognitive dynamics in the conduct of human affairs. *Public Opinion Quarterly,* 1960, *24,* 341–365.

———, G. A. Suci, and P. H. Tannenbaum. *The measurement of meaning.* Urbana, Ill.: University of Illinois Press, 1957.

———, and P. H. Tannenbaum. The principle of congruity in the prediction of attitude change. *Psychological Review,* 1955, *62,* 42–55.

Osler, S. F. Intellectual performance as a function of two types of psychological stress. *Journal of Experimental Psychology,* 1954, *47,* 115–121.

Ovsiankina, M. Die Wiederaufnahme von unterbrochener Handlungen. *Psychologische Forschung,* 1928, *11,* 302–379.

Pallak, M. S., and T. S. Pittman. General motivational effects of dissonance arousal. *Journal of Personality and Social Psychology,* 1972, *21,* 349–358.

Parsons, T. *The social system.* Glencoe, Ill.: The Free Press, 1951.

Passer, M. W. *Perceiving the causes of success and failure revisited: A multidimensional scaling approach.* Unpublished doctoral dissertation, University of California at Los Angeles, 1977.

Patterson, M. L. Stability of nonverbal immediacy behaviors. *Journal of Experimental Social Psychology,* 1973, *9,* 97–109.

———, S. Mullens, and J. Romano. Compensatory reactions to spatial intrusion. *Sociometry,* 1971, *34,* 114–121.

———, and L. B. Sechrest. Interpersonal distance and impression formation. *Journal of Personality,* 1970, *38,* 161–166.

Pavlov, I. P. *The work of the digestive glands.* 2nd ed. Translated by W. H. Thompson. London: Griffin, 1910.

Pavlov, I. P. *Conditioned reflexes.* London: Oxford University Press, 1927.

Pellegrini, R. J., and J. Empey. Interpersonal spatial orientation in dyads. *Journal of Psychology,* 1970, *76,* 67–70.

Pepitone, A. Attributions of causality, social attitudes, and cognitive matching processes. In R. Tagiuri and L. Petrullo (eds.), *Person perception and interpersonal behavior.* Stanford: Stanford University Press, 1958.

———. Some conceptual and empirical problems of consistency models. In S. Feldman (ed.), *Cognitive consistency.* New York: Academic Press, 1966.

———, and M. DiNubile. Contrast effects in judgments of crime severity and the punishment of criminal violators. *Journal of Personality and Social Psychology,* 1976, *33,* 448–459.

Perin, C. T. Behavior potentiality as a joint function of the amount of training and the degree of hunger at the time of extinction. *Journal of Experimental Psychology,* 1942, *30,* 93–113.

Perkins, C. C., and R. G. Weyant. The interval between training and test trials as a determiner of the slope of generalization gradients. *Journal of Comparative and Physiological Psychology,* 1958, *51,* 596–600.

Peterson, P. D., and D. Koulack. Attitude change as a function of latitudes of acceptance and rejection. *Journal of Personality and Social Psychology,* 1969, *11,* 309–311.

Petty, R. E., and J. T. Cacioppo. Forewarning, cognitive responding, and resistance to persuasion. *Journal of Personality and Social Psychology,* 1977, *35,* 645–655.

———, and ———. Effects of forewarning of persuasive intent and involvement on cognitive responses and persuasion. *Personality and Social Psychology Bulletin,* 1979, *5,* 173–176.

Piaget, J. *The moral judgment of the child.* New York: Harcourt, Brace, Jovanovich, 1932.

Picek, J. S., S. J. Sherman, and R. M. Shiffrin. Cognitive organization and coding of social structures. *Journal of Personality and Social Psychology,* 1975, *31,* 758–768.

Pilkonis, P. A. Shyness, public and private, and its relationship to other measures of social behavior. *Journal of Personality,* 1977, *45,* 585–595.

Pliner, P. L. Effects of cue salience on the behavior of obese and normal subjects. *Journal of Abnormal Psychology,* 1973, *82(a),* 226–232.

———. Effect of internal cues on the thinking behavior of obese and normal subjects. *Journal of Abnormal Psychology,* 1973, *82(b),* 233–238.

Polanyi, M. Logic and psychology. *American Psychologist,* 1968, *23,* 27–43.

Pollay, R. W. A model of decision times in difficult decision situations. *Psychological Review,* 1970, *77,* 274–281.

Postman, L., and G. A. Miller. Anchoring of temporal judgments. *American Journal of Psychology,* 1945, *58,* 43–53.

Powell, R. M. Sociometric analysis of informal groups: Their structure and function in two contrasting communities. *Sociometry,* 1952, *15,* 367–399.

Prelinger, E. Extension and structure of the self. *Journal of Psychology,* 1959, *47,* 13–23.

Preston, M. G., and R. K. Heintz. Effects of participatory vs. supervisory leadership on group judgment. *Journal of Abnormal and Social Psychology,* 1949, *44,* 345–355.

Price, K. O., E. Harburg, and T. M. Newcomb. Psychological balance in situations of negative interpersonal attitudes. *Journal of Personality and Social Psychology,* 1966, *3,* 265–270.

Priest, R. F., and J. Sawyer. Proximity and peership: Bases of balance in interpersonal attraction. *American Journal of Sociology,* 1967, *72,* 633–649.

Rachman, S. Clinical applications of observational learning, imitation, and modeling. *Behavior Therapy,* 1972, *3,* 379–397.

Radloff, R. Social comparison and ability evaluation. *Journal of Experimental Social Psychology,* Supplement 1, 1966, 6–26.

Raven, B. H., and J. Z. Rubin. *Social psychology: People in groups.* New York: Wiley, 1976.

Razran, G. H. S. Stimulus generalization and conditioned responses. *Psychological Bulletin,* 1949, *46,* 337–365.

Reisman, S. R., and J. Schopler. An analysis of the attribution process and an application to determinants of responsibility. *Journal of Personality and Social Psychology,* 1973, *25,* 361–368.

Remmers, H. H. Propaganda in the schools: Do the effects last? *Public Opinion Quarterly,* 1938, *2,* 197–210.

Restle, F. *Psychology of judgment and choice.* New York: Wiley, 1961.

Rhine, R. J. The effect on problem solving of success or failure as a function of cue specificity. *Journal of Experimental Psychology,* 1957, *53,* 121–125.

Rodin, J. Effects of distraction on the performance of obese and normal subjects. In S. Schachter and J. Rodin, *Obese humans and rats.* Potomac, Md.: Lawrence Erlbaum, 1974.

———, C. P. Herman, and S. Schachter. Obesity and various tests of external sensitivity.

In S. Schachter and J. Rodin, *Obese humans and rats*. Potomac, Md.: Lawrence Erlbaum, 1974.

Rogers, S. The anchoring of absolute judgments. *Archives of Psychology,* 1941, No. 261.

Rokeach, M. *The open and closed mind.* New York: Basic Books, 1960.

————. *Beliefs, attitudes and values: A theory of organization and change.* San Francisco: Jossey-Bass, 1968.

Rommetveit, R. *Social norms and roles.* Minneapolis: University of Minnesota Press, 1954.

Rosenberg, M. J. Cognitive structure and attitudinal affect. *Journal of Abnormal and Social Psychology,* 1956, *53,* 367–372.

Rosenthal, R. *Experimenter effects in behavioral research.* New York: Appleton-Century-Crofts, 1966.

Rosenthal, T. L., and B. J. Zimmerman. *Social learning and cognition.* New York: Academic Press, 1977.

Rosow, I. The social effects of the physical environment. *Journal of the American Institute of Planners.* 1961, *27,* 127–133.

Ross, E. A. *Social psychology: An outline and source book.* New York: Macmillan, 1908.

Ross, L. The intuitive psychologist and his shortcomings. In L. Berkowitz (ed.), *Cognitive theories in social psychology.* New York: Academic Press, 1978.

————, J. Rodin, and P. G. Zimbardo. Toward an attribution therapy: The reduction in fear through induced cognitive-emotional misattribution. *Journal of Personality and Social Psychology,* 1969, *4,* 279–288.

Rotter, J. B. *Social learning and clinical psychology.* New York: Prentice-Hall, 1954.

————. Generalized expectancies for internal vs. external control of reinforcement. *Psychological Monographs,* 1966, *80* (1, Whole No. 609).

Rubin, Z. Disclosing oneself to a stranger: Reciprocity and its limits. *Journal of Experimental Social Psychology,* 1975, *11,* 233–260.

————, and L. A. Peplau. Who believes in a just world? *Journal of Social Issues,* 1975, *31,* 65–89.

Russell, D. H., and I. V. Robertson. Influencing attitudes toward minority groups in a junior high school. *School Review,* 1947, *55,* 205–213.

Sampson, E. E. Personality and the location of identity. *Journal of Personality,* 1978, *46,* 552–568.

Samuel, W. On clarifying some interpretations of social comparison theory. *Journal of Experimental Social Psychology,* 1973, *9,* 450–465.

Santee, R. T. The effect of attraction of attitude similarity as information about interpersonal reinforcement contingencies. *Sociometry,* 1976, *39,* 153–156.

Sarbin, T. R. Role theory. In G. Lindzey (ed.), *Handbook of social psychology (Vo. 1).* Reading, Mass.: Addison-Wesley, 1954. Pp. 223–258.

————. Role enactment. In B. J. Biddle and E. J. Thomas (eds.), *Role theory: Concepts and research.* New York: Wiley, 1966.

Sargent, S. S., and R. C. Williamson. *Social psychology* (2nd ed.). New York: Ronald Press, 1958.

Schachter, S. Deviation, rejection and communication. *Journal of Abnormal and Social Psychology,* 1951, *46,* 190–207.

————. The interaction of cognitive and physiological determinants of emotional state. In L. Berkowitz (ed.), *Advances in experimental social psychology (Vol. 1).* New York: Academic Press, 1964. Pp. 49–80.

————. *Emotion, obesity and crime.* New York: Academic Press, 1971.

————, and L. Friedman. The effects of work and cue prominence on eating behavior. In S. Schachter and J. Rodin, *Obese humans and rats.* Potomac, Md.: Lawrence Erlbaum, 1974.

————, ————, and J. Handler. Who eats with chopsticks? In S. Schachter and J. Rodin, *Obese humans and rats.* Potomac, Md.: Lawrence Erlbaum, 1974.

————, and J. Rodin. *Obese humans and rats.* Potomac, Md.: Lawrence Erlbaum, 1974.

————, and J. Singer. Cognitive, social, and physiological determinants of emotional state. *Psychological Review,* 1962, *69,* 379–399.

————, and L. Wheeler. Epinephrine chlorpromazine, and amusement. *Journal of Abnormal and Social Psychology,* 1962, *65,* 121–128.

————, et al. Cross-cultural experiments on threat and rejection. *Human Relations,* 1954, *7,* 403–439.

Scheerer, M. Cognitive theory. In G. Lindzey (ed.), *Handbook of social psychology.* Vol. 1. Reading, Mass.: Addison-Wesley, 1954. Pp. 91–142.

Scheier, M. F., A. Fenigstein, and A. H. Buss. Self-awareness and physical aggression. *Journal of Experimental Social Psychology,* 1974, *10,* 264–273.

Scheler, M. *The nature of sympathy.* Translated by P. Heath. London: Routledge & Kegan Paul, 1954.

Schlenker, B. R. Social psychology and science. *Journal of Personality and Social Psychology,* 1974, *29,* 1–15.

————. Self-presentation: Managing the impression of consistency when reality interferes with self-enhancement. *Journal of Personality and Social Psychology,* 1975, *32,* 1030–1037.

————. *Impression management: The self-concept, social identity, and interpersonal relations.* Monterey, Calif.: Brooks/Cole, 1980.

————, R. C. Brown, Jr., and J. T. Tedeschi. Attraction and expectations of harm and benefits. *Journal of Personality and Social Psychology,* 1975, *32,* 664–670.

————, D. R. Forsyth, M. R. Leary, and R. S. Miller. A self-presentational analysis of the effects of incentives on attitude change following counterattitudinal behavior. *Journal of Personality and Social Psychology,* 1980, *39,* 553–577.

————, and M. Riess. Self-presentations of attitudes following commitment to proattitudinal behavior. *Human Communication Research,* 1979, *5,* 325–334.

————, and P. A. Schlenker. Reactions following counterattitudinal behavior which produces positive consequences. *Journal of Personality and Social Psychology,* 1975, *31,* 962–971.

Schneider, D. J. Tactical self-presentation after success and failure. *Journal of Personality and Social Psychology,* 1969, *13,* 262–268.

————, and A. C. Eustes. Effects of ingratiation motivation, target positiveness, and revealingness on self-presentation. *Journal of Personality and Social Psychology,* 1972, *22,* 149–155.

Schopler, J., and J. E. Stockdale. An interference analysis of crowding. *Environmental Psychology and Nonverbal Behavior,* 1977, *1,* 81–88.

————, and D. Stokols. *A psychological approach to human crowding.* Morristown, N. J.: General Learning Press, 1976.

Schutz, W. C. What makes groups productive? *Human Relations,* 1955, *8,* 429–465.

————. *FIRO: A three dimensional theory of interpersonal behavior.* New York: Rinehart, 1958.

————. On group composition. *Journal of Abnormal and Social Psychology,* 1961, *62,* 275–281.

————. *JOY: Expanding human awareness.* New York: Grove Press, 1967.

Schwartz, B. *Psychology of learning and behavior.* New York: Norton, 1978.

Schwartz, J. M., and W. P. Smith. Social comparison and the inference of ability differences. *Journal of Personality and Social Psychology,* 1976, *34,* 1268–1275.

Scott, W. A. Cognitive structure and social structure: Some concepts and relationships. In N. F. Washburne (ed.), *Decisions, values, and groups. Vol. 2.* New York: Pergamon Press, 1962. Pp. 86–118.

————. Conceptualizing and measuring structural properties of cognition. In O. J. Harvey (ed.), *Motivation and social interaction.* New York: Ronald Press, 1963. Pp. 266–288.

————. Structure of natural cognitions. *Journal of Personality and Social Psychology,* 1969, *12,* 261–278.

————. Varieties of cognitive integration. *Journal of Personality and Social Psychology,* 1974, *30,* 563–578.

Scott, W. H., J. A. Banks, A. H. Halsey, and T. Lupton. *Technical change and industrial relations.* Liverpool: Liverpool University Press, 1956.

Sears, R. R. Identification as a form of behavior development. In D. B. Harris (ed.), *The concept of development.* Minneapolis: University of Minnesota Press, 1957.

Secord, P. F., and C. W. Backman. *Social psychology.* New York: McGraw-Hill, 1964.

Seidenberg, B., and A. Snadowsky. *Social psychology: An introduction.* New York: Free Press, 1976.

Senn, D. J. Attraction as a function of similarity-dissimilarity in task performance. *Journal of Personality and Social Psychology,* 1971, *18,* 120–124.

Sensenig, J., and J. W. Brehm. Attitude change from an implied threat to attitudinal freedom. *Journal of Personality and Social Psychology,* 1968, *8,* 324–330.

Severy, L. J., J. C. Brigham, and B. R. Schlenker. *A contemporary introduction to social psychology.* New York: McGraw-Hill, 1976.

Sewell, W. H., P. H. Mussen, and C. W. Harris. Relationships among child training practices. *American Sociological Review,* 1955, *20,* 137–148.

Shaver, K. G. *Principles of social psychology.* Cambridge, Mass.: Winthrop, 1977.

Shaw, Marjorie E. A comparison of individuals and small groups in the rational solution of complex problems. *American Journal of Psychology,* 1932, *44,* 491–504.

Shaw, M. E. A comparison of two types of leadership in various communication nets. *Journal of Abnormal and Social Psychology,* 1955, *50,* 127–134.

————. Implicit conversion of fate control of dyadic interaction. *Psychological Reports,* 1962, *10,* 758.

————. *Scaling group tasks: A method for dimensional analysis.* Technical Report No. 1, ONR Contract NR 170-266, Nonr- 580(11), University of Florida, 1963.

————, and N. Ashton. Do assembly bonus effects occur on disjunctive tasks: A test of Steiner's theory. *Bulletin of the Psychonomic Society,* 1976, *8,* 469–471.

————, and G. J. Bensberg. Level of aspiration phenomena in mentally deficient persons. *Journal of Personality,* 1955, *24,* 134–144.

————, and J. M. Blum. Effects of leadership style upon group performance as a function of task structure. *Journal of Personality and Social Psychology,* 1966, *3,* 238–242.

————, M. E. Briscoe, and J. Garcia-Esteve. A cross-cultural study of attribution of responsibility. *International Journal of Psychology,* 1968, *3,* 51–60.

————, and H. T. Reitan. Attribution of responsibility as a basis for sanctioning behavior. *British Journal of Social and Clinical Psychology,* 1969, *8,* 217–226.

————, and F. W. Schneider. Negro-white differences in attribution of responsibility as a function of age. Research Report No. 8, (NSF, GS-647), University of Florida, November, 1967.

————, and J. L. Sulzer. An empirical test of Heider's levels in attribution of responsibility. *Journal of Abnormal and Social Psychology,* 1964, *69,* 39–46.

————, and T. R. Tremble, Jr. Effects of attribution of responsibility for a negative event to a group member upon group process as a function of the structure of the event. *Sociometry,* 1971, *34,* 504–514.

————, and P. J. Wagner. Role selection in the service of self-presentation. *Memory and Cognition,* 1975, *3,* 481–484.

————, and J. M. Wright. *Scales for the measurement of attitudes.* New York: McGraw-Hill, 1967.

Sherif, C. W. Social distance as categorization of intergroup interaction. *Journal of Personality and Social Psychology,* 1973, *25,* 327–334.

————, M. Kelly, H. L. Rodgers, Jr., G. Sarup, and B. I. Tittler. Personal involvement, social judgment, and action. *Journal of Personality and Social Psychology,* 1973, *27,* 311–328.

————, M. Sherif, and R. E. Nebergall. *Attitude and attitude change: The social judgment-involvement approach.* Philadelphia: W. B. Saunders, 1956.

Sherif, M. A study of some social factors in perception. *Archives of Psychology,* 1935, *27,* No. 187.

————, and C. I. Hovland. Judgmental phenomena and scales of attitude measurement: Placement of items with individual choice of number of categories. *Journal of Abnormal and Social Psychology,* 1953, *48,* 135–141.

————, and ————. *Social judgment: Assimilation and contrast effects in communication and attitude change.* New Haven: Yale University Press, 1961.

————, and C. W. Sherif. *An outline of social psychology.* Rev. ed. New York: Harper & Row, 1956.

Sherman, S. J., K. Ahlm, L. Berman, and S. Lynn. Contrast effects and their relationship to subsequent behavior. *Journal of Experimental Social Psychology,* 1978, *14,* 340–350.

————, and L. Gorkin. Attitude bolstering when behavior is inconsistent with central attitudes. *Journal of Experimental Social Psychology,* 1980, *16,* 388–403.

Siegel, A. E. Film mediated fantasy aggression and strength of aggressive drive. *Child Development,* 1956, *27,* 365–378.

Silverman, I. The resolution and tolerance of cognitive inconsistency in a natural-occuring event: Attitudes and beliefs following the Senator Edward M. Kennedy incident. *Journal of Personality and Social Psychology,* 1971, *17,* 171–178.

————. *The human subject in the psychological laboratory.* New York: Pergamon, 1977.

Simmel, G. Zur Philosophie des Schauspielers. *Logos,* 1920, *1,* 399–362.

————. Sociology of the senses: Visual interaction. In R. E. Park and E. W. Burgess (eds.), *Introduction to the science of sociology.* Chicago: University of Chicago Press, 1921.

Singh, D. Role of response habits and cognitive factors in determination of behavior of obese humans. *Journal of Personality and Social Psychology,* 1973, *27,* 220–238.

Skinner, B. F. *Science and human behavior.* New York: Macmillan, 1953.

————. *Verbal behavior.* New York: Appleton-Century-Crofts, 1957.

Snyder, M. *Individual differences and the self-control of expressive behavior.* Unpublished doctoral dissertation, Stanford University, 1972.

———. The self-monitoring of expressive behavior. *Journal of Personality and Social Psychology,* 1974, *30,* 526–537.

———. Attribution and behavior: Social perception and social causation. In J. H. Harvey, W. J. Ickes, and R. F. Kidd (eds.), *New directions in attribution research.* Hillsdale, N. J.: Lawrence Erlbaum, 1976.

———. Self-monitoring processes. In L. Berkowitz (ed.), *Advances in experimental social psychology* (Vol. 12). New York: Academic Press, 1979.

———, and T. C. Monson. Persons, situations and the control of social behavior. *Journal of Personality and Social Psychology,* 1975, *32,* 637–644.

———, and E. D. Tanke. Behavior and attitude: Some people are more consistent than others. *Journal of Personality,* 1976, *44,* 510–517.

Snyder, M. L., W. G. Stephan, and P. Rosenfield. Attributional egotism. In J. H. Harvey, W. Ickes, and R. F. Kidd (eds.), *New directions in attribution research* (Vol. 2). Hillsdale, N. J.: Lawrence Erlbaum, 1978.

———, and Wicklund, R. A. Prior exercise of freedom and reactance. *Journal of Experimental Social Psychology,* 1976, *12,* 120–130.

Sommer, R. *Personal space.* Englewood Cliffs, N. J.: Prentice-Hall, 1969.

Songer-Nocks, E. Situational factors affecting the weighting of predictor components in the Fishbein model. *Journal of Experimental Social Psychology,* 1976, *12,* 56–69.

Spence, K. W. The differential response in animals to stimuli varying within the same dimension. *Psychological Review,* 1937, *44,* 430–444.

Steiner, I. D. Perceived freedom. In L. Berkowitz (ed.), *Advances in experimental social psychology.* Vol. 5. New York: Academic Press, 1970. Pp. 187–248.

———. *Group process and productivity.* New York: Academic Press, 1972.

———. Attribution of choice. In M. Fishbein (ed.), *Progress in social psychology.* Vol. 1. Hillsdale, N. J.: Lawrence Erlbaum, 1980. Pp. 1–47.

———, R. H. Doyen, and R. Talaber. Some effects of choice and costs on observer's attributions. *Journal of Psychology,* 1975, *90,* 275–286.

———, and N. Rajaratnam. A model for the comparison of individual and group performance scores. *Behavioral Science,* 1961, *6,* 142–147.

Steinman, W. M. Generalized imitation and the discrimination hypothesis. *Journal of Experimental Child Psychology,* 1970, *10,* 79–99.

Stires, L. J., and E. E. Jones. Modesty vs. self-enhancement as alternative forms of ingratiation. *Journal of Experimental Social Psychology,* 1969, *5,* 172–188.

Stokols, D. On the distinction between density and crowding. *Psychological Review,* 1972a, *79,* 275–277.

———. A social-psychological model of human crowding phenomena. *Journal of the American Institute of Planners,* 1972b, *38,* 72–84.

———. Toward a psychological theory of alienation. *Psychological Review,* 1975, *82,* 26–44.

———. The experience of crowding in primary and secondary environments. *Environment and Behavior,* 1976, *8,* 49–86.

———, M. Rall, B. Pinner, and J. Schopler. Physical, social and personal determinants of the perception of crowding. *Environment and Behavior,* 1973, *5,* 87–115.

Storms, M. D., and R. E. Nisbett. Insomnia and the attribution process. *Journal of Personality and Social Psychology,* 1970, *2,* 319–328.

Stotland, E. *The psychology of hope.* San Francisco: Jossey-Bass, 1969.

Stroebe, W., V. D. Thompson, C. A. Insko, and S. R. Reisman. Balance and differentiation in the evaluation of linked attitude objects. *Journal of Personality and Social Psychology,* 1970, *16,* 38–47.

Suls, J., and R. L. Miller, (eds.). *Social comparison processes.* Washington, D. C.: Hemisphere/Halsted, 1977.

Sulzer, J. L. *Attribution of responsibility as a function of the structure, quality, and the intensity of the event.* Unpublished doctoral dissertation, University of Florida, Gainesville, Florida, 1964.

Sumner, W. G. *Folkways.* New York: Ginn, 1906.

———, and A. G. Keller. *The science of society.* New Haven: Yale University Press, 1927.

Tannenbaum, P. H. and R. W. Gengel. Generalization of attitude change through congruity principal relationships. *Journal of Personality and Social Psychology,* 1966, *3,* 299–304.

Tanner, W. P., Jr., and J. A. Swets. A decision-making theory of human detection. *Psychological Review,* 1954, *61,* 401–409.

Tarde, G. *The laws of imitation.* New York: Holt, Rinehart and Winston, 1903.

Taylor, D. The development of interpersonal relationships: Social penetration processes. *Journal of Social Psychology,* 1968, *75,* 79–90.

Taylor, D. A., and I. Altman. Self-disclosure as a function of reward-cost outcomes. *Sociometry,* 1975, *38,* 18–31.

———, ———, and R. Sorrentino. Interpersonal exchange as a function of rewards and costs and situational factors: Expectancy confirmation-disconfirmation. *Journal of Experimental Social Psychology,* 1969, *5,* 324–339.

Taylor, D. W. Problem solving by groups. *Proceedings of the XIV International Congress of Psychology, 1954.* Amsterdam: North Holland Publ., 1954.

Taylor, R. B., and R. R. Stough. Territorial cognition: Assessing Altman's typology. *Journal of Personality and Social Psychology,* 1978, *36,* 418–423.

Tedeschi, J. T., B. R. Schlenker, and T. V. Bonoma. Cognitive dissonance: Private ratiocination or public spectacle? *American Psychologist,* 1971, *26,* 685–695.

Thibaut, J. W., and H. H. Kelley. *The social psychology of groups.* New York: Wiley, 1959.

———, and H. W. Riecken. Some determinants and consequences of the perception of social causality. In H. Proshansky and B. Seidenberg (eds.), *Basic studies in social psychology.* New York: Holt, Rinehart and Winston, 1965. Pp. 81–94.

———, and L. H. Strickland. Psychological set and social conformity. *Journal of Personality,* 1956, *25,* 115–129.

Thomas, D. R., and L. J. Lopez. The effects of delayed testing on generalization slope. *Journal of Comparative and Physiological Psychology,* 1962, *55,* 541–544.

Thorndike, E. L. *Animal intelligence.* New York: Macmillan, 1898.

———. *The psychology of learning.* New York: Teachers College, Columbia University, 1913.

———. *Educational psychology.* New York: Teachers College, Columbia University, 1932.

———. *The psychology of wants, interests, and attitudes.* New York: Appleton-Century-Crofts, 1935.

———. *Selected writings from a connectionist's psychology.* New York: Appleton-Century-Crofts, 1949.

Thornton, D. A., and A. J. Arrowood. Self-evaluation, self-enhancement, and the locus of social comparison. *Journal of Experimental Social Psychology*, Supplement 1, 1966, 40–48.

Thurstone, L. L., and E. J. Chave. *The measurement of attitude.* Chicago: University of Chicago Press, 1929.

Tolman, E. C. *Purposive behavior in animals and men.* New York: Appleton-Century, 1932.

———. Principles of purposive behavior. In S. Koch (eds.) *Psychology: A Study of a science.* Vol. 2. New York: McGraw-Hill, 1959.

———, and C. H. Honzik. Introduction and removal of reward, and maze performance in rats. *University of California Publications in Psychology*, 1930, *4*, 257–275.

Tresemer, D. W. *Fear of success.* New York: Plenum Press, 1977.

Triandis, H., and M. Fishbein. Cognitive interaction in person perception. *Journal of Abnormal and Social Psychology*, 1963, *67*, 446–453.

Trope, Y. Seeking information about one's own ability as a determinant of choice among tasks. *Journal of Personality and Social Psychology*, 1975, *32*, 1004–1013.

———. Extrinsic rewards, congruence between dispositions and behaviors, and perceived freedom. *Journal of Personality and Social Psychology*, 1978, *36*, 588–597.

———. Self-assessment, self-enhancement, and task preference. *Journal of Experimental Social Psychology*, 1980, *16*, 116–129.

———, and P. Brickman. Difficulty and diagnosticity as determinants of choice among tasks. *Journal of Personality and Social Psychology*, 1975, *31*, 918–925.

———, and E. Burnstein. A disposition-behavior congruity model of perceived freedom. *Journal of Experimental Social Psychology*, 1977, *13*, 357–368.

Trotter, W. *Instincts of the herd in peace and war.* New York: Macmillan, 1917.

Turner, R. H. Role taking: Process versus conformity. In A. M. Rose (ed.), *Human behavior and social processes: An interactionist approach.* Boston: Houghton Mifflin, 1962.

Tversky, A. Elimination by aspects: A theory of choice. *Psychological Review*, 1972, *79*, 281–299.

———, and D. Kahneman. Availability: A heuristic for judging frequency and probability. *Cognitive Psychology*, 1973, *5*, 207–232.

———, and ———. Judgment under uncertainty: Heuristics and biases. *Science*, 1974, *185*, 1124–1131.

Upshaw, H. S. The personal reference scale: An approach to social judgment. In L. Berkowitz (ed.), *Advances in experimental social psychology*, Vol. 4. New York: Academic Press, 1969. Pp. 315–371.

———. Judgment and decision processes in the formation and change of social attitudes. In M. F. Kaplan and S. Schwartz (eds.), *Human judgment and decision processes.* New York: Academic Press, 1975. Pp. 201–228.

———. Social influence on attitudes and on anchoring of congeneric attitude scales. *Journal of Experimental Social Psychology*, 1978, *14*, 327–339.

———. Attitude toward the reasons for one's actions: A determinant of perceived freedom. *Personality and Social Psychology Bulletin*, 1979, *5*, 182–185.

———, and L. A. Yates. Self-persuasion, social approval and task success as determinants of self-esteem following impression management. *Journal of Experimental Social Psychology*, 1968, *4*, 143–152.

Valins, S. Cognitive effects of false heart-rate feedback. *Journal of Personality and Social Psychology*, 1966, *4*, 400–408.

———, and A. A. Ray. Effects of cognitive desensitization on avoidance behavior. *Journal of Personality and Social Psychology,* 1967, *7,* 345–350.

Van der Zanden, J. W. *Social psychology.* New York: Random House, 1977.

Volkmann, J. Scales of judgment and their implications for social psychology. In J. H. Rohrer and M. Sherif (eds.), *Social psychology at the crossroads.* New York: Harper & Row, 1951.

Vroom, V. H. *Work and motivation.* New York: Wiley, 1964.

Walster, E. The effect of self-esteem on romantic liking. *Journal of Experimental Social Psychology,* 1965, *1,* 184–197.

Walster, E., E. Berscheid, and A. M. Barclay. A determinant of preference among modes of dissonance reduction. *Journal of Personality and Social Psychology,* 1967, *7,* 211–216.

———, ———, and G. W. Walster. New directions in equity research. *Journal of Personality and Social Psychology,* 1973, *25,* 151–176. Reprinted in L. Berkowitz (ed.), *Advances in experimental social psychology* (Vol. 9). New York: Academic Press, 1976.

———, G. W. Walster, and E. Berscheid. *Equity: Theory and research.* Boston: Allyn & Bacon, 1978.

Walters, R. H., M. Leat, and L. Mezei. Inhibition and disinhibition of response through empathetic learning. *Canadian Journal of Psychology,* 1963, *17,* 235–243.

———, and R. D. Parke. Influence of response consequences to a social model on resistance to deviation. *Journal of Experimental Child Psychology,* 1964, *1,* 269–280.

———, ———, and V. A. Cone. Timing of punishment and the observation of the consequences to others as determinants of response inhibition. *Journal of Experimental Child Psychology,* 1965, *2,* 10–30.

Waly, P., and S. W. Cook. Attitude as a determinant of learning and memory: A failure to confirm. *Journal of Personality and Social Psychology,* 1966, *4,* 280–288.

Watson, G. *Social psychology: Issues and insights.* Philadelphia: Lippincott, 1966.

Watson, J. B. Psychology as the behaviorist views it. *Psychological Review,* 1913, *20,* 158–177.

———. *Behavior: An introduction to comparative psychology.* New York: Holt, Rinehart and Winston, 1914.

———. *Psychology from the standpoint of a behaviorist.* Philadelphia: Lippincott, 1919.

———, and R. Rayner. Conditioned emotional reactions. *Journal of Experimental Psychology,* 1920, *3,* 1–14.

Watson, O. M., and T. D. Graves. Quantitative research in proxemic behavior. *American Anthropologist,* 1966, *68,* 971–985.

Watts, W. A., and L. E. Holt. Persistence of opinion change induced under conditions of forewarning and distraction. *Journal of Personality and Social Psychology,* 1979, *37,* 778–789.

Waxler, C. Z., and M. R. Yarrow. Factors influencing imitative learning in preschool children. *Journal of Experimental Child Psychology,* 1970, *9,* 115–130.

Weiner, B. Achievement motivation as conceptualized by an attribution theorist. In B. Weiner (ed.), *Achievement motivation and attribution theory.* Morristown, N. J.: General Learning Press, 1974.

———, I. Frieze, A. Kukla, L. Reed, S. Rest, and R. M. Rosenbaum. Perceiving the causes of success and failure. In E. E. Jones, D. E. Kanouse, H. H. Kelley, R. E.

Nisbett, S. Valins, and B. Weiner (eds.), *Attribution: Perceiving the causes of behavior.* Morristown, N. J.: General Learning Press, 1972.

———, and A. Kukla. An attributional analysis of achievement motivation. *Journal of Personality and Social Psychology,* 1970, *15,* 1–20.

———, D. Russell, and D. Lerman. The cognition-emotion process in achievement-related contexts. *Journal of Personality and Social Psychology,* 1976, *37,* 1211–1220.

Wellens, A. R., and D. L. Thistlethwaite. Comparison of three theories of cognitive balance. *Journal of Personality and Social Psychology,* 1971, *20,* 82–92.

Wertheimer, M. Some problems in the theory of ethics. *Social Research,* 1935, *2,* 353–367.

Westermarck, E. *Ethical relativity.* New York: Harcourt, Brace, Jovanovich, 1932.

Wever, E. G., and K. E. Zener. Method of absolute judgment in psychophysics. *Psychological Review,* 1928, *35,* 466–493.

Wheeler, L. Motivation as a determinant of upward comparison. *Journal of Experimental Social Psychology,* Supplement 1, 1966, 27–31.

Wheeler, R. H. *The science of psychology.* 2nd ed., New York: Crowell, 1940.

Whittemore, I. C. The influence of competition on performance. *Journal of Abnormal and Social Psychology,* 1925, *20,* 17–33.

Wicker, A. W. Attitudes versus actions: The relationship of verbal and overt behavioral responses to attitude objects. *Journal of Social Issues,* 1969, *25,* 41–78.

———. Undermanning theory and research: Implications for the study of psychological and behavioral effects of excess human populations. *Representative Research in Social Psychology,* 1973, *4,* 185–206.

Wicklund, R. A. Objective self-awareness. In L. Berkowitz (ed.), *Advances in experimental social psychology* (Vol. 8). New York: Academic Press, 1975.

———. Three years later. In L. Berkowitz (ed.), *Cognitive theories in social psychology.* New York: Academic Press, 1978.

———, and J. W. Brehm. Attitude change as a function of felt competence and threat to attitudinal freedom. *Journal of Experimental Social Psychology,* 1968, *4,* 64–75.

———, and ———. *Perspectives on cognitive dissonance.* Hillsdale, N. J.: Lawrence Erlbaum, 1976.

Wilhelmy, R. A. The role of commitment in cognitive reversibility. *Journal of Personality and Social Psychology,* 1974, *30,* 695–698.

———, and B. L. Duncan. Cognitive reversibility in dissonance reduction. *Journal of Personality and Social Psychology,* 1974, *29,* 806–811.

Wilke, W. H. An experimental comparison of the speech, the radio, and the printed page as propaganda devices. *Archives of Psychology,* 1934, No. 169.

Williams, D. C. Attributions of ability and motivation under conditions of performance change. *Representative Research in Social Psychology,* 1975, *6,* 57–62.

Willis, R. H., and M. L. Joseph. Bargaining behavior. I. "Prominence" as a predictor of the outcome of games of agreement. *Conflict Resolution,* 1959, *3,* 102–113.

Wilson, S. R. Ability evaluation and self-evaluation as types of social comparison. *Sociometry,* 1973, *36,* 600–607.

———, and L. A. Benner. The effects of self-esteem and situation upon comparison choices during ability evaluation. *Sociometry,* 1971, *34,* 381–397.

Winch, R. F. *The modern family.* New York: Holt, Rinehart and Winston, 1952.

———. The theory of complementarity of needs in mate-selection: A test of one kind of complementariness. *American Sociological Review,* 1955, *20,* 52–56.

Witkin, H. A., D. R. Goodenough, and P. K. Oltman. Psychological differentiation: Current status. *Journal of Personality and Social Psychology*, 1979, *37*, 1127–1145.

Woodworth, R. S., and H. Schlossberg. *Experimental psychology*. New York: Holt, Rinehart and Winston, 1954.

Woody, E. Z., and P. R. Costanzo. The socialization of obesity-prone behavior. In S. Brehm, S. Kassin, and R. Gibbons (eds.), *Developmental social psychology*. New York: Oxford University Press, 1981.

Wooley, O. W., S. C. Wooley, and R. B. Dunham. Can calories be perceived and do they affect hunger in obese and non-obese humans? *Journal of Comparative and Physiological Psychology*, 1972, *80*, 250.

Wooley, S. C. Physiologic versus cognitive factors in short term food regulation in the obese and non-obese. *Psychosomatic Medicine*, 1972, *34*, 62–68.

Worchel, S., and J. Cooper. *Understanding social psychology*. Homewood, Ill.: Dorsey Press, 1976.

———, and C. Teddlie. The experience of crowding: A two-factor theory. *Journal of Personality and Social Psychology*, 1976, *34*, 30–40.

Wyer, R. S., Jr., and J. D. Lyon. A test of cognitive balance theory implications for social inference processes. *Journal of Personality and Social Psychology*, 1970, *16*, 598–618.

Yalom, I. D., and K. Rand. Compatibility and cohesiveness in therapy groups. *Archives of General Psychiatry*, 1966, *15*, 267–275.

Yang, K., and P. Yang. The effects of anxiety and threat on the learning of balanced and unbalanced social structures. *Journal of Personality and Social Psychology*, 1973, *26*, 201–207.

Yuker, H. E. Group atmosphere and memory. *Journal of Abnormal and Social Psychology*, 1955, *51*, 17–23.

Zajonc, R. B. The process of cognitive tuning in communication. *Journal of Abnormal and Social Psychology*, 1960, *61*, 159–167.

———. *Social psychology: An experimental approach*. Belmont, California: Brooks/Cole, 1966.

———. Cognitive theories in social psychology. In G. Lindzey and E. Aronson (eds.), *The Handbook of social psychology*. Second ed. Vol. 1. Reading, Mass.: Addison-Wesley, 1968. Pp. 320–411.

———, and E. Burnstein. The learning of balanced and unbalanced social structures. *Journal of Personality*, 1965, *33*, 153–163.

Zander, A. *Motives and goals in groups*. New York: Academic Press, 1971.

———. The psychology of removing group members and recruiting new ones. *Human Relations*, 1976, *29*, 969–987.

———, and H. Medow. Individual and group levels of aspiration. *Human Relations*, 1963, *16*, 89–105.

Zanna, M. P., G. R. Goethals, and J. F. Hill. Evaluating sex-related ability: Social comparison with similar others and standard setters. *Journal of Experimental Social Psychology*, 1975, *11*, 86–93.

———, E. T. Higgins, and P. A. Taves. Is dissonance phenomenologically aversive? *Journal of Experimental Social Psychology*, 1976, *12*, 530–538.

Zeigarnik, B. Uber das Behalten von erledigten and unerledigten Handlungen. *Psychologische Forschung*, 1927, *9*, 1–85.

Ziller, R. C. Group size: A determinant of the quality and stability of group decisions. *Sociometry*, 1957, *20*, 165–173.

Zillman, D. Attribution and misattribution of excitatory reactions. In J. H. Harvey, W. Ickes, and R. F. Kidd (eds.), *New directions in attribution research* (Vol. 2). Hillsdale, N. J.: Lawrence Erlbaum, 1978.

Zipf, S. Effects of probability of reward and speed requirement on human performance. *Journal of Experimental Psychology,* 1963, *65,* 106–107.

Zuckerman, M., and L. Wheeler. To dispel fantasies about the fantasy-based measure of fear of success. *Psychological Bulletin,* 1975, *82,* 932–946.

Glossary

Activity In Homans' theory, an alternative term for Skinner's operant; any voluntary behavior emitted by an organism.

Affection Need In Schutz's theory, the need to establish and maintain a feeling of mutual affection with others.

Affiliative Conflict A state of arousal that occurs when both approach and avoidance forces are operating in a social situation.

Anticonformity Behavior in response to normative expectations of the group, but directly opposite to norm prescription.

Assimilation A process in which a new stimulus is integrated into a set of previously experienced stimuli, and thus the internal standard is shifted toward the new stimulus.

Assumed Similarity of Opposites (ASo) The degree to which an individual perceives his most- and least-preferred coworkers as similar.

Attribution The process of perceiving the dispositional properties of objects (including other persons) in the environment.

Attitude A mediating evaluative response to a stimulus object.

Balanced State According to Heider, a state in which unit and sentiment (liking) relations can coexist without stress.

Barrier In Lewin's system, a boundary between regions of the life space which offers resistance to locomotion.

Behavior   In Lewin's system, any change in the life space, that is, any voluntary locomotion of a person in his or her life space.

Behavior Control   In Thibaut and Kelley's theory, a form of power dependence in which person A can control the behavior of person B by enacting behaviors rewarding to B only when B enacts behaviors described by A.

Behavior Sequence   Thibaut and Kelley's unit of analysis, defined as a number of verbal and motor acts which are sequentially organized and directed toward a goal.

Belief   In Fishbein's theory, the probability that there is a particular relationship between the object of the belief and some other object.

Causal Description   Analysis of the underlying conditions that give rise to perceptual experience.

Choice   In Steiner's theory, freedom to select actions or choose among options.

Cognition   That which is known; knowledge acquired through personal experience.

Cognitive Dissonance   An unpleasant psychological state arising from the existence of "nonfitting" or inconsistent relations among cognitions.

Cognitive Script   In Abelson's theory, a coherent sequence of events expected by an individual, involving the individual either as a participant or as an observer.

Cognitive Structure   An organized subset of the attributes an individual uses to identify and discriminate a specific object or event; a set of ideas maintained by a person and relatively available to conscious awareness.

Cognitive Theory   A general orientation that emphasizes central processes in the explanation of behavior.

Commonality of Effects   Consequences that are produced by each of two or more possible actions.

Communicative Act   In Newcomb's theory, a transmission of information from a source to a recipient.

Comparison Level (CL)   In Thibaut and Kelley's theory, the standard against which group members evaluate the attractiveness of the relationship.

Comparison Level for Alternatives (CLalt)   In Thibaut and Kelley's theory, the standard which the individual uses to determine whether or not he or she will remain in a relationship.

Compatibility   In Schutz's theory, a property of a relation between a person and another person, role, or task situation that leads to mutual satisfaction of interpersonal needs. Types of compatibility include the following:

1   *Interchange compatibility.* Compatibility based upon the mutual expression of affection, control, and/or inclusion between two or more individuals.

2   *Originator compatibility.* Compatibility based upon complementarity of needs between the initiator and the receiver of an interaction.

3   *Reciprocal compatibility.* Compatibility based upon the expression of affection, control, and/or inclusion by each group member which meets the needs of others in the group for affection, control, and/or inclusion.

Competition   A social process in which goal achievement by one group member to some extent impedes goal achievement by other group members.

Conflict   In Lewin's system, a situation in which forces in the life space are opposite in direction and about equal in strength.

Congruity Principle   A proposition advanced by Osgood and Tannenbaum which holds that changes in evaluation always occur in the direction of increased congruence with the person's frame of reference.

Contrast Effect   A process in which a new stimulus is perceived as not belonging to the set of stimuli previously experienced, and thus the internal standard is shifted away from the new stimulus.

Control Need   In Schutz's theory, the need to establish and maintain a satisfactory relation with people with respect to power and control of others.

Construct   An explanatory concept; a hypothetical process invoked to account for observed relationships between antecedent and consequent conditions.

Cooperation   A social process in which achievement of a goal by each group member facilitates goal achievement by all other group members.

Coorientation   In Newcomb's theory, simultaneous orientation toward another person and an object.

Correspondence   In Jones and McGillis's reformulation, the degree of information gained regarding the probability or strength of an attribute.

Correspondent Inference   In Jones and Davis's theory, an inference about an underlying attribute based on an action which is assumed to be similar to the attribute.

Cost   In Thibaut and Kelley's theory, those factors which inhibit the adequate performance of a sequence of behavior or factors which restrict the individual's consummation of the rewards of enacting a sequence of behavior. In Homans' theory, rewards foregone by an individual because he or she enacts one activity rather than an alternative activity or activities.

Covert Rehearsal   In Bandura's theory, the internal or "mental" rehearsal of the performance of an observed response.

Crowding   An uncomfortable psychological experience resulting from personal, social, cultural, and spatial factors in social situations.

Decision Verifiability   The degree to which the correctness of a decision or task solution can be demonstrated by logic or by appeal to authority.

Differentiation   In Lewin's system, a process by which the life space becomes separated into functional regions.

Dispositional Properties   Those properties that cause objects and events to manifest themselves in certain ways under certain conditions; the unchanging aspects of the phenomenal world.

Distal Stimulus   The starting point of perception; the object that is experienced as being "out there" in the environment.

Distributive Justice   The fair exchange of rewards and costs in a social interaction; a rule of human exchange stating that each participant of an interaction should expect and receive rewards that are proportional to the costs he or she incurs for participating in that interaction.

Elementary Social Behavior   In Homans' theory, a two-party interaction in which there is a direct and immediate exchange of rewards and punishments between the two parties.

Endogenous Determinants   Term used by Thibaut and Kelley to refer to those determinants of the outcomes of an interaction which arise during the course of an interaction.

Equity   A state of an interpersonal transaction in which the outcomes an individual derives from a given transaction are equal to the inputs invested in that transaction.

Existence   In Lewin's system, the state of having demonstrable effects.

Exogenous Determinants   A term used by Thibaut and Kelley to refer to those determinants of the outcomes of an interaction which are external to the actual process of interaction; the boundary conditions which define the maximum and minimum outcomes which are possible within an interaction.

Expedient Orientation   In Gross, Mason, and McEachern's view, an orientation that characterizes the person whose fulfillment or nonfulfillment of role expectations is based upon the sanctions that might subsequently be administered to him or her rather than upon the legitimacy of the expectations.

Extinction   The progressive decrement in the frequency of performance of a response under conditions of nonreinforcement.

Fate Control   In Thibaut and Kelley's theory, a form of power dependence in which person A can control the outcomes of person B regardless of the behavior that person B enacts.

Favorability Continuum   In Fiedler's theory, the range of group situations with respect to leader advantages.

Force   In Lewin's system, that which causes change.

Frame of Reference   An internal standard against which an individual judges any specific stimulus.

Goal Clarity   The degree to which the requirements of a task are known to the members of the group.

Goal-Path Multiplicity   The degree to which a task may be completed by alternative procedures.

Group Structure   The pattern of relations among the differentiated parts of a group.

Hedonic Relevance   The significance of an action to a perceiver based upon the degree to which the action is gratifying or disappointing to the perceiver.

Hope   In Stotland's theory, an expectation greater than zero of achieving a particular goal.

Human Exchange   In Homans' theory, the exchange of human social activities during interaction.

Impersonal Causality   According to Heider, a situation in which the production of a given outcome does not involve intentionality.

Impression Management   A conscious or unconscious attempt to control images that are projected in real or imaginary social situations.

Inclusion Need   In Schutz's theory, the need to establish and maintain a satisfactory relation with people with respect to association and interaction.

Independence   Behavior that disregards the normative expectations of the group.

Ingratiation   A class of behaviors illicitly designed to influence others concerning the attractiveness of one's personal characteristics.

Latitude of Acceptance   The range of attitudinal positions an individual finds acceptable or tolerable.

Latitude of Noncommitment   All attitudinal positions that are neither acceptable nor objectionable to an individual.

Latitude of Rejection   The range of attitudinal positions that are unacceptable or objectionable to an individual.

Life Space   In Lewin's system, the totality of all psychological factors that influence the individual at any given moment; the person and the psychological environment as it exists for him or her.

Local Stimulus   That part of the stimulus pattern that is of particular relevance to the percept.

Locomotion   In Lewin's system, movement in the life space.

Mand   A stimulus (usually verbal) which specifies or demands the organism's performance of a particular response; in social interaction, a response by a given person which indicates the singular response of another person which will be reinforcing.

Matched-Dependent Behavior   In Miller and Dollard's theory, a form of imitation in which the leader is able to "read" relevant environmental cues but the follower is not; hence the follower is dependent upon the leader for information (cues, signals) regarding appropriate behavior.

Mediation   In Heider's analysis of person perception, the manifestations of the other person's personality which determine the proximal stimulus pattern. Mediation may be (1) *synonymous* (each specific manifestation coordinated to a specific environmental content) or (2) *ambiguous* (each specific manifestation coordinated to more than one specific content).

Method of Construction   A term used by Lewin to refer to an approach to science which considers general laws as statements of empirical relations between psychological constructs or certain properties of them.

Modeling Effects   In Bandura's theory, the acquisition of novel responses by an observer which occurs through observation of the responses of another person.

Moral-Expedient Orientation   According to Gross, Mason, and McEachern, an orientation characterizing a person whose fulfillment of role expectations is jointly based upon the legitimacy of those expectations and the sanctions contingent upon fulfillment or nonfulfillment of them.

Moral Orientation   A term used by Gross, Mason, and McEachern to characterize the orientation of a person whose fulfillment or nonfulfillment of role expectation is based upon the legitimacy of those expectations.

Objective Reality   A situation in which evaluations can be tested by direct examination of the "real world."

Objective Self-Awareness   Conscious attention directed toward self-as-object.

Open System   A situation in which individual group members are free to join or leave the group without destroying its identity.

Operant   A response that operates upon the environment to satisfy the basic needs of the organism and thus leads to reinforcement.

Orientation   In Newcomb's theory, an individual's cognitive and affective mode of relating to others and to objects around him.

Outcome   The result of enacting a given activity (sequence of behavior) jointly with another's enactment of an activity. In Homans' theory, positive outcomes are referred to as profits (rewards are greater than costs) and negative outcomes are referred to as losses (rewards are less than costs).

Outcome Matrix   Thibaut and Kelley's major technique for the analysis of interaction outcomes; a matrix showing the outcomes for each member of a relationship as a function of their joint enactment of behavior sequences.

Person-Behavior Matrix   A descriptive tool in Biddle and Thomas's analysis of role; a matrix which consists of a set of behaviors ordered by both a set of subjects and a set of behavioral classes.

Personal Causality   In Heider's theory, a situation in which a person intentionally produces a given outcome or event.

Personal Space   Usually defined as the area immediately surrounding the person's body that is regarded as personal and private.

Personalism   In Heider's analysis of person perception, a situation in which the perceiver believes that he or she is the target of an action by another.

Phenomenal Description   A delineation of the nature of the contact between a person and his or her experienced environment.

Perturbation   An arousal response generated when an individual is subjected to unexpected or undesirable treatments.

Physical Density   The amount of space per person in any given social situation.

Position   According to Biddle and Thomas, a generally recognized category of persons who are classed together because of common attributes, common behaviors, or common reactions of others toward them.

Primary Environment   The environment in which the person spends much of his or her time, engages in personally important activities, and relates to others on a personal level.

Proximal Stimulus   The perceptual pattern that impinges directly upon the sense organs.

Psychological Conformity   Behavior intended to fulfill normative group expectations as perceived by the individual.

Psychological Reactance   Motivational arousal that occurs when an individual believes a freedom has been threatened or eliminated.

Role Conflict   Conflict which results when the expectations associated with two or more positions which a person occupies are incompatible with one another (inter-role conflict) or when the various expectations associated with a single position which a person occupies are mutually incompatible (intra-role conflict).

Same Behavior   A process described by Miller and Dollard whereby two individuals emit the same response as a function of independent stimulation by the same cue.

Schemata   In Stotland's theory, associations between concepts in an individual's cognitive structure.

Secondary Environments   Environments in which transitory encounters, inconsequential behaviors, and anonymous relations with others occur.

Self-Monitoring   An individual difference variable reflecting degree of concern about situational and interpersonal appropriateness of one's behavior.

Sentiments   A term used by Homans to denote activities which are signs of an individual's feelings and attitudes toward another or others. The same term was used by Heider to denote a liking relation between two persons.

Social Comparison   The act of evaluating one's opinions and abilities by relating them to the opinions and abilities of others.

Social Power   A term variously defined as (1) the quotient of the maximum force which one person can induce on another and the maximum resistance the other person can mobilize in the opposite direction (Lewin), (2) the maximum resultant force that one person can exert on another at a specific time and in a specific direction (Cartwright), and (3) the strength of the force fields which one person can induce on another (French).

Social Penetration   Overt interpersonal behaviors that occur in social interaction and internal subjective processes that precede, accompany, and follow overt exchange.

Social Reality   A situation in which the person must rely upon the opinions of others for evaluation of his or her own opinions and abilities.

Social Role   The set of behaviors expected of an individual by virtue of his or her position in the group; a term also used to refer to the behavioral expectations attached to the person rather than to the group position.

Stimulus   An internal or external event which occasions an alteration in the behavior of the organism. Kimble identified the following kinds of stimuli:

1   *Eliciting stimulus.* A part or a change in a part of the environment which calls forth a specific and almost reflexive response.

2   *Discriminative stimulus.* A stimulus which does not directly elicit a response, but rather sets the occasion or context for the occurrence of a particular response.

3 *Reinforcing stimulus.* A positive (for example, food) or negative (for example, shock) stimulus which is contingent upon the occurrence of a response.

Stimulus Generalization A process whereby a novel stimulus elicits a response which has been previously learned in the presence of another but similar stimulus.

System Strain, Strain Toward Symmetry In Newcomb's theory, a state of psychological tension resulting from the perceived discrepancy of self-other orientations or from uncertainty as to the other person's orientation.

Tact A discriminative stimulus (usually verbal) which sets the occasion for the emission of a response which is not under specified reinforcement control.

Tension In Lewin's system, a psychological state produced by opposing forces in the life space.

Territoriality The assumption of a proprietory orientation toward a geographical area by a person or group.

Theory A set of interrelated hypotheses or propositions concerning a phenomenon or set of phenomena. Types of theories include the following:

1 *Concatenated theory.* A theory whose component propositions form a network of relations which constitute an identifiable pattern.

2 *Constructive theory.* A theory that attempts to map complex phenomena from materials of a relatively simple scheme.

3 *Field theory.* A theory that explains phenomena in terms of relations among specified elements.

4 *Hierarchical theory.* A theory whose component propositions are deduced from a set of basic principles.

5 *Monadic theory.* A theory that explains phenomena by reference to the elements or attributes of elements which are related by propositions.

6 *Principle theory.* A theory derived by the analytic method, starting with a set of empirical data.

7 *Reductive theory.* A theory that attempts to explain phenomena by appealing to lower levels of analysis.

Theoretical Orientation A general approach to the analysis and interpretation of behavior; a system of psychology.

Transorientational Approach A theory that utilizes elements from two or more general orientations in the explanation of behavior or a theory that adopts an orientation which is independent of popular general orientations.

Unit Formation A term used by Heider to refer to the quality of belongingness.

Valence In Lewin's system, a field of forces in the life space which may be either positive or negative in direction.

Vicarious Reinforcement A process by which any observer experiences the rewards and punishments of another; a hypothetical construct inferred from an observer's "no-trial" learning of a response after observing another person make the response.

Vignette In Abelson's theory, an encoding of an event of short duration.

Name Index

Abeles, R. P., 145
Abelson, R. P., 183–184, 199, 223, 328
Adams, C. A., 166
Adams, J. S., 68, 102–104, 107, 108
Adewole, A., 203
Ahlm, K., 276, 277
Aiello, J. R., 355
Ajzen, I., 285–288, 342
Allen, J., 106
Allport, F. H., 41, 52, 381
Allport, G. W., 180, 285
Altman, I., 137, 153–162, 167–170
Anderson, J. R., 181, 190–191
Anderson, L., 290
Anderson, L. R., 217, 385, 388
Anderson, N. H., 283–284
Anrep, G. V., 33
Argyle, M., 353–355, 418
Arkin, R. M., 287
Armstrong, S., 368
Aronfreed, J., 152
Aronson, E., 222, 223, 226, 228, 266, 267
Arrowood, A. J., 267, 269
Asch, S. E., 131, 149, 261

Ashton, N., 382
Atkins, A. L., 276
Atkinson, J. W., 369
Atkinson, R., 391–393, 406
Austin, J. A., 290
Austin, W., 336
Ausubel, D. P., 180, 185, 188–189, 191

Back, K. W., 87, 152, 263, 264, 358
Backman, C. W., 295, 297, 298, 301, 303, 308
Baer, D. M., 43, 45, 47, 53, 54, 56
Baer, R., 231
Baldwin, J. M., 296, 367
Bales, R. F., 72
Bandura, A., 11, 42, 53–67
Banks, J. A., 95
Barchicha, D. C., 59
Barclay, A. M., 226
Barnard, C. I., 131
Barnes, R., 342, 343
Barnett, P. E., 65
Baron, M. R., 33–34

Baron, R. M., 166
Baron, R. S., 269
Bass, M. J., 33–34
Battle, E. S., 173
Beam, L., 95
Bechterev, V. M., 26
Beck, R., 407
Becker, H., 149
Bedell, J., 395, 396
Bem, D. J., 199, 223, 234, 250–257, 398
Bendetti, D. T., 65
Benner, L. A., 269
Bennett, E. B., 281
Bennis, W. G., 367
Bensberg, G. J., 125
Benton, A., 395
Berger, S. M., 65, 269
Berglas, S., 249
Berkowitz, L., 103, 107, 234, 253, 345
Berlyne, D. E., 186, 280
Berman, L., 276, 277
Bersch, P. J., 173
Berscheid, E., 68, 102–108, 226, 328, 339, 342
Bettelheim, B., 174
Biddle, B. J., 296–312
Bieri, J., 182, 276
Bierman, M., 61
Bilodeau, E. A., 33–34
Blau, P. M., 79
Blum, B., 336
Blum, J. M., 384, 388
Bonoma, T. V., 224, 281
Bourne, L., 174
Bovard, E. W., 272
Bower, G. H., 190
Bramel, D., 223, 226, 228, 336
Bredmeier, H. C., 297
Breese, F. H., 367
Brehm, J. W., 182, 199, 221–223, 226–228, 230, 231, 256, 261, 281
Brent, E. E., Jr., 276
Bressler, J., 272
Brickman, P., 203, 377
Bridgman, P. W., 16
Brigham, J. C., 8
Brinberg, D., 287
Briscoe, M. E., 152
Brock, T., 336, 348
Brown, J. S., 33–34, 115
Brown, R., 64, 216, 296
Brown, R. C., 153
Bruch, H., 402
Bruner, J. S., 185–187, 189
Brunswik, E., 111, 138, 187, 284

Bryan, J. H., 64
Buhler, C., 119
Burdick, H. A., 210
Burnes, A. J., 210
Burnstein, E., 203, 217, 282
Burstein, B., 404
Buss, A., 336, 348
Butler, W. M., 388
Butzin, C. A., 284
Byrne, D., 152, 153, 262, 267, 390, 408–410

Cacioppo, J. T., 230, 290
Cahill, H. E., 174
Caine, V. A., 63
Calder, B. J., 285, 336, 342
Campbell, N. R., 7
Canavan-Gumpert, D., 396–397
Cannon, W., 398, 399
Caplow, T., 357, 358
Carnap, R., 137
Carroll, J. S., 181
Cartwright, D., 112, 113, 117, 125–126, 129, 199, 200, 202, 203
Chadwick-Jones, J. K., 79
Champney, H., 367
Chapanis, A., 226
Chapanis, N. P., 226
Chapple, E. D., 72
Chave, E. J., 271
Chemers, M. W., 388
Chodoff, P., 174
Christie, R., 319
Cialdini, R., 336
Clark, L. V., 53
Clore, G. L., 355
Coates, B., 59
Coch, L., 136
Cohen, A. R., 182, 191, 221–222, 226–228, 281
Cohen, M., 173, 281, 282
Collins, B. E., 336
Collins, E. B., 382
Colson, W. N., 162
Conant, J. B., 7–8
Conolley, E. S., 269
Converse, P. E., 295
Cook, S. W., 216
Cooley, C. H., 296, 297, 328
Cooper, J., 5, 222, 224, 225
Costanzo, P. R., 67, 404, 405
Cottrell, L. S., 203
Coutts, L. M., 355
Crockett, W. H., 203

Crutchfield, R. S., 12, 180, 181, 186, 192–197, 205

Dabbs, J. M., Jr., 161
Darley, J. M., 152, 266
Daughtery, B. N., 87
Davidson, E. S., 61, 65
Davis, D., 348
Davis, H., 395, 396
Davis, J. D., 161
Davis, K. E., 87, 150, 151, 233–242, 247–250, 328, 336
Dean, J., 353–355
Dean, R. B., 290
Deaux, K. K., 276, 397, 408
de Carufel, A. C., 204
Dembo, T., 136, 369
Derbyshire, R. C., 357, 358
de Rivera, J., 111
Dermer, M., 339, 342
Desor, J., 163n., 170
Deutsch, M., 112, 126, 131–135, 303, 381
Dewey, J., 296, 328
Dickinson, R. L., 95
Diggory, J. C., 173
Di Nubile, M., 276
Dollard, J. C., 30, 33–38, 41–56, 63, 66–67, 389
Doob, L. W., 131
Doyen, R. H., 281
Duncan, B. L., 223
Dunham, R., 404
Durkheim, E., 296
Duval, S., 313, 346, 348
Dweck, C., 407

Eagly, A. H., 276
Easterbrook, J. A., 173
Edwards, W., 278, 284, 287
Einstein, A., 11
Eisner, J. R., 217, 276
Ellsworth, P. C., 141
Empey, J., 355
Eriksen, C. W., 272
Ervin, C., 152
Esch, J., 204
Esser, A. H., 163n., 170
Eustis, A., 317, 328
Evans, P., 418
Exline, R. V., 141

Falbo, T., 407

Farris, C., 348
Fazio, R. H., 225, 267
Feather, N. J., 369, 392
Feather, N. T., 152, 175
Fenigstein, A., 348
Fenton, M., 231
Fernberger, S. W., 271
Ferster, C. B., 36
Festinger, L., 18, 87, 95, 136, 150, 152, 182, 192, 198, 199, 217–223, 225, 259–269, 303, 358, 369, 398
Fiedler, F. E., 11, 353, 382–388
Fine, R., 348
Firestone, I. J., 170
Fischer, G. W., 204
Fishbein, M., 217, 278, 285–288, 342
Fleming, W. H., 281
Floyd, J., 267
Foa, E. B., 79
Foa, U. G., 79
Ford, C. S., 46
Form, W. H., 153
Frank, P., 13
Frankfurt, L. P., 161, 162
Freedman, J. L., 163n., 226, 227
Freedman, S., 107, 108, 421
Freidman, S., 174
French, J. R. P., Jr., 11, 126–131, 136, 173
Freud, A., 173
Freud, S., 367
Friedman, H. S., 141
Friedman, L., 404
Friend, R., 267
Frieze, I., 393, 405
Fromm, E., 367
Fuller, C. H., 204

Gabrenya, W. K., Jr., 287
Gaes, G., 336
Galanter, E., 189
Garcia-Esteve, J., 152
Gardner, J. W., 261
Garner, K., 396–397
Garner, W. R., 280, 284
Gastorf, J. W., 268
Gebhard, M. E., 174
Geis, R., 319
Gengel, R. W., 217
Gerard, H. B., 5, 173, 263–265, 269, 303, 385
Gergen, K. J., 151, 328, 418
Gerst, M. S., 59
Getzels J. W., 309
Gewirtz, J. L., 43–45, 47, 53, 54, 56, 174

Gibson, J. J., 141
Glass, D., 336
Goethals, G. R., 222, 248, 267, 269
Goetz, T., 407
Goffman, E., 300–301, 313, 315, 328, 334, 335, 338
Goldman, H., 336
Goldman, M., 381
Goldstein, K., 173
Goldstein, S., 174
Golin, S. J., 36
Gollob, H. F., 204
Goodenough, D. R., 183
Gordon, B. F., 266, 267
Gordon, E., 328
Gordon, F. R., 53
Gorkin, L., 223
Gould, R., 261
Gouldner, A. W., 95, 160
Graesser, C. G., 284
Granberg, D., 276
Grant, D. A., 36
Graves, J., 382
Graves, T. D., 355
Gray, D., 141
Graziano, W., 339, 342
Greenberg, C. I., 170
Greene, D., 256, 408
Greenwood, M., 404
Greif, E. B., 64
Griffen, L. M., 166
Groner, N, 166
Gruder, C. L., 267
Grumet, J. F., 248
Grusec, J. E., 55, 58, 59
Guba, E. G., 309
Guetzkow, H., 382
Gullahorn, J. E., 79
Gullahorn, J. T., 79, 87
Gumpert, P., 328, 396–397
Guthrie, E. R., 27, 38
Gutman, G. M., 203
Guttman, N., 33

Haggard, E. A., 173
Hake, H. W., 272
Hakmiller, K. L., 266, 267, 269
Hall, E. T., 167
Hall, J. F., 23, 32–33, 37–39
Halpin, A. W., 384
Halsey, A. H., 95
Hamblin, R. L., 79
Hamburg, D. A., 174
Hammond, L. K., 381

Handler, J., 404
Harackiewicz, J. M., 276
Harari, H., 8, 295, 298
Harary, F., 129, 199, 200, 202, 203
Harburg, E., 209
Hardy, R. C., 388
Hardyck, J., 226
Harris, C. W., 367
Harris, V., 248
Hartup, W. W., 59
Harvey, J. H., 281, 282
Harvey, O. J., 226, 275
Heider, F., 11, 137–153, 192, 198–203, 206, 208, 233–235, 241, 242, 248, 249, 296, 328, 335, 337, 354, 405–406
Heilman, M. E., 230
Heintz, R. K., 272, 384
Heller, J. F., 230
Helson, H., 93
Hempel, C. G., 15
Hendrick, C., 280
Herman, P., 404–405
Higgins, E. T., 223, 225
Hilgard, E. R., 23, 26–27, 34, 181
Hill, J. F., 267
Hillix, W. A., 10, 111, 112
Himmelfarb, S., 284
Hinkle, S., 231
Hochbaum, G. M., 261
Hoerig, J., 336
Hoffman, P. J., 263
Hollander, E. P., 8, 358
Holt, L. E., 291
Homans, G. C., 68–77, 102, 157
Hong, G. K., 166
Honzik, C. H., 27
Horn, C., 203
Horner, M., 313, 315, 391–397
Hornik, J. A., 287
Hottes, J., 395, 396
Hovland, C. I., 33–34, 174, 269, 271–273, 275
Hoyt, M. E., 141, 336
Hughes, J. W., 305
Hull, C. L., 23–24, 27, 29–30, 32–35, 38, 124
Humphrey, G., 52
Hunt, E. B., 185
Hunt, J. G., 388
Hunt, W. A., 273
Hunter, R., 217
Hymovitch, B., 264

Ickes, W., 342, 343, 348
Ingham, A. G., 382

Insko, C. A., 203, 204, 216, 226, 227, 291, 336

Jaccard, J. J., 287
Jacobs, L., 328
James, W., 296, 338, 397–399
Jeffrey, R. W., 59
Jellison, J. M., 281, 282
Jenkins, W. D., 36
Jennings, H., 86
Johnson, C. F., 161
Johnson, P., 404
Johnson, S., 281
Jones, E. E., 5, 87, 150, 173, 216, 233–244, 247–255, 257, 303, 313, 315–328, 336, 338
Jones, R. A., 256, 328
Jones, R. G., 328
Jones, S. C., 267
Jordon, N., 202, 203
Jorgensen, B. W., 87
Joseph, M. L., 101
Jourard, S. M., 160
Judd, C. M., 276
Jurma, W. E., 388

Kahn, R. L., 384, 395, 396
Kahneman, D., 261n.
Kalish, H. I., 33
Kalle, R., 336
Kallhorn, J., 367
Kalven, J., 336, 438
Kanareff, V., 55
Kanfer, F. H., 56, 62
Kanouse, D., 404
Kaplan, A., 8–9, 11–13, 15
Kaplan, M. F., 284
Kardusch, M., 226
Karsten, A., 125
Kasl, S., 173
Katz, D., 384
Kaufman, D. R., 317, 328
Keating, J. P., 166
Keller, A. G., 52
Keller, F. S., 28–31, 33–35, 37–38, 47
Kelley, H. H., 68, 78–101, 104, 150, 157–158, 234, 239, 246–254, 257, 264, 297, 302, 311, 381, 406, 410
Kelly, G. A., 182, 328
Kelly, M., 276
Kemelgor, B., 106
Kenrick, D., 336

Kerchoff, A. C., 87
Kerrick, J., 216, 217
Kessen, W., 8, 10
Kiesler, C. A., 199, 256, 280
Kimble, G. A., 23, 25–26, 28
Kitt, A. S., 297, 302
Kleck, R. E., 355
Klein, S. J., 173
Kleinke, C. L., 141
Kline, T., 269
Knight, D. J., 368
Knower, F. H., 275
Knox, R., 287
Knox, R. E., 203
Koffka, K., 112
Kohlberg, L., 152
Kohler, R., 174
Kohler, W., 112
Koulack, D., 276
Krech, D., 12, 180, 181, 186, 192–197, 205
Kruglanski, A. W., 281, 282
Kuenne, M. R., 174
Kuhn, T. S., 8, 10
Kukla, A., 151, 377, 393, 405
Kunkel, J. H., 79
Kurtines, W., 64

Lambert, W. E., 379
Lamberth, J., 152
Langer, E. J., 166, 257
Lanzetta, J. T., 55
Larder, D. L., 62
Lashley, K. S., 33–34, 111
Latane, B., 152, 266, 268
Lawrence, D. H., 263
Layden, M., 342
Leat, H. M., 62
Leeper, R. W., 256, 408
Lekhyananda, D., 388
Leon, G., 405
Lepper, M. R., 223
Lerman, D., 405–407
Lerner, M. J., 146
Leventhal, G. S., 103, 106, 440
Leventhal, H., 401, 402
Levinger, G., 87, 382
Lewin, K., 111–126, 129, 136, 137, 147n., 154, 174, 181, 369, 383, 417
Lewis, H. B., 131
Liebert, R. M., 61, 65
Liebling, B., 348
Likert, R., 271
Linder, D. E., 256, 284

Lindner, R., 284
Link, W. E., 174
Lippa, R., 339, 341
Lippitt, R., 383
Litwin, G., 391–394
Long, L., 272
Lopes, L. L., 284
Lopez, L. J., 33
Lorber, N., 368
Lorge, I., 379
Lövass, O. I., 62
Luce, R. D., 278
Lundgren, D. C., 368
Lupton, T., 95
Lynn, S., 277
Lyon, J. D., 204

McAllister, D. E., 33
McAllister, W. R., 33
McArthur, L. Z., 249, 404
McCallum, R., 166
McClelland, D., 391–393, 406
McClintock, C. G., 101
McConnell, H. K., 256
McCurdy, H. G., 379
McDavid, J. W., 8, 295, 298
McDonald, F. J., 64
McDougall, W., 3, 40, 52
McEachern, A. W., 304, 309–310
McGarvey, H. R., 271
McGarvey, W., 204
McGee, R. J., 357, 358
McGillis, D., 233–241, 243, 244, 248–250,
    257
McGuire, W. J., 184, 288–291
Mack, D., 404
MacLeod, R. B., 180
McMillan, D. A., III, 217
Mahler, V., 125
Maller, J. B., 131
Mandel, D. R., 166
Mandler, G., 8, 10
Manis, M., 197
Mann, M., 230
Manske, A. J., 275
March, J. G., 278, 381
Marquart, D. I., 379
Marsten, A. R., 62
Martens, R., 162
Marwell, G., 106
Marx, C. H., 10–11, 111, 112
Maslach, C., 400
Maslow, A. H., 173

Mason, J. W., 174
Mason, W. S., 304, 309–310
Masters, J. C., 53
Matterman, J. M., 173
Mausner, B., 395, 396
May, M. A., 131
Mazis, M. B., 230
Mead, G. H., 297, 313, 315, 328, 345
Mead, M., 131
Medow, H., 369
Menlove, F. L., 55, 58, 59
Merton, R. K., 9, 297, 302, 309, 414
Mettee, D. R., 267
Meuwese, W., 388
Meyer, J., 407
Mezei, L., 62
Milgram, S., 170
Miller, D. T., 255, 257
Miller, G. A., 272, 286
Miller, N. E., 27, 30, 33–38, 41–56, 63,
    66–67, 114–115, 173, 354, 355, 389
Miller, R. L., 267, 269
Mills, J. S., 280
Mischel, W., 342
Modigliani, A., 335
Monson, T., 339–342
Morasch, B., 166
Moreno, J. L., 296
Morgan, C. H., 36
Morgan, S., 395, 396
Morton, T. L., 161
Moss, F. A., 226
Mowrer, O. H., 27, 30, 42, 54–56
Mullens, S., 355
Murray, H. A., 154
Mussen, P. H., 367
Mynatt, C., 335

Nachshon, I., 141
Naficy, A., 222
Neale, J. M., 61, 65
Nebergall, R. E., 269–276
Needham, J. G., 272
Neiman, L. J., 305
Neisser, U., 180, 182
Nelson, D., 409
Newcomb, T. M., 86, 87, 91, 150, 160, 192,
    198, 199, 203–209, 262, 285, 295, 297,
    304, 410
Newell, A., 190
Nisbett, R., 255–257, 401, 402, 404
Norman, R. Z., 129
Nosow, S., 153

Nowlis, H. M., 174
Nuttin, J. M., Jr., 199, 224

Oltman, P. K., 183
Orne, M. T., 17
Osgood, C. E., 30, 50, 198, 199, 203,
    209–216, 384
Osler, S. F., 175
Ovsiankina, M., 124

Pallak, M. S., 225, 230
Papageorgis, D., 290
Parke, R. D., 55, 62, 63
Parsons, T., 309
Passer, M., 407
Patterson, M. L., 355
Pavlov, I. P., 24–26, 38–39
Payne, J. W., 181
Peckham, V., 382
Pellegrini, R. J., 355
Pepitone, A., 199, 225, 276
Peplau, L. A., 147, 152
Perin, C. T., 38
Perkins, C. C., 33
Perlick, D., 141
Peterson, P. D., 276
Petty, R. E., 230, 290
Piaget, J., 144
Picek, J. S., 204, 230
Pick, A. D., 141
Pilkonis, P., 343
Pinner, B., 163
Pittman, T. S., 225
Pliner, P., 404
Polanyi, M., 8–9
Pollay, R. W., 280
Postman, L., 272
Powell, R. M., 87
Prelinger, E., 200
Preston, M. G., 384
Price, K. O., 209
Priest, R. F., 87

Rachman, S., 62
Radloff, R., 267
Rajaratnam, N., 379
Rall, M., 163
Rand, K., 368
Ratliff, K., 106
Raven, B. H., 5, 128, 264
Ray, A. A., 256
Rayner, R., 33

Razran, G. H. S., 34
Reed, L., 393, 405
Regan, D. T., 267
Reisman, S. R., 152, 204
Reitan, H., 335
Remmers, H. H., 275
Rest, S., 393, 405
Restle, F., 278
Rhine, R. J., 175
Rice, R. W., 388
Riecken, H., 151
Riess, M., 336
Roback, H., 368
Robertson, I. V., 275
Rodewalt, F., 223, 225
Rodin, J., 256, 401–404
Rogers, H. L., Jr., 276
Rogers, S., 272
Rokeach, M., 154
Romano, J., 355
Rommetveit, R., 305
Roper, G., 269
Rosenbaum, R., 393, 405
Rosenberg, H. J., 199, 286
Rosenfield, P., 257
Rosenthal, R., 17
Rosenthal, T. L., 55, 65
Rosow, I., 152
Ross, D., 62
Ross, E. A., 3, 296
Ross, L, 249, 256, 258, 401
Ross, M., 255, 257, 285, 336, 342
Ross, S., 62
Roth, L., 405
Rotter, J. B., 278, 287, 406
Rubin, J. Z., 5, 147, 152, 161
Rusbult, C. E., 166
Russell, D. H., 275, 405–407

Saegert, S., 166
Sampson, E., 343
Samuel, W., 268
Santee, R. T., 267
Sarbin, T. R., 300, 313
Sargent, S. S., 295
Sarup, G., 276
Sawyer, J., 87
Scalise, C. J., 225
Schachter, S., 87, 152, 254, 256, 263, 264,
    358, 390, 397–405
Scheerer, M., 179, 181, 182, 184, 186, 191
Scheier, M., 348
Scheler, M., 149
Schipper, L. M., 36

Schlenker, B. R., 8, 151, 153, 224, 281, 313, 315, 328–336, 418
Schlossberg, H., 286
Schmitt, D. R., 106
Schneider, D., 317, 328
Schneider, F. W., 152, 355
Schoenfeld, W. M., 173
Schoenfeld, W. N., 28–31, 33–35, 37–38, 47
Schopler, J., 137, 152, 163–166, 170
Schuette, D., 141
Schutz, W. C., 353, 360–368
Schwartz, B., 23
Schwartz, J. M., 268
Scott, W. A., 95, 182–183
Sears, D. O., 226, 227
Sears, P. S., 136
Sears, R. R., 43
Sechrest, L. B., 355
Secord, P. F., 295, 297, 298, 301, 303, 308
Seidenberg, B., 4
Senn, D. J., 87
Sensenig, J., 230
Severy, L. J., 8
Sewell, W. H., 367
Shaver, K. G., 5
Shaver, P., 348
Shaw, J. C., 190
Shaw, M. E., 16, 101, 125, 144, 151, 152, 215, 271, 335, 382–385, 388
Shaw, Marjorie E., 379
Shepard, H. A., 367
Sherif, C. W., 269–276
Sherif, M., 269–276
Sherman, J. A., 43, 45, 47, 53, 54, 56
Sherman, J. J., 276, 277
Sherman, S. J., 204, 223, 335
Shiffrin, R. M., 204
Siegel, A. E., 62
Silver, M., 348
Silverman, I., 17, 226
Silverstone, J., 404
Simmel, G., 141, 296, 354
Simon, H. A., 190, 278, 381
Simon, J. G., 152
Singer, J., 256, 400, 401
Singh, D., 404–405
Sistrunk, F., 395, 396
Skinner, B. F., 23–24, 27, 36, 42, 45, 54–56, 63
Skrzypek, G. J., 388
Smith, K., 231
Smith, W. P., 268
Snadowsky, A., 4
Snyder, M., 313, 315, 337–345
Snyder, M. L., 230, 257

Solomon, H., 379
Sommer, R., 167
Songer, E., 204
Songer-Nocks, E., 288
Sorrentino, R., 162
Spence, K., 23, 30, 174
Stahelski, A. J., 101
Stanley, J. C., 36
Steiner, I. D., 277–282, 317, 328, 353, 377–382
Steinman, W. M., 43, 53
Stephan, W. G., 257
Stephenson, R. M., 297
Stingle, K. G., 43–45, 47, 53, 54, 56
Stires, L., 417
Stockdale, J. E., 137, 163
Stokols, D., 137, 163–165, 170
Stolurow, L. M., 388
Storms, M., 256
Stotland, E., 137, 170–175, 191
Stough, R. R., 170
Strickland, L. H., 303, 325
Stroebe, W., 204
Suci, G. A., 384
Suls, J., 268, 269
Sulzer, J. L., 144, 152
Sumner, W. G., 52, 296
Sundstrom, E., 388
Swann, W., 342
Swets, J. A., 187

Talabar, R., 281
Tanke, E., 342
Tannenbaum, P. H., 150, 198, 199, 203, 210–214, 217, 384
Tanner, W. P., Jr., 187
Tarde, G., 40, 52
Taub, B., 336
Taves, P. A., 225
Taylor, D. A., 137, 153–162
Taylor, D. W., 381
Taylor, M., 151
Taylor, R. B., 170
Teddlie, C., 163n.
Tedeschi, J. T., 153, 224, 281, 336
Telaak, K., 276
Thibaut, J. W., 68, 78–101, 104, 108, 151, 157, 158, 263, 265, 303, 311, 328, 381, 410
Thistlethwaite, D. L., 204
Thomas, D. R., 33
Thomas, E. J., 296–312
Thompson, V. D., 204
Thorndike, E. L., 24–26, 35

Thornton, D. A., 267, 269
Thurstone, L. L., 271
Tittler, B. I., 276
Toffler, B. L., 230
Tolman, E. C., 27, 111, 181, 278
Torrey, J., 264
Tremble, T. R., Jr., 335
Tresemer, D., 394, 396
Triandis, H., 217
Trope, Y., 217, 282, 377
Trotter, W., 52
Turner, R. H., 295
Tversky, A., 261n., 278

Upshaw, H. S., 277, 282, 328
Utne, M., 336

Valins, S., 254, 256, 400, 402
Vander Zanden, J. W., 5
Varela, J. A., 199
Volkmann, J., 271, 272
Vroom, V. H., 278

Wade, M., 33–34
Wagner, P. J., 151
Walbeck, N. H., 64
Walden, T. A., 166
Wallach, M. A., 189
Walster, E., 68, 102–108, 226, 328, 336
Walster, G. W., 68, 102–108
Walters, R. H., 42, 53, 55, 56, 62, 63
Waly, P., 216
Wapner, S., 141
Ware, R., 226
Watson, G., 4
Watson, J. B., 26–27, 33, 38
Watson, O. M., 355
Watts, W. A., 290, 291
Waxler, C. Z., 45
Weiner, B., 151, 393, 405–408
Weinraub, M., 231
Wellens, A. R., 204
Wertheimer, M., 112, 146, 233
Westermarck, E., 149
Wever, E. G., 271
Weyant, R. G., 33
Whalen, C. K., 61

Wheeler, L., 111, 266–268, 396, 401
White, C. J. M., 217, 276
White, R. K., 383
White, V., 162
Whittemore, I. C., 262
Wicker, A. W., 163n., 285
Wicklund, R. A., 223, 226, 228, 230, 313,
    315, 345–349
Wilhelmy, R. A., 223
Wilke, W. H., 275
Wilkins, P. C., 267
Willerman, B., 264
Williams, D. C., 151
Williamsson, R. C., 295
Willis, R. H., 101
Wilson, S. R., 269
Wilson, T., 257
Winch, R. F., 86
Witkin, H. A., 183
Wolfe, D. M., 191
Woodworth, R. S., 286
Woody, E., 404–405
Wooley, O., 404
Wooley, S., 404
Worchel, S., 5, 163n., 248
Wortman, C., 313, 315–328
Wright, J. M., 16, 215, 271
Wyer, R. S., Jr., 204

Yalom, I. D., 368
Yang, K., 203
Yang, P., 203
Yarrow, M. R., 45
Yates, L., 328
Yuker, H. E., 382

Zajonc, R. B., 179, 182–183, 203, 286, 381
Zander, A. F., 353, 356–359, 369–377, 392
Zanna, M. P., 223, 225, 256, 269
Zeigarnik, B., 124
Zeisel, H, 336
Zener, K. E., 271
Ziller, R. C., 381
Zillman, D., 399–402
Zimbardo, P., 256, 400, 401
Zimmerman, B. J., 55
Zipf, S. G., 173, 175
Zuckerman, M., 396

Subject Index

Abilities, social comparison and, 260
A-B-X system, 204–210
  basic definition of, 205–206
  evaluation of, 208–210
  systems of orientation in, 205–206
Acclaiming in impression management, 334–335
Achievement attribution, 397, 405–408
  Weiner's viewpoint on, 405–408
   evaluation of, 407–408
   hypotheses, 406–407
Achievement motivation, 391–393
Act, 190–191
Action, naive analysis of, 142
Actor-observer differences, 255
Actor in role theory, 142
Acts as defined by Jones and Davis, 234
Affection behavior, 363–364
Affection need, 362
Affective leader-group relations, 385
Affiliative conflict theory, 354–356
  basic propositions of, 354
  evaluation of, 355–356
Alter ego, 297

Apologies in impression management, 334
Approach-approach conflict, 113–114
Approach-avoidance conflict, 114–115
Assimilation:
  and anchor effects, 272
  and contrast effects, 272
  social judgment and, 272–273
Associative learning, 24–25, 53
Assumed desirability, factors determining, 237–238
Asymmetry, consequences of, 207–208
Attitude(s):
  and attraction, 408–410
  attribution of, 248–249
  and behavioral intentions, 285–288
   definition of, 285
   nature of, 285–286
    beliefs, 285–286
   theory of, 285–288
    prediction, 286–287
  Byrne's paradigm of, 408–410
   evaluation of, 410
  as cognitive elements, 205

Attribution theory, 232–258
  correspondent inferences (*see*
    Correspondent inferences, theory of)
  dispositional, 232, 234–241
  external, 234, 241–248
    analysis of variance (ANOVA) cube
      model of, 243–244
    of attitude, 248–249
    causal principles in (*see* Causal
      principles in attribution)
    causal schemata and (*see* Causal
      schemata and attribution)
  and self-perception, 250–257
Augmentation principle, 247
Autistic friendliness, 91
Autistic hostility, 91
Avoidance-avoidance conflict, 114

Behavior:
  affection, 363–364
  control, 97, 363
  copying, 47, 51–52
  matched-dependent (*see* Matched-
    dependent behavior)
  same, 47–48
  (*See also* Elementary social behavior;
    Interpersonal behavior)
Behavior sequence, 97
Behavioral intentions and attitudes (*see*
  Attitudes, and behavioral intentions)
Behaviorism:
  distinguished from cognitive theory, 180
  exchange theory and, 69–70
  Watsonian, 26–27
Beliefs and attitudes, 285–286
Benefit, harm and, 148–149

"Can," 142
Causal ascriptions for achievement, 405–407
Causal principles in attribution, 246–248
  augmentation principle, 247
  bases for, 246–247
  covariation principle, 247
Causal schemata and attribution, 244–246
  bases for, 244–245
  multiple necessary schema, 246
  multiple sufficient schema, 245–246
Causality, personal and impersonal, 143–144
Choice, theory of, 277–282
  attribution to others, 281
  comment and evaluation, 281–282
  comparison and, 279
  definition of, 278

Choice, theory of (*Cont.*):
  effects of commitment on, 280–281
  and expected utility of options, 272
  multiple options and selections, 280
  types of, 279
Classical conditioning, 24–26
  vicarious, 65–66
Cognition, definition of, 218
Cognitive consistency, theories of, 199–228
Cognitive dissonance, theory of, 217–228
  consequences of, 219–220
  definition of, 217–219
    sources of, 218–219
  evaluation of, 224–228
    reduction of, 225–226
  implications of, 220–221
  magnitude of, 219
  modifications of, 221–224
  problems of, 225
Cognitive orientation, 179–197
  basic terms of, 181–185
    cognition, 179
    cognitive structure, 181–184
    meaning, 185
    response, 184–185
    stimulus, 184–185
  behaviorism and, 180
Cognitive scripts, 183–184
Cognitive structure, 181–184
  complexity of, 182
  definition of, 182
  integration of, 182–183
  properties of, 182–184
  relatedness in, 182–183
  reorganization of, 195–196
Cognitive theory, 179–197
  basic concepts of, 181–185
  Krech and Crutchfield's, 192–197
  summary of, 196–197
Command, 147–148
Comparison level (CL), 85–86, 93–95
  for alternatives (CLalt), 85–86, 93–95
Compatibility, 364–366
  interchange, 364–365
  originator, 365
  reciprocal, 365
Compatibility theorems, 365–366
Complementarity as a determinant of
  rewards and costs, 87–88
Concatenated theory, 11
Confirmation check, 187
Confirmation completion, 187
Conflict, 113–115
  approach-approach, 113–114
  approach-avoidance, 114–115

Conflict (*Cont.*):
  avoidance-avoidance, 114
  definition of, 113
  field-theory interpretation of, 113–115
Congruity (*see* Principle of congruity)
Consciousness, state of, 345–346
Consensus:
  and attribution, 243–244
  polarized desensus and, 308
  and role relationships, 308–311
Consistency and attribution, 242–244
Constructive method, 113, 115, 117
Constructive theory, 11
Contingency model of leadership
    effectiveness, 382–387
  evaluation of, 386–388
Contrast effect(s):
  assimilation and, 272
  in attribution, 249
Control behavior, 97, 363
Control need, 362
Cooperation and competition, theory of,
    131–135
  definitions of, 132
  hypotheses in, 132–135
Coorientation, 205
Copying behavior, 47, 51–52
Correspondence:
  and assumed desirability, 237–238
  concept of, 235–237
  definition of, 235, 239–240
  and expected effect valence, 240–241
    category-based, 240–241
    target-based, 240–241
  as information gain, 236, 239
  and persons' involvement, 238
Correspondent inferences, 233–241
  theory of, 233–238
    evaluation of, 238–241
Costs:
  determinants of, 86–90
  in equity theory, 103–107
  rewards and, 81–101, 103–107
Covariation principle, 247
Covert rehearsal, 61
Credibility of information, 323–324
Crowding, theories of, 162–170
  model of, 167–169
    basic factors in, 167–168
  setting-specific analysis of, 163–166
Cue search, 187

Decision control, 278
Decision verifiability, 385

Declarative knowledge, 190–191
Defenses of innocence, 333
Desire, pleasure and, 144–145
Differentiation, 182–183
  in achieving balance, 204
  and role concepts, 303
Discounting principle, 247
Discovery learning, 188
Discrimination, 34–35
Discriminative stimulus, 35
Dispositional properties of a person, 142
Dissonance, defined, 218
  (*See also* Cognitive dissonance, theory of)
Distributive justice, 77–78
Drive, 25, 29–31
  in Miller and Dollard's theory, 43–45
  primary, 30, 44
  reduction, 29–31, 44–45
  secondary, 30, 44

Effects:
  commonality of, 235
  consensus about, 243–244
  consistency of, 243–244
    over modality, 244
    over time, 243
  as defined by Jones and Davis, 234
  distinctiveness of, 243
Elementary social behavior, theory of, 69–80
  definition of, 70
Embeddedness, 139
Emotion, two-factor theory of, 397–402
  derivative hypotheses, 398–399
  evaluation of, 399–402
  guiding principle of, 398
  self-perception of, 256, 397–399, 401–402
Emotional self-labeling, 256, 398, 399
Empathetic learning, 55–56
Equifinality, 143–144
Equity theory, 102–108
  defined, 103
  propositions, 105–107
  restoration of, 106–107
Exchange theory and behaviorism, 69–70
Excuses in impression management, 333
Expectancy:
  category-based, 240–241
  target-based, 240–241
  and value, 391–393, 397, 406–408
Explanatory shell, 11–12
  radius of, 12–13
Explication, process of, 137
Extinction, 25, 37–39
  inhibition interpretation, 38–39

Extinction (*Cont.*):
  interference interpretation, 38
  resistance to, 37–38
  vicarious, 66

Fate control, 96–97
  mutual, 98
Favor-doing as ingratiation, 322
Favorability continuum and leadership style,
    386
Fear-of-success theory, 391–397
  defined, 393
  evaluation of, 394–396
  gender nonspecific, 396–397
  hypothesis in, 393–394
Field forces (*see* Force fields)
Field-theoretical orientation, 111–126
  social theories derived from, 126–135,
    137–175
Field theory, 12, 111–126
  applications of, 126–135
  attributes of, 112–116
  basic concepts of, 117–126
  constructs in, 116
FIRO (Fundamental Interpersonal Relations
    Orientation), 360–368
  evaluation of, 367–368
  postulates of, 361
Fluidity, 119
Force fields, 121–125
  driving, 123
  illustrations of, 122
  impersonal, 123
  induced, 123
  related to tension, 125–126
  resultant, 123
  valences in, 122
Frame of reference, 270
Front (in role theory), 300–301
Fundamental attribution error, 249

Generalization:
  in human exchange, 74–75
  response to, 34
  stimulus, 34, 55–56
Generalization gradient, 33
Goal clarity, 385
Goal gradient hypothesis, 113, 123
Goal-path multiplicity, 385
Group aspiration level, 369–371
  assumptions about, 369–370
Group development, 366
Group interaction, 6

Group membership, theory of, 356–360
Group motives and goals, theory of, 368–377
  effects of success and failure on, 371–372
  evaluation of, 376–377
  related to outside pressures, 372–373
Group productivity, theory of, 377–382
  determinants of, 377–378
  evaluation of, 382
  group size and, 381
  and type of task, 378–381
Group tasks, types of, 378–380

Habit strength, 32
Harm, benefit and, 148–149
Hedonic relevance, 238
Hierarchical theory, 11
Hope, theory of, 170–175
  and action, 172–173
  and anxiety, 173
  major propositions in, 171–172
  and schemas, 174
Human exchange, 70–79
  descriptive terms for, 70–72
    activity, 71
    interaction, 71–72
    sentiment, 71
  propositions of, 74–77
  variables for, 72–73
    quantity, 72–73
    value, 72–73

Imitation, theories of, 42–67
  Bandura's, 53–66
  mechanics of, 47–53
  Miller and Dollard's, 42–53
  two-process, 55–56
Impersonal causality, 143–144
Impression management theory, 328–337
  comments on, 335–337
  defined, 329
  predicaments in (*see* Predicaments in
    impression management)
Incentive value of ingratiation, 316–317
Inclusion behavior, 362–363
Inclusion need, 361–362
Incomparability, consequences of
    preventing, 265–266
Incredulity, correction for, 214
Information, credibility of, 323–324
Ingratiation theory, 315–328
  comments on, 327–328
  credibility of, 323–324
  defined, 316

Ingratiation theory (*Cont.*):
  determinants of, 316–320
  effect of, 324–327
  tactics of, 320–323
  uniqueness of, 316–317, 323–324
Inhibition:
  conditioned, 38–39
  and distinctiveness of modeling effects,
    62–63
  reactive, 38
Inoculation theory, 288–291
  assumptions of, 288–289
  defensive variables in, 289–290
  evaluation of, 290–291
Instrumental/operant learning, 23–40
Integration theory, 282–284
  averaging model of, 283–284
  basic operations in, 283
Interdependence, theory of, 80–101
Internal versus external causal ascriptions
    for achievement, 406–407
Interpersonal behavior, types of, 362–364
Interpersonal needs:
  affection, 362
  control, 362
  inclusion, 361–362
Interpersonal relations, theory of, 137–153

Judgment scales, 271–272
Justification in impression management, 333

Knowledge:
  declarative, 190–191
  procedural, 190–191

Latitudes:
  of acceptance, 273
  of noncommitment, 273–274
  of rejection, 273–274
Law of effect (Thorndike), 24
Law of exercise (Thorndike), 24
Leadership, theory of, 382–388
Learning:
  associative, 24–25, 53
  cognitive analysis of, 188–191
  discovery, 188
  empathetic, 55–56
  fundamentals of, 43–47
  latent, 26–27
  meaningful, 188–189
  observational (*see* Observational learning)
  reception, 188

Learning (*Cont.*):
  reinforcement analysis of, 23–49
  response, 54
  rote, 188–189
  social, 41–67
  trial-and-error, 54
  vicarious, 55–66
Legitimacy:
  of ingratiation, 318–320
  of role expectations, 289–299, 309
Levels of analysis, 12–13, 414
Life space, 118–126
  behavior and, 121
  boundaries of, 119–122
  definition of, 118
  differentiation of, 119, 125
  forces in, 121–123
    types of, 122–123
  interdependence of parts of, 118
  locomotion in, 121
  reality-irreality characteristics of,
    119–120
  regions of, 119, 124
    fluidity in, 119
    rigidity of boundaries, 119
  tension and tension systems in, 123–126

Matched-dependent behavior, 47–51
  paradigms for, 48–51
Meaning in cognitive psychology, 185
Meaningful learning, 188–189
Mediation, 138–140
  ambiguous, 139
    overlapping, 139
  synonymous, 139
Mediational learning theories, 23–39
Minitheories, 12, 355, 414
Misattribution of emotional arousal, 401
Modeling, 41–67
  abstract rule transmission, 63–64
  inhibition and disinhibition, 62–63
  innovation and, 64
  and response facilitation, 63
Molar theories, 12
Molecular theories, 12
Moral-expedient orientation in resolving role
  conflict, 309
Moral orientation in resolving role conflict,
  309
Motivation, cognitive analysis of, 191–192
Motive:
  to achieve success, 391–393
  to avoid failure, 391–393
Multifinality, 143–144.

Naive analysis of action, 142
Need achievement, 391–392

Obese externality, 403–404
Obesity-prone behavior, 402–405
    hypothesis concerning, 403–404
    perspective on, 402–405
        evaluation of, 404–405
Objective self-awareness, theory of, 345–349
    comments and evaluation of, 348–349
    propositions of, 346–348
        arousal, 346–347
        avoidance, 347
        reduction of discrepancy, 347–348
        self-evaluation, 347
    as a state of consciousness, 345–346
Observational learning, 42, 57–60
    processes of, 57–60
        attention, 58
        motive reproduction, 59–60
        retention, 58–59
Operational definition, 16
Opinion conformity as a tactic, 321–322
Orientation, 9, 205–207
    field-theoretical (see Field-theoretical
        orientation)
    homogeneity of, 208
    systems of, 206–207
    (See also Cognitive orientation)
Other enhancement, or flattery, 320–321
Other person:
    as perceiver, 140–142
    perception of, 139
    reactions to experiences of, 149
Oughts and values, 146–147
Outcome control, 278
Outcome matrix, 82–86, 96–99
    effective, 85
    given, 85
    transformation of, 85–86
Outcomes:
    in equity theory, 103–107
    experienced, 93
    and inputs, 103
    of interaction, 81–86
    salient, 94
    sampling of, 90

Paradigms, 10
Partitioning:
    of behaviors, 298–303
    of persons, 297–298
        with behaviors, 303–312

Perception:
    cognitive explanation of, 185–188
    of others, 138–140
    perspectives of, 187
Performance decrement and gender,
    394–397
Person-behavior matrix, 305–307
Person-other relationships, 297–298
Person perception, 139
    other person as perceiver in, 140–142
Personal causality, 143–144
Personal space, 167
Personalism, 238
Pleasure, desire and, 144–145
Position in role theory, 303–304
Power, 126–131
    bases of, 128
    field-theory conceptions of, 126–127
    formal theory of, 126–131
    position, 385–386
    strategies of, 100
    types of, 96–97
P-O-X theory, 199–204
    balance in, 201–202
    evaluation of, 202–204
Predicaments in impression management,
    332–334
    remedial tactics for, 333–334
        accounts, 333
        apologies, 334
        defenses of innocence, 333
        excuses, 333
        justifications, 333
Pressures toward uniformity, 264–265
Primacy effect, 92
Primary environments, 164–165
Primitive categorization, 187
Principle of congruity, 210–217
    assertions and, 211–212
    attitudes and, 212
    corollaries of, 214–225
    direction of change and, 212
    evaluation of, 215–217
    pressure and, 213–214
    underlying assumptions of, 210–211
Principle theories, 11
Privacy, 167–168
Procedural knowledge, 190–191
Proximal stimulus, 138
Psychological distance, 123
Psychological reactance (see Reactance,
    theory of)

Rational baseline models, 257

Reactance, theory of, 228–231
  consequences of, 229
  magnitude of, 228–229
  theory of, 228–231
Reception learning, 188
Reductive theories, 11
Reinforcement, 191–192
  cognitive analysis of, 191–192
  law of, 24
  as a modeling effect, 60
  reciprocal, 69–70
  schedules of, 36–37
  secondary, 37
  and social phenomena, 39–40
  varieties of, 35–37
  vicarious, 60
Reinforcement analysis of learning, 23–49
Relational continuity, postulate of, 364
Relationship:
  evaluation of, 93–95
  formation of, 90–93
  power and dependence in, 95–100
Remedial tactics, 333–334
Request and command, 147–148
Response, 28–29
  cognitive definition of, 184
  hierarchy of, 40
  in Miller and Dollard's theory, 46
  strength of, 31–32
Response learning, 54
Responsibility, attribution of, 152
Restraint as an obesity-prone orientation,
    405
Rewards:
  in copying, 51–52
  costs and, 81–101, 103–107
  determinants of, 86–90
  and equity, 103–107
  in matched-dependent learning, 47–51
Role conflict, 308–310
  and fear of success, 393
  legitimacy and sanction in, 309–310
  and moral orientation, 309
  resources of, 309–310
  theory of, 309–310
Role partner, 297
Role performance, 299–301
  and specialization, 310
  uniformity in, 310
Role sanctions, 301–303
  in role conflict, 309
Role theory, 295–313
  language of, 296–312
    conception, 303

Role theory, language of (Cont.):
    conflict (see Role conflict)
    definitions of, 304–305
    demands, 299
    descriptions, 303
    enactment, 301–303
    expectations, 298–299
      norms and, 298–299
      predicted, 298
      prescribed, 299–301
    performance, 299–301
    and person-behavior matrix,
      305–307
    statement, 303
    terms for partitioning behaviors,
      298–303
    types of, 306
  in social psychology, 314–349
Rote learning, 188–189

Same behavior, 47–48
Secondary environments, 164–165
Self-awareness (see Objective self-awareness,
    theory of)
Self-concept and social identity, 329–330
Self-consciousness, 346, 347
Self-focused attention, 346, 347
Self-ideal discrepancy and self-focus, 346,
    347
Self-image, 331–333
  challenges to, 331
  claims to, 331
  expected values of, 331–332
Self-monitoring, theory of, 337–345
  comments on, 344–345
  consequences of, 340–343
  construct of, 338
  hypotheses about, 340–343
  measurement of, 338–340
    scale, 339–340
      validity of, 339
  processes underlying, 343–344
Self-perception:
  and dissonance theory, 234, 250–257
  of emotional state, 399–402
  postulates of, 253–254
  qualifications on, 254–255
  theory of, 234, 250–257
Self-presentation tactics, 322–323, 334–335
  modesty, 323
  self-enhancement, 322–323, 334–335
Sentiment relations, 200
Sentiments, 145–146
Set-point and obesity, 405

Similarity:
  and attraction, 408–410
  as determinant of rewards and costs, 87
  and role, 304–305
Single-principle perspectives, 389–410
Social comparison theory, 259–269
  cessation of, 263–264
  choices of persons for, 261–262
  current status of, 266–268
  group formation and, 265
  modification of, 268–269
  sources of, 260–261
Social facilitation, 41
Social identities, 329–330
  composite, 330
  control over, 331
  protection of, 332
  situated, 330
Social influence, model of, 126–131
Social judgment theory, 269–277
  and assimilation, 272–273
  attitude change and, 275
  basic assumption of, 270
  evaluation of, 276–277
  patterns of acceptance and rejection in,
    274–275
Social learning, 41–67
Social penetration, specific aspects of,
  158–160
Social penetration theory, 153–162
  assumptions of, 154–156
  evaluation of, 160–162
  rewards and costs in, 157
Social power, formal theory of, 126–131
  bases of, 128
  conception of, 126–127
Social psychology:
  definitions of, 4–6
  place in behavioral sciences, 6–7
Solution multiplicity, 385
Space of free movement, 121
Specialization of roles, 310–311
Spontaneous recovery, 25
Stability versis instability causal ascriptions
  for achievement, 406–407
Stimulus:
  cognitive definition of, 184–185
  cue, 45–46
  distal, 138–139
  functions of, 28–29
  local, 139
  proximal, 138
  total, 139

Success, fear of (see Fear of success)
Success expectancy, 397, 407
Successive approximation, 54–55
Symmetry:
  strain toward, 206
  values of, 207

Tactical behavior, 316–328
Tension, 123–125
  reduction of, 124
  systems of, 123–125
    and force, 125
Territoriality, 167
Theory(ies):
  characteristics of a good, 13–15
  current status of, 413–417
  definitions of, 4, 8–9
  functions of, 9–10, 414
  kinds of, 10–12
  middle range, 9
  nature of, 8–9
  orientation and, 9
  and research, 417–419
  scope of, 12
  in social psychology, 7–8
  trends in development of, 416
  (See also specific theory, for example:
    Affiliative conflict theory;
    Attribution theory)
Theory construction, problems of, 15–18
  data reliability, 16–17
  definitions, 15–16
  kind, 18
  scope, 17–18
Transorientational approaches, 353–387
Trial-and-error learning, 54
"Trying," 142

Uniqueness of target (in ingratiation),
  316–317, 323–324
Unit relations, 200

Valence, 113–115, 122
Value, 146–147
  expectancy and, 391–393, 397, 406–408
Vicarious classical conditioning, 65–66
Vicarious emotional arousal, 65
Vicarious reinforcement, 60
Vignettes, 183–184
  types of, 184